Laying the foundation for the new Kamenets Yeshiva, October 6, 1932.
Photo by Rabbi Tzvi Hirsh/Harold Baumrind. Courtesy of the Yudkowsky family and Rabbi Akiva Tendler

Memorial Book of
Kamenets Litovsk, Zastavye, and Colonies
(Kamyanyets, Belarus)

Translation of
Sefer Yizkor le-Kehilot Kamenets de-Lita

Original Book Edited by: Prof. Shmuel Eisendstadt and Mordechai Gelbart

Originally published in Tel Aviv, 1970

JewishGen
מרכז עולמי לגנאלוגיה יהודית
The Global Home for Jewish Genealogy

A Publication of JewishGen, INC
Edmond J. Safra Plaza, 36 Battery Place, New York, NY 10280
646.494.5972 | info@JewishGen.org | www.jewishgen.org

MUSEUM OF
JEWISH HERITAGE
A LIVING MEMORIAL
TO THE HOLOCAUST

Memorial Book of Kamenets Litovsk, Zastavye, and Colonies (Kamyanyets, Belarus)

Translation of *Sefer Yizkor le-Kehilot Kamenets de-Lita*

Editors of Original Yizkor Book: Prof. Shmuel Eisendstadt and Mordechai Gelbart
Project Coordinator: Allen Flusberg
Emerita Coordinator: Jenni Buch
Layout and Name Indexing: Jonathan Wind
Reproduction of Photographs: Sondra Ettlinger
Cover Design: Nina Schwartz

Printed in the United States of America by Lightning Source, Inc.

Library of Congress Control Number (LCCN): 2022931815

ISBN: 978-1-954176-36-2 (hard cover: 450 pages, alk. paper)

About JewishGen.org

JewishGen, an affiliate of the Museum of Jewish Heritage - A Living Memorial to the Holocaust, serves as the global home for Jewish genealogy.

Featuring unparalleled access to 30+ million records, it offers unique search tools, along with opportunities for researchers to connect with others who share similar interests. Award winning resources such as the Family Finder, Discussion Groups, and ViewMate, are relied upon by thousands each day.

In addition, JewishGen's extensive informational, educational and historical offerings, such as the Jewish Communities Database, Yizkor Book translations, InfoFiles, Family Tree of the Jewish People, and KehilaLinks, provide critical insights, first-hand accounts, and context about Jewish communal and familial life throughout the world.

Offered as a free resource, JewishGen.org has facilitated thousands of family connections and success stories, and is currently engaged in an intensive expansion effort that will bring many more records, tools, and resources to its collections.

Please visit https://www.jewishgen.org/ to learn more.

Executive Director: Avraham Groll

About the JewishGen Yizkor Book Project

Yizkor Books (Memorial Books) were traditionally written to memorialize the names of departed family and martyrs during holiday services in the synagogue (a practice that still exists in many synagogues today).

Over the centuries, as a result of countless persecutions and horrific atrocities committed against the Jews, Yizkor Books (Sefer Zikaron in Hebrew) were expanded to include more historical information, such as biographical sketches of famous personalities and descriptions of daily town life.

Following the Holocaust, the idea of remembrance and learning took on an urgent and crucial importance. Survivors of the Holocaust sought out other surviving residents of their former towns to memorialize and document the names and way of life of those who were ruthlessly murdered by the Nazis. These remembrances were documented in Yizkor Books, hundreds of which were published in the first decades after the Holocaust.

Most of these books were published privately, or through landsmanshaftn (social organizations comprised of members originating from the same European town or region) that still existed, and were often distributed free of charge. Sadly, the languages used to document these crucial histories and links to our past, Yiddish and Hebrew, are no longer commonly understood by a significant percentage of Jews today. As a result, JewishGen has undertaken the sacred responsibility of translating these books into English so that the culture and way of life of these communities will be preserved and transmitted to future generations.

In 1986, a group of farsighted JewishGenners started a project to pool their efforts together in groups based upon their ancestors from each town and donate money to get the Yizkor books of their ancestral towns translated into English. As the translated material became available, it was made accessible for free at www.JewishGen.org/Yizkor. Hardcover copies can be purchased by visiting https://www.jewishgen.org/Yizkor/ybip.html (see below).

It is our hope that the translation of these books into English (and other languages) will assist the countless Jewish family researchers who are so desperately seeking to forge a connection with their heritage.

Director of JewishGen Yizkor Book Project: Lance Ackerfeld

About the JewishGen Press

JewishGen Press (formerly the Yizkor Books-in-Print Project) is the publishing division of JewishGen.org, and provides a venue for the publication of non-fiction books pertaining to Jewish genealogy, history, culture, and heritage.

In addition to the Yizkor Book category, publications in the Other Non-Fiction category include Shoah memoirs and research, genealogical research, collections of genealogical and historical materials, biographies, diaries and letters, studies of Jewish experience and cultural life in the past, academic theses, and other books of interest to the Jewish community.

Please visit https://www.jewishgen.org/Yizkor/ybip.html to learn more.

Director of JewishGen Press: Joel Alpert
Managing Editor - Jessica Feinstein
Publications Manager - Susan Rosin

Notes to the Reader

The images in the original book were reproduced from photographs from the time of the first edition. These reproductions were already of poor quality, being pre-war and at least 30 or more years old. As a result the images in the book are not very good and the best achievable.

A reader can view the original scans of the book on the websites listed below.

The original book can be seen online at the Yiddish Book Center website:

https://www.yiddishbookcenter.org/search/collection/NYPL-Yiddish%20Book%20Center%20Yizkor%20Book%20Collection?query=Kamieniec+Litewski&restrict=

or at the New York Public Library Digital Collections website:

https://digitalcollections.nypl.org/items/eb01c3f0-7a71-0133-9ea9-00505686a51c#/?uuid=eb8e8200-7a71-0133-117c-00505686a51c

To obtain a list of Shoah victims from Kamenets-Litovsk the reader should access the Yad Vashem web site listed below; one can also search for specific family names using family name option. These lists are continually updated by Yad Vashem, so it is worthwhile to periodically search these lists.

There is more valuable information (including the Pages of Testimony, etc.) available on this website: https://yvng.yadvashem.org/

A list of all books available from JewishGen Press along with prices is available at: https://www.jewishgen.org/Yizkor/ybip.html

Acknowledgements

I would like to acknowledge those who came before me for translating the Kamenetz-Litowsk Yizkor Book Table of Contents and the Necrology. I thank the staff of JewishGen, particularly Lance Ackerfeld, for uploading my article translations one by one, and for their patience with my errata. I am grateful to other descendants or relatives of Kamenetzers (particularly Gloria Jaffe-Hirsch, Jennifer Mendelson, Perets Mett, Stefan Kozak and Diana Zalph) who spotted typos, corrected name spellings, and identified individuals appearing in photographs in the Yizkor Book. I am grateful to my wife, Rosalind Flusberg, for her love, devotion and encouragement during the five years I spent translating the Yizkor Book articles.

Allen Flusberg

Newton, Massachusetts

February 2022

Credits and Captions for Book Cover

Background:

Kamyanyets in May 2007. Courtesy of Henry Neugass.

Front cover:

Cousins Dobbe Morgenstern (left) and Basha Pochalski, c.1935. Courtesy of Allen Flusberg.

Young men boating on the Leshna (Lyasnaya), March 1932. Courtesy of the Yudkowsky family and Rabbi Akiva Tendler. Photo by Rabbi Tzvi Hirsh/Harold Baumrind.

Unknown soldier Sherman, possibly Moshe Sherman, in Imperial Russian "Polish Division" cavalry uniform, c.1915. Courtesy of Iris Weissman.

Back cover:

Top: *Itzhak (Irving) Gwertzman and friends clowning at the White Tower, c.1930.* Courtesy of Karen Scheer.

Left: *Bracha Pochalski at the cemetery, c.1935.* Courtesy of Allen Flusberg.

Bottom: *Purim at the old Kamenets Yeshiva, March 1932.* Courtesy of the Yudkowsky family and Rabbi Akiva Tendler. Photo by Rabbi Tzvi Hirsh/Harold Baumrind.

GeoPolitical Information

Kamyanyets, Belarus is located at 52°24' N 23°49' E and 187 miles SW of Minsk

	Town	District	Province	Country
Before WWI (c. 1900):	Kamenets-Litovsk	Brest	Grodno	Russian Empire
Between the wars (c. 1930):	Kamieniec Litewski	Brześć nad Bugiem	Polesie	Poland
After WWII (1946 - 1990):	Kamyenets			Soviet Union
Today (After 1990):	Kamyanyets			Belarus

Alternate Names for the Town:

Kamyanyets [Bel], Kamenets [Rus], Kamieniec Litewski [Pol], Kamenets Litovsk [Yid], Kamianiec, Kameniec, Kamenetz, Komenitz, Komenitz D Lita, Kamyenyets Litevski, Kamenets-Litevski, Kamenets-Litovskiy

Nearby Jewish Communities:

Zamosty 1 miles W
Lotovo 2 miles WNW
Abramovo 10 miles NNW
Chernavchitsy 13 miles SSW
Zhabinka 16 miles SSE
Vysokaye 19 miles W
Białowieża, Poland 20 miles N
Sharashova 20 miles ENE
Brest 21 miles SSW
Volchin 23 miles WSW
Terespol, Poland 24 miles SSW
Kleszczele, Poland 25 miles WNW
Hajnówka, Poland 25 miles NNW
Kobryn 26 miles ESE
Janów Podlaski, Poland 29 miles WSW
Niemirów, Poland 29 miles WSW
Orla, Poland 29 miles NW
Pruzhany 29 miles ENE
Linovo 29 miles ENE
Milejczyce, Poland 30 miles WNW
Narewka, Poland 30 miles N

Jewish Population: 2,722 (in 1897)

2012 Border
1940 Border

BELARUS

0 25 50 75   km

0   25 50   75 miles

ESTONIA

Riga

LATVIA

RUSSIA

LITHUANIA

Vilnius

Kaliningrad

BELARUS

Minsk

POLAND

Warsaw

Kamyanyets

UKRAINE

Kyiv

Lviv

Map of Belarus with **Kamyanyets** indicated

Summary of the English Translation of the Kamenetz-Litowsk Yizkor Book

By Allen Flusberg, Translator and Project Coordinator

This Yizkor Book memorializes the Jews of Kamenetz-Litowsk—a *shtetl* in an area that changed hands over the centuries, from Lithuania to Poland to Belarus. It was situated on the banks of the Leshna River, in the shadow of the "Sloop", a 14th-century fortress tower. The Jews of the town took great pride in the Kamenetz Yeshiva, a center of advanced Talmudic learning. Young men from all over the world flocked there to study and to bask in the presence of the renowned Boruch-Ber Leibowitz, the prodigious head of the yeshiva.

The Jewish presence was obliterated by the Nazis during World War II. The Jews of the town were first confined to a ghetto, then expelled and transported to death camps. Only one Jew, Dora Galperin, was hidden by local Christians and survived in and around the town—traumatized by her experience for the rest of her life. A few others who had been expelled survived the brutal conditions of work camps. The small number who returned after the war could not bear their neighbors' animosity and emigrated to Israel and other countries. Nothing remains in Kamenetz of the centuries-long Jewish presence—no living Jew, not even a trace of the Jewish cemetery.

The essays in this Yizkor Book also describe the thriving pre-war Jewish community. There are biographies of mid-19th century Kamenetz adventurers (Menachem-Mendel of Kamenetz, Yisrael Ashkenazi) who settled in Israel in the trying conditions of those times. One essay tells us about the 19th-century career of a fiery orator, the Maggid of Kamenetz, who emigrated to London in 1890. Two writers (Yeḥezkel Kotik, Falek Zolf) contribute colorful autobiographical pieces on life in the town in the late 19th and early 20th centuries. We learn about Kamenetz's travails during World War I: the influx of refugees, the German occupation, the epidemics, the blaze that destroyed much of the *shtetl*, and the bandits—escaped prisoners-of-war who hid out in nearby forests.

Other essays describe Zionist organizations, the hard-working communal volunteers, a successful amateur theatre, a self-trained orchestra that performed when the Kamenetz Yeshiva was dedicated, and the experiences of Jewish pupils attending the Polish elementary school in the 1920s. Several articles tell us about the last Chief Rabbi of the town, the charismatic Reuven Burstein, who perished in Auschwitz; he was an enlightened, tolerant leader with a profound religious interpretation of Jewish history. Another tells the story of a brilliant PhD mathematician from Kamenetz, Ayzik Gorny, for whom "Gorny's Theorem" was named; he was teaching in a French university in 1940, yet shared the fate of his fellow Kamenetzers—sent from France to his death in Auschwitz. And we are told about the achievements of those who had left: the proud, new lives of the immigrants to Israel; and the philanthropic accomplishments of the immigrants to America. Both groups joined hands to memorialize the town and to write the Yizkor Book. Finally, a detailed necrology, authored by Meir Bobrowski, lists all the Kamenetzers, more than 1,700 in number, who perished at the hand of the Nazis.

Note on Transliterations of Names

My transliteration of family names has varied between English or German spellings (e.g., Rudnitzky) and Polish spellings (e.g., Rudnicki). In certain cases, the Yizkor Book did not vocalize the vowel-letter "aleph" occurring in Yiddish names, forcing me to make an educated guess as to whether such occurrences were pronounced "a" or "o". Finally, I endeavored to transliterate proper names and Hebrew words occurring in Hebrew text according to the Israeli pronunciation, but proper names and Hebrew words occurring in Yiddish text according to the Ashkenazi Litvak pronunciation used by the Jews of Kamenetz.

Note on Reference to Page Numbers

All page numbers appearing in braces (e.g. *[Page 27]*) refer to the page numbers in the original Yizkor Book. Similarly, cross references in the footnotes to other articles in the Yizkor Book are cited by the page numbers of the original Yizkor Book, rather than those of the English translation.

TABLE OF CONTENTS

Comunal Workers, Writers and Teachers in Kamenets-Litowsk

Committee members of Kamenetz-Litowsk townspeople organization who passed away in Israel

In the Holocaust

Social Life in Kamenets

Memories from Kamenets Before the Destruction

Persons in Town

Destruction and Ruin

Dedication

I dedicate this translation to the memory of my mother and aunt, sisters Dobbe and Chaika Morgenstern (a.k.a. Dorothy Flusberg and Helyn Reichenthal), who were fortunate enough to leave their native Kamenetz for America in 1938. And most of all I dedicate this translation to their mother Sarah and two other sisters, Golda and Mashke Morgenstern, who tried to leave but never made it out, perishing instead with all the other Jews of Kamenetz at the hands of the Nazis. May their memories and those of all the other Kamenetzers who were put to death by the Nazis be a blessing.

Allen Flusberg

February 2022

Memorial Book of Kamenets Litovsk, Zastavye, and Colonies (Kamyanyets, Belarus)

52°24' / 23°49'

Translation of
Sefer Yizkor le-Kehilot Kamenets de-Lita

Edited by: Prof. Shmuel Eisendstadt and Mordechai Gelbart

Published in Tel Aviv, 1970

Acknowledgments:

Project Coordinator

Allen Flusberg

Emerita Coordinator: Jenni Buch

This is a translation from: *Sefer Yizkor le-Kehilot Kamenets de-Lita*;
Memorial book of Kamenets Litovsk, Zastavye, and colonies.
Ed. Prof. Shmuel Eisendstadt and Mordechai Gelbart. Tel Aviv, Kaminiec and Zastavye communities in Israel and the U.S., 1970, "Orli", Rehov Akiva Eiger 8, Tel Aviv.

Note: The original book can be seen online at the NY Public Library site: Kamieniec Litewski

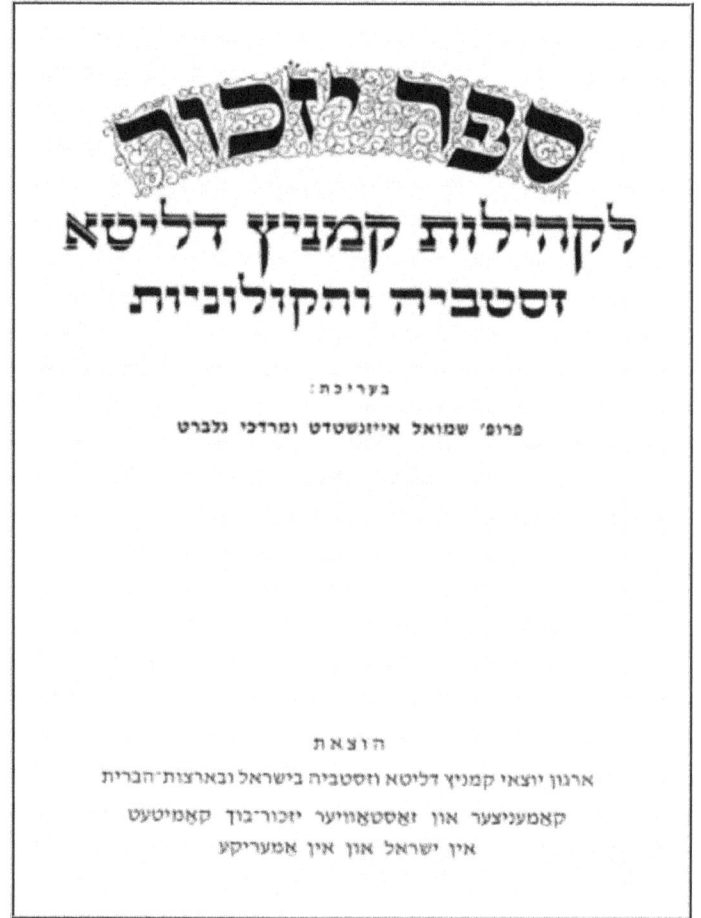

ספר יזכור

לקהילות קמניץ דליטא
זסטביה והקולוניות

בעריכת:

פרופ' שמואל אייזנשטדט ומרדכי גלברט

הוצאת

ארגון יוצאי קמניץ דליטא וזסטביה בישראל ובארצות־הברית

קאמעניצער און זאסטאווייער יזכור־בוך קאמיטעט

אין ישראל און אין אמעריקע

[Page 8]

Let Us Remember and Not Forget[1]

By the Committee of Kamenetzers in Israel and the USA

Translated by Allen Flusberg

Memorial and candle lighting in memory of the martyrs of Kamenetz by our fellow townspeople in Israel at the dedication of the Memorial Plaque (p. 9) [Hebrew].
Our fellow townspeople in Israel at the Yizkor Service and candle lighting in memory of our martyrs, at the dedication of the memorial plaque on Mt. Zion in Jerusalem [Yiddish][2].

[Page 9]

ב"ה

יברכך ה' מציון וראה בטוב ירושלם כל ימי חייך

וזאת התעודה

לוח זכרון לקדושי קהילות

קמניץ-ליטובסק

זסטביה והסביבה

שנרצחו ע"י הנאצים
בשנים ת"ש-תש"א
הי"ד תנצב"ה

המציחים יוצאי קמניץ-ליטובסק וזסטביה
בישראל ובתפוצות

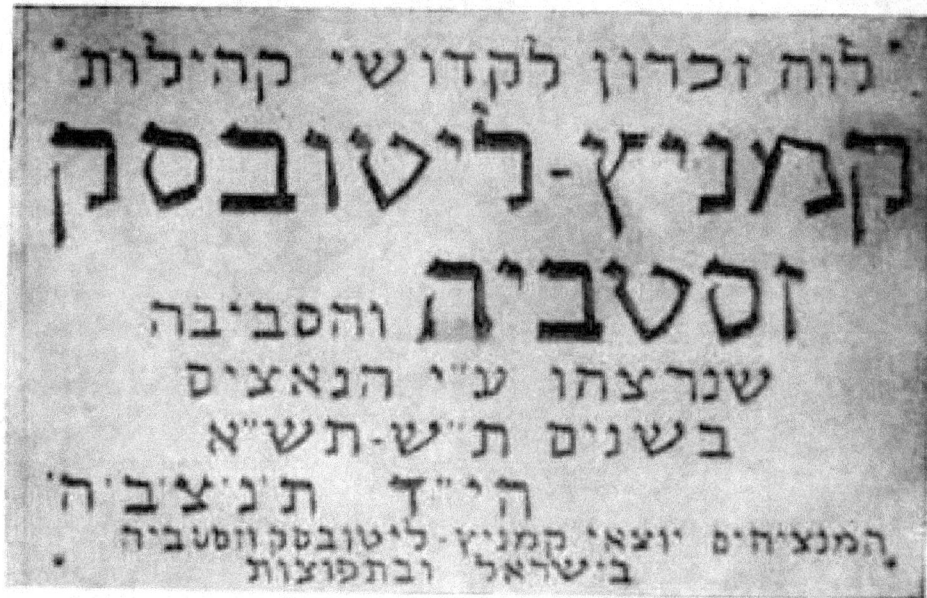

ניתן בהר ציון ... ה'תשכ"ג שלום על ישראל
– 19. 8. 63 –

ישראל

Memorial Plaque. Certificate[3][4]

[Page 10]

Let us remember and not forget: Our townspeople at a memorial service in Tel Aviv

[Page 11]

With tremulousness and reverence, we are publishing this book in memory of the martyred innocents of our town.

We shall not forget you, dear parents, who in spite of hardships and burdens of your day–to–day lives, and despite persecutions by various regimes that came and went in our town, you did not refrain from toiling to educate your children in Torah and good deeds. You sent your sons and daughters to the Land of Israel so that they should build up the Land and live there freely as proud Jews. How great your contribution to the establishment of the State of Israel has been, even though the Nazi murderer prevented you from ever seeing it established and developed.

We shall not forget you, brothers and sisters, you and the little ones of our town, gentle and innocent, who were brought away to be slaughtered, though blameless of any wrong.

We shall not forget you, Jewish religious scholars and teachers, headed by Rabbi Reuven Burstein and Rabbi Boruch–Ber Leibowitz, who educated the youth for a life of religion and tradition, for good deeds, and for love of fellow Jews.

We shall not forget the community leaders of Kamenetz, whose concern for their fellow man led them to establish and sustain institutions for Torah, culture and social welfare.

We shall not forget the youth organizations, which in spite of their ideological and political differences remained loyal to their people; they aspired to immigrate to Israel, to participate in its upbuilding, and to ensure its independence.

[Page 12]

We shall not forget the common folk of our town who toiled by the sweat of their brow to support their families.

We shall surely remember all of you.

We shall not be silent nor be silenced in recounting what the savage Nazi beasts perpetrated.[5]

This book will serve as a historical document for researchers and scientists who will someday, when the time is right, delve into it; and from it they will be able to understand the character of the communities of Kamenetz, Zastavya and the Colonies, all destroyed, never to arise again.

This memorial book will be an eternal lamp for those who were annihilated, for their spirit and their memory; and it will connect us and our children after us to our origin. From it they will learn about their parents and ancestors, about their lives and the circumstances of their lives, about their suffering during various periods.

This book will tell the story of annihilation and valor, of the struggle against the bloodthirsty Nazi beast, of their longings, during their last moments, for a life of freedom in Zion. The future generations will know where they came from; they will be proud of their ancestors, and they will bind their souls forever to the bond of the life of our nation.

Footnotes:

1.   From *Kamenetz–Litovsk, Zastavije and Colonies Memorial Book*, edited by S. Eisenstadt and M. Galbert, published by the Israel and America Committee of Kamenetz Litovsk and Zastavya, (Orly, Tel Aviv, Israel, 1970), pp. 8–12. A Yiddish translation of the Hebrew text of this article appears on pp. 346–348 of this volume. It is nearly identical to the Hebrew; any differences are noted below.
2.   As noted, the photograph on p. 8 has two captions, one originally in Hebrew and the other in Yiddish.
3.   Text translates as follows:
b.h. [*b'ezrat haShem* = with God's help].
May God bless you from Zion, and may you see the good of Jerusalem all the days of your life [Ps. 128:5].
This certifies that the following plaque has been placed on Mount Zion on the 30th day of the month of solace [Av], 5723, August 19 1963. Peace upon Israel [Ps. 128:6].
A remembrance plaque for the martyrs of the communities of Kamenetz–Litowsk, Zastavya and the surrounding area, who were murdered by the Nazis in the years 5700–5701 [1939–1941]. May God avenge their blood; and may their souls be bound in the bond of life. Immortalized by those in Israel and the Diaspora who hail from Kamenetz–Litowsk and Zastavya.
Israel. [Signed,] Dr. S. Z. Kahane.
4.   The plaque was erected in *Martef haShoah*, the Chamber of the Holocaust, the first Holocaust museum established in Israel (1949). It is located on Mount Zion in Jerusalem. Its walls are covered with hundreds of plaques, each of which memorializes the Jewish victims of a European community. Rabbi Dr. Shmuel Zanwil Kahane, who signed the certificate, had led the effort to establish this museum. See the following link (retrieved November 2019): https://en.wikipedia.org/wiki/Chamber_of_the_Holocaust
5.   This paragraph occurs in the Yiddish translation but is absent in the original Hebrew.

[Page 13]

An Eternal Memorial for Our Town and Our Martyrs[1]

By Simcha Dubiner,
Chairman of the Kamenetzer Organization in Israel

Translated by Allen Flusberg

In this Memorial Book we will return in our minds to the streets and alleyways of our town, so dear to us. We will peer into every Jewish household and recognize the faces of fathers and mothers, children and grandchildren, the faces of friends. We shall memorialize their names, engraved in our hearts, and we shall remember them in the bitterness of their despair, on the threshold of their terrible annihilation.

We, the few orphaned who have remained alive, will preserve in our hearts the memory of our dear martyrs and of our past, in all its diversity.

This Memorial Book will serve as a faithful testimony to future generations of the lives and actions of the members of our generation, and as an eternal monument to our martyrs.

Footnote:

1. From *Kamenetz–Litovsk, Zastavije and Colonies Memorial Book*, edited by S. Eisenstadt and M. Galbert, published by the Israel and America Committee of Kamenetz Litovsk and Zastavya, (Orly, Tel Aviv, Israel, 1970), p. 13

[Page 14]

List of Committee Members of
Kamenetzers in Israel Since Its Founding[1]

Translated by Allen Flusberg

Simcha Dubiner	Faivl Shragai Dubiner
Baruch Kotik	Rachel Weingrod
Chaya Krakowski	Chana Wissotzky
Pinchas Ravid	Isaac Zlatas
Perl Abramson	Chaim Zlotnik
Baruch Eliyahu Gurfein	Shmarya Solnitza
Asher Glezer	Aharon Kotik
Dov Shmida	Yocheved Kotik
Dov Tzedek	Yaakov Kaminski

The Editorial Board

Leah Aloni-Bobrowski, z.l.[2]	Chaya Krakowski-Karabelnik
Leibl Goldberg / Levi Sarid	Pinchas Ravid-Rudnitzki
Simcha Dubiner	P. Rabi-Rabinowitz, z.l.
Baruch Kotik	Dov (Bertchik) Shmida

Footnotes:

    1.   From *Kamenetz–Litovsk, Zastavije and Colonies Memorial Book*, edited by S. Eisenstadt and M. Galbert, published by the Israel and America Committee of Kamenetz Litovsk and Zastavya, (Orly, Tel Aviv, Israel, 1970), p. 14

    2.   z.l. is an acronym for *zichrono/a livracha* = of blessed memory

[Page 15]

Editor's Introduction[1]

by Professor Shmuel Eisenstadt

Translated by Allen Flusberg

Kamenetz-Litowsk was a typical Jewish town in which Torah, secular knowledge and manual labor existed side by side. Because of its geographic proximity to Brisk-Litowsk[2], it was always under the influence of that traditional, large Jewish center. The study of Torah found a faithful home in the local yeshiva of Kamenetz, which was headed by influential rabbis who were scholarly and virtuous. And secular knowledge, spreading along a trajectory from west to east, took root here as well.

At the very same time as the voices of Torah study and prayer rose upward from the yeshivas and study houses, they were joined by a call for immigration to the Land [of Israel] coming from the assembly and meeting halls—a call for *hachshara* [training], manual labor, and *tikkun olam* [pursuit of justice and liberation to improve the world].

The terrible Holocaust that destroyed the massive glorious Jewish presence in Eastern Europe also reached into the gates of Kamenetz-Litowsk and Zastavya, cutting down this beloved, humble branch from the great flourishing Jewish tree of Lithuania and Poland. This book can serve as a spiritual monument to the pure and innocent martyrs who perished by the hands of the perpetrators of this genocide.

Only a small number of the articles of this wide-ranging book have been composed by experienced writers who originated in the town. Most of the articles are instead memoirs—simple and honest accounts—true-to-life descriptions of the day-to-day, modest and troubled life that once existed and has vanished. For our generation and future ones, this can serve as a faithful memorial book containing a series of essays on the bloody history of our people in Europe during the twentieth century.

From my father, of blessed memory, who was born in Chemeri, located near Kamenetz[3], I heard stories about the life of the town during my childhood, and I willingly took upon myself the task of completing the editing of this collection of memoirs that my good friend Mordechai Galbert had put a great deal of effort into, having collaborated with the honored committee members of the Kamenetzers of Tel Aviv. Each of them contributed his part to the success of this collection. And a special mention must be made of the members of the Committee of Kamenetzers in the United States—headed by their president, Avraham Shudroff—who actively volunteered so much of their time. All of them worked hard and contributed generously to support memorializing their fellow townspeople. They also raised funds from the Kamenetzers of the United States to make it possible to publish this Memorial Book.

[Page 16]

May this book serve as a perpetual memorial lamp for all who have been faithful to their destroyed native town and to their fellow townspeople who were exterminated by the oppressors of the Jews. May it also serve as a reminder for the next generation—the generation of redemption—which continues to struggle with a proud bearing and great devotion to the life of our people, to their land and their martyrs.

Footnotes:

    1.   From *Kamenetz-Litovsk, Zastavije and Colonies Memorial Book*, edited by S. Eisenstadt and M. Galbert, published by the Israel and America Committee of Kamenetz Litovsk and Zastavya, (Orly, Tel Aviv, Israel, 1970), pp. 15-16.

    2.   Brisk or Brest-Litowsk, located 40km south of Kamenetz.

    3.   There is currently (2020) a place named Chemeri about 8km east of Kamenetz. See the following essay by Eisenstadt, pp. 124-126 of this volume, "It Happened in Kamenetz-Litowsk".

[Page 18]

Committee Members

Translated by Allen Flusberg

Mrs. Rimon, Yeshaya Rimon, Avraham Shudroff, Y. Koscikiewicz-Grunt, Dov Aloni, Mr. Kamini,
Esther Dubiner, Simcha Dubiner, when Shudroff participates as a delegate to the 25th Zionist Congress
in Jerusalem, 1960

At that time Avraham Shudroff sets in motion the Committee of the Organization of Kamenetzers in Israel, which decides to publish a Memorial Book dedicated to the memory of the martyrs of our town. Upon his return to America he initiates the Book Committee there, starts it going and heads it throughout.

[Page 19]

Committee Members, Organization of Kamenetz-Litowskers in Israel

Laybl Goldberg.
(Sarid)

Chaya-Krakowski-Karabelnik.

Simche Dubiner

Bertchik Schmidt. (Shmida)

Pinchas Rudnitzki -Ravid

Asher Glezer

Baruch Kotik

[Page 20]

Chaya Krakowski-Karabelnik during her visit to America in the years 1962-63

Chaim Rubin, V. Kustin, M. Visotzky, Rivka Liptzig, Chaya Hurwitz-Goldberg, Isser Goldberg, Ch. Kagan, Ch. Mendelson, S. Hurwitz, A. Shudroff, Y. Sheinfeld[1]

Footnote:

1.   The visitor from Israel, Chaya Krakowski, is sitting, 2nd from left. The others are listed from right to left, first those standing, followed by those sitting.

[Page 21]

History of our Town

Beginnings of the Town Kamenetz–Litowsk and Its Jewish Settlement[1]

By Levi Sarid (Laybl Goldberg)

Translated by Allen Flusberg

Dedicated to the memory of my martyred parents, Kalman and Rachel–Leah; my innocent brothers Noah and Yisrael–Yitzhak; my pure, martyred sisters Shifra, Rivka and Bracha, who were exterminated by the impure Nazis.

The beginning of Kamenetz–Litowsk occurred in the Middle Ages, during the period of the dawn of nations and states that burst on the scene among wildly overgrown roads, forests, muddy swamps, rocky wildernesses and broad wild plains.

This town that we knew—in the hinterland, far from the railroad line—is actually crowned with an ancient, eventful history. In its early years it was a central city whose founders apparently anticipated great things from it. But from the beginning of the 18th century, its star began to dim, and it remained a typical town that preserved its essence and form like other towns of Lithuania of our period, still stuck in the world and tradition of the Middle Ages. So, too, has it been preserved in our memories—we of the last generation of its Jewish residents.

Few among its natives who are today dispersed throughout the world know that this town—with its dilapidated cottages, suspended here and there on cliffs; with its rows of miserable shops that were built like cages—had also experienced a splendid past, in the shadows of kings and princes. From a historical perspective Kamenetz–Litowsk appears as a major city on the central crossroads of Poland–Lithuania, leading from the far north of the State of Poland–Vilna and its surroundings—to its south, bustling with life and international trade. It provided protection and defense to the important central city of that time–Brest–Litowsk[2], which served as an essential hub of continental trade with the East. Brest was a vital intersection in the trade routes between distant countries and states. From it the roads branched out to the inner states that made up ancient Poland: the Polish Crown, Ukraine, Russia and Lithuania.

[Page 22]

The Chronicles tell of the establishment of the city in the year 1276. They explain that the city of Kamenetz was established for the security needs of Brest–Litowsk, which the Lithuanian and Russian tribes were fighting over. This opinion is expressed[i],[ii] by Latkowski, the historian of ancient Lithuania. From the document cited by Latkowski concerning the war between the Lithuanians and the Romanovyches[3] before the ascension of Poland–Lithuania, the place Kamenetz is depicted as one of the strategic points over which a fierce battle was fought in 1262. According to this document, Mendog[4] sent an army that fought near Melnic and Kamenetz. Latkowski identifies these places with Mielnik in Podlachia[5] and Kamenetz–Litowsk[iii].

The association between these places occurs about one hundred years later, when Janusz the prince of Masovia[6], who was the son–in–law of Kistut [Kęstutis], conquered the cities Drochitzin [Drohiczyn] (Podolski)[7], Suraż[8], Melnic and Kamenetz.

The historian of the Kobryn area, Severin Wisołuch[iv], who was descended from the Lithuanian *szlachta* [nobility], rejects the opinion of Latkowski, and strongly expresses the opinion that Kamenetz refers to Kamin Kashyrskyi[9], on the border of Polszia–Poland. But it appears that Latkowski is right that the ancient battle was concentrated in the areas of Podlachia, and it can be assumed that Kamenetz was the name of a village in that area, on whose foundations the city was built.

According to the chronicles known to us from the archives of the Volyn[10] principality, the founder of the city of Kamenetz was Vladimir Vaselewicz, the ruler of Volyn, who resided at that time in Brest. He was also called the philosopher, and was the ruler of Vladimir Volynsk[11] (Ludmir). The chronicle recounts: After Brest was destroyed by the Tatars (apparently, during their second invasion in 1259), it was decided to establish a line of fortifications that would protect Brest from the hinterland. It should not be forgotten that the 13th century was renowned as the period in which urban settlements of Poland and Lithuania were established, and thus this document may perhaps be viewed as an additional source for the establishment of the city.

In 1276 Vladimir sent his officer Oleszko to find a suitable location for the establishment of a fortified city. After the latter had located the designated place, Vladimir, too, arrived with his retinue—a group of Boyars[12], young nobles from Brest—and he set up his headquarters there. According to the above chronicles, they chose a rocky peak on the banks of the Leshna River, which is referred to in all the sources as Greater Leshna[v]. They immediately began to clear the thick forests that surrounded the peak, and the city called Kamenetz thus began its existence in 1276.

To defend against attacks by the Tatars (the last attack by the Tatars was in 1287, and it was blocked by the Poles near Krakow[13]), they began constructing a large fortress, which is known to us as the "Slup"[vi]. Once it was completed its height reached 37 meters (17 *sazhen*[14]), and its circumference 35 meters (16 *sazhen*). Within the fortress they arranged oak stairs, which, remarkably, have resisted rot and destruction to this very day. They constructed openings in the walls of the fortress tower for firearms barrels, and similarly they built a system of canals that led to the river, so that supplies and men could be conveyed to the tower. The fortress is referred to as the "White Fortress"[vii]. In medieval times the word for fortress was locally pronounced "ordos"[viii], which denoted fortress in Latin. The surrounding forests were also afterwards called "the forests of the White Fortress", and from this is derived also the name of the forests of Bialowieza[15], after the name of the fortress of Kamenetz.

It should be noted that the forests of Kamenetz and Bialowiez are mentioned side–by–side in the above chronicles. An official empowered by the Grand Duchy of Lithuania, whose domain was over the Bialowiez and Kamenetz wilderness, was appointed over them both. During some periods the permanent residence of this high official was located in Kamenetz (e.g. Philip Machewicz at the end of the 16th century, who was called the woodsman of the forests of Bialowiez and Kamenetz)[ix].

[Page 23]

Kamenetz is denoted by two different names in the sources from the 14th century: Ruthenian Kamenetz[x] and Volynian Kamenetz[xi]. For those who are not well–versed in the history of Poland and Lithuania—it should also be pointed out that in the first few centuries of the second millennium, Volyn was an integral part of Lithuania; it was detached from it only after it was annexed to the Polish Crown before the unification of Lithuania and Poland[xii] in 1569[16]. Kamenetz was connected to Volyn by the main highway that led from Vilna to Lvov[17] and passed through the province Masovia on the west and the area to the east of Narew[18], known in the ancient history of Poland as the place of "the Great Swamps". The important crossroad was Novyi Dvor[19]. In the 16th century this road was called the Great Highway[xiii]; and from there [Novyi Dvor] the path continued west to Pruzhany[20], Szereszew[21] —which was then part of the province of Kamenetz[xiv] —and from Kamenetz the road continued on to Brest, then to Lubomil[22], and from Lubomil to Red Russia and to its capital, Lvov.

Kamenetz was annexed to the Duchy of Lithuania at the beginning of the 14th century, and was the capital of a province that bore its name; this was a large *starostwo*[23], whose eastern border was the province of Kobryn (then the duchy of Kobryn), with Pruzhany on the north. According to a document dated April 26, 1380, Witold[24][xv] transferred the village of Szereszowa [Szereszew or Šarašova, see above] to his friend Mikolai Nasut Szampert. The Nasut family was a dynasty of dukes who greatly influenced Jagiello, and Szereszowa appears here as an estate that was located within the domain of Kamenetz[xvi]. After Gedimin[25], the founder of Greater Lithuania, was wounded in the Battle of Wielowa, during the war against the Saxon Knights, he bequeathed his estate to his seven sons; and Kamenetz and its surroundings went to his second son Kiestut[26][xvii]. During his reign the attacks by the Teutonic Knights reached their climax. The first attack by the Teutons on Kamenetz occurred in 1375, under the leadership of the Belgian *Komtur* [Commander] Theodor von Elsner. The Chronicle mentions the abundance of spoils that Theodoric took in captives, cattle and horses. In this battle Kamenetz was badly damaged, but the Teutons were unable to conquer it; they did not destroy this important strategic location. In the intense attacks that were repeated in 1319 they took the city and held it for a short time, but at the end of that year they were forced to retreat from it[xviii].

[Page 24]

During the period of the war of inheritance between the brothers Kiestut and Jagiello, Janusz the prince of Masovia, who was the son–in–law of Kiestut, conquered the city of Drohiczin, Melnik and Suraż, and finally Kamenetz, which was, according to the claim of Janusz, included in the dowry of his wife Danuta, who was Kiestut's daughter. It may be assumed that Janusz reached Kamenetz along the above–mentioned "Great Highway". Jagiello then lay siege to Kamenetz in 1383; and after conquering the fortress and the city, he stayed there for a while. According to the treaty between him and Witold, the Grand Duke of Lithuania, Kamenetz was transferred to Witold as a possession, and starting then (1384) it was incorporated into the Duchy of Lithuania. As a part of the Brisk region, Kamenetz had fallen into the possession of Witold as an inheritance from his father Kiestut. (At that time Witold also obtained Grodno[27]; and in 1388, four years after the treaty, he provided the Jews of Brisk with the first charter of their rights).

After Witold conquered Kamenetz, it became a central location within the entire region, and together with Brisk and Kobryn it was considered an important provincial capital of Lithuania. Indeed, this is how they are depicted in the documents from that period. Its location on the main highway from Krakow to Vilna and its envelopment by the forests of Lithuania gave it a unique value. For this reason, we see that from the 15th to the 17th century it served as a meeting place for the king's council, particularly in the summer season. These council meetings were accompanied by royal hunting excursions that the king and the Lithuanian nobility participated in. It was in Kamenetz that the historic meeting between Pope Alexander V's emissary and Jagiello and Witold took place. This meeting occurred during the great papal schism[28] between Gregory XII, Benedict XIII and Alexander V. Alexander's *legatus* (emissary) came to Kamenetz to ask Jagiello, who was then living in the city, to have Poland and Lithuania join his camp, which supported the unification of the Catholic Church that was then split between the three popes.

It was also here in Kamenetz that Casimir of Jagiellon[29] spent some of his time while he was heir to the throne and Grand Duke of Lithuania[xix]. During his many journeys within Lithuania he spent time in Kamenetz. When he was also the king of Poland, he would conduct council meetings there with the Polish nobility, and, accompanied by the noblemen, he would of course go on hunting excursions.

For some time Kamenetz was withdrawn from the Brisk region and was instead annexed to Podlachia[30]. But in 1569 the city was returned to the Brisk district, and since then this situation has not changed. As stated above, Kamenetz was a *starostwo* [administrative unit] and was considered a royal possession. In 1525 Kamenetz was granted the status of a voivodeship[31][xx][xxi][xxii]. This status provided it with rights, in addition to the Magdeburg Rights[32] that apparently had been granted it—together with Brisk, Grodno and other cities—in 1496. The administration of the city was thereby extended, and the *Woit*[bailiff] served as a chief municipal judge; and from this we can conclude that in the beginning of the 16th century there already existed in Kamenetz an elected city council headed by a mayor, and the *Woit* served as administration head and chief municipal judge; he was also the head of the *lavniks* [aldermen], beside whom there were also city councilors, headed by a mayor[xxiii].

[Page 25]

All the settlements along the Leshna River lay within the domain of the Kamenetz *starostwo*. It should be noted that the heads of the *starostwo* were among the most important of the nobility of the Polish state, and they apparently leased the city and the surrounding area from the monarchy. The research historians see the Kamenetz *szlachta* [nobility] as greatly influential, with inroads in the royal court. These were the magnate families Tiszkewicz and Pac (Pacewicz), whom we meet in the 16th century as *starostas* [administrative officers] of Kamenetz (or Oklepaczy); they also served as *voivodes* [governors]. Pac was a *voivode* of Minsk, and the Tiszkewiczes also officiated as finance ministers of Lithuania (*Podeskerwy*).

King Casimir of Jagiellon, who was especially fond of our town, wrote letters to Pac (Pacewicz) about land disputes over surrounding villages, between them and the Tiszkewiczes. A dispute of this type, which lasted for decades, was over the village of Kiwaticz. During these conflicts, property was set on fire and subjects were murdered. Intervening in the dispute, the crown prince wrote to Pac[xxiv]. Zygmunt I[33] also sent notifications on this subject, threatening the Pacs with legal remedies[xxv].

Thus we find well–known families of the *szlachta* [nobility] residing on estates in the vicinity of Kamenetz: Radziwill[34] (Czemery and vicinity) and Sapieha (in the vicinity of Szustokowo–Wysokie[35]). In the 16th and 17th century we find a lower–rank aristocracy near Kamenetz whose descendants became famous in later periods, such as the Kościuszko family. (The residents of Kamenetz recall Stoipiczewo well, as it was located on a hill on the left bank of the Leshna River, in Bliniewicz and in the village of Sechnowic, between Kamenetz and Žabinka[36]).

From documents found primarily in Acts of the Historical Committee of Vilna, particularly in Volume 6, we learn of stiff competition and hostile relationships that existed between the high–ranking nobility and the burghers of Kamenetz–Litowsk. As is well known, the city received a special ordinance granting it Magdeburg rights and voivodeship rights. These rights guaranteed administrative and jurisdictional autonomy to the city. The burghers were exempt from the specific services to the king, including even army service. They had a special privilege, granted by King Zygmunt I in the year 1528, giving the burghers a special right to utilize timber in the surrounding forests for building materials and firewood[xxvi]. The forests of Kamenetz were considered crown property and were referred to as such in the documents mentioned above[xxvii]. This privilege served as a background for disputes that sprung up and lasted for decades. In these documents we read how the burghers were conspiring against the nobles' subjects. There were cases in which they murdered them in the streets of the city[xxviii]. A striking example of this type of case was the long judicial proceedings between Anna Koszczuszko of Stoipiczewo and the burghers who had killed two of her subjects.

In addition, some of the members of the Polish high nobility, such as Sapieha, Radziwill and Pac, were involved in conflicts with the burghers of Kamenetz. These disputes, very typical of that period, provide a small example of the relations that existed between the *szlachta* and the monarchy. On one side were the burghers of Kamenetz, supported by the king; and on the other side the nobles, who were defending their *szlachta* rights. A dispute of this type came up in Kamenetz in 1600. The monarchy was represented by Jan Pac, the *voivoda* [governor] of Minsk; the *starosta* [administrator][37] of Kamenetz, Castellan Grogery Woina; and the prosecutor of the Grand Duchy of Lithuania, Malchaer Kamenskyi[xxix][xxx]. In this dispute, Zygmunt III of the House of Waza sided with the *mieszczanies* [burghers]. Sapieha, the *voivoda* of Homel, did not appear, instead sending as his representative his confidant Bogdan Cholomowski. In the letter that Sapieha sent, he complains against the government of the crown that it had robbed him of parts of the

Kamenetz forests. The dispute was over the woods in the vicinity of the village of Czemery, where Anna Radziwill resided, this area having been given to her as a gift by Sapieha. Sapieha appealed against the very right of the kingdom to litigate against his *szlachta* in the *szlachta's* judicial institutions; he refused to sit at the same table with the Kamenetz burghers, since he viewed it as a wrong against the laws of the land[xxxi]. The prosecutor claimed that only the king himself was the giver of laws, and that it had been clarified to the king that the burghers were simply trying to obtain timber for their own use and were not claiming any ownership; if Sapieha had any claims, he should be appealing to the *Sejm* [parliament].

[Page 26]

A more complex legal dispute took place between Radziwill and the monarchy over the forests, this time in the section between Kamenetz and Czernowczicz. Here, too, the burghers had felled trees, having relied on the privileges granted them by Zygmunt I and Zygmunt III. The forest was located near the villages of Demnic and Liska, where the little river Wisznia flows into the Leshna. Radziwill did not appear at the hearing, either, instead sending a delegate, who relied on documents he had in his possession from the time of Aleksander (1501–1508), according to which the land and the forest belonged to him. The prosecutor for the monarchy brought evidence that the particular section of forest mentioned in Radziwill's appeal belonged to the crown. The legal decision was interesting: they were ordered to "draw up" the land in dispute, and send it to the king for a decision—that is, they had to draw up a map.

It appears that the city suffered badly as a result of the great wars with the Cossacks, and for that reason it appears that the in 1661 the problem of Kamenetz appeared on the *Sejm*'s agenda. The *Sejm* decided to provide several reliefs to both the burghers and the Jews. A separate decision by the *Sejm* also provided a special privilege to the Jews[xxxii]. With extraordinary warmth, the decision takes into account the city's destruction and ruin (*desolasjonem*), and it releases the Poles and the Jews from taxes for a period of 4 years, except for the levying of the *mita* (*mojt*) that was demanded as a customs tax on crossroads, bridges and city entrances. Similarly they were still obligated to provide customs tax on merchandise (an old customs tax on merchandise transiting from one district to another, and a new customs tax—*pobur*—that was initiated in 1501 on exported merchandise). They were also obligated to pay *czopowa*—beverage payments that were one of the large sources of income of the Polish government. It should be noted that the lease for most of these taxes and customs taxes were in the hands of the Jews; and the largest tax collectors were mainly Jews who resided in Brisk, who were known as the lessees for the royal taxes and customs tax.

[Page 27]

The status of the town of Kamenetz took a sharp turn in the middle of the 18th century. The city and its vicinity lost their royal status and became the property of a nobleman—the well–known nobleman Wielhorski[38], the most important officer in Lithuania, who was a politician and diplomat. Even before that a change had occurred in Kamenetz's status in the area.

At the end of this period, after the partition of Poland took place[39], the noblemen living in the vicinity were leaving after having sold their estates to local buyers.

In the middle of the 19th century (1878) the city had a population of 6855 residents, among which 5900 (90%) were Jews (including six village communities).

The Beginning of the Jewish Settlement in Kamenetz (To the Mid–18th Century)

It is not easy to write about the history of the Jewish community of our town. The dearth of Jewish documents is onerous. With the exception of a few lines in Dubnow's work, *Pinkas Medinat Lita* [Records of the Lithuanian Council][40], I was not able to find any document from those ancient times. It is particularly burdensome that we are cut off from the sources of records, containing Jewish documents—these are located in archives that we have no access to, such as those of Brisk, Grodno, and others. Thus there was no other possibility but to recount the history of the Jewish settlement in the town according to the non–Jewish documents, which are mainly in the document centers of the institutions of the government of Poland, located in this country. But these documents and similar ones reveal very little of the Jewish way of life during those ancient times.

Reports on the Jewish settlements in our vicinity appear only at the end of the 14th century. As stated above, the Jews of Brisk were given a privilege by Witold in 1388, but it can be assumed that even before that there existed a Jewish presence in Brisk. We have clear reports on this region only from the end of the 15th century, but here as well one can assume that Jewish communities existed in the area even earlier. (Kobryn appears as an organized community at the beginning of the 16th century). It should be noted that in 1495 the Jews were expelled from Lithuania, at the time of the Lithuanian Duke and Crown–Prince Alexander; but after he was crowned King of

Poland he allowed the Jews to return (1503), and their houses and property were given back to them in return for an annual tax (*powrotny*).

Thus one may assume that the Jewish settlement of Kamenetz began in very early times. Jews are first mentioned in a document from the year 1525 (see below). It is not plausible that during the process of establishing cities in backward Lithuania—at a time when the Jews were given an opportunity not only to deal in trade and monies, but also to purchase estates and to work in every trade—that the Jews were not present in an important town that is located on crossroads and in proximity to a big city as important as Brisk–Litowsk. In a document taken from Lithuanian records, published by the historian G. Bershadsky[xxxiii], *Yevrei* [Jews] are mentioned as tavernkeepers, but the document is obscure, and we cannot conclude from it whether the reference was to a Jewish settlement in the town or to isolated tavernkeepers. It should be understood that one can assume that the Jews were in a community, which, if not large, must have at least reached a quorum of ten [the minimum required for communal prayer]. It follows that there was a Jewish community in Kamenetz still earlier. In this very document the following is stated: "On the 26th of February, 1525, the town of Kamenetz receives the rights of voivodeship in addition to the Miburg (Magdeburg) rights of the *starostwo* [province] Kamenetz. So also the burghers (*mieszczanies*) receive the rights to the taverns that were previously leased to the Jews."[xxxiv][xxxv]

[Page 28]

The development of the towns of Lithuania, as those of other lands, caused the rise of the burgher class, but in Lithuania the rise of this class occurred more slowly than in other parts of Poland. First they received the status of voivodeship, which also provided the town with a town court that was headed by a *woit* [bailiff or sheriff]. The Miburg (Magdeburg) rights were given to the *starostwo* of Kamenetz even earlier. As stated above, one would think that the Magdeburg rights, which granted administrative independence to Kamenetz, were given at nearly the same time as similar rights were granted to other cities in Lithuania, such as Brisk, Grodno, Luck, Polock, Minsk and others (1496). But the detail that is most interesting is that the right to tavern leases *was now handed over to the burghers*. Undoubtedly the dispossession of the Jews from their taverns is closely connected to the granting of specific rights of voivodeship status to the Christian burghers. It is inconceivable that the Jews would have given up their livelihoods of their own free will. It can be assumed that it was a result of the burghers' battle with the Jews of the city.

The Jewish community continued to exist in Kamenetz and its surroundings throughout all of the 16th century. A 1565 document of the *lustracja* [survey] in the Kamenetz *starostwo* requires the Jews living in the town of Sarawka, in the province of Kamenetz, to pay a tax, as follows: Eliezer (Lazar)—3 zlotys [gold coins]; Naḥum—3 zlotys; Chiczko—3 zlotys; Pesaḥ—2 zlotys; Stopko—3 zlotys; coming to a total of 14 zlotys. We learn from this that there was a Jewish community not only in Kamenetz, but also in the little towns of the province. In Jewish documents the Jews of Kamenetz are first mentioned at the time of the formation of the Lithuanian Council; that is: with the withdrawal of Lithuania from the Council of the Four Lands[41], a specific sum of tax was imposed on the Jews of Lithuania; they were required to pay it to the Lithuanian treasury minister (*podskarbi*) in the year 1623 (5383). This matter is what led to the formation of the Lithuanian Council.

In the Lithuanian Council, 3 communities and their surrounding areas were represented: Brisk, the main community; Grodno; and Pinsk[42]. Kamenetz was included in the Brisk communities. But Kamenetz did not merit the same position of respect attained by its neighbors Wysokie and Pruzhany, where the Council actually held meetings several times.

We read in the Council Records of Lithuania, in the regulations of the Council of the year 5430 (1670) that met in Selc, that they were obligated to pay six hundred Polish zlotys to the nobleman Judicki.

[Page 29]

The historical Charter of Main Rights of the Jews of Kamenetz, from the year 1635 (December 11), was given to them by King Wladyslaw IV[43]. It was ratified by his brother John Casimir[44] (1661), and then ratified again by King Michael Wiśzniowiecki[45] in the year 1670[46]. This privilege provides several concessions: (a) a market day in addition to that of Saturday; (b) the right to erect a synagogue, on the condition that it should not be taller or more beautiful than the Christian churches of the area; (c) permission to build a bath house on city land; (d) permission to set up a cemetery in the city or outside it; (e) the right to freely exercise in trade and labor, and also to purchase estates in the town and to construct houses. The *mieszczanies* [burghers] are warned not to disturb the Jews, neither in their lives nor in their activities to implement the concessions provided to them in the privilege. The privilege threatens that if they conduct any such disturbance, they will be responsible for the consequences and will have to pay fines. Additionally, in the Charter of Rights of Michael Wiśzniowiecki, the size of the fine to be imposed on the *mieszczanies* in case of damage caused to the Jews is also given in detail. Citing the earlier statement by Wladyslaw IV, a paragraph is inserted that had disappeared from the Charter of Rights of John Casimir: "If the *mieszczanies* will dare to disturb the Jews, they will be required to pay a fine of 5000 zlotys, which will be divided between the claimants and the government."

The privilege also refers to the Sovereign Charter of Rights of the Lithuanian Jews. It is conceivable that this is the Sovereign Charter of Rights that was granted to the Jews of Lithuania in 1629, according to which it was permissible to engage in crafts without belonging to the Christian crafts guilds (*cech*)—and this was in addition to their rights in trade and running taverns.

An interesting fact is that in 1633 Wladyslaw IV, who was known for his favorable relationship with the Jews, decreed restrictions on the Jewish craftsmen that permitted them to tailor garments for Jewish customers only, and that allowed them to freely sell only ready–made garments—and similarly to be occupied only in those crafts that Christian craftsmen were not organized in.

It is therefore noteworthy that *the Jewish craftsmen of Kamenetz were among the first in Lithuania* to receive privileges to freely engage in crafts at a time when the Jewish craftsmen in the other towns of Lithuania were restricted in their rights[xxxvi].

The account of the relationship between the Jews and the burghers in Kamenetz reveals an enmity and hatred on the part of the burghers towards the Jews. The Christian burghers of Kamenetz were brazen, and they were engaged in battle with both the nobles and the Jews. Just as in the other cities of Poland and Lithuania, the Jews of Kamenetz won the support of the nobles, as was indicated from the first document from 1525, which transferred the taverns from the Jews of Kamenetz to the burghers. Let us note the harsh language that Wladyslaw IV employed in the privilege from the year 1635: "We hereby inform our *starosta* [administrator] in Kamenetz and also city offices: we declare it to be our will that all that is written in this privilege should be fulfilled, and we command not to violate[xxxvii] the liberties of the Jews that were provided to them by us."

[Page 30]

The absence of any monetary value of a fine imposed on the burghers in the event that the Charter was violated by them—missing from the privilege of John Casimir—is also evidence of the harsh battle of the Christian burghers against the Jews; the insertion of this clause into Wiśniowiecki's Charter of Rights should be understood as evidence that the burghers were not carrying out the privilege. They were undoubtedly fighting with all their might to prevent the privilege from being implemented.

At the end of the 17th century (1693) the Magistrate of Kamenetz presented a protest, signed by 40 town burghers, against the Councilor[xxxviii] Andree Piablewicz, who had given the Jews a lease on the *copowa* (tax on drink) without the knowledge of the other Councilors or of the entire Magistrate.

It should be noted that during the reign of King John Sobieski (1674–1696)[47] there was a central policy supporting the Jews as in previous times. Thus we see that the finance minister Sapieha handed over the lease on the customs tax of Kamenetz to Isaac Noigmowicz and Yeshayahu Jakubowicz (1693). In that period Kamenetz still served as a provincial capital with a customs house at the crossing between the Brisk region and the region of Podlachia. In the same document Kamenetz appears together with the important cities of Brisk, Pinsk and Jalowo[48], to which little towns are attached[xxxix]. One of the *prykomorkis* that belonged to Kamenetz was Palisziszcz[49]. The *mieszczanies* [burghers] were not sitting on their hands, and throughout the entire period of Sobieski's reign they sought out all possible pretexts against the privileges of the Jews of the town. In 1684 the *komornik* [bailiff] proposes to record in the Vilna Records Book a privilege that John III (Sobieski) granted the city of Kamenetz according to the request of its magistrate. In this document the king verifies charters of rights that were granted to the city by Alexander, Zygmunt I, Zygmunt III and others. The document mentions the Kamenetz burghers' legal suit, adjudicated back in 1631, against the *voivoda* [governor] Ostap Tiszkewicz (owner of the villages Klepaczi and Paszeki), when he violated the privileges that had long before been granted to the city. John III confirms the rights of the city management and decrees that the Jews living in the city must subject themselves to the city authorities and its jurisdiction. In his decree, Sobieski writes that the Jews must obey the city courts and carry out all the obligations that the city burghers are subject to.

But we should not be misled by any of this. Reading between the lines of the above documents, we learn about good relations between the Jews and their neighbors. The Jews resided in Kamenetz and its surroundings—and one may assume in the villages, as well. In documents from the year 1733 we read about a Jew from the village of Ḥolobork[xli] and similarly of a Jew who lived on a Church estate[xlii]. From wills appearing in Kamenetz municipal documents we learn of business negotiations between the Christians and the Jews. For the most part the nobles and estate owners in the region freely engaged in business dealings with the Jews, with no restrictions—something the *mieszczanes* found intolerable.

[Page 31]

In the beginning of the 18th century, during the rule of the Saxon king Augustus II[50], we begin to see that the conditions are changing: the significance of the town drastically declines, and near it there was now a *starostwo* in Klepaczi, that belonged to Tiszkewicz, and managed the entire area along the Bialowieze border. Hard times came to the Jews of Poland and Lithuania; blood libels and other fabrications became common occurrences. The political reactionaries, mainly the *Kler* [clergy], spread superstitions among the people, regaling them with terrifying tales of Jewish witches who had made a pact with demons—and thus persecution of the Jews became commonplace. In particular they frightened the people that the Jews had cast an evil eye on the crops. An echo of this period comes to us from Kamenetz, as well. A document dated 17 June 1718 recounts: "In Kamenetz–Litowsk, two Jewish women accused of witchcraft were imprisoned. Chaika Shmulicha hid a pot containing odd substances in the trash. These included: flour, poppy seed, eggs, barley, and other things. Chaika Shmulicha claimed that she did this at the request of another Jewish woman, Yospe. Yospe claimed that she had hidden it in order to cure her daughter of an illness. This Yospe, the wife of a musician[xlii], wept and said that she had been at a *znacherke* [sorceress], who had instructed her to prepare it at night and place it in a hidden place for safekeeping from the evil eye, to protect it from the view of wicked people. The two of them were taken to the fortress under guard." We do not know what became of these two Jewish women, but this libel also follows the pattern of fabrications against the Jews of Brisk and its surroundings when the Jews of Brisk were swamped by blood libels and accused of aid to the Swedes (1703).

The war of the Kamenetz residents against the Jews finally bore fruit: the burghers protested before King Augustus II—opposing the privilege from the year 1679—that "the Jews of Kamenetz are living lives of comfort and convenience[xliii] in the city: they are serving brandy, mead, beer and other strong drinks; they are doing business freely and opening shops in the marketplace within the city itself; they are trading in houses, estates and church property; they are selling textiles and dry goods, both retail and wholesale[xlv] by the length[xliv]; and they are selling ornamental goods of various kinds. They are also distributing their merchandise in the Old City and lowering the rents—and all of this is causing pain and suffering to the Kamenetz burghers."

In his response to these charges, King Augustus II the Saxon ordered that the Jews should be forbidden from building courtyard apartments and from dealing in liquor. Additionally, he ordered the *starostas* [administrators] to limit the Jews' business in shops. This protest of the burghers relied on the privilege that had been granted to the city by Michael Wiśniowiecki, the same king who had ratified the privileges to the Jews of Kamenetz and had even extended them. We saw above that in 1684 the *mieszczanes* [burghers] presented a complaint on the granting of over–extensive rights to the Jews, and they also referred to the privilege that had been granted to the burghers. Although this seems somewhat puzzling, it should not surprise us once we consider how privileges were being granted to the Lithuanian Jews by the Polish kings. The Jews used to obtain these privileges at the cost of much toil and great sums of money. It was for this reason that they were described as "geese that lay golden eggs" in that period, as well—for every approval of a privilege or a new grant involved handing over "golden eggs" to the king, to the members of his chancellery, to the voivodeship officials, and to others.

[Page 32]

And thus the situation we are familiar with was created, that general and particular privileges were granted in contradiction to other privileges that kings were granting to burghers. The main goal of the latter privileges, obtained by the burghers, was to limit, as much as possible, the Jewish economic activity with its competitive nature. Sometimes the two sides reached a compromise agreement; but the burghers could not maintain whatever restrictions had been agreed to, because the realities of life were too powerful for them. And so they would try to get the authorities to intervene; but the Jews would, in return for money, receive new concessions.

From the details of the above protest we learn that Kamenetz was then divided into two parts: the Old City and the New City. It is easily understood that the western part of the city was the Old City; it included Litowski Street and its vicinity. The Jewish part of the city included the center and all the side–streets near the large Beit Midrash [House of Study], which faces the Leshna River—including the Talmud Torah, the bathhouse, etc.

We also learn that the magistrate of Kamenetz was a very powerful and influential institution. Its arrogance was unparalleled. It did not even take orders from the *voivoda* [governor], often turning instead directly to the king. This is the source of the difficult struggle for existence that was the lot of the Kamenetz Jews. We can easily envision how the *mieszczanes* battled against the Jews—and particularly against the Jewish peddlers, who would be going around through the villages and estates, illicitly selling merchandise. And the taverns that served as the source of the Jews' livelihood were like thorns in the burghers' flesh. From the above documents we hear an echo of the accusations by the Polish anti–Semites, of the sort made by well–known anti–Semites such as Stanislaw Macinski and others.

The Jewish population of Kamenetz numbered several hundred. This can be deduced from a document dated 1705: "The *szkolnik* (*gabbai* [synagogue functionary]) Szymon from the community of Brisk presented the budget of the head tax of the communities and of the towns of the Brisk region. In the meeting a sum of 1384 zlotys was levied on Brisk; on Kobryn—315 zlotys; on Pruzhany—485 zlotys; on Kamenetz—250; on Melcz—100; etc." In the beginning of the 18th century, during the period of Jewish central autonomy, the Jews payed Lithuania a total head–tax of 60,000 zlotys. But with the annulment of autonomy in the year 1764, the communities were required to pay 2 zlotys per head for each person older than one year. It can thus be assumed that in that [earlier] period the calculation was based on one zloty per head of age one and over. Since the Jews of Lithuania were then paying a total head–tax of 60,000 zlotys, it is reasonable to estimate the number of Jews in Kamenetz at the beginning of the 18th century as 200 souls over one year old. This was, then, a small community, but by the scale of that period a community of this size was considered important.

The history of the Jews of Kamenetz has not yet been written. As stated above, documents on its internal life—the daily life, the culture, the economic struggle, the rabbis and the religious scholars—are unavailable to the present author. But even the little information that has been presented here has borne witness to a Jewish community fighting for its historical existence.

[Page 33]

Translation of the Royal Privilege—from the year 1661—Granted to the Jews of Kamenetz by Jan Kazimierz, King of Poland[51]

In the year one thousand, six hundred and sixty–one A.D., on the 20th of January—in the court office of the city of Brisk, before Hieron Kazimir Alenski, standard–bearer and under–*starosta*—the Jews Berek and Boruch, heads of the Jews of Kamenetz, personally presented a letter from his gracious royal highness, which is a privilege written on parchment, written in the Lesser Council of the Grand Duchy of Lithuania. It was given to the Jews in Kamenetz and copies made in the records of the city of Brisk. It states the following:

Jan Kazimierz [John Casimir], King of Poland, by the grace of God etc. With this letter we proclaim: In order to increase and enhance the prosperity and welfare of our subjects, we are interested that our cities shall have control not only over population but also over all branches of trade; and for that purpose, marketplaces have been set aside in the cities. Hearkening to the words of our officials of the royal court, who are with us, and who have advised us—and in keeping with the needs of the people of the religious and secular classes, also in keeping with the needs of our Jewish subjects who dwell in Kamenetz—we declare that in addition to the market day taking place in our city Kamenetz every Saturday, there shall be an additional market day every Tuesday, so that henceforth there shall be two market days in our city Kamenetz, and so shall it be in perpetuity, without causing any losses to nearby cities.

To demonstrate our royal grace to those Jews of Kamenetz, following the example of other cities and towns in our kingdom, we permit them to establish a study hall and a Jewish synagogue on the lot belonging to the Jew Beyrech Smuszkowicz, located near the lot of the burgher Chrostowski, or in some other location on someone else's property, with the condition that it may not be greater in either height or beauty than the churches and Russian churches of the city.

We also permit them to establish a bathhouse on a city lot that has already been purchased from a man of great fame, Jakob Kusznier. And they may also establish a cemetery on a lot, either in the city or outside it. And finally we grant them every liberty to open shops and taverns, and to occupy themselves in all crafts, to purchase estates and city lots. And in order that they do not suffer therewith any hardships or losses[xlvi] at the hands of our burghers, we impose a fine following the letter of our brother Wladyslaw IV—whose memory we hold sacred—from the 11th of December, one thousand six hundred thirty–five according to our calendar. And we hereby proclaim and additionally emphasize with all our strength and inform thereof to our citizen the *starosta* [administrator] in Kamenetz from now and henceforth, and we also inform the authorities of the city, and command to safeguard the liberties we have granted to the above Jews in the Charter of Rights to the Jews of the Grand Duchy of Lithuania without any interference whatsoever.

Given in Warsaw, in the *Sejm* elected by the crown, on this day, the 16th of June, year one thousand six hundred sixty–one, in the 13th year of the reign of our Polish and Swedish lord, King Jan Kazimierz; and the king has signed it in his own hand: Jan Kazimierz.

The Secretary of the Grand Duchy of Lithuania brought this letter to be recorded in the books of the city of Brisk.

[Page 34]

Footnotes by original author (Sarid):

i. Chronicles of Volyn by "Polska Starozytna"
ii. Latkowski, "Mendog", pp. 424.
iii. *"Wojewawsza okolo Kamenica I wojewawsze tjeze nedeli okolo Melnic"* [voivodeship near Kamenica and tjeze nedeli voivodeship around Melnic]
iv. Wisołuch —Ateneum Wleńskie 1928–1929. *Rozwój granic powiatu kobryńskiego do połowy XVI wieku* [= Development of the boundaries of the Kobryn district up to the mid–16th century (Polish)].
v. *Ta welikaja Lasna–Akty zdawalnie Wyllukoju Arche Geografyczeskoju*
vi. *"Stolp Kamenecky"*
vii. *"Album Oordi"* [= the white fortified tower (Latin)]
viii. In the Middle Ages the Latin word *ortus* [fortified tower] was pronounced ordus.
ix. "The *puszcza* [woods of] Kamieniecka and the *puszcza* Białowieska"
x. *Camenec ruthenicale.*
xi. *Camenec volynskie.*
xii. *Unia Lubelska* [= Union of Lublin].

xiii. *Droga velikaia gostiniec kotoryi ydet z Kamenca do Novavo Dvora* [= The great road *gostiniec kotryi ydet* from Kamenec to Novavo Dvora].

xiv. *Droga velikaia gostiniec kotoryi ydet z Kamenca do Szereszewa* [= The great road *gostiniec kotoryi ydet* from Kamenec to Szereszew].

xv. Aleksander Alias Witold.

xvi. *Dzierżawa Kameniecka*

xvii. See Wisołuch, op. cit. *Wsłupowaty sia w Kiestutowy hordy w Beresty Kamence* etc.

xviii. See the entry Kamenetz–Litowsk in *Słownik Geograficzny Polski*.

xix. *Weliki kniaz Kazimier korolewicz.* [= Great Prince Casimir the King]

xx. See *Acts of the Archeographic Committee in Vilna*, Volume 6, starting on p. 200.

xxi. *Voitowstwo*

xxii. See G. Barshadski, *Rusko–Evreisky Archiv*, from the document records of the Lithuanian Matrika, Book 12, T 2. And see below in the section on the history of the Jewish settlement of Kamenetz; and see also the above Acts, p. 566.

xxiii. See G. Barshadski, *Rusko–Evreisky Archiv*, from the document records of the Lithuanian Matrika, Book 12, T 2. And see below in the section on the history of the Jewish settlement of Kamenetz; and see also the above Acts, p. 566.

xxiv. *Namestnik panu Kameneckemu*

xxv. Letter of July 20, 1532, and see Wisołuch, op. cit.

xxvi. *Wolny wyrub po ugrowanie I po drowa na budowanie.*

xxvii. *A kgrunt samyi korolewskoj mylozty nalezyt.*

xxviii. *otaia ulica litowskala*

xxix. *Pan Malchaer Kamenskyi ukazał nam dekret ewo korolewskoyi myłosty ostywszy na stronu mieczan kameneckich.*

xxx. *Pan Malchaer Kamenskyi ukazał nam dekret ewo korolewskoyi myłosty ostywszy na stronu mieczan kameneckich.*

xxxi. *Welikyie bezprawie I gwałt (fundament slacheckovo prawa)*

xxxii. *Miasta naszego Kamienca Litowskiego desolationem mając w respekcie od podatku na lat cztery, tak mieszczan jako I Żydow uwalniamy, excepte płacenia myt cel takoż I czopowego* [= The desolation of our city of Kamieniec Litowski, having suspension of the tax for four years, we free the townspeople as well as the Jews, except for paying tolls as well as…]

xxxiii. *Book of Documents of the Lithuanian Matrika*, Book 12, Volume 2.

xxxiv. *Odkup*

xxxv. *Evrei*

xxxvi. See Dr. Esther Notik, "Jewish Craft in Lithuania", YIVO Shriften [writings], etc. Also R. Mahler, "History of the Jews in Poland", pp. 307–8.

xxxvii. *Inviolabiter.*

xxxviii. *Rajca* [= councilman (Polish)].

xxxix. *Prykomorki.*

xl. *Żyd holoborski*

xli. *Żyd co na cerkwnej siedzi*

xlii. *muzykantsza*

xliii. *Pożywajut*

xliv. *Na łokcie*

xlv. *Kustkami.*

xlvi. *Praepeditiones* [= hindrance (Latin)].

[Page 35]

1661 г.

Изъ книги за 1660—1662 годы, стр. 1013—1016.

200. Привилегія короля Яна Казиміра городу Каменцу.

Король Янъ Казиміръ даетъ всѣмъ обывателямъ города Каменца, какъ духовнымъ, такъ и свѣтскимъ, а также и евреямъ, слѣдующую привилегію: кромѣ субботняго торговаго дня, дается имъ еще другой торговый день—вторникъ каждой недѣли; торгъ долженъ производиться безъ ущерба другимъ прилежащимъ мѣстечкамъ. Кромѣ того, евреямъ, какъ этого, такъ и другихъ окрестныхъ городовъ и мѣстечекъ—возволяется воздвигнуть на одномъ изъ плацовъ Каменца синагогу (божницу), но съ тѣмъ, чтобы

она высотою и великолѣпіемъ не превосходила костеловъ и церквей; тутъ же, на которомъ либо изъ городскихъ плацовъ, они могутъ устроить себѣ и кладбище. Въ заключеніе король даетъ обывателямъ право на всякія вольности—въ торговлѣ, корчмахъ, ремеслахъ, въ пріобрѣтеніи плацовъ, земель и домовъ въ городѣ—такъ, какъ это изложено въ листѣ предшественника его, брата, короля Владислава четвертаго.

Лѣта отъ Нароженья Сына Божого тысеча шестьсотъ шестьдесятъ второго, мѣсеца Генваря двадцатого дня.

На врадѣ кгродскомъ Берестейскомъ, передо мною Іеронимомъ Казимеромъ Еленскимъ, хоружимъ и подстаростимъ Берестейскимъ, постановившисе очевисто Беркъ и Берахъ, жиды старшіе Каменецкіе, листъ его королевское милости, привелей на паркгаминѣ писаный, зъ канцелярыи меньшой великого князства Литовскаго вынесеный, жидомъ Каменецкимъ на рѣчь нижей въ немъ выражоную служачій, ку актикованю до книгъ кгродскихъ Берестейскихъ подалъ, который въ словѣ до слова такъ се въ собѣ маетъ: Jan Kazimierz z Bożey łaski król Polski etc. Oznaymuiemy tym listem naszym, komu by o tem wiedzieć należało. Do gruntownego pomnożenia dostatków między poddanemi naszemi, iż wiele na tem należy, aby miasta nasze, nie tylko frequentia ludzi, ale też z obopólnemi handlami obfitowały, a

czego, że targi w miastach postanowione nie poślednią są przynętą, zatym, przychylaiąc się do przyczyny panów rady urzędników dworu naszego, przy boku naszym będących, łaskawie skłoniliśmy się do tego, żeś my, wygadzaiąc potrzebie dla duchownego, iako y świeckiego stanu ludzi, tudzież żydów poddanych naszych, w Kamiencu mieszkaiących, do dnia sobotniego targowego, w mieście naszym Kamienieckim odprawuiącego się,—drugi dzień wtorkowy, w każdy tydzień, przydali y postanowili,—iakoż y ninieyszym listem naszym przydaiemy y postanowiamy taki: iż odtąd dwa dni targowe w każdy tydzień w mieście naszym Kamiencu odprawować się, wiecznemi czasy, sposobem zwyczaynym maią, iednak bez przeszkody innych miast naszych przyległych. Nad to, tymże żydom Kamienieckim, chcąc przykładem inszych miast y miasteczek naszych łaskę naszą królewską oświadczyć, pozwalamy im szkołę, bożnicę żydowską, na placu żyda Beyrcha Szmerzkowicz, po

[Page 36]

dle placu urodzonego Chrostowskiego leżącym, lubo gdzie indzie u kogokolwiek nabywszy, wystawić,—tak iednak, aby wyniosłością y apparentią do kościołów y cerkwi nie równała się. Przy tym pozwalamy im łaznię na placu mieyskim od sławetnego Jakowa Kusznierza iuż nabytym. zbudować y oney zażywać; także kopiszcze. na placu swym. lubo w mieście. lubo za miastem nabytym, mieć: na ostatek, daiemy im moc wszelakich wolności: w handlach, szynkach, w rzemiosłach. w nabywaniu placów, gruntów y domów mieskich zażywać. W czym, aby żadney od mieszczan naszych Kamienieckich nie ponosili trudności. ani praepediciey, winę w liście świętey pamięci króla iego mości Władysława czwartego, pana brata naszego. de data w Warszawie. dnia iedenastego miesiąca Decembra, roku Panskiego tysiąc sześćset trzydziestego piątego. reassumimus et interponimus vigore praesentium. Co do wiadomości urodzonemu staroście naszemu Kamienieckiemu teraznieysze-

mu, y napotym będącym. tudzież urzędowi mieyskiemu tamecznemu przywodząc, chcemy mieć y rozkazuiemy. abyście pomienionych żydów Kamienieckich przy wolnościach im ad praesens nadanych y w przywileiu generalnym żydom w. x. Lit-go wyrażonych inviolabiliter zachowali, dla łaski naszey. Na co dla lepszey wiary ręką się naszą podpisawszy, pieczęć w. x. Lit-go przycisnąć roskazaliśmy. Dan w Warszawie. na seymie walnym coronnym. dnia szesnastego, miesiąca luniy. roku Panskiego tysiąc sześćset sześćdziesiąt pierszego. panowania naszego Polskiego y Szwedzkiego—trzynastego roku. У того листу его королевской милости привилею подпис руки его королевской милости и писарское тыми словы: 'Jan Kazimierz Król: Andrzey Kazimierz Zawisza. pisarz w. x. Lit-go. Которыи же тоть иисть его королевской милости. ку актикованю поданый, есть до книгъ кгродскихъ Берестейскихъ уписанъ.

[Page 37]

1670 г.

Изъ книги за 1671 — 1672 годы, стр. 2180.

499. Подтвердительная привилегія короля Михаила, данная Каменец-гимъ жидамъ.

Король Михаилъ подтверждаетъ привилегію своего предшественника Яна Казиміра, данную Каменецкимъ жидамъ на слѣдующія льготы: 1) на два торговыхъ дня въ теченіи каждой недѣли; 2) на постройку синагоги (божницы), но только съ условіемъ, чтобы она величиной своей и великолѣпіемъ не превосходила костеловъ и церквей; 3) на пріобрѣтеніе плаца для кладбища и бани; 4) на свободное занятіе торговлею и ремеслами и 5) на право пріобрѣтенія плацовъ и земель. Подлинная привилегія отъ 16-го Іюня 1661 года; подтвердительная — отъ 20 Апрѣля 1670 года.

Лѣта отъ Нароженья Сына Божого тысеча шестьсотъ семьдесятого, мѣсеца Мая десятого дня.

На врадѣ кгродскомъ Берестейскомъ, передо мною Еримъ Станиславомъ Умястовскимъ—стольникомъ Венденскимъ, подстаростимъ Берестейскимъ, постановившисе очевисто жидъ мѣста его королевское милости Каменца, листъ свой конфирмаційный, отъ его королевское милости даный жидомъ Каменецкимъ, на речь въ немъ ниже менуную, ку актикованью до книгъ кгродскихъ Берестейскихъ подалъ, въ тые слова писаный:

Michał. z Bożey łaski król polski etc. Oznaymuiemy tym listem przywileiem naszym, komu by o tem wiedzieć należało. Pokładany był przed nami przywiley pergaminowy. ręką naiaśnieyszego króla imści Jana Kazimierza. antecessora naszego podpisany, y pieczęcią mnieyszą w. x. Lit. zapieczętowany, cały. zupełny y żadney wątpliwości w sobie nie maiący, żydom Kamienieckim służący, y doniesiona nam iest prożba, abyśmy takowy przywiley mocą y powagą naszą królewską in omnibus suis intro contentis zmocnili y stwierdzili. który od słowa do słowa tak się w sobie ma:

Jan Kazimierz. z Bożey łaski król polski etc. Oznaymuiemy tym listem naszym. komu by o tem wiedzieć należało. Do gruntownego pomnożenia dostatków między poddanemi naszemi. iż wiele na tym należy, aby miasta nasze nie tylko frequentią ludzi, ale też zobopólnemi handlami obfitowały; do czego że targi w miastach postanowione nie poślednią są przynętą: zatem przychylaiąc się do przyczyny panów rad y urzędników dworu naszego, przy boku naszym będących. łaskawie skłoniliśmy się do tego, żeśmy wygadzaiąc potrzebie tak duchownego, iako y świeckiego stanu ludzi.—tudzież żydów poddanych naszych. w Kamieńcu mieszkaiących, do dnia subotniego targowego w mieście naszym Kamienieckim odprawuiącego się. drugi dzień wtorkowy w każdy tydzień przydali y postanowili. Jakoż y ninieyszym listem naszym przydaiemy y postanawiamy tak, iż odtąd dwa dni targowe w każdy tydzień w mieście naszym Kamieńcu odprawować się wiecznemi czasy sposobem zwyczaynym maią, iednak bez przeszkody innych miast na-

[Page 38]

szych przyległych. Nadto tymże żydom Kamienieckim, chcąc przykładem innych miast y miasteczek naszych, łaskę naszą królewską oświadczyć, pozwalamy im szkołę, bożnicę żydowską na placu żyda Beyrecha Smuszkowicza, podle placu urodzonego Chrostowskiego leżącym, lubo gdzie indziey, u kogokolwiek nabywszy, wystawić, tak iednak, aby wyniosłością y apparencią do kościołów y cerkwi nie równała się. Przytem pozwalamy im łaźnie na placu mieyskim, od sławetnego Jakóba Kusznierza iuż nabytym, zbudować y oney zażywać: także kopiszcze na placu swym, lubo w mieście, lubo za miastem nabytym, mieć. Naostatek daiemy im moc wszelakich wolności w handlach, szynkach, w rzemiosłach, w nabywaniu placów, gruntów y domów mieyskich zażywać, w czem aby żadney od mieszczan naszych Kamienieckich nie ponosili trudności, ani praepediciey, winę w liście świętey pamięci króla iego mości Władysława czwartego, pana brata naszego, de data w Warszawie, dnia iedenastego miesiąca Decembra, roku Pańskiego tysiąc sześćset trzydziestego piątego, reassumimus et interponimus vigore praesentium. Co do wiadomości urodzonemu staroście naszemu Kamienieckiemu teraźnieyszemu y napotym będącym, tudzież urzędowi mieyskiemu tamecznemu przywodząc, chcemy mieć y rozkazuiemy, abyście pomienionych żydów Kamienieckich przy wolnościach, im ad praesens nadanych, y w przywileiu generalnym żydom, w. x. Lit. wyrażonych, inviolabiter zachowali, dla łaski naszey. Na co dla lepszey wiary, ręką się naszą podpisawszy, pieczęć w.

x. Lit. przycisnąć rozkazaliśmy. Dan w Warszawie, na seymie walnym koronnym, dnia szesnastego miesiąca Junii, roku Pańskiego tysiąc sześćset sześćdziesiąt pierwszego, panowania naszego polskiego y szwedzkiego trzynastego roku. Jan Kazimierz król: Andrzey Kazimierz Zawisza — pisarz w. x. Lit. Pieczęć zawiesista mnieysza w. x. Lit.

My tedy Michał król, do prożby takowey, iako słuszney, łaskawie się skłoniwszy, zwysz inserowany przywiley we wszytkich onego punktach, clausulach y obowiązkach mocą y powagą naszą królewską zmacniamy, stwierdzamy y in casu contraventionis albo praepeditionis przez mieszczan, żydom Kamienieckim uczynioney, winę y zarękę pięciu tysięcy złotych polskich, per medium na nas y na delatora w liście króla iego mości Władysława czwartego założone y warowane, odnawiamy y reassumuiemy. Na co dla lepszey wiary, ręką się naszą podpisawszy, pieczęć w. x. Lit. przycisnąć rozkazaliśmy. Dan w Warszawie, dnia dwudziestego miesiąca Kwietnia, roku Pańskiego tysiąc sześćset siedmdziesiątego, panowania naszego pierwszego roku.

У того листу его королевское милости конфирмаційнаго, при печати завѣсистой великаго княжства Литовскаго, подпись рукъ тыми словы: Михаł король: Валеріанъ Станиславъ Юдыцкі, архидіакон Вилеński — писарь w. x. Lit. Который же тотъ листъ конфирмаційный, черезъ жидовъ Каменецкихъ до актъ гроду Берестейскаго поданый, есть до книгъ игродскихъ Берестейскихъ прыняятъ и уписанъ.

Translator's Footnotes:

1.   From *Kamenetz–Litovsk, Zastavije and Colonies Memorial Book*, edited by S. Eisenstadt and M. Galbert, published by the Israel and America Committee of Kamenetz Litovsk and Zastavya, (Orly, Tel Aviv, Israel, 1970), pp. 20–38. The present translation of the article written in Hebrew incorporates elements of the Yiddish version of this article, appearing on pp. 357–375 of this volume. (The English versions appearing on pp. 12–25 and pp. 26–28 of the original English section of this volume, which skip over some details, have been

consulted as well.) Note that Sarid's original footnote numbers have been placed in braces (i.e. "curly brackets" { }). His footnote citations are provided at the end of the text of this translation.

2. Brest–Litowsk (called Brisk by the Jews) is located ~40km south of Kamenetz.

3. See the following link, retrieved October 2020: https://en.wikipedia.org/wiki/Daniel_of_Galicia

4. Mendog, also known as Mindaugas, king of Lithuania (c. 1203–1263). See the following link, retrieved October 2020: https://en.wikipedia.org/wiki/Mindaugas

5. Mielnik, Poland lies 60km west of Kamenetz–Litowsk. Podlachia is the name of the province it is in.

6. Janusz I (c. 1350–1429). See the following link (retrieved October 2020): https://www.wikiwand.com/en/Janusz_I_of_Warsaw

7. Drohiczyn, Poland, lies on the Bug River, about 90km west of Kamenetz.

8. Suraż, Poland, is located about 90km northwest of Kamenetz.

9. Kamin Kashyrskyi, Ukraine, in the Volyn Oblast, is located about 130km southeast of Kamenetz.

10. Volyn or Volin, also written Volhynia, is an area currently (2020) in northwest Ukraine, bordering on both Poland and Belarus. See the following link (retrieved October 2020): https://en.wikipedia.org/wiki/Volhynia

11. Volodymyr–Volynskyi, Ukraine, is located ~200km south of Kamenetz.

12. See the following link (retrieved November 2020): https://en.wikipedia.org/wiki/Boyar

13. For details, see the following link, retrieved October 2020: https://en.wikipedia.org/wiki/Third_Mongol_invasion_of_Poland

14. The *sazhen* is an old Russian unit of measurement, equivalent to a fathom (7 feet). See the following link (retrieved October 2020): https://en.wikipedia.org/wiki/Obsolete_Russian_units_of_measurement

15. *Bielo* = white in Slavic languages

16. This union created the Polish–Lithuanian Commonwealth, to be ruled by a single elected monarch who would carry out the duties of both King of Poland and Grand Duke of Lithuania. The country was to be governed by a common senate and parliament (*Sejm*). See the following link (retrieved October 2020): https://en.wikipedia.org/wiki/Union_of_Lublin

17. Lvov = Lviv, Ukraine, lies 600km south of Vilna (Vilnius, Lithuania).

18. Narew, Poland lies 150km northwest of Kamenetz

19. Novyi Dvor, Belarus, lies ~70km northeast of Kamenetz.

20. Pruzhany, Belarus, is located ~50km northeast of Kamenetz.

21. Szereszew = Šarašova, Belarus, located ~35km northeast of Kamenetz

22. Luboml', Ukraine is located ~100km south of Brest, Belarus; Lviv, Ukraine is located ~180km south of Luboml'.

23. A *starostwo* was an administrative unit headed by an official call a starosta. See the following link (retrieved November 2020): https://en.wikipedia.org/wiki/Starostwo

24. Witold (c. 1350–1430) was also known as Vytautas. See the following link (retrieved October 2020): https://en.wikipedia.org/wiki/Vytautas

25. Gediminas (c. 1275–1341). See the following link, retrieved October 2020: https://en.wikipedia.org/wiki/Gediminas

26. Also known as Kinstut or Kęstutis (c. 1297–1382). See the following link (retrieved November 2020): https://en.wikipedia.org/wiki/K%C4%99stutis

27. Grodno, Belarus, is located ~160km north of Kamenetz.

28. The split lasted from 1378 to 1417. See the following link (retrieved October 2020): https://en.wikipedia.org/wiki/Western_Schism

29. Casimir IV Jagiellon (1427–1492). See the following link (retrieved October 2020): https://en.wikipedia.org/wiki/Casimir_IV_Jagiellon#Grand_Duke_of_Lithuania

30. Podlachia (or Podlasie) is a historical region in the eastern part of Poland, along the middle stretch of the Bug River, between Masovia in the west, Polesia and Volhynia in the east, the Narew River in the north and the Chelm Land in the south. See the following link, with maps (retrieved October 2020): https://en.wikipedia.org/wiki/Podlachia

31. A voivodeship is equivalent to a province, headed by a voivode (governor). See the following link, retrieved November 2020: https://en.wikipedia.org/wiki/Voivodeships_of_Poland

32. Magdeburg rights were a set of town privileges primarily targeted at regulating trade. See the following link (retrieved October 2020): https://en.wikipedia.org/wiki/Magdeburg_rights

33. Zymunt or Sigismund I (1467–1548), King of Poland and Grand Duke of Lithuania 1506–1548. He was the son of Casimir IV. See the following link (retrieved October 2020): https://en.wikipedia.org/wiki/Sigismund_I_the_Old

34. See the following link (retrieved October 2020): https://en.wikipedia.org/wiki/Radziwi%C5%82%C5%82_family

35. Shastakova, Belarus, lies 18km west of Kamenetz. Wysokie = Vysokaye, Belarus, is located 12km west of Shastakova and ~30km west of Kamenetz

36. Žabinka is located ~20km southeast of Kamenetz.

37. See the following link (retrieved October 2020): https://en.wikipedia.org/wiki/Starosta

38. This appears to be Michal Wielhorski (c. 1730–1794). See the following link (retrieved November 2020): https://en.wikipedia.org/wiki/Micha%C5%82_Wielhorski_(elder)

39. 1772–1795. See the following link (retrieved November 2020): https://en.wikipedia.org/wiki/Partitions_of_Poland

40. Written by Simon Dubnow (1860–1941) in 1925. See the following link (retrieved October 2020): https://en.wikipedia.org/wiki/Simon_Dubnow#Published_titles

41. See the following link (retrieved October 2020) for details: https://en.wikipedia.org/wiki/Council_of_Four_Lands

42. Pinsk, Belarus is located ~180km east of Kamenetz.

43. Wladyslaw IV Vasa (1595–1648) ruled over Poland and Lithuania from 1632 until his death. See the following link (retrieved October 2020): https://en.wikipedia.org/wiki/W%C5%82adys%C5%82aw_IV_Vasa

44. John II Casimir Vasa (1609–1672) ruled over Poland and Lithuania from 1648 until he abdicated in 1668. In Polish he is called "Jan Kazimierz". See the following link (retrieved October 2020): https://en.wikipedia.org/wiki/John_II_Casimir_Vasa

45. Michael I Wiśniowiecki (1640–1673), ruled over Poland and Lithuania from 1669 until his death in 1673. See the following link (retrieved October 2020): https://en.wikipedia.org/wiki/Micha%C5%82_Korybut_Wi%C5%9Bniowiecki

46.　Yiddish version reads 1670; Hebrew version reads 1679, apparently a misprint, since Michael died in 1673 (see previous footnote). The original Russian–Polish document, shown on p. 37, is indeed dated 1670.

47.　John III Sobieski (1629–1696), who ruled over Poland and Lithuania. See the following link (retrieved October 2020): https://en.wikipedia.org/wiki/John_III_Sobieski

48.　Jalowo = Yalovo, Belarus, is located ~40km northeast of Kamenetz.

49.　Hebrew version: Palisziszcz, probably Pelishche, Belarus, located ~12km southeast of Kamenetz. Yiddish version: Milaicicz.

50.　Augustus (August) II, "Augustus the Strong" (1670–1733), who ruled over Poland and Lithuania 1697–1706 and 1709–1733. See the following link (retrieved October 2020): https://en.wikipedia.org/wiki/Augustus_II_the_Strong

51.　See duplicate of originals of this document and the charter of 1670 (in Russian and Polish) on pp. 35–38.

[Page 47]

Torah Institutions in Kamenets-Litowsk

Rabbi Yehoshua Hakohen Blumenthal z.tz.l.[1],[2]

by David Hakohen Burstein[3]

Translated by Allen Flusberg

I will write a bit about the history of our father, Rabbi Yehoshua Hakohen Blumenthal, may the memory of the righteous in the world to come be a blessing. He was born in the city of Yugustov[4] to his father, our teacher and rabbi Reuben z.l.[5] From his early years he was a great prodigy, and he studied Torah in the yeshiva of the great Chatam Sofer[6], z.tz.l. Our father was first appointed as rabbi of the town of Lazdei[7] in the province of Suvalk[8], and afterwards he became rabbi of the district city Mariampoli[9]. My father became engaged in a serious dispute with the freethinkers [non-observant Jews] who were living there. At that point he already had one child, a gifted son. Because of the great anguish the dispute inflicted on him, this gifted son, with whom my father was very close, died. Right after the seven days of mourning for his son had ended, on the very next morning, my father suddenly loaded his books and other belongings onto a wagon and returned to his town, Lazdei.

When the people of Lazdei heard that their saintly, prodigious rabbi, Yehoshua Hakohen, was on his way back, all of them—young and old, men, women and children—came out a great distance[10] from the city to joyfully greet him. He stayed there several years in peace and quiet. Then declaring that he wished to live in Lithuania, where the people were more God-fearing, he moved to Bialystok[11] and founded a high-school yeshiva[12] there. When he would give his lectures, there was not enough room in the *Beit Midrash* for everyone who had come to hear him speak; people would be standing outside around all the windows of the *Beit Midrash* to hear his amazing *pilpul*[13]. At that time he was famous everywhere, referred to as Rabbi Yehoshua'le the Sharp.

Our father was seeking to live a tranquil life, but then the incident of the eighteen geese suddenly crept up on him. At that time there used to be women in Bialystok who sold slaughtered geese. Once a very poor woman salted[14] the meat from eighteen such slaughtered geese together. Afterwards a nail was found in the head of one of the geese in a manner that made that goose non-kosher. By then the geese had all been mixed up together, and it was no longer possible to distinguish from their heads which of them was the non-kosher one. However they did find a nail puncture in the side of one of the geese, opposite its head. This woman went to inquire about the [kosher] status of the geese. She came to our father and asked him for a ruling, but she neglected to inform him that she had already asked [a different rabbi] and the goose[15] had been ruled not kosher. Our father declared all the geese to be kosher with the exception of the one that had the nail puncture in its side. Then the elderly ritual judge [who had made the original ruling] started a terrible dispute with our father; but our father stated that had he known that this question had been asked of someone else beforehand who had ruled it non-kosher he would not have responded [to the woman] at all. The next morning all my father's students dispersed to all the *Batei Midrash*[16] of the town, each of them carrying a slice of fried meat taken from the other seventeen geese, and they ate them publicly in front of everyone who had attended the morning services there. Then the controversy really flared up and turned into a major storm that lasted a long time, until the responsum of the great scholar of that generation, Rabbi Shmuel Avigdor[17] z.tz.l of Karlin, came back, stating that he agreed with everything my father had said. Our father left Bialystok and went to Yanova[18], and from there to Kamenetz in the year 5627[19].

[Page 48]

All his life he studied and taught; he would wake up every night at 1 AM and spend the time studying until it was time for the Morning Prayers. On the night of the holy Sabbath [Friday night], when he would get up at midnight to study, our saintly mother Sarah daughter of Gavriel would also have to get up with him; she would sit at the table, watching over him to make sure he did not move the candle[20].

He was a man of incomparably excellent character: he never lost his temper and he loved his fellow man like himself. Although he was impoverished during all of his last years, money did not matter to him at all. When someone poor came to his door, he would take all the money he found in his own pocket and give it to this poor person. His salary in Kamenetz-Litovsk was one kopek[21] per week from each household, although not everyone would pay.

He went up to Heaven on the 11th of Shvat, 5640[22]. Before his death he said to my saintly mother, "Are you aware that in another four days my little Avraham'le[23] will be bar mitzvah?" He was 65 years old when he died.

Footnotes:

1. From *Kamenetz-Litovsk, Zastavije and Colonies Memorial Book*, edited by S. Eisenstadt and M. Galbert, published by the Israel and America Committee of Kamenetz Litovsk and Zastavya, (Orly, Tel Aviv, Israel, 1970), pp. 47-48.

2. z.tz.l. = may the memory of the righteous be a blessing

3. Note in original: "Excerpted from the book by Rabbi Reuven Burstein". (The full name of the author, who perished in the Holocaust, was Reuven David Hakohen Burstein.) The book referred to is *Divrei Radach* (=Words of Radach, acronym for Rabbi David Hakohen), Warsaw, 1927. An electronic copy of the book can be viewed in the following link (retrieved October 2018): https://www.otzar.org/wotzar/Book.aspx?100829&.

4. Augustów, Poland, located 200km north of Kamenetz

5. z.l. = of blessed memory

6. "Chatam Sofer" was the pen name of Rabbi Moshe Sofer (Schreiber) (1762-1839). The original yeshiva he founded was located in Pressburg (Bratislava, Slovakia), 800km southwest of Kamenetz. See the following link, retrieved October 2018: https://en.wikipedia.org/wiki/Moses_Sofer#Pressburg_(Bratislava)

7. Lazdei = Lazdijai, Lithuania, located 250 km north of Kamenetz

8. Suwalki, now a region in Poland

9. There are 3 cities with this name. Mariampol, Poland is 70km southwest of Kamenetz; Marijampole, Lithuania, lies 300km north of Kamenetz, not far from Lazdei; and Mariampol, Belarus is 600 km northeast of Kamenetz.

10. Hebrew: "several parasangs", a parasang being about 4 km

11. The city of Bialystok, now in Poland, lies 100km northwest of Kamenetz

12. Hebrew: *yeshiva gedolah*, a religious studies school for teen-aged boys

13. *Pilpul* = an approach based on keen-edged analysis to reconcile apparent contradictions in the Talmudic literature. See the following link (retrieved October 2018): https://en.wikipedia.org/wiki/Pilpul

14. A technique of salting to drain the blood is a necessary condition for the meat to be considered kosher.

15. According to the more detailed version in *Words of Radach* that this essay is excerpted from (see Footnote 3), the first rabbi consulted had ruled that all the geese were to be considered non-kosher.

16. *Batei Midrash* (plural of *Beit Midrash*) = study halls, where synagogue services were held

17. Rabbi Shmuel Avigdor Rabinowich (1806-1866) was a well-respected expert in Jewish law who served as rabbi of the city of Karlin from about 1855 until his death. See the following link (in Hebrew), retrieved October 2018: https://he.wikipedia.org/wiki/%D7%A9%D7%9E%D7%95%D7%90%D7%9C_%D7%90%D7%91%D7%99%D7%92%D7%93%D7%95%D7%A8_%D7%AA%D7%95%D7%A1%D7%A4%D7%90%D7%94

18. Yanova = Janów Sokolski, Poland is located ~40km north of Bialystok, and 150km north of Kamenetz.

19. The Jewish year 5627 corresponded to 1866-1867.

20. Moving the candle being forbidden on the Sabbath. But since he was concentrating on his studies by candlelight, he might have inadvertently forgotten that it was the Sabbath.

21. kopek = Russian penny, a hundredth of a ruble. From the silver content of the ruble (~18 grams) and the US dollar (24 grams) in ~1880, it follows that a kopek was equivalent to 3/4 of a US cent in 1880. Because of inflation, an 1880 kopek would have the buying power of US$0.18 in 2018. See the following links, retrieved October 2018: https://en.wikipedia.org/wiki/Ruble#Imperial_ruble_(14th_century_%E2%80%93_1917; http://www.coinflation.com/coins/1878-1921-Silver-Morgan-Dollar-Value.html; http://www.in2013dollars.com/1880-dollars-in-2018?amount=1

22. 11 Shvat 5640 = January 24, 1880 (Gregorian calendar)

23. The reference is to his son Avraham Aharon Burstein, whose biography appears on pp. 55-57 of this volume.

[Page 49]

My Grandfather,
Rabbi Moshe Yitzhak of Kamenetz-Litowsk[1],[2]

by Moshe Rabinowitz

Translated by Allen Flusberg

My grandfather, the great scholar Rabbi Moshe Yitzhak Rabinowitz, z.tz.l.[3], was born in Vilna [Vilnius] in the year 5604 (1833)[sic][4], to his father, the righteous great scholar Rabbi Naphtali Hertz, a man of good character and great wisdom; and to his mother, the righteous *Rabbanit* [Rabbi's wife] Chena the daughter of the famous rabbi, Luminary of the Diaspora, our great teacher, Rabbi Yehuda Abelson of Neustadt[5], who wrote the following in his well-known book *Zichron Yehuda*: "My son-in-law, the great learned Rabbi Naphtali Hertz, perfect in all virtues, deserves honorable mention[6]."

My grandfather was a great Torah scholar. Even in his youth he was famous for having amazing talent, and he was one of the Torah titans. The Prodigy of Bielsk said of him in his book *Divrei Emet*: "For nearly sixty years I was one of those who often visited the home of Rabbi Naphtali Hertz and his sons, among them the great scholar Rabbi Moshe Yitzhak; in Vilna they were known as great prodigies." And Rabbi David Tebele Ephrati, in his book *Toldot Anshei Shem* [Chronicles of the Famous Personages] in the year 5635[7] refers to him as "my relative, the great, prodigious Rabbi Moshe Yitzhak."

For nearly thirty years he officiated as the Rabbi of Kamenetz-Litowsk, a small town that was located far away from any main city. Yet there were learned laymen in Kamenetz, and its rabbinate was imposing and famous.

In the 19th-century towns of Lithuania the life of a rabbi was hard. The Jews of the towns did not provide them with material luxuries. Their lives were difficult and filled with suffering, and sometimes they did not even have enough to eat. Rabbis of that era led miserable lives, yet they accepted it all with love. My grandfather was one of them. He was a symbol of love for the Jewish people; he was well-liked and well-accepted for his good nature and his simplicity. He was the spiritual shepherd of his flock.

He was well-versed in the entire Talmud, having gone through it in sequence many times. And with respect to his religious-court rulings the Torah-world rabbis would take his judgments seriously. There was a story told of a litigant who lodged a complaint with the greatest rabbi of the generation, Rabbi Chaim Brisker[8], over a religious-court ruling my grandfather had made. The great Rabbi of Brisk responded as follows: "I rely on the Kamenetz Rabbi, for he is a great Torah scholar."

His home was open to everyone, and prestigious Torah scholars would often visit him. Even rivals were received with open arms. He dedicated himself completely to study and worship[9], while paying attention throughout to the needs of his townspeople.

During the winter of the year 5668[10] my grandfather passed away in Kamenetz, where he was laid to rest. His brothers were: Rabbi David Tevel Katzenelboigen[11], Chief Rabbi of St. Petersburg, and Rabbi Tzvi Yehuda Elboim, Chief Rabbi of Chicago, z.tz.l.

Footnotes:

1. From *Kamenetz-Litovsk, Zastavije and Colonies Memorial Book*, edited by S. Eisenstadt and M. Galbert, published by the Israel and America Committee of Kamenetz Litovsk and Zastavya, (Orly, Tel Aviv, Israel, 1970), p. 49.
2. For complementary essay by the same author (originally in Yiddish) see pp. 405-407 of this volume.
3. z.tz.l. = *zecher tzadik livracha* = may the memory of the righteous be a blessing
4. 5604 = secular years 1843-44
5. Neustadt-Schirwindt (Wladyslavow). See Jewish Encyclopedia, *Neustadt-Schirwindt (Wladyslavow)*, at the following link (retrieved January 2020): http://www.jewishencyclopedia.com/articles/11481-neustadt-schirwindt-wladyslavow. It is currently called Kudirkos Naumiestis, Lithuania, located about 200km west of Vilnius and 300km north of Kamenetz. See the following link (retrieved January 2020): https://en.wikipedia.org/wiki/Kudirkos_Naumiestis
6. Hebrew *yizacher latov* = should be remembered/mentioned for good things
7. 5635 = secular years 1875 (publication year of this book)
8. Chaim Brisker = Rabbi Chaim Soloveitchik (1853-1918) of Brest-Litovsk [called "Brisk" by the Jews], located 40km south of Kamenetz. For a short biography, see the following link (retrieved October 2018): https://en.wikipedia.org/wiki/Chaim_Soloveitchik
9. Hebrew: *yoshev al haTorah v'al haAvoda*
10. Winter of 5668 = secular year 1907-1908
11. David Tevel (1850-1930) was St. Petersburg Rabbi from 1908 to 1930. See the following link (retrieved January 2020): https://www.jewishvirtuallibrary.org/katzenellenbogen-david-tevel

[Page 50]

Rabbi Reuven David Hakohen Burstein,
May God Avenge His Blood[1]

by Rabbi Yehuda Gershuni

Translated by Allen Flusberg

A day of turmoil and confusion for the Jews of Kamenetz–Litovsk, a day of rage and fury, a day on which the firmament above wept bitterly, mountains and hills wailed, and the earth trembled and quaked: this was the bitter, harsh day on which [human] cruelty exceeded that of wild beasts.

My heart goes out to you, Kamenetz, for your rabbis and your enlightened scholars, for your merchants and laborers, for all the members of your community, whose souls were all as pure as that of Heaven. They may have gotten into disagreements, but they esteemed one another: for when trouble came upon any of the town residents, the entire community would gather in the synagogue, utilizing their powerful weapon of interrupting the Torah reading on the Sabbath[2]. They would not leave the synagogue until the matter was properly settled and requisite aid was given.

Among the pearls of the Kamenetz community there stood out the remarkable personage of the community rabbi of Kamenetz–Litovsk, the prodigious and saintly sage, Rabbi Reuven David Hakohen Burstein, may God avenge his blood. He stood head and shoulders above everyone; his soul had been fashioned beneath the Throne of Glory. He was pure of mind and sharp–witted, with a gentle soul and good lineage.

Rabbi Burstein was descended from distinguished families of the people of Israel. His most prodigious father, the saintly Rabbi Yehoshua Hakohen Blumenthal, of blessed memory, was the rabbi of the city of Lazdei[3] and the city of Mariampol[4]. He was also the head of the yeshiva and head of the court in Bialystok[5]; and at the end of his life he served as rabbi of Kamenetz–Litovsk.

The brother of Rabbi Burstein was Rabbi Aharon Burstein, the prodigy of his generation, someone with a profound comprehension comparable to that of the *Rishonim*[6]. He was referred to as the prodigy of Tavrik[7]. When he was 18 years old he became the head of the Slabodka Yeshiva[8]. During the First World War, when Rabbi Aharon Burstein was deported to Russia, the philanthropist Shoshana Persitz[9] of Moscow used her own money to found a yeshiva in the city of Bogorodsk[10], on the condition that Rabbi Aharon Burstein should deliver his Talmud lectures there in Hebrew. And at the end of his life he was appointed head of the Rav Kook Yeshiva in Merkaz Harav[11] in Jerusalem. To this very day the people of Jerusalem speak of his wondrous and miraculous genius, his proficiency and his conduct.

[Page 51]

Aside from greatness in Talmud, Rabbi Reuven David Hakoken Burstein was extremely proficient in the Biblical text, in grammar. He was also a master of *Aggadah*[12]: just as he was proficient in the plain meaning of the Biblical text he was also sharp in Biblical exegesis. While I was studying at the Kamenetz Yeshiva I would occasionally visit Rabbi Burstein. Once I asked him the following: it is a well–known fact that in the yeshivas no one studies *Nach*[13], only *Gemara, Rishonim* and *Poskim*[14]. And so when had he found the time to learn so much *Nach*, as well as the *Rishonim*'s commentaries on them? And Rabbi Burstein answered that during the holiday seasons, when all the yeshiva students were busying themselves in the joy of the holiday as was customary in the yeshivas, he would sit and go over *Nach* with the commentaries of the *Rishonim*. Rabbi Burstein published a wonderful two–volume work on *Halacha*[15] and exegesis; it was called *Divrei Radakh*[16]. His work demonstrates the clarity of his penetrating understanding of all difficult matters, in all the subjects of the Torah.

He inherited the power of innovation from his teachers, who were world luminaries: the great prodigy Rabbi Yitzhak Yaakov Rabinowitz of Ponevezh[17] and Rabbi Chaim Halevi Soloveitchik[18]. From the former he inherited his sharpness, and from the latter the capability of analysis. His good qualities were those of pure–minded Torah scholars. He valued and was fond of all people, every human being: he accepted everyone with welcoming open arms and with kindness. Among all his spiritual qualities there stood out grace, beauty and good nature. He was glad to do good to all and to help individuals. He spoke gracefully and mildly, weighing his words with forethought. I was always surprised by the amount of patience he displayed. Once a visitor asked him whether his patience was an innate familial trait that he had inherited—or was it an ability attained by self–imposed training, through the power of Torah knowledge and introspection. For this had been the practice of the greatest rabbinical scholars throughout the generations, to refine their deeds and purify their souls, in order to be esteemed and thereby magnify respect for God and his Torah. This very idea was taught by our sages, who wrote (Yoma 86): "Of a rabbinical scholar who acts good–naturedly and modestly, people say 'Happy is his father who taught him Torah, happy is his teacher who taught him Torah, and woe to those who have not studied Torah; see how pleasant the manners and proper the deeds are of someone who has learned Torah.' And of such a person it is said, 'Israel, it is through you that I am exalted' (Isaiah 49)."

To this question Rabbi Burstein replied as follows: "The quality of patience that I practice has no particular advantage, but the 'essence of the law' [basic, obligatory law] requires it. For the sages of the Talmud defined the requisite measure of patience of those who head the community, saying, 'To what extent is the community leader supposed to carry the burden of the community? In the way the nursing mother carries her infant (Sanhedrin 7a)'[19]". And he explained this metaphor in the name of the prodigious Netziv[20], as follows: When the mother is carrying her nursing baby in her arms, and it happens that he has a bowel movement, as infants do, and he dirties her and her clothing, making him repugnant—what does the mother then do? Does she angrily toss her baby down because of his repugnant deed? God forbid, the very opposite: she good–willingly and gently cleans him, dressing him in fresh clothing. And afterwards she takes the child into her arms and nurses him, and also willingly and lovingly kisses him, speaking to him tenderly and pleasantly. So the relationship between them has not been harmed; in fact the stench has actually strengthened the love.

This allegory was used by the Talmudic sages to describe the responsibility of the community leader, who is required to carry the burden of the community on himself. And if a member of the community upsets him, or even insults him, it is forbidden for the leader to angrily reject him or to chase him away. The very opposite: he should bring him closer, responding to his issue by kindly explaining whatever he should be made to understand, until he leads him onto the desirable path, the path of honor and ethical behavior.

In his book Rabbi Burstein extensively dwells on the meaning of *kiddush hashem* [sanctifying the name of God]. One has the feeling that it is as if he foresaw that he was destined to become a burnt sacrificial offering, together with the rest of the Jewish community of Europe, at the hands of the contaminated unclean ones, may their names be blotted out. He quotes the Talmudic statement in Menahot 29: "When Moses went up to Heaven, he saw the Holy One, Blessed be He, sitting and drawing crowns[21] on the [Torah] letters. He said to Him, 'Master of the Universe, who is holding you back [from leaving your writing as it is, without crowns]? ' He answered, 'There is a certain person, named Akiva son of Joseph, who will live many generations from now, and who will someday expound heaps and heaps of laws from every single stroke…' Moses said to Him, 'Lord of the Universe, let me see his teachings, and let me see his reward.' God said, 'Turn around'. Moses turned around and saw them weighing out his [Akiva's] flesh at the market stalls.[22] Moses said, 'For this teaching, this is the reward?' God replied, 'Be silent, this is my decree.'" All the commentaries wavered as they grappled with God's reply. Did Moses not know that this was God's decree? What deeper meaning does this statement hint at?

[Page 53]

Rabbi Burstein delved deeply into this subject to ascertain the Talmud's message. He explained it as follows: During the period in which the people of Israel dwelled in their land, there were times when the people were influenced by the foreign culture of idol worship. Yet there was then no threat against the continued existence of the nation and its spiritual values, no danger that it would assimilate into the other nations and cease to exist: for a people dwelling in its own land, a people whose kings and officials came from among them, could not assimilate into other nations and lose their very existence.

But after the destruction of the Temple, when the Jewish people were scattered among the nations and hatred of the Jews broke out in all its intensity, the dispersed people were no longer immune from the great danger to their existence in the face of decrees, persecution and forced conversion, in spite of all the decrees of the Men of the Great Assembly and the Talmudic sages to arm the people with spiritual values, with fences [around the law] to maintain their existence. To preserve our existence the Jewish rabbis saw fit to instill within us the concept of martyrdom.

All Jews are obligated to martyr themselves in circumstances that come under the rule of "be killed rather than transgress"[23]. And from this derives the long history of the devotion that characterizes us after the destruction of our land, a devotion that began with Rabbi Akiva and the rest of the ten martyrs executed by the Roman regime, and continued into the Jewish exile from Spain and others.

This teaching was introduced by the great Jewish sages after the destruction of the land, and they were the first to be killed for the sanctification of the Divine Name—to serve as models of self–sacrifice to the Children of Israel, to bequeath some of their strength to them, to impart some of their spirit to their generation and to future generations, for the sake of national survival.

This virtue was infused in the nation's bloodstream and in that of their children. The tradition of martyrdom served the nation by preserving its existence from those times unto this very day.

There is a story from the Crusader period, of a certain city in Germany in which most members of the Jewish community were martyred for the sanctification of the Name, tortured to death. But among them were some who could not stand up to this challenge and converted [to Christianity]. The rabbi of the city, the martyr Rabbi Yechiel of blessed memory, slaughtered with his own hands his son, who was a groom at the time, for the sanctification of the Name; afterwards the rabbi killed himself, sanctifying the Name of Heaven. When those who had converted saw this terrible deed, they regretted what they had done and changed their minds, saying that it was better to die with these martyrs than to live with the unclean ones; they were then all martyred. This story became known throughout all the Jewish communities, whereupon they all became willing martyrs for the sanctification of Heaven, for Rabbi Yechiel's deed had become a model of devotion and self–sacrifice for the Jews.

[Page 54]

And with this he explained God's reply to Moses: It was for this reason that Rabbi Akiva was destined to teach this path of self–sacrifice and martyrdom to all of the Jewish people. It was for the purpose of preserving the Jewish people that Rabbi Akiva and the rest of the ten martyrs, executed by the Roman regime, were obligated to fulfill this decree.

His pure words shine like the glow of the firmament, connecting the annals of our people's history with the Divine pledge to secure our continued existence. They reveal Rabbi Reuven Burstein's exalted spirit and the deep insight of his thinking on the continued survival of our people.

A generation of knowledge has been destroyed before our very eyes with a cruelty that has had no equal in our people's history. From the terrifying bereavement wrought by the crematoria, from the mounds of ashes of their burned bodies—those of the most worthy of our young people—Israel courageously and vigorously flowered anew: in blood and fire Israel rose up in its land in order to preserve the eternal flame of our people, never to be extinguished.

What connection exists between the destruction of the diaspora and the revitalization of our people in our land—this remains a divine, unfathomable mystery. And yet we can console ourselves with the knowledge that the sun has not set on Israel. May the souls of the pious and righteous radiate like the glow of the firmament; may our sacred communities that were martyred for the sanctification of God's Name obtain their final rest seeing that the eternal destiny of Israel is indeed not false; and may they obtain their vengeance by seeing our land rebuilt. "And I shall avenge their blood that has not been avenged, and God will dwell in Zion."[24]

Footnotes:

1.   From *Kamenetz–Litovsk, Zastavije and Colonies Memorial Book*, edited by S. Eisenstadt and M. Galbert, published by the Israel and America Committee of Kamenetz Litovsk and Zastavya, (Orly, Tel Aviv, Israel, 1970), pp. 50–54.
2.   Someone in need of community help might interrupt the synagogue services at the beginning of the Torah reading to demand a fair and open hearing.
3.   Lazdijai, Lithuania is located 250km north of Kamenetz.
4.   There are 3 cities with this name. Mariampol, Poland is 70km southwest of Kamenetz; Marijampole, Lithuania, lies 300km north of Kamenetz, not far from Lazdei; and Mariampol, Belarus is 600 km northeast of Kamenetz.
5.   The city of Bialystok lies ~100km northwest of Kamenetz
6.   *Rishonim* = the earlier interpreters of the Talmud
7.   Tavrik = Taurage, Lithuania, located 400km north of Kamenetz
8.   The Slabodka Yeshiva was located in Slabodka, Lithuania, 250km north of Kamenetz.
9.   See the following link (retrieved September 2018): https://en.wikipedia.org/wiki/Shoshana_Persitz
10.   Bogorodsk, Russia is located 400km east of Moscow and 1500km northeast of Kamenetz
11.   Merkaz Harav Kook is a religious–Zionist yeshiva, located in Jerusalem. See the following link (retrieved September, 2018): https://en.wikipedia.org/wiki/Mercaz_HaRav
12.   *Aggadah* = Biblical exegesis, particularly on the narrative of the Bible
13.   *Nach* = Acronym for Prophets and Writings, the second and third parts of the Hebrew Bible (the Torah, or Five Books of Moses, being the first part).
14.   *Gemara* = Talmud. *Rishonim* = commentaries written by the earlier interpreters of the Talmud. *Poskim* = writings of the *Poskim* (= adjudicators), the later rabbis who settled Jewish law based on the Talmud, *Rishonim*, and other precedents.

15.   *Halacha* = Jewish law

16.   *Divrei Radakh* = literally "Words of *Radakh*", *Radakh* being an acronym for **R**euven **D**avid ha**K**ohen.(Burstein). The book was published in Warsaw in 1927. It can be viewed at the following link (retrieved October 2018): https://www.otzar.org/wotzar/Book.aspx?100829&

17.   Ponevezh = Panevezys, Lithuania, located ~400km north of Kamenetz. For a short biography of Rabbi Yitzchak Yaakov Rabinowitz (1854–1918), see the following link (retrieved October 2018): http://www.hevratpinto.org/tzadikim_eng/137_rabbi_yitzchak_yaakov_rabinowitz.html

18.   Rabbi Chaim Soloveitchik of Brest–Litovsk (1853–1918). For a short biography, see the following link (retrieved October 2018): https://en.wikipedia.org/wiki/Chaim_Soloveitchik

19.   The Talmudic passage paraphrased here (Sanhedrin 8a) cites Moses' statement in Num. 11:12.

20.   Netziv = acronym for Rabbi **N**aphtali **Tz**vi **Y**ehuda **B**erlin (1816–1893), who headed the Volozhyn Yeshiva. See the following link (retrieved September 2018): https://en.wikipedia.org/wiki/Naftali_Zvi_Yehuda_Berlin

21.   Crowns = crown–like patterns of short strokes drawn at the edges of particular alphabetical letters of the Torah

22.   Rabbi Akiva ended his life as one of ten martyrs who were tortured and executed by the Romans during the religious persecution by the Roman Emperor Hadrian following the Bar Kochba rebellion (~135 CE). In a liturgical poem read in the synagogue on Yom Kippur, their deaths are described as a willing sacrifice that they accepted after ascertaining that it was God's preordained decree. See the following links (retrieved September 2018): https://en.wikipedia.org/wiki/Ten_Martyrs, https://www.chabad.org/library/article_cdo/aid/2751091/jewish/The-10-Martyrs.htm

23.   Three transgressions come under this rule: murder, idolatry and incest. See the following link (retrieved October 2018): https://en.wikipedia.org/wiki/Self-sacrifice_in_Jewish_law

24.   Joel 4:21. An alternative translation: "And I shall cleanse their blood that has not been cleansed…".

[Page 55]

Rabbi Avraham Aharon Hakohen[1]

by Rabbi Reuven David Hakohen Burstein[2]

Translated by Allen Flusberg

And the following is the life story of my brother, the saintly prodigy[3] z.tz.l[4]. He was remarkably gifted as a child; and when his wondrous talents amazed my prodigious father, the latter, fearing the evil eye, attempted to keep it hidden. He even prevented the boy's teachers from singing his praises. Nevertheless everyone knew the secret, for this child was not only a prodigy, he was a genius from the day he was born. In his deep comprehension of all aspects of Torah and wisdom, even when he was a child, he was like a great, brilliant elder. And in addition to his prodigious capabilities he was also extremely diligent during his childhood, like our father z.tz.l. From the very day that he began studying in *cheder*[5] at the age of four, and until the day he died, he never stopped, studying day and night without pause.

The well–known calamity that befell him in the town of Shavil[6], leaving him within a hairsbreadth of being hanged, was actually a consequence of his disciplined diligence in Torah study. It took place at the beginning of the war [World War I]. When the Germans entered the town of Tavrig[7], which was on the border, my brother fled with his family to Shavil. The Germans entered Shavil as well, but afterwards the Russians fought them off; the Germans retreated from Shavil and the Russians came in. My brother paid no attention to what was occurring in the town; he stood behind his lectern with his open *Gemara*[8] on it, studying out loud with great diligence in his usual manner. But then Russian Cossacks came by and saw him swaying back and forth and talking to himself. They said: "This man must be a spy who is passing information with signals to the Germans. They put him in a dungeon and he was sentenced to hang. On the morning of the third day all had been prepared for the hanging. His wife and children already knew that the Russians were about to hang their father, their crown and glory—this weak, ill man who had no more on him than skin, bones, and an enormous brain. His family members were all stretched out on the floor of the house with their heads down, towards the ground, too weak to even weep. Meanwhile the men of the town Shavil, to their everlasting disgrace, did nothing to try to rescue him, each of them being afraid for his own life. But God in Heaven was using this as a trial, to test the people of Shavil, and at the last moment He roused the spirit of a young girl, daughter of the religious judge from Tavrig; she had also fled with her entire family from Tavrig to Shavil. Entering the *Beit Midrash*[9] while the entire congregation was praying *shacharit*[10] together with their rabbi, Rabbi Atlas, she called out in a loud voice: "Why are you silent? Is this the right time for you to be praying, while the prodigy of Tavrig is being led to the gallows? None of them answered her, for the silence of the fear of death had fallen upon them. They did not make a move, each of them fearing for his own life. Then the precious girl left them and ran over to the [Russian] general, castigating him with appropriate words over the great mistake that they were about to make; she spoke to him of the responsibility for the blood of a saintly, pure man that they were taking upon themselves. And God made her words find favor in the general's eyes. I have also heard that this girl was accompanied by a certain [Christian] priest, who swore by all that was holy to them that this man was entirely innocent. Then the general said to the girl: "Take him out of the dungeon quickly, but under the condition that he must leave the city right away. So she took him out and immediately hired a wagon, sending him to the city of Glubaka[11]. And may God recompense her well for this good deed she carried out with great devotion, saving the life of a lofty, righteous man and rescuing him and his entire family from a terrible misfortune.

[Page 56]

When our father died, my brother was thirteen years old. He left to study in Suchowola[12], where the family of my mother, of blessed memory, lived. He studied there for only half a year. When he returned from there the prodigious Rabbi Libtchik[13] Keidaner, who was then the rabbi of Wysoko–Litovsk[14], located near Kamenetz–Litovsk, took a liking to him, and he took him in to groom him as his youngest daughter's future husband. He brought him into his home immediately and they studied together. My brother was fifteen years old when they were married. At that point Rabbi Libtchik z.tz.l announced that this new son–in–law of his knew more than the rest of his rabbinical family put together—him and his other sons–in–laws, all great rabbis, as well as his son the rabbi, of blessed memory. One year and three months later, my brother's father–in–law, the great Rabbi Libtchik z.tz.l died, leaving my brother with absolutely no means of support; at the time I was ten years old and was being supported by my brother while I was studying at the Wysoko yeshiva. Since his father–in–law had died on him, my brother, who was now suffering from hunger and want, told me: "What can I do for you, my dear brother, when I haven't even a penny for myself? I was then compelled to eat "day meals"[15]. And when my brother was seventeen years old he left Wysoko for Keidan[16], district of Kovno, the birthplace of his father–in–law, z.tz.l, to study there. He studied there with amazing, superhuman diligence, almost 20 continuous hours daily, studying out loud with no break. While he was studying his voice was so pleasant that many of the townsmen would gather around the *Beit Midrash* every day, to listen to the sweet sound of his studying. They refrained from entering the *Beit Midrash* so as not to interrupt him; instead they stood outside, unable to tear themselves away from the lovely melody of his learning.

All his life my brother would jokingly relate that a certain shoemaker in Keidan turned him into a studious Torah scholar. And this was the story: My brother was staying as a guest in the home of a shoemaker who would wake up early each morning to engage in his craft—repairing shoes belonging to the townsfolk by hammering nails into them, or sewing new shoes together. The noise prevented my brother from sleeping, so he would get up and go to the *Beit Midrash* to study. One day when the shoemaker went there to look for him, he heard his pleasant voice of study, and he liked it so much that he preferred to be there listening rather than working. The next day the shoemaker woke up earlier to get his work done even sooner, so that he could go to the *Beit Midrash* with my brother after my brother woke up. But when the shoemaker began working, my brother was unable to sleep and got up too. The next day the shoemaker got up even earlier, as did my brother, until finally my brother was waking up in the middle of the night. It was then that he began to have a malady of the heart that put stress on him for the rest of his life, and from it he developed a chest illness called asthma that [eventually] cost him his life.

[Page 57]

When he was about 18 years old he was given the position of Yeshiva Head at the Slabodka Yeshiva[17], where everyone referred to him as the prodigy from Wysoko. And truthfully my brother was already then a giant of learning. His understanding was profound; and his logical reasoning was concise, like that of the *Rishonim*[18]. He also had an amazing memory; he was extremely studious and never forgot anything that he had learned. There is no doubt that someone like him would have been considered one of the Torah prodigies even in the previous generation.

Because of differences of opinion between him and the administrators of the Slabodka Yeshiva, he left the yeshiva for Kelm[19] to study there. There he suffered again from poverty and want. Then a great conflict broke out in his town, Wysoko–Litovsk, against their rabbi, Rabbi Shimshon of blessed memory, who had been selected as town rabbi to succeed Rabbi Libtchik, my brother's father–in–law. The townspeople who opposed their new rabbi rose up and wrote to my brother, inviting him to return to the town to take the position of town rabbi, which, they said, was rightfully his. They also sent him an official document stating that he was now the town rabbi. Knowing of his dire situation, they had thought he would jump at the opportunity, but they were completely mistaken. He turned their proposal down, bringing up their rebellion against their rabbi and the discord against him that they had created. Meanwhile my brother's family was still residing in Wysoko, living in dire straits, until my brother was appointed rabbi of the small city of Tzitevian[20] near Kelm. He was then 24 years old. He stayed there a year–and–a–half until he was appointed rabbi of Riteve[21], where he stayed five years, and then moved to Aniksht[22]; and from there he went to Salant[23], and from Salant to Shadova[24], and from Shadova to Tavrig. And in Tavrig he officiated in his position for about 23 years. During the war [World War I] they were all expelled from the town deep into Russia. The philanthropist Shoshana Persitz[25] of Moscow used her own money to found a yeshiva in the town of Bogorodsk[26], where she requested my brother be the head of the yeshiva on the condition that he should give his discourses in the Holy Tongue [Hebrew]. I do not know how long this yeshiva lasted in this town, but afterwards it moved, with my brother, to the town of Saratov[27], and in the end it fell apart completely. My brother took a position as town rabbi of Cherkasy[28], where twice there were terrible, frightful murders committed by the Ukrainians against the Jews. At that time the murderers pursued my brother, but he managed to get away by going into the home of a Gentile physician. The murderers chased after him into the house, as well; the physician's wife held them back for a while, but they overpowered her. While this was going on my brother had managed to climb out through a window and escape.

When the roads to the district of Kovno[29] were open again my brother quickly returned to his town of Tavrig, where he was overcome by asthma. The doctors told him that his illness would ease up in the Land of Israel, so he hurried to go there. But not only did he not improve, his condition actually worsened. And in addition he had to serve as Yeshiva Head at the Yeshiva Merkaz Harav[30] in Jerusalem, and to give his Talmud lectures there. At the end of a year–and–a–half his life came to an end there before he had reached the age of 59, so he did not merit a long life in Jerusalem as he had hoped. When he was still a youngster he had told me that were he to have a choice he would prefer being the rabbi of some village in Israel to being the rabbi of a city outside Israel.

Footnotes:

1. From *Kamenetz–Litovsk, Zastavije and Colonies Memorial Book*, edited by S. Eisenstadt and M. Galbert, published by the Israel and America Committee of Kamenetz Litovsk and Zastavya, (Orly, Tel Aviv, Israel, 1970), pp. 55–57.
2. Rabbi Avraham Aharon Hakohen died in Israel in 1925. His brother Rabbi Reuven Burstein, the author of this essay, perished in the Holocaust. This essay appears to have been extracted almost verbatim from the dedication section of Rabbi Reuven David Burstein's book, *Divrei Radach* (=Words of Radach, acronym for **R**euven **D**avid Ha**k**ohen), Warsaw, 1927. An electronic copy of the book can be viewed in the following link (retrieved October 2018): https://www.otzar.org/wotzar/Book.aspx?100829&
See also previous essay in this Yizkor Book, "Rabbi Reuven David Hakohen Burstein, May God Avenge His Blood", by Rabbi Yehuda Gershuni, pp. 50–54.
3. The term *gaon* (translated here as prodigy), used many times throughout this essay, has been omitted in the translation where it has been deemed superfluous.
4. z.tz.l is an acronym for *zekher tzadik livracha* = may the memory of the righteous be a blessing. It is used many times throughout the original essay and, where judged superfluous, has been omitted in this translation.
5. *cheder* = religious school for young boys
6. Shavil (or Shavel) = Šiauliai, Lithuania, located 500km north of Kamenetz
7. Tavrig (or Tavrik) = Taurage, Lithuania, located 400km north of Kamenetz and 100km southwest of Shavil
8. *Gemara* = Talmud volume
9. *Beit Midrash* = House of Study (of religious tracts), also often used as a synagogue
10. *Shacharit* = the morning prayer service
11. Glubokoye, Belarus, which lies 450km northeast of Kamenetz and 330km southeast of Shavil
12. Suchowola, Poland is located ~170km north of Kamenetz.
13. In the original article the Hebrew spelling of the name varies between "Libtchik" and "Libtzik" (i.e. either with or without an apostrophe after the letter tzadi). In *Divrei Radach* (see Footnote 2) it is spelled "Libtzik".
14. Wysoko–Litovsk (Vysokaye, Belarus) is located ~30km west of Kamenetz.
15. Day meals = meals taken at homes of townspeople who would invite poor yeshiva students to dine with them according to a weekly schedule, each home on a different day of the week
16. Keidan = Kedainiai, Lithuania, located ~50km north of Kovno (Kaunus, Lithuania), and ~400km north of Wysoko–Litovsk
17. The Slabodka Yeshiva was located in Slabodka, Lithuania, 130km south of Keidan and 250km north of Kamenetz.
18. *Rishonim* = earlier medieval interpreters of the Talmud
19. Kelm = Kelme, Lithuania, ~200km northwest of Slabodka
20. Tzitevian = Tytuvenai, Lithuania, 18km east of Kelm
21. Riteve = Rietavas, Lithuania, 60km west of Kelm
22. Aniksht = Anyksciai, Lithuania, 150km east of Kelm
23. Salant = Salantai, Lithuania, 100km northwest of Kelm
24. Shadova = Seduva, Lithuania, ~60km northeast of Kelm
25. See the following link (retrieved September 2018): https://en.wikipedia.org/wiki/Shoshana_Persitz
26. Bogorodsk, Russia, is located 400km east of Moscow
27. Saratov, Russia, located on the Volga River, lies ~600km south of Bogorodsk and ~800km southeast of Moscow
28. Cherkasy, Ukraine is located 1100km west of Saratov and 900km south of Moscow
29. Kovno = Kaunas, today a county of Lithuania with its capital in the city of Kaunas. Tavrig is located ~100km west of Kovno.
30. Merkaz Harav Kook is a religious–Zionist yeshiva, located in Jerusalem. See the following link (retrieved September, 2018): https://en.wikipedia.org/wiki/Mercaz_HaRav

[Page 58]

Rabbi Meir-Tzvi Putchinski, z.tz.l.
Head of Yeshiva in Kamenetz-Litowsk[1]

by Rabbi Yakov Bobrowski
(Head of Yeshiva "Ḥafetz-Ḥaim" in Baltimore, United States)

Translated by Allen Flusberg

In his youth he [my grandfather] learned Torah from Rabbi Pinḥas Michael, rabbi of the community of the city of Antopali[2] and the author of *Divrei Pinḥas,* a commentary on the entire Talmud. Studying Torah day and night, he excelled in his studies and became famous as a prodigy throughout the entire area.

When he grew up and was ordained as a rabbi, he was appointed as a yeshiva head in our town. The townspeople related to him with great respect and courtesy, referring to him as "Rabbi Meir Hirsch[3], Head of the Yeshiva".

The yeshiva was crammed with students, and he taught several generations of them. They had flocked to him from Kamenetz and beyond, some from nearby and some from far away, for him to teach them Torah. Among his students one should mention especially the Prodigy of Tavrik[4] and his brother Rabbi Reuven Burstein[5]. The latter served for many years as the community rabbi of our town Kamenetz; he perished in Auschwitz together with the members of his community.

In those days the study method in most of the yeshivas was based on the technique of *pilpul*[6]—to derive one thing from another and to make never-ending successive interpretations. My grandfather, Rabbi Meir Hirsch, had a different way of understanding the Talmud and the *Poskim*[7]. He would explain the statements of the *Tanaim* and *Amoraim* [earlier and later rabbis of the Talmud] with sweeping logic, and without extreme *pilpul*. I heard a great deal about his power of teaching and the simplicity of his explanations from his students in Kamenetz.

Rabbi Avraham Stempanitski told me the following story: "Once your grandfather happened to overhear a dispute in the synagogue between two sharp students. He listened as they used *pilpul* to argue about the significance of a single, solitary word, to which each of them attached a "deep meaning". Calling the two students over, he gently explained to them the principles of studying Torah—whose interpretation provides knowledge of the *halacha* [practical Torah law]—are to understand the principles of the law and the context using logic and reason, and not through just *pilpul* that does not amount to anything."

Footnotes:

1. From *Kamenetz-Litovsk, Zastavije and Colonies Memorial Book*, edited by S. Eisenstadt and M. Galbert, published by the Israel and America Committee of Kamenetz Litovsk and Zastavya, (Orly, Tel Aviv, Israel, 1970), p. 58. "z.tz.l" stands for *zecher tzadik livracha* = May the memory of the righteous be a blessing.
2. Antopali = Antopol or Antopal, Belarus (near Kobryn), ~70km southeast of Kamenetz
3. Hirsch (Yiddish) is equivalent to Tzvi (Hebrew) = deer.
4. The "Prodigy of Tavrik" refers to Rabbi Avraham Aharon Hakohen. See the article about him, written by his brother, Rabbi Reuven Burstein, on pp. 55-57 of this Yizkor Book.
5. See the following two articles in this Yizkor Book: Y. Gershuni, "Rabbi Reuven David Hakohen Burstein, May God Avenge His Blood", pp. 50-54; Ch. Z. Mendelson, Rabbi Reuven Burstein, z.tz.l., pp. 409-410.
6. *pilpul* = a method of keen-edged analysis of Talmudic literature
7. *Poskim* (= adjudicators) were post-Talmudic rabbis who settled Jewish law based on the Talmud and other precedents.

[Page 59]

The Yeshiva of Kamenetz-Litowsk[1]

by Yeḥiel Belizowski

Translated by Allen Flusberg

From the mists of the past, memories of my experiences in the Kamenetz-Litowsk Yeshiva come back to me. I can no longer recall what led me to come to this particular town—far from where I was born—to study in a yeshiva that was small compared to many others located throughout Lithuania.

One fine day in the year 1910, I arrived at the Yeshiva of Kamenetz and presented myself to the Heads of the Yeshiva, who welcomed me with open arms. My very first issue was how to obtain "days". It was customary then that each yeshiva pupil—particularly if he was from a poor family—received his meals at the tables of townspeople, each of whom supplied him with a meal one day a week [a "day"]. Even students from wealthier families, who could afford to support themselves without difficulty, were also eating "days", apparently adopting this practice to fulfil the statement: "You shall eat your bread in salt and drink water in small measure."[2]

In those days I was very young and inexperienced, and in addition I was shy; and so it is understandable that obtaining "days" was as hard for me as splitting the Red Sea. I did not have the nerve to knock on a door to imploringly ask the lady of the house if she would kindly and good-naturedly be willing to provide one "day" a week of meals to a yeshiva pupil. Many of the yeshiva students tried hard to set themselves up for "days" as quickly as they could. Since the competition was obviously stiff, each of them hustled to beat the others to secure meals for himself. I was at a loss and desperate, not yet having obtained even a single "day". But then I got lucky— some enterprising yeshiva student came by and offered to "sell" me seven of his "days". Energetic and brazen, he had secured a total of fourteen "days" rather than the seven he actually needed, so that he could sell the other seven. I was pleased to have been given this opportunity and gladly went along with the transaction.

I had no idea that the townspeople—and especially the housewives of Kamenetz—were eagerly waiting for students to come by to ask for "days"; they were glad to support Torah students, so that by fulfilling this important *mitzva* [commandment] they would be sure to earn themselves a share in the Next World.

[Page 60]

Near the yeshiva there was a small candy store. The proprietress was an elderly widow with a refined nature and a good heart. She did her best to create a pleasant, home-like atmosphere in her shop. The yeshiva students, who had been severed from their parents' homes while still in need of parental love and care, found in this shop a place to relax and some solace for their pining souls. And so a student might be quite pleased when he arrived for his "day" meal at a lady's house—but the lady, busy with something else, offered him some money in lieu of a meal. He would spend that money on candy in the widow's shop.

The yeshiva students were young, ranging in age from 12 to 14, and so needed guidance from the heads of the yeshiva. There were no class schedules, no set hours. The pupils studied from early morning to late into the night. They ate their meals hastily, so as not to waste time that could have otherwise been applied to studying Torah. Most of the pupils were studious and diligent. Once or twice a week they studied all night, until it was time for morning prayers. Those nights were termed *mishmar* [night watch]. Obviously not all those who attended *mishmar* were able to stay awake; many of them fell asleep before midnight, stretched out on study-hall benches.

The two Heads of the Yeshiva, Rabbi Hirsh and Rabbi Moshe, stuck around in school as late as they could—not only to supervise, but also to help the students with advice, with instructions and with explanations of what they were studying.

Rabbi Hirsh and Rabbi Moshe were brothers, but they were very different from each other physically and in other aspects. Rabbi Hirsh was short and thin, alert and agile, sharp-witted and devoted heart and soul to Torah study. In contrast, Rabbi Moshe was portly and clumsy; his speech was calm and patient, and his knowledge of Talmud was unparalleled.

Rabbi Hirsh devoted himself to spiritual matters, which were under his supervision. Rabbi Moshe took care mostly of administrative matters—he was in charge of funding for the school, and it was he who made the final decision on how much financial aid each student received.

These two brothers lived together peacefully and affectionately, with great respect for one another. They would refer to one another in the plural, calling each other "you" instead of the familiar form "thou"[3]. They explained it as their way of showing respect for Torah learning. Both were extremely charitable; they were God-fearing and modest. They loved the Torah and treated all people with respect. They never imposed their authority over the students and were not overly strict; rather they spoke to them gently, in calm voices. In return the pupils treated them with respect and esteem, and studied diligently.

This town also had its share of brave Jewish heroes. Any Gentiles who might have considered rampaging on market days were afraid of these mighty Samsons and did not dare go after the Jews.

I will always remember Kamenetz-Litowsk with a trembling heart and with great nostalgia.

Jewish Kamenetz-Litowsk is gone and no longer exists. May its memory be an everlasting blessing.

Footnotes:

    1.   From *Kamenetz-Litovsk, Zastavije and Colonies Memorial Book*, edited by S. Eisenstadt and M. Galbert, published by the Israel and America Committee of Kamenetz Litovsk and Zastavya, (Orly, Tel Aviv, Israel, 1970), pp. 59-60.

    2.   *Pirkei Avot* [Ethics of the Fathers] 6:4—an excerpt from a maxim directed at those who spend their time toiling in Torah study.

    3.   In Yiddish the single and plural forms of the second person are different, and the plural form is used for a single person as an expression of respect.

[Page 61]

The "Knesset Beit Yitzhak" Yeshiva[1]

by Leah Bobrowski-Aloni (Tel Aviv)

Translated by Allen Flusberg

The "Knesset Beit Yitzhak" Yeshiva, also known as the Yeshiva of Kamenetz-Litovsk, was founded in the year 5657 (1897) in Slobodka[2], a suburb of Kovno[3], which was the capital of Lithuania. The yeshiva was founded by Rabbi Hirsch Rabinowitz, and it was named in memory of his father, Rabbi Yitzhak Elchanan, the rabbi of Kovno. Rabbi Moshe Denishevski, the rabbi of Slobodka, also devoted himself to establishing and maintaining the yeshiva.

In the year 5664 (1904), after the yeshiva had been in existence for seven years, Rabbi Boruch Ber was brought in—following the recommendation of Rabbi Chaim Soloveitchik of Brisk—to officiate as head of the "Knesset Beit Yitzhak" Yeshiva.

With the outbreak of the First World War in the year 5674 (1914), the yeshiva experienced its first tribulation: the directors and members of the yeshiva were forced to leave Slobodka and to move to the city of Minsk (in White Russia[4]).

When the battlefront approached Minsk, the yeshiva moved further east, settling in 1917 in the city of Krementchug[5]. After the World War ended, the "Knesset Beit Yitzhak" Yeshiva was forced to leave Krementchug when the Bolsheviks got the upper hand. And because the Lithuanian government also refused entry to the members of the yeshiva, it was only after much effort that they succeeded in reaching Vilna and renewing their study there.

The Jews of Vilna, headed by the great Rabbi Chaim Ozer Grodzenski, treated Rabbi Boruch Ber and the members of his yeshiva with respect and affection. From the years 5680 to 5686 (1921[sic]-1926) the "Knesset Beit Yitzhak" Yeshiva resided in Vilna. However, the desire to escape from the hustle and bustle of the big city motivated the yeshiva management to move from Vilna to a small town, a quiet cul-de-sac. And thus the yeshiva arrived in our town, Kamenetz-Litovsk, in Elul 5666 (1926).

The community of Kamenetz-Litovsk, as well as the residents of Zastavya and the colonies, received the arrivals joyfully and with great respect. That day was like a town holiday, a day when everyone took off from work. Everyone was dressed in holiday clothing.

[Page 62]

They marched out, young and old, with the young people's orchestra leading the way. When this procession reached the outskirts of town, a chair of honor, upholstered in velvet, was brought out, and Rabbi Boruch Ber was asked to sit on it. The chair was raised high in the air, and Rabbi Boruch Ber was carried aloft in the procession with singing, dancing and orchestral music, all the way to the yeshiva building.

That evening a holiday meal was arranged in several homes along Brisk Street in honor of the yeshiva students. Chaya-Golda the cook had her hands full, although she was also helped by other women of the town. The people of Kamenetz welcomed the members of the "Knesset Beit Yitzhak" Yeshiva and did all they could to make their settling-in pleasant and to provide everything they needed.

The people of Kamenetz had a great affection for Rabbi Boruch Ber, whose saintliness illuminated the community and its residents, and whose reputation made our town famous throughout the entire Jewish world.

The years in which the "Knesset Beit Yitzhak" Yeshiva resided in Kamenetz turned out to be its most productive period. And the number of yeshiva students steadily increased until the temporary quarters of the yeshiva were too small to accommodate all who came to study Torah there.

When the lack of space in the yeshiva building was brought to the attention of Mr. Gershon Galin, a native of Kamenetz who was now living in the United States, he took upon himself the task of erecting a new, spacious building in our town to house the "Knesset Beit Yitzhak" Yeshiva. Mr. Galin visited Kamenetz for this purpose. He purchased a parcel of land and contributed the first sums to the building fund.

Rabbi Boruch Ber with the heads of the yeshiva and yeshiva students[6]

[Page 63]

On the 12th of Elul 5692 (1932)[7], the building foundation was laid in a great celebration. All the townspeople were there, and many residents of Zastavya and the colonies contributed significant sums that were beyond their means.

On the eighth day of Hanukkah 5697 (1937) [sic][8] the dedication of the yeshiva was joyously celebrated. Rabbis and leaders from the entire region participated, as well as the entire community of the town, who were so proud of their new yeshiva building.

This was the final "*Simchat Torah*"[9] for the Kamenetz Yeshiva…On the outbreak of the Second World War the yeshiva students were forced to disperse to many different lands. Among these students, some reached Israel and others the United States.

The magnificent yeshiva building that had been erected with so much toil was taken over by the Russians, and to our great sorrow it was converted into a movie theatre.

Footnotes:

1.   From *Kamenetz-Litovsk, Zastavije and Colonies Memorial Book*, edited by S. Eisenstadt and M. Galbert, published by the Israel and America Committee of Kamenetz Litovsk and Zastavya, (Orly, Tel Aviv, Israel, 1970), pp. 61-63.
2.   Slobodka = Slabodka, Lithuania, 250km north of Kamenetz
3.   Kovno = Kaunas, Lithuania, which lies some 80km NW of Slabodka
4.   White Russia = Belarus
5.   Krementchug = Kremenchuk, Ukraine, 900km southeast of Kamenetz, and 800km southeast of Minsk
6.   Banners read (in Yiddish): Cornerstone-laying celebration of the Knesset Beit Yitzhak Yeshiva, Kamenetz.
7.   12 Elul 5692 = September 13 1932.
8.   Eighth day of Hanukkah 5697 = December 16 1936; eighth day of Hanukkah 5698 = December 6 1937.
9.   *Simchat Torah* = Rejoicing of the Torah, a holiday celebrated yearly immediately after the holiday of Sukkot with Torah processions, dancing and singing. A similar rejoicing celebrated the dedication of the yeshiva building.

[Page 64]

Rabbi Baruch Dov Leibowitz,
Head of the Yeshiva of Kamenetz-Litovsk[1]

by Rabbi Yitzhak Edelstein[2]

Translated by Allen Flusberg

The area where the prodigious Rabbi Baruch Dov[2], of blessed memory, grew up was the city of Slotzk[3], where he was born in the year 5626[4]. In the city of his birth Baruch Dov experienced an atmosphere filled with the light of the Torah and a tradition of prodigiousness. In Slotzk the officiating rabbis were Torah prodigies. Young Baruch Dov studied in *cheder*[5] until he was accepted as a student by R.[6] Yisrael Yonah's, who had also been the teacher of the great Rabbi Chaim Soloveitchik[7] when the latter was a child. While he was still studying with R. Yisrael Yonah's, Baruch Dov was already displaying erudition and a keen sharpness in his own original innovative interpretations. In these innovations, which he also put into writing, he was like a fountainhead. At the age of fourteen he gave a lecture on *halacha*[8] in the Slotzk synagogue. Elderly men, some in their eighties, stood in awe before the young boy with the penetrating gaze who astonished them with his sharp *pilpul*[9] and his remarkable proficiency

[Page 65]

The young Baruch Dov reached Volozhin[10] when he was 16 years old. He stood before the genius Rabbi Chaim Soloveitchik and lectured before him on his innovative, exceedingly subtle Torah interpretations. In the first period of Baruch Dov's studies in Volozhin his yeshiva peers would taunt him for his pilpulism. As time passed Baruch Dov acclimated to the Volozhin Yeshiva and became close friends with the other students, all gifted, with great capabilities—the cream of the Torah youth. He grew close to his teacher, the great Rabbi Chaim, who viewed him as his spiritual heir and as the one student who was most capable of absorbing his teaching and his spiritual virtues. Baruch Dov was very attached to his teacher. When the great Rabbi Chaim would go out for a walk, Rabbi Baruch Dov would accompany him to hear the novel interpretations that he spoke of as he walked. As time passed Rabbi Baruch Dov grew even closer to Rabbi Chaim and was strongly influenced by his spirituality.

Rabbi Baruch Dov was appointed Yeshiva Head of "Knesset Beit Yitzhak" in Slobodka[11] in in the year 5664[12]. After that appointment his work and activity teaching Torah spread far and wide. During the First World War (1914), the "Knesset Beit Yitzhak" yeshiva was exiled to Minsk. When the war front approached Minsk, the yeshiva moved to Krementchuk[13]. During the hardships of the war his students found a safe haven with Rabbi Baruch Dov, who cared for them like a father. It is said that during the three days of battles between the Bolsheviks and the militia gangs, Rabbi Baruch Dov was sitting and teaching his Talmud classes in a cellar. Deep underground, in the shadow of death, he was able to clarify various issues in the Talmud that had now become clear to him. Then, after much difficult wandering along back roads, Rabbi Baruch Dov reached Poland together with his yeshiva, settling in Vilna.

For five years Vilna served as a way station for the Yeshiva "Knesset Beit Yitzhak". Rabbi Baruch Dov, with his passionate will and enthusiasm to disseminate Torah teaching, came to the conclusion that he should move his yeshiva to a small, quiet town, where the atmosphere would be conducive to the dissemination of Torah and piety. Following the advice of the saintly prodigy, the author of "Chafetz Chaim"[14], may the memory of the righteous be a blessing, Rabbi Baruch Dov chose the town of Kamenetz, which was near Brest-Litovsk.

In the year 5686[15] Rabbi Baruch Dov moved his yeshiva to Kamenetz. Starting then the town of Kamenetz was transformed into a "kingdom of Torah" as the yeshiva entered its age of glory. Great Torah scholars, the best of the yeshiva world, began to flock to the yeshiva, knocking on its doors and longing to be accepted within. The image of the yeshiva "Knesset Beit Yitzhak" in Kamenetz is described as follows by one of its best students, Mr. Shmuel Warshad (who perished in the period of the Holocaust): "Even while you are standing outside you hear the sound of Torah study breaching the high walls of the yeshiva building, echoing far, far away…and when you enter the yeshiva you see before you a large choir of more than three hundred tempestuous souls that have crystalized into a single unit, from whom there sounds a marvelous medley of tunes. You have before you a miniature gathering of the exiles: the yeshiva is packed with youth from all of the Jewish Diaspora. The boys sitting here are from Poland, America, Germany, England, Belgium, Denmark, Switzerland, Hungary, as well as from the Land of Israel. What a feeling of seriousness and deep responsibility has seized each and every one of them. And the atmosphere is that of the fervor of Torah learning: blazing eyes, brows furrowed in deep thought, open books, and the lively give-and-take discussions of Talmudic subjects."

[Page 66]

The yeshiva hall was never empty, not for a moment. After the *sedarim*[16] and between them, in the early morning hours, late into evening, and during the daytime, the young men are to be found in the yeshiva, learning and studying. In its regal tranquility, nighttime in the town of Kamenetz creates a special atmosphere that is particularly conducive to contemplating and analyzing all that has been learned during the day. Late into the night, when all the townspeople are fast asleep, the voices of the yeshiva students pour out into space, the sing-song of *gemara* study ringing out into the infinite vastness. There are those among the townsmen who come to the yeshiva specifically at night; they sit glued to their seats for hours at a time to absorb those eternal musical notes that are so full of longing. And even when the students go out to walk and get some fresh air together, they continue discussing words of Torah, using sophistry to triumph over one another in analysis of *halacha*.

Rabbi Baruch Dov presided over all the members of the yeshiva. He guided their path, his pure and fatherly spirit hovering over them and enveloping them. Rabbi Baruch Dov's house, a simple and humble place, was situated at the edge of the little town of Kamenetz, on Litwak Street. The members of the yeshiva were drawn to this house as if by magic cords. Rabbi Baruch Dov was vigilant about each yeshiva member, whether young or old, and was ready to serve them at any time. All day and even well into the night, his home bustled with words of Torah. Tirelessly, nonstop, Rabbi Baruch Dov provided his students with water drawn from his pure wellspring of Torah.

It was the desire of this great saintly prodigy to continue to live in Kamenetz in tranquility, but he encountered the fury of a serious economic crisis. In spite of his age and the precarious state of his health, he took the staff of wandering in his hand and traveled to America, to ask for help and to find a reliable source there that could keep the yeshiva going. Wherever he went in America he was received royally. The lectures he gave in the synagogues made a completely unforgettable impression. The administration of the Rabbi Yitzhak Elchanan Yeshiva[17] in New York sought to keep him there, offering him a position as head of the yeshiva. Rabbi Baruch Dov, however, replied as follows: "My students in Kamenetz hunger for bread, and you would like to take me away from them?" The members of the Rabbinical Agudah of America[18] also pleaded with him to stay there and officiate as their leader and president, but he didn't accept this offer either. He was attached to his yeshiva in Kamenetz with every fiber of his being.

Once he had returned from America, a new era in the life of the yeshiva began. The yeshiva grew in size and quality, all under the influence of Rabbi Baruch Dov, who continued giving his profound classes before hundreds of students, old and new. He found philanthropists who contributed to putting up a new building, and during Hanukkah of the year 5697[19] the new building was dedicated in splendor with the participation of dozens of renowned rabbis from Lithuania and Poland.

[Page 67]

In Elul of the year 5699[20] the Second World War broke out. The Germans invaded Poland; the danger approached Kamenetz, causing fear and panic throughout the town. Even in this time of distress, Rabbi Baruch Dov did not lose his equilibrium, his mental stability, his staunch faith in God. That evening the members of the yeshiva came into Rabbi Baruch Dov's house to recite *Tehillim*[21]. There was a sense of relief when the prayers ended.

In the month of Heshvan of the year 5700[22], the Soviet Union proclaimed that Vilna was being handed over to Lithuania. Rabbi Baruch Dov decided to move the yeshiva to Vilna. Just before he left his house he kissed the walls that had absorbed his spiritual life; within them he had disseminated Torah for so many years. In the middle of the night a caravan of horse-drawn wagons left Kamenetz, headed for Vilna. Rabbi Baruch Dov sat in one of the wagons, curled up in a coat, surrounded by yeshiva students. He lived to deliver a number of discourses in the yeshiva transplanted to Vilna. Ten days before he passed away, he gave his last lecture with fervor and alertness, with as much energy as he had displayed in his early years. No one could tell that his days were numbered. But very quickly he fell ill, and on the fifth of Kislev of the year 5700[23], he expired, his pure spirit leaving his body. All of the House of Israel mourned this great, irreparable loss.

Rabbi Baruch Dov's wife, Fayge, used to grumble about her husband's behavior. She would complain to him that he was ignoring his health, not watching out for himself with respect to how he ate. It would happen quite often that when Rabbi Baruch Dov would find out that a yeshiva student was ill, he would not leave him to fend for himself. He would take him to his own home, where he would feed him the breakfast, lunch and supper that his wife had prepared for him. When her son Leib, of blessed memory, traveled to Radin[24] to study in the Chafetz Chaim Yeshiva, the Rabbi's wife, Fayge, decided to accompany her son so that she could pour her heart out to the Chafetz Chaim[25] himself. Certainly the Chafetz Chaim would decide who was right. When she arrived in Radin she went straight to the Chafetz Chaim. He was then busy, in the middle of a discussion with his yeshiva students. When he noticed that a woman had entered the house, he inquired who she was, and the moment he heard that she was Rabbi Baruch Dov's wife he stood upright in a gesture of respect, stating emphatically: "A colleague's wife is equivalent to the colleague himself."[26] When the students saw their rabbi standing upright, they too stood up to show their respect. Taken by surprise by the honor they were bestowing on her, the woman completely forgot all the complaints against her husband as she suddenly experienced the great importance of her Rabbi Baruch Dov. "Now I see that it is worthwhile to tolerate everything from him," she murmured, as if to herself.

Our teacher, the prodigious Rabbi Baruch Dov, was one of those people who possess a sacred spirit that arises from within their souls, purifying and refining the air around them—so that whoever comes near senses that he is standing in a place of holiness. He made a powerful, deep impression on everyone, for everything he said and everything he did was natural, upright and honest. The name "Rabbi Boruch Ber" encapsulated a treasure of desirable virtues, those of a person who had risen up the ladder of Torah and piety. He was a great genius who was affable, virtuous, truly humble and honest, devoid of any taint. This is how this great nurturing prodigy lived and how he departed from this world, as a man who was always soaring upward to the sacred and exalted, a mighty giant whose thoughts always dwelled in the wellsprings of eternity, and whose entire life consisted of a medley of Torah, prayer and lovingkindness.

Translation of Hebrew: Talmud Torah and Yeshiva Ohel Moshe, founded by Meir Kohn in the year 5684[27],
and named after: R. Yoel Moshe, son of R. Avraham Abba of blessed memory, who passed away on the first day of Shavuot 5680[28];
and his wife, the lady Kayla daughter of R. Moshe of blessed memory, who passed away on 12 Heshvan 5677[29].

Footnotes:

1. From *Kamenetz-Litovsk, Zastavije and Colonies Memorial Book*, edited by S. Eisenstadt and M. Galbert, published by the Israel and America Committee of Kamenetz Litovsk and Zastavya, (Orly, Tel Aviv, Israel, 1970), pp. 64-68.
2. See the other article in this Yizkor Book on Rabbi Baruch Dov (Y. Turetz, "R. Boruch Ber and his Great World-Renowned Yeshiva", p. 408), in which he is referred to as Boruch Ber. The Hebrew name "Dov" (= bear) is equivalent to the Yiddish name "Ber" (= bear).
3. Slotzk = Slutsk, Belarus, located ~300km east of Kamenetz, and ~100km south of Minsk, Belarus
4. The Jewish year 5626 corresponds to the secular year 1885-1886.
5. *cheder* = religious school for young boys
6. "R." here probably stands for "Reb", an honorific title akin to "Mr." in English
7. Rabbi Chaim Soloveitchik of Brest-Litovsk (1853-1918). For a short biography, see the following link (retrieved October 2018): https://en.wikipedia.org/wiki/Chaim_Soloveitchik
8. *halacha* = Jewish law
9. *pilpul* = a method of keen-edged analysis of Talmudic literature
10. Volozhin = Valozhyn, Belarus, located ~300km northeast of Kamenetz and 80 km west of Minsk. It was the seat of the Volozhin Yeshiva.
11. The Slobodka (or Slabodka) Yeshiva was located in Slabodka, Lithuania, 250km north of Kamenetz.
12. 5664 = secular year 1903-1904.

13.   Krementchuk = Kremenchuk, Ukraine, 900km southeast of Kamenetz, and 800km southeast of Minsk

14.   Rabbi Yisrael Meir Kagan (1839-1933), an influential and prodigious rabbi and ethicist, known as the "Chafetz Chaim" (sometimes spelled "Chofetz Chaim"), after the name of his most famous book on ethical behavior. See the following link (retrieved November 2018): https://en.wikipedia.org/wiki/Israel_Meir_Kagan

15.   5686 = 1925-1926

16.   *sedarim* = plural of *seder* = a give-and-take study session conducted jointly by a pair of students. See the following link (retrieved November, 2018): https://en.wikipedia.org/wiki/Yeshiva

17.   Yitzhak Elchanan Yeshiva = Rabbi Isaac Elchanan Theological Seminary (RIETS). See the following link (retrieved November, 2018): https://en.wikipedia.org/wiki/Rabbi_Isaac_Elchanan_Theological_Seminary

18.   Rabbinical Agudah of America = *Agudath Harabonim* = Union of Orthodox Rabbis of the US and Canada. See the following link (retrieved November, 2018): https://en.wikipedia.org/wiki/Union_of_Orthodox_Rabbis

19.   Holiday of Hanukkah, 5697 = December 9-16, 1936

20.   Elul 5699 = August-September, 1939

21.   *Tehillim* = excerpts from the Book of Psalms, recited in times of distress

22.   Heshvan 5700 = mid-October, 1939.

23.   5 Kislev 5700 = November 17, 1939

24.   Radin = Radun, Belarus, ~200km north of Kamenetz. It was the site of the Chafetz Chaim Yeshiva.

25.   "Chafetz Chaim" = Rabbi Yisrael Meir Kagan. See Footnote 14.

26.   See Shevuot 30b for an anecdote describing the obligation felt by the 3rd-4th-century Rabbi Nachman to stand up in a gesture of respect for the wife of his colleague, Rabbi Huna.

27.   5684 = secular year 1923-1924

28.   1st day of Shavuot, 5680 = May 23, 1920

29.   12 Heshvan 5677 = November 8, 1916

[Page 71]

Public Life in Kamenets-Litowsk

On the Life of the Young People in Kamenetz-Litowsk[1]

by Yehudit Koscikiewicz-Grunt (Petah-Tikva)

Translated by Allen Flusberg

Kamenetz was never fortunate enough to have a high school, and very few of the young people managed to study at high schools located in nearby cities. Instead, the majority of the young people studied with private teachers, took examinations and thereby obtained a general and professional education.

Our young people were aware of all that was taking place not only in the Jewish world, but also in the world in general. In particular they were closely following the increasing number of political trends in Poland and in all of the Diaspora. They were quick to organize *Tze'irei Tzion* [Zion Youth], Gordonia[2], Revisionist[3] and even Communist groups; and more than once the Polish police arrested young men at their meetings and put them in jail.

The Kamenetz theatre was very well respected. Among the many vibrant young people, there were always young girls and boys that were gifted with theatrical talents and could put on plays in amateur groups. Asher Saperstein[4], a suave and well-liked teacher, was unanimously chosen head stage manager. The leading comedian, who participated with great success in all the plays, was, of course, Mr. "Bubil Mazik", who had an extended family and was a carpenter by trade.

At first the plays were performed in the school auditorium or in a large, private house; but afterwards, when the number of attendees increased, Mr. Motye Reznik, who had a barn in his yard, agreed to let the performances take place in his barn. It was a huge building that had once housed a large number of horses; but as the years passed the animals had been taken away, and the barn was now empty.

The young people invested a great deal of labor in the barn to transform it into a theatre. They put up a large stage, as well as benches, constructed of planks, that were brought in to fill seating in the barn to capacity. And they thus created a special, central building for theatre in Kamenetz.

More than once a bench broke and collapsed during a performance, spilling everyone sitting on it onto the floor; but the play would always continue as if nothing had happened. Some children used to find hidden corners on some side planks up in the attic, and when no one was looking they would sneak up there without tickets. Sometimes, in the middle of a play, they would lose their footing and fall down into the audience; but they would stay there, protected by the audience, until the performance was over.

Some of the noteworthy plays that were put on, to name a few, were: "The Sale of Joseph", "Chasya the Orphan", and Goldfaden's "Shulamith". Nowadays in Israel I sometimes get together with many of these amateur actors, and we reminisce about those idyllic, good old days.

[Page 72]

Owners of professional stage groups—though not first class—would occasionally visit our town. For us, each of these visits was a great experience that left a deep impression. And obviously our barn, the "Central Theatre Building of Kamenetz", also took in traveling troupes that came from elsewhere to perform.

I must mention that all the profits from these performances were contributed to various charities and distributed as well to support the solitary and isolated needy. Let's hear it for the young people of Kamenetz, dear to all of us!

Zionist preachers and modern lecturers did not overlook Kamenetz, either. Most of the lectures on the topics "Rebirth of Israel" and "The Return of the Jewish People to Zion" would take place in schools, synagogues, and even outdoors.

Young people boating on the Leshna River

Summers were interesting enough and pleasant. The surroundings, the view, the river and the "Slup"[5] enchanted all who came; and there were always many guests who were there to visit family. But in the winter…when winter came, we were overcome with boredom. No wonder our adolescents, always looking around for some relief, would try to flee from Kamenetz, whether to move to a large city, to leave Poland altogether, or to wander overseas to Argentina, Cuba, and America. But the greatest aspiration among all of us had always been, and remained, to get to the Land of Israel!

Footnotes:

1. From *Kamenetz-Litovsk, Zastavije and Colonies Memorial Book*, edited by S. Eisenstadt and M. Galbert, published by the Israel and America Committee of Kamenetz Litovsk and Zastavya, (Orly, Tel Aviv, Israel, 1970), pp. 71-72.
2. Gordonia was a Zionist youth movement, founded in Poland in 1925, that rejected Marxism, emphasizing instead manual labor and the revival of the Hebrew language. See the following (retrieved October 2019): https://en.wikipedia.org/wiki/Gordonia_(youth_movement). See article on p. 77-79 of this volume: P. Ravid-Rudnicki, "The Gordonia Movement in Kamenetz-Litowsk".
3. Zionist Revisionism was a movement founded in the 1920s by Ze'ev Jabotinsky. It rejected socialism and favored the establishment of a Jewish state encompassing all of mandatory Palestine, including Transjordan. See the following (retrieved October 2019): https://en.wikipedia.org/wiki/Revisionist_Zionism#Jabotinsky_and_Revisionist_Zionism.Also see article on p. 80 of this volume: B. Kotik, "Beitar and Tzohar Movement in Kamenetz-Litowsk".
4. See p. 131 of this volume for a short biography by P. Ravid-Rudnicki, "Asher Saperstein".
5. The "Slup" or "Sloop", also known as the White Tower, was a 13th-century, picturesque fortress located in the town. It is visible in the background of the photograph of the boaters on p. 72. A close-up photograph can be found on p. 25 of the original English section of this Yizkor Book.

[Page 73]

HeChalutz (Pioneer Movement) in Kamenetz-Litowsk[1]

by S. Dubiner (Petah–Tikva)

Translated by Allen Flusberg

The longing for the Land of Israel became deep–seated within the hearts of the Jewish youth of Kamenetz as the young people began to understand that it would not be possible to continue living as our ancestors had for generations. Within the Zionist youth movement there was a desire for *aliya* [immigration to Israel], yet only very few actually went.

After the end of the First World War, people began thinking about immigrating to the Land of Israel with the goal of starting new lives. There was a need for them to undergo physical and mental training to become fit for lives of productive labor. *HeChalutz* called for learning a productive trade, going back to working the land, renewing the life of the nation, preparing for agricultural life in the Land of Israel, and immigrating there.

Many of the Kamenetz youth embarked on productive work where they lived, while others traveled to places of *hachshara* [training] in *HeChalutz* centers. A few of the members of *HeChalutz* from Kamenetz, I among them, were sent to Pinsk to prepare themselves for *aliya* to the Land. The working conditions were difficult. We labored from sunrise to sunset. The equipment was primitive, food was meager and we received very little spending money. Many learned to be carpenters, locksmiths and electricians. Cooperatives were set up for these types of work. All physical labor that was not professional, such as felling trees and the like, were accepted as training for *aliya*. At the end of the training period each *chalutz* [pioneer] was entitled to appear before the *aliya* Committee. There was an *aliya* Committee in Kamenetz, and no one could obtain a certificate [for *aliya*] without its endorsement. The applicant also had to have some knowledge of the Hebrew language and the history of Zionism.

The members of *HeChalutz* in Kamenetz practiced what they preached: many of them immigrated to the Land of Israel, put down roots and excelled wherever they worked, whether in an urban or rural setting.

Footnote:

1. From *Kamenetz-Litovsk, Zastavije and Colonies Memorial Book*, edited by S. Eisenstadt and M. Galbert, published by the Israel and America Committee of Kamenetz Litovsk and Zastavya, (Orly, Tel Aviv, Israel, 1970), p. 73.

[Page 74]

Poalei-Zion (United with Tz.S.) in Kamenetz-Litowsk[1]

by Chaya Krakowski-Karabelnik

Translated by Allen Flusberg

Like many other Jewish communities of Lithuania and Poland that were not very large, Kamenetz had few organized cultural institutions and few regular, recognized schools. There was no theatre there, nor was there any fixed amateur acting group. There was no movie theatre, either. Instead, groups of young people who were good at singing, playing music, dancing and acting would occasionally get together, under the direction of the brothers Asher and Shlomo Saperstein, and with help from the local youth would put on theatrical plays. Since there was no suitable building in the town to serve as a theatre, they would use a warehouse that they had adapted for this purpose.

Each play generated a good deal of interest among the townspeople, entertaining them and transporting them away from their bland daily routine. Moreover the plays served as an opportunity to collect money for various community causes.

In contrast with the town's dearth of regular cultural and artistic activity—and perhaps actually because of it—nearly all the townspeople were members of one or another of all the political movements that existed in Poland at that time, particularly the various Zionist and socialist movements. Each movement sponsored lectures, discussion periods and educational activity. Our lives were vibrant and rich in action, especially in the framework of the Zionist movements, which focused their activities on training for immigrating to the Land [of Israel] and for productive labor in the historical homeland.

In that respect the work conducted by the *Poalei Zion* party, united with Tz.S.[2], excelled. The local branch was organized in 1925 by a group of members of *HeChalutz*[3] and by several others who had been part of *HaShomer HaTzair*[4], among them myself. The founders of the branch and its first members were: Yosef Kotik (Ben-Efraim) and Tuvya Savitzki, who later passed away in Israel; Faygl Riveles, who passed away in America at a young age; Avraham Bleichbard, who later joined Kibbutz Dafna; Shmerl Solnitze; and myself.

At first we were an illicit, underground organization; we would meet at one-another's homes, disguising our activities as family celebrations. Although in fact our party was officially legal, we had not been able to obtain a license from the authorities because we lacked the requisite three adult members to take responsibility for our activities, as required by the authorities. We would therefore send patrols outside during our meetings on the lookout for the police, who might raid us and falsely accuse us of communism. Under these conditions we used to conduct study classes; organize indoctrination[5] activities and the distribution of party periodicals; engage in training for aliya; and browse through circulars and instructions that we had received from party headquarters.

[Page 75]

In 1926 we began public activity after we received a license from the authorities: two members had managed to correct their birth records and were now considered adults by the police, and a third member, Yankl Neimark, who actually was an adult, had arrived from outside the town to work in a tannery.

The first public meeting took place in Manish's house on Brisk Street. Two representatives of the party's district committee participated: Comrade[6] Rogzhanski, who later came to live in Kamenetz for a while; and Comrade Sheinman from Brisk [Brest-Litowsk]. Starting at that time we extended our work. New members from among the working class joined our ranks. We rented an apartment and invited speakers from the central and district committees: Comrades A. Palushka, Arachov, and Bayla Klatnitzki (the latter perished during the Holocaust]; we used to organize literary evenings, during one of which Comrade Perlov participated. Occasionally we would have an open forum for the audience, set aside for topical questions. We would also set up question-and-answer evenings.

The activity of *Poalei-Zion* generated a great deal of interest among the townspeople and attracted large crowds to its meetings.

Our first members who left for training in Pinsk were: Tuvya Savitzki; Yosef Kotik (Ben-Efraim); Sh. Solnitze; and Simcha Dubiner; the latter later moved to *Hitachdut*[7].

Our members were active in *HeChalutz*, in *Kapai* (Fund of Workers of the Land of Israel[8]), and in distributing the shekel[9].

In the promotional-information meetings of the party the following members of the Central Committee participated: Minkowski, A. Bialopolski and others. Lectures were given on the ideological path of the party.

When Shlomke Saperstein and Yisraelke Freier joined our ranks, they added their intellectual strengths to the party, and we then decided to participate in the election for Town Council.

Additional members who left for training were Faygl Riveles and Yaakov Mikey. The latter immigrated to Argentina because of difficulty getting a certificate that would entitle him to immigrate to Israel. After living in Argentina for three decades, he sold all his property, came to Israel and settled here. He lost his life here after a short time in a traffic accident that took place while he was traveling to work.

In 1927 *Poalei Zion* appeared in a joint list with the Association of Craftsman (the *Hantwerker-Ferein*) in elections for Town Council, and we got our member Shlomke Saperstein elected as our representative. Later he immigrated to Israel and settled in Petah-Tikva; and after several years he passed away here.

[Page 76]

Under the influence of *Poalei Zion*, the youth movement *Freiheit* [Freedom] was established in 1926. Among its founders were: Ben-Tzion Sapir, Chaim Ruchmes, Shayne Shmukler, Avraham Yagalkowski, Tova Solnitze, as well as others. In order to run the *Freiheit* youth work, Comrade Yisrael Rogzhanski would occasionally come from the district (Brisk). After a short while the activity of *Freiheit* expanded, attracting many of the young people in the town, particularly those who worked in tailoring, shoemaking, carpentry and other crafts. The young people in *Freiheit* began studying, participating in classes and training themselves for activities of the movement. Outings and meetings were organized with other members of the *Freiheit* movement from the vicinity of Kamenetz. These young people became accomplished in Jewish history and in knowledge of the Land of Israel. They participated in party events and carried out the party's assignments.

Text written on photograph reads: 1ˢᵗ Convention of the Freiheit Org. and Ch.S. Force in the Brisk Region…
(translation is tentative, some letters being difficult to decipher; the third line is illegible)

The Kamenetz townspeople considered the *Poalei Zion* party and the *Freiheit* youth movement that was associated with it leftist, and they therefore refrained from including *Freiheit* representatives in the local committee of the JNF (Jewish National Fund). Understandably our members protested to the JNF Board of Directors in Warsaw. And when Comrade Bialopolski, who was a member of both the Central Committee of *Poalei Zion* (united with Tz.S.) and of Poland's JNF Board of Directors, came on a visit to Kamenetz, our members petitioned him; but he was not comfortable coming out openly against the other members of the JNF Committee, and so he made no decision on the matter. But the *Freiheit* movement did not give up its right to be represented and active in the local committee of the JNF. After some time passed another member of Poland's JNF Board of Directors, Rabbi Menachem[10] Hager of blessed memory, visited the town. A *Freiheit* delegation approached him, the writer of these lines being one of them; and he ruled that *Freiheit* should have representation in the local JNF committee. And after that we participated in additional activity, working for the JNF, together with agents of the other movements.

Only a small number of those young people were privileged to immigrate to Israel. Most of them perished during the Holocaust period.[11]

May their memory be preserved among us forever!

Translator's Footnotes:

1.   From *Kamenetz-Litovsk, Zastavije and Colonies Memorial Book*, edited by S. Eisenstadt and M. Galbert, published by the Israel and America Committee of Kamenetz Litovsk and Zastavya, (Orly, Tel Aviv, Israel, 1970), pp. 74-76. In the title, *Poalei Zion* = Zionist Workers, and the abbreviation "Tz.S." stands for *Tzionit Sotzialistit* = Zionist Socialist (see Footnote 2 below). This article, written in Hebrew, also appears in Yiddish on pp. 419-422 of this volume. The Yiddish article is essentially the same, and the present translation of the Hebrew also relies on the Yiddish version for clarification as necessary.

2.   *Tzionit Sotzialistit* (=Zionist Socialist) movement. See the following link (in Hebrew, retrieved February 2020): https://he.wikipedia.org/wiki/המפלגה_הציונית-סוציאליסטית

3.   *HeChalutz* (= The Pioneer) was a Jewish youth movement that trained young people for agricultural settlement in the Land of Israel, as described in the following link (retrieved February 2020): https://en.wikipedia.org/wiki/HeHalutz

4.   *HaShomer HaTzair* (= The Young Guard) was a youth movement that encouraged immigration to the Land of Israel and agricultural work in kibbutzim (communal agricultural settlements). See the following link (retrieved February 2020): https://en.wikipedia.org/wiki/Hashomer_Hatzair#Early_formation

5.   From Hebrew *hasbara* = promotional information, indoctrination

6.   Hebrew *Chaver* = fellow member or comrade. Wherever it appears as a title before someone's name in this article it has been translated "Comrade".

7.   *HitAchdut* (= Federation). For information on this party in this period see p. 276 of *Social and Political History of the Jews in Poland 1919-1939*, by Joseph Marcus.

8.   On *Kapai*, an acronym for *Kupat Poalei Eretz Yisrael*, see the following link (in Hebrew, retrieved February 2020): https://he.wikipedia.org/wiki/קפא"י

9.   The "shekel" referred to here was a symbolic banknote that was sold throughout all Jewish communities. It gave the bearer the right to vote for Zionist-Congress delegates. See the following links (retrieved January 2020): https://www.jewishgen.org/yizkor/ostrow/ost298.html, http://www.jta.org/1931/05/26/archive/election-day-in-palestine-thirty-thousand-shekel-payers-electing-30-delegates-to-zionist-congress

10.   First name "Menachem" added in Yiddish version

11.   Yiddish version adds: Their young lives were cut off at the beginning of their paths, before they could realize the lofty ideals they had strived for.

[Page 77 - Hebrew] [Page 423 - Yiddish]

The Gordonia Movement in Kamenetz-Litowsk[1]

by Pinḥas Ravid-Rudnicki, Haifa

Translated by Allen Flusberg

Like all the other cities and towns of Poland, Kamenetz was blessed with political parties and pioneer-Zionist youth movements. One that stood out in particular among the youth movements—and that could claim seniority for being the first to have been established in the town—was the Gordonia Movement. It was founded by Laybl Shostakowski and Moshe[2] Bilecki (both of blessed memory), as well as Yaakov Kolodicki (may he live a long life), who is now in Argentina. The three of them were members of the Tz.S. Association Party[3], and for that reason our movement was under the auspices of that party for a while.

Gordonia was established in the year 1926, right after the "Hebrew Circle" Union was disbanded; its goal had been to promulgate the Hebrew language among the local youth, but it had drawn only a very small number of members. As soon as Gordonia opened, however, it began attracting the local youth, especially the student population, into its ranks.

Having no dedicated meeting place, we would get together twice a week in members' homes, where we would hear a lecture on a pioneer-Zionist topic given by one of the founders, followed by a discussion. One could see how involved everyone was, particularly during the open discussions that were conducted in the form of "questions and answers"—or, as we called them back then, "*kestl ovnt*" [box evenings]—referred to as such because each member could write a note about a question or issue that he was concerned about, and deposit the note into a special box designated for this purpose. The discussions that followed would encompass all the questions and issues that had appeared on the notes. These meetings would end with various announcements, and after that the administration, consisting of 5 to 7 members, would meet to address various organizational problems.

This situation lasted for a while, until finally we found a roof over our heads: first, as sub-tenants in the General Zionist *Histadrut* [Workers' Organization] auditorium, and then later in our very own meeting place. The cultural-educational program that had previously been run by older members was handed over to a younger group of members: Laybl Nowinski[4] (of blessed memory), Laybl Goldberg/Sarid (may he live a long life) and the present author. The educational program, run according to a fixed schedule, was extended to cover different age subgroups.

At that time the head administration of Gordonia was established in Lodz[5] (it later moved to Warsaw), in addition to the administration that already existed in Lvov, covering East and West Galicia[6]. The connection with the head administration and also with the regional administration in Brisk[7] contributed significantly to the continuing operation of our branch. Everything was well organized to run smoothly. We were circulating periodicals written by the head administrations, and similarly we were receiving the announcements and letters that were serving as directives to all the branches of the movement and lifting our morale.

[Page 78]

Writing on photograph:
Staff of Gordonia Organization of Kamenetz-Litowsk.
Kamenetz, 28 Nisan 5690.[8]

Our local Gordonia Movement had entered a smooth routine as its membership underwent steady growth. Its framework expanded with the establishment of additional groups for different ages. More instructors were recruited from among its members; evening lessons in Hebrew were set up; and we started a drama club that put on shows not only in Kamenetz, but in other nearby towns, as well. A newspaper, affixed to walls, began to appear regularly in Hebrew and Yiddish; and parties and banquets were scheduled for celebrations. Commemoration services were organized to memorialize important figures in the Zionist and Socialist movements, such as A.D. Gordon, Dr. T. Herzl, Yosef Trumpeldor, of blessed memory, and others. Whenever one of the members of the head administration came to visit our branch, we made sure to schedule a public lecture that would draw a large audience.

The scope of the movement's activities was not limited to culture and education. Members were also active in collecting contributions for the various national funds. The emptying of coins from the little blue collection boxes of the Jewish National Fund was done on a monthly basis mostly by the members of Gordonia, something that raised the movement's prestige within the entire Zionist community of the town.

We played an important cultural role, as well. Our members were represented in the administration of the *Tarbut* library, in public "Literary Trials" [mock trials][9] and also in other various cultural appearances.

[Page 79]

Like any pioneer youth movement, the Gordonia Movement of Kamenetz did not restrict itself to the spiritual and cultural development of its members; it also concerned itself with encouraging their personal fulfillment through *aliya*. It is no coincidence that this activity later began to bear fruit as some of the members of the movement left for training, in preparation for their immigration to the Land of Israel. As time passed several members were indeed approved for immigration. We would hold festive farewell parties for members who were about to depart on *aliya*; those left behind took leave of these fortunate individuals with evident envy.

The movement's days of glory continued for some time. We still recall those days, when the movement was bustling with vigor, and the outside walls of the auditorium resonated with the sound of pioneer singing and dancing late into the night. During spring and summer, we used to often have organized hikes into the woods and to scenic points in the vicinity, mostly on Sabbaths and holidays. The most outstanding and memorable one—which became a tradition—was on *Lag BaOmer*[10]. Our members, wearing their distinct uniforms and loaded down with supplies for the outing, would file out in formation from the outskirts of town, marching toward the Prusky Forest, a distance of about 10km from Kamenetz. There they spent the entire day relaxing in the great outdoors and discussing the significance of this date. As evening was approaching, the outing would end with *Hora* dancing, followed by a march back to town. The march, with its singing, flag-waving and burning torches, left an indelible impression on everyone in the town.

Writing on top of photograph reads:
Gordonia Organization of Kamenetz, on the Lag BaOmer outing of 5692 [May, 1932].[11]

As stated above, the activity of the movement branched out in various directions. On its initiative a pioneer training program for Gordonia members from various regions of Poland was set up in our town. We made sure the group would have financial stability by arranging employment for its members. The very existence of this group breathed new life into our local branch, and it also made a significant impression on all of the town.

The Kamenetz Gordonia members participated in the regional meetings that were held in the Polesia province[12], and also in the regional summer camps. Two such meetings were held in Kamenetz, hosted by our local group. At one point there was also a summer camp meeting in the village of Kruhel, situated in the vicinity of Kamenetz.[13] Our movement also sent its delegates to national conferences.

Memories of that period are engraved in the minds of former members who are now in Israel and the Diaspora.

The members of the movement viewed fulfilling their objectives [to go on *aliya*] as their main goal, but unfortunately only a small number of them made it. It is painful that most of them were subject to a bitter, cruel fate, perishing with the other Kamenetz Jews in the Holocaust.

Translator's Footnotes:

1. From *Kamenetz-Litovsk, Zastavije and Colonies Memorial Book*, edited by S. Eisenstadt and M. Galbert, published by the Israel and America Committee of Kamenetz Litovsk and Zastavya, (Orly, Tel Aviv, Israel, 1970), pp. 77-79. This Hebrew-language article also appeared in Yiddish on pp. 423-428 of this Yizkor Book. The Yiddish version has been used to supplement the Hebrew version. Any significant differences between them are mentioned in footnotes.
2. Yiddish version: Eliyohu, apparently an error, since the Necrology (translated at the end of this Yizkor Book) lists a Moshe Biletski (an alternative spelling of Bilecki), but no Eliyahu Biletski.
3. *Hitachdut Tz.S.* or (as sometimes written) *Tz.S. Hitachdut* = Zionist Socialist Association
4. Yiddish version: Gubinski, apparently a misprint, since the Necrology (translated at end of this Yizkor Book) lists a Laybl Novinski, but no one named Gubinski.
5. Lodz, Poland is located about 350km west of Kamenetz.
6. Galicia is a region straddling present-day Poland and Ukraine. See the following link (retrieved July 2021): Galicia (Eastern Europe) – Wikipedia. Lvov (in Galicia), is now Lviv, Ukraine, located about 350km south of Kamenetz.
7. Brisk = Brest-Litowsk, a city located about 40km south of Kamenetz.
8. 28 Nisan 5690 = April 26, 1930
9. See the article on pp. 131-132 of this Yizkor Book, "Binyamin Bogatin".
10. *Lag BaOmer* [=33rd Day of Omer] takes place some 33 days after the first day of Passover. See the following link (retrieved July 2021) on the history of *Lag BaOmer* and its reinterpretation by the early Zionists: Lag BaOmer - Wikipedia
11. From p. 425 of Yiddish version of this article.
12. Polesie Voivodeship, encompassing much of the historical region of Polesia, was a province of Poland between 1921 and 1939. Today it is divided between Poland, Belarus, Ukraine and Russia. See the following link (retrieved July 2021): Polesia - Wikipedia
13. Kruhel is about 5km southwest of Kamenetz. See the following link (retrieved July 2021): village Kruhel at map (Kamianiec county, Brest region) (radzima.net)

[Page 80]

Beitar and *HaTzohar* [Zionist Revisionist] Movement in Kamenetz-Litowsk[1]

by Bunia Kotik

Translated by Allen Flusberg

These movements[2] had a large number of members. The most active members were: Lipa Horwitz z.l.[3], Binyamin Bogatin z.l., Yosef Kotik Ben Dov z.l., Alexander Kotik z.l; and the following who are still alive—may they live and be well—Dov Miletzki and myself—Bunia Kotik.

In the year 1930, members of Beitar appeared in the streets of the town in their uniforms for the first time, drawing the townspeople's attention. One of the ideas that we were emphasizing was that our Jewish youth was fit for a movement that supported the slogan "a healthy mind in a healthy body". But clearly our main aspiration was to renew our national life in our eternal homeland.

Beitar educated its members to stand up tall and be courageous. The movement encouraged its members to fulfil the obligation of safeguarding the dignity of all people in general—and of the Jewish people in particular.

I recall the proud march of the Beitar group into the forest, accompanied by a Hebrew marching song and music played with pride by the local Beitar band. The Jews of Kamenetz walked along these marching boys and girls with fond looks, as if to say "How good looking our Beitar youth is!"

The blustery, stormy Beitar group of Kamenetz-Litowsk quickly turned into a center for some of the youth of our town. Members learned the history of the Jewish people and the geography of the Land of Israel. There were talks on ethical values and societal life. In another wing they were studying the Hebrew language and literature; every Beitar member was required to know Hebrew.

In the year 1932 we had a fundraising campaign to support acquiring a ship for the Jewish navy that was under the leadership of Jeremiah Halpern[4]. The Jews of Kamenetz contributed generously. This was what the Jewish public of Kamenetz-Litowsk was like.

In the year 1933 I left my brothers and sisters, my fellow members of the movement and my fellow townspeople, in order to immigrate to the Land of Israel.

When I reached the Homeland, I continued my membership in Beitar. I am still doing communal work for the movement from where I live, in Givatayim.

Translator's Footnotes:

1. From *Kamenetz-Litovsk, Zastavije and Colonies Memorial Book*, edited by S. Eisenstadt and M. Galbert, published by the Israel and America Committee of Kamenetz Litovsk and Zastavya, (Orly, Tel Aviv, Israel, 1970), p. 80.
2. The Zionist Revisionists rejected socialism and Marxism, supporting instead a more right-wing nationalist form of Zionism. See the following links, retrieved July 2021: Betar – Wikipedia; Hatzohar - Wikipedia
3. z.l stand for *zichrono livracha* (= of blessed memory)
4. Halpern (1901-1962), a staunch Revisionist, was one of the driving forces behind the establishment of an Israeli Navy. See the following link (retrieved July 2021): Jeremiah Halpern - Wikipedia

[Page 83]

Memories before the Holocaust

During the Years of the First World War[1]

by Leah Bobrowski-Aloni (Tel Aviv)

Translated by Allen Flusberg

Total Mobilization

I can still recall the day on which the First World War broke out in August 1914; and I remember the day they announced a total mobilization, throughout all of Russia, including, of course, our town Kamenetz-Litowsk and its vicinity.

A large number of wagons arrived from the surrounding villages to transport the men who had been mobilized to the train station in Žabinka, located about 20km from our town.

It was disturbing to watch so many people saying goodbye to each other in tears. Once the wagons began leaving to take the men away, those left behind wept much more loudly. Everyone was crying out: "God in Heaven—who knows if we will live to see our dear ones again when they return from the war". And indeed, many did not come back, among them fathers of infants and small children.

Those not quite old enough to be drafted into the armed forces were taken away to labor at excavation and fortification construction, whether nearby or far away. Most of these did return home, glad to still be alive.

And in this way Kamenetz very slowly began to get used to a state of war.

Aid to the Refugees

When Jewish refugees from towns that were near the front began passing through Kamenetz-Litowsk on their way to the Russian interior, they stayed over in Kamenetz for a while. The Jews of Kamenetz rose to the challenge, to make sure these people found lodging and food during their stay in our town.

Our town Kamenetz was not blessed with restaurants, and the taverns of our town were meant for farmers from the surrounding villages. The Jews were not accustomed to eating in taverns that sold mostly liquor, whiskey, salted fish and similar items.

The caravans of refugees were directed to the hallways of the synagogues and the *shtiblach* [small prayer rooms] that adjoined them. No fund for refugee aid existed. The entire burden of arranging care for the refugees fell upon the townspeople who lived near the synagogue. In practice, this is what happened: every family that could prepared a hot meal with bread and vegetables on a daily basis, serving it to the refugees, wherever they were.

[Page 84]

One evening, when our father returned from the synagogue after the evening prayer, he told us that a group of refugees, including women and children, had just arrived in town, and had been put up in "Shepsil's *Beit Midrash*" [House of Study]. Our father urged us to quickly prepare a cooked dish with potatoes in the largest pots we had in the house. And he hurried out to purchase loaves of bread, salted fish and more.

Right away we all joined forces to help, and meanwhile our father returned with all the necessities he had bought. Everything was ready for a dinner meal. We added tea and hot cocoa for dessert. We brought along plates, spoons, forks and knives; and, bearing all this "cargo", we set off to the place where the refugees were being housed—the *Beit Midrash* named after Shepsil.

Most of the families who lived nearby did the same, each according to its generosity, ability and available supplies. And in this way the Jews of Kamenetz welcomed all the refugees who had left their homes for a new haven, out there in the great Russian Steppes.

The Front Draws Near

In the first year of the war we did not experience any notable suffering in our town. Most of the Kamenetz residents were able to make a living in spite of the war. A few of the merchants were actually expanding their business and growing rich from their profits.

Starting July 1915, however, we began to notice that the front was approaching. Every night we would hear cannons thundering in the distance. And there were rumors going around in our town about atrocities committed by the Cossacks against the Jewish population.

Most of the Christians who lived in and around Kamenetz hurriedly left their homes, heading out on journeys to towns and villages in the interior of Russia. But when we Jews tried to leave the town to get farther away from the front, we came up against a great number of difficulties. The civil and military authorities did not grant us permission to leave, and even prohibited us from traveling by train. Meanwhile caravans of refugees from nearby towns and villages were reaching us. The fear of what lay ahead and the rumors about what the Cossacks were doing preyed on our minds.

Within the Front

The thundering sounds of cannons were getting louder. On the horizon we could see smoke rising from fires; every night it looked as if the glowing skies themselves were on fire (from the actions of the retreating army). Our trepidation intensified every day.

Those who owned horses and wagons loaded as much of their belongings on them as they could, in spite of the prohibition, and set out from their homes without a clear destination in mind. The streets and roads leading away from town filled up and became more and more crowded. Soon we were all stuck in a traffic jam, unable to move forward or to find a place that we could turn into, while behind us and in front of us were the two warring army encampments. When the shots that were reaching us from nearby became unbearably intense, we abandoned the wagons that were loaded with all our belongings, and we fled for shelter from the bullets buzzing overhead.

[Page 85]

Most of the day was spent in an atmosphere of miraculous incidents. Bullets rained down on us from all directions without hitting us. Some of the bullets came to their "final resting place" inside pots of cooked food. And a truly incredible miracle occurred: a bullet passed right near the head of a Jewish man, tearing only the brim of his cap and leaving the rest of it undamaged.

The men, fathers of our families, sat on the ground, reading chapters of Psalms and praying all day long: "…God, hear my prayer, and may my cry reach You…"[2].

The Occupation of Kamenetz

At dusk battalions of the Austro-Hungarian army entered our town. They occupied the town and all the surrounding villages. We were saved, and we breathed a sigh of relief, seeing that the war had not harmed us so very badly. The townspeople came out into the streets to welcome the occupiers.

As they shouted victoriously, the soldiers were offered bread and salt, as well as other foods: a royal reception, "as befits a king"[3]. There was great joy, for we had been spared from the terrible Cossacks, who had been prevented from carrying out their heinous acts.

But in the middle of that night a great and bitter cry rang out from many of the houses of the town. The cries continued, growing even louder. We were terrified, afraid to open a door, to go outside and find out what was happening. It had to mean that the Cossacks had returned and retaken the town, and were now avenging themselves against everyone…

At dawn we found out the truth: the Hungarian soldiers who had been welcomed so royally when they had marched into town—those very same soldiers had come out at midnight to make home visits, robbing and pillaging.

Although all of these soldiers were given the ultimate punishment by their officers—they were sent to the front on that very day—we did not calm down for quite some time, remaining anxious day and night.

Slowly but surely, we made our peace with our adverse fortune. And once things had quieted down, the refugees we had been housing returned to their former abodes. Only a few families from Brest-Litowsk remained in Kamenetz; as we knew, the Russians had expelled all the Jews of Brest from the fortified city.

What the Front Gave Us

A short while after the occupation began our Kamenetz was overcome by a great disaster. A cholera epidemic raged through the town, killing many of the townspeople within a few short weeks. The disease moved from one house to the next, making all family members ill; and there were no doctors or medications, none whatsoever. Everyone was terrified, thinking his hours were numbered. We had no idea how to protect ourselves from this *choli ra*, which was indeed bad, worse than anything.[4]

We did hear about a singular cure that had been "discovered" nearby: "In the cemetery conduct a wedding ceremony for a couple who were about to get married, and the plague will cease…"

Once the front moved away from our area, the epidemic slowly diminished, and then it went away completely.

[Page 86]

But we were all in shock when we found out about the calamity that had befallen the family of my student, Avraham Shudroff. His young parents, Esther and Moshe, had both been stricken with cholera, and both of them passed away overnight. They left behind five children, now orphans, and the children's elderly grandmother.[5]

During the Occupation Period

An Austrian battalion replaced the Hungarian fighting battalion. For about eight months the Austrians scrupulously observed the rules of war. Their attitude to us Jews was tolerable. But we were cut off from all of the world, and especially from the business centers from which we had always been getting our supply of various provisions and clothing. Traveling from one town to another without a special permit was now strictly prohibited, and whoever tried to break this law was severely punished.

With no alternative, we began to take advantage of the potato fields and vegetable gardens that the farmers who had lived nearby had abandoned when they fled to Russia. To feed their families, the Jews of Kamenetz began ploughing and sowing, cultivating sections of farmland in the town and around it.

Meanwhile the shortage of clothing grew daily, especially for families with many children. Our dear mother was forced to unstitch our mattresses and to replace the mattress covers with jute fabric. From the old, soft mattress covers she sewed shirts for the boys, while for the girls she sewed dresses from the bedsheets, after first dyeing them blue. I decorated my sisters' dresses with Stars of David embroidered in red, with the addition of the word "Zion"—decorations they took great pride in.

Those families that had been supporting themselves with money that used to be sent to them from their husbands and other relatives in the United States were not able to receive any help from them during the years of occupation. They suffered more than anyone else, cut off from their loved ones during all those years.

Our Youth

Our enterprising young people set up a community kitchen for the needy. All of them committed themselves to collecting food that had been contributed from our town's "farmers", and to collecting the townspeople's generous monetary contributions to support the community kitchen. In addition, many of the young people rolled their sleeves up to do volunteer work in the kitchen.

Members of the Drama Club set aside all income from the shows they were performing to support this kitchen, which was our pride and joy.

A large number of families obtained meals and other food from the community kitchen for many months, getting it all delivered to their homes—as much as they needed.

I would like to point out something special about this activity: our young people took pains to help even those who preferred to silently remain hungry, rather than ask for charity. For those families the food they needed was delivered to them covertly, as anonymous giving[6].

Translator's Footnotes:

1. From *Kamenetz-Litovsk, Zastavije and Colonies Memorial Book*, edited by S. Eisenstadt and M. Galbert, published by the Israel and America Committee of Kamenetz Litovsk and Zastavya, (Orly, Tel Aviv, Israel, 1970), pp. 83-86.
2. Psalms 102:2.
3. Esther 2:18
4. Play on words: *choli ra* = bad illness in Hebrew
5. See p. 318 in the Necrology section of this volume.
6. Hebrew *matan beseiter* (based on Prov. 21:14). The Talmud describes matan beseiter as a high form of charity in which the donor and recipient are unknown to one another (Baba Batra 9b). The recipient is spared the embarrassment of accepting charity from someone he knows, and the donor cannot expect future compensation from a recipient who does not know his identity.

[Page 87]

Kamenetz-Litowsk During the First World War[1]

by Yehudit Koscikiewicz-Grunt (Petah Tikva)

Translated by Allen Flusberg

I remember the outbreak of the First World War, when I was less than 9 years old. Very quickly we found ourselves under Austrian rule, which afterwards was replaced by German rule. We hadn't yet come round when the cholera outbreak took place. I recall the panic that ensued, with no physicians and no medications. There was one particular night on which many Jews suddenly died. I remember it well because some of them were relatives of ours. Our partner Guterman died that night, leaving behind 3 daughters, now orphans, with no mother; they stayed with us for a while. In the Shudrowitzki (Shudroff) family both parents died that night, leaving behind 5 young boys, the youngest of whom was less than a year old. Their grandmother Malka Szczupak took them in.[2] They were not the only ones; many others died during this terrible epidemic. In spite of the great danger, the Jews of Kamenetz helped one another at that time, even though they did not know what the morrow might bring. And because of that I remember the devotion of our forefathers to each other, a quality that contributed a great deal to our upbringing.

I remember how after the cholera epidemic we had a typhus epidemic. This one also spread like lightning. At that time the Germans had already reopened the only government hospital that existed in Kamenetz, and they ordered that everyone who was ill should be brought to the hospital. Of course, since each family was taking care of small children, people were happy about this help, hoping that they would be cured and that further spread of the illness would be avoided. But very quickly we found out from the nurses and aides working in the hospital at the time that they were not giving the patients any medical help, but rather were abandoning each to whatever lay in store for him. Naturally after people heard this news, they stopped sending those who were sick to the hospital, in spite of the Germans' search of homes for typhus patients. The ill were cared for at home without any medication and with no physician. The primitive treatment was laying on cold sheets in the winter and on ice in the summer, but obviously the dedicated care of parents and family members saved many patients. I, too, was ill then, and for a long time I lay in a dark room; they hid the door to the room behind a cupboard when the Germans came by to search for ill people.

[Page 88]

When the typhus epidemic was spreading like wildfire through the town, many people fell ill. In our home. my brother Meir and my sister Rachel were sick. Then one night a fire broke out, and initially no one actually noticed the fire, which was rapidly spreading in three directions, and so no one came out to help put it out. The reason was that in those days there was a curfew in town confining us to our homes from 9 PM until 6 AM. Among the Germans on duty during the curfew was a guard named Putermann, a real villain. Many a time Putermann had used various subterfuges to nab curfew violators. He would seize people he had tricked into leaving their homes, bring them to the police station, and beat them fiercely. More than once someone was sent away for hard labor without his family members even knowing for a long time where he was; and many a time such arrested people would return broken, crushed and ill. So given Putermann's reputation for such tricks, the town residents did not rush out immediately when calls for help first rang out. But on that night the fire was real, and by the time people came out to help it was too late. The houses were all constructed of wood; the fire spread in three directions, and half the town burned down. The next morning, there we were with two typhus patients in the fields outside town. We had with us a few belongings that we had managed to rescue, but we had no roof over our heads. Half the townspeople were in the same situation. After a while some of the Jews decided to leave for nearby villages whose residents had fled to Russia when the war came and left their homes unoccupied.

The Jews who remained in the town and those who had moved to the villages became concerned about how they would make a living. The Kamenetz Jews were shopkeepers, traders and craftsmen. There were also big businessmen who were involved in exporting goods out of the country: for example, they would ship wood to Germany, as well as shrimp, eggs and various forest seeds. There were also two breweries in town, one in Zastavya and the other in Kamenetz proper; there was an oil factory and flour mills. The war had taken away their livelihoods. At first people went out into the fields to gather the grain and potatoes that the Gentiles had not had a chance to harvest before they had fled; and after there was nothing left to gather in the fields they began to sow and plant in order to grow crops and have something to eat.

And then a new kind of trouble came. Kamenetz was located near the Bialowieza Forest, whose woods—and particularly all the villages that were in these woods—were well known throughout Russia. The soldiers who had deserted and were left behind from the war were hiding out there. Among them were Bilachowic and Patalor gangs, as well as all kinds of bandits. For the most part they would roam at night in search of food; and in this manner they began to loot and kill. Among those who were killed by these murderers were two of my aunts: my father's sister Chasha Leder, and my mother's sister Chaya Gerber, and there were many other victims. Once these bandits actually came into our town. This situation continued until 1919, when the Poles arrived in our town.

In 1920 (albeit for only a short time, perhaps two months), Kamenetz also experienced the lightning war between Poland and Russia. The Jews of Kamenetz suffered then, as well, especially the young people. Some of these young people fled to Russia, while others were jailed and mistreated, suspected by the Poles of being Bolsheviks.

After this period the Poles took over our region and began to impose order. Everyone began to go back to work and to conduct business.

[Page 89]

The Kamenetz Jews were very devoted to one another, and the mutual aid was remarkable. Seeing this devotion was a major influence on our upbringing. Those of us still left alive recall many of the good qualities of our parents and of the people around us who were so dear to us.

We who were adolescents during the war went through a very difficult period then. Aside from periods of school cancellation that took place during the war, we went through crises of a different kind: for 4 or 5 years, each time a regime was replaced by a new one, we were forced to adapt to a new language of study. Except for Jewish studies, we switched from Russian to German and then from German to Polish. It is obvious that these changes impeded our progress in learning. Yet many of these adolescents attained great achievements, some by studying at home, others with the help of private teachers, and still others outside the home.

A Talmud Torah in Our Town

Footnotes:

1.   From *Kamenetz-Litovsk, Zastavije and Colonies Memorial Book*, edited by S. Eisenstadt and M. Galbert, published by the Israel and America Committee of Kamenetz Litovsk and Zastavya, (Orly, Tel Aviv, Israel, 1970), pp. 87-89.

2.   See p. 318 in the Necrology section of this volume; also article by Leah Bobrowski on pp. 83-86 of this volume.

[Pages 90-91]

Some of My Memories[1]

by Rabbi Yaakov Bobrowski (New York)

Translated by Allen Flusberg

During the period in which I was a yeshiva student, before the new Kamenetz Yeshiva building had been built, we studied in the *Beit Midrash* [House of Study] *HaChoma*[2]. One summer day, at dusk, between the *Mincha* [afternoon] and *Maariv* [evening] prayer services, I was sitting near the window. As I gazed through it, I saw a crystal-clear sky merging with the forests and the river on the horizon. And I, so young, was completely captivated by the beauty of nature: Earth and Heaven "that You established"[3], God of Israel…

And so, although deeply engrossed in the world of the mind—pondering the profundities of the back-and-forth exchange of views within the section of Talmud I was studying—I now felt uplifted as I also contemplated the strength and power of the Creator of the Universe—"The heavens recount the glory of God, and the firmament tells of His deeds"[4];…But all at once Rabbi Baruch Ber[5], Head of the Yeshiva, was standing next to me. And when he perceived the depth of my contemplation and the inspiration I was feeling, he spoke to me with admiration: "Happy are you, Yaakov, and fortunate, that you were born in this charming little town. Now I understand why Kamenetz has so many scholars who are native to this place. It is because Nature and Torah become integrated here, elevating one another. 'Your very air's alive with souls'[6]. These clear skies, this fruitful earth—these are what produced all these prodigies: the author of *Birkat Rosh*[7]; Rabbi David Karlin[8], author of *Yad David*, a commentary on the Rambam[9]; and the Prodigy of Tavrik[10], who served as Rabbi and Head of the Yeshiva *Mercaz HaRav*[11]."

Indeed, it was in this atmosphere that my parents were born and raised, and it was within this aura that all the residents of Kamenetz-Litowsk, Zastavya and the Colonies lived.

My father, R. Avraham, of blessed memory, had not had any opportunity to complete his studies, in spite of his many talents. The economic situation of his family had prevented him from being "exiled to a place of Torah". As a villager he was forced to engage in garden and field work. Yet all his life a love for Torah and for the wisdom of Israel was lodged within him. He found an outlet by ensuring his sons and daughters were well-versed in Torah. His sons he sent to yeshivas; and by hiring private teachers in Kamenetz he educated his daughters in both Hebrew and general studies.

When the yeshiva *Knesset Beit Yitzhak* moved from Vilna to Kamenetz, my father worked hard in support of the yeshiva. When Rabbi Baruch Ber and Rabbi Grozowski left on a mission to America, my father was given the task of overseeing building the rabbi's house. My father fulfilled this task with devotion and dedication—with no desire to benefit from it.

At that time, I was studying at the *Beit Yosef* Yeshiva[12] in Bialystok[13]. One day Rabbi Baruch Ber invited my father over to his house and suggested bringing me back to Kamenetz to study in the *Knesset Beit Yitzhak* yeshiva. Rabbi Baruch Ber proposed that he himself would guide and supervise me during my studies in the yeshiva, as a way of thanking my father for all he had done for the yeshiva. And thus, thanks to my father, I was destined to become one of the students of the prodigious Rabbi Baruch Ber.

My mother was a gentle person with lofty ideals. All her life she devoted herself to improving her children's lot. Her love for us reached the level of self-sacrifice. I still recall the following: when the Second World War broke out, I had been drafted into the Polish army, and I was near sites of battles against the accursed Nazis. In 1939, on the holiday of *Hoshana Rabba*[14], I went over to my parents' house in Kamenetz. We discussed the prevailing chaotic situation that was approaching us. And then we heard that all the yeshivas in the area were about to move and to converge on Vilna, the "Jerusalem of Lithuania"[15]. My mother begged me to leave Kamenetz immediately and to join up with the Mir[16] yeshiva students. "There you will be rescued from death and destruction," she said. Since my mother was seriously ill at that time, I was reluctant to abandon her in the depressed state she was in (three months before her death). My mother realized this and said, "I am ordering you to fulfil the commandment of honoring your mother by obeying me when I tell you to leave here at once. Your father also agrees with me."

The very next day I said goodbye to my mother and father, as well as everyone else. I left my home and family forever…

Footnotes:

1. From Kamenetz-Litovsk, Zastavije and Colonies Memorial Book, edited by S. Eisenstadt and M. Galbert, published by the Israel and America Committee of Kameńetz Litovsk and Zastavya, (Orly, Tel Aviv, Israel, 1970), pp. 90-91.
2. See article by Bobrowski-Aloni, "The 'Knesset Beit Yitzhak' Yeshiva," pp. 61-63 of this volume.
3. Paraphrase of Psalms 99:4
4. Psalms 19:2
5. For more on Rabbi Baruch Dov (or Boruch Ber) Leibowitz, see the following essays in this volume: Edelstein, "Rabbi Baruch Dov Leibowitz, Head of the Yeshiva of Kamenetz-Litovsk," pp. 64-67; Turetz, "Rabbi Boruch Ber and His Great World-Renowned Yeshiva," p. 408.
6. An excerpt from Yehuda Halevi's Hebrew poem, "Zion, Do You Wonder?" Translation into English by Hillel Halkin, retrieved May 2020 from the following link: http://nextbookpress.com/download/The_Selected_Poems_of_Yehuda_Halevi.pdf
7. *Birkat Rosh* is a commentary on the tractates *Berachot* and *Nazir* of the Babylonian Talmud. Its author was Rabbi Asher HaKohen, the mid-19th-century rabbi of Sarasova, Belarus (located about 35km northeast of Kamenetz). See the following link: (in Hebrew, retrieved May 2020): https://hebrewbooks.org/14746 and https://he.wikipedia.org/wiki/%D7%98%D7%99%D7%A7%D7%98%D7%99%D7%9F
8. The reference is to Rabbi David Friedman (1828-1917), Chief Rabbi of Karlin. See the following link, retrieved May 2020: https://www.rabbimeirbaalhaneis.com/Rabbi%20Dovid%20Friedman.asp
9. The reference is to the work *Mishne Torah*, written by Maimonides (the Rambam). *Yad David* is a commentary on a section of this work, "Laws of *Ishut* (Relationships between Men and Women)".
10. See the following essay in this volume: Burstein, "Rabbi Avraham Aharon HaKohen," pp. 55-57. Tavrik is Taurage, Lithuania (located 400km north of Kamenetz), where Avraham Aharon HaKohen officiated as rabbi.
11. Mercaz HaRav is a yeshiva in Jerusalem where Avraham Aharon HaKohen officiated as Yeshiva Head. See the following article (retrieved May 2020): https://en.wikipedia.org/wiki/Mercaz_HaRav#Roshei_Yeshiva
12. For more information on this yeshiva, which was part of the Novardok network of *Mussar* yeshivas, see the following link (retrieved May 2020): https://en.wikipedia.org/wiki/Novardok_Yeshiva
13. Bialystok, Poland is located ~100km northwest of Kamenetz.
14. *Hoshana Rabba* occurs on the seventh day of Sukkot (Tabernacles). In 1939 it fell on October 4.
15. See article "Vilnius" at the following link (retrieved May 2020): https://en.wikipedia.org/wiki/Vilnius
16. Mir, Belarus (~200km northeast of Kamenetz) was the site of the Mir ("Mirrer") Yeshiva that was transplanted to Vilna in 1939 and from there to Shanghai. See the following link (retrieved May 2020): https://en.wikipedia.org/wiki/Mir_Yeshiva_(Belarus)

[Page 92]

Memoirs from My Home and from the Town Kamenetz–Litowsk[1]

by Pinḥas Ravid-Rudnicki, (Haifa, Kiryat Eliezer)

Translated by Allen Flusberg

The town of Kamenetz, known as Kamenetz–Litowsk, lies approximately 40km away from Brisk [Brest] on the Bug River, in Poland (presently in Russia [2]). Its name came from the large number of stones (*kamień* = stone in Polish) it was endowed with, and it is no wonder that all its inner roads were paved with stones. Standing gloriously within the town was a tall, circular brick tower, about which people had spun various yarns. One was that it had been built at the command of a nobleman who had invested his entire inheritance in it. This tower (which was called the *Sloop* in the local language), also served as a lookout and fortress for warring armies before the Polish state had been reestablished. From a different perspective, this tower served as a derogatory name for the Jewish populace of the town: if an outsider wanted to tease or insult a Kamenetz resident or to make fun of his vanity, all he had to do was to refer to him as a "Kamenetz *sloop*".

JNF Committee of Kamenetz–Litowsk.
Standing: Mendel Szczytnitski, Baruch Ostron, Tuvia Savitzki, Chaim Zlotnik.
Sitting: A Kotik, A.Y. Bleichbord, Shmaryahu Solnitza, Zelig Trestinitzer, Y. Greenblatt.

[Page 93]

The population of the town, nearly all of which was Jewish, amounted to around 7000 residents (of which there were about 500 Jewish families). Its Christian residents lived on a particular street that we called *die Goyeshe Gass*–that is, Gentile Street. The relationship between the two communities was completely proper, and so the Jewish community lived in peace and quiet. Two rows of wooden buildings, all in the same style, stood out in the center of town. They included a haberdashery, a grocery, a merchandise store, a paint store, iron store and the like. The vast majority of the Jewish population made its living from trade, but a significant number were craftsmen: tailors, shoemakers, saddlers, tanners, etc. The residents looked forward to Thursday–the weekly market day–and especially to the *yeridim* [market fairs], during which farmers from nearby villages flocked into town to sell their wares and to make all their purchases at once. These were the days of "recovery" for the town residents. However, there was also a slow season during summer, when the farmers were busy harvesting their crop. During that period the shopkeepers would sit around at their market stalls yawning in boredom, with nothing to do.

Like every typical small town in Poland, Kamenetz had its wealthy, its poor and its middle class. In any event no one who lived there was starving, since the concern to provide for others was very well developed in the town. Collecting money and organizing various funds for philanthropic purposes were some of the virtues of the Jews of the town. More than once the Sabbath Torah reading was interrupted in the synagogue [3] until a committee was formed to provide for various needy people. Feelings of mutual care and concern about others were well developed among the residents. There was also an institution in the town, *Linat Tzedek*, whose purpose was to provide aid and medical equipment for ill people with limited means.

There were no modern schools in the town. Most of the boys were educated in *cheders*, *talmud torah*, and yeshiva [4]; and alternatively, by private teachers, some with no degree. By contrast, the girls were sent to the Polish public school (*Powszechna*) [5]. After some time had passed, steps were taken to establish a *Tarbut* Hebrew school and a kindergarten; and several boys and girls were sent to the nearby city of Brisk [Brest] to continue their studies in the *Tarbut* Gymnasia [6]. The thirst for knowledge awakened a desire among the young people of the town to obtain a higher education on their own; their self–development was helped substantially by a community library that was supervised by the local Zionist movement. In addition to the young people, adults who aspired to higher education in Hebrew, Yiddish, Polish and Russian also used the library.

[Page 94]

However, the highlight of the town's community life was undoubtedly the Zionist parties, especially the pioneer youth movements, which included the best of the local youth: those who were seeking an outlet for their secret desire, their yearning to free themselves from the narrow framework of their lives. They aspired to begin a new life–a creative life in the land of our forefathers. Among the parties the following stood out: *Hitachdut Tz.S.* [7], *Poalei Tzion Yamin* [8], and General Zionists [9]. And from among the youth movements: *Gordonia* [10], *Freiheit* [11], and *Beitar* [12]. Within the youth clubs you could have met on a daily basis groups that were preparing themselves for a pioneering life in the Land of Israel. More than a few of them went off to training camps, where they spent several years until they could immigrate to Israel. The fact that a sizable fraction of the young people, pressed for time, did immigrate to North and South America, cannot be denied. However, the great majority of the young people who obtained a Zionist and pioneer education preferred to immigrate to the Land of Israel. I recall that when someone was fortunate enough to obtain a certificate [entry visa] or a "request" from the Land of Israel, his joy was unbridled–and how his friends would be jealous of him, that he had managed to leave our secluded little town. The farewell parties that were held for these emigrants brought out the bond the young people had for the Land of Israel.

Since I was one of the founders and one of the instructors of the *Gordonia* movement, it is only natural that most of my memories are concentrated around this movement. It was preceded by *HaPina Halvrit* [the Hebrew Corner], which was founded by a small group of young people with the goal of increasing use of the Hebrew language among its members in practice. *HaPina* did not last very long because it did not have the right atmosphere and because it lacked the older generation's communal support. The absence of a local Hebrew school was an additional factor that led to its collapse. In the year 1926, if I remember correctly, the *Gordonia* youth movement was established. From the time it was founded, this movement was viewed positively by most of the young people of the town, who found their way to it and joined as members. A wide range of cultural and social activities took place within it; and a sizeable fraction of its members went off for training and even immigrated to Israel by various routes. A visit to our branch by a representative of the head office always turned into a major town event: the branch leadership would make sure to arrange a public lecture on a timely subject, and this lecture would draw a large audience. Valid pioneer Zionist activities within this movement, and similarly in other youth movements, also made their mark in circles of the older generation, most of whom had initially looked on them unsympathetically and had some reservations about the Zionist movement altogether—fearing that the boys would, God forbid, want to move away from the path of righteousness. But with the decline of the economic situation of the Jewish population in the State of Poland in general, and in the smaller towns in particular—as a result of the official economic policy—the attitude toward the pioneer youth who "dared" to bring nearer the messianic–like time of Jewish salvation [13], became more favorable…

I will not forget the first time I left for training in the Volyn Region [14]. While I had been there for a while, I received a letter from home, in which they wrote that one of my closest friends, who had recently gone on *aliya* to the Land of Israel with the goal of settling there, had returned and was giving the Land a bad name in our town. This news got me so upset that when I returned home I refused to get together with the *yored* [15] and stayed away from him completely.

Innumerable difficulties piled up one after another when it came to my immigrating–the most problematic was the small number of available certificates. I stayed home, waiting, for a number of years, while my passport was renewed over and over again; and finally, I went out for *hachshara* [training] in Zagłębie [16], until I managed to immigrate to Israel in 1938, just one week after the Nazis entered Vienna. But I was still around long enough to see Polish students in Warsaw attacking Jews and plucking their beards out; and in Vienna, which we passed through on the way to Trieste, we saw the fluttering swastikas and experienced the refusal of the residents to serve us water to drink.

[Page 95]

After I had lived for half a year in the *kvutza* [communal agricultural village] Ma'ale HaḤamisha (then known as "Ma'ale") [17], and afterwards in the *moshava* [agricultural village with private property] Karkur [18], bad news began arriving from home—then news of annihilation with the outbreak of World War II and the entry of the Germans into Poland. Our communications with home were cut off for a while, but were renewed with the entry of the Red Army into that area as a result of the Molotov–Ribbentrop Agreement [19]. The postcards and letters I received from there foretold how the previous life of the town was coming to an end, but it did not occur to us that they were about to be completely annihilated. These letters, which I still have in my possession, are a faithful testament to their lives at the end, before they were sent on their final journey to death. Communications with home were cut off completely once the Red Army retreated and Nazi Germany took over all parts of Poland. The fate of my family members was like that of the other Jewish residents of Kamenetz and of all of Poland, a fate dictated by the Nazi beast of prey—with the exception of one brother and one sister and their families, who had been in Argentina for some time. And miraculously my niece Dvora survived the Auschwitz concentration camp; she came to Israel first and is now with her family in the United States [20]; while her father—my brother Yoel, of blessed memory—perished in the Pruzhany Ghetto [21], according to what I have been told.

Kamenetz, My Town, I Will Surely Remember You

Like from within a nightmare, you spring forth and appear before my eyes—you, my serene little town. Days pass, years go by, and every now and then you come to mind again. It is indeed difficult to think back to that era. It is very much like picking at an old wound that has healed outwardly and gone away. In reality, however, it does not heal and never ever gets better. As the years go by, the years since the calamity that was visited upon you, my town, and upon the other Jewish habitations in the occupied countries—so does the magnitude of the heinous crime stand out even more before us, a crime that was inflicted on the myriads and millions of our people by a supposedly cultured, enlightened nation. This slaughter, perpetrated in cold blood and with thorough planning to commit genocide, will never be forgotten; and the mark of Cain on the brows of those guilty of the murder will not easily be removed, perhaps not ever.

I will surely remember your quiet, serene Jewish community life from before the Holocaust; is it even necessary to recapture each and every detail of the exuberant life of that era? When I think back upon you, I see you as if you are still alive: the life of the town, with all its lights and shadows, its organizations and institutions, its leaders and active members, all come back to me; a life of culture and educational institutions, parties and Zionist pioneer youth movements, a diverse rainbow of various types in the town, etc. All these were expressions of the Jewish community life in Kamenetz and Zastavya.

[Page 96]

Indeed, my little town, living in you was like being in a quiet river whose waters flow gently, with no concern about a coming storm. Under these conditions of serenity, whether imaginary or real, everything within you was normal. Merchants, shopkeepers and peddlers were bargaining–or sitting at their stands with nothing to do during the slow season, the time of sowing and reaping. Craftsmen and laborers were busy with their work. The young people were immersed in their studies: reading, composing literary sentences, and the like. The yeshiva students were immersed in the sea of Talmud; and you, my town, were completely enveloped, as if in your own secrets. Apparently, you were content and satisfied with the combination of Torah and labor, the sacred and secular that were integrated and interwoven within you.

You, my town, were blessed with Torah educational institutions and budding secular educational institutions. Within you were libraries and mutual–aid institutions such as a cooperative bank, *Linat Hatzedek*, and others. Various charity funds were set up in you for the purpose of raising money to distribute to those requiring assistance in their time of need. Charity was indeed a characteristic feature that your Jewish residents were blessed with. Their concern for others was foremost. Their hand was always ready to give to any charity, and they contributed significantly to national funds. Their commitment to the redemption of their people and their land was outstanding.

I will always remember your community volunteers, whose entire activities were provided gratis, with no thought of compensation. Among your leading personalities the following stood out: the local rabbi, Rabbi Reuven Burstein; R. [22] Yosef Vigutov; and R. Chaim Schmidt, of blessed memory. With respect to Rabbi Burstein, the Jews of Kamenetz were proud to have a modern rabbi, an affable man with an aristocratic bearing, the chief rabbi of the congregation who was tolerant of other people's opinions [23]. The second one [Vigutov] was a committed community volunteer and congregation head, graced with a warm heart, benevolent to all who turned to him with requests. The third one [Schmidt] was one of the representatives of the congregation in the town, a philanthropic person who led a progressive life. So, my town, you did not lack Torah–knowledgeable, active community volunteers. And in your last years your greatest crown was the *yeshiva gedola* [24] Knesset Beit Yitzhak with its rabbis, principals and students. The glory of the yeshiva was the rabbi who headed it, Rabbi Baruch–Ber Leibowitch, who was so diligently immersed in the study of Torah that he knew next to nothing about secular life.

You, my town, like other cities and towns, were blessed too with parties as well as Zionist and pioneer youth movements. Within you were General Zionists, the *Tz.S. HitAchdut, Poalei–Tziyon Yamin*, not to mention the Bund [25] and Communists. Among the youth movements were *Gordonia, Freiheit* and *Beitar*. Some of the active members of these movements managed to immigrate to the Land of Israel, but the vast majority died in the Holocaust. Among those, we recall the names of Binyamin Bogatin, Lipa Hurwitz, Moshe Biletzky, Freidl Winograd, Berl Welhandler and many, many others. With respect to the first two of these, that is Bogatin and Hurwitz, we had the opportunity to appear in public debates with them more than once, in mock trials and the like. Our differences of opinion, due to quarrels between parties, did not prevent us from respecting and valuing rivals who supported other viewpoints.

[Page 97]

I recall the last years before the Holocaust came. The economic situation in the town was worsening. The young people began to seek ways to emigrate to countries across the sea. Most were knocking at the gates—yearning to immigrate to the Land of Israel. Some went out for training to prepare themselves for lives of labor in the Land. Unfortunately, this period did not last very long. The first signs of the approaching Holocaust began to appear, however nebulously, and the ground literally began to burn under the young people's feet. When I returned from *hachshara* in the Zagłębie and Upper Silesia region, a short time before the Nazis invaded Austria in 1938, I came across Polish slogans written on walls and bulletin boards: "Have pity on a poor animal—have mercy on a living creature"; and next to it a vociferous slogan: "Beat the Jews—death to those who suck our blood!" In spite of the paradoxical inconsistency between these slogans, they did reflect the prevalent situation of that period. The groundwork had been laid for the Holocaust that was fast approaching.

Half a year after I immigrated to the Land of Israel, the Second World War broke out, and the spasms of death of our dear ones there began: first, as they were concentrated in the ghettos of Kamenetz and Pruzhany, and later when they were transported to the death camps and exterminated. At first, while they were under Soviet rule, we were still able to receive letters from them and to maintain a connection with them somehow. But reading between the lines we could discern the bad news of what lay in store for them. Afterwards our connection with them was completely cut off, and we found out about their ultimate, utter annihilation.

My town, I will surely remember you; and the images of our dear ones, the martyrs of Kamenetz–Litowsk and Zastavya, will remain engraved in our hearts for generations to come.

Footnotes:

1.   From *Kamenetz–Litovsk, Zastavije and Colonies Memorial Book*, edited by S. Eisenstadt and M. Galbert, published by the Israel and America Committee of Kamenetz Litovsk and Zastavya, (Orly, Tel Aviv, Israel, 1970), pp. 92–97.

2.   When this original article was written, the town was in the Soviet Union. Since 1991, after the Soviet Union disintegrated, the town has been in the independent state of Belarus.

3.   Someone in need of community help might interrupt the synagogue services at the beginning of the Torah reading to demand a fair and open hearing.

4.   *cheders* = religious–studies elementary schools for young boys; *talmud torah* = religious–studies school for older boys and young teenagers; yeshiva = school teaching religious studies, mostly Talmud, to older teenagers and young men.

5.   See article by Gurvitz, pp. 450–451 of this volume, "The *Powszechna* School".

6.   The *Tarbut–Gymnasias* (high schools) were part of the Zionist–Hebrew educational network. See the following link (retrieved March 2020): https://www.yadvashem.org/yv/en/exhibitions/vilna/before/education.asp

7.   *Hitachdut Tz.S.* or (as written below) *Tz.S. Hitachdut* = Zionist Socialist Association

8.   *Poalei–Tziyon Yamin* = Zionist Workers Right. The term "Right" was added after a right–left schism in the Zionist Workers party. Zionist Workers Right later evolved into the Labor Party of Israel. See the following link (retrieved June 2020): https://en.wikipedia.org/wiki/Poale_Zion.

9.   General Zionists took up the cause of Zionism while endeavoring to be less ideological about socialism, Marxism, etc. See the following link (retrieved June 2020): https://yivoencyclopedia.org/article.aspx/General_Zionists.

10.   On the *Gordonia* movement, see the article on pp. 77–79 in this volume by Ravid, "The *Gordonia* Movement in Kamenetz–Litowsk."

11.   *Freiheit* (*Dror* in Hebrew) = Freedom, a Zionist Socialist youth movement

12.   *Beitar* (or *Betar*) was a non–socialist Zionist youth movement, founded in 1923 by Ze'ev Jabotinsky. See the following web site (retrieved June, 2020): https://en.wikipedia.org/wiki/Betar.

13.   Hebrew *leKarev et haKetz* = bring the end–time near

14.   This region was in Poland between the two World Wars. Volyn has been in Ukraine since 1945. It lies ~200km southeast of Kamenetz.

15.   *yored* = someone who emigrates from the Land of Israel (literally "one who goes down", as opposed to an immigrant to Israel, who is called an *oleh* = one who goes up). The term *yored* has a negative connotation in Modern Hebrew.

16.   Zagłębie = coalfield (Polish). From the mention of Upper Silesia below (p. 97), this appears to be the Upper Silesian Coal Basin, Poland, ~ 400km southwest of Kamenetz.

17.   Ma'ale HaHamisha, located ~15km northwest of Jerusalem, was founded in 1937 by a *Gordonia* group. See the following link (retrieved June 2020): https://en.wikipedia.org/wiki/Ma%27ale_HaHamisha

18.   Karkur is now (2020) Pardes–Hana–Karkur, ~60km north of Tel–Aviv and ~50km south of Haifa.

19.   This agreement (1939) divided Poland between Germany and the Soviet Union; Kamenetz became part of the Soviet Union.

20.   See article by Dvora Rudnitzky on pp. 540–549 of this volume: "What I Lived Through in the Ghettos and Concentration Camps".

21.   Pruzhany, Belarus is located approximately 50km northeast of Kamenetz (see map on p. 160 of this volume). Many of the Jews of Kamenetz were expelled by the Germans to Pruzhany.
See the following article by Dora Galpern on pp. 550–556 of this volume: "The Kamenetz Ghetto" (A Testimony); also the article by Dvora Rudnitzky, cited in Footnote 20.

22.   R. = *Reb*, a title akin to "Mr." in English.

23.   See the two biographies of Rabbi Burstein in this volume: pp. 50–54, Y. Gershuni, "Rabbi Reuven David Hakohen Burstein, May God Avenge his Blood"; and pp. 409–410, Ch. Mendelson, "Rabbi Reuven Burstein, z.tz.l.".

24.   *yeshiva gedola* = religious–studies school for older teenagers and young men. See the following link (retrieved October 2018): https://en.wikipedia.org/wiki/Yeshiva

25.   The *Bund* was an evolving Jewish socialist/Marxist organization that supported cultural autonomy for the Jews within the countries of Eastern Europe, rather than a homeland in Palestine. It also favored Yiddish, rather than Hebrew, as the cultural language of

the Jews. See the following links (retrieved June 2020): https://en.wikipedia.org/wiki/Bundism; https://yivoencyclopedia.org/article.aspx/Bund.

[Page 98]

Shlomo Zelig and His Sons[1]

Translated by Allen Flusberg

It is true that the distinguished members of the community and its volunteer workers were the glory of each and every Jewish city and town in Poland before the Nazi Destruction. Yet we should not at all look down on the *amcha* [common folk], who were embedded in the background life of the town and stood out in the human landscape of the population.

In Kamenetz-Litowsk, Shlomo Zelig and his two sons were without any doubt part of the latter group. Shlomo Zelig was the town guard—or more precisely, the hired guard of the shopkeepers. His job was to monitor the two rows of shops located in the center of town—to prevent robberies and vandalism. More than once, when we came back late at night from a party or from an outing sponsored by a youth movement, we encountered him, curled up in a blanket and dozing—in either a standing or sitting position—on the steps of one of the shops. When we came by he would stir, make some small talk with us, and try to keep us there for a little while—to give him some entertainment and make his hours of boredom more pleasant. He was a simple man, uneducated, but he was a fount of folk wisdom; in spite of his age, he was aware of everything that was happening around him, and he would react to everything in his own unique way. Educated people his age were not close with him, and they treated him with some disapproval. So no wonder then that he was able to find some commonality with the young people, and he preferred to pour his heart out to them.

He used to get paid for his work directly by the owners of the shops. More than once one of the shopkeepers either held back or put off payment for some reason or other. Shlomo Zelig did not react immediately. However, on the very next morning, that shopkeeper would find the lock on his door smeared with tar or with cattle manure. The shopkeeper would hustle to pay his debt and make sure to never go through this experience again.

As part of his job as a guard, he had to check in at the local police station every night to prove that he was carrying out his job. One night he didn't show up at the station the way he usually did. The next day the police commander asked him for an explanation, and he answered, "*Pan komendant velyky sobaka*"[2], i.e., "The honorable commander a big dog." He was trying to say that a big dog that had been lying next to the entrance had scared him away, and so he did not dare come near. It was no more than his poor command of Polish that was responsible for his wording, but all the same it gave rise to laughter and hilarity throughout the entire town.

[Page 99]

His two sons, Arye and Ḥaim, were very different from him, being somewhat adventurous characters. They had never received any education and were illiterate. They worked as porters—a profession that was not particularly popular among the young people. The two of them were sturdy, brawny fellows. Hardly anyone would dare start up with them, afraid of what those strong arms could do to them. Many a time we, who had been preparing for a life of labor in Israel, looked at them with admiration, watching them toil at loading or unloading sacks of salt and flour, barrels of salted fish, crowbars, oil barrels and the like. I recall that, for various jobs they carried out as contractors, they used to keep count by making chalk marks on one of the walls, so that they could confirm how many sacks or barrels they had unloaded from a wagon from the number of chalk lines they had drawn. Many a time, pranksters would quietly sneak up to the wall and erase some of these lines, sometimes even causing them to lose earnings.

The townspeople's attitude to them was polite. To some extent they viewed them as defenders of Jewish honor against Christian roughnecks, somewhat like the heroes of Zalman Shneur, typified by Noah Pandre[3]. It is no wonder that for any event in town that charged an admission fee—such as a play in a theatre or any kind of party—they were always allowed in for free. So after all was said and done they were treated like privileged characters—for among the young people, nearly all of whom were, in practice, complete loafers, they were the only ones toiling at hard labor.

And so a kind of indiscernible connection was forged between them and the pioneer youth. Their derision for the intellectuals and pseudo-intellectuals, or even for notables and people with pedigree, always resonated with the young people, even though the "loafers who were pioneers" received saucy epithets from them, as well. Yet they did appreciate the difference in virtue between this type of young people and other types who distanced themselves completely—in both word and deed—from the concept of physical labor.

Recalling these toiling laborers and others like them gives us a sharp pain in our hearts, realizing that they were not fortunate enough to be among those who built up the Land—for our young State would have especially benefited from their broad shoulders.[4]

Footnotes:

1. From *Kamenetz-Litovsk, Zastavije and Colonies Memorial Book*, edited by S. Eisenstadt and M. Galbert, published by the Israel and America Committee of Kamenetz Litovsk and Zastavya, (Orly, Tel Aviv, Israel, 1970), pp. 98-99.
2. The language appears to be the local dialect used by the peasant farmers, which is said to be similar to Ukrainian.
3. Zalman Shneur, sometimes spelled Salman Schneour (1887-1959), was a prolific author of novels in Hebrew and Yiddish. Noah Pandre was the protagonist of one of his novels.
4. See the following articles in this Yizkor Book for some details from the Holocaust period on Shlomo-Zelig's sons: p. 553 of "The Kamenetz Ghetto", by D. Galpern,; p. 564 of "Kamenetz in 1945", by Ben-Moshe.

Alterke[1]

by Pinḥas Ravid-Rudnicki

Translated by Allen Flusberg

Like most Diaspora towns, our town had its very own eccentric, an odd person. His name was Alterke.[2]

The children of the town loved to start up with him and make fun of him. When they would see him passing by in the street, they would throw stones towards him: certainly not to hurt him, God forbid, but rather to provoke him a bit. But in fact this was something that actually pleased Alterke: it let him become the center of attention as he began shouting at and cursing the children who were provoking him.

No one knows how Alterke came to our town or where he came from, at least not any of the young people. The older people of the town must have known his "family pedigree", but no one ever revealed the secret. Nor was his age known, and on that subject there were various guesses of all kinds. But how was it possible to estimate Alterke's age when his cruel fate did not provide him with any sign of a beard? Some said he was about fifty and even about 60, and others thought he was older or younger than that.

[Page 100]

Alterke had a unique position: seeing to it that the streets were clean. Whenever City Hall would assign him the job of town crier, to make public announcements—particularly when some distinguished delegation was expected in town—he would urge townspeople to sweep the parts of the streets that their houses were adjacent to. But there were also incidents in which Alterke would suddenly appear and convey an order to the community for an urgent cleanup campaign, as if the president himself, in all his glory, was about to make an immediate appearance. In the end it would turn out that there really was no truth to it: there was no such order, and no important personality was about to arrive in town. When the townsfolk gathered around Alterke and asked him for an explanation for the cleanup "order", he answered with a grin: "Aren't you glad that I made you clean up the town a bit? Let it be in honor of the Sabbath that is coming soon…"

But this was not Alterke's only job. He had "franchises" that he would not give up to anyone, not for all the riches in the world. It was Alterke's priority that the following items were in his possession: the keys to the *shul* (main synagogue); the four velvet-covered poles used in wedding ceremonies; and the two pillows that they would place the male infant on during the circumcision ritual. Still there was always some prankster who would sneak into the place where these articles were kept hidden and take them away. When Alterke would find out he would pace through the streets, crying like a baby, until the "stolen" objects were returned to him.

Alterke

[Page 101]

With the beginning of the emigration of the young people overseas, and in particular with the increase in the pioneer aliya to the Land [of Israel], Alterke became more and more depressed. It was as if he foresaw that his job in the town would be coming to an end, and his loyal allies would be leaving him to his own devices. It was painful to look at him and see him stooped over, leaning on his cane. For the town this was the beginning of the end of the era of great fame, in which Alterke had played so distinguished a role.

Footnotes:

1.   From *Kamenetz-Litovsk, Zastavije and Colonies Memorial Book*, edited by S. Eisenstadt and M. Galbert, published by the Israel and America Committee of Kamenetz Litovsk and Zastavya, (Orly, Tel Aviv, Israel, 1970), pp. 99-101.
2.   Alterke (or Alter'ke) = diminutive of Alter, a common Jewish first name that is interpretable as "Old Man". Hence "Alterke" can mean "little old man".

[Page 102]

Memories and Yearning[1]

by Yakov Kaminski

Translated by Allen Flusberg

With great reverence and with pain in my heart, I recall my native town Kamenetz-Litowsk and its people, my townspeople who once were and are no longer. Kamenetz was widely known as "Kamenetz *Slup*", a nickname derived from the ancient, large fortress [the *Slup*] with a circular shape that stood in the middle of town. Then our town became famous throughout the Jewish world thanks to the renowned, preeminent yeshiva, with its hundreds of students, that was located in Kamenetz. It was headed by one of the greatest scholars of our generation, Rabbi Baruch Ber, may the memory of the righteous be a blessing.

Kamenetz was a typical Jewish town. Nearly all of its residents were shopkeepers and artisans, who labored from morning until evening to provide some bread for their children. But their greatest concern was providing their children with an education, which in those days was obtained in the *Ḥeders*, *Talmud-Torahs* and yeshivas[2]. Only a few of the children attended the Polish state school; and a very small number of children whose parents were affluent were sent to Brisk-Litowsk[3] to study in the Hebrew high school established by *Tarbut*[4].

As fresh winds of change blew through the Jewish streets of the cities and towns in Poland, the Zionist idea began winning over the young people. In our town the youth also started organizing branches of the various movements, like Gordonia[5] and Beitar[6], and began training for *aliya* [immigration] to the Land of Israel. Slowly but surely their parents were influenced by their children's actions and started supporting the national funds that the young people were managing. In the last year before the terrible Holocaust, dozens of these youths began to immigrate illegally (no immigration certificates) to the Land of Israel after receiving word from me and from my friend Beryl Miletski that we had reached Israel safely. Unfortunately, most were overtaken by the Nazi beast before they were able to fulfil their dream.

Thinking about lovely little Kamenetz arouses in me yearnings for and memories of my family members who were martyred in the Holocaust. I had left my father, mother, brother and three sisters behind, as well as my good friends Velvl Glezer and Raya Shostakowski, of blessed memory. I can still see them and all the other townspeople, and I cannot forget them. Human language is incapable of articulating my feelings about the terrible Holocaust that was visited upon our brothers and sisters: the men and women, the old people and young children, who were tormented and martyred for the sanctification of God's Name and the Jewish people, saturating the earth of Kamenetz with their blood. It is very difficult to come to terms with this awful reality, that all my cherished relatives and the other people of my town—the town where I was born, spent the years of my childhood and grew up—were exterminated and are no more.

Footnotes:

1.   From *Kamenetz-Litovsk, Zastavije and Colonies Memorial Book*, edited by S. Eisenstadt and M. Galbert, published by the Israel and America Committee of Kamenetz Litovsk and Zastavya, (Orly, Tel Aviv, Israel, 1970), pp. 102.
2.   *Ḥeder* = school providing elementary religious education. *Talmud-Torah* = a religious boys' high school. In the present context "yeshiva" refers to a school of advanced religious study.
3.   Brest-Litowsk, a city located about 40km south of Kamenetz.
4.   *Tarbut* was a Zionist-Hebrew educational network. See the following link, retrieved January, 2021: Educational Institutions - The Interwar Period - The Jerusalem of Lithuania: The Story of the Jewish Community of Vilna (yadvashem.org)
5.   See article by P. Ravid on pp. 77-79 of this Yizkor Book, "The Gordonia Movement in Kamenetz-Litowsk".
6.   See article by B. Kotik on p. 80 of this Yizkor Book, "Beitar and Hatzohar [Zionist Revisionist] Movement in Kamenetz-Litowsk".

[Page 103]

Kamenetz, Where I Was Born[1]

by Penina Felayev-Bobrowski

Translated by Allen Flusberg

I remember our town Kamenetz as a place of Torah and wisdom, in which hundreds of young men, yeshiva students, were seated studying Torah in the Advanced Yeshiva that had been founded by Rabbi Baruch-Ber, of blessed memory.

I recall the Leshna River with its clear water, in which we used to bathe on the hot summer days, and in which the housewives would wash their laundry. In my mind's eye I can still see the *Slup* [medieval tower] standing upright on a hill and towering high, immersed in a sea of legends and mystery.

And the market with its shops all around it, in which many of the Kamenetz townspeople eked out a living from one another and from their Gentile neighbors who lived in the surrounding villages. And the library in which I spent many hours working as a librarian together with my friend Malya Greenblatt, of blessed memory. And during early evening hours, just after sunset, everyone would cease his labor, and the Kamenetz residents would go out to breath some fresh air and to enjoy some friendly conversation.

I left Kamenetz, the town where I was born, in the year 1939, about one month before the Second World War broke out. At that time we knew about the existence and organization of the Nazis and their leader Hitler, may his name be blotted out, and about their hatred for the Jewish people. But we did not imagine then that these beasts of prey might destroy a third of our people.

In Kamenetz anti-Semitism was intensifying from day to day. On the streets of the town we would many a time hear someone say "*Żydzi do Palestyny* (Jews, off to the Land of Israel); there is no place for you here." Our young people were very depressed. Many times we gathered together, especially during evenings, to consult with each other, either in my parents' home or in the home of my uncle, R.[2] Yisrael Grunt, may their memories be a blessing. We would discuss what we might do in the event of a pogrom. Rumors were spreading that the Christians were getting ready to riot against the Jews during one of the monthly fairs that took place in the town.

We were all overcome with gloom as the days passed slowly. Rumors of the war that was coming shocked and upset us, but we could see no solution, and so we were consumed with despair.

I decided to immigrate to the Land of Israel, and I set out on my way. After many days of being tossed on the ocean waves in the rickety ship *Parita*, I arrived with many other *olim* [immigrants to Israel] like me on the beach of Tel Aviv[3], into the bosom of my sisters' families. Here I found out, to my great sorrow, that Chaya, the daughter of my uncle R. Alter Puczinki, who had set off on her way to the Land of Israel, had been sent back from the Romanian border; and thus she, too, perished at the hands of the accursed Nazis, together with all our other relatives.

All was annihilated without a trace—my Kamenetz was destroyed together with all its Jewish residents: women and children, the young and old, all were cut off and are no more.

I will never forget them.

Footnotes:

1.   From *Kamenetz-Litovsk, Zastavije and Colonies Memorial Book*, edited by S. Eisenstadt and M. Galbert, published by the Israel and America Committee of Kamenetz Litovsk and Zastavya, (Orly, Tel Aviv, Israel, 1970), p. 103.
2.   R. stands for *Reb*, an honorific similar to English "Mr."
3.   For more on the landing of this steamer on the Tel Aviv beach on August 23, 1939, with 700 refugees on board, see the following links (retrieved November 2020):
   https://en.wikipedia.org/wiki/Aliyah_Bet#cite_ref-FRUS1096_10-0;
   https://www.jewishvirtuallibrary.org/the-irgun-rsquo-s-role-in-illegal-immigration

[Page 107]

Comunal Workers,
Writers and Teachers in Kamenets–Litowsk

About the *Maggid* of Kamenetz,
Rabbi Ḥaim Zundl Maccoby, of Blessed Memory[1]

by P. Rabi[2],[3]

Translated by Allen Flusberg

The *Maggid* [Orator, Preacher] of Kamenetz, R.[4] Ḥaim Zundl, son of Simḥa Maccoby, was born in 1856 in a village near Kobryn[5]. While still a child Ḥaim Zundl was known for his sharp mind. He never tolerated any injustices from anyone. While still in *ḥeder*[6], when he would see someone mistreating someone else, he would berate him to his face. Already then, the way he would fight for fairness and justice was indicative of the "nationalist orator" he would become in the future.

When Ḥaim-Zundl started out in *ḥeder* he showed signs of being a prodigy. At six years of age he began to study the Prophets, which he became very enthusiastic about. And after several years, when he had already begun to study *Gemara* [Talmud], he never put aside his *Tanach* [Bible]. At the age of 12 he moved to Brisk-Litowsk[7], where he studied in the local yeshiva for 3 years.

When he was sixteen, Ḥaim-Zundl married the daughter of R. Mordechai Blecher, a distinguished man from Pruzhany. His father-in-law promised to cover his provisions for an extended period on the condition that he would study to become a rabbi. Meanwhile, Ḥaim-Zundl began to learn languages and to read secular books.

A disagreement between Ḥaim-Zundl and his father-in-law forced him to leave the latter's house: When he wanted to give his first *drasha* [lecture] in Pruzhany[8], his father-in-law forbade him. What did Ḥaim-Zundl do? He put up notices that on a particular day a *maggid* would be giving a talk, but he did not specify the *maggid's* name in the notices. The audience came to the *Bet Midrash*[9], waiting for the *maggid* to appear. When no *maggid* came to lecture, Ḥaim-Zundl went up to the podium and announced that since the *maggid* had not shown up, he was requesting permission to speak in his place. And in this very first lecture of his he demonstrated the capability and oratory talent that he was later renowned for after he became the *Maggid* of Kamenetz.

[Page 108]

During the Intermediate days of Passover, 5634[10], R. Ḥaim-Zundl was appointed *maggid* of Kamenetz-Litowsk, and from then on he became known as "The *Maggid* of Kamenetz". When he was 25 years old the *maggid* was sent by the central committee of *Ḥovevei-Tzion*[11] on a mission to travel through the cities of Russia as a "nationalist *maggid*". He would go from one city to another and preach on the rebuilding of Zion and Jerusalem. His lectures greatly helped enlist supporters for the idea of *Hibbat-Tzion*.

How profound an influence R. Ḥaim-Zundl Maccoby had on the people of his generation can be seen from the words of Rabbi Tz. H. Orliansky[12] in his book *Toldot Ḥayai* [My Autobiography]. He wrote as follows: "I was then about ten years old, and I was studying in the *Bet Midrash* of a small city, Janova[13]. I recall that in the winter of 5634 [1873-1874] a young yeshiva student, about twenty-three years old, went over to the *shamash* [beadle] of the old *Bet Midrash* and said that he was a *maggid* and that he would like to lecture after the *minḥa* [afternoon] prayer service. The *shamash* then announced that a *maggid* would speak that evening. After the prayer service this young man went up to the podium and said that he was the *maggid* of the town of Kamenetz that was near Brisk. He started his lecture at 4 PM and finished at 10 PM. And after that he spoke again on Friday night after dinner until midnight; and at dawn of the next morning from 5 AM until the morning prayer service began. And after that—in the afternoon, and again after the afternoon service. All the townspeople, men and women, from one end of the town to the other, came to hear his lectures—and even residents of the nearby villages came, as if they were grabbing in the very last rain of the season. This young man was a source of huge inspiration for me, and afterwards I would always be picturing him and thinking about him—the *Maggid* of Kamenetz…"

For nine years the *maggid* travelled around the entire country and preached to the Jewish Diaspora. There were occasions when entire groups of *Maskilim* [progressives], lay scholars and those who appreciated good *drash* [learned lectures] would follow him around, travelling from one city to the next in order to hear him give more and more learned talks. He founded more than three hundred new societies dedicated to settling the Land of Israel; the largest and foremost associations, located in Odessa, Vilna, Minsk, Kovno, Bialystok, Kiev etc., were founded by him. The newspapers *HaMaggid*, *HaTzefira* and *HaMelitz* considered him the greatest nationalist preacher of his generation.

Yet Ḥaim-Zundl had no small share of foes: rabbis and community leaders who were opposed to *Hibbat-Tzion*. On one occasion Ḥaim-Zundl was invited by the *Maskilim* and scholars of Navahrudak[14] to give a nationalist lecture. The city rabbi, Rabbi Michl HaLevi Epstein (author of the book *Aruch HaShulḥan*)[15], one of the foremost opponents of the idea of settling the Land of Israel, prohibited him from giving any lectures. Between the *minḥa*[afternoon] and *maariv* [evening] service the large *Bet Midrash* filled up and was crowded, and the congregation was standing packed together in a stifling crush, with hundreds of people left outside in the courtyard of the *Bet Midrash*, unable to enter. Those who had gathered there were shouting in unison that if the *maggid* did not give his lecture they would not take it quietly—they were going to wreck the *Bet Midrash* and the entire city. When the rabbi saw that the congregation did not accept his "decree", he ordered the *gabbais* [functionaries] of the *Bet Midrash* to go to the inn where the *maggid* was staying and ask the *maggid* to come to preach to the congregation.

As a matter of principle and in practice R. Haim-Zundl was a vegetarian. He was also very strict in the religious laws of eating and dressing. He never wore leather shoes; instead he purchased rubber shoes as a special order from a factory. He was also persecuted by the government, which refused to give him a passport, since he had not paid the 300-ruble fine[16] that they had imposed on him because of his younger brother, who had run away from army service.

[Page 109]

In the year 1890 he made his way to England, where he was appointed *Maggid* of the *Oraḥ Tzedek* Society. The Jewish Chronicle wrote the following about his first lecture [in London]: "He gave a terrific lecture. The hall was completely full; Jewish women from wealthy families of 'the City' attended, as well as important, prominent men. The *maggid* did not limit himself to speak before the Jews of London only; he made himself available to respond to the demand of other large cities that invited him to visit their many congregations. He made a name for himself among all the Jews of Britain." Rabbi Tz. H. Masliansky[17], the famous orator of American Jewry, wrote the following in his "Memoirs": "The *Maggid* of Kamenetz inspired all the hearts of his audience. Indeed, he was a terrific and genial speaker. He had an amazing talent for oratory, and a great deal of erudition in both ancient and modern Hebrew literature. When he came to London several years ago, he was able to focus the interest of all English Jews around himself. It was because of his wonderful talent and the feelings of his Jewish heart—a heart that was alert to all that touched upon Zion and its rebuilding, and to all that was holy in the eyes of the people."

He became a British citizen. The citizenship document was presented to him by the congregation Netzaḥ Israel at a banquet in his honor chaired by the Chief Rabbi.

Lord Rothschild once invited him to visit him in his house, and after a long conversation during the visit, he wrote him two checks, each for £100[18], asking the rabbi to keep the first for himself and distribute the second among the poor people of the East End of the city. The rabbi accepted the second check with great thanks, but he refused the first check, explaining that he was opposed to taking personal donations.

He was offered the position of Dayan [religious judge] to replace the deceased Dayan, Reverend Spiers[19]. But he had to turn down this important, respectable position because, as a vegetarian, he would feel uncomfortable ruling on the *kashrut* [ritual fitness] of meat…After a difficult but very active life, having accomplished so much for the Jewish people of Russia and England, he passed away in 1916, in the prime of life, at the age of about 60.

Footnotes:

1. From *Kamenetz-Litovsk, Zastavije and Colonies Memorial Book*, edited by S. Eisenstadt and M. Galbert, published by the Israel and America Committee of Kamenetz Litovsk and Zastavya, (Orly, Tel Aviv, Israel, 1970), pp. 107-109.
2. Footnote in original reads: "Collected and compiled [by Rabi], based on the book Imrei-Ḥaim". This collection of writings by Maccoby is introduced by a biography authored by the publisher, M. Mansky, on which this article is based. The book is available at the following website (in Hebrew, retrieved Aug 2020): https://www.hebrewbooks.org/pdfpager.aspx?req=2831&st=&pgnum=1&hilite= The translator of the present article has referred to Mansky's book to clarify some of the text in this article.
3. Biography of author, Pinḥas Rabi (Rabinowitz), may be found on pp. 157-158 of this volume.
4. R. = *Reb*, a title similar to English "Mr."
5. Kobryn, Belarus, is located ~35km southeast of Kamenetz.
6. *ḥeder* = religious school for young children (also spelled *chayder*, *cheider*)
7. Brisk = Brest, 40km south of Kamenetz
8. Pruzhany, Belarus, is located ~50km northeast of Kamenetz.
9. *Bet Midrash* = study hall, often also used as synagogue
10. April, 1874
11. *Ḥovevei-Tzion* = Lovers of Zion, also known as *Hibbat-Tzion* (= Love of Zion), was a late-19th-century movement encouraging Jews to found settlements in the Land of Israel. See the following link (retrieved Sep 2020): https://en.wikipedia.org/wiki/Hovevei_Zion
12. Tzvi Hirsh Orliansky (1864-1940)

13.   Janova = Jonava, Lithuania, 20km northeast of Kovno (Kaunas, Lithuania), about 400km north of Kamenetz

14.   Navahrudak, Belarus, is located ~200km northeast of Kamenetz.

15.   Yechiel Michl Epstein (1829-1908). See the following website (retrieved Sep 2020): https://en.wikipedia.org/wiki/Yechiel_Michel_Epstein

16.   See the following link (retrieved July 2020): https://kehilalinks.jewishgen.org/lida-district/wages.htm. In 1900, a typical worker might earn 180 rubles yearly, hence 300 rubles would be equivalent to nearly two years of salary of such a worker. From a different perspective, in 1900 1 ruble was worth US$0.78. The inflation in the period 1900-2019 was a factor of 31, hence 300 rubles of the year 1900 would be equivalent to $7,000 in 2019 dollars (see the following link, retrieved July 2020: https://westegg.com/inflation/).

17.   Tzvi Hirsch Masliansky (1856-1943). See the following website (retrieved Sep 2020): https://www.clevelandjewishhistory.net/silver/masliansky-biography.html

18.   In 1900, £100 was equivalent to $500 (See the following link, retrieved September 2020: https://www.exchangerates.org.uk/articles/1325/the-200-year-pound-to-dollar-exchange-rate-history-from-5-in-1800s-to-todays.html). Accounting for inflation, £100 would be equivalent to approximately $15,000 in 2019 dollars (see Footnote 16).

19.   Dayan Bernard Spiers (1835-1900). See the following websites (retrieved September 2020): https://www.geni.com/people/Reverend-Dayan-Bernard-Dov-Ber-Spiers/6000000025793863483; https://jewishmiscellanies.com/2020/04/26/the-threefold-cord-by-dayan-bernard-spiers-london-wertheimer-lea-co-1891/

[Page 110]

Menachem Mendel of Kamenetz–Litowsk[1]
5593–5594 (1833–1834)[2]

Translated by Allen Flusberg

R.[3] Menachem–Mendel, son of Aharon of Kamenetz–Litowsk was born around the year 5560 (1800). He went up to Israel in Elul, 5593 (1833), and died in Jerusalem in 5633 (1873).[4]

During a cholera epidemic that swept through the town, he made a vow that if he survived the epidemic he would go up to the Land of Israel. On the Eve of the New Moon of Tammuz 5593 (18 June 1833[5],[6]) he fulfilled his vow and, together with his wife and son, traveled from the town to Odessa, where they arrived a month later. From there they sailed on an Italian ship on the 10th of Av (26 July 1833), and after three days arrived in Constantinople [Istanbul]. After staying there for nine days they set sail on the Mediterranean Sea and arrived in Haifa on the 1st of Elul (16 August 1833). Since there was not a single Ashkenazi Jewish community there at that time, they sent a message to the *Kolel* [Community] of Safed to let them know they had arrived. From Safed someone was sent to hire donkeys for them and bring them to Safed.

R. Menachem–Mendel settled in Safed and joined the Community of the *Perushim*[7], followers of the Gaon of Vilna[8], headed by R. Yisrael of Shklov[9]. At the time there was a community of 2000 Jewish families in Safed, serving as a hub for immigration of *Perushim* from Lithuania and Hasidim from Reisin[10] and Poland. R. Menachem–Mendel had hoped to support himself from the money that he had brought along, but he was not to live in the country in peace and quiet. Three months after his arrival his son died in a plague[11] epidemic. He describes this event in plain but poignant language: "And thanks to God who rescued me and my wife from this; but my son died then, meriting burial in the Land of Israel on the New Moon of Kislev."[12]

What pious innocence emerges here in his voice! A father who has lost his child tells how his son died of plague, but notes that this personal calamity is outweighed by the great merit of being buried in the Holy Land!

Nine months after he arrived a terrible calamity befell the Jews of Safed: the *fellahin* [peasant farmers] who lived around Safed rebelled against Pasha Ibrahim, who was then governing the country in the name of his father Mohammed Ali, ruler of Egypt.[13] The rebels attacked the Jews of Safed on the 8th of Sivan, 5594 (15 June 1834), robbing, pillaging, wounding and tormenting; and the riots continued for over a month. The Jews of Safed had not yet fully recovered from this misfortune when an earthquake took place on the 24th of Tevet 5594 [sic][14] (1 January 1837). In this earthquake more than two thousand people were killed and the city was devastated, becoming little more than rubble.

[Page 111]

After these events R. Menachem–Mendel was left "naked, without clothing" and found it necessary to leave the country for a while. The leader of the *Perushim*, R. Yisrael of Shklov, gave him permission to leave, asking him to join the emissary of the *Perushim*, R. Natan Neta, son of Menachem–Mendel of Shklov, who was then leaving for Lithuania to encourage the Jews there to send monetary aid to the Land of Israel. They set out from Israel at the end of the summer of 5598 [1838] via Constantinople and Odessa.

In the year 5600 (1840), while he was on this mission, R. Menachem–Mendel printed in Vilna a short book called *Korot Haitim* [Events of the Times][15], in which he described his coming up to the Land, his short visit to Jerusalem and Hebron, and the frightening incidents that had taken place in Safed. In a particular chapter entitled *Maalot HaAretz* [Advantages of the Land], he realistically described the lifestyle of the Land of Israel in detail and with a keen eye: the climate; types of food; the vegetables and the fruits; how food was customarily cooked and baked; the utensils; trade and craft; weights and coins; prices; customs of the Sephardim; the graves of the righteous; as well as a short dictionary of Arabic providing requisite everyday vocabulary.

In his book he intended to encourage the Jewish people to send aid to the Jewish *Yishuv*[16], "each person according to what he has been blessed with and can afford"; and "whoever has the means…let him take his bag of coins and leave for the Holy Land." He also described how he himself had gone up to Israel and how he had visited Jerusalem and Hebron, "so that all the people may know how one can get to the Land of Israel." And in addition he hoped to reestablish himself from the sales of the book.

[Page 112]

In the year 5602 (1842) he returned from his mission and settled in Jerusalem, where he opened the very first hotel.[17] This hotel served as a temporary lodging place for new immigrants.

"It was a hostel that welcomed rent–paying guests, as well as a temporary lodging place for new immigrants before they found permanent places to settle in the country. At the same time it served as a free place of lodging for quite a few impoverished guests." One of the old–time residents of Jerusalem, R. Yosef HaLevi Horowitz, goes on to recount that it served not only poor lodgers, but also religious scholars of Jerusalem who had no means of support; these would be coming and going to this unique "hotel" and sitting down for meals together with all of R. Menachem–Mendel's family members.

Although the "hotel" was created to provide livelihood, the owners of the business, R. Menachem–Mendel of Kamenetz and his wife, Tzipa, fulfilled the commandment of hospitality selflessly, as a labor of love.[18]

For many years this "hotel" and "restaurant" were unique in Jerusalem. In one or two of Montefiore's trips to Jerusalem with his wife, food was brought for him from R. Menachem–Mendel's kitchen.

R. Menachem–Mendel's wife, Tzipa, was the housewife, the Jewish woman of valor who managed all of the business. It was to Tzipa's credit that her husband was able to spend most of his time engaged in the study of Torah and in prayer services.[19]

Their son Eliezer Lipa, born in the year 5605 [1845], followed in his parents' footsteps: After many years (in the year 5640 [1880]) he opened a modern hotel, the first one run by Jews, in Jerusalem. It was called the "Kaminitz Hotel" or the well–known "Eshel Yerushalayim".[20]

Footnotes:

1. From *Kamenetz–Litovsk, Zastavije and Colonies Memorial Book*, edited by S. Eisenstadt and M. Galbert, published by the Israel and America Committee of Kamenetz Litovsk and Zastavya, (Orly, Tel Aviv, Israel, 1970), pp. 110–112. Footnote in original: Transcribed following *Sefer Mea Shana* [= Centennial Book] and *Masaot Eretz Yisrael* [= Journeys to the Land of Israel].
2. The years 5593–5594 (1833–1834) in the title are apparently the first years he spent in Israel.
3. R. stands for *Reb*, an honorific similar to "Mr." in English.
4. For additional information, see the Encyclopedia Judaica article "Baum, Menahem Mendel Ben Aaron of Kamenetz", available at the following link (retrieved January 2020): https://www.encyclopedia.com/religion/encyclopedias–almanacs–transcripts–and–maps/baum–menahem–mendel–ben–aaron–kamenetz
5. All secular dates in the original article follow the Gregorian calendar; but note that the official calendar used by the Russian authorities in Kamenetz–Litowsk at the time was still the Julian calendar.
6. 1 Tammuz 5593 = 18 June 1833. The first day of the New Moon of Tammuz is a day earlier, 30 Sivan, hence the secular date of the Eve of the New Moon was 16 June.
7. *Perushim* = those who had separated themselves. A large group of Perushim left Lithuania and settled in the Land of Israel in the beginning of the 19th century. See the following link, retrieved January 2020: https://en.wikipedia.org/wiki/Perushim
8. Eliyahu son of Shlomo Zalman of Vilna (1720–1797), known as the Vilna Gaon, was a prodigious scholar who led the Jewish opposition to the Hasidic movement. See the following link (retrieved January 2020): https://en.wikipedia.org/wiki/Vilna_Gaon
9. Yisrael son of Shmuel of Shklov (~1770–1839), a follower of the Vilna Gaon, emigrated to Israel. See the following link (retrieved January 2020): https://en.wikipedia.org/wiki/Yisroel_ben_Shmuel_of_Shklov
10. Reisin = Ruthenia. See the following link (retrieved January 2020): https://en.wikipedia.org/wiki/Rusyns
11. Hebrew *dever* = plague, pestilence
12. November 12–13, 1833.
13. See following link (retrieved February 2020) for more details on this insurrection: https://en.wikipedia.org/wiki/Peasants%27_revolt_in_Palestine
14. 24 Tevet 5594 = Jan 5 1834; 24 Tevet 5597 = Jan 1 1837. Apparently the misprint is the year 5594, which should read 5597, as can be confirmed from the account given in Menahem–Mendel's book *Korot HaItim* (see Footnote 15), as well as the following link (retrieved February 2020): https://en.wikipedia.org/wiki/Galilee_earthquake_of_1837
15. The book *Korot HaItim* (written in Hebrew) can be read at the following link, retrieved January 2020: https://benyehuda.org/read/2695
16. *Yishuv* = pre–state Jewish communities of the Land of Israel, particularly in the Ottoman period. See the following link (retrieved February 2020): https://en.wikipedia.org/wiki/Yishuv
17. This hotel was located near the Tower of David in the Old City of Jerusalem. See the following link (in Hebrew, retrieved January 2020): https://he.wikipedia.org/wiki/מנחם_מנדל_מקאמיניץ
18. Hebrew *lishma* = for its own sake
19. Hebrew *yashav…al haTorah vehaAvoda*
20. Also known as "Hotel Jerusalem", it was the first modern hotel in West Jerusalem that was under Jewish ownership. What is left of the building entrance can be seen in a parking lot behind Neviim Street [Street of the Prophets] 65. See the following links, retrieved January 2020: https://en.wikipedia.org/wiki/Street_of_the_Prophets#Hotels
https://commons.wikimedia.org/wiki/File:Kaminitz_Hotel_Street_of_Prophets_02.jpg
A more detailed history of the hotel, in Hebrew, can be found at the following link (retrieved January 2020): https://he.wikipedia.org/wiki/מלון_קאמיניץ

[Page 113]

R. Yisrael Ashkenazi[1]
One of the First Settlers in Yesud HaMaala

Translated by Allen Flusberg

In the year 5644[2], a young man named Yisrael Ashkenazi of Kamenetz–Litowsk, a member of the family of R.[3] Fishl Salomon[4] of Brisk–Litowsk[5], set out to go up to the Land of Israel.[6] He was a diligent young man, adept in and experienced at agricultural labor—and he had a talent for taking action. As soon as he reached the moshava [agricultural village], he energetically applied himself to the work and began to organize all the other settlers to follow his lead. Following R. Yisrael's advice they enlarged the orchard, dug a well, ploughed the land up thoroughly and planted various vegetables. And thus the first settlers' labor started out under R. Yisrael's sensible, experience–based guidance.

The poverty and suffering of these first settlers was great; one of the women of that group tells how they were going around barefoot and without clothing. Yisrael Ashkenazi, the instructor who was carrying the burden of the work—he himself would go down to the sea, take off his garment, wash it while naked (pardon the expression), then dry it in the sun, put it back on and go home.

As an agricultural laborer for R. Fishl Salomon, Ashkenazi received a salary that consisted of a postage stamp and a packet of smoking tobacco. After many trials and tribulations, Ashkenazi became independent and began to set up his own private farm; this farm of his served as a model for all the farmers of the moshava.

He was one of the first to defeat the northern wilderness, the swamp wilderness of the Ḥula—the place where Yesud HaMaala[7] was established. From morning to evening R. Yisrael, dressed in a long *tallit–katan*[8], strode behind his plough as his lips murmured holy psalms.

The Turkish government did not grant them *rukhsas*[9] [permits] to build houses. R. Yisrael saw that the Arabs were living in huts that were made of reeds they had brought from the Ḥula swamp. It dawned on him that huts did not require any building permit. When he told his comrades what he was thinking, they agreed it made sense. Carrying tools, all of them went out to the lake, where they collected reeds and bound them into sheaves. They made rafts out of them and floated them along the lake back to the moshava. After a relatively short time, two rows of reed huts, plastered with clay and whitewashed with lime, stood on the shore of the Sumkhi Sea [Ḥula Lake].

R. Yisrael's hut played multiple roles. It served as a dwelling for him and his household; as a shed for hay and for bags of flour; as a place of shelter for nursing calves; and as a shelter for hens sitting on eggs and on newly hatched chicks. The mats spread out on the ground of the hut served as beds for the people living there. In the middle of the night R. Yisrael would wake up to sit in a corner, studying the Book of Zohar by the light of a little lamp to conduct *Tikkun Ḥatzot*[10].

[Page 114]

Blackwater fever[11] severely afflicted the members of Yesud HaMaala. However, R. Yisrael used to say that "fever is not an illness". The fever burning within him would not prevent him from going out to work during a part of the agricultural season that demanded fervent, immediate attention.

All the days of his life, all of the sixty years that he lived in the moshava, he labored with a plough, a scythe, and a pitchfork. And in his old age he worked in his famous fruit orchard, also with a hoe. He was straight–backed, tall and never hunched over—an oak tree whose roots had been planted on streams of water.

Armed with a rifle, R. Yisrael also knew how to defend his possessions. One dark night R. Yisrael's mules were stolen from his yard. He knew full well that this was the work of a well–known local robber. He armed himself and went straight to the robber's house at a time of night when he knew that the robber would be out doing his usual work on the roads. And indeed, he did find his mules tied to the trough in the robber's yard—the robber had been so convinced that no one would dare cross the threshold of his yard that he had not even bothered to hide the mules. R. Yisrael brought the mules back to his own yard.

But the robber could not forgive this violation of his "honor": a Jew had boldly entered his lair, removed his prey and departed unharmed! And so one night the robber, crawling like a viper, sneaked into the moshava, stabbed R. Yisrael in the back with a dagger, and fled. For many months R. Yisrael had to lay in a sickbed, until he mended and recovered his strength.

In 1920[12] the Druze rebellion against the French broke out in Syria. An echo of the disturbances reached the Ḥula region as well. Gangs of bandits organized to attack field laborers and shepherds—to rob the former of their animals and the latter of their flocks. After the attack on Tel–Ḥai[13] and the murder of Trumpeldor and his comrades[14], the attacks by these gangs intensified. In the moshava of Yesud HaMaala information arrived that a gang of bandits was prowling around in the mountains adjacent to the moshava's land. The farmers were hesitant to go out to work in the fields. Then R. Yisrael stood up and said: "If we stop working in the more distant fields today, the gang will realize it and then come to the fields closest to the moshava tomorrow; and then the day after they will put a siege around us within the moshava itself. We must continue our labor, and God will come to our aid."

The next day R. Yisrael and his son, Alter, went out to plough. The son led the pair of mules, and R. Yisrael carried a German rifle; he took along a Book of Psalms as well. R. Yisrael set up a position for himself in the field while his son began ploughing. He continued ploughing until the afternoon. Suddenly a volley of shots, coming from three directions, were fired on R. Yisrael and his son from the mountains. R. Yisrael returned fire towards the attackers. Fearing for his son he left his position, going towards the mountain in order to get closer to him. The shots had killed the mules, and when the son crawled towards his father he found him in the middle of the field, wounded in the leg. The son dragged R. Yisrael along until they got to the slope, which the enemy's bullets could not reach. In the end help came from the moshava, and R. Yisrael was brought to the hospital. He had held a plough in one hand and a weapon in the other.

[Page 115]

Around then the poet Naphtali Imber[15] was roaming around in the fields of the Galilee while the poem *HaTikva* was forming in his mind. The poet wandered along the length of the Jordan River and was mesmerized by the blue of the Sumkhi Sea. His feet carried him further, into the valley, and as he continued to walk, singing, his feet began sinking into the soft clay that led to the swamps. As the poet pulled one foot out of the mud, his other leg sank in above the knee. He began to realize that he was going to drown. Beads of cold sweat enveloped his face, and his hair stood on end. How could he ever be rescued? Just as Imber was preparing himself for the worst, the voice of a man reached his ears: "Mister, what has happened to you?" It was R. Yisrael, who had come to the edge of the swamp. Right away R. Yisrael threw Imber a rope, telling him "Tie it tightly around your waist." R. Yisrael began pulling hard on the rope; slowly dragging the poet out. After a half hour the poet was laying exhausted next to R. Yisrael.

R. Yisrael lifted Imber up, placed him on his shoulders, and began marching home with his "load" as the clay and mud were dripping from him. At home R. Yisrael washed Imber off himself, put him to bed and revived him.

The figure of R. Yisrael combined a pioneering spirit with a will of iron. He was a symbol of labor. When they first brought a combine into the moshava, the elderly R. Yisrael came over and stroked it with his hand…In R. Yisrael's times there had been no combine, no machines—everything had been done by hand, with oxen. There was no road, no permanent place to live, only wilderness. He was a man of the earth, a pioneer and the instructor of the encampment.

In the year 5673[16] a delegation of the most prominent rabbis of the country, Rabbis Kook[17], Sonnenfeld[18], Ḥarlap[19] and Horowitz[20], paid a visit to the Galilee in order to repair and strengthen the religious situation in the settlements. One of their stops was at Yesud HaMaala. A festive meal was set up in their honor in the home of R. Yisrael. When the rabbis were about to leave the moshava to continue on to Metula[21], a group of people, both young and old, gathered around them to accompany them as they left. And when the rabbis mounted their horses, these people formed a large circle around them. Rabbi Kook was very moved by the sight and burst out singing, *El Yivne HaGalil* [God will build the Galilee][22] as the large group of people coalesced around the rabbis, singing along and dancing to *El Yivne HaGalil*. And as they sang Rabbi Kook made his horse prance to the beat as he himself participated, his face glowing with joy and devotion.

R. Yisrael Ashkenazi's mother, Gitl Chaya, used to live in a separate room. She owned a cow that she herself milked every day. On the last day of her life, the eve of the New Moon of Nisan, 5669[23], she managed to milk the cow. Then she called her son Yisrael and complained she wasn't feeling well. Yisrael wanted to help her into bed, but she went into bed herself, without his helping hand, and after a few minutes she passed away at the age of 95.

Footnotes:

1. From *Kamenetz–Litovsk, Zastavije and Colonies Memorial Book*, edited by S. Eisenstadt and M. Galbert, published by the Israel and America Committee of Kamenetz Litovsk and Zastavya, (Orly, Tel Aviv, Israel, 1970), pp. 113–115.
2. 5644 = secular year 1883–1884
3. R. = *Reb*, a title similar to English "Mr."
4. In 1883, Ephraim Fishl Salomon (1849–1924) had purchased the land for Yesud HaMaala from the Abu family of Safed. He led the group that settled there. See the following link (in Hebrew, retrieved Aug 2020): https://he.wikipedia.org/wiki/%D7%90%D7%A4%D7%A8%D7%99%D7%9D_%D7%A4%D7%99%D7%A9%D7%9C_%D7%A1%D7%9C%D7%95%D7%9E%D7%95%D7%9F
5. Brest–Litowsk, which lies ~40km south of Kamenetz
6. For more information on Yisrael Ashkenazi, see the following link (in Hebrew, retrieved Aug 2020): https://dubrovin-farm.com/
7. Yesud HaMaala lies 13km northeast of Safed.
8. *tallit–katan* = four–cornered garment with fringes at the corners, ritually worn during the day to fulfil the Biblical commandment (Numbers 15:38–39) of placing fringes on the four corners of one's garment. See the following link (retrieved Aug 2020): https://en.wikipedia.org/wiki/Tallit#Tallit_katan
9. *rukhsa* (Arabic) = *ruhsat* (Turkish) = permit or license
10. *Tikkun Ḥatzot* = custom of arising during the night to recite prayers lamenting the destruction of the Jerusalem Temple. See the following link (retrieved Aug 2020): https://en.wikipedia.org/wiki/Tikkun_Chatzot
11. Blackwater fever is a complication of malaria. See the following link (retrieved Aug 2020): https://en.wikipedia.org/wiki/Blackwater_fever
12. The Franco–Syrian War took place in 1920. See the following link (retrieved Aug 2020): https://en.wikipedia.org/wiki/Franco-Syrian_War
The Druze rebellion against the French—a later rebellion—broke out in 1925 and lasted until 1927. See the following link (retrieved Aug 2020): https://en.wikipedia.org/wiki/Great_Syrian_Revolt
13. Tel–Ḥai (which has been absorbed into Kfar Giladi) lies 25km north of Yesud HaMaala.
14. In March 1920, Yosef Trumpeldor and some of his men were killed defending Tel Ḥai, in the Northern Galilee, against Shiite militias. See the following link (retrieved Aug 2020): https://en.wikipedia.org/wiki/Tel_Hai
15. Naftali Herz Imber (1856–1909), the author of the poem *HaTikva* that became the Zionist Hymn and then later Israel's national anthem, spent the years 1882–1887 in the Land of Israel. See the following link (retrieved Aug 2020): https://en.wikipedia.org/wiki/Naftali_Herz_Imber
16. 5673 = secular year 1912–1913
17. Abraham Isaac Kook (1865–1935), later the first Chief Rabbi in Mandatory Palestine. He was the leader of this 1913 rabbinical delegation to the Galilee, whose purpose was to strengthen Jewish observance in the remote settlements. See the following link (retrieved Aug 2020): https://en.wikipedia.org/wiki/Abraham_Isaac_Kook
18. Rabbi Yosef Ḥaim Sonnenfeld (1848–1932), who led the Ḥaredi community in Jerusalem. See the following link (retrieved Aug 2020): https://en.wikipedia.org/wiki/Yosef_Chaim_Sonnenfeld
19. Rabbi Yaakov Moshe Ḥarlap (1882–1951) was a disciple of Rabbi Kook. See the following link (retrieved Aug 2020): https://en.wikipedia.org/wiki/Yaakov_Moshe_Charlap
20. Rabbi Yonatan Binyamin Horowitz (1862–1940). See the following link (in Hebrew, retrieved Aug 2020): https://he.wikipedia.org/wiki/%D7%9E%D7%A1%D7%A2_%D7%94%D7%9E%D7%95%D7%A9%D7%91%D7%95%D7%AA
Rabbi Horowitz wrote an account of the rabbis' journey to the Galilee. Entitled Eileh Masa'ai, (in Hebrew), it is available for reading or download at the following link (retrieved Aug 2020): https://www.hebrewbooks.org/36617
21. Metula lies 30km north of Yesud HaMaala.
22. *El Yivne HaGalil* was a late–19th–century song of unknown authorship, often accompanied by a *hora* dance. See the following link (in Hebrew, retrieved Aug 2020): https://he.wikipedia.org/wiki/%D7%90%D7%9C_%D7%99%D7%91%D7%A0%D7%94_%D7%94%D7%92%D7%9C%D7%99%D7%9C
23. 29 Adar 5669 = March 22, 1909

[Page 116]

The Writer Moshe Eliyahu Jacques-Zhernensky,
of Blessed Memory [1],[2]

by Leah Aloni-Bobrowski

Translated by Allen Flusberg

Moshe Eliyahu Zhernensky was born in Kamenetz-Litowsk to parents who were God-fearing, humble and learned in the Torah, scions of religious judges and rabbis. When he was young, he studied in the yeshivas of Brest-Litowsk[3] and Novogrudok[4]. After being educated in Torah in these yeshivas he continued wandering until he reached distant Slobodka[5], in order to bask in the

Mussar[6] teaching—at the advanced yeshiva Knesset-Yisrael[7]—taught by the Old One, the brilliant Natan Tzvi Finkel[8], may the memory of the righteous be a blessing.

His material life was extremely difficult, and he supported himself in great deprivation. His aspiration for knowledge, study and a secular education roused his pure heart, and in secret he began reading secular books.

[Page 117]

At that time he found a loyal friend in the yeshiva, Natan Greenblatt-Goren[9], a native of Slobodka, who was also one of the progressives, and when they met and realized that both of them were reading secular books that were forbidden in the yeshiva, they made a pact to keep their activities secret. They also vowed to speak to one another in Hebrew only for the rest of their lives (a vow they did indeed keep). For two years he lived a double life: studying in the yeshiva by day, and delving into secular books by night. This behavior was fraught with great "danger", however, because there were "yeshiva snoops" who were ambushing anyone who was pursuing secular knowledge. For this reason, Zhernensky decided to leave the yeshiva, and he moved from Slobodka to Kovno[10], moving into a house whose owners had gone abroad. He had found an apartment, but not a way to earn a living. And yet even though he was going about hungry, he was living in a world of absolute nobility, immersed in reference and science books.

When his misery became unbearable, he left Kovno and made his way to Vilna[11]. But he did not find peace of mind in Vilna, either; he had no bread to eat and was unable to replace his tattered clothing. It was then that he decided to move to a small town in Podolia[12], where he had been invited to serve as a teacher.

In this town he recovered from the indignity of hunger and suffering. He taught Hebrew to teenagers, who liked him as a teacher and instructor with good qualities. He still longed to get a higher education, however. After much wandering and hardship, he reached Odessa[13]. His humility and shyness prevented him from obtrusively inserting himself among the prominent, but he quickly gained a reputation in the Hebrew circles of the city. Two of the Great Ones, Ussishkin[14] and Lewinsky[15], invited him to teach their children Hebrew.

At that time his oldest brother, D.Y. Zhernensky, got a job as a clerk in *Moriah*[16], and through him Moshe Eliyahu got close to Bialik[17] and Rawnitzki[18], the founders of *Moriah*. In that period, he began to write and publish articles in *HaOlam*[19]. Afterwards he and his friend, Natan Goren, published the collection *Tal*, and a literary anthology *Pekaim* in memory of U.N. Gnessin[20], who had passed away that year. He was also one of the pillars of *Shacharit*, which was published by him, Natan Goren and Dr. S. Eisenstadt (may the latter continue to live a long life). While he was living in Odessa, he used to visit his parents in Kamenetz-Litowsk twice a year, on Passover and on the High Holy Days. At those times he showed a great deal of interest in the education of our town's young people; occasionally he would assemble us as a group, encouraging us to learn the Hebrew language and arousing in us a great deal of interest in the Land of Israel and Zionism. He would also particularly emphasize that we should aspire to a higher education, which we could only attain by leaving our town.

About a year before the First World War broke out, he fulfilled his aspiration to obtain a higher education in the sciences: he left for France, enrolled in the Sorbonne and dedicated himself completely to knowledge and science. And at that time he was publishing notes in *HaTzefira*[21].

The war uprooted all his dreams, and again he was cast into misery, torment and suffering as a prisoner in Germany. After the war he settled in Germany, got married and took up literary work in *HaTekufa* (published by Stybel)[22]and in the company Eshkol. He became well known in literary circles and published his first book of essays, *MiSaviv*.

[Page 118]

When Hitler came to power, he left Germany and immigrated to the Land of Israel, something he had longed to do from the very first days of his youth. Here he went through the suffering of absorption—acclimation to a new land. His job as a proofreader in the newspaper *HaBoker* frustrated him; he left it after some time and moved to Jerusalem. The entire time he lived in Israel he was really tormented in a vise of stress and deprivation.

One day, after the Second World War had ended, my husband and I visited him at his home in Jerusalem. We told him about how our townspeople's organization was aspiring to publish a special book that would be dedicated to the memory of our fellow townspeople who had perished during the Holocaust. Excited by the idea of erecting a monument to the martyrs of our town, Zhernensky expressed his willingness to help edit the book. And although his economic situation was so difficult, he stated twice, emphatically: "But not for any compensation."

Moshe Eliyahu was always huddled in the shadows, staying on the sideline, and carrying his yoke of suffering within him. He lived and died like his humble ancestors, who were also able to silently bear the hardships they lived in. He passed away in Jerusalem on the 17th of Elul, 5708, corresponding to 21 September 1949 [sic].[23]

May his memory be a blessing.

Footnotes:

1. From *Kamenetz-Litovsk, Zastavije and Colonies Memorial Book*, edited by S. Eisenstadt and M. Galbert, published by the Israel and America Committee of Kamenetz Litovsk and Zastavya, (Orly, Tel Aviv, Israel, 1970), pp. 116-118.
2. The last name "Jacques" was a pseudonym that he used. See a short biography at the following link (retrieved Aug 2020): https://www.encyclopedia.com/religion/encyclopedias-almanacs-transcripts-and-maps/zhernensky-moshe-eliyahu
3. Brest-Litowsk, Belarus is located about 40km south of Kamenetz.
4. Novogrudok = Navahrudak, Belarus, located about 200km northeast of Kamenetz.
5. Slobodka = Slobotka (Vilijampole), Lithuania, located about 350km north of Kamenetz. It is also spelled "Slabodka".
6. Mussar (or Musar) is the name of a Jewish movement that arose in Eastern Europe in the 19th century; it combined religiosity and study with a strong emphasis on ethical behavior. See the following link (retrieved Aug 2020): https://en.wikipedia.org/wiki/Musar_movement
7. For a history of the yeshiva, see the following link (retrieved Aug 2020): https://en.wikipedia.org/wiki/Yeshivas_Knesses_Yisrael_(Slabodka)#:~:text=Yeshivas%20Knesses%20Yisrael%20was%20a,century%20until%20World%20War%20II.
8. Finkel, known as "the *Alter* [Old One] of Slabodka", was the founder of the Knesset-Israel Yeshiva. See the following link (retrieved Aug 2020): https://en.wikipedia.org/wiki/Nosson_Tzvi_Finkel_(Slabodka)
9. Natan Goren (1887-1956) was a Hebrew writer, journalist and essayist. See the following link (in Hebrew, retrieved Aug 2020): https://he.wikipedia.org/wiki/%D7%A0%D7%AA%D7%9F_%D7%92%D7%95%D7%A8%D7%9F
10. Kovno = Kaunas, Lithuania, located 6km southeast of Slobodka, on the other side of the Neman River.
11. Vilna = Vilnius, Lithuania, about 100km east of Kovno
12. Podolia is a region in southwestern Ukraine, bordering on Moldova. It lies about 800km south of Vilna, and about 600km southeast of Kamenetz. See the following link (retrieved Aug 2020): https://en.wikipedia.org/wiki/Podolia
13. Odessa, Ukraine lies about 150km southeast of the southeastern edge of Podolia.
14. Menachem Ussishkin (1863-1941) was a Zionist leader who headed the Jewish National Fund. See the following link (retrieved Aug 2020): https://en.wikipedia.org/wiki/Menachem_Ussishkin
15. Elḥanan Leib Lewinsky (1857-1910) was a Zionist leader, writer and publisher who spent the last years of his life in Odessa. See the following link (retrieved Aug 2020): https://www.encyclopedia.com/religion/encyclopedias-almanacs-transcripts-and-maps/lewinsky-elhanan-leib
16. *Moriah* was a Hebrew publishing house founded in Odessa by Bialik, Rawnitzki and several others in 1901-1902. See the following link (retrieved Aug 2020): https://yivoencyclopedia.org/article.aspx/Moriah
17. Chaim Nachman Bialik (1873-1934), a writer whose Hebrew poetry led him to be recognized as Israel's national poet. See the following link (retrieved Aug 2020): https://en.wikipedia.org/wiki/Hayim_Nahman_Bialik

18.   Yehoshua Ḥana Rawnitzki (1859-1944), an author and editor in Hebrew and Yiddish who lived in Odessa for many years. See the following link (retrieved Aug 2020): https://en.wikipedia.org/wiki/Yehoshua_Hana_Rawnitzki

19.   *HaOlam* was a weekly Hebrew periodical, published beginning in 1907. See the following link (retrieved Aug 2020): https://www.jewishvirtuallibrary.org/haolam

20.   Uri Nissan Gnessin (1879-1913), a pioneering writer of modern Hebrew literature. See the following link (retrieved Aug 2020): https://en.wikipedia.org/wiki/Uri_Nissan_Gnessin

21.   *HaTzefira* (or *HaTsfira*) was a Hebrew-language newspaper published in Poland. See the following link (retrieved Aug 2020): https://en.wikipedia.org/wiki/Ha-Tsfira

22.   *HaTekufa* was a Hebrew literary magazine that appeared quarterly. See the following link (in Hebrew, retrieved Aug 2020): https://he.wikipedia.org/wiki/%D7%94%D7%AA%D7%A7%D7%95%D7%A4%D7%94

23.   17 Elul 5708 corresponds to September 21, 1948.

[Page 119]

Falek Zolf, of Blessed Memory[1]

by Zelda Saperstein

Translated by Allen Flusberg

Falek was one of the few in our town who excelled in his talent and intelligence. Falek Zolf, a dear person. Falek Zolf: affable and pleasant, the *maskil* [enlightened] and Judaic scholar, the teacher and educator, the writer and author. Falek Zolf, persistent and diligent, who had strong feelings for his family, his people and his land.

Falek Zolf, of blessed memory

Yes, Falek Zolf is no more. The pain is deep; he is hard to forget.

I was in contact with Falek Zolf for seven years. I started exchanging letters with him in the United States. His letters were interesting: Each letter was an entire book; each word was a pearl. There were times when I had a strong desire to put what he had written into a frame so that they would remain forever. In his last letter to me he describes his illness. A letter 12 pages long, packed with descriptions. Falek describes his illness somewhat jokingly and somewhat with complete despair. His illness was very serious. Apparently Falek died of a malignant disease. He wrote to me that he had gone to the hospital because of a heart attack. The doctors discovered that he had a spot on his lung—or, as he expresses it in his letter—"*a flekl oif die lungen*" [a little spot on the lungs]. This, he thought, was a great joke! For when he was a young boy in Zastavya his friends used to compose songs making fun of his odd name, such as "Falek, flekn flekl" (as he also mentions in his book *Oif Fremde Erd* [On Foreign Soil]). And so a *flekl* [spot] was teasing him once more; but not as a joke, in a very tragic manner, for this *flekl* did him in before his time. He had surgery twice, once on his lungs and a second time on his stomach. His heart, though weak, sustained it, and he wrote to me as follows: "*Die harinte mein harts hot geshvigen*" [my lady heart was silent]. Falek survived the two surgeries, and returned home very pleased…but his happiness did not last very long. Falek passed away. After years of suffering and despair he was gone. His path through life was not a bed of roses, not easy at all. Falek suffered physically, but he did have a satisfying spiritual life. As I wrote above, he was a persistent scholar throughout his life. Aside from his professional work in education, he would sit for days and nights, writing and studying literature. As we know, Falek wrote two books about Kamenetz: *Oif Fremder Erd* [On Foreign Soil] and *Die Letste fun a Dor* [The Last of a Generation]. In addition, he wrote educational and psychological articles. He wrote stories for children, and more recently he wrote a journal of his life, *A Teacher's Journal*. And during his illness he added a word to its name, renaming it *An Ill Teacher's Journal*.

[Page 120]

He sent me two articles that he had written in Hebrew; they were clipped from newspapers. In these articles of his he describes in a general way how things look around a teacher after he dies. While he was writing these articles he was still healthy, but apparently he had a premonition that something terrible was about to happen. When I wrote back to him, I commented with two questions: For what reason is he thinking so much about death? And where did he get such a deep and rich Hebrew from? After all, he has always lived outside Israel and does not hear our language spoken on a daily basis; so how did he obtain such a culturally rich, fluent facility in Hebrew?

Falek replied to me in the words of Bialik[2]:

"The light I've achieved did not come for free.
I've gouged it out of my own rock and stone
And carved it out of my heart.
Nor have I borrowed or stolen it from anyone,
For it comes from me myself, it lies within me."

Adding: "I did not sit around with folded arms for the 34 years I lived in Canada. *Asiti laylot k'yamim* [I toiled by night as by day]" (these were his own words).

All his life Falek longed to come to Israel and see the Land of our Forefathers with his own eyes—but he did not achieve it.

Footnotes:

1. From *Kamenetz-Litovsk, Zastavije and Colonies Memorial Book*, edited by S. Eisenstadt and M. Galbert, published by the Israel and America Committee of Kamenetz Litovsk and Zastavya, (Orly, Tel Aviv, Israel, 1970), pp.119-120.
2. Chaim Nachman Bialik (1873-1934) is considered the national poet of Israel. Many have tried their hand at translating this famous poem, which has also been put to music. For some other translations see the following (retrieved July 2020): http://www.soulandgone.com/2014/05/03/hayim-nahman-bialik-lo-zakhiti-be-or-min-ha-hefqeir/,https://lyricstranslate.com/en/lo-zakhiti-baor-min-ha-hefker- For more on Bialik, see the following link (retrieved July 2020): https://en.wikipedia.org/wiki/Hayim_Nahman_Bialik

[Page 121]

Baruch Eisner, of Blessed Memory[1]

by H. K.

Translated by Allen Flusberg

Baruch Eisner, a native of Kamenetz-Litowsk. was an intellectual, an enthusiastic Zionist and someone who was active in communal affairs. His public activity was focused mainly on the adolescents, whom he would guide and encourage to seek a higher education. Sometimes he would gather the young people together to speak to them about Hebrew authors and also about literature, both Hebrew and general. He would try to imbue them with a love for Zion.

Baruch was one of the founders of the town library that served as a reliable source of knowledge for most of the youth. It was through his effort that new books were occasionally acquired, to the great satisfaction of the readers, especially the young people. With his pleasant demeanor and politeness, and in his great devotion to educating the younger generation, he was a model for all his peers.

Baruch made plans for the establishment of educational facilities in which Kamenetz children of all ages would be schooled. But he was not fortunate enough to achieve these aspirations of his. Several years before the First World War, at a young age, he passed away from a harsh ailment.

May his memory be a blessing forever!

Footnote:

1.   From *Kamenetz-Litovsk, Zastavije and Colonies Memorial Book*, edited by S. Eisenstadt and M. Galbert, published by the Israel and America Committee of Kamenetz Litovsk and Zastavya, (Orly, Tel Aviv, Israel, 1970), p. 121.

[Page 122]

Yosef Vigutov and Bendet Winograd[1][2]

by R. V.

Translated by Allen Flusberg

Social life was better in little Kamenetz than in many of the other little towns of Poland. Individuals' concern for the community was very well developed in our little town, and there were many Jews who unceasingly gave of their time to benefit the community. Some of these personalities whom I remember well were Yosef Vigutov, Bendet Winograd, and others. Yosef Vigutov headed all the associations, but Bendet Winograd also worked hard for the benefit of the community. He was always ready to help others, and it was never too much for him: he worked to benefit *Linat Hatzedek*[3], provided aid for those in need, and before Passover worked for *Maot Chittim* (money for the needy to purchase *matzot* [unleavened bread] for Passover).

Yosef Vigutov

[Page 123]

As in every little town in Poland, the Jews—particularly the Jewish shopkeepers—always had run-ins with the police. The shopkeepers kept their stores partially open on Sundays, something that was forbidden by Polish law; but on Sundays many farmers came to town from the surrounding areas where they lived, and the main livelihood of the town was derived from these farmers. The policemen used to walk on patrol, giving out fines (violation summonses), and so there was a need for someone to mediate between the town residents (i.e. the Jews) and the police. Bendet Winograd was one of the few townspeople of his generation who could speak Polish. Most of the Jews of the town did not know Polish, but rather Russian or Ukrainian, the languages in which they could communicate with the farmers who lived nearby. Thus Winograd was someone who could readily mediate between the Jews and the police, and he always had his hands full providing this service.

It once happened that the police arrested three Zionist youths whom they suspected were Communists. But thanks to Bendet Winograd's patient dedication in interceding with the police officer, they released all three of them.

There was a Polish hospital in Kamenetz that was not particularly sophisticated. Its physician was a Polish doctor whom the Jews of the town did not have much confidence in, and so in practice the Jews of the town had no physician at all. Jewish communal volunteers, among them Bendet Winograd, worked hard to bring in a Jewish doctor who would move to the town—for very few Jewish doctors were interested in settling in small towns.

There was also a training group[4] in Kamenetz. Since there were not many opportunities for work available in the town, the material situation of the group was difficult, and for the most part its members required aid. Bendet Winograd was also ready to help them as well as he could.

There were many other cherished Jews in the town who were always ready to provide aid to others. The Nazi beast destroyed them all.

Blessed be their memory, all of them!

Footnotes:

     1.   From *Kamenetz-Litovsk, Zastavije and Colonies Memorial Book*, edited by S. Eisenstadt and M. Galbert, published by the Israel and America Committee of Kamenetz Litovsk and Zastavya, (Orly, Tel Aviv, Israel, 1970), pp. 122-123.
     2.   See also article on pp. 505-506 of this volume, "R. Yosef Vigutov", by Ch.Z. Mendelson
     3.   *Linat Hatzedek* was an institution whose purpose was to provide aid and medical equipment for ill people with limited means. See the article by P. Ravid in this volume, "Memoirs from My Home and from the Town Kamenetz-Litowsk", pp. 92-97 of this volume.
     4.   Hebrew: *plugat hachshara*

[Page 124]

It Happened in Kamenetz-Litowsk[1]

by Professor Shmuel Eisenstadt, Tel Aviv

Translated by Allen Flusberg

My father, Yosef Meir, was a scholar and a *Maskil*[2]. He participated in the *Chovevei-Zion* Conference in Katowice[3] in 1884[4]. And he was one of the founders of the *Poalei-Zion*[5] movement in Russia in 1898. He had been born in the village of Chemeri[6], near Kamenetz Litowsk; where his father R. Yaakov Ber had leased an estate from Count Grabowski.

From the beginning of his youth in the village of his birth he thirsted for Torah and Haskalah, and he was searching for a way to improve his knowledge and resolve the issues that had arisen in his mind. At that time his relative R.[7] Yekutiel Rabinowitz was working as the manager of a flour mill in Kamenetz-Litowsk; he had become well known as a scholar and as one of the pioneers of Haskalah. The 16-year-old Yosef Meir had a burning desire to meet this remarkable relative of his in person and to get his help in his studies. And so, on a spring day of the year 1881, the young boy set out on foot to Kamenetz from his father's estate in Chemeri in order to visit the home of R. Yekutiel Rabinowitz.

R. Yekutiel received him warmly, and with hugs and caresses he seated him on the wide sofa. As he looked at the youngster with gleaming eyes, he sat down opposite him and began speaking, as follows: "I have already heard about your thirst to extend your knowledge, and I have also known that your path would eventually lead you from your isolated village to my house. Please feel free to come to our home often and to consider yourself like a member of the family. As you know very well, 'It is not the shy person who learns'[8], and 'Turn it over and over'[9]."

"Thank you, *Rebbe* Yekutiel, for your warm words and your encouragement. Had I been shy I would not have come here to pester you. I truly need your guidance and your advice," replied Yosef Meir in a voice that shook with emotion.

"First of all, my dear Yosef Meir, do not call me *Rebbe*, a title that comes with a degree of rabbinical garb…Tell me Yosef Meir, simply what kind of help you need; what is bothering your thoughts the most?"

[Page 125]

"You probably know," began Yosef Meir in a more courageous tone, "that all these years I have been studying with R. Simcha Grunem, who lived in my father's estate until Passover of the last year. I learned *Shas*[10] and *Poskim*[11] thoroughly. He was a first-rate Talmud teacher. He put me on a learning path that followed generations-long tradition; but articulating and thinking about the material was up to me, and many a time I found myself stalemated. Initially I tried to ask R. Simcha Grunem one or two questions; but although he is sharp and well-versed, he was unable to properly address my questions. I did not want to embarrass him, and so I stopped asking…"

"You acted correctly, Yosef-Meir: you refrained from committing a great ethical wrong. For *Rebbe* Simcha Grunem could not explain something to you that his teachers had not explained to him. As it says, 'Rabi did not teach it, so how could Rabbi Ḥiya have known?'[12]" *Rebbe* Yekutiel added, in almost a whisper, "And still more: had you asked *Rebbe* Simcha Grunem for a clear explanation of a very difficult Biblical verse, particularly in the Book of Job, he would have mumbled on and on but not been able to explain it properly; and no wonder, for during the long rabbinical era the method of study in the old *Beit Midrash* [House of Study] went awry, particularly in Poland. The first thing taught to little children was not the Bible, but rather the Talmud. The children began their studies with the Tractates Gittin and Kiddushin[13], and even that was taught without extensive explanation. There was only a dry page of Talmud with the commentary of Rashi[14], and later that of *Tosefot*[15] and *Maharsha*[16]; and without distinguishing between one topic and another or between one period and another, so that the students completely lacked any concept of the nature and topography of the Land of Israel, or of Jewish history; and also of the grammar of the Hebrew language and of the language of the Babylonian and Jerusalem Talmuds…"

Rebbe Yekutiel felt he had sufficiently delved into the matter, although he could have continued on and on; but his lunch break was coming to an end, and Yosef Meir also had to leave, so that he could get home before dark. So he summarized his thoughts succinctly, saying:

"I brought all this up, my dear Yosef Meir, as an example. The reason for the developmental delay of the Haskalah Movement goes much deeper. Our generation received, as a heritage from the Ghetto Era, one-sided spiritual riches that had lain folded up within the confines of the *Beit Midrash*. Most of our people were separated from the world, distanced from secular knowledge. We had frozen our own spiritual riches, clothing them in a narrow, religious garb, and we had been fearful of any cultural development and contact with what lay outside. The thinkers and philosophers who did arise among us were forced to separate themselves from the ghetto and to distance themselves from their own people, who stigmatized them as heretics and unbelievers."

"It is incumbent upon the Jewish youth," added R. Yekutiel with particular emphasis, "to learn and to become familiar with the spiritual assets of the world: philosophy, history, and literature; and primarily natural sciences, since our people have distanced themselves from nature, from all that grows and blooms, flourishing around us."

[Page 126]

And as he extended his hand, warmly parting from his young relative with a fond smile, he said: "Come to me, my dear boy, during some evening next week; you can stay over with us, and I will tell you about the great luminaries of science, about Darwin and Humboldt[17]. And I will also give you books to take home so that you can look through them and study them. For out of Kamenetz will come forth teaching[18]," he ended, his face beaming even more, as he kissed Yosef Meir on the forehead.

Translator's Footnotes:

1. From *Kamenetz-Litovsk, Zastavije and Colonies Memorial Book*, edited by S. Eisenstadt and M. Galbert, published by the Israel and America Committee of Kamenetz Litovsk and Zastavya, (Orly, Tel Aviv, Israel, 1970), pp. 124-126.
2. *Maskil* = a supporter of the Haskalah Movement; a progressive
3. Katowice, Poland, is located 500km southwest of Kamenetz.
4. For more details on this conference, see the following link (retrieved March 2020): https://en.wikipedia.org/wiki/Katowice_Conference
5. *Poalei Zion* = Workers of Zion, a Socialist-Zionist movement. See the following link (retrieved March 2020): https://en.wikipedia.org/wiki/Poale_Zion. On the beginnings of the movement throughout the Pale of Settlement in the Russian Empire in 1898, to some extent in response to the rejection of Zionism by the Jewish Bund movement, see the following link (in Hebrew, retrieved March 2020): https://he.wikipedia.org/wiki/פועלי_ציון
6. There is currently (2020) a place named Chemeri about 8km east of Kamenetz.
7. "R." usually stands for *Reb*, a title similar to English "Mr." But see below: it can also denote *Rebbe* (teacher) or Rabbi.
8. Pirkei Avot (Ethics of the Fathers) 2:5
9. Pirkei Avot 5:22. This maxim is generally understood to mean that one should "turn" the Torah this way and that, delving into it from different perspectives, for all wisdom lies in it.
10. *Shas* = acronym for Six Orders (of the Talmud)
11. *Poskim* = post-Talmudic literature settling Jewish law (literally adjudicants, referring to the authors of these works)
12. "Rabi" or "Rebbi" here refers to Rabbi Judah haNasi [the Prince or Patriarch] (~135-217 CE), head of the Jewish court, who wrote the Mishna, a succinct compilation of Jewish Law. The quotation is from the Babylonian Talmud, Nida 62a. Ḥiya was Judah's student.
13. In Gittin (=Divorce Documents) and Kiddushin (=Betrothal, Marriage Documents), much of the subject matter is laws of contracts.
14. *Rashi* = a concise, plain, virtually indispensable commentary on the Talmud, written mostly in Hebrew and some Aramaic by Rashi (Shlomo Yiẓḥaki, an 11th century scholar who lived in Troyes, France), and printed in the inner margin of volumes of the Talmud, with the text of the Talmud in the center of the page.

15.   *Tosefot* (= additions), a commentary on the Talmud that poses and resolves difficult questions on the text, comparing and contrasting texts of different tractates. It was written by Rashi's scholarly successors, including some of his grandchildren. It is printed in the outer margin of volumes of the Talmud, so that the Talmudic text is encompassed by *Rashi* and *Tosefot*.

16.   *Maharsha*, a commentary on *Rashi* and *Tosefot* of the Talmud, written by Shmuel Eidels (1555-1631). The name Maharsha is an acronym, standing for "Our teacher, the Rabbi Shmuel Eidels". See the following link, retrieved March 2020: https://en.wikipedia.org/wiki/Maharsha.

17.   Alexander von Humboldt (1769-1859), a Prussian scientist, explorer, naturalist and geographer, who wrote works on botanical geography and extensively explored the Americas. See the following link (retrieved March 2020): https://en.wikipedia.org/wiki/Alexander_von_Humboldt

18.   A play on the words of Isaiah 2:3, "For out of Zion will come forth teaching".

[Page 127]

Zelig "the Bookbinder"[1]

by Pinhas Ravid-Rudnicki

Translated by Allen Flusberg

A proper memorialization of a community that was destroyed by the Nazi foe should include a eulogy for its finest members. In the dreary life of the little town these people did not stand out very much. After all they were only single individuals—but perhaps it would be better to describe them as singular individuals. What characterized them was that they were unappointed, unadorned volunteers, who became committed, heart and soul, to the pioneer-Zionist movement. Since achieving this idyll was their vision, they endeavored to intellectually prepare others for the redemption of the People and their Land. More than a few of the former residents of the little town were rescued from the Inferno of the Holocaust thanks to these individuals, who had urged and goaded them to hasten their immigration. And yet they themselves remained to the last, like captains on the deck of a burning ship. They perished with all the other members of the community, sharing their tragic destiny of utter annihilation.

[Page 128]

In the town of Kamenetz-Litowsk one of these singular individuals was Zelig *der Einbinder* [the Bookbinder].

He got this name from his profession, bookbinding, in which he was involved in his earlier years—and the name stuck. His real family name was Trastnitzky[2], and in later years his actual business was distributing daily newspapers that were published in the capital city, Warsaw. Most were in Yiddish and a small number in Hebrew. As the agent for the newspapers *Heint*, *Moment*, *Hatzefira*, *Heintike Nayes*, *Radio*, etc., Zelig became an expert not only in distributing newspapers to the few individual subscribers, but also in forming subscription groups that consisted of 2-3 people who shared a single subscription. Once one of them finished reading a newspaper, he would pass it along to the others in the group.

It is no wonder that Zelig's job led him to know everyone in the town—and that almost everyone knew him, too. However, his activity was not limited to this profession of his, for making a living was not his main concern. He was quite willing to devote much of his time and energy to the Movement. When I use the term "Movement", I am not referring to any particular "movement", for Zelig the Bookbinder did not hold any particular narrow, isolated view when it came to activity supporting the revival of the People and their Land. Every Zionist organization that was active—whether to collect money for the nationalist funds, to arrange indoctrination sessions, or to send members for training and aliya [immigration to Israel]—all were dear to his heart and benefited from his support. His home was always open to potential candidates for aliya and to all advocates of the Zionist idea. He loved to quiz anyone he conversed with in knowledge of the land, in the annals of Zionism, etc. If he thought it necessary, he would explain anything that needed to be explained, preaching on the personal fulfilment that the pioneers experienced.

There were many indoctrination sessions in the town, particularly by the pioneer youth movements. Similarly, there were public fundraising events, lectures to raise money for various funds. There was practically no meeting of this type that Zelig did not attend. Being in an indoctrination session or in a meeting to solicit contributions made him feel very much like a fish in water. He would enjoy it when Zionist "stock" rose in the town; his face would then beam with endless joy.

However, Zelig was strict, a stickler when he came up against someone who deviated a bit from the original idea of national revival— for example, if in a conversation with someone he heard words and sentences that he interpreted as heretical to this idea. In particular he would be shocked by the melding of Zionism with Communism, Heaven forbid. On this point he showed no mercy: he poured his wrath out on these heretics and was able to avenge himself upon them when it was their turn to go on aliya. He insisted that these candidates not be given the requisite recommendations by the Zionist institutions on the aliya questionnaires in the applications unless they agreed to atone for their sins with "ransom", i.e., one-time respectable contributions to the funds. Thus it was no wonder that each candidate for aliya would breathe a sigh of relief when Zelig gave him his stamp of approval, indicating he was fit to immigrate.

[Page 129]

Sermonizing, particularly to the members of the pioneer youth movements, was the main activity he was noted for. The leaders of these movements "suffered" from him, more than just a little, when he vehemently attacked them for their gentle approach to educating the younger generation. He demanded unlimited devotion to the Zionist idea. When he saw the young people dancing the *hora* pioneer dance, he would sigh, muttering "ho-ra!"[3]...As I recall, when a member of the *Merkaz heḥalutz* [Pioneer Center] one visited the town for a meeting, Zelig's colorful image was described to him by several of the attendees. The visitor suggested that we "immigrate" him— ship him off to Israel—as quickly as possible, so that we could "rid ourselves" of him and breathe freely…For by nature Zelig was very unbending, unable to change with the times.

Zelig was accustomed to "sticking his nose" into everything. There was not a single Zionist town event that he was not involved in. For example, holding elections for *halutz*-branch committee members would give Zelig the opportunity to propagandize in support of a candidate he favored, and to pour fire and brimstone on a candidate he disliked. He was also able to absorb derisive insults from others with little concern and no qualms. His spontaneous response to everything was consistent, substantive and uncompromising.

Zelig appeared to be headstrong. In his role as the reprimanding "preacher at the gate"[4], he acquired both friends and opponents. He ridiculed the loafers who were strutting about like fine gentlemen; instead, he esteemed the young people who were engaging in physical labor. Yet since it was not in his nature to hand out compliments, very few merited his praise.

When I returned to the town from *hachshara* [pioneer training] in the beginning of the year 1938, a short time before I left on aliya to Israel, I found that the youth movements and the Zionist organizations there were in a state of complete stagnation. Their ranks had been thinned, emptied of youth leaders and counselors who had gone on aliya or were preparing themselves to go. This fact indirectly influenced Zelig's role, reducing it to a minimum. There is no doubt that in his heart he longed for the good old days when the pioneer Zionist activity was vibrant and thriving.

The Holocaust wiped out all the Jewish townspeople, organizations, and volunteer workers of our little town Kamenetz-Litowsk, leaving not even a remnant—nor did it spare Zelig. May his memory remain preserved among us!

Translator's Footnotes:

　　1.　　From *Kamenetz-Litovsk, Zastavije and Colonies Memorial Book*, edited by S. Eisenstadt and M. Galbert, published by the Israel and America Committee of Kamenetz Litovsk and Zastavya, (Orly, Tel Aviv, Israel, 1970), pp. 127-129.

　　2.　　Or "Trasnitzer", as recorded in the Necrology section of this Yizkor Book (p. 263 and English translation of the Necrology appearing at the end of the book).

　　3.　　*ho-ra* = oh, bad (Hebrew}, a play on words.

　　4.　　See Amos 5:10, Isaiah 29:21

Isaac Shostakowski[1]

Translated by Allen Flusberg

His activity in the Zionist Movement and in the *Tarbut*[2] Institute began a bit late. For many years he did not engage in any community work of any kind, not because of any indifference to public needs, but simply because no suitable area of activity—one in which he could invest his abundant energy with passion— presented itself. And then one day a lecturer came to our little town to speak on behalf of the National Committee of *Tarbut*. He gave a public talk on the need to establish a Hebrew-language school locally. As is well known, the vast majority of the boys of the town had been receiving a religious education in the *ḥeders* [at the level of beginning elementary schools] and the yeshivas, while nearly all the girls were attending the Polish public school. To attain the goal of setting up a [secular] Hebrew school, a committee, headed by Isaac Shostakowski, was assembled. Under his leadership, the committee energetically undertook laying the groundwork for the project.

However, it was no sooner than the undertaking had begun that it confronted a serious challenge: the heads of the town's yeshivas declared war—a religiously obligatory war[3]—against the enterprise, aiming all their attacks on the committee members. The townspeople were divided, some supporting and others opposing the campaign. A veritable culture war—with all the little things that come along with it[4]—had been unleashed. Yet even under these circumstances, Shostakowski demonstrated his abilities as an exceptional, bold public leader. He performed his mission fearlessly, taking on every job or role he was given. Afterwards it was not long before he was elected local head of the Zionist *Histadrut* [Federation], and he remained in this position, continuing to serve with great devotion.

[Page 130]

We, the members of a pioneer youth movement, held him in great esteem, even though we experienced a parting of the ways in some respects. Who knows how many fruitful years of activity supporting Zionism and establishing Hebrew culture in the town he might have been able to contribute had it not been for the approaching Holocaust?

During the short period of Soviet control of the town[5] following the Molotov-Ribbentrop Pact[6], the Soviets began expropriating all the assets of private-property owners. According to eyewitness accounts, Shostakowski had the audacity to protest against this expropriation. The authorities of the new regime had him shot, putting an end to his life.

Translator's Footnotes:

　　1.　　From *Kamenetz-Litovsk, Zastavije and Colonies Memorial Book*, edited by S. Eisenstadt and M. Galbert, published by the Israel and America Committee of Kamenetz Litovsk and Zastavya, (Orly, Tel Aviv, Israel, 1970), pp. 129-130.

　　2.　　*Tarbut* [= Culture (Hebrew)] was a network of secular Hebrew-language schools in Poland (between the two World Wars) with tens of thousands of enrolled students. See the following link (retrieved March 2021): Tarbut - Wikipedia

　　3.　　Hebrew *milḥemet mitzva*

　　4.　　Hebrew *lechol perateha vedikdukeha*

　　5.　　1939-1941

　　6.　　This alliance between Nazi Germany and the Soviet Union allowed these two countries to partition Poland. Kamenetz was in the part that was annexed to the Soviet Union. The pact ended when Germany invaded the Soviet Union in 1941. See the following link (retrieved March 2021): Molotov–Ribbentrop Pact - Wikipedia

Ze'ev (Velvl)-Ḥaim Kirschenbaum[1]

Translated by Allen Flusberg

Z. Ḥ. Kirschenbaum was an unpretentious Hebrew teacher who taught dozens of the youth of the town, providing them with a basic knowledge of literature, *Tanach* [Bible], and Jewish history. There was no Hebrew school in our town, but his private lessons served as an excellent alternative. He implanted in his students a burning love for our people and for the Land of Israel. Even before the pioneer youth movements arose, he was good at inspiring us, heart and soul, with a desire for redemption—of our people and our land.

He was proud when he observed that what he had taught his students had borne fruit. Many a time, when he would run into one of his former students in the street, he would quiz him briefly on meanings of newly coined words in modern Hebrew and on deciphering Biblical verses.

As soon as the Gordonia movement was established, it organized evening Hebrew classes for some of its members; and naturally Z. Ḥ. Kirschenbaum was invited to serve as teacher.

During some events that we celebrated—such as: the anniversary of Dr. Herzl's death, the commemorations of the Balfour Declaration and of the ground-laying of the cornerstone of the Hebrew University of Jerusalem, etc.— Kirschenbaum used to give a public speech in the Large Synagogue. Since he was an emotional man, he would get excited and speak very passionately. When he would finish and get off the stage, he would approach some of his former students, feeling compelled to ask them what they thought of his speech. He would be overjoyed if they said they liked it.

As mentioned above, he was a modest person who never sought to stand out—and it was actually for this very reason that his students and everyone else who came in contact with him liked him.

[Page 131]

Like so many others, he was destined for a cruel and bitter fate in the Holocaust, perishing together with our other townspeople.

Translator's Footnote:

1.   From *Kamenetz-Litovsk, Zastavije and Colonies Memorial Book*, edited by S. Eisenstadt and M. Galbert, published by the Israel and America Committee of Kamenetz Litovsk and Zastavya, (Orly, Tel Aviv, Israel, 1970), pp. 130-131.

Asher Saperstein[1]

Translated by Allen Flusberg

Asher Saperstein, too, was a well-known Hebrew teacher in the town. His best class was the *Tanach* (Bible) class that he taught with a pleasant melody and interesting explanations. He had a social personality and approached his students in a friendly and intimate manner that would win them over and get them to like him.

His home served not only as a classroom, but also as a meeting place for the amateur actors of the town, who used to put on various plays that he directed. Later the Gordonia movement organized a troupe of this type; it, too, was stage-managed by him. He also served as the prompter during the plays. And he would compose various monologs that he used to integrate into the program of the plays.

In the last few years before I immigrated to Israel, I didn't have a chance to talk to him very often; but when I did run into him, I enjoyed his crisp, critical analysis of community affairs. And he always had a special place in my heart for all the kindness he showed me in the old days, when we were young.[2]

He, too, was cut off, his life taken, with all the other victims of the Holocaust.[3] May his memory be a blessing!

Translator's Footnotes:

1. From *Kamenetz-Litovsk, Zastavije and Colonies Memorial Book*, edited by S. Eisenstadt and M. Galbert, published by the Israel and America Committee of Kamenetz Litovsk and Zastavya, (Orly, Tel Aviv, Israel, 1970), p. 131.
2. Hebrew: *shamarti lo ḥesed neurim* (after Jeremiah 2:2)
3. Asher Saperstein was expelled from Kamenetz to Pruzhany and later perished in Auschwitz. See the following article in this Yizkor Book: Y. Portnoy, "From the Ghettos to the Concentration Camps", pp. 183-188 (Hebrew) and 534-439 (Yiddish).

Binyamin Bogatin[1]

Translated by Allen Flusberg

Binyamin Bogatin came from a prominent family. His father was a dentist who, when he grew old, served as a senior official in the branch of the Jewish Cooperative Bank in the town. His mother was educated and had a noble character. He and his sister Esther-Ḥana, who lives here in Israel (and may she live a long life), served as an example of excellent upbringing for the other young people. Among the local youth Binyamin stood out as an intelligent and educated young man.

In spite of the Polish education—far removed from Jewish tradition—that he received in his parents' home, he became interested in the Jewish movement for national liberation. At first he did not have a well-defined perspective. We were glad that he was contributing his intellectual capability, and we worked together with him in the educational activity of the Gordonia Movement[2]. As time passed, he grew closer and came around to be with us more often, joining our group of young people. We were very pleased by his friendship, and we enjoyed spending time together. Many a time we held discussions and debates on politics, literature, society, etc.

When a branch of *Beitar*[3] was established in our town, our paths diverged somewhat. He became more sympathetic to this movement, and before long he moved over to it and became one of its leaders—a deputy commander. In spite of his radical turn to the right, we continued to think highly of him because of his virtues and personal qualities. In mock trials that we held, we appeared together with him on the same stage. He approached everything seriously, practically and methodically; and the conclusions he reached as a prosecutor in such trials were well founded.

[Page 132]

After his father had died and his sister had immigrated to Israel, we used to meet from time to time at his home. I recall that when his mother became ill and her serious condition demanded continuous care, several of us pitched in to take turns caring for her at night, to ease his heavy burden. Once, when I was on duty with her, she woke up, and in a weak voice turned to me and said: "A pity that you're wasting all this strength for nothing—my days are numbered and my end is near." And indeed, shortly thereafter she passed away.

After I immigrated to Israel, I found out that Binyamin had later moved to the nearby city of Brisk[4], where he had to some extent made a place for himself.

He, too, was one of the victims of the Holocaust.

Translator's Footnotes:

1. From *Kamenetz-Litovsk, Zastavije and Colonies Memorial Book*, edited by S. Eisenstadt and M. Galbert, published by the Israel and America Committee of Kamenetz Litovsk and Zastavya, (Orly, Tel Aviv, Israel, 1970), pp. 131-132.
2. Gordonia, founded in Poland in 1925, was a Zionist youth movement that rejected Marxism, emphasizing instead manual labor and the revival of the Hebrew language. See the following (retrieved October 2019): https://en.wikipedia.org/wiki/Gordonia_(youth_movement). See article on pp. 77-79 of this volume: P. Ravid-Rudnicki, "The Gordonia Movement in Kamenetz-Litowsk".
3. *Beitar* (or *Betar*) was a non-socialist Zionist youth movement, founded in 1923 by Ze'ev Jabotinsky. See the following web site (retrieved June, 2020): https://en.wikipedia.org/wiki/Betar. Also see article on p. 80 of this volume: B. Kotik, "*Beitar* and *Tzohar* Movement in Kamenetz-Litowsk".
4. Brisk [Brest-Litowsk] is located ~40km south of Kamenetz.

[Page 133]

Hershl Tzvi Saperstein[1]

by Haya Krakowski-Karabelnik

Translated by Allen Flusberg

Hershl was born in Kamenetz-Litowsk. His parents, Avromche and Fayga Nehama, ran a business. He was the third of four brothers. All four were well known in the town for their self-initiative and ability. They were considered part of the intellectual circle of the town.

Like his other brothers, Hershl Tzvi was a teacher, and for a while he served together with his brothers as a teacher in the Jewish[2] school. I, too, was one of his students.

He was known for his good temperament and relaxed attitude. He was usually cheerful and happy—humming a tune as he walked down the street.

[Page 134]

He was one of the few Yiddishists[3] in Kamenetz. He supported the Left Zionist Workers[4], who were essentially inactive in the town after the First World War. He was among the remnant of that movement in Kamenetz.

Hershl Tzvi had a broad knowledge of literature, particularly in the Yiddish language. Devoted to its promulgation, he was glad to contribute whenever an opportunity arose to take an active part in this endeavor.

He was one of the few Kamenetz townspeople who was rescued from the inferno of the Holocaust.

We were aware that he was about to immigrate to Israel from one of the refugee camps in Germany. And indeed, on the day after he immigrated in 1948, I happened to run into him on Allenby Street in Tel Aviv. Our chance meeting brought him unbridled joy.

To our great sorrow, he never had the chance to put down roots in Israel. Soon after his arrival, he was having great difficulty adjusting to life here. And then the heart disease he suffered from after he got to Israel overwhelmed him, and he died, childless, in mid-1949.

May his memory be a blessing!

Footnotes:

     1.   From *Kamenetz-Litovsk, Zastavije and Colonies Memorial Book*, edited by S. Eisenstadt and M. Galbert, published by the Israel and America Committee of Kamenetz Litovsk and Zastavya, (Orly, Tel Aviv, Israel, 1970), pp. 133-134.
     2.   Hebrew: *Ivri* (= Hebrew; in context probably means Jewish)
     3.   Yiddishists generally supported a Jewish cultural identity with Yiddish, rather than a revived Hebrew, as the cultural language of the Jews. See the following (retrieved January 2021): Yiddishist movement - Wikipedia
     4.   See the following (retrieved January 2021): Labor Zionism - Wikipedia

[Page 135]

Leibl (Arye) Pomaranchik[1]

By Asher Glezer

Translated by Allen Flusberg

He was a modest man, God-fearing and learned—not only in Torah and Judaism, but also in modern secular knowledge, and especially in Hebrew and arithmetic.

As they say, "I have learned something from each of my teachers";[2] but, of the little I still remember, I have not retained as much from any other *melamed* or teacher. And I recall a particularly boring school day—when I was told that on that very day R.[3] Leibl was going to be giving a class in Hebrew grammar—how unable I was to contain my excitement.

All the time that I was his student I never saw him hit any child. And I recall that once a boy—who was from the poorer class of society—came to the Talmud Torah school in the winter, wearing a very meager outfit. R. Leibl went straight to the *gabbai* [functionary in charge of charity], R. Michael Kaplanski, to try to see to it that the boy received some better clothing so that he could come to school, rather than having to stay home.

Anyone who passed by the window of his house late at night could see him sitting bent over some book, studying.

Footnotes:

     1.   From *Kamenetz-Litovsk, Zastavije and Colonies Memorial Book*, edited by S. Eisenstadt and M. Galbert, published by the Israel and America Committee of Kamenetz Litovsk and Zastavya, (Orly, Tel Aviv, Israel, 1970), p. 135.
     2.   Psalms 119:99, as interpreted in *Pirkei Avot* (Ethics of the Fathers) 4:1
     3.   R. stands for *Reb*, a title similar to "Mr." in English

R. Nuske the *Melamed*[1]

by Asher Glezer

Translated by Allen Flusberg

R.[2] Nuske (R. Nosson [Natan] Kravitsky) was fortunate to have passed away a few short years before the Nazis invaded our little town, Kamenetz-Litowsk in the province of Brisk. He apparently merited this good fortune for his sublime, good qualities and for being a God-fearing, charitable Jew who got along well with all people great and small, his pupils. (R. Nuske passed away on the 23rd of Av[3] in the year 1934.)

R. Nuske's funeral was large—for so many of the townspeople wanted to pay him their last respects with a final, unrequited kindness. R. Yosef Vigutov[4], the representative of the Jews of the town who was quite learned in Judaism, delivered a powerful eulogy. Yet with all his words of praise he was unable to articulate R. Nuske's small, everyday acts that had been engraved in all our minds, especially those of his young students.

He had a long, white beard that was always carefully combed. His black cap, with its short brim, never departed from his head. All of his simple clothing was neat, and he was accustomed to making sure that his shirt was clean and unwrinkled.

[Page 136]

We, his students and others who respected him, knew him as someone who was meticulous about Jewish observances, down to the finest details. And we were therefore careful when we were around him, so as not to upset or infuriate him. But there were two things he was particularly strict on: the observance of Yom Kippur [Day of Atonement] and the preparations for Passover.

On Yom Kippur the Mayer-Hersh Synagogue was packed. R. Nuske was careful not to start *Barchu*[5] before three stars were visible in the sky; only after that would he slowly begin reciting the evening service and prepare himself for *Havdala*[6] while his wife was standing at his side with a reverent gaze.

R. Nosson lived in a poor home. In the front room there was a table and stools, where we, his pupils, used to sit, drinking up his teaching with great thirst.

In his home they would bake *matzot* [unleavened bread] on the day before Passover— a great experience. R. Nuske was especially strict and would recruit his finest students for the job; and more than once I, too, was fortunate enough to participate in the baking of the *matzot*.

R. Nuske would also see to it that charity was collected for the widows and orphans. For this purpose he himself would go to the houses of the wealthy on Fridays—from one house to the next—thereby feeling the pain of the impoverished children who did not have any bread in their homes.

He was a dear man, and his memory will always be with me.

Footnotes:

1. From *Kamenetz-Litovsk, Zastavije and Colonies Memorial Book*, edited by S. Eisenstadt and M. Galbert, published by the Israel and America Committee of Kamenetz Litovsk and Zastavya, (Orly, Tel Aviv, Israel, 1970), pp. 135-136. *Melamed* = teacher of small children.
2. R. stands for Reb, a title similar to English "Mr."
3. August 4, 1934
4. For more on Yosef Vigutov, see the following articles in this Yizkor Book: Mendelson, "R. Yosef Vigutov", pp. 505-506; R.V., "Yosef Vigutov and Bendet Winograd", pp. 122-123.
5. *Barchu* refers to the beginning of the evening prayer service, in this case right after Yom Kippur ends. Visibility of three stars indicates it is dark enough to be sure that the previous day has ended. In this case the evening service is recited at the end of a 25-hour fast, when hunger is gnawing at most people, but the evening service is customarily completed before breaking the fast.
6. *Havdala* = blessings marking the end of a Holy Day and the beginning of an ordinary day when labor is permissible

[Page 137]

Efraim Kotik, Sr.[1]

by Baruch Mordechai Kotik

Translated by Allen Flusberg

I recall that right after the Austrians conquered Kamenetz[2], and the town was full of Austrian soldiers, a soldier stole a gold watch that belonged to our neighbor, Isaac Steinberg. My father caught him, took the stolen object away from him and returned it to its owner.

Starting with the beginning of the German occupation all employment ceased in our town; anyone who had a horse and wagon would fell some timber in the forest and bring it for sale near my father's house. My father was prepared to encourage and help each of them to the extent that he could.

Both Jews and non-Jews would turn to my father to settle disagreements and mediate between two claimants.

He was a devoted, enthusiastic Zionist who sent his children to Israel and was prepared to part from them even though he was in poor health. He himself wanted very much to immigrate to Israel, but did not merit it: two weeks after he passed away, he received an immigration permit.

May his memory be a blessing!

Footnotes:

1. From *Kamenetz-Litovsk, Zastavije and Colonies Memorial Book*, edited by S. Eisenstadt and M. Galbert, published by the Israel and America Committee of Kamenetz Litovsk and Zastavya, (Orly, Tel Aviv, Israel, 1970), p. 137.
2. During World War I

[Page 141]

Committee members of Kamenetz-Litowsk townspeople organization who passed away in Israel

Zahava Gershuni[1]

by Rabbi Yehuda Gershuni

Translated by Allen Flusberg

Zahava-Golda (née Sher) was born in Kamenetz-Litowsk. She was a member of the very first committee formed by those who hailed from Kamenetz-Litowsk, Zastavya and the Colonies.

When Zahava was one year old her mother died, leaving her as a lonely orphan who went through much suffering during her childhood. At a young age she joined the Zionist youth movement, and she remained devoted to Zionism until the end of her life.

In 1933 the two of us immigrated together to the Land of Israel, settling in Jerusalem. Everyone who knew Zahava liked her. She was so very generous that she tried to help those in need all the time, beyond her ability. She was a mother not only to her daughters, but to every depressed child. There was an impoverished family living in our neighborhood. The children of this family were hungry most of the time and left on their own. My very merciful wife Zahava used to bring them clothing and food to revive their spirit.

[Page 142]

When she found out that one of our friends was in dire need, she did not rest until that friend came over to us, and she cared for him like a devoted mother. She especially dedicated herself to the education of our little daughters. She used to say: "Education in the Land of Israel is the siren of our spirit. Our entire aim is to bring about the renewal of our people in their land, a renewal that can be accomplished only through proper and basic education."

With a strong love for our people and culture, she took care to ensure that Hebrew was the only language spoken in our home.

Because she died young, Zahava did not merit the full pleasure of seeing our daughters educated.

When she felt her end approaching, she called out in a choking voice, "I don't want my daughters to also be left orphans!"

May her memory be a blessing!

Footnote:

1.   From *Kamenetz-Litovsk, Zastavije and Colonies Memorial Book*, edited by S. Eisenstadt and M. Galbert, published by the Israel and America Committee of Kamenetz Litovsk and Zastavya, (Orly, Tel Aviv, Israel, 1970), pp. 141-142.

[Page 143]

Yehuda Rappaport[1]

by Asher Glezer

Translated by Allen Flusberg

Yudl (Yehuda Rappaport, of blessed memory) was forty-one years old when he gave his soul back to the Creator on the 27th of Elul 5719 (September 30, 1959).

I knew Yehuda from the time we were children; we studied together in *cheder*[2]. After he was grown he continued his studies in the Yeshiva of Kletsk[3]. I have been told that he received certification as a *shochet* and *bodek*[4], and he became well known for his good qualities, his humility and generosity.

In 1949 Yehuda and his wife reached Israel (via Cyprus). His two children, Yosef and Asher, were born here. For several years Yehuda was a committee member in the Organization of Kamenetzers in Israel.

The night before he passed away, he was still baking bread in the bakery that he had worked hard to establish near the train station of Lod, the city of immigrants. In the early morning hours he did not feel well, and he asked to be taken to Hadassah Hospital. But the doctor concluded that he was in immediate mortal danger and that it was imperative to bring him to a nearer hospital. He was brought to the hospital in Tzrifin[5]. On that very day he suffered a heart attack; his heart could not withstand the pressure and gave out.

Yudl, who in the past had experienced and survived so much suffering and torment, did not make it this time, and his life ended before his time.

May his memory be a blessing!

Footnotes:

1. From *Kamenetz-Litovsk, Zastavije and Colonies Memorial Book*, edited by S. Eisenstadt and M. Galbert, published by the Israel and America Committee of Kamenetz Litovsk and Zastavya, (Orly, Tel Aviv, Israel, 1970), p. 143. See also the following related article on pp. 561-568 of this volume: Ben-Moshe, "Kamenetz in 1945".
2. *cheder* = religious-studies school for small children
3. Kletsk, Belarus, located about 200km northeast of Kamenetz-Litowsk. For some details on the Kletsk Yeshiva, see the following link (retrieved February 2020): https://en.wikipedia.org/wiki/Aharon_Kotler.
4. Ritual slaughterer and inspector of meat for *kashrut*
5. Tzrifin, Israel is located about 4km west of Lod. The hospital there, formerly known as Assaf HaRofeh, was renamed Yitzhak Shamir Medical Center in 2017.

Tuvya Savitzki[1]

by Ḥaya Krakowski-Karabelnik

Translated by Allen Flusberg

Tuvya was born to religiously observant parents in Kamenetz. His father was a synagogue *gabbai* [charity functionary] whose modest salary was not large enough to support his family. They did also have a tavern that the farmers who lived in the surrounding area used to frequent on Sundays and during town fairs.

Tuvya did not adapt to his situation, and his parents' livelihood was not to his liking. Not wanting to continue his studies in a yeshiva, as his father wished him to do, he was going through a psychological crisis.

[Page 145]

When *HeHalutz*[2] was established in our town, it was as if he had found a path to redemption. He joined the movement, and at a later time he joined the *Poalei-Zion* [Zionist Workers] (united with Tz.S. [Zionist Socialist])[3] party, becoming one of its active members. Together with a number of comrades he set out for training in Pinsk[4], so that he would be able to immigrate to the Land of Israel. But for various reasons his *aliya* [immigration to Israel] was delayed, and he returned home from the training program.

He didn't stay in Kamenetz very long, however, and left for Warsaw. There he worked for a period of time in a locksmith shop, continuing to train himself for *aliya*. His living conditions in Warsaw were very difficult, and he came back home again without having obtained an immigration certificate. And once again he was unable to adapt to his situation.

After marrying Tova Solnitze, he decided to immigrate to Israel in *Aliya Bet*[5]—for the time being by himself—and to make a home for himself in the Land of Israel. And in 1934 he fulfilled this dream of his.

His absorption—adaptation to the country—was difficult. Meanwhile his wife, who had remained behind in Kamenetz, gave birth to a son. Tuvya had still not found adequate work and was actually going hungry, and so he did not dare bring his family to the country.

On the eve of the outbreak of World War II he was working as a watchman.

His wife and son, who had not managed to immigrate to Israel, perished in the Holocaust together with all the other Kamenetz martyrs.[6]

In Israel Tuvya served on one of the committees of the Organization of Kamenetzers, but he did not live to see the memorialization of his fellow townspeople. His heart was unable to physically withstand the hardships he had lived through, and he passed away very suddenly in Tel Aviv in the year 1948.

May his memory be preserved among us!

Footnotes:

1.   From *Kamenetz-Litovsk, Zastavije and Colonies Memorial Book*, edited by S. Eisenstadt and M. Galbert, published by the Israel and America Committee of Kamenetz Litovsk and Zastavya, (Orly, Tel Aviv, Israel, 1970), pp. 144-145.
2.   *HeHalutz*, sometimes spelled *HeChalutz* (= The Pioneer), was a Jewish youth movement that trained young people for agricultural settlement in the Land of Israel, as described in the following link (retrieved February 2020): https://en.wikipedia.org/wiki/HeHalutz
3.   See the article by Krakowski-Karabelnik on pp. 74-76 of this Yizkor Book, "Poalei-Zion" (United with Tz.S.) in Kamenetz-Litowsk
4.   The city of Pinsk, Belarus is located about 170km east of Kamenetz.
5.   *Aliya Bet* = name of a wave of *aliya* during the British Mandate, starting in the 1930s and ending with the independence of the State of Israel in 1948. This immigration was illegal or restricted by British law at the time. See the following web site (retrieved April 2021): Aliyah Bet - Wikipedia
6.   Tuvya's wife, Tova Savitzki is listed in the Hebrew/Yiddish Necrology on p. 268 under the name "Toiba Savitzki". The English translation of the Necrology (at the end of this Yizkor Book) transposed the *vav* and *bet* of the name "Toiba" and listed it as "Tuvya".

[Page 146]

Yeshaya Rimon[1]

By Pinḥas Ravid-Rudnicki

Translated by Allen Flusberg

A short announcement appeared in the press on the sudden death of our fellow townsman, Yeshaya Rimon, one of the old-time prominent townspeople, who had continued the tradition of the best of the previous generation, incorporating a fusion of Torah and secular knowledge. I recall the heartfelt memorial speeches he gave many times at the yearly gatherings to honor the martyrs of Kamenetz and Zastavya. His words were saturated with pain and anguish for the loss of the living town—a town that once was and is no more, a town whose living song was interrupted in mid-stanza.

For a while Yeshaya Rimon, of blessed memory, served as the head of the Committee of Townspeople from Kamenetz and Zastavya. He carried out this volunteer position faithfully, working hard for long hours to memorialize our martyrs.

But he did not live to see the actual publication of the collection of essays in this memorial book. And so, as fate would have it, this book is now serving as a memorial not only to our martyrs, but also to the remnant of our beloved townspeople, who, like him, felt the pain of the loss—of their townspeople and all the other Jews who perished in the period of the Holocaust.

May his memory be a blessing!

Footnote:

    1.   From *Kamenetz-Litovsk, Zastavije and Colonies Memorial Book*, edited by S. Eisenstadt and M. Galbert, published by the Israel and America Committee of Kamenetz Litovsk and Zastavya, (Orly, Tel Aviv, Israel, 1970), pp. 146.

[Page 147]

Shimon Kotik[1]

By Leah Aloni-Bobrowski (Tel Aviv)

Translated by Allen Flusberg

Shimon, who was born in Kamenetz-Litowsk, was the son of Matke and Yudl Kotik. He received a traditional and general education in the town, and for a few years he also attended a high school in Brisk-Litowsk[2]. When he grew up, he saw no future for himself in Kamenetz and decided he would leave. He studied Hebrew and general knowledge of the Land of Israel. He joined the first group of pioneers from our town, all of whom immigrated to the Land of Israel together. When he got here, he found a job as a policeman in Safed. He viewed himself in this line of work as serving in an important public position. Shimon understood that as a policeman he would be able to help others, and indeed he helped many people find work. In that period, when the Jewish population was struggling — practically empty-handed — for security, Shimon many a time also helped purchase arms.

[Page 148]

In Safed he started a family, but he did not enjoy a happy family life for very long. The first calamity he suffered was the sudden, untimely death of his wife. He was left alone, depressed and hopeless, with his little daughter.

It was not very long before his only daughter passed away, too.

It was very hard for Shimon to carry this painful burden of loneliness. With the encouragement of family members, he married his cousin Neḥama. They left Safed and moved to Kiryat-Ḥaim[3], where a son and daughter were born to them.

Shimon was promoted to sergeant. In the defense of the Jewish population, he held high-level public positions, placing himself at risk more than once in very dangerous situations.

But the path his life took was littered with grief and tragedy. During the Israeli War of Liberation [Independence], his only son was killed in the war, in defense of his native land. This tragedy depressed Shimon to the very core. It was hard for him to recover, to get over his bitter fate; and the great sorrow he experienced made him physically ill. As he lay on his deathbed in the hospital, his devoted wife Neḥama died, too.

He did not live very long after that. He passed away suddenly while in the middle of his morning prayers, standing as he did every day wrapped in his *tallit* [prayer shawl] and *tefillin* [phylacteries].

May his memory be a blessing!

Footnotes:

1. From *Kamenetz-Litovsk, Zastavije and Colonies Memorial Book*, edited by S. Eisenstadt and M. Galbert, published by the Israel and America Committee of Kamenetz Litovsk and Zastavya, (Orly, Tel Aviv, Israel, 1970), pp. 147-148.
2. Brisk = Brest-Litowsk, a city located about 40km south of Kamenetz.
3. Kiryat-Ḥaim was then (c. 1930) a new town about 10km northeast of Haifa. It was annexed to Haifa in 1950.

[Page 149]

Meir Bobrowski[1]

by Dov Aloni (Tel Aviv)

Translated by Allen Flusberg

Meir was the son of Avraham and Tama in Kamenetz-Litowsk. During his childhood—from the age of five until his bar-mitzva—he received a traditional Jewish education, in classes taught by a series of *melamdim* [children's teachers] in the "Four *Heders*". He did not have the inclination to continue his studies in yeshivas. He received a secular education—in Russian and German—from private "licensed" teachers who used to occasionally be in Kamenetz. Mainly he devoted himself to both mathematical science and humanities, studying them intensively day and night.

[Page 150]

During the Russian-Polish war[2] he was compelled to quickly leave his parents' home to save himself from the Poles when they occupied Kamenetz. Using back roads, he crossed the border and arrived all alone, with no near relatives, in Soviet Russia. Lonely, cut off from all his family members, he suffered the indignities of hunger, disease and cold weather. In spite of all his agony he aspired to study for examinations, obtain a high-school diploma, and enroll in one of the schools of higher education or in a university. But because of his decision not to join the Communist Party he was never able to fulfill this aspiration.

During those days of torment, he needed to find some kind of work to support himself. Fortunately, he was able to get a job in a stationery cooperative. He worked in this cooperative for several years, until he obtained a new job as manager of a large regional warehouse containing various food supplies. His material situation improved greatly, but his social life was unsatisfying. He made up his mind to leave Russia when the opportunity presented itself. To make sure he would be able to carry out this ambition of his someday, and taking into account that Russia was sealed off and did not allow its people to leave, he chose not to put down roots: instead of starting a family, he remained all alone—solitary and lonely.

During the years of the Second World War, Meir was drafted into the Red Army. For a long time he served as a translator from German to Russian. When the war intensified, he was sent to the front to fight against the Nazis. He was gravely wounded and lost his left leg. In this condition he clearly did not find any fulfilment in living in this land, where he felt like a stranger[3]. He decided that he would leave Russia—come what may—and when he was released from the hospital he got around on crutches and refused to work, claiming: "I am an invalid; I am ill, and lack the strength to work. I have no relatives in Russia. Let me leave the country to join members of my family, with whom I will live, and they will support me for the rest of my life."

Meir knew that in the Land of Israel, which he longed to go to, he had four sisters, all of whom had families, and that they would certainly welcome him into to their homes and family circles, so that in his last years he would find support and achieve a tranquil life. After much effort for many years, while he was living in Fergana[4], he succeeded in getting an immigration certificate to the Land of Israel from the Russian government, which "permitted" him, after three years of treatment, to unite with his family members. And after he received the requisite sum of money that would completely cover the trip expenses from the Chief Rabbi of Moscow, Rabbi Shlomo Shliffer—who was a personal friend of his brother-in-law, the author of this article—he arrived the year that the State of Israel declared independence, welcomed by family members in Israel. On crutches, he was carrying with him a passport with the very first visa from the government of Communist Russia.

Once he was in Israel, however, he did not sit around with folded hands. He studied Hebrew for two years in our house, and the third year he was accepted as a student in the most advanced class of the Ulpan [for learning Hebrew] in Jerusalem. When he came afterwards to Tel Aviv he passed an examination, and he got a job managing the catalogue of the electric company in the Reading Power Station[5], to the satisfaction of the company management. He worked there for 18 consecutive years, until the day he died.

[Page 151]

In Israel he also found community work that particularly interested him, and he devoted much of his time to it. He was chosen to serve on the Committee of the Kamenetz-Litowsk and Zastavya Organization; and when the Committee decided to publish a book dedicated to the memory of the martyrs who perished in Kamenetz during the Holocaust, he was one of the first to serve on the editorial staff of the book. He decided to visit every single one of the Kamenetzers who now resided all over Israel, to obtain testimony from them that would provide the most updated list of the martyrs. And despite his difficulty getting around on one leg, he went up and down many flights of stairs in all the apartment houses the Kamenetzers lived in, wherever they were. He took down detailed testimony from them about every one of those who had perished, by family, by name and by profession. He also contacted the Organization Committee of the Kamenetzers in the United States, asking them to add whatever they knew to this list. And when with tremulousness and reverence he handed this list of his—of the many names of those who had perished—to the members of the editorial board, they offered to compensate him for his travel expenses. He was offended and stated: "This work of mine, so precious to each and every one of us, I am dedicating and offering as a memorial to our townspeople and to their memory."[6]

All the suffering and anguish that he experienced in Russia affected his health and damaged his heart. On Friday, the 15th of Kislev 5729[7], during the afternoon, while he was in a *Kupat Ḥolim*[8] clinic—in the presence of doctors, nurses and a crowd of people who were there for doctor's visits—he suddenly collapsed and died: a quick, painless and easy death.[9]

May his memory be a blessing for all of us forevermore.

Footnotes:

1.   From *Kamenetz-Litovsk, Zastavije and Colonies Memorial Book*, edited by S. Eisenstadt and M. Galbert, published by the Israel and America Committee of Kamenetz Litovsk and Zastavya, (Orly, Tel Aviv, Israel, 1970), pp. 149-151.
2.   1919-1920. For details, see the following link (retrieved October, 2020): https://en.wikipedia.org/wiki/Polish%E2%80%93Soviet_War
3.   Hebrew: *al admat nekhar* (Psalms 137:4), in a strange or foreign land
4.   Fergana is the name of a region and city in Uzbekistan. Uzbekistan was a republic of the Soviet Union at that time (the1940s); it did not obtain independence until 1991.
5.   The Reading Power Station is on the Yarkon River in Tel Aviv.
6.   Bobrowski's list of martyrs can be found on pp. 251-278 of this volume: "List of Jews of Kamenetz-Litowsk, Zastavya and the Colonies, Who Perished at the Hands of the Nazis, May Their Memory Be Blotted Out", by Meir Bobrowski.
7.   15 Kislev 5729 = December 6, 1968
8.   *Kupat Ḥolim* = Funds for the Ill, the National Health Insurance organizations of Israel
9.   Hebrew: *mitat neshika* = death by a kiss (from God), a description of the easy death said to be the manner in which the righteous die.

[Page 152]

Yehudit Koscikiewicz[1]

by Leah Aloni-Bobrowski

Translated by Allen Flusberg

Yehudit was born in Kamenetz-Litowsk, the daughter of Yisrael and Ḥana Grunt. She received her traditional and general education from private tutors, just like all the other girls of the town. During World War I, when a Hebrew-German school was established in the town, she was one of the first students there, and she excelled in her studies. After the war ended, she continued her studies in one of the gymnasia high schools of Brisk-Litowsk[2].

After she married her fiancé, Yeḥezkel Koscikiewicz, she settled down to start a family in Brisk-Litowsk.

[Page 153]

Yehudit was not satisfied with her life in Poland, where anti-Semitism was growing stronger from day to day. She decided to immigrate to Israel together with her husband and her little daughter. But it was a very long road between making this decision and implementing it, because Israel was then experiencing an economic crisis and a job shortage. In 1932 she went to Israel all by herself— as a tourist— even though she was the mother of a three-year-old daughter. After she had checked out the situation and become intoxicated with the life of freedom in Israel, she decided not to return to Poland. She took on all kinds of jobs and worked hard, so that her husband and daughter should be able to immigrate as soon as possible.

After much effort—and with the help of relatives in the country—her husband and daughter arrived in Israel. For a short time they lived in Tel Aviv, and afterwards the Koscikiewicz family moved to Petaḥ Tikva.

Yehudit was very sociable and liked helping others. With her pleasant demeanor, she was a good conversationalist who was always accessible to anyone seeking advice and wisdom. And indeed she helped many people out with great devotion. Her home was a meeting place for the large number of Kamenetzers and other people she knew, as well as new close friends she had made in Israel. She would genially and affectionately invite her guests in—including any who had come from far away and sometimes stayed for a long time. These qualities helped her acquire many devoted friends.

Thanks to its energetic effort—and with some help from friends—the Koscikiewicz family set up an electrical appliance shop in Petaḥ Tikva, from which they made their living.

For many years Yehudit worked hard and suffered through the difficulties of absorption [adaptation to Israel], but she never complained, instead accepting all her hardships with equanimity.

As time passed these hardships began to ease up, but then her husband suddenly died, before his time. She bore the burden of widowhood in silence.

Yehudit was an active member of the Kamenetzer Committee and was a member of the editorial board for the publication of this Memorial Book to honor the martyrs of our town. She was particularly dedicated to arranging the necrologies that would perpetuate the memory of those who perished and those who passed away.

Our hearts ache, not wanting to come to terms with the reality that our Yehudit is no more, and that we must add a necrology to her memory as well[3].

She passed away in the early hours of Tuesday, January 21 1969.

With her death her only daughter, Zahava, and her daughter's husband Binyamin, as well as her three grandchildren—Aya[4], Avi and Yeḥezkel (who is named after her husband)—and her sister Rachel—the only one left from among the older generation of the family—have all been bereaved. She loved them all so much, and they loved their mother and grandmother with an eternal love.

Her family members and her many friends followed behind her bier and shed bitter tears over her untimely death.

We will not forget you, Yehudit. Rest in peace! And may your memory be an everlasting blessing.

Footnotes:

1.   From *Kamenetz-Litovsk, Zastavije and Colonies Memorial Book*, edited by S. Eisenstadt and M. Galbert, published by the Israel and America Committee of Kamenetz Litovsk and Zastavya, (Orly, Tel Aviv, Israel, 1970), pp. 152-153.
2.   Brisk (or Brest) Litowsk is a city located about 40km south of Kamenetz.
3.   See Necrology section, p. 294 of this Yizkor Book.
4.   In the Necrology section, p. 294, her name is given as Chaya.

[Page 154]

A Farewell to Leah Aloni, of Blessed Memory[1]
(after the burial in the Holon Cemetery, Sunday 21 Tishri 5730 [sic][2])

by Gideon Hausner

Translated by Allen Flusberg

We take our leave from a lady to whom we can wholeheartedly give the honorary title of "a mother in Israel". For Leah Aloni was a mother who merged the best Jewish-family tradition with all the lifestyles of our times. Whoever visited her home invariably admired the prevailing splendid family relationships between parents, daughters and granddaughters, all of whom lived together in a common apartment—not because they had to or were forced to, but rather because they loved and respected one another, and so they liked being together.

[Page 155]

Leah was a beloved wife, loving and sympathetic, who accompanied her husband on the entire trajectory of his life, from the little town in the Diaspora where she became attached to Zionism and the Hebrew language—and further along the way, with all its geographic twists and turns. Yet this path went straight, naturally and consistently: *aliya* to Israel, school-teaching, and educating many generations of pupils. Thus she walked alongside her spouse in all he did, for their lives were a joint enterprise, and they saw themselves as bound together in everything. Even the letters they wrote to friends were signed by both of them, for they were a pair of comrades who labored side-by-side. And they worked as a team—whether at home, within society, or in school.

Leah was a gifted educator. Once I happened to go with her to the school that she had taught in. It was after she had already retired. And so I saw the children who remembered her dashing over and hugging her with affection and admiration. I saw her fellow teachers greeting her with respect and appreciation. I saw that she had left love and admiration behind in her wake.

In the last few years, I collaborated with her on the educational project of memorializing—within Israeli schools—the communities that had been destroyed in the Holocaust. She was enthusiastic about this educational program that was intended to provide Israeli youth with an existential connection to the past of the people that had been destroyed. Leah implemented this project, as well, at the side of the love of her youth. She worked on it tirelessly, travelling to schools in various parts of the country, acting and encouraging others to be active, giving speeches and rousing the hearts of students, teachers and principals with the fire of her enthusiasm for the project that she was so attached to. She was very pleased when her little town Kamenetz-Litowsk was the first to be commemorated by her school in Tel Aviv.

What words of solace can we offer to her husband, Dov, who is now bereaved of the love of his youth; to her daughter, son-in-law and granddaughters, who have lost a mother; to her bereaved sisters; and to the entire family? I have no words of comfort for them, nor for myself. One can only hope that her husband and family will manage to continue to live according to Leah's spirit. I am sure that were she able to speak to us from beyond, she would say to all of us: "Continue! Guard the glowing ember of love of family and of our people, and may the same spirit dwell among you as has until now."

Let us strive to fulfil this command and to cling to the values that Leah believed in. And in this way her soul will be bound in the bond of life.

Rest in peace, Leah Aloni; your family and friends will fulfil your command.

Footnotes:

    1.   From *Kamenetz-Litovsk, Zastavije and Colonies Memorial Book*, edited by S. Eisenstadt and M. Galbert, published by the Israel and America Committee of Kamenetz Litovsk and Zastavya, (Orly, Tel Aviv, Israel, 1970), pp. 154-155.

    2.   Friday, 21 Tishri 5730 = October 3, 1969. See the next article in this Yizkor Book by Shraga Aloni, p. 156, which states that Leah's funeral took place on Sunday, 23 Tishri 5730, i.e., 2 days later. Perhaps it was Leah Aloni's death that took place on 21 Tishri.

[Page 156]

Leah, My Sister-In-Law—My Sister![1]

(Delivered at her Graveside on 23 Tishri 5730[2])

by Shraga Aloni

Translated by Allen Flusberg

I knew you as a refugee after the First World War, when you left you parents' home in Kamenetz-Litowsk, serving together with my only brother, Dov, as a Hebrew-language classroom teacher[3], in the *Reali* [Natural Science] *Gymnasia* [high school] in Kovno[4].

After two years of respectable work, both of you left your positions in Kovno, immigrating together to the Land of Israel during a difficult period for *aliya*. This was what you had been yearning for—to get to Israel, come what may.

In spite of your own hardship establishing yourselves in Safed, in Rishon LeZion and even in Tel Aviv, you showed concern for your family in Kamenetz-Litowsk; and, taking full responsibility, you brought over your three sisters, your parents as tourists as a first step[5], and your brother Meir from the Soviet Union[6].

We, who originated in my native town of Yezne[7], also found sanctuary in your home in Safed—I, our elderly mother, my grandfather who is turning 116 this year, family relatives, friends and acquaintances; you took care of all of us and helped see to it that we establish ourselves in Israel. And you also did much volunteer work in the organization for those who came from the Diaspora.

You were one of the veteran classroom teachers in the country—a skill you passed down to your only daughter—and hopefully, as the years pass your other descendants will also be blessed with the talent of teaching. You helped your husband Dov—to whom we wish a long life—with the commemoration in Israeli schools of the martyrs of the communities, on the initiative of our honorable Knesset Member and attorney, Mr. Gideon Hausner.

How great is our sorrow and how devastating it is that, following his physicians' orders, your husband—my brother, Dov—is not with us here, attending your funeral.

Together, all of us grieve your sudden death—woe unto us that you have been taken from us in so untimely a fashion. May you rest in peace!

Footnotes:

    1.   From *Kamenetz-Litovsk, Zastavije and Colonies Memorial Book*, edited by S. Eisenstadt and M. Galbert, published by the Israel and America Committee of Kamenetz Litovsk and Zastavya, (Orly, Tel Aviv, Israel, 1970), p. 156.

    2.   23 Tishri 5730 = Sunday, October 5, 1969

    3.   Hebrew: *mora meḥanekhet* (general class teacher, as opposed to teacher specializing in a subject)

    4.   Kovno = Kaunas, Lithuania, 350km north of Kamenetz

    5.   See p. 281 of the Necrology section of this Yizkor Book.

    6.   See the article "Meir Bobrowski", by Dov Aloni on pp. 149-151 of this Yizkor Book.

    7.   Yezne = Jieznas, Lithuania, located about 40km southeast of Kaunas (Kovno) and 300km north of Kamenetz

[Page 157]

Pinhas Rabi (Rabinowitz): In His Memory[1]

by M. K.

Translated by Allen Flusberg

Pinḥas, who had such a zest for life, who saw only the good in life, who was always filled with the joy of creation, who believed in the good hidden within people, who used to drive the mundane away from our lives—he, too, is gone, no longer with us.

Pinḥas Rabinowitz was born in Kamenetz in the year 5657[2]. His father was the prodigious, saintly Rabbi Moshe Yitzḥak[3] of blessed memory, who was the chief rabbi of the town, a member of a large, multibranched family of great Torah scholars, such as the *Maharal* of Prague[4], the *Maharam* of Padua[5], etc.

He was educated at home by his rabbi father, a home in which Torah scholars were always present. Within the walls of his father's house he absorbed the wisdom of life, the beauty and courage of Jewish life—passed down for many generations—the dreams of a persecuted people that had lived throughout most of the years of its exile in sorrow and hardship. All these impressed on him the dreams of generations of Jews and the path they had followed.

[Page 158]

At a very young age he was bereaved of his father the rabbi, and the hardship of life affected him in the little town of Kamenetz[6]. His lot was that of other Jews of the town who could not afford to indulge themselves, who experienced a hard life of suffering. Most of them sometimes went hungry. They were good, simple Jews whose difficult lives were always illuminated by a longing for consolation and redemption. And it was this light that left its impression on young Pinḥas and on the entire course of his life.

And in this atmosphere, among the youth of the little town, there arose a yearning for redemption. The threads leading to the old-new homeland had been woven, and then these young people became aware that there was substance in this new life, that there was a path to redemption and deliverance for the persecuted nation that they were part of.

The striving for and streaming to the land of our forefathers had already begun. But the first ones, among them young Pinḥas, did not arrive on a magic carpet. They experienced days and nights deprived of food and sleep. And it was along a circuitous path that Pinḥas finally reached the Land in 1920.

He lived in the country for fifty years. His life encompassed a series of events and uncertainties. He experienced many crises during these years, but he always emerged from them honorably.

He was among the first who, as soon as he had set foot upon the soil of the homeland, went to the *kvutza* [agricultural communal settlement][7] of Degania[8], and recognized that the kibbutz lifestyle could provide a life of substance. He worked as a construction laborer, seeing in it a fulfilment of the idea of building up the country. He went through many years of being up on scaffolds during both fierce summers and rainy winters. This hard labor exhausted his strength. He also experienced years when there was no work and times of unemployment, but he was always full of life, for he saw this lifestyle as a fulfilment of his dreams.

He was one of the founders of the Ohel Theatre[9], and he viewed his appearances in it as an educational role. True to himself, he battled against exploitation all his life, and he was a conscientious worker. Whatever he believed in, he believed with all his heart and soul.

He did not live in the past, but there were moments in his life when, with trepidation and longing, he began to talk about his childhood—of his little town Kamenetz and all that he had experienced there. At those moments gloom and grief melted away from his face, and we would experience with him the life of the little town in its times of joy and sorrow.

He departed from us quietly, silently. May the clumps of earth of our homeland, which he loved so dearly, give him sweet comfort.

Footnotes:

1.   From *Kamenetz-Litovsk, Zastavije and Colonies Memorial Book*, edited by S. Eisenstadt and M. Galbert, published by the Israel and America Committee of Kamenetz Litovsk and Zastavya, (Orly, Tel Aviv, Israel, 1970), pp. 157-158.
2.   5657 = secular year 1896-1897
3.   See the following articles in this volume: Moshe Rabinowitz, "My Grandfather, Rabbi Moshe Yitzhak of Kamenetz-Litowsk", p. 49; "Rabbi Moshe Yitzchok Rabinowitz, of Blessed Memory", pp. 405-407.
4.   *Maharal* is an acronym for Judah Loew the son of Bezalel (died 1609), Chief Rabbi of Prague. See the following link (retrieved September 2020): https://en.wikipedia.org/wiki/Judah_Loew_ben_Bezalel
5.   *Maharam* is an acronym for Meir ben Isaac Katzenellenbogen (~1482-1565), chief rabbi of Padua. See the following link (retrieved September 2020): https://en.wikipedia.org/wiki/Meir_Katzenellenbogen
6.   See the following article in this volume: Y. Post, "Kamenetz-Litowsk, Where I've Never Been," pp. 500-501; also the Necrology section, p. 329 of this volume
7.   The *kvutza* was the forerunner of the kibbutz
8.   Degania is located at the southern tip of the Sea of Galilee. See for example the following link (retrieved September 2020): https://en.wikipedia.org/wiki/Degania_Alef
9.   The Ohel Theatre was established in 1925 as a socialist, collective theatre; members combined acting with agricultural and industrial labor. See the following link (retrieved September 2020): https://en.wikipedia.org/wiki/Ohel_Theater#History

[Page 160]

In the Holocaust

Map of Routes
from Kamenetz-Litovsk to Death Camps[1]

Translated by Allen Flusberg

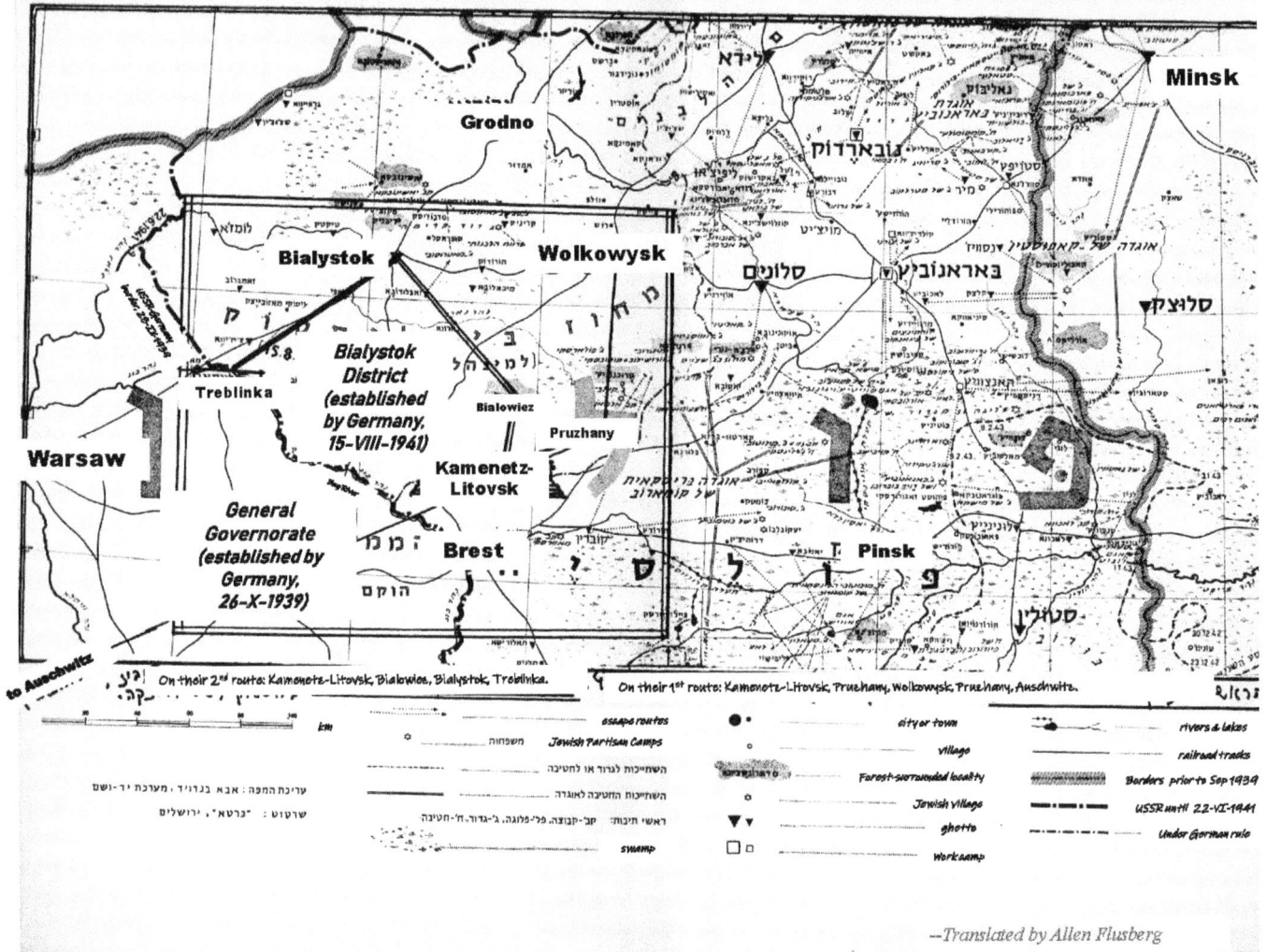

--Translated by Allen Flusberg

Footnote:

1.   The map shows the two routes taken by the Jews of Kamenetz to the Death Camps. First most of the Jews were expelled from Kamenetz to Pruzhany. Route (1): for those who never returned to Kamenetz after the expulsion, the route ran from Kamenetz to Pruzhany, then to Wolkowysk, then back to Pruzhany, and finally to Auschwitz. Route (2): for those who stayed in or clandestinely returned from Pruzhany to Kamenetz, the route ran from Kamenetz to Bialowiez, then to Bialystok, and finally to Treblinka.

[Page 163]

The Prayer[1]

By Arye Sarid

Translated by Allen Flusberg

As the axe swung over my father's head
I didn't cry out: Father! Oh, Father, alas!
In the forests of Bialowież rhinos[2] then meandered
Within the preserve guarded by watchmen.

As my sister and brother cried out and wailed
I didn't raise a hand, didn't clench my fists,
The horses were then tranquil in the clover-filled pasture
As an elderly watchman prayed for their welfare.

While my dear ones were loaded onto the wagon—
Bereaved creatures, starved for weeks
Whose lips murmured: Oh, my God, where is God?
They were then playing Bach and Handel in Kfar Yeḥezkel…[3]

…Then my mother dragged her wounded wing
Her ripped body—a shelter for her son,
Toward me then the torn face turned—
The silent prayer of my shot relatives…

Footnotes:

1. From *Kamenetz–Litovsk, Zastavije and Colonies Memorial Book*, edited by S. Eisenstadt and M. Galbert, published by the Israel and America Committee of Kamenetz Litovsk and Zastavya, (Orly, Tel Aviv, Israel, 1970), p. 163.
2. The bison of these forests (about 20km north of Kamenetz) are endangered and have been referred to by analogy as "Europe's black rhinos".
3. Kfar Yeḥezkel is a *moshav* in the Jezreel Valley, about 10km southeast of Afula.

[Page 165]

The Destruction of Kamenetz[1]

By Dora Galperin

Translated by Allen Flusberg

(Based on letters to Leah and Dov Aloni; Translation [into Hebrew] by Leah Aloni-Bobrowski)

Note by translator: *an English translation of the Yiddish article this Hebrew translation was based on appears on pp. 91-104 of the English section of this Yizkor Book, "The Tragedy and Destruction of Kamenetz", by Dora Galperin. The English translation appears to be based on both the Yiddish original and the Hebrew translation.*

Footnote:

1. From *Kamenetz–Litovsk, Zastavije and Colonies Memorial Book*, edited by S. Eisenstadt and M. Galbert, published by the Israel and America Committee of Kamenetz Litovsk and Zastavya, (Orly, Tel Aviv, Israel, 1970), pp. 165-173.

[Pages 174-182]

My Life in the Ghettos and Extermination Camps[1]

By Dvora Rudnitzky-Singer (New York)

Translated by Allen Flusberg

Note by translator: the original Yizkor Book contains 3 versions of this article: the first in Yiddish (pp. 540-549); a translation of the Yiddish into Hebrew by Leah Aloni-Bobrowski (the present article, pp. 174-182); and an English version (pp. 105-116 of the English section). The three versions are essentially identical. One discrepancy is the date on which the 3rd transport from Pruzhany arrived at Auschwitz. According to the Yiddish version (p. 544) and the Hebrew version (p. 177), it was February 23, 1943; the English version (p. 110) gives the date as February 3, 1943.

This article may be read in the original English version on <u>pp. 105-116</u> of the English section.

Footnote:

1.   From *Kamenetz–Litovsk, Zastavije and Colonies Memorial Book*, edited by S. Eisenstadt and M. Galbert, published by the Israel and America Committee of Kamenetz Litovsk and Zastavya, (Orly, Tel Aviv, Israel, 1970), pp. 174-182.

[Pages 183-188]

From the Ghettos to the Concentration Camps[1]

by Yitzhak Portnoy, Kfar Saba

Translated by Allen Flusberg

Note by translator: This Hebrew–language version is a translation of the Yiddish–language article entitled <u>"From the Ghettos to the Concentration Camps"</u>, by Yitzhak Portnoy, pp. 534–549. Minor differences between the two articles have been noted in footnotes of the English translation of the Yiddish.

Footnote:

1.   From *Kamenetz–Litovsk, Zastavije and Colonies Memorial Book*, edited by S. Eisenstadt and M. Galbert, published by the Israel and America Committee of Kamenetz Litovsk and Zastavya, (Orly, Tel Aviv, Israel, 1970), pp. 183-188.

[Page 189]

A Tear for the Loss of My Townspeople[1]

by Leah Aloni-Bobrowski (Tel Aviv)

Translated by Allen Flusberg

(Based on Testimony by Witnesses)

Night, darkness; the shadow of death, silence. By bad luck, the first Nazi shell struck and went through the window of the house belonging to one of my students, Chaya'ke Horowitz, killing her on the spot, while she slept. Chaya'ke is gone.

At dawn the calamity became known throughout our entire town. Family members, close friends and neighbors gathered together and came, standing in grief, as fright and terror enveloped the house. They were trembling and weeping, crying and shaking, and the tears were tears of bitterness.

"If only we would have died in your place, our young child, the first victim. How fortunate for you that your death spared you from all the torment awaiting each and every one of us, our daughters, our little children and infants—may your memory be a blessing." This was how everyone lamented her.

And with their arrival the chapter of Nazi torture began, a torment that was well planned: robbery and looting wherever they could, and in addition beatings with clubs and whips—not discriminating by gender or age—meted out to young and old, women and children, the ill and the dying.

The "first roundup": about one hundred men were seized in the streets of the town for hard labor. The names of only a small number of them are known to us, as follows:

R. Avraham Stempanitzki, an elderly man, age 83 (the uncle of Fishka Cohen from Fijja[2], near Petah-Tikva); Chaim Yoffe, a 15-year-old boy, son of Tamar and Moshe; R.[3] Yitzhak Leib Stempanitzki, a modest man, 55 years old (the brother of Elchanan Stempanitzki from Fijja, near Petah-Tikva); R. Shalom Galprin, a man who all his life faithfully attended to community needs (the cousin of Simcha Dubiner of Petah-Tikva); Shlomo Mandelblat, the secretary of the town, an enlightened, cultured person who was well liked, good looking, and well-dressed when he appeared in public; R. Shimon Buchalter, the brother-in-law of Yosef Vigutov. May their memory be sacred to all of us.

Pruska Forest, located on the outskirts of our town, was a meeting place for the young people; in the shade of the trees they would get together, one group here and another there, to share "secrets" of their lives as they looked ahead to their future plans, some this way and some that way…

[Page 190]

Sometimes I used to come to this forest with students of the school and with my teacher colleagues. During the "Days of Omer"[4] we would go there with "bows and arrows"[5], and we would tell our students at length about the miracles, heroic acts, salvation and battles that took place in those days and at this time. We would rouse their spirits for Zion, a longing for redemption of the "land that our ancestors desired"…

And this time the first one hundred men were brought to this forest, where they were all murdered by the defiled Nazis.

And what did the foul Nazis do with the bodies of our martyrs after this cruel, atrocious massacre? Were they buried in a common grave? Were they burned? Where? Only the birch and pine, the mute, eternal trees of the forest—they are the only ones who know…

After the "first shell" and the "first roundup", the accursed Nazis began to become even more savage. They created an atmosphere of fear in the town and all around it; they continued to rob in any way that occurred to them; and they systematically starved the people by reducing the available vital food. They set trained dogs on every passerby, and they seized townspeople day and night and put them to death with no rhyme or reason. This endless savagery lasted a very, very long time.

And on one of those black days the Nazis announced their command to our townspeople: "The Jews are ordered to leave Kamenetz-Litovsk and go to the ghetto of Pruzhany."[6] Without uttering a single word some of the Jews left, accompanied by the Nazi beasts of prey, who treated them with horrific cruelty along the entire way.

The brilliant rabbi Reuven Burstein[7] (the brother of the prodigy of Tavrig[8]) came along with all of them, he and the members of his family as well as those attached to him, his congregation.

When they reached the ghetto many of them had been beaten and were wounded. They were hungry and thirsty, exhausted, barely alive.

It was very crowded. People being transferred from nearby towns were arriving from morning to evening. These people were broken and crushed and had nothing. Many were brought on stretchers; sickness was breaking out left and right. The food shortage kept getting worse.

The Pruzhany residents did all they could to make things easier for their refugee brethren. But with the increase in population of the ghetto and the worsening situation of the Pruzhany residents, they reached a state of helplessness in a matter of days—to their great sorrow and grief.

In these days of trouble and hardship, the esteemed, faithful and dedicated town rabbi, Rabbi Burstein, did much for his congregation. He organized multiple groups to study Torah and *Aggadah*[9]; with this action he endeavored to make his congregants forget their troubles, if only for a little while. People who had arrived from other towns also joined them, coming to listen to words of Torah, to obtain encouragement and strength from these "clandestine meetings".

And on one of these terrible days, about 250 men were seized in the streets of the ghetto and sent to work on fortifications in Slovakia. Among them were a few dozen people from Kamenetz. Those left behind waited in vain for their return; all of them were put to death there.

[Page 191]

In the end some tried to leave the Pruzhany ghetto to return to Kamenetz, to live again "in der aygener haym"[10]. The "loyal guards" among the Nazis clandestinely were given "gifts", redemption money from anyone who desired, and so they allowed people to go back to Kamenetz when no one was looking.

But then came the last act of fury—a decree that descended on them quickly.

And the bitter, black day arrived. The impure Nazis had decided to liquidate the remnant of the fugitives, come what may. One bright day, in the light of the rising sun, farmers from the surrounding area were rushed to our town with their wagons, and the final command rained down on the heads of all our townspeople, young and old, children and infants: "Jews! You must appear immediately in the town square! No one may remain in his house! The ill and little ones will be transported in the wagons. Those who hide will be shot in their hiding places. Come immediately and leave!" And thus the Jews were taken out of the ghetto.

Everyone understood that this time there was no escape. Those who were dear to us came and gathered to leave the town, following the order, as they were surrounded by the S.S. soldiers. There was no one to save them, no one to rescue them.

The Christians residents of the area were eyewitnesses to this atrocity. We know of the death march from a Christian woman who recounted that when my father, Avraham, passed by the onlookers who had gathered around, he proudly proclaimed: "Tremble with fear! Our sons and daughters in the Land of Israel will avenge our spilled blood!"[11]

From Kamenetz they were brought along the direction of Visoko-Litovsk[12], to the Bialowiec forest (where many died of starvation). All the rest were brought to Bialystok, to Treblinka[13], where they were murdered and annihilated.

The Jews in the Pruzhany Ghetto were transported to Auschwitz. Among them were people from Kamenetz, with Rabbi Reuven Burstein and his family at their head. All of them perished in the gas chambers. The entire community of Kamenetz, including its great ones and its holy people, all the members of our families and our dear ones, perished and are no more, gone forever.

May the memory of our townspeople remain hallowed in all of our hearts; may their souls be bound in the bond of eternity and of our tears, together with the tears of the entire ancient House of Israel.

Yitgadal veyitkadash shemay rabba![14]

Footnotes:

1.   From *Kamenetz-Litovsk, Zastavije and Colonies Memorial Book*, edited by S. Eisenstadt and M. Galbert, published by the Israel and America Committee of Kamenetz Litovsk and Zastavya, (Orly, Tel Aviv, Israel, 1970), pp. 189-191.
2.   Fijja, now (2018) in eastern Petah-Tikva, Israel (within the neighborhood of Kiryat Alon)
3.   R. = *Reb*, an honorific similar to English "Mr."
4.   Omer, a period of seven weeks between Passover and Shavuot (Pentecost)
5.   A custom on the 33rd day of Omer
6.   Pruzhany is located approximately 50km northeast of Kamenetz.
7.   See biographies of Rabbi Reuven Burstein on pp. 50-54 (Y. Gershuni, "Rabbi Reuven David Hakohen Burstein, May God Avenge His Blood") and pp. 409-410 (Ch. Mendelson, "Rabbi Reuven Burstein, z.tz.l.) of this Yizkor Book.

8.   See the following article on pp.55-57 of this Yizkor Book: R. Burstein, "Rabbi Avraham Aharon Hakohen".
9.   *Aggadah* = exegetic and homiletic interpretations of the narrative part of the Bible
10.   Yiddish phrase inserted in quotation marks in this Hebrew essay, meaning "in one's own place"
11.   See photograph of Avraham Bobrowski (father of the author of this article) on p. 281 of this Yizkor Book, where it is mentioned that Avraham had visited Israel for two months in 1940.
12.   Wysokie-Litewski (Polish name) = Vysokaye, Belarus (30km west of Kamenetz)
13.   See map with notations on p.160 of this Yizkor Book
14.   *Yitgadal veyitkadash shemay rabba* = May the great Name [of God] be exalted and hallowed. These are the first few words of the Aramaic *Kaddish* prayer that is recited by mourners.

After the Destruction

[Page 195]

Kamenetz after the Destruction[1]

By Asher Ben-Moshe (Tel Aviv)

Translated by Allen Flusberg

Note by translator: *This article was a translation into Hebrew of the Yiddish article appearing on pp. 561-568. The Hebrew translation,*
by Leah Aloni-Bobrowski, is essentially identical with the Yiddish article with a few exceptions that are noted in the footnotes of the English translation of the Yiddish article.

Footnote:

1.   From *Kamenetz–Litovsk, Zastavije and Colonies Memorial Book*, edited by S. Eisenstadt and M. Galbert, published by the Israel and America Committee of Kamenetz Litovsk and Zastavya, (Orly, Tel Aviv, Israel, 1970), pp. 195-199

[Page 200]

A Journey to the Past[1] [2]

by Dov (Bertchik) Shmida

Translated by Allen Flusberg

Survivors

I remember that just after the war ended two brothers, cousins of mine from Pruzhany[3] who had survived Auschwitz, paid me a visit. They were fearful, their nerves on edge. Their stories were fragmentary and not of this world. What they said sounded more like descriptions of Gehenna, the hell of the afterlife: something that no living human had ever experienced.

Although every one of their stories was about Pruzhany Jews, families I had known and real people I was acquainted with, I did not really react to their words; for deep down inside I did not believe that what they had said could be accurate. I listened and remained quiet, stunned: I couldn't absorb their words, because none of it seemed plausible.

Later we received Dora Galperin's first letters,[4] which shook me to the core, for they came from there, straight from the Valley of Tears. They mentioned names of relatives and townspeople who were lost and exterminated. Dora's letters were first–hand accounts: they told of the backstreets and oppressiveness, of the dead bodies in the streets and starvation within the houses. Her letters shocked me to the very depths of my soul. However, the sense of loss of everyone, of all the people who were dear to me, was not yet there. My heart did not want to believe and my tears did not yet come, for deep in my heart there was still some hope: perhaps in spite of everything someone had been rescued: someone from my family, from the town, from among my friends or even from among acquaintances.

The Journey

In the summer of 1965 I received word that I had been given permission to participate in a seminar on fishing that would take place in the Soviet Union. The first thought I had upon hearing this news was to visit Dora and to hear the horrible story directly from her; and also to make a trip to the graves of my forefathers in my hometown of Kamenetz. I knew that there were no graves left and that nothing had remained, yet my heart demanded that I should see it with my own eyes. After arranging a special visa in the Soviet embassy, I was given permission to visit Brisk[5], where I would be able to get authorization to travel to Kamenetz. Then I decided that on my way to the Soviet Union I would take a three–day side trip to visit Dora in Poland and to hear from her the story of the fate of the Kamenetz townspeople.

[Page 201]

Dora

When I met Dora in the Warsaw airport I felt as if I had actually returned to Kamenetz: to my childhood, and to all my relatives and acquaintances.

Throughout that night, as we traveled by train from Warsaw to Gliwice[6], we did not even close our eyes. I listened and sighed as she told her story, her eyes welling with tears. Her Polish husband, a sensitive and compassionate man, also did not close his eyes. He listened to the conversation in Yiddish, understanding the momentousness as she relived the collapse of decency and humaneness.

The story of my little town of Kamenetz is no different from stories about other towns and cities in Poland and throughout Europe: the murders, the shutting up into ghettos, the hunger and suffering that pierced the heavens; peasants' wagons loaded with women and children as the men plodded along behind, surrounded by murderous Ukrainian and German militias; the train that led to extermination without leaving a single person alive, someone who could tell the world where the train had gone to and what the last moments had been like.

The next day we went to pay a visit to Auschwitz, and along the way Dora poured out her own story: how she was saved by the Gregorowski family; how she hid out in cellars and attics; her hiding place over the stove, in barns and in horse stables.

Auschwitz

We reached Auschwitz and all the conversations ended; there were no more questions. Our senses were paralyzed by the sight of the blocks, outer walls, death walls and soot–covered chimneys. Death strolled about between the barracks. There was nothing but a choking feeling, endless sighs, and tears running down our faces, for our hearts were broken. It was as if we were present at a large, solemn funeral.

When we left Auschwitz, it was almost superfluous to discuss the fate of Kamenetz after seeing the giant cemetery of our entire people. There was nothing to talk about anymore.

Dora also told me about her bitter fate after the liberation, about her year of imprisonment in Brisk, about how she moved to Poland, exhausted; and how her kindhearted and compassionate husband rescued her from the very jaws of death that lay in wait even there, in liberated Poland.

Dora is not the same Dora whom we knew before, the pretty, cheerful girl with the mischievous spirit and fiery vivaciousness. The Dora I met up with in Poland is the embodiment of all the grief, pain and torment that our town underwent. She did indeed remain alive, but without the ability to free herself from all that she had experienced, all that Kamenetz had undergone. And yet she did not actually see the bitter end with her own eyes.

[Page 202]

When we said goodbye to each other in the train station, she told me that she hadn't believed that she would ever meet a living soul from Kamenetz again, even though she was quite aware that there were hundreds of Kamenetz Jews scattered throughout the world. For to her it felt as if they were all dead, that nothing was left, nothing but nightmarish memories.

*Dora Galperin and Dov (Bertchik) Shmida
in front of Block 27*[7]

[Page 203]

Brisk

On September 17 1965, I got on the international train Moscow–Berlin–Amsterdam. I was on my way to Brisk, which is the last stop on the Russian side of the Russian–Polish border. All night I did not close my eyes, and the conductor in the train car couldn't understand why I was not sleeping even though I was in a luxurious sleeping car. The conductor brought me tea all night, asking me where I was headed. I answered that I was going to Brisk, that I was a Jew who was born near there. "Yes," she replied in a compassionate voice, "You are excited to return to your hometown (*na rodino*), but you will not meet up with a single one of your Jews there, because Hitler murdered them all."

The express train flew past all the stations: Smolensk[8], which aroused a memory of battles, and Minsk[9], which brought back the memory of a large Jewish city. It was dawn and we were already passing Baranovichi[10], where as a child I studied in the little yeshiva. Racing along at 120 km per hour, not stopping at any station, the train rapidly passed Kartuz–Bereza[11], a famous Jewish town well–known for its Polish prison camp; and then Linova, the train station of Pruzhany[12], where I used to spend my summer vacations. And now we were passing Žabinka[13], the train station of my Kamenetz. The train slowed down as it entered the suburbs of Brisk.

The sun rose. It was a beautiful summer day; from far away the *Przechodni* crossing bridge was visible; and there I was, already in the Brisk train station: the same building, the same clock in front, the controller at the doors. However in the entrance there were only large red flags and red stars fluttering from the towers of the station.

My heart was beating hard with emotion, for it was in Brisk that I had studied and spent the best years of my adolescence: in *Tachkemoni*[14], in *Gordonia*[15] and in the *Tarbut*[16] high school.

I make all the formal arrangements in the Intourist office and start out on foot along Unya–Lubelska (now Lenin) Street to the address that I had on Yagelony (now Moscow) Street, where the sisters Clara and Genya Ehrlich, who hail from Kamenetz, now live.

Until the moment when I reached the line of shops that I remembered well, on the corner of Dombrowska Street, I thought that I had gotten lost and come to a strange city. The Soviets constructed and erected many buildings that changed the appearance of the city fundamentally. Some of the streets that had been side–streets were transformed into central streets, and among them were Yaglonska and Sharoka.

However the former city center, which had been completely populated by Jews, has remained standing, without any change and without a single house or sidewalk being missing; but what is missing from it are the Jews of the city of Brisk, where more than thirty thousand Jews used to live, a community that gave the city its character and its mold.

For three days straight I stroll around Brisk in a state of shock…

[Page 204]

At first I am drawn to the Large Synagogue on Dombrowska, standing neglected and serving as a shabby movie theatre. Right near it is the rabbi's house, and a bit further away the *Tachkemoni* School. Strangers are strolling around, walking along the streets and into the houses, houses I know so well that it feels as if it was just yesterday that I was living in an apartment here. I don't see a single familiar face among them. Strangers who don't seem to belong here gaze out from the windows, walk through the courtyards, and stare at me as if I am the stranger.

I walk around for all three of those days in the streets that I know so well: Topolowa, Kashiwa, Bialostocka, Dombrowska, and Zigmontowska, the streets I had walked around in for 6 years, on my way to the *Tachkemoni* School, to *Tarbut*, to *Gordonia*, to relatives and friends. Everything has remained the same: the sidewalks, the houses, the shutters, the courtyards; only the people are strangers from elsewhere, as if they have been brought to this place unnaturally. Where are the people I know? Where are my friends? Where are the Jews of Brisk?!!

I felt as if none of this was real, that something basic was missing, that life itself had been uprooted from these streets. Is it not unnatural and inhuman not to meet a single acquaintance throughout this entire city? Not one friend?!

The Monument

Two sights have been deeply engraved in my heart, and I will never forget them:

On Daluga Street I searched for the large common grave, where the last ten thousand Jews of Brisk had been murdered. The place is abandoned, built up with yards and temporary structures. It was hard to find the paths that led to the grave, which is marked by a shabby concrete monument. The memorial plaque on the monument bears the following inscription, written in Russian: "Here lie buried Soviet citizens who were murdered by the Fascist beasts". This is all that is stated about Brisk Jewry.

As I stood next to the monument, a young boy, 13–15 years old, came over to me and said: "Citizen! Did you know that the people who lie here were buried alive, and to this very day the earth trembles here every single night…" My eyes did not well up with tears, for my heart had turned to stone; and only my feet trembled as they stood upon the blood that had not been covered over.

The next day I asked the Brisk survivors: "What has remained of all the glorious Jewry of Brisk? Has the Brisk cemetery survived?" "Yes," answered one of my friends (one of the seven Jewish natives of Brisk who still live there), "Come with me and I will show it to you!" He brought me to Staczekwicza Street, to a yard whose sidewalk and the rest of the yard was paved with Jewish gravestones. The house located in this yard had been occupied by the Gestapo during the German occupation. As an everlasting memorial, these beasts had paved the yard and the sidewalk with gravestones from the Jewish cemetery.

The Nazi beasts murdered and destroyed, and those who came to Brisk afterwards and liberated it obliterated every trace and every sign of the flourishing life that had still existed here in every lane and every house 25 years ago; this is the story that I heard from the tiny remnant of the Jews of Brisk, and this is the reality that I saw with my very own eyes. Not a single Jewish inscription, not one Hebrew memorial.[17]

[Page 205]

Yet the sidewalk [paved with gravestones] cries out: "Remember, do not forget!"

The strangers strolling along the streets appear passive; but when they are made aware that I am a Jew they become hostile, for this reminds them of an unpleasantness, something that preys on their conscience. However one can neither deceive history nor silence a conscience.

My Hometown Kamenetz on September 20, 1965
[Pages 206-208]

Note by translator: *The sections entitled "My Hometown Kamenetz on September 20, 1965", "My Kamenetz", "The Only One who Greeted Me with Tears", and "Effacing the Memory and the Past", appear in the English version of the article, beginning on p 176 of the English part of this Yizkor Book. There are only a few differences between the three versions (Yiddish, Hebrew and English).*[18] [19] [20] [21]

Footnotes:

1. From *Kamenetz–Litovsk, Zastavije and Colonies Memorial Book*, edited by S. Eisenstadt and M. Galbert, published by the Israel and America Committee of Kamenetz Litovsk and Zastavya, (Orly, Tel Aviv, Israel, 1970), pp. 200–208.
2. This Hebrew article is essentially the same as the Yiddish essay, by the same author, also entitled "A Journey to the Past," on pp. 569–578 of this volume. The present translation relies on both versions; any differences are highlighted in footnotes. An English version originally in this volume, "My Journey to Kamenetz in 1965", by Dov (Bertschik) Schmidt, pp. 175–183 of the English section, did not include several sections that appear in the Hebrew and Yiddish versions (see below).
3. Pruzhany is located approximately 50km northeast of Kamenetz. See map on p. 160 of this Yizkor Book.
4. See Dora Galperin, "The Tragedy and Destruction of Kamenetz", pp. 91–104 of the English section of this Yizkor Book.
5. Brisk is the Yiddish name (acronym) for Brest–Litovsk, a city 40km south of Kamenetz. In 1965 it was a major border crossing between Brest (in Belarus, a state of the Soviet Union) and Poland. It is presently (2019) the border crossing between Brest (Belarus) and Poland.
6. Gliwice, Poland is located about 50km northwest of Auschwitz.
7. Plaque on building reads as follows (in Yiddish): "In this block there will be a permanent exhibit dedicated to the Jewish resistance and annihilation".
8. Smolensk (in Russia) lies 700km northeast of Kamenetz. It is presently (2019) about 100km east of the border between Russia and Belarus.
9. Minsk, the capital of Belarus, is located about 300km northeast of Kamenetz.
10. Baranovichi, Belarus, lies about 200km northeast of Kamenetz.
11. Bereza Kartuska, now (2019) Byaroza, Belarus, lies about 100km east of Kamenetz.
12. See Footnote 3.
13. Žabinka, Belarus is located 30km southeast of Kamenetz. The train was headed toward Brisk (Brest), which is located ~50km south of Kamenetz.
14. *Tachkemoni* = a religious–Zionist school with secular studies
15. *Gordonia*, a Zionist youth movement founded in the 1920s, emphasized settlement in Israel and revival of the Hebrew language. See the following Web site (retrieved August, 2019): https://en.wikipedia.org/wiki/Gordonia_(youth_movement)
16. *Tarbut* was a network of Hebrew–language schools established in Poland in the 1920s. See the following Web site (retrieved August, 2019): https://en.wikipedia.org/wiki/Tarbut
17. This entire paragraph is absent in the Yiddish version
18. On p. 176 of the English version, two of the people accompanying the author to Kamenetz are named Clara Sapir and Misha Serba. In both the Hebrew and Yiddish versions the names are given as Clara Ehrlich and Misha Sarver, respectively.
19. On p. 177, the English reads "houses…of Shmuel Golobchick and David Rosenstock." The Hebrew version reads "house…of Shmuel Golobchick and that of the wagon driver (the Roznashchik)".
In the same paragraph, the English reads "Only Hayim Shayke and Hana Bobro are missing…" The Hebrew version reads "only Hayim, Shayke and Hana, my friends, are missing…" This entire sentence is absent in the Yiddish version.
20. On p. 178, the English version reads, "When we met, Yuzek was even more moved than I." The Hebrew version adds "After a short visit to "Shepsil's Beis Medresh" and the narrow lanes of "Chava the Milchikeren [the dairy lady]", I felt confused, as if I was in shock. Yuzek was even more moved than I." The Yiddish version reads "After passing Shepsil's Beis Medresh and the narrow streets, where Chava the Milchikeren lived, I made a short visit to Yuzek Gregorowski…I was in shock and confused. Yuzek Gregorowski was very overcome with emotion."
21. On p. 178, the English version reads "The Great Synagogue (Der Mayer) together with the Talmud Torah was converted into a factory." Both the Hebrew and Yiddish versions read instead "…was converted into a brewery."

Fallen in the Homeland

[Page 211]

Michael Kotik, of Blessed Memory[1]

Translated by Allen Flusberg

Another link in the golden chain of the Hagana[2] was broken when Michael was killed in the Judean Hills, in the battle over Castel[3] during the War of Liberation [Independence] of the year 1948.

Michael, son of Shimon and Neḥama Kotik[4] was born in Safed on January 8, 1929. He attended the Hebrew Reali School[5] in Haifa. When he ended his studies in 1947, he enlisted in the Palmach. With every bit of the loyalty and ideological innocence of youth, he fought in the battles for the liberation of our homeland and for the independence of Israel. He fell in battle on the Eve of Passover 5708[6] in Nabi Samwil[7], and he was buried in Kiryat Anavim[8].

May his remains find peace!

May his soul be bound in the bond of the renewed life of Israel!

Footnotes:

1. From *Kamenetz-Litovsk, Zastavije and Colonies Memorial Book*, edited by S. Eisenstadt and M. Galbert, published by the Israel and America Committee of Kamenetz Litovsk and Zastavya, (Orly, Tel Aviv, Israel, 1970), p. 211.
2. The Hagana [= Defense] was originally a paramilitary force set up to defend the Jewish population of Mandatory Palestine. It was transformed into the core of the Israel Defense Forces. See the following link (retrieved April 2021): Haganah - Wikipedia
3. This was the battle for control of the road from Jaffa to Jerusalem. See the following link (retrieved April 2021): Castel National Park - Wikipedia. See also L. Collins and D. LaPierre, O Jerusalem! (Simon and Schuster, 1988) and the following link (retrieved April 2021): Battle for Jerusalem - Wikipedia
4. See the following article by Leah Aloni-Bobrowski on pp. 147-148 of this Yizkor Book, "Shimon Kotik".
5. See the following link: The Hebrew Reali School in Haifa - The Hebrew Reali School in Haifa
6. 14 Nisan 5708 = April 23, 1948
7. Nabi Samwil is located about 8km northwest of central Jerusalem.
8. Kiryat Anavim is a kibbutz located about 10km west of Jerusalem, adjacent to the town of Abu Ghosh. A military cemetery is located at the northeast corner of the kibbutz; many of those who fell in the battle for opening a road to Jerusalem are buried there.

[Page 212]

My Dear Son, Efraim[1]

By Baruch Mordechai Kotik

Translated by Allen Flusberg

He was a captain in the Israel Defense Forces. He fell on his watch, while carrying out his duty, on the 18th of Adar, 5723.[2]

Already in his youth, Efraim stood out in his noble-mindedness and his readiness to help others all the time. In school he would lend support or help any student who had either physical or psychological issues. His friends were drawn to him and enjoyed his company; he was at the center of his circle. He also excelled in his studies in the Marom-Zion Yeshiva in Jerusalem, winning first prize twice for his knowledge of Talmud. And when at the completion of his studies he joined *Bnei Akiva*[3], he was the spirit of the group. Before he joined the army he was working as a trainee in Kibbutz Be'erot Yitzḥak[4].

[Page 213]

After a period of basic training, he was sent to a radar course. After he completed this course, he participated in the harsh battles near Mitla during the Sinai Campaign[5], and, risking his life under fire, he evacuated the wounded from the battlefield. After the Sinai War he was sent to officers' school, and when he finishing this course he continued to serve in the army as a lieutenant. After completing his military service he went back to Kibbutz Be'erot Yitzḥak, but after a period of time he returned to the military and was appointed a training officer.

He was married on Thursday, 18 Ḥeshvan 5723[6]; on Thursday, 18 Adar of that same year he was slain, not meriting to establish a Jewish family life.[7]

May his memory be a blessing!

Footnote:

    1.   From *Kamenetz–Litovsk, Zastavije and Colonies Memorial Book*, edited by S. Eisenstadt and M. Galbert, published by the Israel and America Committee of Kamenetz Litovsk and Zastavya, (Orly, Tel Aviv, Israel, 1970), pp. 212-213. The phrase *haben yakir li Efraim* [= "My Dear Son, Efraim"] is from Jeremiah 31:20.

    2.   18 Adar 5723 = March 14, 1963

    3.   Bnei Akiva is the youth wing of the Mizrachi (religious Zionist) movement. See the following link (retrieved April 2021): Bnei Akiva - Wikipedia

    4.   Be'erot Yitzḥak is a religious kibbutz located in central Israel, near Yehud, about 6km south of Petaḥ Tikva.

    5.   In the Sinai Campaign (1956) Israel responded to Egypt's nationalization and blocking of the Suez Canal by invading and occupying the Sinai Peninsula, while Britain and France, coordinating with Israel, landed paratroopers along the Suez Canal. Mitla is the name of a pass between mountain ranges (located about 50-100km east of Suez, Egypt) where harsh battles took place. See the following links (retrieved April 2021): Suez Crisis - Wikipedia; Mitla Pass - Wikipedia

    6.   18 Heshvan 5723 = November 15, 1962

    7.   For more information see the following link (in Hebrew, retrieved April 2021): סרן אפרים קוטיק - אתר יזכור (izkor.gov.il). This source adds that several months after Efraim Kotik's death his wife gave birth to his son, who was named after him.

[Page 216]

Activities of the Organization of Former Residents of Kamenetz[1]

by Leah Bobrowski-Aloni and Haya Krakowski-Karabelnik

Translated by Allen Flusberg

(Standing [sic]). Last on left—Pinḥas Rabi
From right to left: Leah Aloni-Bobrowski, Ḥaya Krakowski-Karabelnik, Simḥa Dubiner, Yeshaya Rimon

[Page 217]

    With the end of the Second World War, reports of the destruction of the Jewish communities of Europe began reaching Israel. And very soon we ascertained that all the members of our town, Kamenetz-Litowsk, Zastavya and the Colonies, had been taken out of the ghetto, and that the accursed Nazis and their lackeys took them away to some place and murdered them all.

When we received this chilling report, we gathered together in Tel Aviv on the 4th day of Adar 5705—February 17, 1945—and we decided to establish an organization of former residents of Kamenetz-Litowsk and the surrounding area.

The first committee that was elected included the following: Yeshaya Rimon (chairman); Leah Aloni (vice-chairman and treasurer); Ḥaya Krakowski (secretary); and members Dov Zhernensky, Simḥa Dubiner (Petah Tikva), Golda Sher-Gershuni (Jerusalem), and Aharon Kotik (Haifa). The committee was assigned the task of examining, investigating and unearthing—by all possible means—what had become of our parents, brothers and sisters of Kamenetz-Litowsk, Zastavya and the Colonies. Our hope was that perhaps some of them had been rescued with the help of their Christian neighbors, or perhaps others had managed to flee to the forests and had survived.

The organization members made contributions that were meant to be sent to aid those we were hoping had survived; and as a first step we collected 100 Palestinian lira (pounds) that were dedicated to this goal.

We could not imagine that the Nazi beast of prey had been so brutally cruel that it had annihilated thirty-four thousand Jewish communities, including the communities of Kamenetz, Zastavya and the Colonies.

After many investigations, we found out from the HIAS[2]-ICA[3] organization known as HICEM[4] that some of our townspeople who had managed to escape from the Nazi occupation were in Russia and Shanghai. We immediately contacted our fellow townspeople who were in Shanghai and made arrangements for HIAS to send them packages of clothing and food supplies as aid. And in addition, we tried to locate their relatives in Israel so that they could help them out.

When the lone survivors reached Israel—and among them one woman who was rescued from the Auschwitz concentration camp— each of them received a loan from our fund, which, in the interim, had grown larger from additional contributions. Most of the survivors paid the loan off after they had undergone absorption in Israel and had found jobs.

Among those who were rescued and reached Israel after the Holocaust was our townsman Tz.S., who had arrived with a serious heart ailment. He found absorption [adjusting to Israel] very challenging; eventually his heart disease worsened and we had to hospitalize him in a sanitorium. The committee tried to cover some of his hospitalization expenses, and was able to pay a significant part of the expenses until the day he died.

[Page 218]

We were unable to sit idly by, always feeling we had a sacred duty to establish a memorial to our cherished fellow townspeople who had been put to death, exterminated and burned alive in Auschwitz, Treblinka and the forests of Bialowieza[5], leaving behind no trace of where they had been buried.

Already in the year 5705 [1945], several of the committee members proposed to perpetuate the memory of our martyrs by publishing a "Yizkor Book" dedicated to their memory, following a well-defined plan. Unfortunately, this proposal was shelved at the time.

In the year 5709 [1949], the head office of the Jewish National Fund [JNF] announced a plan to plant groves of trees, dedicated to the martyrs, in the Jerusalem Hills. Any organization that contributed 1000 Israeli liras[6] would plant a grove of 1000 trees in the name of their destroyed community, and the grove would commemorate the community with a specially inscribed marble plaque. The members of our first committee decided to participate in this project and to plant a grove commemorating the martyrs of our town and the surrounding area. Up to that time we had raised only 65 liras. We got several of our townspeople to join this important activity by planting trees in memory of their relatives. We thereby succeeded in collecting about 500 Israeli liras. But according to the rules of JNF we were not able to obtain and set up our marble plaque in the Martyrs' Forest as long as we had not yet collected 1000 liras for the 1000-tree grove.

Planting of the grove of trees commemorating the martyrs of Kamenetz-Litowsk in the Forest of the Martyrs
From right: Dov Aloni, Leah Aloni, Yehudit Grunt-Koscikiewicz, Meir Bobrowski and Ḥaya Krakowski-Karabelnik

[Page 219]

In the year 5710 [1950], Mr. Yaakov (the son of Moshe Zevil) Savitzky, of blessed memory, visited our country from New York, where he lived. When we met with him, we told him about the planting of the grove commemorating the martyrs of our town, and about the difficulties we were having raising sufficient funds. After he returned to New York he immediately sent us the money we needed to complete the funding, and so the grove was planted.

Shortly thereafter Yaakov Savitzky passed away in New York without ever having had the opportunity to visit Israel once more to see the grove. May his memory be a blessing!

Today our grove stands prominently in the Jerusalem Hills, with the following inscribed on its marble plaque: "In Memory of the Communities of Kamenetz-Litowsk and the Surrounding Area".

On Monday, the 29th of Av, Eve of the New Month of Elul, 5723 [August 19, 1963], we set up a plaque memorializing the martyrs of our town in one of the halls of the "Chamber of the Holocaust"[7] on Mount Zion in Jerusalem. Kostin and Sheinfeld of the United States contributed toward the plaque. More that forty of our townspeople came from all corners of Israel to participate in the impressive ceremony.

While Mr. Abraham Shudroff, the committee chairman of Kamenetzers in the United States, was paying a visit to Israel, the proposal to publish a Yizkor Book memorializing our martyrs was brought up again—this time with the support of our fellow townspeople in the US—and this time the proposal was ratified. In the year 5722 [1962] we published a special preview sample of this Yizkor Book. Four hundred copies of the preview were printed and distributed among our townspeople in Israel and the Diaspora.

At one of the Yizkor services memorializing the martyrs of Kamenetz-Litowsk in the JNF Building in Tel Aviv

[Page 220]

At the grove of trees commemorating the martyrs of Kamenetz, on Holocaust Memorial Day

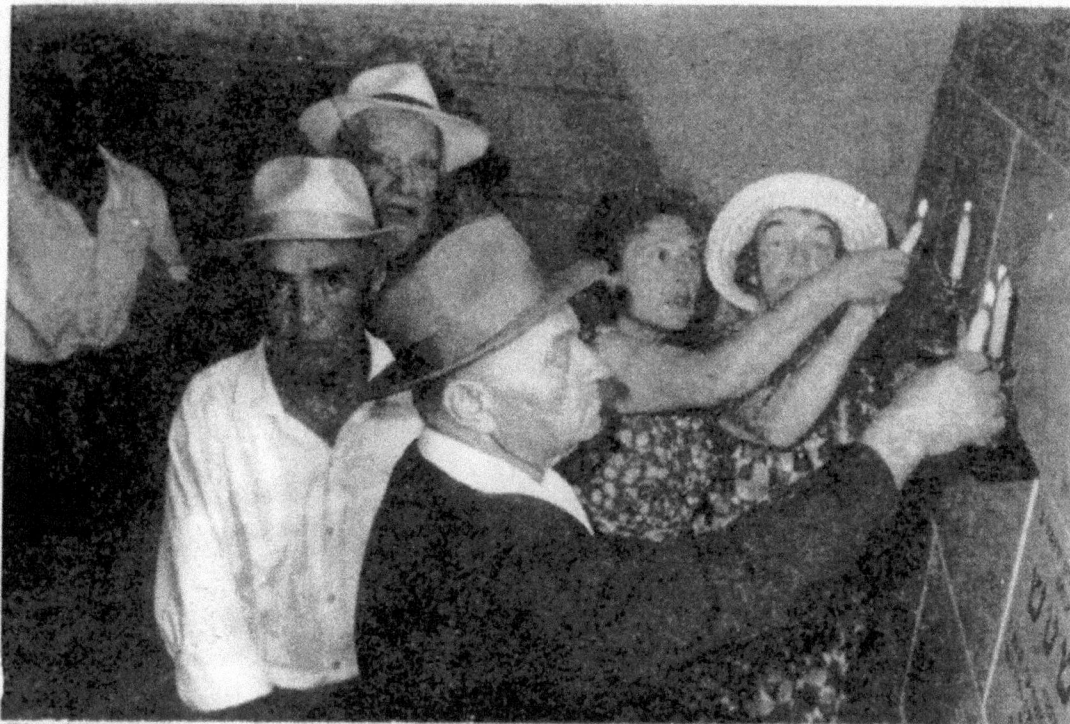

Lighting of candles at the memorial plaque on Mount Zion

[Page 221]

In the year 5723 [1963] Attorney Gideon Hausner, the prosecutor in the trial of Eichmann (may his memory be blotted out), made a proposal to the Israeli schools that they should perpetuate the memory of the Jewish communities that had been destroyed in the Holocaust period. The Bialik *mamlachti* [state secular] school of Tel Aviv was the first to respond, choosing to memorialize the community of Kamenetz-Litowsk, Zastavya and the Colonies. This effort was led by Leah Bobrowski-Aloni and her husband, both of whom had been teaching in that school for many years.

In an impressive ceremony that took place on the 12th of Heshvan 5724 [October 30, 1963], many distinguished public figures came to participate and to pay their respects to our martyrs. They were joined by many of our townspeople. The members of the committee: Chairman Simḥa Dubiner, Leah Aloni, Ḥaya Krakowski, Pinḥas Rabi and Arye Goldberg-Sarid, spoke from the podium on the history and institutions of our community, a community that was destroyed and is no more.

The organization committee decided to erect a memorial to the martyrs by establishing a "library of the Holocaust" within the school. One bookcase has been dedicated to works on the Holocaust, contributed by the Kamenetzers in Israel and the Diaspora in memory of their family members who had perished. Each book contains a page dedicated to a family member who perished, with the signature of the contributor. We hope that the number of books and contributors to this memorial library will grow with the participation of all our townspeople, wherever they may be.

In this library there is also an "Album of Kamenetz-Litowsk, Zastavya and the Colonies". This album preserves photographs of our town's institutions, and each of the townspeople can add photographs of his parents and family members, so that they may be preserved.

A strong bond between our organization and this school has persisted. We conduct our yearly memorial services in the auditorium of the school, with the participation of the students.

We acquired a "perpetual lamp" from the Yad Vashem management board. It bears a special inscription on its six candlesticks memorializing the six million Jews who perished in the Holocaust.

During the yearly assembly meeting of Yad Vashem of the year 5725 [1964-65], a memorial scroll was presented by the school to Ḥaya Krakowski-Karabelnik, who was representing our organization. The scroll bore the signatures of the principal of the Bialik school and its students. The scroll reads as follows: "We declare that our school has taken upon itself the mission to perpetuate the memory of the Kamenetz-Litowsk, Zastavya and Colonies communities that were destroyed during the Holocaust period by the impure Nazi soldiers and their followers…The students will do their best to continue the activity they have begun—to perpetuate the memory of the living, active community as it was before the Holocaust; and also to preserve the memory of its suffering, struggle and annihilation during the Holocaust."

Because of its primary role in this program, our community's name has been mentioned in other schools during memorial assemblies, as well as in newspapers, both in Israel and the Diaspora.

[Page 222]

During the last few years, we have devoted much time and unceasing energy to the publication of a book memorializing our martyrs. We have been able to concentrate a maximum number of lists, articles and photographs that are printed in the book. Thanks to the cooperation of our fellow townspeople in the United States, this long-awaited book is coming out; and we hope that copies of it will soon be found in all our townspeople's homes, wherever they may be, as well as in institutions and public libraries in Israel and the Diaspora.

The members of the organization's committee have for years been in close touch with the sole survivor of the ghetto, Dora Galperin. The dozens of letters that we received from her have provided a trustworthy testimony on the lives of the Jews in the Kamenetz ghetto up to their very last day, as described in this Yizkor Book in three languages.

The tree-planting ceremony in the grove dedicated to the Kamenetz-Litowsk martyrs, the erection of a memorial plaque on Mount Zion, and the arrangement of the commemoration ceremony in the Bialik school of Tel Aviv were organized through the laudable instigation and diligence of Dov Aloni, for which the organization committee here expresses its special thanks.

Footnotes:

1.   From *Kamenetz-Litovsk, Zastavije and Colonies Memorial Book*, edited by S. Eisenstadt and M. Galbert, published by the Israel and America Committee of Kamenetz Litovsk and Zastavya, (Orly, Tel Aviv, Israel, 1970), pp. 217-222.
2.   HIAS is an acronym for "Hebrew Immigrant Aid Society", which was based in New York.
3.   ICA or JCA is an acronym for "Jewish Colonization Association", which was based in London.
4.   HICEM, based in Paris, was a combined office of HIAS and ICA. In 1945, it was assisting family searches for survivors and helping survivors repatriate and/or immigrate. See the following link (retrieved June 2021): Collection: Records of HIAS-HICEM Main Office in Europe | The Center for Jewish History ArchivesSpace (cjh.org).
5.   The Bialowieza Forest (located in 2021 on the border between Belarus and Poland) is at its closest point about 20km north of Kamenetz.
6.   The Israeli lira of 1949 was pegged at par to the British pound. 1000 British pounds would have been equivalent to US$2,780 in 1949. Thus, taking inflation into account, 1000 Israeli lira would be equivalent to US$30,000 in 2021. See the following links (retrieved June 2021): Palestine pound – Wikipedia; Israeli pound - Wikipedia
7.   The Chamber of the Holocaust, a museum established in 1949, is located on Mount Zion in Jerusalem. See the following link (retrieved June 2021): Chamber of the Holocaust - Wikipedia.

[Page 225]

Commemoration Ceremony for the Community of Kamenetz-Litowsk and Zastavya[1]

Translated by Allen Flusberg

Student at Bialik School in Tel Aviv during ceremony commemorating our community[2]

[Page 226]

S. Dubiner in the Bialik School Commemoration Ceremony

[Page 227]

מדינת ישראל
משרד החנוך והתרבות
מחוז תל-אביב

יפו, כ' בתשרי תשכ"ד
8 באוקטובר 1963
מס' 2218/21

לכבוד
מר דב אלוני
ארגון יוצאי קמניץ-ליטובסק
רח' שור 17, דירה 3
תל-אביב

שלום !

א. נ.

ברצון הננו מאשרים את הצעתכם, כי אחת מכיתות ח' בביה"ס הממלכתי
ע"ש ח.נ. ביאליק בתל-אביב תאמץ את זכרה של עירכם קמניץ-דליטא.

זכורה לי אישית עירכם זו מימי שבתי בעיירתי סוויסלוץ שבפולין. הייתה זו
עיר ספוגה יהדות שרשית ומקורית, אשר הניבה כוחות חלוציים-ציוניים מפרים
ומעצבים את חזון-הגאולה. ברוכים תהיו על מאמצי ההנצחה לזכרם של קרבנות
אלה, אשר נרצחו ונהרגו בידיהם הטמאות של הנאצים ימ"ש.

על פרטי הסידורים — בואו נא בדברים עם מנהל ביה"ס מר מ. גוריון.

בברכה
יעקב ניב
מפקח המחוז

Letter [in Hebrew] from School District Supervisor, Yaakov Niv, to Dov Aloni, authorizing Bialik School ceremony to perpetuate the memory of the Kamenetz-Litowsk community [see English translation below].

State of Israel
Office of Education and Culture
Tel Aviv District.

Jaffa, 20 Tishri 5724
8 October 1963
Number 2218/21.

To:
Mr. Dov Aloni
Organization of Kamenetzers
Shor Street 17, Apartment 1
Tel Aviv.

Dear Sir,

We are pleased to accept your proposal that one of the eighth-grade classes in the H.N. Bialik State School of Tel Aviv will adopt the memory of your town Kamenetz Litowsk.

I personally recall your town from when I lived in my town Swislocz in Poland[3]. Your town was steeped with a deep-rooted fount of Jewishness—nurturing pioneer-Zionist forces that were fruitful in shaping the vision of redemption. You are to be commended for your efforts to commemorate these victims, who were murdered by the impure hands of the Nazis—may their memory be blotted out.

With respect to details of the project, please be in touch with the school principal, Mr. M. Gurion.

Best wishes,

Yakov Niv
District Supervisor

English translation of letter from Yaakov Niv appearing on p. 227[2]

[Page 228]

Haim Nahman Bialik School of Tel Aviv

[Page 229]

Principal[4] of H.N. Bialik School of Tel Aviv speaking during the commemoration ceremony

[Page 232]

Gideon Hausner speaking at the commemoration ceremony

[Page 234]

During the commemoration ceremony

[Page 236]

Recitation of Yizkor during the commemoration ceremony

[Page 239]

***During the exhibit, Kamenetzers view the reproduction that school pupils made to commemorate the Kamenetz
community***

[Page 241]

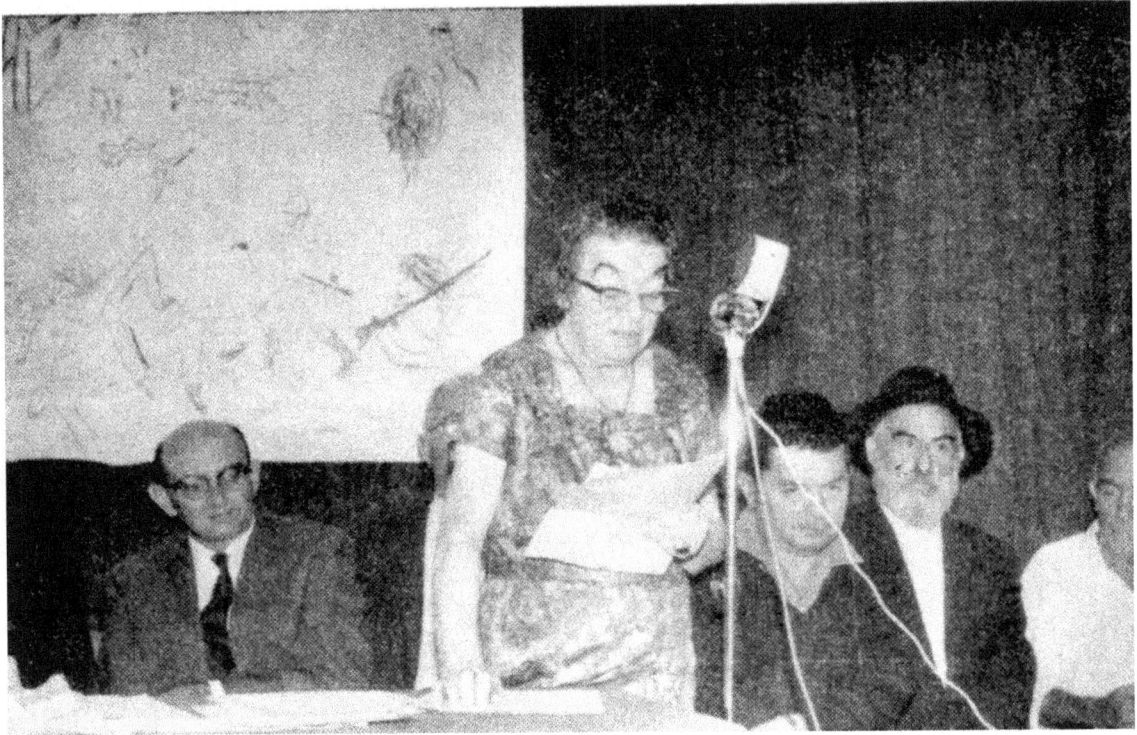

Leah Bobrowski-Aloni speaking during the commemoration ceremony

[Page 244]

Ḥaya Krakowski-Karabelnik during the commemoration ceremony

[Page 246]

At the commemoration ceremony

[Page 606]

The commemoration ceremony for the Kamenetz martyrs, in the Bialik School in Tel Aviv.

[Page 614]

Students of the Bialik School, convened to perpetuate the memory of the Kamenetz martyrs.

[Page 618]

Student choir of the Bialik School performing during the ceremony

[Page 248]

We Shall Not Forget![5]

A hush had fallen over the auditorium. The eighth-grade pupils, the teachers and the honored guests that had come to the assembly sat there in silence. Sad memories had been aroused and came back to all those who had come from that community—noticeable from hushed sobs that every now and then could be heard in the silence. All of us knew what the goal of our meeting had been: to remember! To remember all the events that our people experienced during the Second World War: the war atrocities, our innocent six million brothers and sisters who died in gas chambers and extermination camps. To remember and not forget! We must not forget them, and that is why we have assembled here.

We, the students of Grade 8, Class 4 at the H.N. Bialik School, have taken upon ourselves to adopt the community of Kamenetz-Litowsk and Zastavya. Before the Second World War this community teemed with life, labor and industry; and the yearning for redemption became deeply rooted in the hearts of its people. This community no longer exists—it was wiped out and has perished—the Nazis having destroyed it together with the other Jewish communities. But we will not forget this community. Although it is not within our power to bring it back to life, we are still able to erect a monument to it within our hearts. We will learn a great deal about this community, we will visit the remnant of those who came from there and are now in the Land of Israel, and we will be prepared to hungrily devour whatever they have to tell us about it.

I have been sitting among my fellow students listening to the speeches of our guests who were trying to transport us in our imagination to a different world, a world that was all suffering and agony: concentration camps, extermination chambers, ghettos; children next to their dead mothers; broad areas sown with the bones of many children who had never experienced the taste of life, who had never taken pleasure in the splendor of nature and the warmth of the sun. Children who came into this world in dark cellars and sewers. As I was sitting and listening, a powerful emotion of compassion for my brethren was roused in me, as well as frightful feelings of great hatred for the raving Nazi beast that drowned its victims in rivers of blood.

—**Naava Kozraz**
A student of Grade 8, Class 4 of the H.N. Bialik School
From the booklet "Remember!" by the students of the H.N. Bialik School on the commemoration of the Kamenetz-Litowsk community and its martyrs

Footnotes:

1. From *Kamenetz-Litovsk, Zastavije and Colonies Memorial Book*, edited by S. Eisenstadt and M. Galbert, published by the Israel and America Committee of Kamenetz Litovsk and Zastavya, (Orly, Tel Aviv, Israel, 1970), pp. 225-240 (Hebrew), and pp.601-626 (Yiddish translation by Ḥaya Krakowski and Pinḥas Ravid). Most of this article appeared in the original English section of this Yizkor Book, pp.149-174, under the following title: "*Yad Vashem* Martyrs' and Heroes' Memorial Authority, Ceremony of Perpetuating the Memory of the Community Kamenetz-Litovsk-Zastavye by the Hayim Nahman Bialik State School in Tel Aviv on October 30th, 1963." See the original English section, which hones closely to the Yiddish translation (which in turn differs only slightly from the Hebrew version); and see below for photographs appearing in both followed by a translation of Hebrew text omitted from the original English section.
2. Banner in photograph reads "Perpetuation of the martyred community destroyed in the years of the Holocaust."
3. Śvislač, Belarus, located 100km north of Kamenetz
4. The principal's name is given in the Hebrew version as Moshe Gurion.
5. This section was left out of both the Yiddish translation and the original English version.

[Pages 251-278]

List of Jews of Kamenetz-Litowsk, Zastavya and the Colonies, Who Perished at the Hands of the Nazis, May Their Memory Be Blotted Out[1]

By Meir Bobrowski[2]

Translated by Allen Flusberg

Note by translator: an English translation of this list, converted into a searchable, alphabetically arranged list of names, appears at the very end of this volume under the title "Necrology"[3]

Footnote:

1. From *Kamenetz–Litovsk, Zastavije and Colonies Memorial Book*, edited by S. Eisenstadt and M. Galbert, published by the Israel and America Committee of Kamenetz Litovsk and Zastavya, (Orly, Tel Aviv, Israel, 1970), pp. 251-278
2. See Aloni's biography of Bobrowski on pp. 149-151 of this volume.
3. The translator has found an error in the English Necrology Section: Tova Savitzki (see p. 145 of the article by Krakowski-Karabelnik on Tuvya Savitzki) is listed in the Hebrew/Yiddish Necrology on p. 268 under the name "Toiba Savitzki". The English incorrectly lists her as "Tuvya Savitzki." Toiba (or Tova) was the wife of Tuvya Savitzki, who emigrated to Israel.

[Page 281]

Kamenetz Yizkor Book Necrology[1]
Translated by Allen Flusberg

We will surely remember you, our loved ones!

Our mother **Tama**—died in Kamenetz on Friday, 18 Shvat 5701.[2] Our father **R.**[3] **Avraham son of Shmuel Tevye and Golda Sessil (nee Bobrowski)**, who perished at the hand of the Nazis in 5702[4], h.y.d.[5] (Our parents merited making a 62-day visit to Israel in the year 5700[6].)

Grandmother **Zlata** of blessed memory, widow of **Rabbi Meir Hirsh Potchenka**, head of the Kamenetz-Litovsk Yeshiva. Died in Kamenetz in the month of Shvat, 5689.[7]

Our brother **Mordechai** and his wife **Yente daughter of Leah and Nachum Grunt.** And their daughter **Zlata-Zahava.**
Perished in the year 5702, h.y.d.

Our brother **Moshe** and his wife **Libb née Shatz**, and their son **Shmuelik Tuvya.**
Perished in the year 5702, h.y.d.

Mourning them:
Leah and her husband Dov Aloni and their family in Israel;
Chaim and his wife Rachel Bobrowksi and their family in the US;
Chava and her husband Yaakov Yatchekovski and their son in Israel;
Meir Bobrowski in Israel. Rabbi Yaakov and his wife Chaya Bobrowski in the US;
Shifra and her husband Shmuel Mezukar and their family in Israel;
Penina and her husband Aharon Felayev and their family in Israel.

[Page 282]

In memory of our unforgettable brother,
Meir Bobrowski z.l.[8], son of **Avraham and Tama**
Who passed away before his time on Friday, 15 Kislev 5729, Dec 6, 1968

Left in mourning and sorrow:
His sister Leah and her husband Dov Aloni
His brother Chaim Bobrowski with his wife Rachel, United States
His sister Shifra, with her husband Shmuel Mezukar
His sister Chava Yatchekovski
His brother, Rabbi Yaakov Bobrowski with wife Chaya, United States
His sister Penina and husband Aharon Felayev and their families

In memory of our martyrs, h.y.d.

My parents: **Chaya-Malka (Bubul)** and **Aharon-Zeev (Alter) Greenblatt**
My sisters: **Rachel** and her husband **Shmuel Zilberberg**;
Malya Greenblatt
My brothers **Yosef**, his wife **Henye**, and their children **Isser and Malya Greenblatt**.
Avraham Greenblatt

We will never forget
Perl Greenblatt-Abramson, Israel
Itche Greeenblatt and family, US
Moshe Greenblatt and family, Argentina

[Page 283]

As an Everlasting Remembrance

Our parents:

Arye Leib Haberman (died in America 3 Shvat 5711, 10 January 1951) and **Nishe Reznick-Haberman** (died in America 15 Av 5726, 1 August 1962 [sic][2])

Brother: **Yosef Huberman** (fell in battle in Italy, 1944)

In sorrow:
Chana, Yitzchok Sheinfeld and family, America
Yisroel Haberman and family, Canada

[Page 284]

As an Everlasting Remembrance

Our parents
**Tuvya and Menucha Kozak
a.h.**[10]
Sister **Deena**
Her husband **Pesach Gurinski**
Their children: **Chaye Sara and
Itke**
Brothers: **Yitzchok, Nechemya**
and **David** with his wife **Nechama
and children**
Sister **Frume** and her
husband **Shlomo Lindbaum**
Children: **Betzalel Avrohom
Meir**,
Moshe Tzvi and daughter
sister **Manya** and
husband **Yaakov Kalbkof**
and children **Frume, Sara, Liebe,
Tzirl and Dobbe**
Perished at the hands of the Nazis,
h.y.d.

In sorrow:
Chaya and Isser Goldberg-Kozak (New York)
Shmuel Kozak

[Page 285]

Shmuel Chaim (Shmuelke) Kozak, son of Tuvye and Menucha
Died in New York, 28.10.1966, 14 Heshvan 5727

In sorrow:
His wife Rochel and children (New York)

Rivka Lipchik

Founder and president of the Kamenetz-Litovsk "Society for Clothing the Poor", vice-president of the Yizkor Book Committee in New York, America. Died 31 December 1967

[Page 286]

As an Everlasting Remembrance

To Our Unforgettable

Shraga Feivl Tendler a.h.

Died 26 Tammuz 5727 (August 3, 1967) in New York

In sorrow:
His wife, children, brother and sister
New York

[Page 287]

As an Everlasting Remembrance

To My Unforgettable Husband

Avrohom Hurvitz a.h.

Passed away: 9 Shvat 5711 (26 January 1951)

In sorrow:
**His wife Sarah and children
Chaya, Zelda and Asher**
In New York

[Page 288]

As an Everlasting Remembrance

To Our Dear Parents

**R. Yekusiel and Sara-Rivka
Kaufman-Garfinkel**
h.y.d.

Perished at the hands of the Nazi murderers

In sorrow:
Son, **Moshe Garfinkel**
Daughter, **Shifra Birnbaum**
Canada

[Page 289]

Our brother

Bebl Garfinkel

Died in Winnipeg, Canada
In the year 1961

In sorrow,
Brother: **Moshe**
Sister: **Shifra Birenbaum**

**To the memory of my father
R. Aharon Tzvi Gurfein** z.l.
And my righteous mother **Shifra** z.l.

My father was learned in the Torah and a charitable man. He participated actively and with dedication in public affairs. The words of our sages were constantly on his lips, and he was always fond of their *midrashic* analysis [exegesis]. He studied our Torah, a Torah of life and lovingkindness; it encompasses all, so "do not step away from it".[11]

My dear mother, may her soul dwell in Paradise, supported refugees during the days of misfortune, providing them with needed food as well as she could.

And we mourn the slaughter of our brothers and sisters that took place when the bloodthirsty German foe, may their names be blotted out, entered Kamenetz-Litovsk.

Over these I weep! My eyes, my eyes shed tears, for there is no one who can console me.[12]

From their son, **Baruch**, and his family

[Page 290]

As an Everlasting Remembrance

Pessl Singer

Died in Kamenetz, 2 Shvat, 5698 (1938)

R. Yitzchok Singer a.h.

Died in Kamenetz, 2 Nisan, 5679 (1919)

In Sorrow:
Their children, Simcha and Eliyohu Singer and families, New York (America)

Footnotes:

1.   From *Kamenetz-Litovsk, Zastavije and Colonies Memorial Book*, edited by S. Eisenstadt and M. Galbert, published by the Israel and America Committee of Kamenetz Litovsk and Zastavya, (Orly, Tel Aviv, Israel, 1970), pp. 281-340.
2.   18 Shvat 5701= February 15, 1941. The translator has found a discrepancy between this date and the information provided by Rabbi Yaakov Bobrowski in his article "Some of My Memories", pp. 90-91 of this Yizkor Book, where it is implied that his mother's death took place in early 1940, rather than 1941.
3.   R. (Hebrew ר') is generally an abbreviation for *Reb*, an honorific similar to English "Mr."
4.   5702 = 1941-42
5.   h.y.d. = *Hashem yikom damam* (= may God avenge their blood)
6.   5700 = 1939-1940
7.   Shvat 5689 = January-February, 1929
8.   z.l. = *zichrono livracha* (= of blessed memory)
9.   15 Av 5726 = 1 August 1966
10.   a.h. = aleihem hasholom = may they rest in peace
11.   Pirkei Avot 5:22
12.   Lamentations 1:16

[Page 291]

Kamenetz Yizkor Book Necrology (cont.)

As an Everlasting Remembrance

Golda Topolowski, z.l.

(born 1881, Died in America, 1961)

R. Meir Topolowski z.l.

(Born 1873, Died in America 1956)

In sorrow:
Chaya Kopski, Dorothea and Yosef Topolowski (America)

[Page 292]

**As an Everlasting
Remembrance**

Our dear
Eliyohu Milgram
Vice-President
of the Kamenetz Yizkor
Book
(Born 1900, Died June
1962)

His dear mother,
Chaye-Feige
(died 1 January, 1948)

And his brothers:
**Zalman, Leibl and
Velvl**
(died in America)

In sorrow:
**Wife, children, grandchildren
and their family** in New York

[Page 293]

As an Everlasting Remembrance

Our father, **Mordechai Reznik**

Brothers: **Mendl, Elchonon** and **Beril** with his wife, **Baltsche** and child
Brother: **Sholom Reznik (Matte's son)**, died in Russia in 1956
Sister: **Gitl** and **Alter Chazanowitz** and child

In sorrow:
Leah Reznik-Tendler and family, Laizer Reznik—America

[Page 294]

We Weep Bitterly for the Death of our Dear Martyrs

Our father, R. Yisrael son of **R. Menachem Mantcha Grunt**, z.l., a well-known businessman, energetic and generous;

Our mother, **Chana** daughter of **R. Meir Putchinski z.l.**, a noble woman, active in the community, kind and devoted to all people.

Brothers and sisters, together with their little children, 16 people on our father's side. Woe unto us, that they fell victim to the Nazi murderers.

May their memory be a blessing!

Yehudit Grunt-Koscikiewicz and her family
Rachel Grunt-Stempenitzki and her family

We are steeped in mourning and grief

Upon the death of our dear, unforgettable parents before their time

Father, grandfather **Yechezkael Koscikiewicz z.l.**

Mother, grandmother **Yehudit Koscikiewicz, née Grunt z.l.**, who died on Tuesday, 2 Shvat 5729 (21 January 1969)

May their memory be an everlasting blessing

Daughter: **Zahava and her husband Binyamin Stolomitzki**
Grandchildren: **Chaya, Avi and Yechezkael**

[Page 295]

As an Everlasting Remembrance

My brother, not forgotten **Velvel Kustin, and his wife**

Perished at the hands of the Nazi-German murderers

In sorrow:
His sister **Peitche Kaplan** (Argentina)

[Page 296]

We will remember forever

Mirtche and Shoul'ke Gurinski

And their little daughters, **Rivka and Rachel, h.y.d.**

Perished at the hands of the Nazi murderers

In Sorrow:
Velvel Kustin and brothers (America)

[Page 297]

As an Everlasting Remembrance

Our brother, **Leibl Kustin**

And his wife **Rachel**

Perished at the hand of the Nazi murderers

In sorrow:
Sarah and Velvel Kustin and family (America)

[Page 298]

As an Everlasting Remembrance

Yehuda Rappaport
Came on Aliya in the year 1949
Died 5 Tishri 5720—1959

His parents **Yosef and Leah**
And his eight brothers and sisters
Who perished together with the Jews of Kamenetz

In mourning:
His wife Ella
His sons Yosef and Asher Rappaport

To the memory of

My husband and our father **Shraga (Feivel) Katz**
Died 3 Heshvan 5724, October 21 1963

His father **R. Yosef Katz**, who died in Kamenetz.

His 2 brothers and his brother-in-law died in the US.

His mother **Yenta Katz, 3 brothers and a sister** perished together with the Jews of Kamenetz.

My father, **R. Moshe Geier**
Died 4 Adar 1920 in Kamenetz

My mother **Rivka Geier and 21 members of the Geier family**,
all perished in the Holocaust

My brother **Chaim Geier** died in the US

In mourning:
Dina Katz née Geier
Yehudit Katz
Moshe, Dalia and their son Shraga Katz

To the Memory of

Our father **R. Shmaryahu**
Son of **R. Yeshayahu-Natan Stempenitzki**
Died in Kamenetz 21 Iyar 1922, age 56

Our mother **Sara**, who perished
Our brother **Binyamin**,
who fell in World War I at the age of 20

Our brother **Arye-Leibl**,
who died in the US, 27 Nisan 1951, age 46

Our sister **Tama**, her husband **Moshe Yaffe**
and their children

Our brother **Asher**, his wife **Devora and their**
children

Our brother **Yeshayahu**

Who perished with the martyrs of Kamenetz

In mourning:
Yocheved Meltzer-Stepnitzki and family, US
Pesya (Peshka) Cohen-Stempenitzki and family,
Israel

To the Memory of

My family members who perished in the
Holocaust

My father, z.l. **R. Yitzhak-David**,
the ritual slaughterer,
son of **R. Avraham-Simcha Stofitchevski**

My brother **Nachum**
and my sisters **Sara and Chasha**

My wife **Chaya z.l., nee Gurfin**

My children: **Aharon-Tzvi, Avraham-Simcha,**
Shifra and Leah

My **mother z.l.** who died in the year 5700

May their memory be a blessing

Left in sorrow and grief
Moshe Moriah (Stofnitchevski) [sic], Ramat-Gan

Moshe Stofitchevski Moriah died 21 Tevet
5728[13] in Israel

As an everlasting memorial

To my dear parents
R. Yitzhak and Beila Levin z.l.

My brothers **Aharon, Feivel (Shraga)**

My sister **Reizl**
Who perished with the martyrs of Kamenetz

My brother, **Rabbi Arye z.l.** and his family
Who perished in the Warsaw Ghetto t.n.tz.b.h.[14]

In grief
Their daughter, Rachel Levin-Slonimski
And her family — Israel, Ramat-Gan

Weeping bitterly for

Reizl née Gordon
and David Shpigelman
Reichl née Gordon
and Nechemia Eisenstein

And their children **Nachum, Esther and**
Moshe

Who perished in the Holocaust

Our grandfather and grandmother
Gershon-Moshe and Malka Gordon z.l.

In mourning:
Moshe Gordon, Washington
Sonya Grun née Gordon, New York
Esther Mendelson née Shpigelman, Israel

[Page 300]

As an Everlasting Remembrance

My cousins
Chaya, Itte, Yehudis and Golda-Reizl Mandelblatt, h.y.d.

Who were cruelly put to death together with the Jews of Kamenetz
at the hand of the Nazi murderers

In Sorrow:
Sinne and Rachel Sawitzki (Mandelblatt) and family (America)

Footnotes:

13. 21 Tevet 5728 = 22 January 1968
14. t.n.tz.b.h. = *tihye nafsham tzerura bitzror hachaim* = may their souls be bound in eternal life

[Page 301]

Kamenetz Yizkor Book Necrology (cont.)

As an Everlasting Remembrance of our Parents

Yosef Mandelblatt (the writer)
Died 1945

and his wife **Nechama**
(died 1948 in New York)

In sorrow:
Their children —
Chatzkl, Chemka, Rachel, Chaim, Binyomin
And families, New York

[Page 302]

As an Everlasting Remembrance

R. Hershl Geier

One of the Heads of the Yeshiva
"Chofetz Chaim" in Radom

Perished at the hands of the Nazi murderers

In sorrow:
Eliyohu Singer, America

**As an
Everlasting
Remembrance**

**Isaac
Pomerantz**

Son of **Tzippe
and Feivl**

Perished at the
hands of the Nazi
murderers

In sorrow:
Relatives in America

[Page 303]

As an Everlasting Remembrance

The Family Yagalkowski, h.y.d.

Who perished at the hands of the Nazi murderers

In sorrow:
Their son and brother Avrohom Yagalkowski (America)

[Page 304]

As an Everlasting Remembrance

Mindl Lopates

And daughter Esther and son-in-law

Perished at the hand of the Nazi murderers

In sorrow:
Lopates Family-Circle (America)

[Page 305]

As an Eternal Memorial

My dear father **Zalman Hersh Chayit**

Sister **Sheve with her husband and two children, h.y.d.**

Perished at the hand of the Nazi murderers

In sorrow:
Eliyohu Chayit (America)

[Page 306]

As an Everlasting Remembrance

Our dear parents, not forgotten—

Devoted father **Yitzchok Shlomo z.l.**
(died in America, 1920)

Dedicated mother **Chaye Sarah z.l.**
(died in America, 1952)

In sorrow:
Chaim Zeev Mendelson
And family in America
Avraham David Mendelson
And family in Israel

As an Everlasting Remembrance

My generous father—

The well-known businessman **R. Chaim Polakevitch**
Died on the first day of Elul 1930 in Kamenetz-Litovsk

My mother **Sarah-Gitl**, not forgotten

Brother **Yaakov**, sisters **Kayla and Rachel, together with their families**

Sisters **Rayzl and Mirke**

All perished with the martyrs of Kamenetz
at the hands of the German murderers

May their memory be a blessing

In sorrow:
Chaya Mendelson-Polakevitch
And family(New York)

[Page 307]

In Memory of

My dear parents **Golda and David Krevtchik**

Brothers: **Eliyahu with his wife and children**
Meir
Hershl
Gottlieb

All of whom perished in the Holocaust

Mourning for them:
Their daughter and sister
Chana Kretzmer (Krevtchik) and her family members
Israel, Moshav Netaim

In Memory of My Family Members

My mother, **Chaya-Gitl z.l.**
Who died before the War

My father **Yosef Kravitzki**

My brother **Tzvi, his wife Manya née Liev**

And their daughter **Gitl**, age 2

My sister **Kayla**, age 14

My brother **Moshe**, age 12

My aunt **Frume** and her son **Yisrael Goldshul**, age 21

Who were exterminated by the Nazis

In grief
their daughter and sister
Sonya Kravitzki-Gereshtenski
Israel, Tel Aviv

To the members of my family
Who were murdered by the Nazi beasts
with the Jews of Kamenetz-Litovsk in 1942

My parents, **R. Chaim and Rachel Schmidt**

My sister **Malka** and her husband **Shlomo Dolinski**
and their son **Shmuel (Mulik)**

My sister **Dina** and her husband **Lipa Horvitz**
and their son **Shmuel (Mulik)**

My sister **Shoshana (Rayzele)**

My uncle and aunt **Mordechai (Motye)**
and **Yehudit Aharonowski and their children**

My aunt **Sara** and her husband **Ben-Tziyon Zub and their
children**

My uncle Daniel and his entire family

My aunt **Sara and Yaakov (Shayne Chaye's)**

I will not forget them

Dov (Bertchik) Shmide
and his family Israel, Haifa, 5728[15]

In memory of my dear ones

My father **Moshe Tzvi Blaichbord z.l.**
Who died 22 Kislev 5693[16], age 72

My mother **Sara-Dina z.l.**
Who died 7 Tevet 5680, age 52

My sister **Malka Blaichbord-Nuselvitch**
Died 10 Elul 5680, age 29

My sister **Chana Widomlanski**
Died 8 Iyar 5699[17], age 42

All in Kamenetz

My sister Trayna with her family members

And our other relatives died in the Holocaust

Memorializing them,
their only son and brother
Avraham Yitzhak Blaichbord
Israel, Kibbutz Dafna

[Page 308]

**As an Everlasting Remembrance
To our friends**

Isaac Wolhendler

And his wife **Malka**

Who perished at the hands of the Nazi-murderers

In sorrow:
Shimon Birnboym (America)

[Page 309]

As an Everlasting Remembrance

Our dear **Esther Birnboym**
(**Chaya Sara Tendler**'s daughter)

Who perished at the hands of the Nazi murderers

In sorrow:
Dr. Meir Tendler (America)

[Page 310]

As an Everlasting Memorial

Our unforgettable mother-grandmother
Malka Glezer

Who was murdered with the Jews of Kamen. by the Nazi murderers

In sorrow:
Son, Shmuel; daughter, Gitl;
Granddaughter, Libbe Polyakevitch (America)
Grandson Asher Glezer and family (Israel)

To the memory of

Our mother and grandmother **Malka Glezer, h.y.d.**, whose memory is sacred to all of us. Over her noble and devoted soul, dedicated and devoted to all, who perished together with all the Jews of Kamenetz in the Holocaust at the hands of the unclean, accursed Nazis

We mourn:
Her son Shmuel Glezer and his wife
Her daughter Gitl
Her granddaughter Libbe Polyakevitch (US)
Her grandson Asher Glezer and members of his household (Israel, Tel Aviv)

To the memory of

My father, **R. Moshe-Nachum Glezer**, who died in Kamenetz 11 Tishri 5698—1938 [sic][18]

My mother, **Esther-Brayna**

My sister **Chana, her husband Yonah-Shmuel, and their children: Dov, Chaya and Moshe**

My sister **Sara, her husband Mordechai Mintz and their children**

My brother **Arye-Leib; my brother Eliezer;**

My sisters **Bayla, Chaya and Tzipora**

All of whom perished in the Holocaust

Weeping bitterly
Asher Glezer and family

Footnotes:
15. 5728 = 1967-68
16. 22 Kislev 5693 = 21 December 1932; 7 Tevet 5680 = 29 December 1919; 8 Iyar 5699 = 27 April 1939; 10 Elul 5680 = 24 August 1920
17. 8 Iyar 5699 = April 27, 1939
18. 11 Tishri 5698 = September 16, 1937; 11 Tishri 5699 = October 6 1938

[Page 311]

Kamenetz Yizkor Book Necrology (cont.)

As an Everlasting Remembrance

Our Family: Parents **R. Aharon and Leah, h.y.d.**

Father and brother **Yoel**

Mother and sister-in-law **Esther and brother Zavele, h.y.d.**

Sisters: **Bayla, Chashe. Brothers: Moshe Zuske and Yossel, h.y.d.**

All of them perished at the hands of the Nazi murderers

In sorrow:
Chaye-Sara Rudnitzki-Bandar and family
Yaakov Rudnitzki and family, Buenos Aires
Dvora-Rudnitzki-Singer and family, New York
Pinchas Ravid-Rudnitzki and family, Haifa

[Page 312]

As an Everlasting Remembrance

To my dear parents **Arye and Golda Pomerantchik**

To my sisters **Rivka and Sara'le**;

and to my brother **Mordechai**

Who perished in a cruel manner with all the Jews of Kamenetz during the Holocaust

We have been left in mourning and grief
Your daughter **Leah and Avraham Pomerantchik**
And her family — Tel-Aviv

As an Everlasting Memorial

We shall remember and not forget:

My parents: **Bendit son of Zeev Winograd and Malka née Horvitz**

My sisters: **Kayla and Fraydl;**

My uncle: **Baruch Horvitz and his family h.y.d.**

Who perished at the hands of the Nazis

Weeping bitterly
Rachel Vered-Winograd and her family

[Page 313]

In Everlasting Remembrance

Of our dear family: **Yitzchok Leib Eisner**

His wife **Rivka**

His daughters **Bluma and Zlate**

And **two grandchildren — h.y.d.**

Who perished at the hands of the Nazi murderers

In sorrow:
Chaya Gitl Rosen, America
Liba Greenman, America
Hershel Eisner, America
Shimon Eisner, Canada
Dobbe Garfinkel, Canada

[Page 314]

As an Everlasting Memorial

Our parents, sister and family **R. Yaakov-Pinchas and Dobbe-Yehudis Kagan, h.y.d.**

(**Yankl Alter Pini's**, active in the Kamenetz community)
Who died in America August 11, 1955, age 83

Sister **Sheine-Chaya, children Hindele and Yitzchok-Chaim'ke**

Perished at the hand of the German murderers

In sorrow:
Chatzkel Kagan
And **Mindel Kagan (Shudroff)**, New York
Sirke Kagan-Wofniarski, Haifa

[Page 315]

In memory of

My father: **R. David son of Elchanan Stempenitski**
Who died at a ripe old age in Petah-Tikva, 4 Tishri 5715[19]

My mother: **Sirka-Chaya daughter of R. Yitzhak Stoler**
Who died in Kamenetz, 1 Tishri 5699 [20]

In mourning:
Elchanan Stempenitski and his family

**As an Everlasting Remembrance
To the Martyrs of our Family and Dear Ones**

My brother, **Shmuel Golomborski, his wife and children**, who
perished in the Bialystok Ghetto;

Aunt **Bayla Golomborski, with the members of her family,**

My cousin, **Bovel Gich, with family members,**

My cousin **Elka with her family members,**
Who perished with the Jews of Kamenetz

And to my mother, **Chava Golomborski**, died 17 November 1964
in Israel

To my husband, **Chaim Stoler (Rokeach)**, died 30 September
1968 in Israel

To my sister **Miriam Goldberg**, died 5 May 1958 in Israel

To my cousin, **Friedka Golomborski**, who was killed in an
accident

In mourning:
Bovel Stoler-Golomborski and household members, Tel Aviv

[Page 316]

As an Everlasting Remembrance

Father **David** (died January 1938), mother **Zisl Galpern**, perished

Brother **Sholom**, his wife **Sara** and children **Yitzchok and Dobbe**

Brother **Maml**, his wife **Fira and child**

Sister **Faygl**, her husband **Avrohom** with their son and daughter

Sister **Bashke**, her husband **David** with two children

Sister **Chaya**

All cruelly put to death by the Nazi murderers

Left in sorrow:
Dobbe Galperin and family
Osna Yamner and family (America)

[Page 317]

In Memory of the Goldberg Family, h.y.d.

On the death of my dear ones:

My parents, **Kalman and Rachel-Leah Goldberg**, good honest people

My brothers **Noah and Yisrael-Yitzhak**, pioneers and Lovers of Zion

My sisters **Shifra, Rivka and Bracha**, the pure, martyred girls

Who were murdered by the defiled Nazis,
and their burial place is not know

Mourning, and bearing his gloomy agony forever
Their surviving son **Arye (Laybl) Goldberg**
And his family members

[Page 318]

Yizkor!

We recall with awe

Our dear parents **R. Moshe and Esther Shudrowitzki** a.h.

Who were tragically and so young torn away from us
in Kamenetz on the Eve of Sukkot[21] 1915

Our dear grandmother **Malka**
daughter of **Eliyohu Shtzupak** a.h.
Died in Jerusalem, 1948

Our younger brother **Yekusiel**, a.h.
Who died in Brisk[22], 1928, age 14 years

We will hold their memory dear forever

In sorrow:
Sons, brothers and grandchildren:
Avrohom, Hirshl, Eliyohu and David Shudroff and families (New York)

As an Everlasting Remembrance

My father, **R. Moshe-Eliezer Katchalski** a.h. (a scribe s.t.m.[23])
Died in Kamenetz 26 Adar 1929

My mother **Rochel** died during the last days of the ghetto.

My brother **Michael with his wife and 4 children**,

also my brother **Eliyohu Chaim** with his **wife and child**

Perished at the hands of the Nazis, may their names be blotted out.

In sorrow:
Daughter, sister
Shoshke Katchalski and family (New York)

[Page 320]

As an Everlasting Remembrance

My dear brother

Motl Shmukler

And his children:
**Moshe, Temme Fraydke and
Yache**—h.y.d.

All perished at the hands of the
Nazi murderers

In sorrow:
Chaim Shmukler, America

Footnotes:

19. 4 Tishri 5715 = 1 October 1954
20. 1 Tishri 5699 = 26 September 1938
21. September 22 1915 = 14 Tishri 5676, Eve of Sukkot
22. Brisk = Brest-Litovsk
23. s.t.m. = *soifer tefillin mezuzois*, a scribe who writes the scroll text for phylacteries and *mezuzas*

[Page 321]

My Dear Wife

Sima Rayzl Shmukler

Died in America 26 Elul 5726,
11 September 1966

In sorrow:
Chaim Shmukler, America

[Page 322]

Our dear parents:

R. Chaim (beloved cantor of Kamenetz) and **Gitl Yoffe, z.l.**

Brother **Moshe Yoffe with his wife** and children: **Shmeril, Chaim and Shlomo**

Sister **Trayna Dolinski**, children **Malka and Chaya**

Sister **Rayzl Dolinski**, husband **Moshe** and son **Chaim**

All perished at the hands of the Nazi-murderers   .

Terry Trayna Ever—born 15.2.1956

Died in New York 7.3.1961,
a granddaughter of **Aharon Meir and Leah'ke Yoffe**

In sorrow:
Aharon Meir and Leah'ke Yoffe and family (New York)

[Page 323]

As an Everlasting Remembrance

Our mother

Toibe Ashkenazi

Sister **Bracha**, her husband **Avrohom Kanolik**
and their children **Gitel'e and Yitzchok'l**

Brother **Yaakov Ashkenazi together with his wife**

And our grandfather **Yeshaya Ashkenazi**

All perished at the hands of the Nazi-murderers

In sorrow:
Daughter Sarah Ashkenazi and her husband Velvl Kustin,
Son Shlomo Ashkenazi and family in America,
Daughter Bella Ashkenazi-Faygenblum and family in Israel

[Page 324]

Bella Faygenblum née Ashkenazi z.l.

A noble and beautiful woman, tender and graceful. She was bound to her family, and she devoted her best years to bringing up her daughter.

She never complained about her fate and her difficult life. At the twilight of her life she found encouragement and joy in her two granddaughters, who were strongly bound to her.

She died before her time, at the tender age of 52. She left behind a daughter, a son-in-law and two granddaughters, as well as a brother and sister in the United States, stunned by the tragedy and refusing to be comforted.

May her memory be a blessing!

Her daughter, in mourning,
Rachel Golan (Faygenblum) Israel

[Page 325]

In Eternal Remembrance

Yisroel Pomerantz

His wife **Fayge-Chaya and her mother**
And their **children, h.y.d.**

Perished at the hands of the Nazi murderers

In sorrow:
Mindl Kagan, Dovid Shudroff America

[Page 326]

In memory of our sister

Perl Goldstein

And her husband **Yosef, and their children**

All perished at the hand of the Nazi murderers

[Page 327]

As an Everlasting Remembrance

Our father

R. Anshel Sheinfeld

Active in the community, charitable, Sabbath observant and gabbai in the synagogue, died 23 Sivan 1943 in New York.

Our brother **Tzvi Arye (Hersh Layb) Sheinfeld**

Died 1963 in New York

In sorrow:
Sheinfeld children and grandchildren

My dear parents

Chaim and Frayde Sheinfeld

Sisters **Bashe and Perel'e h.y.d.**

All perished together with all the Kamenetz Jews
at the hands of the Nazi murderers

In sorrow:
Son, **Yitzchok Sheinfeld and family** New York

[Page 328]

As an Eternal Remembrance!

Our family

Morgenstern-Pochalski[24]

Perished at the hands of the Nazi murderers

In sorrow:
Dobbe and Chaika[25] Brooklyn, New York

[Page 329]

To the Memory of

Our dear mother: *Rabbanit*[26] **Gitl**, wife of **Rabbi Moshe-Yitzhak Rabinowitz** of Kamenetz, who died at a ripe old age in Israel, 8 Adar 1941, in Tel Aviv.

Our brother and uncle: **R. Arye-Layb** son of Rabbi **Moshe-Yitzhak Rabinowitz** (born in the year 5633[27]) and his wife **Rayze**, who perished in the Brisk Ghetto in the year 5702[28] h.y.d.

Our brother and uncle: **Shaul** son of Rabbi **Moshe-Yitzhak Rabinowitz**, died at a ripe old age in Tel Aviv in the year 5720[29].

Our brother and father: R. **Naphtali Hertz** son of Rabbi **Moshe-Yitzhak Rabinowitz**, died at the age of 27 on 13 Kislev 5688[30]. Buried in the Trumpeldor Street Cemetery in Tel Aviv.

Pinchas Rabi (Rabinowitz)
Yona Eisenstein (Rabinowitz)
Moshe Rabinowitz
And their families

[Page 330]

The American Yizkor Committee

Strongly expresses its sorrow for the loss of our esteemed
fellow-townsman and coworker on the Yizkor Book

Mrs. **Itke (Ida) Lipchik a.h.**

(died 28 Nisan 5729, 20 March 1969)

She was the wife of our esteemed Committee Member

Sholom Lipchik

And a mother of 2 sons.

We will hold her memory dear

Avrohom Shudroff, president
Sarah Hurwitz, corresponding secretary

Footnotes:

24. The translator recognizes several individuals. Sitting, from left: Sarah Morgenstern, Zune Pochalski (died 1940), Pochalski daughter (likely Riva), Bracha Pochalski, Golda Morgenstern (Sarah's daughter). Standing from left: Pochalski son, Pochalski son, Pochalski daughter (likely Basha), Pochalski son, Pochalski daughter (likely Liba), Pochalski son, Masha Morgenstern (Sarah's daughter). The Pochalski sons were named David, Hershel, Abba and Rephael; they and their sisters were children of Zune and Bracha (née Morgenstern) Pochalski..

25. Dobbe née Morgenstern (Dorothy Flusberg) and Chaika née Morgenstern (Helyn Reichenthal) were Sarah Morgenstern's daughters

26. *Rabbanit* = title used for a rabbi's wife (Hebrew)

27. 5633 = secular year 1872-73

28. 5702 = secular year 1941-42

29. 5720 = secular year 1959-60. The translator has discoverd a discrepancy between p. 330 of the original Yizkor Book and a gravestone inscription: the names of the brothers, "Shaul" and "Naphtali-Hertz", are swapped in the Yizkor Book. Shaul Rabinowitz died in 1927 and was buried in the Tel Aviv Trumpeldor Cemetery, as is evident from the photograph of his gravestone available at the following link (retrieved January 2020): https://billiongraves.com/grave/. Naphtali-Hertz Rabinowitz is the brother who died at a ripe old age in 1959, and was the father of Moshe Rabinowitz, author of the articles appearing on pp. 49 and 405-407 of this Yizkor Book. (In the latter article the author states that his father's name was Naphtali.)

30. 13 Kislev 5688 = 7 December 1927. See previous footnote.

[Page 331]

Kamenetz Yizkor Book Necrology (cont.)

As an Eternal Remembrance

Our parents: Father **Shmuel**, who died in America on the 23rd of May 1949

Mother **Bracha Forer**, died 13 November 1922 in Kamenetz,

Leaving us as young orphans

In sorrow, the remaining daughters and son:
Leah'ke Yoffe and family
Chaitche Chayet and family
Dob'ke Kessler and family
Yitzchok-Zelik Forer and family, America
Faygel Podravanek and family, Israel

[Page 332]

As an Everlasting Remembrance!

My dear parents, **Laybl and Esther Dolinski**

With pain and sorrow I recall my lifelong companion

Nosson Panski
(died 2 February 1965)

His memory will be with me always

In sorrow:
Dvora Dolinski-Panski New York

[Page 333]

As an Everlasting Remembrance

Our father: **R. David Timianski a.h.**
Died before the war [World War II]

Mother: **Gitl, h.y.d.**

Brother, sister and their children h.y.d.

Perished at the hands of the Nazi murderers

In sorrow:
The sole survivor **Zlata Gers-Timianski and her family**
New York (America)

[Page 334]

As an Everlasting Remembrance

Tzvi Hersh Gers (Gershkowitz)
Died 5 September 1968, 12 Elul 5729 [sic] [31]

In sorrow:
Wife Zlata, son Avrohom Moshe and Dr. Shlomo Gers

[Page 335]

In Memory of Our Martyred Parents

My mother, **Sarah** daughter of **Simcha David and Bayla Mekler**

My father **Moshe** son of **Shalom Dubiner**

Our dear brothers **Hershl and Layzer**

Our unforgettable sister **Bayla**

Who perished at the hands of the Nazis in the year 5702[32], h.y.d.

Mourning them:
Esther and Simcha Dubiner and family in Israel
Yisrael and Shifra Koval and family in Argentina
Shalom Dubiner and family in Argentina
Mordechai Dubiner and family in Israel
Chaya Tzevardlik and family in Israel
Feivl Dubiner and family in Israel

Amitzur Dubiner z.l.

It is difficult and bitter to think of, and even more difficult to put into writing, words about Amitzur, who passed away at a young age and left behind a wife, two children, an extended family and many friends and acquaintances mourning him.

As a scion of a nationalist family, Amitzur was drawn to the Beitar[33] Group from the very beginning of his youth in the Land; he was educated in the spirit of the movement and he in turn educated hundreds of young people in its bosom.

He endeavored to link his young life with a practical tie to the landscape of our homeland. He was drawn to agricultural studies, and as a matter of course this is what brought him to the Weizmann Agricultural School. He studied diligently and was one of its first graduates.

At the graduation party of the school, which was located in the heart of the Arava[34], he was asked by Kaddish Luz—who in those days was serving as the Minister of Agriculture, and now for many years has been serving as chairman of the Knesset—how it came to be that a city boy like him had decided to come there, to continue his studies in this desolate place. Amitzur's reply, conscientious and to the point, was:

"My forefathers were also the first to settle on the arable fields of Petah Tikva, and it appears that this spirit of being the first is in my blood as well."

Amitzur's acquaintances and friends knew him as a cheerful sociable person, who brought joy to the people around him. Justice and integrity were particularly embedded in his character.

After Amitzur completed his service in the Israeli army as an officer, he went to live in various border settlements, and eventually he settled in Kfar-Arif, where he set up his farm and home.

His fruitful life ended while he was still young.

With love and much grief in their hearts, his parents, wife **Rachel**, son **Avi**, daughter **Orit**, brother **Yosef** and family, sister **Penina** and family, will all carry his unforgettable memory.

[Page 337]

It is difficult to think of, and even more to write about **Amitzur**, who departed from us in his youth, at the tender age of only 28. He left behind a wife, two children, an extended family, and many friends and acquaintances who mourn him.

As a scion of a nationalist family, Amitzur was attracted to the Beitar Group from a very young age. He clung to its ideas, was educated and educated others—hundreds of young people—in the bosom of the movement that he believed in with all his heart.

His attraction to agriculture brought him as a matter of course to the Weizmann Agriculture School, and Amitzur was one of its first graduates.

In the graduation party of the school, which was located in the heart of the Arava, he was asked by Mr. Kaddish Luz—now the Knesset Chairman, but then the Agriculture Minister—what made him, as a city boy, come to this desolate place to continue his studies. His spontaneous answer was that his forefathers were the first to settle on the arable fields of Petah Tikva, and this spirit of being the first was apparently in his blood.

And indeed his family was one of the oldest, extended and well known in Petah Tikva and throughout the entire Land, and Amitzur was faithfully following in its path.

His acquaintances and friends knew him as a cheerful, sociable person, who brought joy to the people around him. In particular he pursued and fought for justice and integrity, characteristics embedded in him.

After he completed his army service with the rank of officer, he went to live in various border settlements, whether Mevo'ot Beitar, Amatzya or Yad Arba'a Asar; and eventually he moved to Kfar Arif, where he settled down and set up his farm and home.

His friends and acquaintances will certainly not be able to forget him. They will always picture him as young, cheerful and proud, as befits a member of the national movement.

Chanoch Bar Lavi, *Herut*

[Page 338]

With Great Pain We Weep for the Death of

Shmuel (Sam) Glezer

Our glorious crown has fallen.
He died in New York in the year
1970
At the age of 72

A true man of the people, full of wisdom of life, with deep vision and a generous heart to take up and address various human problems. He was a dedicated associate and a good friend, who gave up much time and energy to help out wherever he could. All those who were in his presence, and those who were closely associated with him, especially the three families to whom he served as a father, were left orphaned.

A pity for the loss!

In deep sorrow:
His wife, **Mina Glezer**
His sister **Gittel and her son Lipa Polyakevitch**, New York
His nephew **Asher Glezer with his wife and children** Tel Aviv, Israel

[Page 339]

To the Memory of

My mother, **Rachel Krakowski, née Eisenstein**
To my aunt, **Mania Eisenstein née Gelerstein**
To my cousins, **Simcha'le and Gitel'e**, the pure children who were murdered with the martyrs of Kamenetz-Litovsk by the impure Nazis in the year 1942.
To my uncle, **Aharon Eisenstein**, who was murdered in the Warsaw Ghetto.
To my father, **Tzvi-Nachum Krakowski** who died in Brisk-Litovsk.
To my brother, **Simcha Krakowski**, who died a young man, age 21, in Warsaw.
To my uncle **Yisrael Eisenstein**, who died in Kamenetz.

May their memory be a blessing!

Chaya Krakowski-Karabelnik and family
Tel-Aviv, Israel

As an Everlasting Remembrance

To our Dear

Yitzchok David Shudroff

Who died 20 Av 5730—22 August 1970

In sorrow:
His wife **Mindl**
Sons **Moshe and Michael**
Brother **Avrohom Shudroff**
(president of the Book Committee in America), New York

Golda Rosanski-Riveles

Golda Rosanski-Riveles and her sister Faygl of blessed memory, were among the first active members of Poalei-Tziyon.[35] After her wedding she settles in America and continues her party work in the Histadrut campaign and in the Pioneer Women. It is decided to house the pioneer movement "Habonim" in America within her home. In 1955 she and her husband visit Israel for the first time. After two further visits they decide to settle in Israel. In the year 1971, when they have already prepared themselves to take the trip that will fulfil their dream, Golda suddenly becomes ill and, on July 3, dies in New York before her time.

Left in deep sorrow:
Her husband: **Yisroel Rosanski**
Daughters: **Tzafira and Cecille**
Three grandchildren
Sister: **Malka**
Brothers: **Aharon and Nachum**

As a Remembrance

The friend of my youth,
who died before her time

Golda Rosanski (Riveles),

in New York
On 10 Tammuz 5731, July 3 1971

In deep sorrow:
Chaya Krakowski-Karabelnik

And her husband and daughter Israel, Tel Aviv

Footnotes:

31. 5 September 1968 = 12 Elul 5728
32. 5702 = secular year 1941-42
33. Beitar (or Betar) was a Revisionist Zionist movement, a predecessor of the Herut and Likud political parties. See the following (retrieved June, 2019): https://en.wikipedia.org/wiki/Betar
34. Arava = desert-like area of Israel, running along the Israeli-Jordanian border south of the Dead Sea
35. Poalei-Tzion (or Poale Zion) is the name of a Labor Zionist organization. See the following (retrieved June, 2019): https://en.wikipedia.org/wiki/Poale_Zion

YIDDISH SECTION

Poem of the Murdered Jewish People[1]

By Yitzchok Katznelson, May God Avenge His Blood

Translated by Allen Flusberg

…An entire world looked on
As during days bright
And during nights dark
Via trains and on foot
They led my people to their death;
A million children, as they were put to death,
Stretched their hands out to them—
And it did not move them…

Footnote:

1.   From *Kamenetz-Litovsk, Zastavije and Colonies Memorial Book*, edited by S. Eisenstadt and M. Galbert, published by the Israel and America Committee of Kamenetz Litovsk and Zastavya, (Orly, Tel Aviv, Israel, 1970), p. 342. Katznelson perished in Auschwitz in 1944. See the following (retrieved October, 2019): https://en.wikipedia.org/wiki/Itzhak_Katzenelson.

[Page 346]

Let Us Remember and Not Forget[1]

By the Committee of Kamenetzers in Israel and the USA

Translated by Allen Flusberg

A memorial service for the martyrs of our town on Yom Hashoa [Holocaust Memorial Day]

[Pages 347-348]

[***Note by translator***: *The Yiddish text of this article was a translation of the Hebrew text of the article appearing on* pp. 8–12 *of this volume. The translator from Hebrew to Yiddish was Chaya Krakowski–Karabelnik. See the English translation of pp. 8–12 in this volume; any differences between the Hebrew and Yiddish are noted there.*]

Footnote:

      1.   From *Kamenetz–Litovsk, Zastavije and Colonies Memorial Book*, edited by S. Eisenstadt and M. Galbert, published by the Israel and America Committee of Kamenetz Litovsk and Zastavya, (Orly, Tel Aviv, Israel, 1970), pp. 346–348

[Page 349]

A Monument to Our Destroyed Hometown[1]

by Avraham Schudroff

Translated by Allen Flusberg

Note from translator: A translation of this Yiddish article appears in the English-language section of this Yizkor Book, p. 9 ("Foreword" by Abraham Schudroff). The following two photographs appear on p. 352 of the Yiddish version.

Jewish prisoners being led to work by the Nazis

During the Yizkor Meeting and candle-lighting ceremony
for the Kamenetz martyrs on Mt. Zion in Jerusalem

Footnote:

1.   From *Kamenetz-Litovsk, Zastavije and Colonies Memorial Book*, edited by S. Eisenstadt and M. Galbert, published by the Israel and America Committee of Kamenetz Litovsk and Zastavya, (Orly, Tel Aviv, Israel, 1970), pp. 349-352.

[Page 353]

Introductory Remarks[1]

by Professor Shmuel Eisenstadt

Translated by Allen Flusberg

It was no accident that I took upon myself the redaction of the Kamenetz-Litowsk Memorial Book, for I have been transported back to the world of my origins and of my early youth by this history of the Kamenetz Jewish community and of its tragic destruction—after many long years of life struggles and accomplishments.

On a summer day of 1893, I came to Kamenetz accompanied by my beloved mother, may she rest in peace. We had come there from the estate of my grandfather, *Rebbe*[2] Yakov Ber—the estate was located in Chemeri, near Kamenetz[3]. A child of only seven, I strolled through the quiet streets of Kamenetz, gazing at first upon the amiable faces of the ordinary Jewish people, and looking at the *Slup* [Medieval fortress-tower], about which we had been told so many children's stories.

A little later I began to understand what kind of intellectual sources my dear father, may he rest in peace, had been nourished on. Although he had spent his childhood years in Chemeri, where he had grown up, he was actually a scion of scholarly laymen and community leaders of Brisk.

While raising me my father had told me much about Kamenetz, about its lay scholars and intellectuals, and how this town had been influenced intellectually by nearby Brisk. And later, when I was deeply immersed in the study of our people's history, I developed a strong bond with my kindred brothers and sisters of Kamenetz and the surrounding area.

It became clear to me that the profound national spirit and the studious and worldly activism of the small Kamenetz community had been derived mainly from the fact that this *shtetl*, like other Jewish settlements in the country, lay on the great historical route of our people, as they moved from west to east—from Spain, France and Germany towards Poland and Lithuania.

[Page 354]

During the long and difficult Jewish struggle for survival, Jewish culture deepened and solidified here. Here also the institutions of national Jewish autonomy—the Council of the Four Lands[4]—at one time took hold.

The destruction of Kamenetz-Litowsk is a most tragic and bitter chapter within the greater history of the Jewish destruction. It is a story of the downfall and eradication of a modest but daring nucleus of Jewish culture and sociability, which might otherwise have developed further, spawning welcome and desirable intellectual forces within our people. Every page, every single line of this Kamenetz-Litowsk Memorial Book, cries out bitterly—each in its own way—over this loss.

May our people know and remember what it has lost as a result of the blood-soaked hands of the Nazi murderers!

May the children, grandchildren and great-grandchildren of the Kamenetz Jews, wherever they may be, know and remember their origins with pride and sorrow, and may they continue to carry on their ancestors' banner!

May the bloody foe—the enemy of our people and of humanity—not be forgotten, nor forgiven for the blood they shed—the blood of the elderly, women and children—including the blood of the Kamenetz Jewish community annihilated by them

Footnotes:

1.   From *Kamenetz-Litovsk, Zastavije and Colonies Memorial Book*, edited by S. Eisenstadt and M. Galbert, published by the Israel and America Committee of Kamenetz Litovsk and Zastavya, (Orly, Tel Aviv, Israel, 1970), pp. 353-354. In a footnote in the original article, the author, Eisenstadt, makes the following statement: "I took over completing the redaction of the Kamenetz-Litowsk Memorial Book, which had for the most part been done by my friend, Mendl Gelbart. He deserves my heartfelt thanks."
2.   *Rebbe* can in this context be an honorific akin to the English "Mr.", or it can mean "Rabbi".
3.   There is currently (2021) a place named Chemeri about 8km east of Kamenetz. See also the essay by Eisenstadt on pp. 124-126 of this Yizkor Book, "It Happened in Kamenetz-Litowsk".
4.   See the following link (retrieved October 2020) for details: https://en.wikipedia.org/wiki/Council_of_Four_Lands

[Page 357]

The Past of our Destroyed Home

History of Kamenetz-Litowsk and Its Jewish Settlement[1]

By Levi Sarid (Laybl Goldberg)

Translated by Allen Flusberg

Note from translator: this Yiddish article is identical to the Hebrew article with the same title and by the same author on pp. 21-28. See the English translation of that article.

The following figure appeared on p. 375 of the Yiddish article.

A Street in Kamenetz

Translator's Footnote:

1.   From *Kamenetz-Litovsk, Zastavije and Colonies Memorial Book*, edited by S. Eisenstadt and M. Galbert, published by the Israel and America Committee of Kamenetz Litovsk and Zastavya, (Orly, Tel Aviv, Israel, 1970), pp. 357-375.

[Page 400]

The First School in Zastavya[1]

by Falek Zolf[2]

Translated by Allen Flusberg

A group of friends and I began to think about establishing a modern school for the Jewish children of Zastavya. At that time only a few middle-class boys were studying in the small number of private *Ḥayders* [religious schools for children] that were left in Zastavya.

What a modern Yiddish school should consist of and how it should operate—this I had already seen in the Russian city Yaroslavl, beyond Moscow[3], where I wound up as a result of the war [World War I]. I had been exiled there, homeless, together with several hundred other Jewish families from war-torn territories.

I had resolved that I must establish a school for the children of Zastavya. But the question was: where in this burnt-down town could I find a suitable space, the requisite furniture and other items? Where could I get teachers? And where could I get young people who would want to help this enterprise along? The few young people who had survived and remained in Zastavya were about to leave— some to the Land of Israel and others to America. The situation was not a happy one; but I was too taken with the idea of a school to give up so quickly.

I went over to see "the Saperstein brothers"[4]—as they were known in the neighboring town of Kamenetz—with my plan to establish a Yiddish school in the little suburb of Zastavya.

Intelligent young men, the Saperstein brothers were former non-matriculated students who before the war had been preparing themselves to take examinations for an *Attestat Zrelosty*[5]. They were so enamored with my proposal that their eyes practically lit up with delight. They were captivated by the thought of becoming the pioneers of an all-Yiddish school.

[Page 401]

Right away Asher, the oldest of the four Saperstein brothers, ran off to fetch a bottle of whiskey and a snack—some salted herring. We all drank a *l'ḥaim* [toast] to the life of the first new school in the suburb of Zastavya.

We got right down to work. First, we rented half a house from a fellow-Jew who had just finished putting up its roof. We hammered a board together and blackened it to use it as a blackboard—reasoning that once we had a blackboard, we would soon have a school, as well. Then we all chipped in to purchase some wooden planks. After planing them down, we used them to construct tables and benches, making sure they were long enough to accommodate a large number of children.

The older boy students helped out, hammering nails wherever needed—and in places where there was no need for them, as well. The girls decorated the classroom with colored paper and hung portraits of Yiddish authors on the walls; they had cut these pictures out of old Yiddish newspapers. Outside the front door we hung a sign on which we had written *Die Zastavyer Yiddishe Folks-Shule* [The Zastavya Yiddish Public School] in giant block letters.

The parents—and even more so the children—were inspired, especially since we were not asking them to pay any tuition. We also provided all the requisite teaching supplies—to the extent that such items were even available then. All these things were funded by a special subsidy from the American Joint[6]. And in addition to their salaries, the teachers were given a bonus: a provision of food *payok* [rations] from the *Kinder-Kich* [Children's Kitchen], which the Polish-American Committee was providing[7].

The school reinvigorated our quiet, darkened little suburb. A new Yiddish song, with an old-new Yiddish melody, resounded throughout the Jewish street and echoed in every Jewish home. The children embraced the school the way a small child clings to its caring mother. They showered us teachers with a great love that warmed our hearts and encouraged us to be strong for the work that lay ahead.

[Page 402]

All the responsibility of keeping the school going lay on my shoulders, since I was the principal; but in addition, I also had to serve as a teacher of *Tanach* [Bible] and history. I will never forget the day I stood face-to-face with my young neighbors, the children of my little *shtetl*, to lecture to them for the first time. At the time, this was one of the happiest moments of my life.

(From Falek Zolf's Book, *Zichroinos* [Memoirs])

Translator's Footnotes:

1.   From *Kamenetz-Litovsk, Zastavije and Colonies Memorial Book*, edited by S. Eisenstadt and M. Galbert, published by the Israel and America Committee of Kamenetz Litovsk and Zastavya, (Orly, Tel Aviv, Israel, 1970), pp. 400-402.

2.   The name of this author is spelled "Zalf" in the Yiddish of this article; elsewhere, however, it is spelled "Zolf". See the article by Zolf on pp. 462-470 of this Yizkor Book, "The Revisor [Auditor]", specifically Footnote 2.

3.   Yaroslavl, Russia is located about 250km northeast of Moscow.

4.   See the following two biographies in this Yizkor Book: P. Ravid-Rudnicki, "Asher Saperstein", p. 131; and Ḥaya Krakowski-Karabelnik, "Hershl Tzvi Saperstein", pp. 133-134.

5.   Maturation certificate (Russian); likely similar to a high-school equivalency certificate

6.   American Jewish Joint Distribution, a relief organization based in New York City. See the following link (retrieved January, 2021): American Jewish Joint Distribution Committee - Wikipedia

7.   See the following article: M.L Adams, "Herbert Hoover and the Organization of the American Relief Effort in Poland (1919-1923), *European Journal of American Studies* 4-2 (2009), available at the following link (retrieved January 2021): Herbert Hoover and the Organization of the American Relief Effort in Poland (1919-1923) (openedition.org)

[Page 405]

The Religious life in Kamenets-Litowsk

Rabbi Moshe Yitzchok Rabinowitz, of Blessed Memory[1] [2]

by Moshe Rabinowitz

Translated by Allen Flusberg

Kamenetz was a little Jewish *shtetl* with its share of pain and pleasure. It also had its share of disputes, of synagogue charity functionaries who were striving to hold sway. And there were many stories about the town. I was with my father, may he rest in peace, for nearly fifty years; and as he was always steeped in memories of the little town, his fount of stories about Kamenetz never ran dry.

The Bays-Medresh [House of Study] of Rabbi Moshe Hersh, of blessed memory,
and the synagogue of Rabbi Moshe Yitzchok Rabinowitz, of blessed memory

[Page 406]

My father also told me a great deal about my grandfather [Moshe Yitzchok Rabinowitz], who had served as the Rabbi of Kamenetz. He had been a great prodigy who happened to wind up in Kamenetz, a town of diverse learned laymen. It was said that when my father's brother, the Rabbi of St. Petersburg, Rabbi David Tevel[3], came to visit, they would go outside together for a stroll, and people used to remark that it was two angels, with the spirit of God resting on them, that were walking around in the town.

With respect to my grandfather's prodigious scholarship, the following story was told: After my grandfather had presented his ruling at the end of a particular *Din-Torah* [religious-court hearing], one of the litigants was not pleased. This man thereupon brought his case to the brilliant Rabbi Chaim Soloveitchik[4], the Rabbi of Brisk[5], who told him that the Kamenetz Rabbi was a great scholar whose ruling should be relied on.

My grandfather's home was always filled with Torah scholars, since rabbis from outside Kamenetz as well as ordinary learned laymen were constantly coming over. And thus my grandfather's children, among them my father and my Uncle Laybke, absorbed Jewish wisdom, sharp reasoning, the beauty of Jewish life, and the Torah scholarship that had been passed down for many generations.

My father and Uncle Laybke were very different from each other. My uncle was uninhibited, one "who stands before kings"[6]; he would mesmerize his listeners with rhetoric that was simultaneously beautiful and meaningful. He was always ready to do anyone a favor, never refusing to help a fellow Jew. He was the finest example of someone who interceded on behalf of the Jews. When he spoke, it was in "words that come from the heart and penetrate the heart". He was a modern Jew whom everyone was fond of. Christians who knew him also treated him with respect, and many a time he brought glory to his people.

Although he never attended high school, he spoke Russian and Polish well.

When the image of my Uncle Laybke[7] comes back to me, it seems to me that people were more admirable and more sincere in those days. Within him "Torah and greatness were combined". I had the good fortune to spend time with him during my adolescence. I often accompanied him on his walks, and every one of his words and ideas were gems, for he had "a mouth that utters pearls". He was a true religious scholar.

If my Uncle Laybke was the representative of the family, then my father was the modest, unassuming one[8], the humble one, the one whom the family referred to as "good Naphtali"[9]. He was willing to do anything for everyone, to help out even beyond what he was capable of. He was zealous about putting all his heart and soul into the things he truly believed in.

[Page 407]

At a young age he was already subscribing to *HaMelitz*[10] (which in the 1890s was a usual [sic][11] step for the son of the Town Rabbi). He was already a Zionist in his youth, and he was among the first to buy the "shekel"[12].

He was active in the Jewish community, doing much for Jewish religious education. He was one of the founders of Mizrachi, the "Mizrachi Schools of Brest Litowsk." Many times he prioritized his Zionist work and neglected his family. He was one of "those who faithfully occupy themselves with the needs of the community"[13], and in his later years he was fortunate enough to come to the Land of Israel and realize his ideological goals.

He had a dignified old age. People would gaze at this emaciated man, whose physical body, little more than skin and bones, had such a great soul within it. He was a rarity, the Last of the Mohicans of a fine generation of Jews. They lived in God's little world, these admirable people, harming no one, always seeing the best in people. They were the righteous intercessors[14] for the Jewish people, pleading only for peace. I would say he was one of the 36 righteous ones in whose merit the world exists[15].

He lived in a generation of the sword, of wars that exterminated a large fraction of the Jewish people. How much he suffered, how many troubles and torments he lived through during his long lifetime! With his own eyes he saw how a third of his people went to the crematoria to be exterminated. But he also saw the beginning of the redemption[16], and he believed that our redeeming messiah would soon be arriving. My father would also readily accept all that came his way, whether good or bad[17]. He left this world calmly and quietly, without suffering[18]. He was never a burden on anyone, not during his lifetime and not even when he was taken away from us.

Translator's Footnotes:

1. From *Kamenetz-Litovsk, Zastavije and Colonies Memorial Book*, edited by S. Eisenstadt and M. Galbert, published by the Israel and America Committee of Kamenetz Litovsk and Zastavya, (Orly, Tel Aviv, Israel, 1970), pp. 405-407.
2. For complementary essay by the same author (originally in Hebrew) see p. 49 of this volume.
3. David Tevel (1850-1930) was St. Petersburg Rabbi from 1908 to 1930. See the following link (retrieved January 2020): https://www.jewishvirtuallibrary.org/katzenellenbogen-david-tevel
4. Rabbi Chaim Soloveitchik of Brest-Litovsk (1853-1918). For a short biography, see the following link (retrieved October 2018): https://en.wikipedia.org/wiki/Chaim_Soloveitchik
5. Brisk (Jewish name for Brest-Litowsk) is a city located 40km south of Kamenetz.
6. Proverbs 22:29
7. According to p. 329 of the Necrology Section of this volume, Laybke (Arye-Leib) perished in Brest-Litovsk during the Holocaust.
8. Hebrew *nechbo al hakaylim (nechba al hakelim)* (I Sam. 10:22) = hiding behind the baggage (referring to Saul's behavior when he was first chosen as king).

9.   Naphtali was the author's father's name.

10.   *HaMelitz* was a Hebrew-language newspaper that reflected the ideology of the *Haskalah* (progressive, enlightened) movement. See the following link (retrieved January, 2020): https://en.wikipedia.org/wiki/Ha-Melitz

11.   Possibly a typographical error in the original for "unusual"

12.   The "shekel" referred to here was a symbolic banknote that was sold throughout all Jewish communities. See the following links (retrieved January 2020): https://www.jewishgen.org/yizkor/ostrow/ost298.html, http://www.jta.org/1931/05/26/archive/election-day-in-palestine-thirty-thousand-shekel-payers-electing-30-delegates-to-zionist-congress

13.   Hebrew quotation from a Sabbath blessing for those who volunteer their time to support the needs of the community or congregation.

14.   Hebrew *melitzay yosher*

15.   Based on the belief that there are perpetually 36 living Hidden Righteous Ones, unknown and often unappreciated, even though it is only in their merit that the world does not come to an end. See the following link (retrieved January 2020): https://en.wikipedia.org/wiki/Tzadikim_Nistarim

16.   Aramaic *at'chalta d'geula*, a term dating from Talmudic times (e.g. Babylonian Talmud Megilla 17b). Religious Zionists have used this term to refer to the birth of the State of Israel. See the following link (retrieved January 2020): https://en.wikipedia.org/wiki/Atchalta_De%27Geulah

17.   Yiddish: *un oif altz flegt er zogen "omayn"* = he would say "amen" to everything.

18.   Hebrew *bemiso shebineshiko* (*bemita shebineshika*) = death by a kiss (from God), a description of the easy death said to be the manner in which the righteous die.

[Page 408]

Rabbi Boruch Ber
and His Great World-Renowned Yeshiva[1]

by Rabbi Yitzchok Turetz, of Blessed Memory

Translated by Allen Flusberg

It was a great honor for Kamenetz when the town was selected as the site of a place of Torah, the world-renowned yeshiva (previously "Knesses Bais Yitzchok" of Kovno[2], then later housed in Lukishok, Vilna[3]), with its young unmarried students, its great Torah scholars, and their great rabbi, the Head of the Yeshiva, Rabbi Boruch Ber Leibovitch, of blessed memory.[4]

When he arrived in Kamenetz from Vilna-Lukishok, Rabbi Boruch Ber was given a reception with singing and orchestral music. The sound of Torah study[5] rang out day and night.

A few years before the destruction wrought by the Second World War, they built a new building to house the Great Yeshiva. All the town residents expressed great joy for being fortunate enough to have such a yeshiva in their midst.

The day on which the building was dedicated was a holiday. They carried Torah scrolls in a procession to Rabbi Boruch Ber's house and to the new building. All the windows of the houses were lit up with candles and lamps[6]; everyone flocked to the yeshiva. The doors to the houses stayed unlocked, like in the days of the pilgrimages, when everyone would rely on the verse "no one will covet your land"[7]. In addition the Jews who lived in the surrounding villages gathered around the yeshiva.

It is a sacred labor to immortalize the memory of the community in which all these great sages had taken root—generations of prodigies and righteous ones, including the last rabbi, the wise and saintly prodigy, the local rabbinical authority, Rabbi Burstein, may God avenge his blood.

Aside from the *yeshiva gedola* "Knesses Bais Yitzchok", there was also a *yeshiva ketana* and a *talmud torah*[8], headed by Rabbi Leib, who was the son-in-law of the *moreh horo'o*[9] Rabbi Shlomo Chaim Garfinkel. The community leaders Mr. Alter Liptzik-Greenblatt and Mr. Avrohom Yeshaya-Noson's Stempnitzki were in charge of materially supporting the *yeshiva ketana* and the *talmud torah*.

Kamenetz with its religious scholars, great rabbis, yeshivas and its *beis-midroshim*[10], which were always packed—what has become of it!

This was the type of Holy of Holies that Kamenetz was, with all the treasures of the Jewish people.

Translator's Footnotes:

1.   From *Kamenetz-Litovsk, Zastavije and Colonies Memorial Book*, edited by S. Eisenstadt and M. Galbert, published by the Israel and America Committee of Kamenetz Litovsk and Zastavya, (Orly, Tel Aviv, Israel, 1970), p. 408.
2.   Kovno = Kaunas, Lithuania, located 100km west of Vilnius
3.   Lukishok was originally a suburb of the city of Vilna (=Vilnius, Lithuania). Vilnius currently has a street, a square and a city park that bear the name Lukiškių. See the following link (retrieved October 2018): https://en.wikipedia.org/wiki/Luki%C5%A1k%C4%97s_Square
4.   See also a more extensive biography of Rabbi Boruch Ber that appears in this Yizkor Book: Y. Edelstein, "Rabbi Baruch Dov Leibowitz, Head of the Yeshiva of Kamenetz-Litovsk", pp. 64-68.
5.   Hebrew/Yiddish "*kol torah*"
6.   It was the eighth day of Hanukkah, 5697 (mid-December, 1936), when lit candles would be visible in every window. See L. Bobrowski-Aloni, "Yeshivat 'Knesset Beit Yitzhak'", pp. 61-63 of this Yizkor Book.
7.   Exodus 34:24, encouraging the Israelites not to be concerned about leaving their homes and possessions unguarded during the three yearly pilgrimage festivals
8.   *yeshiva gedola* = school for religious studies for older teen-agers; *yeshiva ketana* for younger boys (late elementary-school and early teens); and *talmud torah* for still younger boys (early elementary-school age). See the following link (retrieved October 2018): https://en.wikipedia.org/wiki/Yeshiva
9.   *moreh horo'o* = an expert in Jewish law who is consulted for legal decisions
10.   *Beis-midroshim*= Yiddish plural of *beis medresh*, a study hall, typically doubling as a small synagogue

[Page 409]

Rabbi Reuven Burstein, z.tz.l.[1][2]

by Ch. Z. Mendelson

Translated by Allen Flusberg

Rabbi Reuven Burstein, z.tz.l: a tall patriarchal figure with a noble face enveloped by a short, black beard with a few white hairs. His proud bearing demanded respect; even non-Jews would deferentially take their hats off as they passed him in the street. He was not only greatly learned in religious subjects—someone who was constantly sitting and studying in the religious courtroom—but also knowledgeable about secular subjects. He was beloved and esteemed by all. Even the government authorities of our town dealt with him in a dignified manner.

The rabbi and his wife, with his son and daughters

The image of how our town welcomed him as the new rabbi —after the death of our previous rabbi, the great scholar Rabbi Rabinovich—is truly unforgettable, as is the profound sermon that he delivered then, on *Shabbes Hagodol*[3]. All of the most learned and nearly all of the other townspeople had come to hear the new rabbi's first sermon; they were standing cheek to jowl. Then a sacred hush fell over the sanctuary as the rabbi, wrapped in his *talllis*[4], slowly walked up the few stairs to the Holy Ark. Leaning on his lectern, he opened his sermon with a timely *pilpul*[5] concerning the Passover regulations. He brought up contradictions from within the vast sea of Talmud and then resolved them, rendering everything consistent. Held in suspense, the audience was spellbound, hanging on every word. After he had completed his sermon, several of the finest scholars deferentially accompanied him down to his seat at the eastern wall, near the Holy Ark. And everyone wished one another *mazel tov*[6].

His household consisted of his wife, two daughters and a son. They too were treasured and beloved for their courteousness and scholarship. All of them perished in Auschwitz.

Translator's Footnotes:

1. From *Kamenetz-Litovsk, Zastavije and Colonies Memorial Book*, edited by S. Eisenstadt and M. Galbert, published by the Israel and America Committee of Kamenetz Litovsk and Zastavya, (Orly, Tel Aviv, Israel, 1970), pp. 409-410.
2. z.tz.l. = may the memory of the righteous be a blessing
3. *Shabbes Hagodol {Shabbat Hagadol)* = the Sabbath immediately preceding Passover.
4. *tallis* = prayer shawl
5. *pilpul* = a method of keen-edged analysis of Talmudic literature
6. *mazel tov* = congratulations

[Page 411]

Rabbi Shlomo Ḥaim,
Head of the Yeshiva[1]

Translated by Allen Flusberg

I experience a shiver of reverence when I recall the name Rabbi Shlomo Ḥaim[2], the Head of the Yeshiva, under whom I studied before I left to go abroad. He was a personage with an imposing appearance and many good qualities, someone for whom the only real way to be triumphant in one's life was through Torah study and good deeds. He was of medium height, a bit bent over, his face graced by a thick, black beard. I remember how unobtrusively he would enter the brick building where he lectured to us on Talmud every day. With remarkable simplicity, he would analyze and clarify the most difficult passages of the vast sea of Talmud. His voice was quiet and calm, but also clear and intelligible. He related to us students like a father. Never becoming angry, always maintaining an affectionate smile on his noble face, he would patiently explain everything that we had trouble understanding.

He was extremely modest, never trying to impress anyone with his great erudition and moral stature. Every evening he could be found sitting in a corner next to the Holy Ark, where he would study late into the night.

But his greatest virtue was the way he fulfilled the commandment of honoring his father. He behaved with remarkable love and respect for his father—a great prodigy who was the chief rabbi of Zastavya (a suburb of Kamenetz). I remember how I would always glance at them when they used to pass the *Hoif*[Szkolna Street in Kamenetz[3]] onto the crossing that connected Kamenetz and Zastavya, where I lived. He would be leading his elderly father by the hand with such love and fondness, discussing Torah matters as they walked together.

He and his household—his wife and two daughters—shared the gloomy fate of all our martyrs.

Translator's Footnotes:

1. From *Kamenetz-Litovsk, Zastavije and Colonies Memorial Book*, edited by S. Eisenstadt and M. Galbert, published by the Israel and America Committee of Kamenetz Litovsk and Zastavya, (Orly, Tel Aviv, Israel, 1970), p. 411.
2. The reference is to Rabbi Shlomo Ḥaim Garfinkel. See the following article, authored by Rabbi Yitzchok Turetz, on p. 408 of this Yizkor Book: "Rabbi Boruch Ber and his Great World-Renowned Yeshiva".
3. See article by Ben Moshe, p. 561 in this Yizkor Book, "Kamenetz in 1945".

[Pages 412-415]

Yom Kippur in Our Little Town[1]

by Ch. Z. Mendelson

Translated by Allen Flusberg

A translation of this Yiddish article appears in the English-language section of this Yizkor Book, pp. 69-72 ("The Day of Atonement in Our Town", by H. Mendelsohn [New York]).

The following figure appears on page 413 of this Yiddish article:

Holzsynagoge in Kamenez-Litowsk

The Kamenetz synagogue[2]

Translator's Footnotes:

1.   From *Kamenetz-Litovsk, Zastavije and Colonies Memorial Book*, edited by S. Eisenstadt and M. Galbert, published by the Israel and America Committee of Kamenetz Litovsk and Zastavya, (Orly, Tel Aviv, Israel, 1970), pp. 412-415.
2.   The German text just below the photograph translates as "Wood Synagogue in Kamenetz-Litowsk".

[Page 419]

Social Life in Kamenets

[Pages 419-422]

Poalei-Zion (United with Tz.S.) In Kamenetz[1]

By Chaya Krakowski-Karabelnik

Translated by Allen Flusberg

This article (in Yiddish) is essentially identical to the Hebrew article of the same title on pp. 74-76 of this volume. Any differences are mentioned in footnotes in the translation of that article.

Translator's Footnote:

1.   From *Kamenetz-Litovsk, Zastavije and Colonies Memorial Book*, edited by S. Eisenstadt and M. Galbert, published by the Israel and America Committee of Kamenetz Litovsk and Zastavya, (Orly, Tel Aviv, Israel, 1970), pp. 419-422.

[Page 429]

Memories from Kamenets Before the Destruction

Longing and Grief for the Town of My Birth[1]

by Avrohom Shudroff (New York)

Translated by Allen Flusberg

Note from translator: A translation of this Yiddish article appears in the English-language section of this Yizkor Book, pp. 43-45 ("Yearning and Mourning for My Home Town", by Abraham Shudroff).

Translator's Footnote:

1. From *Kamenetz-Litovsk, Zastavije and Colonies Memorial Book*, edited by S. Eisenstadt and M. Galbert, published by the Israel and America Committee of Kamenetz Litovsk and Zastavya, (Orly, Tel Aviv, Israel, 1970), pp. 429-430.

[Page 431]

Our *Shtetl*[1]

by Simcha Dubiner (Petah Tikva)

Translated by Allen Flusberg

My *shtetl* [little town] Kamenetz-Litowsk, whose population was mostly Jewish, bubbled with vitality. The Gentiles lived on three streets—separately from the Jews. The Jews, who were mostly shopowners and craftsmen, supported themselves from customers who lived in the nearby poor villages. The majority of the Jews in the shtetl toiled away incessantly to make a living; only a small number of them were affluent.

During my childhood, the standard places of learning in the *shtetl* were the *ḥayder* [religious school for very young boys] and the lower yeshiva [school for somewhat older boys]. If anyone wanted to give his son a more advanced education, he would send him to a higher-level yeshiva in Brisk[2], Bialystok[3] or Baranowicze[4]; the graduates of those advanced yeshivas became the intelligentsia and culturally active people of Kamenetz.

For as long as I can remember, our *shtetl* had a tradition of mutual material support. There were different types of volunteer societies that the *shtetl* relied on. Someone who was seriously ill would be visited by members of the *Bikur Ḥoilim* Society to take care of him all night. An indigent older girl who needed to celebrate her marriage—particularly if she was an orphan—was not left in the lurch; she would receive help from a *Hachnosas-Kala* Fund, created for the purpose, to provide her with a wedding.

I cannot forget the days of Sabbath Eve in our little Kamenetz. The Sabbath-Eve atmosphere used to begin by Thursday. The housewives would go shopping to buy strings of fish from the Gentiles. To honor the Sabbath, each woman would get the very best she could afford.

Friday mornings they would bake dough with grated potatoes; and many homes would open their doors to yeshiva students, offering them a portion of dough and sour cream that would revitalize them.

[Page 432]

The diligent housewives would be preparing all kinds of Sabbath dishes, tastefully cooked; and sweet fragrances of the cooking food would waft through the air.

The homes were cleaned and spruced up. The children were washed and combed with motherly charm, all in honor of the Sabbath.

During the Friday afternoon hours, the sweet sound of little boys chanting rang out in the Sabbath-Eve silence. Each boy would be going over the weekly Torah portion, as well as the page of Talmud that he had learned that week—all out loud.

Jews were winding down their work, about to leave it behind. The weekday noise was subsiding, the shops were being closed, and the town square was clearing out. An atmosphere of spirituality was taking hold in the *shtetl*, from one end to another. A *neshomo yesayro*[5] [additional soul] was awakening in everyone, whether young or old.

And then—along all the streets and lanes, Jews were slowly walking to the synagogue. As each person entered the synagogue, his eyes would be dazzled by the figure of the town rabbi, Rabbi Reuven Burstein, of blessed memory, with his luminous, stately appearance. Soon the soft, rhythmic sounds of heartfelt prayers were carried throughout the town on the evening air.

And afterwards Jewish families, whether large or small, were gathering in their well-lit homes around tables that had been set for the occasion, joined in camaraderie with their invited guests, the yeshiva students and others in need of a meal.

After the Friday-evening meal, the older people would relax, perhaps perusing religious books; and the young people would go out to take walks and have a good time carrying on; others would spend the time conversing about public matters. Those who belonged to political parties would gather in groups, while others would get together at the library and devote themselves to reading books or newspapers. And later at night many of us would go over to Zelig the bookbinder[6], who used to take us outside, into the open air, and give talks on astronomy as he pointed to the stars above. Other times he would passionately tell us the latest news from the Land of Israel—something that would revitalize us and intensify our longing.

That is what Friday nights were like in Kamenetz.

[Page 433]

Right after the rise of Polish independence, the economic situation in Kamenetz, just as in the other poor little towns, took a turn for the worse. And when the time of Grabski[7] came—when we Jews practically lost our ability to make a living from *luft parnosos* [trading in intangibles]—at that time, from among all the parties that were active in our town, the *HeHalutz* organization split up. Meanwhile, the dozens of unemployed young men no longer wanted to, nor were able to, tolerate the hardships they were experiencing and the angry looks their non-Jewish neighbors were giving them. And so they began to prepare themselves to immigrate to the Land of Israel. Soon a *hachshara* [training] program was established, and the Jewish youth took up learning to become productive laborers. Some of them taught themselves farm work, while others were sent to work in sawmills and other such places outside Kamenetz.

It was not only through physical labor that the Jewish youth of Kamenetz were preparing themselves to immigrate—they were adapting themselves mentally and intellectually, as well. They were studying the Hebrew language diligently; and they were familiarizing themselves with the geography, history and literature of the Land of Israel. These young people were now walking around with earnest and dreamy looks on their faces, constantly absorbed in the books they were reading. They were being influenced by Yehuda HaLevi, Bialik, Ahad Haam and other Hebrew authors.

Translator's Footnotes:

1. From *Kamenetz-Litovsk, Zastavije and Colonies Memorial Book*, edited by S. Eisenstadt and M. Galbert, published by the Israel and America Committee of Kamenetz Litovsk and Zastavya, (Orly, Tel Aviv, Israel, 1970), pp. 431-433.
2. Brisk = Brest-Litowsk, Belarus is located 40km south of Kamenetz
3. Białystok, Poland is located 100km northwest of Kamenetz
4. Baranowicze = Baranovichi, Belarus, located 200km northeast of Kamenetz
5. *neshomo yesayro [neshama yetera]* = "additional soul" that provides the proper Sabbath spirituality, said metaphorically to enter a Jew's body at the onset of the Sabbath
6. See pp. 127-129 in this volume, "Zelig the Bookbinder", by P. Ravid.
7. Władysław Grabski (1874-1938), prime minister of Poland 1923-25. He instituted a drastic currency reform that led to a tariff war with Germany. See the following link (retrieved February 2021): Władysław Grabski - Wikipedia

[Pages 435-443]

Kamenetz—As I Remember You[1]

by Dvora Dolinski-Panski, New York

Translated by Allen Flusberg

Who will remember Father's sigh
Who will remember Mother's last moan!
(from the poem *Mir Kumen Um* [We Are Perishing] by Chava Rosenfarb[2], Lodz)

Note from translator: The above poem introduced the Yiddish article beginning on p. 435, but was not translated in the English section. The remainder of this article appears in English translation on pp. 46-55 of the English section of this Yizkor Book. One uncaptioned photograph that appears on p. 436 is reproduced here, together with the translation of the paragraphs preceding it and following it to provide context for it; the translation of those paragraphs has been copied directly from the English section.

I find in my memory materials for a family chronicle, memoirs and in the main, recollections of a little town that was alive, a townlet with its images and human types. I remember bright and shady figures, a gallery of portraits of tailors, cobblers, smiths and other craftsmen; religious teachers, school teachers, cantors; the water-carrier, the bath-house 'attendant, the beadle. A popular saying, which stated that "every town has its madman" applied also to Kamenetz. We had our Alterke though it must be said that he was not completely crazy. In other words, he was harmless to the inhabitants of the town. Alterke was short, skinny and his face deathly pale; his eyes were dull; he always wore a stained, sweaty cap and a long coat; he used to hang out near the municipality building where he swept the rooms. He also performed another function in the town: whenever a circumcision ceremony took place he had to set the pillow on which the boy rested.

Each one of these types and figures had his own specific charm; each one of them cherished the traditional folklore and possessed hidden talents. There were religious Jews, though some of them had been tinged by the "Has kala" (Enlightenment) movement and were also partly interested in worldly affairs. And there were free-thinkers who derived their pleasure from reading the works of modern Jewish authors and dreamed about better days to come. Kamenetz was just one of the many towns and townlets spread all over White Russia and Poland where the majority of the Jewish population lived in hard and painful conditions; it embodied, in miniature, the whole Jewish national existence with all its shades – from the extreme right to the extreme left. Tradition and a profound Jewish religious feeling reigned supremely at home and in the sphere of social life. The synagogue was a meeting place for young and old. All problems, including the political, were solved there. On the other hand, it is a fact that the strict and fanatical adherence to tradition brought in its wake some petrifaction of Jewish life. In spite of it, Kamenetz was not an ignorant town belonging to the dark ages but adjusted itself to the modern world. There were parties and circles striving toward other aims; they had their own vision of a better future for the Jewish people and the working masses. All this added color and warmth to our existence.

Translator's Footnotes:

> 1.   From *Kamenetz-Litovsk, Zastavije and Colonies Memorial Book*, edited by S. Eisenstadt and M. Galbert, published by the Israel and America Committee of Kamenetz Litovsk and Zastavya, (Orly, Tel Aviv, Israel, 1970), pp. 435-443. See also p. 332 of the Necrology section of this volume.
> 2.   Chava Rosenfarb (1923-2011), who emigrated to Canada after surviving the Lodz Ghetto, Auschwitz and Bergen-Belsen, wrote many poems describing her experiences. See the following link (retrieved February, 2020): https://en.wikipedia.org/wiki/Chava_Rosenfarb

[Page 444]

My Little Shtetl Kamenetz-Litowsk[1]

by Malka Kurtchanski-Polyakevitch

Translated by Allen Flusberg

I was born and grew up in Kamenetz, located 25 kilometers away from the train station Zhabinka[2]. As small as this *shtetle* [little *shtetl*] was, it had an even tinier suburb, Zastavya, connected to Kamenetz proper by a wooden bridge. The entire *shtetl* and its suburb were enveloped by meadows, fields, woods and gardens. And that bridge brings back a memory of the early days of my youth, when on moonlit nights (this was before electric lighting came to the town) the young people would congregate on the bridge, enjoying each other's company as the panoramic views beckoned and teased.

The rows of shops around the town square met all the vital needs of the peasant farmers who lived in the surrounding villages. These farmers came once a month, with their horse-drawn wagons carrying all their village produce; and from this trade the *shtetl* drew its living.

The *shtetl* was able to support *bays-medroshim*[3], as well as a yeshiva where young bachelors, both local and outsiders, studied. Wagon-drivers also spent time studying there late into the night. Everyone helped support the students who were outsiders by taking turns providing them with meals on a fixed weekly schedule[4].

There were no schools in the *shtetl* except for a *narodnaya uczylieszcze* (state school), where Jews were not permitted to study. Nonetheless the young people were culturally advanced, and we had a library of Yiddish, Hebrew and Russian books. People would study languages privately with tutors who came from other towns. The parents, especially mothers, strenuously saw to it that their children also learned the national language.

When I was very young the *Haskala*[5] movement arrived and spread through the town, arousing nostalgic feelings for the Land of Israel. And so we studied modern Hebrew, as well, with private tutors.

[Page 445]

Then in 1914 the First World War broke out. The Germans occupied our area for almost a full three years. The local population that had fled began returning to their homes. During the state of war the situation was oppressive. Everything was suppressed. Ill children were roaming around aimlessly in the streets, hungry and filthy. When packages sent by the JOINT[6] began arriving this situation eased up somewhat. The Germans, working with the Jewish community, decided to open a school, where the children could spend several hours a day under the supervision of the teachers-educators. There they were taught Yiddish, Hebrew and German.

Translator's Footnotes:

1. From *Kamenetz-Litovsk, Zastavije and Colonies Memorial Book*, edited by S. Eisenstadt and M. Galbert, published by the Israel and America Committee of Kamenetz Litovsk and Zastavya, (Orly, Tel Aviv, Israel, 1970), pp. 444-445.
2. Zhabinka (or Žabinka) is southeast of Kamenetz
3. *Bays-medroshim* is the plural of *bays-medresh* = house of study, where men study Talmud and hold prayer services
4. Yiddish *teg* = days. From one weekday to the next each student went from one participating home to another for meals, according to a weekly schedule.
5. *Haskala* = enlightened (progressive, modernization)
6. JOINT = American Jewish Joint Distribution Committee. See the following link (retrieved July, 2015): https://en.wikipedia.org/wiki/American_Jewish_Joint_Distribution_Committee.

[Page 446]

Once Upon a Time in My Shtetl Kamenetz[1]

by Sarah Hurwitz

Translated by Allen Flusberg

I remember how the Jews lived a quiet, sheltered life there so many years ago. I can still recall the Friday evenings with the Sabbath candles that had been lit at the proper time in the Jewish homes, and the Jews hurrying so as not to be late for *Kabbolas Shabbes* [the service to welcome the Sabbath]. Through the doors and windows of the Houses of Study one could hear them singing *Lechu Neranena* and *Lecha Dodi*[2]. Everyone felt transformed by the Sabbath spirit: all the worries and concerns were gone, since it was forbidden to talk about business matters on the Sabbath.

Most of our *landsleit*[3] were shopkeepers, as well as laborers and merchants, whether on a small or large scale. I remember how we had a fair on the fifth of every month. Merchants from other towns would arrive to buy and sell horses, cows, etc. They would bring along various merchandise to sell: the *Pruzhin antshares* brought hand-made clay pots, which were displayed near the shops; the used-clothing dealers brought garments; the blacksmiths brought carts; the furriers brought their Gentile-style fur caps; and various other merchandise, as well. Blind beggars would be sitting around between the shops, on their knees, singing and begging the passersby to throw a few pennies into their caps.

Aside from the fair we had a market day every Thursday. On this day the village peasants would bring various products to the town to sell: dried-out sponges, grains, potatoes, wood, young calves, geese, ducks, blackberries from the forest, sheep's wool, linen that had been fashioned by hand from hand-planted flax, pig-hair bristles, all kinds of fruits and many other products. After taking payment for their merchandise, they would use the money to buy items from the shopkeepers, who would make their living selling to them. Most of the peasants would then go into the taverns and spend all of their money on liquor. After that they would arrive inebriated in the store to get a pound of sugar and a small bottle of oil on credit, and then go home to their village.

[Page 447]

It was interesting that the Gentiles knew the timetable of Jewish holidays.[4] On the eve of Yom Kippur they would bring chickens to the town to sell for *Kappores*[5]; on the eve of *Sukkes*[6] they would bring wagons of *s'chach*[7] to cover the *sukka*[8]; and on the eve of *Hoshanna Rabba*[9] they would bring *hoshanes*[10].

In the freezing weather and blizzards of winter, when the peasants could not set out on the roads to town, we shopkeepers would not have any sales nor anything to do. Instead we used to get together to hear the latest news: had the car already arrived from Zhabinka[11] or from Brisk[12], and what news they had brought. Much later, when I was already in America, we heard that Kamenetz now had sidewalks and electricity.

The peasants trusted us; they used to ask us for remedies for the ill. The women peasants who had husbands in America or sons serving in the army would have us write letters for them in Russian, and in return they would bring us valuable gifts.

The shopkeepers had to endure indescribable misery from *uriadniks*[13] and from the *strazhnikes*[14]. When we saw them coming from far away, we signaled to each other that a "button" was coming ([referring to] the brass buttons). They would give us a ticket, with a fine of several rubles, for any minor infraction.

The shops were closed all day on Sundays. When the Gentiles came out of church and wanted to purchase something, we would go into the shop to bring the merchandise out. We would arrange for the door of the shop to be locked from the outside by a neighbor while we were inside. Once a *strazhnik* observed someone being locked up inside a shop, and he didn't let the shopkeeper out of there all day; but then two peasants got into a fight, and when the *strazhnik* went away to impose order, the shopkeeper hurriedly left his store.

When the license inspector arrived in Kamenetz, a panic ensued. Every storeowner ran out of his shop, as if from a fire, carrying with him the small amount of merchandise he had. None of the shopkeepers actually knew what his license allowed him to be selling. And so we cleared the shelves off so well that the inspector would nearly faint when he had a look.

Even the schoolteachers were required to have licenses, and they would abandon the *cheder*[15] until the inspector left.

[Page 448]

Just as suddenly the excise-tax collector would show up, and he would search the taverns and the snuff stores to find anyone with merchandise that was missing excise bands. He frightened all the shopkeepers; for who among them was completely aboveboard?

The young people had a place to go, with a library, where they could have a pleasant time. Although the town was quite small, the majority were educated and intelligent.

*

The First World War broke out. All the young men of Kamenetz were mobilized, bachelors and married men, and they were immediately sent to the front. Those who had horses rode on them, drafted into forced labor. Many of them never came back, probably starving to death there. They left behind widows, *agunes*[16] and orphans. The town stopped getting mail and the telegraph lines were down. Then there was shooting, and bullets whizzed over our heads; when the shooting stopped the Germans entered our town. By then we did not have enough food to give our children, and we were living in a perpetual state of fear for what the morrow might bring. By 6 PM every day we were all afraid to even go outside into the street. When someone was seized for forced labor, he would believe his life was over. There was a German named Putermann that everyone was afraid of, like fire. Whoever had a hidden stash of potatoes or some food supplies in his house or cellar was considered the wealthiest person. Several shopkeepers buried some salt, soap or sugar in pits. With great trepidation they used to trade it to the village Gentiles for a little food.

The Germans took every family out of their house for disinfection and also brought them to bathe in the bathhouses. At that time typhus and cholera were going around and spreading. People were dropping like flies. During the epidemic a young couple also perished on the very same day: Moshe and Esther Shedrowitzki (parents of Avrohom Shudroff), who left behind 5 little children, all boys, ranging in age from 2 to 10.

The provisions that had been depleted during the war returned little by little.

[Page 449]

After that Kamenetz endured another war. The Polish police arrived, and again men were being rounded up for forced labor. Everyone was seized with fear, as there was nowhere to hide: they were searching even the attics and the cellars. We had gone from one war to another. The arriving soldiers, Russian, Polish and others, cleaned everything out. People were afraid to go out into the street. Money no longer had any value. First there was the Kerensky[17] currency notes and afterwards zlotys. When America opened its doors and everyone began emigrating, American dollars started coming in: and from America they sent packages of clothing and food to Yosef Vigutov, of blessed memory, to distribute to the poor. The majority of the people were barefoot and without clothing; their feet were swollen from hunger. The young women and adolescent girls were wearing Gentile *andrakas* [andaraks, peasant skirts] with wooden shoes.

Translator's Footnotes:

1. From *Kamenetz-Litovsk, Zastavije and Colonies Memorial Book*, edited by S. Eisenstadt and M. Galbert, published by the Israel and America Committee of Kamenetz Litovsk and Zastavya, (Orly, Tel Aviv, Israel, 1970), pp. 446-449.
2. These are chanted or sung during the *Kabbolas Shabbes* or *Kabbalat Shabbat* (=Sabbath Welcoming) synagogue service.
3. *landsleit* = people originating from the same area
4. Since the Jewish calendar is lunar, the holidays shift around on the solar calendar by as much as 3 weeks from year to year.
5. *Kappores* (Hebrew: *Kapparot* = atonements), a ritual carried out on the day before Yom Kippur (Day of Atonement), in which each Jew would wave a purchased live chicken around his head, reciting "…may this chicken be my atonement (*kapporos*)…." Males waved

a rooster, while females waved a hen. The chicken would be slaughtered, and either the meat or its monetary value given to charity. Since the middle of the 20th century the ritual has in many circles been carried out by waving money, rather than a chicken. See the following link (retrieved November, 2019): https://www.chabad.org/holidays/JewishNewYear/template_cdo/aid/989585/jewish/Kaparot.htm

6.   *Sukkes* (Hebrew *Sukkot* = Tabernacles), seven-day autumnal holiday on which booths are erected as temporary dwellings in which meals are eaten.

7.   *s'chach* = plant materials used to thatch booths on Tabernacles holiday (see previous footnote)

8.   *sukka* = tabernacle or booth

9.   *Hoshanna Rabba* = seventh day of Tabernacles holiday

10.   *hoshannes* (Hebrew *hoshanot* = willow branches used ritually on *Hoshanna Rabba*)

11.   Zhabinka (or *Žabinka*) is located 30km southeast of Kamenetz. The nearest train station to Kamenetz was located there. See article by D. Shmida, "Journey to the Past", p. 203 of this volume.

12.   Brisk (Jewish name for Brest-Litowsk) is a city located 40km south of Kamenetz.

13.   *uriadniks* = government officials (Ukrainian)

14.   *strazhnikes* = security guards (Ukrainian, Polish), law-enforcers

15.   *cheder* = religious school for small children

16.   *agunes* = "fettered" wives (Hebrew *agunot*) whose husbands have disappeared; according to Jewish law they may not remarry without evidence that their husbands are dead.

17.   In 1917, between the abdication of the Czar and the Bolshevik Revolution, Kerensky headed a short-lived moderate socialist Russian government that issued new currency. See the following link (retrieved November 2019): https://en.wikipedia.org/wiki/Alexander_Kerensky

[Page 450]

The *Szkola Powszechna* [Polish Public School][1]

by Chaya Gurvitz-Goldberg (New York)

Translated by Allen Flusberg

The first and only general Polish school in Kamenetz after Polish sovereignty was instituted consisted of 7 grades.

During the first few years of its existence the school did not have the most essential sanitary facilities available, not even drinking water. For this reason we had to go to the neighbors of the *Hoif*[2] during recess. All the Jews of the area exhibited a great deal of patience and kindness. Mostly we utilized the generosity of the family Chaim Polyakevitch, who lived near the school.

Whoever wanted to continue studying Polish after completing the seven *Powszechna* grades would have to move to one of the larger cities. For economic reasons very few could manage this.

The teaching staff consisted of Christian teachers only; the relationship between the students and teachers was always strained, a mixture of respect and fear. There was no shortage of a feeling of anti-Semitism.

Since the last scheduled session was set aside for the subject "religion", we were fortunate enough to have a Jewish teacher in the school once a week, Rivka Gevirtzman (a sister of Yitzchok Gevirtzman). For a while she was also my private Hebrew tutor, and she was the first to acquaint us with modern Hebrew.

[Page 451]

At this opportunity I would like to cite a statement that I am extracting from my graduation album. Written by a Kamenetz intellectual, Binyomin Bogatin (the brother of Chana Bogatin), it ends with the following words: "…and a longing for all that is gone and will never be again." A sort of prophecy that has become a frightening reality, though at the time it was not meant that way; and certainly the destruction was not foreseen, a destruction that lay in wait for those near and dear to us in the tranquil and modest little town of Kamenetz.

Translator's Footnotes:

1.   From *Kamenetz-Litovsk, Zastavije and Colonies Memorial Book*, edited by S. Eisenstadt and M. Galbert, published by the Israel and America Committee of Kamenetz Litovsk and Zastavya, (Orly, Tel Aviv, Israel, 1970), pp. 450-451. *Szkola* = School (Polish). *Powszechna* = universal or common (Polish).

2.   "The Hoif" was the Jewish name for the street that the school was on. See the following article: Ben-Moshe, "Kamenetz in 1945", pp. 561-568 of this volume.

[Page 452]

Years of My Youth in Kamenetz-Litowsk[1]

By Hatzkel Kagan

Translated by Allen Flusberg

Note from translator: This Yiddish article is identical with an English version, with the same title and by the same author, appearing on pp. 73-84 of the English section of this Yizkor Book. The following three photographs were in the Yiddish version:

[Page 453]

Members of the Town Council of Kamenetz

[Page 458]

The first bus that changed the way people traveled
Right to left: the proprietors Mendel Reznik and Asher Stempnitzki; and their driver

[Page 460]

A yerid [fair] day in Kamenetz

Translator's Footnote:

1.   From *Kamenetz-Litovsk, Zastavije and Colonies Memorial Book*, edited by S. Eisenstadt and M. Galbert, published by the Israel and America Committee of Kamenetz Litovsk and Zastavya, (Orly, Tel Aviv, Israel, 1970), pp. 452-461.

[Page 462]

The *Revisor* [Auditor][1]

by F. Zolf[2], of Blessed Memory

Translated by Allen Flusberg

Falek Zolf, who was born September 18, 1896 in Zastavya, founded the first Yiddish folkschul [public school] there. In 1927 he immigrated to Canada, and became a teacher in the Winnipeg folkschule [Yiddish school]. He was also active as a Yiddish writer. In his books, "Oif Fremder Erd" [On Foreign Soil] (Premiered by YIVO, (1945)), and "Die Letste Fun A Dor" [Last of a Generation] (1952), he describes characters and personalities from the destroyed little towns of Poland and Lithuania. He also published a book on Jewish writers (1946), as well as a play for children that was performed in Jewish schools of America and Canada.[3]

Every summer, as soon as the muddy roads that led to our little town dried up, and all nature bloomed and grew, flooded with golden rays of the sun—it was then that my parents began to be fearful of the Russian Czar. As soon as we heard from afar the faintest sound of a jingling bell—which indicated that a notable was riding nearby, a Russian *natchalnik* [official]—at that point my father would turn white as a sheet, and every hair of his thick blond beard would begin to quiver. Right away he would dismiss the *chayder* [boys' religious school]; the students would scatter in all directions, like a flock of frightened birds. My mother would be standing at the chimney, holding her wooden cooking spoon, frozen in place with anxiety, unable to move a muscle. Until—with God's help—the *natchalnik* passed by peacefully, and the sound of the jingling bell died away; only then did they recover.

[Page 463]

It was the revisor [auditor] that they were so afraid of. Every single year he would come down from the provincial capital, or "all the way from St. Petersburg", to demand from my father "the three-hundred-ruble penalty" for not delivering his eldest son, Layzer, to military conscription. And when his second son, Moishe-Ber, also thumbed his nose at the Russian Czar, making a run for it all the way to America—then my father's debt to the *kazna* [royal treasury] increased to a sum of around six hundred rubles[4]. At that point the Czar became quite insistent on demanding this large payment from my father the *melamed* [schoolteacher].

The author, Falek Zolf, of blessed memory

So when lovely summer came around, you could count on it—that one day the assessor, or the auditor, would suddenly come by, and would inventory all our household possessions: the bedding, the inherited copper pans, the brass candlesticks, the mortar-and-pestle, and all the other items…so as soon as people heard that a "button" was coming from the big city, everyone was seized with fear, there being a large number of such "debts owed the Czar" in our little town. Only when, with God's help, the lovely summer faded away, and the cool, wet autumn came along with its rains, inundating all the byways and trails with a thick, sticky mud—only then did my parents sigh with relief; then we little children could also sleep securely, with our heads on our mother's pillow.

[Page 464]

But it was not only on account of the deep, sticky mud that my father's meager, hard-earned belongings were rescued from falling into Gentile hands: for the most part we could thank the town's Jewish *tchlen* (member) of the *meshtchonsker uprave* (tribunal), Yudl Kotik. He was a scion of the well-known Kotik family of Kamenetz, which had high-handedly held sway over the entire town for many generations. The *korobka* [box] was always in their hands, the taxes and other state revenues. Whatever they said had to be taken into account, and so for that reason people in Kamenetz referred to them as "the Czar's *gvordia* [guards]" (see Yechezkel Kotik, "My Memories").

Yudl Kotik was also—like his grandfather and great-grandfather before him, who were the *naborshchtikes*, the *parnosim* [community leaders]—well-connected with the Russian *natshalstude* [authorities]. With several of them he was a close friend. Every *natchalnik*, every important person who came from the district or from the government on government business, first stopped off for a visit to Yudl Kotik's home, which was located at the very center of the market square. This particular house took on the character of a Russian salon. Often the important people of the town would gather there, the Russian intelligentsia, such as: the Russian priest, the Jewish doctor, the Polish apothecary, the police chief, the postmaster, the *sudya* (judge), as well as others. They would play cards and chess; they would drink whiskey and wine, as well as tea from the large samovar—followed by tasty Jewish dishes, which Yudl's wife, Matke, the renowned *ayshes chayil* [active, resourceful wife], had prepared for them in advance for the occasion. Yudl Kotik's children were also the first in the town to attend the Brisk gymnasia [high school]; they wore uniforms with silver buttons, spoke Russian and whistled Russian melodies. So whatever the issue was—whether it was trouble for the community, or a personal disaster, or a government decree—people ran to Kotik, the intercessor, to ask him to write a "petition to the Czar". When a ruling against a Jew was passed, a "protocol"—they would run to Kotik as well. In some cases he would hear people out in a dignified manner, with esteem, as if he himself was actually the governor.

[Page 465]

So this Yudl Kotik—like a person of great wealth, who philanthropically supports certain community institutions—took it upon himself to protect my father's meager belongings—to keep them from falling into the Czar's hands. As soon as he would sense that a revisor was coming to town to demand "the three hundred rubles" from the Jews, he would immediately send a special messenger over to Zastavya to tell us to "clear out the *chometz*"[5] as soon as possible.

Right away our entire home would undergo a commotion, an upheaval. My father's older students and neighbors who had come running over were grabbing things—one a quilt, another a pillow, a third a kneading trough, a fourth a set of books—and taking them away to their own houses. The only things they left behind were: the large table with the big flaps hanging from it; the teetering wooden bed, one of whose legs was held up by a block of wood; and the sleeper benches, stuffed with bags of straw, known as "*senikes*". After such a "*chometz* inspection", our tiny little apartment looked like it had just been ransacked, undergone a pogrom…And to give the picture a realistic, finishing touch, our father would take a religious book in hand, sit down at the table, and make it look like he was studying it. My mother would grab a pot and pluck feathers; and as for us little children, she would hand us hard pieces of bread, which we then chewed with particular relish…

With Yudl Kotik accompanying him, the revisor would appear, with his thick briefcase under his arm; he was quite certain that he was about to enrich the royal Russian treasury. But as soon as he observed the extent of our father's poverty, which now lay before him naked and uncovered, he would remain standing at the threshold, afraid to step in any further…and in order to fulfil his obligation to the Czar, he would ask my father:

"How do you support yourself and your *semeistava* (household)?"

"From a city allowance," my father would answer without raising his head up.

"And where are your sons?"

"I don't know, scattered about somewhere in the world, seeking food…," my father would reply with a deep sigh.

Yudl Kotik, who by nature was a jokester—and who, in addition, was now quite pleased that his trick on the Russian revisor was working so well—would on his part add the following:

"Certainly, for such an *utchani Yevdeii* [learned Jew], which is what this Srul Zholf is, it would be a great act of rectitude if his Royal Highness the Czar would provide him with a few rubles for the Sabbath…"

[Page 466]

The revisor would sit down on a small stool, and tell a couple of respectable homeowners to write down that—as for the abovementioned Srul Zholf—he regretfully did not find anything of value in his home, since he is—forgive the expression—a full-fledged pauper[6]. And therefore he [the revisor] is now compelled to go away empty-handed…And so it went, year in and year out.

But as soon as my father became the owner of his own property, a cottage my mother inherited—which was moved into town from the village of Luskele—the following question came up: what will happen now? If, God forbid, the Czar in St. Petersburg finds out that my father has suddenly come up in the world and now has a house of his own, will he come and take it away? All right, when it comes to movable objects—the few items he had in his household—you can, as always, find a way out. But when it comes to a house, you can't stash it away with a neighbor!

After a long deliberation with my mother, my father ran off to R.[7] Meir Pasternak, a very respectable householder of the town—so respectable that more than one house was registered in his name. My father set up a *kinyan* [property transfer agreement] with him, stating that this house also belongs to him [Pasternak]. And so as soon as the revisor came around to my father, a panting R. Meir Pasternak came running over with the *kuptche* (sales agreement) in his hand, in which it was written explicitly in black on white, and signed by witnesses, that this particular house is his *imushtchestva*, his own property—and as an indication, he was paying even the *nalogen*, the taxes, on this property; so that my father was nothing more than his *bidner kamernik*, his tenant…

Then one time an incident took place, one that for years afterwards people were talking about in the town of Kamenetz and in the village of Zastavya—incidentally heaping unending praise on Yudl Kotik's wisdom and his sharp mind. The incident was as follows:

Suddenly, one bright summer day, a revisor arrived in Kamenetz, one who was completely different from all the previous revisors. He was still a young pup with a pair of thin, blond, moustaches—the son of a wealthy, corpulent villager. He had graduated from a Russian school, but did not succeed in becoming a *tchinovnik* [functionary]. With great gratitude to his Czar the Father, who did him so great a kindness [appointing him as revisor], he took it upon himself to serve him body and soul. So now on his first mission he wanted to show that—never mind that all the previous revisors who came before him had furnished reports stating that my father "Srul Zholf" is, may it not befall us, a true *bednyak* [pauper], who does not possess even a broken clay vessel of his own—he was actually going to manage to collect from him, in one fell swoop, the entire six hundred rubles, to make up for those two absconded sons of his who had avoided military service.

[Page 467]

He had come to our town after having made this decision, but he was careful not to tell anyone; he was afraid that the town's *khitry Zhides* [crafty Jews] might somehow pull a fast one. It was almost as if he had a premonition of what was going to happen…

By mistake he wound up staying in a poor inn. He went about gloomily, angrily—not speaking to anyone at all. From time to time he took a quick walk through the streets, around the town market square, and past the shops. He was looking around, searching—probing with those bitter, angry eyes that cast a pall of terror on everyone.

And as much as the clever, crafty Yudl Kotik utilized every novel method under the sun to extract the revisor's secret—why he had come here—he did not succeed. More than once he tried to hint to him, that, just the opposite, may the esteemed gentleman say what it is he desires, what is going on with his staying over in the town—that he, as a member of the town tribunal, can meet him halfway, help him out with all that he needs, as he has always done with all the revisors who came before him…But none of it did any good: the Gentile remained obstinate, like a young horse the first time it is hitched to a wagon.

Meanwhile, within town, people were now panicking: who knows what sort of troubles this non-Jew[8], may his name be blotted out, will bring upon the town? This is what the Jewish shopkeepers and tavernkeepers were whispering to one another.

Right away some of them began to get rid of their *treifene s'choira* [illicit merchandise]: one his packets of cheap tobacco with no license labels; a second his flasks of *kvass* and whiskey; a third the packages of matches and similar types of goods that Jews used to make their living from. Schoolteachers, who according to the law also had to have licenses, dismissed the *chayders* [schools]. Jews didn't know if they were coming or going[9]. They were frightened by every rustling sound, scared of their own shadows. Everywhere clusters of people were standing around whispering, while others listened attentively, hanging on every word. They were giving each other advice—how to outsmart this particular new revisor, the *melech chodosh* [new king][10]...

The town was quaking. Some people were loitering around the inn the revisor was staying at. They were spying, probing—perhaps they would find something out over there...For surely this gentleman was not going to be able to stay here another day while the town still didn't know what he was up to and what he wanted...And hours and days were passing—lasting, it seemed, as long as the Jewish exile had endured...

[Page 468]

But then, completely unexpectedly, the deliverance finally came. It was during dusk, between the *mincha* [afternoon] and *maariv* [evening] prayer services, when the shepherds were already leading their flocks back from pasture. The *adon hakol* [His Eminence] suddenly sent for Yudl Kotik, asking him to go for a stroll with him "to the bridge"—the most beautiful walk through the town. Yudl Kotik was very pleased with this invitation. Understandably, it gave him great pleasure that finally the young, angry gentleman was, after all, coming to him—the influential man of the town.

And when the town saw that these two great men—on one side, Kotik the Jew, with his cane in his hand and his fat cigar in his mouth; and on the other side, the Gentile *natchalnik* with the thick briefcase under his arm—had set out for a walk, they all breathed a sigh of relief. They realized this was a sign that everything, God willing, was about to resolve itself for the good...

And so the two of them were ambling along, with measured steps, following the path that led to the suburb of Zastavya[11]. As they got to the bridge, the revisor began to reveal his secret, that he now intended to go to "Zamosty" [Zastavya], to the "*Yevrei* [Jew] Srul Zholf", for an inventory...

When Yudl Kotik heard this, the poor man became very upset—he hadn't counted on something like this happening. But what should he do now? He couldn't leave the revisor there and run over to the schoolteacher, Yisroel Luskeler, to tell him that they were about to make an inventory of his ragged bedding! It didn't bother him so much that a misfortune was about to befall a poor Jew; but rather, more importantly, he was concerned that his entire reputation as the protector of his little Jews was now completely at stake...

[Page 469]

But all at once—like a miracle from Heaven—Shaya the carpenter, with his stork-like long legs, came hurrying by. He had his tool bag slung over his shoulder and his little saw and plane in his hand; he was on his way home to Zastavya, after working in town. An idea suddenly occurred to Yudl Kotik. He very humbly begged pardon of his exalted guest, with whom he was walking, that he was about to leave him alone for a moment; and with rapid strides he caught up with Shaya the carpenter. Grabbing him by his coat, he began to shake him angrily, yelling at him, half in Yiddish and half in the Holy Tongue [Hebrew]:

"Hey, you rascal! You are not too *choileh* [ill] to take your *raglayim* [legs] with your shoulders and *moidiya zein* [inform] the *Yehudi* [Jew], the *gemora melamed* [Talmud teacher], that right now the *adon hakol* is coming over to inspect for *chometz*! Remember, if you don't do it, I'll have you thrown into *chad-gadya* [jail]!

Although he was not so sharp, Shaya the carpenter quickly understood what was expected of him. In his fright, he tried to mumble something, but then right away he took off running.

And when the revisor asked Yudl Kotik what he had been shouting at the Jewish workman, the clever Yudl Kotik quickly, on the spot, came up with an explanation that went as follows:

"A while back," he said, "I hired him to come by and raise the *uprave* (magistrate) balcony, but he hasn't shown up. And, in addition, he owes a considerable amount of *nalogen* (tax), so I wanted him to pay it off with his labor. He's been hiding out from me. Now I've caught him, so I gave him a piece of my mind, that *paskudnyak* [rascal]!"

Meanwhile the carpenter Shaya was walking fast, and whoever he happened to meet along the way he instructed to run as fast as possible to let our family know. Each of these messengers ran ahead of the other; and immediately my father came running from the *Bays-Medresh* [House of Study][12] with a bunch of young men, drafted for the occasion. Quickly they grabbed all of our meager household furnishings and carried them off to our neighbors. Before long, almost nothing was left in our little house but four empty walls.

[Page 470]

And so the new young, proud revisor—who was so haughty and so certain that this time he would surely succeed in coming up with my father's real *motnya* [assets]—wound up, poor soul, leaving empty-handed.

For a long time Kamenetz, Zastavya and other nearby little towns laughed and joked about how the clever, sharp-witted member of the tribunal, Yudl Kotik, had led the new, proud revisor down the garden path.

Translator's Footnotes:

1. From *Kamenetz-Litovsk, Zastavije and Colonies Memorial Book*, edited by S. Eisenstadt and M. Galbert, published by the Israel and America Committee of Kamenetz Litovsk and Zastavya, (Orly, Tel Aviv, Israel, 1970), pp. 462-470. Footnote at end of this article reads: "From F. Zolf's book *Zichroinos* [Memoirs]".
2. The name is spelled "Zalf" rather than "Zolf" in the original Yiddish of this article, possibly a printer's error. The correct spelling appears to be "Zolf". See for example the following link (retrieved July 2020): http://yleksikon.blogspot.com/2016/07/falik-zolf.html. See also the Hebrew biography/obituary in the article by Z. Saperstein on pp. 119-120 of this volume, "Falek Zolf, of Blessed Memory".
3. This biographical paragraph introduced the original Yiddish article.
4. See the following link (retrieved July 2020): https://kehilalinks.jewishgen.org/lida-district/wages.htm. In 1900, a typical worker might earn 180 rubles yearly, hence 600 rubles would be equivalent to more than 3 years salary of such a worker. From a different perspective, in 1900 1 ruble was worth US$0.78. The inflation in the period 1900-2019 was a factor of 31, hence 600 rubles of the year 1900 would be equivalent to $14,500 in 2019 dollars (see the following link, retrieved July 2020: https://westegg.com/inflation/).
5. In analogy with removing all the *chometz*, i.e. leavened food, from the home just before Passover
6. Yiddish: *kabtsen in sieben polles*
7. R. = *Reb*, similar to English "Mister"
8. Yiddish: *orel* = uncircumcised male (here used derogatorily)
9. Yiddish: *Yidden senen arumgegangen vie on kep* [= Jews were going about as if without heads]
10. In the sense of Exodus 1:8, "There arose a new king over Egypt who did not know Joseph..."
11. Zastavya was separated from Kamenetz by the bridge over the Leshna River.
12. At that time of day, men would be sitting in the *Bays-Medresh* after the afternoon prayer service had ended, waiting until it was dark enough to begin the evening prayer service.

[Page 471]

Memories of My Town[1]

by Shifra Mazover-Bobrowski, Rishon-Letziyon

Translated by Allen Flusberg

One day my mother brought me to the *Hayder* [boys' religious school], to the teacher Shayele, to learn prayer-book Hebrew. The teacher began to teach me to say, by heart, *modeh ani*[2], *krias shma*[3] and various blessings: a blessing for hearing thunder, for seeing lightning, for seeing a rainbow, and all the blessings for different kinds of foods; also, the Sabbath blessing "when the dear, holy Sabbath ends".

We would hurry to finish, so that the boys that stayed in the *Hayder* all day, learning *Humesh* [Pentateuch] and Rashi [11th-century commentary on the *Humesh*], could continue their studies. My two brothers, Moyshke and Mordechai, of blessed memory, were students in this *Hayder*. I recall how my mother would send me to bring them snacks; on my way back, I would run over to the Adolen Hill and roll down from the top—in summer over the sand and in winter over the ice. For us children flying down this Adolen Hill was exhilarating.

On Fridays I would be sent to Zune the Baker, carrying the *tscholent*[4], to make sure it was brought to him on time to have it sealed in the oven. Along the way I could hear the pounding of cleavers—the sound of gefilte fish being made for the Sabbath.

Moyshe-Haim the water carrier used to carry yokes on his shoulders, supporting two buckets of fresh river water for tea. He would come to us at dawn, when we were still washing our hands with *negl-vasser* [water for morning handwashing] from the copper ladle.

My mother used to feel sorry for him and say: "Come, Moyshe-Ḥaim, put the buckets down—and have a warm *ulnik* [grated potato casserole] made by Frayde the *ulnitske* [*ulnik* maker]."

Poor Moyshe-Ḥaim would take the *ulnik* in his hand and say that he still had a lot of river water for tea to deliver that morning—and then he would run off.

[Page 472]

I recall how in our *shtetl* [little town], right after Purim[5], they began baking matzos [unleavened bread] for Passover. This baking would take place in what were called *szwalnies* [sewing workshops], located in the poor part of town. Two long planed-down planks, supported from below by two barrels, formed what looked like two long tables; and around them stood about 20 destitute girls holding wooden rollers, with which they were rolling nice, round matzos. A young boy stood at a small table using a *redl* tool [a small, indented wheel] to perforate each matzo. In an adjoining room a woman was sitting with flour in a copper wash basin, kneading.

Once when I came to see how they baked matzos, one of the girls showed me how swollen her hands were from rolling for days on end. For an entire month they would be rolling all day, while standing on their feet. I said that I would come to help out a bit. I didn't know how to "stretch out" the matzo, and the girls taught me how. They were very glad whenever I showed up. My mother had told me that when you do a good deed, you should not talk about it; and so I never told anyone what I had been doing—even in my own home no one knew.

The husband of Sara-Mindl, the undergarment seamstress, was a Ḥasid who wore a *shtraiml* [fur hat], *kapote* [caftan] and *gartl* [loose belt tied around the waist]. On Simchas Torah[6], in the Ḥasidic *shtibl* [small, one-room synagogue], he would climb up on a table to dance. I remember that once, when I was hurrying away from the *szwalnie*, Sara-Mindl's husband was standing there [drawing water from a well]. I immediately saw how hard he was struggling to turn the *kibel* [*kurbel* = crankshaft]; I ran over to [grab] the other handle, and just then the shaft released and unwound into the well. My hands were badly bruised by the [spinning] handle. At the nearby home of Itche Artchech, they applied cold water to my fingers. It was a week before Passover, and the worst part of it was that because of the injury I couldn't go help the poor girls who were working in the *szwalnie*.

On Purim, a friend of mine and I would open my relatives' charity boxes and hand the money over to a lady charity volunteer, who would distribute it to poor brides[7].

When we were little girls, two of us would go to keep watch over an ill person all night. *Linas HaTzedek* [a charity organization to aid the sick] used to provide us with an icepack for the patient's head and a hot-water bottle in case his belly ached. I recall that one night the ice ran out, which meant someone had to go to Ahron-Moyshe's cellar to hack off some more ice. I was afraid to go alone, but we were also afraid that if we both went the sick person might die while we were gone. And so the two of us sat there until morning, crying. At dawn they sent me to get Avrome the *feldsher* [medic]. He used to heal the sick, and he had medications for everything: a salve to apply to the neck, *bankes* [cupping glasses], giving a *klizme* [enema], and making the patient drink castor oil mixed with some pickled-cucumber juice. When, Heaven forbid, none of the above helped, he would prescribe *piavkes* [leeches], so that the ill person would have no choice but to get better…

[Page 473]

Orphanage with the management and teaching staff[8]

[Page 474]

I can remember when the assistant would come by carrying a lantern during the evenings of Ḥanukkah[9], when the ground was all muddy, asking for Ḥanukkah *gelt* [money][10].

I also recall that when a male baby was born, the *melamed* [teacher of small children] and his entire *Ḥayder* [class of children] would come on the Friday night before the circumcision; this was called the *vachnacht* [watch night][11]. The *melamed* and all the children would read *krias shma* near the mother and baby. The grandmother would also be there. In return for coming, each boy would receive a fistful of *arbes* [chickpeas] which had been arranged on an entire tray, spread out on a white tablecloth, together with little candies. Verses from *shir hamaalois* [A Song of Ascents, Psalms 121][12] had been hung on the windows and doors of the room where the baby was.

There were also theatre shows in our town. The performers were mostly amateur actors from Brisk [Brest-Litowsk, 40km south of Kamenetz]. Sometimes the performances took place in a barn that belonged to Ahron-Moishe Galpern. We would also have other forms of entertainment there.

Images of Moyshe-Ahron the *meshugener* [crazy] come back to me—how we used to see him only at night, wandering around in courtyards. I was very frightened by his eyes and his glance, but he never actually bothered anyone.

I also remember the times in my little *shtetl* Kamenetz, when the army draftees would carry on all night, playing various pranks, just before they began their military service. This used to take place around *Sukkos* [Tabernacles—September-October].

The village Gentiles who were serving in the Polish military also would cause trouble when they were on their way out of our little *shtetl*, quite drunk.

Translator's Footnotes:

1. From *Kamenetz-Litovsk, Zastavije and Colonies Memorial Book*, edited by S. Eisenstadt and M. Galbert, published by the Israel and America Committee of Kamenetz Litovsk and Zastavya, (Orly, Tel Aviv, Israel, 1970), pp. 471-474.
2. *modeh ani* = prayer recited when one wakes up (I thank You, Living, Eternal King, for compassionately returning my soul…)
3. *Krias shma* = Hear O Israel, the Lord is our God, the Lord is One (Deut. 6:1), the Jewish declaration of monotheistic faith
4. *tscholnt* = Sabbath stew, already brought to a boil, placed in an oven on Friday to continue stewing over Friday night, and removed fully cooked after the following morning, to be eaten warm on the Sabbath. Since the fire is not lit, tampered with or adjusted on the Sabbath, this form of cooking is not considered to violate the commandment of Exodus 35:3, "You shall not kindle any fire in your dwellings on the Sabbath." This was generally the only warm food permissible on the Sabbath. See the following link (retrieved February 2021): Cholent - Wikipedia
5. The Purim holiday occurs one month before Passover.
6. *Simchas Torah* = Rejoicing of the Torah, a joyful holiday with much celebration and dancing
7. A Purim custom / commandment is donating charity to the poor (Esther 9:23). See the following link (retrieved February, 2021): Purim - Wikipedia
8. Sign in photograph reads: *Ochronka dła sieroł starozakonnych* (= Jewish orphanage school [in Polish]; *bays yesoimim* = orphanage [in Hebrew/Yiddish]).
9. Winter (December) festival
10. See the following link (retrieved February 2021): Hanukkah gelt - Wikipedia
11. See the following link (retrieved February 2021) for variant customs: Vach nacht - Wikipedia
12. See the following link (retrieved February 2021): The Shir Lamaalot - Lifecycle Events (chabad.org)

[Page 477]

Prewar Kamenetz[1]

by Yitzchok Sheinfeld (Brooklyn, New York)

Translated by Allen Flusberg

Translator's note: Most of this article appeared in an English version in the English section of this Yizkor Book, pp. 85-90, under the title "Kamenetz—The Memories of My Youth", by Izhak Sheinfeld. That English version is missing the following paragraphs, translated here from Yiddish

In 1935 a new mayor came to Kamenetz, and he introduced new decrees. One of the new edicts was "sharvarag"[2]: every household had to provide one day of labor for the town once a month—road construction, gathering rocks, digging, moving the dug-up dirt, etc. During the short days of winter, the work would continue after darkness fell. When the Jewish members of the town council protested to the mayor, the Friday work hours were shortened, so that the Jews would not have to violate the Sabbath.

In the years 1936-1937 the activity of the Zionist organizations declined and almost completely fell apart. There was a group of young men who were still collecting money for the *Keren Kayemes* [Jewish National Fund, JNF] and turning it over to the Kamenetz JNF treasurer, Yosef Greenblatt. He used to send the money to the JNF Headquarters in Warsaw. That group of young men were: Yitzchok Sheinfeld, Yosef Feldman, Noach Goldberg, Reuven Szczytnicki and Yaakov Weitzhendler.

[Page 478]

Our friend, Yisroel Goldshal (a native of Pinsk), was at that time teaching at the *Tarbut-Gymnasia*[3] in Pinsk. In 1939 he became a teacher in Kamenetz, teaching children Hebrew.

During discussions with Yisroel Goldshal about reviving the Zionist Movement in Kamenetz, we decided to found a branch of *HaShomer HaTzair*[4]. Yosef Feldman was appointed branch head, and Yitzchok Sheinfeld branch secretary, whose duties included correspondence with the Warsaw headquarters. Noach Goldberg became the deputy branch head, and Reuven Szczytnicki the treasurer.

The government created difficulties and did not grant permission to open a location for meetings and to legalize *HaShomer HaTzair*. We held meetings in members' homes.

During Sabbath mornings, our group of *HaShomer HaTzair* invited the General Zionists to Mordechai Chaim in the bakery. We asked Isaac Shostakowski, Velvl Chaim Korshnboim and Yosef Greenblatt to help us legalize the organization. Berl (Berele) Fisher came to our aid and joined our ranks. At that time, after completing a leadership seminar, he had just returned to Kamenetz. Berele Fisher participated in our discussions and classes, and helped bring in new members from an even younger generation. The Zionist movement came back to life.

Then pressure on Jews began to be felt in Kamenetz, as well. Christian restaurants opened up, shops and cafeterias. Jewish shopowners lost some of their livelihood. The government demanded higher taxes and also loans, which were hard to comply with.

At 10 AM the passenger bus from Brisk[5] used to arrive. Groups of people would gather and wait at Zelik the bookbinder, so that he would distribute the newly arrived newspapers to his readers. The Bund newspaper, *Folkstzeitung*, was often confiscated. The newspapers *Moment, Heint, Heintike Nayes, Radio* and *Dos Neier Wort* were read by the majority of the Jewish population. The Workers' Library, which was also called the *Y.L. Peretz Library*, was closed by the authorities, and the majority of the books were confiscated. The former officials of the library were temporarily arrested.

[Page 479]

As always, the Kamenetz youth endeavored to emigrate, particularly to the Land of Israel. Unfortunately, only a small number made it. Whoever was able to immigrated to other free countries.

When I got to America, I could not forget the precious poor Jews. During the Second World War, when I was in the American army, in Africa, I met Jews from Poland, but could not find anything out about the fate of the Jews of Kamenetz.

Translator's Footnotes:

1. From *Kamenetz-Litovsk, Zastavije and Colonies Memorial Book*, edited by S. Eisenstadt and M. Galbert, published by the Israel and America Committee of Kamenetz Litovsk and Zastavya, (Orly, Tel Aviv, Israel, 1970), pp. 475-479.
2. *szarwark, scharwerk*: = crowd labor, crew work. See the following link (in German, retrieved March 2020): https://de.wikipedia.org/wiki/Scharwerk
3. The *Tarbut-Gymnasias* (high schools) were part of the Zionist-Hebrew educational network. See the following link (retrieved March 2020): https://www.yadvashem.org/yv/en/exhibitions/vilna/before/education.asp
4. *HaShomer HaTzair* (= The Young Guard) was a youth movement that encouraged immigration to the Land of Israel and agricultural work in kibbutzim (communal agricultural settlements). See the following link (retrieved February 2020): https://en.wikipedia.org/wiki/Hashomer_Hatzair#Early_formation
5. Brisk (Jewish name for Brest-Litowsk) is a city located 40km south of Kamenetz.

[Page 480]

Memories[1]

by Shashke Visotzky

Translated by Allen Flusberg

I left my town of Kamenetz-Litowsk in 1930, in the full bloom of youth. At the time my greatest hope and desire was to return quickly.

As a child, I used to gaze at the large, beautiful synagogue with great awe and reverence. I believed I could hear the voices of angels singing songs of praise from the synagogue during evening.

My father, Moishe Eliezer Katzalski, the Kamenetz *soifer* [scribe], used to sit around day and night, either studying or writing a Torah scroll. The only time he was distracted was when he went out for a walk with Rabbi Burstein, the wise, intelligent Rabbi of Kamenetz.

I started attending school during the First World War, a short time before the German forces pulled out of Kamenetz. Our teachers then were: Kumersteiner and Chvat for German; Leah Bobrowski and Malka Polyakevitch for Hebrew; and Unterman for Jewish history and singing.

We were then suffering from hunger and disease, yet we did still go to school; and we were singing and dancing. Our youthfulness simply overcame our deprivation. Then our need was alleviated somewhat by the food from the [community] kitchen and the packages of food and clothing that began arriving from America.

After the Germans left the Bolsheviks came into our town, so we studied Russian and Hebrew. Our teachers at that time were: Leah Bobrowski for Hebrew and Dvora Dolinski for Russian. Once the Poles captured our town, we had to study Polish in the *Powszechna*[2] School. But we continued to study Hebrew in a private school that was run by the Saperstein brothers: Velvel Saperstein taught Hebrew, Shloimo'ke Saperstein taught Russian, and Herschl Saperstein taught Yiddish.

[Page 481]

We decided to set up our own library, for which each child in our school paid one groschen per week. To bring in more money for books, we used to sell raffles for tickets to shows that we performed; and with this money we were able to buy the best books. And this is how the "I.L. Peretz[3] Children's Library" was established.

We also let other children of the town—whoever wanted to— read our books. We had good books and a large number of readers. The library management included the following: Moishe Greenblatt, Chaya Krakowski, Golda Sher; and later also Lipa Horowitch, myself and several other boys and girls, whose names I do not recall.

The school studies did not go far enough for us. Several of my friends left for Bialystok, the girls to complete high school there, and the boys to study in the Yeshiva. And incidentally, one of the Bialystok Yeshiva students, Meir Visotzky, later became my husband.

Later many of these boys and girls threw themselves with the same fervor into the work of raising money for the Jewish National Fund (JNF). Kamenetz became well known for the large sums of money it collected for the JNF. And let me make mention here of two very dedicated and stalwart workers who supported the Zionist organization: Zelig the bookbinder and Yosl Greenblatt.

After each of the Zionist gatherings, we used to sing Zionist songs and dance a *hora* with great passion.

At that time *HeChalutz*[4] was also established in Kamenetz under good leadership. Meir Visotzky, who was then my friend, was one of those leaders. A large number of the members of the Zionist organization and *HeChalutz*, both male and female, are now in Israel

Translator's Footnotes:

1.   From *Kamenetz-Litovsk, Zastavije and Colonies Memorial Book*, edited by S. Eisenstadt and M. Galbert, published by the Israel and America Committee of Kamenetz Litovsk and Zastavya, (Orly, Tel Aviv, Israel, 1970), pp. 480-481.
2.   The State, public school. See article on pp. 450-451 of this volume, "The *Szkola Powszechna*", by Chaya Gurvitz-Goldberg.
3.   The library was named after I. L. Peretz (1852-1915), a Yiddish-language author and playwright. See the following link (retrieved April 2020): https://en.wikipedia.org/wiki/I._L._Peretz.
4.   *HeChalutz* (= The Pioneer) was a Jewish youth movement that trained young people for agricultural settlement in the Land of Israel, as described in the following link (retrieved February 2020): https://en.wikipedia.org/wiki/HeHalutz. See also the article by S. Dubiner on p. 73 of this volume, "*HeChalutz* (Pioneer Movement) in Kamenetz-Litowsk".

[Page 482]

A Religious-Court Hearing at the Rabbi's[1]

by Chaya Sara Binder-Rudnitzki (Argentina)

Translated by Allen Flusberg

Although I have already lived in Argentina for more than half of my life, I still cannot forget Kamenetz, the town I was born in, and where I spent my childhood together with my nearest and dearest. In my mind's eye I still see it as it was, with all the charm of an authentic Jewish *shtetl*[2]: its streets, alleyways and houses; the *Slup* [Medieval tower] with its tall walls, the subject of so many legends—yet no one could determine exactly what purpose it had been built for. The Kobryn, Brisk and Litowsk Streets; Shosay Street, a valley where we had recently lived after the great fire, when half the town burned to the ground; the town square, with the two rows of shops, where the Jewish shopkeepers used to sit and wait long hours for customers that rarely came by. The shopkeepers' only hope was the monthly fair that would reinvigorate them and bring in a bit of a living to the *shtetl*; but even that was in fact of little value after the high taxes that the government demanded were taken into account. In spite of the difficult economic situation and the oppressiveness, Jews lived securely, giving charity from their very last penny, helping out the needy, supporting institutions, and lifting up their morale.

Kamenetz was not considered one of the really tiny *shtetls*. It had fine young people who were always striving for a higher purpose. They were Zionists—among them General Zionists[3], Poalei-Tzionists[4], members of Gordonia[5] and Beitar[6], most of them Gordonia. They led culturally creative lives. They were in contact with great personalities who visited our *shtetl*, among them Pinchas Lubianker (Lavon)[7]. Many of these pioneer youth are now in Israel and occupy important positions.

[Page 483]

Kamenetz became well known for its great Yeshiva, which prepared and graduated many rabbis, among them US American, Canadian, and a few from the Land of Israel.

Kamenetz had its fine homeowners, synagogue functionaries and craftsmen. It had a few Houses of Study, several synagogues, a kindergarten, and two very well-respected rabbis. One of them, Rabbi Burstein[8], whose outlook was more worldly, gave his children a secular education and lived an aristocratic life. Since I was a close friend of his youngest daughter, I once had an opportunity to listen to a *din-Torah* [a religious-court hearing] at his home.

The case was that of a village girl who was accusing a former yeshiva student of pursuing her with professions of love. The two of them, not so very young anymore, make a curious spectacle. The yeshiva student: pale, of medium height, with dreamy, brown eyes and a refined appearance, is dressed simply but neatly. He feels quite uncomfortable with the present situation, and he gazes at the girl with some embarrassment, but without any anger. Very nervous, he tries to be calm as he recounts that when he happened to come to the village and saw her, he immediately fell in love with her, and for this reason remained there as a schoolteacher. She always responded to him with a smile and a warm look—until a short time ago, when she underwent a complete transformation. And although a yeshiva student is not allowed to carry on a love affair, he is unable to conceal his feelings for her.

The girl, a short brunette, certainly not ugly, expressed contempt for him and categorically refuted what he had said. But it was apparent that everyone there sympathized more with the young man.

Sitting in the next room as an unseen onlooker, I observed the rabbi's bearing, his dignified appearance and wise smile. He must have been thinking: two grown people who are making fools of themselves. To this very day I cannot forget the words of wisdom spoken by Rabbi Burstein with confidence as he ended the two-hour-long *din-Torah*.

Translator's Footnotes:

1. From *Kamenetz-Litovsk, Zastavije and Colonies Memorial Book*, edited by S. Eisenstadt and M. Galbert, published by the Israel and America Committee of Kamenetz Litovsk and Zastavya, (Orly, Tel Aviv, Israel, 1970), pp. 482-483.
2. *shtetl* = small town.
3. General Zionists were members of *Tzioni-Klall*, a Zionist party that was not affiliated with either the Social Zionists or the Religious Zionists. In the 1930s it split into two factions, one favoring cautious cooperation with the British in Palestine and the other advocating stronger opposition. See R. Medoff and C. Waxman, *The A to Z of Zionism*, "General Zionists" (Scarecrow Press, 2009).
4. *Poalei-Tzion* = Workers of Zion (Hebrew), or Zionist Workers, a Jewish Marxist-Zionist party. See the following (retrieved December 2019) for more information: https://en.wikipedia.org/wiki/Poale_Zion.
5. Gordonia was a Zionist youth movement, founded in Poland in 1925, that rejected Marxism, emphasizing instead manual labor and the revival of the Hebrew language. See the following (retrieved October 2019): https://en.wikipedia.org/wiki/Gordonia_(youth_movement).
6. See article on p. 77-79 of this volume: P. Ravid-Rudnicki, "The Gordonia Movement in Kamenetz-Litowsk".
7. See the following (retrieved December, 2019): https://en.wikipedia.org/wiki/Pinhas_Lavon
8. See pp. 409-410 of this Yizkor-Book volume: Ch. Mendelson, "Rabbi Reuven Burstein"; pp. 50-54 of this volume: Y. Gershuni, "Rabbi Reuven David Hakohen Burstein, May God Avenge His Blood"; pp. 189-191 of this volume, L. Aloni-Bobrowski, "A Tear for the Loss of My Townspeople"; p. 105 of the English Section of this Yizkor Book, D. Rudnitsky-Singer, "My Life in Ghettos and Concentration Camps". Two articles in this volume are excerpted from Rabbi Burstein's writings: pp. 47-48, "Rabbi Yehoshua Hakohen Blumenthal" and pp. 57-59, "Rabbi Avraham Aharon Hakohen"..

[Page 484]

Memoirs[1]

by Rachel Sofer-Renkevitch (America)

Translated by Allen Flusberg

My *shtetl* [little town] Kamenetz-Litowsk, is located 35km away from the city of Brisk [Brest-Litowsk]. It resides on the banks of the Leshna River, whose water was utilized by the entire *shtetl*. Water carriers derived their livelihoods from bringing water to the wealthier homes. During the winter, when the river froze over, boys used to skate on the ice. In the summer the housewives washed their laundry in it; the young people would boat there, and on the hottest days people used to bathe in the river. A wide, sandy path ran along one side of the river; and the other side was flanked by broad green meadows.

Not far from this river, on a lofty hill with leafy trees, there stood a narrow, tall tower with masonry walls, the *Slup*. As you got closer to it, you would see that it stood in a valley, from which canals constructed of masonry led to various small streets of the town. Once you went through the iron doors of the *Slup*, you could climb a staircase all the way to the very top. From up there you had a view of the entire area surrounding the town, over quite a distance. In the summer, when the hill was overgrown with grass, people who lived nearby would go up the hill to lounge around as part of their Sabbath relaxation.

When a guest came to the town, he would be brought to visit the *Slup* as a historical fortress. And if someone wanted to slight a person in jest, he would call him a "Kamenetz *Slup*".

* * *

The town had a synagogue and study halls, several small prayer houses, a Ḥasidic *shtibl* [one-room synagogue], a town rabbi, a cantor, a ritual slaughterer—as well as all else that had been retained from many generations of a deep-rooted Jewish way of life.

[Page 485]

Two rows of wooden shops stood in the middle of the market. From these shops nearly half the Jews of the *shtetl* derived their livelihoods. Every Sunday and Thursday the peasant farmers from the surrounding villages would ride in, bringing grain, fruit, fowl and similar items to sell. With the money they received in return, they would purchase all their necessities in the Jewish shops; and whatever money was left they would spend on getting drunk in the taverns.

There was no working class in the *shtetl*—this was a convention of the period in which people maintained that "in our family, thank God, there are no laborers". There were merchants, private teachers, schoolteachers, brokers, and members of various other idle vocations.

Our tiny *shtetl* was isolated from the outside world. The railroad was 20km away. Mail used to arrive with the driver who drove passengers to the Žabinka train station. The driver's wife, Sara Leah, would take letters along when she felt like it. Newspapers were delivered once a week to the wealthier people—and even for them, only jointly for two or three families who shared a subscription.

The yeshiva was located in the larger study hall. There many young bachelors—long-term, assiduous scholars—studied. They would eat "*teg*"[2] at the homes of townspeople who provided meals for them in turn, each for a single day of the week. When someone passed the study hall at night, he could see from afar little flames and the flicker of wax candles, at whose light a young student would be chanting the sorrowful, pining melody, "*mai ko mashma lon*"[3].

There was a *Ḥovevei Tzion* [Lovers of Zion][4] movement, one of whose members was Zelig the bookbinder[5]. Various pamphlets and party newspapers used to be delivered to him, and the other members would get together there.

There was a drama circle that performed plays, bringing joy and culture to the *shtetl*. In those days Kamenetz had a library with a significant number of books—in Yiddish, Russian and Hebrew. The young people read, contemplated, and dreamed of a more beautiful, better morrow, knowing that the world did not end at the outskirts of the little *shtetl*—that roads led to new, unfamiliar territory beyond distant horizons that were opening before them.

[Page 486]

When the First World War broke out and the Germans occupied the area, life became even more paralyzed. In what was then already their brutal, systematic way, they suppressed all signs of life outdoors at night with a 9 PM curfew. And on one such night a fire broke out. Before anyone had any idea what was happening, half the *shtetl* was in flames, and the inhabitants had to abandon their homes with all their belongings and property. This event led to a state of fatal impoverishment and need, as well as a terrible struggle for material existence. When the war ended and the townspeople became aware of how profound the sorrowful economic situation had become, the young people set off in droves to the big, wide world: some to the Land of Israel, others to the Soviet Union—but most of them to America.

Those who remained behind continued to keep the thread of traditional Jewish life going under the rotten fascist Polish government, living without a present and with no prospect of a better future. They hungered and languished in a state of absolute material scarcity.

By the time the Second World War broke out and the Nazi brute entered my *shtetl*, its ground had already been tilled and sown with a savage anti-Semitic hatred of the Jews.

Translator's Footnotes:

1.   From *Kamenetz-Litovsk, Zastavije and Colonies Memorial Book*, edited by S. Eisenstadt and M. Galbert, published by the Israel and America Committee of Kamenetz Litovsk and Zastavya, (Orly, Tel Aviv, Israel, 1970), pp. 484-486.
2.   *teg* = days
3.   *mai ko mashma lon* (Aramaic) = what does this come to teach us, i.e., what are its ramifications that we would not have known otherwise (a common Talmudic phrase)
4.   The "Lovers of Zion" organization, founded in 1884, a forerunner of Zionism, promoted Jewish immigration to the Land of Israel and the founding of agricultural settlements there. See the following link (retrieved March 2021): Hovevei Zion - Wikipedia
5.   See article by P. Ravid-Rudnicki on pp. 127-129 of this Yizkor Book, "Zelig 'the Bookbinder'"

[Page 487]

Unpleasant Recollections[1]

by Dobbe Halpern (America)

Translated by Allen Flusberg

Bands of Robbers in Zastavya During the First World War

At the end of the First World War, the situation in our shtetl [little town] and the surrounding villages was steadily deteriorating. The Germans were already aware that their cause was lost and that they would now have to retreat from the territory they had occupied; and so they stopped bothering to maintain order.

At this time gangs of robbers and murderers appeared in the shtetl and in the entire surrounding area. Most of them were Russian prisoners who had escaped from the German [prisoner-of-war] camps that were in the Bialowieza Woods[2] and other locations. They would demand money and provisions, terrorizing the Jewish population in particular. No one could travel beyond a few kilometers from the town; they would attack anyone on the roads, taking everything away and often leaving the victims naked. Anyone who stood up to them would be risking his life.

My uncle, Mayshe Dubiner, lived in the village of Shishki. Once a group of robbers came to him and demanded money. My uncle didn't have the sum they were demanding available. Realizing that he was in great danger, he begged off, suggesting instead that they travel with him to Kamenetz, where he could raise the money. When they arrived at our house everyone fled, leaving only me with my uncle. Then after one of the gang had received the money I asked him for a receipt for the entire amount. He complied, signing his name "*Chornaya Ruka*"[3], i.e. "Black Hand".

[Page 488]

Often they would also rob Germans who lived in the villages. The Germans knew who the robbers were, but when it came to blaming someone they would blame the Jews.

Once, on a very cold winter day, a group of armed Germans came into our shtetl claiming that some Kamenetz Jews had robbed them during the night. They demanded as penalty a large sum of money from the entire community; and should the money not be brought to them within an hour, they would set the whole town on fire, from one end to the other. To show that they meant it, they placed straw sheaves and flammable material on all the streets.

Many people in the town were ill with typhus at that time; they were carried out of the houses. The Germans didn't let anyone escape and the air filled with the sounds of mothers and children wailing. Several prominent men, among them my father, David Galpern, immediately set off to collect money. The rabbi and (to make a distinction[4]) the priest persuaded the Germans to wait until the sum they had demanded could be collected. Several hours passed before we no longer had to be in fear of a conflagration. And after this incident we never saw the Germans again in Kamenetz-Zastavya.

In Independent Poland

When Poland became an independent state, and when Kamenetz and its vicinity became part of it, the Kamenetz Jews breathed a sigh of relief, hoping that the Polish government would protect them from the bands of robbers. But it didn't take long to find out that we had been completely mistaken. It turned out that the commandant and his police force were the very same bandits that had been beating Jews in the streets.

Once a group of us, boys and girls, had gotten together at the home of Laybl Wystoker. Suddenly the commandant, whip in hand, appeared, beating everyone in sight. Gedalyahu Shustukowski z.l.[5], Berl Kaplanski z.l., and the teacher Gelerstein a.h.[6] were the ones who were beaten the most. When the bully got close to me I noticed that he was very drunk. I pushed him so hard that he fell over, and quickly I ran away. After getting home via backyards and side streets, I immediately hid in a neighbor's attic.

[Page 489]

I recall another incident: a Zastavya Jew came to sell some cucumbers in the town marketplace. He was carrying them in a sack, tossed over his shoulders. The Polish police from the police station beat him badly. Hearing his screaming, the neighbors ran to the pharmacist, who was the town mayor, and asked him to rescue the Jew. But the Polish mayor refused. When my father, who was then deputy-mayor, heard what was happening, he quickly ran to the police station to ask that they rescue the Jew from the savagery of the Polish police. Ignoring his position as deputy-mayor, they hit him too, and he came home all beaten up. But this incident aroused in him a strong wish to help the downtrodden. The clashes that often took place with the Polish police gave him the desire to labor for the common good.

When parcels of provisions for the neediest Jews of Kamenetz-Zastavya would arrive from America, my father a.h., together with Yaakov Kagan, who had a horse-and-buggy, would ride off to Brisk[7] to bring groceries back to people in the shtetl. The needs of the local Jews were so dire that he willingly overlooked the unrest along the roads.

Translator's Footnotes:

1. From *Kamenetz-Litovsk, Zastavije and Colonies Memorial Book*, edited by S. Eisenstadt and M. Galbert, published by the Israel and America Committee of Kamenetz Litovsk and Zastavya, (Orly, Tel Aviv, Israel, 1970), pp. 487-489.
2. The edge of the Bialowieza Forest is about 30km north of Kamenetz.
3. Russian
4. Yiddish/Hebrew *lehavdil*
5. z.l. = *zichraynay livrocho* = of blessed memory
6. a.h. = *olov hasholom* = may he rest in peace
7. Brisk = Jewish name for the city of Brest-Litovsk, 35km south of Kamenetz.

[Page 490]

Unforgettable[1]

by Zlate Timyansky-Gers (New York)

Translated by Allen Flusberg

Although I left Kamenetz in the year 1929, I still can, even today, see the little town clearly in my imagination.

Like all Jewish children of that period, I, too, attended *chayder* [Jewish religious school for young children]. The *melamed* [teacher] was R.[2] Shlomo Rudnicki—who was called R. Shlomo "Lisker", after the village that he came from. In *chayder* we were learning the Hebrew alphabet and *Ivri* [Biblical Hebrew]. We studied secular subjects, like Yiddish, Russian and afterwards also Polish, with private teachers. But an especially beloved institution of learning that we used was the library, for it provided a glimpse of the outside world.

In the library the young people who were still studying—as well as a significant part of the workforce—would gather during their free time to read newspapers or books dealing with social issues. The leaders of existing cultural circles and parties made it their meeting place. It served as the beating pulse of both Jewish and general culture.

Theatrical shows also used to be produced in the town. The star performers were mostly amateurs from Brisk[3]. At certain times the performances were staged in a barn belonging to Itche Palyakewicz (Itche the *Tsegelnik* [brickmaker]). The young people took great interest in these shows.

The arrival of a cantor, a maggid [preacher] or a Zionist speaker into town would generate a special holiday-like atmosphere. The large *bays-medresh* [study house] would then be completely packed with an audience. At such events little disagreements would also sometimes occur, but without having a bad effect on the almost always peaceful coexistence among the Jews of the town.

During summer evenings, especially on Sabbaths, the young people would go out for walks along the market street, where the circle of shops were located.

[Page 491]

In the period of the general economic crisis, during the 1930s, a large number of Kamenetz Jews began leaving the town, off to the Land of Israel and America. But to our great misfortune, most of the Jews of the town remained there and were murdered by the Nazis.

Jewish Kamenetz, my native town, full of the dreams of my youth—how can I ever forget you?

Translator's Footnotes:

1. From *Kamenetz-Litovsk, Zastavije and Colonies Memorial Book*, edited by S. Eisenstadt and M. Galbert, published by the Israel and America Committee of Kamenetz Litovsk and Zastavya, (Orly, Tel Aviv, Israel, 1970), pp. 490-491.
2. R. stands for *Reb*, an honorific similar to English "Mr."
3. Brisk = Brest-Litowsk, a city ~40km south of Kamenetz.

[Page 492]

The Orchestra[1]

by Aharon Meir Yoffe (America)

Translated by Allen Flusberg

In 1925, a certain group of people who were musical proposed starting an orchestra, but realized that it would be expensive and difficult to implement: we would have to purchase instruments and to bring in a director who could both teach us and conduct. Through various sources we found out that a particular landowner who had once—years earlier—conducted an orchestra, had retained various instruments in his possession. We decided to each contribute a particular amount of money—two zlotys per week—and to establish two groups to teach ourselves how to play, thereby making it possible to bring in more money. We also decided to go to the mayor and propose that the orchestra would be part of the firemen's brigade, so that we could obtain a subsidy from the municipality.

Shloimke Mandelblatt, who served as a secretary in the municipality, put in a good word for us on the project. After a few weeks it was all taken care of, and we established the orchestra. With much effort and energy we trained ourselves, and one fine morning we went out on a "march" around town. Everyone was amazed that we had completed so great an undertaking in such a short time.

At that time fellow townspeople approached us for a favor: since a very great yeshiva, headed by Rabbi Boruch Ber Leibovitch (one of the great Talmudists), was about to move to Kamenetz—and since the town would very much like to welcome them festively—might the orchestra greet them with music as they entered the town? We immediately agreed. We went out to the town outskirts via Brisk Street, waiting for them to arrive. Then we accompanied them into town with music, up to the *Bays-Medresh* [House of Study] building, which had been designated to house the yeshiva; and from there we continued on to the house that had been set aside for the Head of the Yeshiva.[2]

[Page 493]

The Firemen's Orchestra[3]

[Page 494]

Later the town began constructing a new building for the yeshiva on Brisk Street, and the orchestra again participated in collecting money in support of it.

The orchestra also played at evening dances, *bliml-teg*[4], etc.

But then I left my little town, and for me all that is left are the memories.

Translator's Footnotes:

1. From *Kamenetz-Litovsk, Zastavije and Colonies Memorial Book*, edited by S. Eisenstadt and M. Galbert, published by the Israel and America Committee of Kamenetz Litovsk and Zastavya, (Orly, Tel Aviv, Israel, 1970), pp. 492-494.
2. See the following parallel account by L. Bobrowski-Aloni in this volume: "The *Knesset Beit Yitzhak* Yeshiva", pp. 61-63.
3. In the photograph, the author (Aharon Meir Yoffe, a.k.a. Harry Jaffe) is standing in the back row, third from the right (as identified to the translator in 2021 by the author's daughter, Gloria Jaffe Hirsch).
4. *bliml-teg* = flower days (Yiddish): outdoor, public celebrations, serving as fundraisers.

[Page 495]

Our Little Town and Its Livelihoods[1]

by Ḥ. Z. Mendelson

Translated by Allen Flusberg

Life in our *shtetl* [little town] of Kamenetz-Litowsk went by peacefully and quietly. The town's outward appearance was no different from that of other nearby *shtetls*: Many wooden houses, and several masonry houses on sloping ground. A main street, as well as several smaller streets. Open, unheated shops extending across the main street to the market square. In summer the stall-keepers sat there to sell their produce: various fruits, vegetables, and especially cucumbers, which our *shtetl* was known for because they were so abundant. In winter, warmed by coal pots, the stall-keepers sat there, too, selling a variety of baked goods. They were waiting impatiently for the market days, which took place twice a week—Sunday and Thursday—as well as for the special market fairs, from which these shopowners derived most of their livelihoods.

To provide some idea of the difficult economic situation in our *shtetl* in those days, I will now endeavor to recreate from memory a market day, as I recall it from my childhood years:

At the very crack of dawn, the retailers would go out to meet the peasant farmers, who would be coming into town in horse-and-wagons. These retailers were checking out what the farmers had brought with them, to see what they might be able to earn from it—perhaps they might actually be able to get a better deal before the farmers raised the prices of their produce as more potential buyers showed up—a strategy that rarely worked.

[Page 496]

The neighing of the horses and clatter of the iron wheels on the stone pavement; the tumult of throngs streaming into the *shtetl* on foot: all that noise and commotion made our *shtetl* seem more like a city besieged by foreign armies than a tranquil, peaceful little town. Gradually the market-day was getting under way. Suddenly our merchants and shopowners—who ordinarily would be sitting around, half asleep, in the sun in summer and next to their coal pots in winter—were transformed into truly masterful tradesmen. At first they would go from wagon to wagon to poke around and sniff things out—for there was no shortage of buyers, and each of them was trying to find a way to outbid the others in offering price. Haggling would begin in an undertone and quickly go up several decibels. If that didn't work, they used their last resort, the clap of a hand: the buyer would clap to signify a higher bid, and the seller would respond with a clap to indicate he was lowering his price. And so they would agree on a price, and the deal was sealed.

Once they were done selling their goods, the peasants would set off to the shops to buy whatever they needed: some shoes, a peasant coat, a kerchief as a gift for the wife, and other small items. And now the real war of competition would rage. Every shopkeeper was shouting, whining—dragging a customer over to his own stall—trying to demonstrate in any which way that his merchandise was better, nicer and stronger than that of his competitor. But this didn't pass so uneventfully, for these customers were responsible for more than a few losses before they made any purchase: despite the shopkeeper's careful scrutiny to make sure this non-Jew[2] did not swipe anything, and in spite of the watchful eyes of the entire household, all standing guard—a pair of shoes or something else quite often vanished into thin air.

They used to tell lots of stories, communicating in a mixture of Polish, Yiddish, and even Hebrew.

The peasants would end the market day in the taverns. There they would satisfy their hunger and thirst with liquor accompanied by a snack, from which the tavernkeepers made their living. And thus, half-drunk, the peasants would be singing as they left the *shtetl*. Now life was about to return to an even keel—tranquil and genteel.

[Page 497]

In the town there were also shopkeepers who derived their livelihoods exclusively from aristocrats, the landed gentry who lived nearby. But these were not ordinary shopkeepers who waited around all day for a customer. To most of them—like David Halpern, Hershl Dmitrewski, also Motke Kotik—customers came with a degree of courtesy; it was no small matter to do business with the aristocrats! With the aristocrats you didn't clap your hands the way the ordinary peasants and shopkeepers did. When the *poritz* [aristocrat] climbed down from his *britchke* [buggy], the shopkeeper would greet him with an affected smile. First the two of them would have some tea and a light bite together; and only when it came time for the actual sale did they go over to the merchandise. The shopkeeper's entire household would participate, presenting and extolling the merchandise, and just making small talk with the *poritz*—in either Russian or Polish, of course. And after the sale was completed, they would say their goodbyes most amiably. Perhaps surprisingly, however, none of these businessmen was wealthy. Their economic situation was no better that that of the ordinary shopkeepers—possibly even worse. They had a very limited number of customers, and most of the sales were on credit.

There were various kinds of merchants in the marketplace: small-time merchants, who might buy inexpensive items, such as a bit of pig's hair, some eggs, a rooster, or the like—nothing more valuable because of their limited ability to lay out enough money. But there were also real merchants who used to buy everything possible: cattle, grain, etc. It is worthwhile to mention several by name because of the unique traits each had. I remember them from my early youth in Mayer-Hirsch's *Bays Medresh* [Study Hall that served as a synagogue], where they were always attending prayer services after I returned from the Yeshiva of Krynki[3].

I can remember what a Sabbath prayer service in Mayer-Hirsch's *Bays Medresh* was like: The *Bays-Medresh* is packed, and the eastern wall[4] is occupied by the most prominent men. Aharon-Hirsch, a learned layman who owns a dry-goods store, is sitting there: his patriarchal, snow-white beard gives him a stately appearance. And there, standing in the corner near the Holy Ark, is Layzer-Moishe, who also owns a dry-goods store; he is the son-in-law of the previous rabbi. He is a great Judaic lay scholar who is actually also acquainted with secular knowledge. Sitting between them is old grey-haired Tzadik, known as "*Anustn*" ["A While Back"]. He got this nickname because he liked to tell all kinds of stories about events that had taken place in our *shtetl*, and he would always add that the event had taken place "a while back". And when someone asked him: "*Reb* [Mr.] Tzadik, when did this particular event actually occur?" he would say: "Oh, around 50 or 60 years ago!…"

[Page 498]

And there is Aharon-Yosef the grain merchant, an agile man of medium height, who is always endeavoring to be the one who goes up to the *omed* [prayer-service lectern] to lead the prayers. His father, a quite elderly man in his late 90s, is sitting next to him. And before the prayer service can start, there begins what might be viewed as haggling over who is going to go up to the *omed*. Truthfully, each of them really wants to. But the one who is the most concerned is Aharon-Yosef the grain merchant—who is always afraid someone else may get there before him. For this reason, he is almost always the first to go up to the *omed*. He *davens* [leads the service] with heartfelt feeling in his own lovely and unique Sabbath melody. After the service ends, when everyone is wishing him a "*Gut Shabbes*" [Good Sabbath] as they congratulate him on how nicely he had *davened*, he beams with happiness. In addition, his elderly mother is taking great pleasure and pride in his performance, commenting "Certainly no small thing, such *davenen*!"

Who can recall them all? Yet each was an entire world of Torah and wisdom within himself.

Translator's Footnotes:

1.   From *Kamenetz-Litovsk, Zastavije and Colonies Memorial Book*, edited by S. Eisenstadt and M. Galbert, published by the Israel and America Committee of Kamenetz Litovsk and Zastavya, (Orly, Tel Aviv, Israel, 1970), pp. 495-498.
2.   Yiddish/Hebrew *orel* [*arel*] = uncircumcised, a derogatory term

3.   Krynki, Poland, located about 100km due north of Kamenetz, near Bialystok.
4.   The eastern wall was preferred because it faced Jerusalem, towards which everyone faced during the main prayers.

[Page 499]

Life in Kamenetz[1]

by Yakov Aronowicz (Buenos Aires)

Translated by Allen Flusberg

Kamenetz-Litowsk, geographically located between Brisk-Litowsk and Pruzhany[2], was a Jewish town that was just like all the other Jewish towns. Its Jewish population was not very large—500 families in all—yet a full-blooded Jewish life flourished there in every way. There were 10 study houses[3], a Talmud Torah [religious school for older children], and a *shtibl* [small synagogue] for Ḥasidim. There Jews prayed and studied, strictly observing the beautiful religious life, until they perished in the Holocaust.

The Kamenetz Rabbi, Rabbi Reuven Burstein of blessed memory, was a great religious scholar—the scion of a rabbinical family—and also an intellectual[4]. And many of the large number of respectable middle-class Jews of the town were very religiously learned.

Kamenetz had an illustrious synagogue, hundreds of years old, containing a Holy Ark [where Torahs are kept] that was considered an artistic marvel: people would come from far and wide to visit the synagogue and view its ark. But the synagogue burned down during the great Kamenetz fire that took place during the First World War[5]. Afterwards on the site of this synagogue they built the Talmud Torah, where many children studied, including children who did not live in the town. And Kamenetz Jews, none of them wealthy, would provide meals for these nonresident children.

For the most part the Jews of Kamenetz made their living selling merchandise from shops; very few of the Jews were craftsmen, and only a small number of them were laborers. Nevertheless, they managed to support the famous *yeshivo ketano*[6], headed by the very learned Rabbi Shlomo Chayim. A special building was erected for this yeshiva, funded by Kamenetz and American Jews.

There were many intellectuals, teachers and writers in Kamenetz. There were political parties of all persuasions, the majority being Pioneer Zionist.

50 years ago Kamenetz already possessed a Jewish library with a robust membership as well as ordinary readers. Most of the books were in Hebrew, and some in Russian.

Translator's Footnotes:

1.   From *Kamenetz-Litovsk, Zastavije and Colonies Memorial Book*, edited by S. Eisenstadt and M. Galbert, published by the Israel and America Committee of Kamenetz Litovsk and Zastavya, (Orly, Tel Aviv, Israel, 1970), p. 499.
2.   Kamenetz is about halfway between these two cities. Brest-Litowsk (called Brisk by the Jews) is located ~40km south of Kamenetz; Pruzhany, Belarus, is located ~50km northeast of Kamenetz.
3.   *botay-medroshim* (Yiddish plural of *bays-medresh*) = study houses that often doubled as synagogues.
4.   See the following articles of this Yizkor Book: Y. Gershuni, "Rabbi Reuven David Hakohen Burstein, May God Avenge His Blood" (pp. 50-54); Ch. Mendelson, "Rabbi Reuven Burstein" (pp. 409-410).
5.   On the fire, see the following articles of this Yizkor Book: Y. Koscikiewicz-Grunt, "Kamenetz-Litowsk During the First World War" (pp. 87-89); Y. Post, "Kamenetz-Litowsk, Where I've Never Been" (pp. 500-501).
6.   *yeshivo ketano* (yeshiva ketana) = a high-school-level school for religious studies

[Pages 500-501]

Kamenetz-Litowsk, Where I've Never Been[1]

By Yosef Post (New York)

Translated by Allen Flusberg

Although I've never been there, I have "gotten to know" the *shtetl* [little town] of Kamenetz—and not only just recently. For nearly forty years I have been seeing the *shtetl* through the eyes of my wife Chana (Chana Kuptchik), daughter of Faygl and Herschl, who had lived in their beloved town, the place where they had been born. More than once it has seemed to me that I am strolling through the streets of Kamenetz with my wife and her family; not only do I see the *Slup* [ancient medieval tower]—I see the row of shops, I see their grandfather's windmill in Zastavya; and in addition I feel I know a large number of the residents, practically by name.

I see the synagogue in all its glory and splendor: its extraordinarily beautiful Holy Ark, with its crafted woodwork, and the two lions, looking very much alive, standing guard over the descending stairs. This synagogue was comparable with the most beautiful temples of the world.

Such a love for a native *shtetl* does not fall under the framework of ordinary nostalgia: it is a portion of one's life that accompanies a person all the way into very old age and perhaps beyond, to all eternity.

Only recently did I become acquainted with friends from the Kamenetz-Litowsk Book Committee, with whom I became quite close.

From our forty years of "roaming" around Kamenetz, we could report hundreds of episodes about the *shtetl*; but one episode, which my wife never tires of telling about, occurred in the aftermath of the fire, during the First World War, when about seventy-five houses burned down, and dozens of families were forced to move in with others in the remaining houses. Together with several other families, my wife's family moved into Shidlowski's house. When it got too crowded there, they, together with Rachtche Sofer and her family moved into a loft on Brisk Street, over Rochel Geier's tavern. The old *rebbetzin* [rabbi's wife][2] and her three children, Pinye, Shoulke and Chayene, had already been living there beforehand. The apartment, consisting of two rooms and a kitchen, was now housing eleven people, yet they lived there together as nicely as if they had been a single family. They were under the supervision of one mother—the very clever and warm woman, *Rebbetzin* Rabinowitch. To this very day I still hear about her little aphorisms that gushed with down-to-earth wisdom.

I can still also hear the singing from back then, resounding outside during the Sabbaths of summer, as the streets filled with strolling young people—a sound that will never be heard again.

Footnotes:

1. From *Kamenetz-Litovsk, Zastavije and Colonies Memorial Book*, edited by S. Eisenstadt and M. Galbert, published by the Israel and America Committee of Kamenetz Litovsk and Zastavya, (Orly, Tel Aviv, Israel, 1970), pp. 500-501.
2. See p. 329 of this volume, in article entitled "Kamenetz Yizkor Book Necrology".

Persons in Town

[Page 505]

R. Yosef Vigutov[1][2]

by Ch.Z. Mendelson[3]

Translated by Allen Flusberg

Among the people learned in Torah and the leading members of the community in our *shtetl* [little town], there were also Jews who, aside from their Torah knowledge, were also dedicated heart and soul to the welfare of the community. One of these, who achieved an outstanding reputation throughout the region, was the Torah-learned volunteer worker R.[4] Yosef Vigutov of blessed memory, who together with other esteemed members of the community, such as R. Avrohom Shaya Nosson and R. Hirsh Rudnicki, led the assistance work in our town.

During the period in which the Germans captured our *shtetl* [during the First World War] and immediately began to confiscate the entire wealth of the region—already in those days the Germans were conducting their effort of plunder with great brutality. There stood out in particular a member of the military who would, with sadistic pleasure, beat Jews whom he came across while he was riding his horse; he was accompanied by his assistant, Chwat, a son of the German teacher Chwat, of whom it was rumored that they were *meshumodim* [Jewish converts to Christianity].

But worse than that in that period was when the farmers became so impoverished that they had nothing more to bring to town to sell. In addition, monetary support that a large fraction of the population used to receive from their relatives in America was suspended. Consequently, the economic situation in our town deteriorated from one day to the next, until the majority of the population was actually starving. They didn't even have clothing to wear: they were wearing wooden shoes, as well as garments fabricated from German coats that had been purchased from German soldiers.

At that time, we needed someone to lead an assistance program, someone with a truly warm Jewish heart who would be prepared to sacrifice his own needs to benefit the public welfare. The monthly support that our *shtetl* was receiving from the JOINT was not nearly enough to aid those in need, not even partially.

[Page 506]

I vividly recall the heart-rending spectacles at R. Yosef Vigutov's house. His home was always full of people who had come to ask for aid. They were all crying out, begging, pouring out their bitter hearts, describing the great deprivations that they were experiencing. R. Yosef, whose desire it was to help everyone, would grimace with pain; for as great as the needs were, the available funds were limited. Yet no one left emptyhanded, whether he received a note that would get him bread from the baker, or a few German marks in cash. Nor did R. Yosef forget the impoverished individuals who were too ashamed to ask.

I remember him well: a tall man, running around worriedly all the time, deep in thought—ignoring his own livelihood, which he obtained from a tavern. Every evening would find him sitting at home, studying Torah late into the night. This was the kind of aid workers that our little town had—who can forget them!

Translator's Footnotes:

1. From *Kamenetz-Litovsk, Zastavije and Colonies Memorial Book*, edited by S. Eisenstadt and M. Galbert, published by the Israel and America Committee of Kamenetz Litovsk and Zastavya, (Orly, Tel Aviv, Israel, 1970), pp. 505-506.
2. See also article on pp. 122-123 of this volume, "Yosef Vigutov and Bendet Winograd", which contains a photograph of Yosef Vigutov.
3. The printed version of the Yizkor Book lists the author as Pinchos Ravid-Rudnicki. A handwritten note next to this name corrects the name of the author to Ch. Z. Mendelson.
4. R. stands for *Reb*, a title similar to English "Mr.".

[Page 507]

Avrohom Hersh Kotik[1]

by Zalman Reisen

Translated by Allen Flusberg

Avrohom Hersh Kotik was born in Kamenetz-Litowsk on the 3rd of Elul[2], 1868. He was the son of Yechezkel Kotik. At the age of four he had already begun learning from children's teachers. Later he moved to Kiev with his parents. In 1881 he enrolled in a Warsaw state gymnasia (high school), but he was expelled from the school in 1886 because of revolutionary activity. Much later, in 1898, he completed his education at the Warsaw University as a pharmacist.

From the very beginning of his youth he took part in the socialist movement, leading the propaganda and enlightenment effort in Russian. But realizing that the Jewish workers did not understand any Russian, he got the idea that there was a need to create a popular scientific literature in Yiddish.

In 1894, together with A. Breslern, he began publishing a series entitled *Visenshaftliche Folks-Bikher* [Popular Science Books], of which the first was entitled "What Life Was Like for People Several Thousand Years Ago". This publication played a certain role in the years of the Jewish workers' movement before the *Bund*[3] was founded and immediately afterwards.

After a break of several years (1900), A. H. Kotik renewed his publishing activity in Bialystok, where he also served as a teacher. He established the publishing company *Folks-Bildung* [Popular Education], where Avrohom Reisen and afterwards Y. Ch. Brener served as secretaries.

[Page 508]

In 1904 Kotik settled in Minsk, where he founded a *Yiddishist*[4] Center, one of the first that would occupy itself with putting together a Yiddish grammar, Yiddish textbooks, etc. Members of the center included David Kasel, Sarah Reisen, and Yosef Tzipkin, to name a few. Zalman Reisen was then working under Kotik as a secretary. In July 1905 Kotik was arrested for his connections to the *Bund*, but he was released during the October events[5].

In 1906 he gave lectures on Yiddish literature for the Warsaw Jewish night courses. In 1912 he became the editor-in-fact of the weekly supplement of the [newspaper] *Heint*, called the "House Doctor".

During the First World War he and his entire family were forced to wander across various cities of Russia as the representative of the newspaper *Russkiye Vedomosti*[6]. In 1920 he returned to Poland as director of the information section of the public-health medical organization of the Joint[7].

In February, 1924 he came to America, but because of the limitations on immigration he was forced to leave the country in 1926. He went off to Moscow, where he took a position in the education department.

In his versatile activity and creative work, Kotik also published journalistic and popular science articles in various Yiddish and Russian newspapers. He wrote about culture and school issues, bibliography, economic issues, social hygiene, and the like.

(From Zalman Reisen's Lexicon, as abridged by Chaya Krakowski)

Translator's Footnotes:

1.   From *Kamenetz-Litovsk, Zastavije and Colonies Memorial Book*, edited by S. Eisenstadt and M. Galbert, published by the Israel and America Committee of Kamenetz Litovsk and Zastavya, (Orly, Tel Aviv, Israel, 1970), pp. 507-508.
2.   August 21, 1868 (Gregorian)
3.   The Jewish Labor Bund was a secular Jewish socialist party in Eastern Europe. See the following link, retrieved July 2020: https://en.wikipedia.org/wiki/General_Jewish_Labour_Bund
4.   The *Yiddishist* movement emphasized the central role of the Yiddish language in culturally uniting the Jews of Eastern Europe. See the following link, retrieved July 2020: https://en.wikipedia.org/wiki/Yiddishist_movement
5.   In October 1905, Czar Nicholas II of Russia, pressured by an insurrection, signed the October Manifesto, agreeing to basic civil rights, political parties, and a legislative parliament. See the following link, retrieved July 2020: https://en.wikipedia.org/wiki/1905_Russian_Revolution#Start_of_the_revolution
6.   This Russian liberal daily newspaper was published in Moscow until 1918. See the following link, retrieved July 2020: https://en.wikipedia.org/wiki/Russkiye_Vedomosti
7.   Joint is the American Jewish Joint Distribution Committee, an American-based Jewish relief organization that was providing postwar assistance to the Jewish communities of Eastern Europe in the 1920s. See the following link, retrieved July 2020: https://en.wikipedia.org/wiki/American_Jewish_Joint_Distribution_Committee

[Page 509]

R. Shepsl *Soifer* [the Scribe][1]

by Prof. Shmuel Eisenstadt (Tel Aviv)
(From My Father's Memoirs)

Translated by Allen Flusberg

My father, Yosef Eisenstadt, recounts the following in the memoirs of his youth in Chemeri[2]:

On the eve of every holiday, my father, R.[3] Yaakov Ber, used to send charity from his estate to Kamenetz and the surrounding littles towns—not less than 18 rubles to each of them, to be distributed among the poor people of each place. He also used to send wagons, laden with potatoes from his own fields, to the *gabbais*[4] of Kamenetz, to distribute to poor families for Passover.

*

When I was only seven years old, I was already quite aware that there was a *soifer* [scribe] living in Kamenetz who wrote scrolls for Torahs, *tefillin* [phylacteries] and *mezuzes* [door-posts]. He name was R. Shepsl. We children were very fond of him because he was funny and told great stories. Although very poor, he was always jolly and good-natured; and he was a treasure house of sayings and ideas.

And when R. Shepsl's source of income dried up completely—because townspeople who had no children stopped commissioning him to write Torah scrolls—he was not at all flustered, and he decided to set off on a journey to the Land of Israel. Townspeople who knew him well provided him with expenses for the trip.

After a year had passed he returned to Kamenetz, bringing with him all the best of things: a few bags of earth from the Land of Israel[5]; Torah *Atzei Chayim*[6], made of cedarwood from Lebanon; pomegranates from the vicinity of Jericho; coconuts; and most of all, an endless stockpile of stories about the wonders that he experienced on his journey to the Land of Israel.

[Page 510]

R. Shepsl, always a welcome guest at our house, used to visit our estate quite often. He was treated like a gentleman and a scholar, and he would always stay over for several days. My father received him very respectfully and rewarded him with a few rubles and a flask of wine for *kiddush* and *havdola*[7]. On each of his visits to our estate that took place after he had returned from the Land of Israel, he would tell us children his wondrous stories. And in our imaginations, we used to think of him as a kind of reincarnation of the prophet Elijah.

Translator's Footnotes:

1.   From *Kamenetz-Litovsk, Zastavije and Colonies Memorial Book*, edited by S. Eisenstadt and M. Galbert, published by the Israel and America Committee of Kamenetz Litovsk and Zastavya, (Orly, Tel Aviv, Israel, 1970), pp. 509-510.

2.   There is currently (2020) a place named Chemeri about 8km east of Kamenetz.

3.   R. = *Reb*, a title similar to English "Mr."

4.   *gabbai* = synagogue treasurer functionary, who, among other duties, collected contributions and organized the provision of charity to the needy

5.   There is a Jewish burial custom outside Israel to place earth from the Land of Israel in the grave with the body. See the following link (in Hebrew, retrieved Aug 2020):
https://he.wikipedia.org/wiki/%D7%A2%D7%A4%D7%A8_%D7%90%D7%A8%D7%A5_%D7%99%D7%A9%D7%A8%D7%90%D7%9C

6.   *Atzei Ḥaim* (singular *Etz Ḥaim*) = two poles with handles that Torah scrolls are mounted on to facilitate rolling the scrolls forward or backward to the section that is to be read. See the following link (retrieved Aug 2020): https://en.wikipedia.org/wiki/Etz_Chaim

7.   *kiddush, havdola (havdala)* = blessings, accompanied by wine, for welcoming the Sabbath and taking leave of the Sabbath, respectively

[Page 511]

Shlomo Mandelblatt,
May God Avenge His Blood[1]

by Leah Aloni-Bobrowski (Tel Aviv)

Translated by Allen Flusberg

Shloimke was born in Kamenetz-Litowsk. His parents were Nechama and Yossl Mandelblatt; the latter was a writer who for many years was a Yiddish-Russian teacher in our town. Even as a child, Shloimke was an excellent student. At the age of 12 he was already actively working alongside his father in the Yiddish-Russian classes, but all this did not satisfy him—he was striving for an education.

He taught himself from textbooks until the First World War broke out. When the Germans occupied Kamenetz at that time, no one needed the Russian language anymore, and the writer Yossl and his family were left without any livelihood. But Shloimke did not lose courage. Right away he began to study German diligently, and he was very successful. It didn't take very long for Shloimke to obtain a position as a secretary and translator for the German military authority in Kamenetz, a job that greatly improved his family's economic situation.

[Page 512]

During the course of his work in the headquarters of the German command, he tried as hard as he could to help the citizens of Kamenetz, whether Jewish or Christian. When the First World War ended and the Germans retreated from our area, Shloimke was again unemployed.

As soon as the Polish state came into existence and incorporated our shtetl, Shloimke began to study again. With much difficulty he acquired Polish textbooks and intensively devoted himself to learning the Polish language. He studied while concealed in an attic, just as many of the Jewish youth of Kamenetz were doing, because the cruel Polish police commander, a Jew hater, would beat any Jew whom he came across.

When Shloimke was convinced that he knew both written and spoken Polish well, he began to seek a practical occupation. He went to the Polish police headquarters and spoke directly to the Polish police commander, the Jew hater, offering his services as secretary and translator in the Polish military authority. The police commander responded with derision, expecting to bestow a bit of a beating on him, but Shloimke was not flustered. He reminded the police commander that the majority of Kamenetz's citizens were Jews and *Provoslavna* [Eastern Orthodox] who did not know the Polish language, and so the Polish police headquarters would need a translator who could lighten the work load of the police authorities. After he had said this, the police commander gave him a sheet of paper and asked him to write the following in Polish: "All the Jews are Communists and enemies of the Polish Fatherland, and they should all be shot." Shloimke responded boldly and emphatically: "I am a Jew and I will not write those words about my people!" The commander softened a bit and said: "Then write whatever you wish."

Shloimke wrote down his resumé, in which he noted that in that very same building he had also worked as a German secretary and translator. He said that if the commander wanted someone to vouch for his honesty, he could ask the Catholic citizens of Kamenetz, many of whom Shloimke had helped in their interactions with the German police.

[Page 513]

Once the commander was convinced that everything that Shloimke had said and written was true, he called Shloimke in and said: "You will be my secretary!" And when Shloimke began working in the Polish headquarters, the savage commander stopped beating Jews. Shloimke became the Jews' patron: whoever needed help came directly to him, and he rescued many Jews from various troubles and evil decrees. He served both the Jewish and Christian population with great faithfulness.

When they held the very first election for the local municipality of Kamenetz, the local government appointed Shloimke Mandelblatt as the town secretary in the municipality,[2] even though a candidate who was Polish was competing against him. Shloimke was a personality who was well liked by all the citizens of Kamenetz, both Jewish and Christian. A man of profound understanding, he knew how to adapt to all the different types of people that he dealt with throughout the course of his work in the municipality. His competence and tactfulness made it possible for him to remain in his position for many long years, from his difficult start all the way to his tragic end.

Shloimke was married to Chaya-Sara Chazanowitz. They led a tranquil, dignified family life.

When the Nazi murderers took over Kamenetz, the Mandelblatts' oldest son, Reuven, was among the first 100 victims.[3]

Chaya-Sara, Shloimke and their children all perished at the hand of the German murderers, together with all the other Jews of Kamenetz and Zastavya.

May their memory be a blessing.

Translator's Footnotes:

    1.   From *Kamenetz-Litovsk, Zastavije and Colonies Memorial Book*, edited by S. Eisenstadt and M. Galbert, published by the Israel and America Committee of Kamenetz Litovsk and Zastavya, (Orly, Tel Aviv, Israel, 1970), pp. 511-513.
    2.   See for example A. Yoffe, "The Orchestra", pp. 492-494 of this volume.
    3.   See D. Galpern, "The Kamenetz Ghetto (A Testimony)", pp. 550-556; also D. Galpern, "The Tragedy of Jewish Kamenetz", pp. 91-104 of the original English section (both in this volume), where several of the victims are listed by name, and additional information on Mandelblatt in 1941 is provided.

[Page 514]

Dr. Ayzik Gorny,
May God Avenge His Blood[1]

by N. N.

Translated by Allen Flusberg

Dr. Ayzik Gorny was born in Kamenetz. His parents made it possible for him to receive a traditional upbringing as well as a secular education. Right after the First World War—when he was 13 years old—he got into the 5th class of the Hebrew Gymnasia in Bialystok, where his parents had also taken up residence. But two months later his father died.

After his father's death, the economic situation of the bereaved family worsened considerably. But Ayzik continued learning, spending hours on mathematics, preparing himself for his studies. It should be noted that after his father's death he recited *kaddish*[2] for him several times a day, and even studied a chapter of Mishna[3] to honor his memory.

[Page 515]

At the age of 17 he left to study in university—first in Switzerland and then in France—where he studied mathematics, and obtained a doctorate. He was given a university chair in France[4].

In spite of the fact that outside the country Dr. A. Gorny was not living in a traditional Jewish environment, he courageously kept his Jewish name, and he participated in circles that were active in nationalist funds that supported building up a free national home in the Land of Israel.

During the Second World War, on Yom Kippur[5] of 1942, he was sent to Auschwitz by the Nazis, who had occupied France. And he never returned from there.

Dr. Ayzik Gorny published mathematical works that can be found in the mathematics faculty of the Jerusalem University. In that faculty, a conference was held on October 8, 1963, in which Prof. S. Mandelblatt of England[6] memorialized Dr. Ayzik Gorny, referencing a number of the works of the scholar who had been put to death.[7]

Translator's Footnotes:

1. From *Kamenetz-Litovsk, Zastavije and Colonies Memorial Book*, edited by S. Eisenstadt and M. Galbert, published by the Israel and America Committee of Kamenetz Litovsk and Zastavya, (Orly, Tel Aviv, Israel, 1970), pp. 514-515.
2. The *kaddish* prayer is recited by mourners during synagogue prayer services
3. The Mishna, written down around 200 CE, is a compilation of the laws of Judaism. It is customary for mourners to study chapters of Mishna to honor the memory of the deceased.
4. Gorny's position was at Clermont-Ferrand University, located ~400km south of Paris. See the following article: M. Audin, "Mathematiques à Strasbourg-Clermont-Ferrand (1939-44)…" (in French, retrieved September 2020) at http://irma.math.unistra.fr/~maudin/MathAuvergne.pdf. This article, which summarizes a 1993 university colloquium on the period of German occupation, adds the following details about Gorny: "The thesis of Ayzik Gorny was the longest mathematics thesis during the period 1914-1945—359 pages long! Its subject was the theory of functions of a real variable, with Szolem Mandelbrojt. Although he [Gorny] was a young man [in 1939-1940], he had not been mobilized [by the French army, fighting against Germany] because he was a foreigner…He was an assistant in the Faculty of Sciences of Clermont-Ferrand…[In 1940-41, in response to anti-Semitic decrees,] Gorny was remunerated unofficially as a library employee at a salary that was certainly meager; it was a handout within a solidarity network that apparently worked well…[By 1942] Gorny had already disappeared from the landscape; arrested before October 1941, he left Drancy for Auschwitz in Convoy 37, on September 25, 1942. " Drancy, located near Paris, served as an internment camp for Jews before they were transported to Auschwitz.
5. Yom Kippur of that year occurred on September 21, 1942. In the Holocaust Survivors and Victims Database of the US Holocaust Memorial Museum, the date of the convoy that brought Ayzik Gorny to Auschwitz is given as September 25, 1942. See the following link (retrieved September 2020): https://www.ushmm.org/online/hsv/person_view.php?PersonId=5328794
6. It is possible that the reference is to Szolem Mandelbrojt (1899-1983), a mathematician who appears to have been Gorny's thesis advisor (see Footnote 4).
7. See the following: A. Gorny, "Contribution a L'Étude des Fonctions Dérivables d'une Variable Réelle" [Contribution to the Study of Differentiable Functions of a Real Variable], *Acta Math.* 71, pp. 317-358 (1939), available at the following link (retrieved September 2020): https://projecteuclid.org/euclid.acta/1485888266. The theorem derived by Gorny in this paper has become known as "Gorny's Inequality". See for example C. Fabry, "An Elementary Proof of Gorny's Inequality", *Proc. Royal Soc. Edinburgh, Sec. A: Mathematics*, 105, pp. 345-349 (1987).

[Page 516]

Yankl Zlates[1]

by M. Naiman

Translated by Allen Flusberg

During the First World War, a very large number of people were suffering from hunger, fear and illness in Kamenetz. Families stayed together as a group and suffered together. At that time Yankl Zlates of Zastavya lost his entire family (except for one brother, Avrohom Moishe and family, who later died at the hands of the Nazis); and he, the youngest of his brothers, was starving. He was sleeping in attics and walking around in tattered clothing.

When he grew up, however, he became a capable young man. He organized labor meetings and spoke before the workers, explaining to them that they should join a union, so that together they could fight for better working conditions. Not all the workers listened to him, but Yankl did not give up. After a hard day of labor, together with Bentze Safir, Layzer Kagan and many other workers, he would go out to round the workers up at work, so that they would not work 10 hours or more a day. Yankl and the others wanted to fight for an 8-hour workday. It was difficult to make this happen, but organizing the workers in unions was successful. After a great struggle the workers there became conscientious members of professional unions.

Yankl was also one of the first to come up with the idea that the town must have a library. Together with Moishke Greenblatt, Moishke Visotzky, Gitl Sofer and Hiyene the Rebbetzin's[2], he founded the first Jewish workers' library. This library brought the town joy: every evening young boys and girls would come to the library to read books and also to meet their friends. These were lovely, pleasant years.

After that Yankl was selected as a councilman, representing the workers of Kamenetz, while Yosl Vigutov[3] became the representative of the shopkeepers and businessmen. Matuchnik was then the mayor of the municipality and Shloimke Mandelblatt[4] was the secretary.

[Page 517]

Yankl was always watching out to make sure that the poor segment of the population was not burdened by too much tax. The mayor and the secretary always paid attention to what he had to say, and many times they also followed his opinion. He was kindhearted and did many favors for poor people.

Later, Yankl, together with Yosl Vigutov were selected as councilmen to the Assembly in Brisk [Brest-Litowsk][5]. Once a month the councilmen from the impoverished little towns used to come to Brisk for the sessions, to defend the interests of their towns.

Yankl died in Brooklyn on July 10, 1963.

Translator's Footnotes:

1. From *Kamenetz-Litovsk, Zastavije and Colonies Memorial Book*, edited by S. Eisenstadt and M. Galbert, published by the Israel and America Committee of Kamenetz Litowsk and Zastavya, (Orly, Tel Aviv, Israel, 1970), pp. 516-517.
2. See Y. Post, "Kamenetz-Litowsk, Where I've Never Been," pp. 500-501 in this volume. This Hiyene (or Chayene) appears to have been the daughter of Gitl Rabinowitz, the widow of the former Chief Rabbi of Kamenetz, Moshe Yitzchok Rabinowitz. See p. 329 of the Necrology section of this volume; also the following two articles in this volume by M. Rabinowitz: "Rabbi Moshe Yitzchok Rabinowitz, of Blessed Memory", pp. 405-407; "My Grandfather, Rabbi Moshe Yitzhak of Kamenetz-Litowsk", p. 49.
3. See the following two articles, both in this volume: R.V., "Yosef Vigutov and Bendet Winograd", pp. 122-123; Ch. Mendelson, "R. Yosef Vigutov", pp. 505-506.
4. See the following article on pp. 511-513 in this volume: L. Aloni-Bobrowski, "Shlomo Mandelblatt, May God Avenge His Blood".
5. Brest-Litowsk, Belarus is located about 40km south of Kamenetz.

<u>Destruction and Ruin</u>

[Pages 521-533]

The Destruction of Kamenetz
at the Beginning of the Second World War[1][2][3][4]

by Dora Galperin
(From her letters to Leah and Dov Aloni)

Translated by Allen Flusberg

*This Yiddish article was translated into English in the article entitled "The Tragedy and Destruction of Kamenetz",
by Dora Galperin, pp. 91-104 of the English section of this Yizkor Book.*

A group of Jews just before their execution
(This photograph was found in the possession of a German soldier)

Translator's Footnotes:

1.   From *Kamenetz-Litovsk, Zastavije and Colonies Memorial Book*, edited by S. Eisenstadt and M. Galbert, published by the Israel and America Committee of Kamenetz Litovsk and Zastavya, (Orly, Tel Aviv, Israel, 1970), pp. 521-533.

2.   The words at the end of the Yiddish title, "At the Beginning of the Second World War", are apparently a misprint; they should have appeared as the title of the first section of the article, as is evident in both the Hebrew (p. 165) and English translations. It appears that the English translation was based on both the original Yiddish and the Hebrew translation.

3.   On page 524 of the Yiddish version and p. 167 of the Hebrew version, the following statement is made: "They were Issachar-Velvel Freier from Kobrynska Street, his daughter Beyla, Zuna Pochalski's son-in-law, and a man from Warsaw, Dr. Gelberg's guest." The English version misspells the name "Freier" as "Freizer" and the name "Zuna Pochalski" as "Zina Porolska."

4.   In the Yiddish version, the last sentence of the article is missing the following words "…and the life in the Russian paradise." These words appear in both the Hebrew and English versions

[Page 534]

From the Ghettos to the Concentration Camps[1]

by Yitzhak Portnoy, Kfar Saba

Translated by Allen Flusberg

At the end of 1942, the Germans gave an order that everyone from Kamenetz had to move into the Ghetto of Pruzhany[2], but a few days later we found out that not everyone would be moving at the same time. When Kamenetz residents began arriving in the Prozhany Ghetto, I met the following: (1) Sholom Kaminski. (2) Yitzchok the *shochet* [ritual slaughterer] (Yitzchok Stupicewski), with his family. (3) David Bash with his family. He perished in Auschwitz. His wife had died in the Pruzhany Ghetto; his oldest son had been sent to the Bielowieza Forest[3] to do forest work, and from there he vanished to this very day. (4) Kaufman (a bagel baker), who had a son Shlomo (a shoemaker); and his son–in–law from Chernovchytz[4], Shiya Fishbein, with his wife and daughter. Later they illicitly went back to the Kamenetz Ghetto. (5) My friend Bentze Sorkes (who was called Bentze Kashemachers) with his children; they lived on the small street that Shepsel's *beis medrash*[5] was on. They had a shop in Rad[6]. His wife was named Sara[7] (the daughter of Itzel the butcher; she was an aunt of Berchyk Schmidt[8]). They, too, illicitly returned to the Kamenetz Ghetto several weeks later. (6) Leibel Pomeranczik with his family (his daughter lives in Tel Aviv); he was a *rebbe*[9] in Kamenetz. They had a linen shop in Rad[10]. They went back to the Kamenetz Ghetto, as well. (7) The family of Noske (the *melamed*[11]), who were seized as he fled back to Kamenetz; they brought them to the Pruzhany Gestapo. (I don't know what became of them.) (8) The family of Saperstein (the teacher) was also there.[12] (9) I also knew a very young man from Kamenetz, who was called Yosl Katchkele (I think he was a tailor). I don't remember his family. He perished somewhere.

Within the ghetto people did not speak to one another; they only gazed into each other's eyes.

[Page 535]

My brother Shmuelke Portnoy also came to me from Kamenetz, bringing along his pregnant wife, as well as his father–in–law (Koppel the tailor) and mother–in–law. A few weeks later they illicitly returned to the Kamenetz Ghetto. She gave birth to a child there, and after that she went to the mother–in–law. Koppel remained in Pruzhany for a longer while, and in the end went to the Kamenetz Ghetto.

My brother Shmuel also told me that the son of Koppel the tailor, whose name was Leizer Dulinski, happened to be in Brisk[13] during the period when Kamenetz was taken. There he was taken together with the first group of Brisk residents that were seized, and on that very day they were executed in the vicinity of Brisk.

When the Germans entered Kamenetz, they seized 100 Jews and shot them somewhere near Kamenetz[14]. Nachman Olshanski (son–in–law of the butcher, Nisl) was in that first group seized.[15]

When my brother saw that they were seizing people and killing them, he hid behind a gravestone in the old cemetery in Adolina.

My brother told me that Gedalia Shostakowski and Boruch Leib (the son of Nisl the butcher) were members of the Kamenetz *Judenrat*[16]. I met Boruch Leib in the Pruzhany Ghetto. He told me that he had illicitly[17] come to conduct business with the Pruzhany *Judenrat* on Jewish interests, to aid the Kamenetz and Pruzhany ghettos.

Bertzik's father, Chaim Novitzkevitcher[18], was hidden away by Gentiles of Novitzkevitch.[19] When he heard that all the Kamenetz Jews were being taken away, he went back to his family in the Kamenetz Ghetto, and he perished with them and with all the other Kamenetz Jews.

In the Pruzhany Ghetto there was a young Kamenetz boy who was working in a bakery. When I got to Israel and met up with people from Kamenetz, it turned out that that young boy was Rappaport[20], and that he had been sent to Auschwitz together with the Pruzhany Jews and had survived. He returned to Kamenetz[21] and then[22] went to Israel, where he died several years ago.

From Pruzhany the Jews were taken away in groups, 3000 people in each group. In my group I didn't meet anyone who was from Kamenetz. They brought us to the Linova[23] train station in wagons belonging to Gentiles from the surrounding villages. Just as we got off the wagons in Linova, the Gentiles gave the horses the whip and rode away, to make sure that the Jews should have no chance to take their belongings off the wagons.

[Page 536]

In Linova they put us in train boxcars, packed together and without water. Along the way many people gave the SS men gold watches and other valuables in return for a glass of water. Some gave their children urine, mixed with a little sugar, to drink. No one knew what kind of death we were going to. This trip lasted three days. Along the way many died of anguish, unable to take all that was happening to them. Some jumped out of the boxcars at the edge of the forests around Tchenstochov[24]; their fate is not known.

When we got to our destination, the SS men opened all the boxcar doors and cried out: "Everyone out without luggage!" This was in Birkenau, where I spent six weeks. There people were dropping like flies. Whoever was not able bodied, and also women with small children, were immediately brought in buses to the crematoria[25]. There were incidents in which grandmothers took their grandchildren so that their daughters could be among those able to work.

From Birkenau I was sent in a group to the Kabier Camp[26], not far from Auschwitz. There I worked in the forest. There were four work teams in our group, each of which consisted of 40 to 50 men. I didn't see anyone from Kamenetz in my group. In Kabier my job was felling trees. The four teams had four kapos, Germans who were former criminals. They were our bosses. There was also a fifth kapo who was in command over them. My kapo was a real murderer.

Every day they would take away one or two Jews and shoot them dead. In this manner I saw them shoot my brother–in–law, Velvel Ragovitch, as well as Velvel Goldberg (a son of Reuven the butcher of Pruzhany). I was there for five months.[27]

[Page 537]

At the end of these 5 months they liquidated the camp and brought us to Auschwitz. When we arrived in Auschwitz they assigned us to the "Rasko" *Kommando* [slave–labor detail], near the main road that led to a park entrance. The work day lasted from 7 AM to dusk. At noon we sat down wherever we were. Few of us had anything to eat and all of us were under guard. After having been in Birkenau, we noticed a strong odor of burning human flesh.[28] In Auschwitz, where I spent 6 weeks, I met two brothers–in–law and nephews (few of whom survived).

In the *Appellplatz*[29] they began rounding up the stronger men for work. I wound up among them, and they sent us to Buna–Werk (I.G. Farben Industries)[30], a few kilometers from Auschwitz. There they had central heat; the food was much better, because work there was hard[31]. I lost the middle finger of my right hand there; the hospital there was called K.B. The physician was a Polish Jew. After four weeks they sent me back to my work *Kommando*. My kappo was named Karol (a German Jew from a Dutch transport); he was good to everyone. We received our food according to the numbers tattooed on our arms.

Once when they noticed that I had two sweaters, I was punished with 25 lashes.

I remained working in Buna–Werk until the Russian army approached, after which I was evacuated to a nearby camp.

We arrived in Buchenwald[32] in January, 1945. I was in Buchenwald for two weeks; from Buchenwald they took us to the Zweiberger camp that was near Halberstadt. In Zweiberger I spent barely three months, under very difficult conditions. There people were dropping like flies because of the terrible hunger. Mornings they gave out coffee, one portion for three or four people. Often the man in charge of the coffee (a German) would knock over the coffee pot with his foot, and then order us to go to work. We would sleep on the ground. When we got back from work, we had to grab a blanket. The lice would feed on our bodies, making us itch. 90% of the people perished. We dug large pits, and every night after the count we had to toss the dead into the pits and carry the caskets back. We had no strength left after having carried the caskets, two men carrying each. We used to put disinfectant on the corpses.

[Page 538]

On the Road, After Escaping

On the road my friend Budgash said that we should stay, and it was no longer important where we went, as we could die anyway.[33] But I encouraged my friend, and he came along with me. Along the way we came across a pile of potatoes, and there lay nearby the dead body of a concentration–camp inmate. We continued on and saw a strong military force moving in disarray on the main highway, so we went back some distance along a side road leading to a river near a village. When dogs began to bark loudly in the village, we crossed over to a different street; we lay down in the grass next to a fence and fell asleep.

When we woke up it was light out. It was at the beginning of April, 1945. Not far from us a German civilian holding a stick was taking a walk. I wrapped my blanket around me and went over to him, asking for a piece of bread. The German pointed in the direction of our transport and told me to go there.[34]

We started off on the same road and in a few minutes came upon a group of Ukrainian women, who advised us to get ourselves into the forest, for very soon we would be liberated. We asked them for some food, and some of them gave us pieces of bread with boiled potatoes. They warned us of the bad foreman[35] who would be coming along right away, and they went off into the field…

We sat down to eat. Later another man who had escaped from the same transport, a French Jew, joined us. I gave him a piece of bread. He told us that he was going to a Polish acquaintance who was working for a German, and promised he would be back to join us as we headed into the forest. Right away we saw the work foreman, who started making us go back with him[36]. Along the way the French Jew was caught, too. He [the foreman] brought us to a group of about 100 men, who had also escaped from a transport; here we met up with four friends who had escaped with us and had gotten separated along the way. They were starving. The SS men in charge of us handed us over to civilian guards[37]. From this we understood that we would soon be liberated. Right away a German woman came with a sack of bread to distribute to us. We all pounced on the sack, each of us trying to grab it for himself. One or two men got into a fight, and as a result one man fell down and died.[38]

[Page 539]

Afterwards a few buses came with[39] civilian forces and picked us up. A bit later we were stuck on the road because of intense bombardment by the American artillery. The drivers and guards fled into the woods, with us behind them. After the shooting ended we drove on, but right away there was another bombardment by the American artillery, and we stopped not far from the town of Fanderslebn, next to a large barn. Our guards scattered and we ran over to another shed to look for potatoes. When the shooting quieted down we entered the town without any guards and spread out to look for food. A few residents of the town were walking through the streets carrying white flags. Right away the Americans arrived and gave us some bread, chocolate, cigarettes and boiled potatoes. We noticed a camp of Yugoslavs and went in; there we got some more food. At night we slept in a barn.

A few days later they put us up in a movie theatre where a sign at the entrance read: "For Jews and Poles only. No Germans allowed." We were already completely free, but I felt lonely without my family.

When I heard that the Americans were pulling out and the Russians were going to be coming in, I left on a train headed for France. In Nordhausen they asked everyone where they were from. As a Polish Jew I was detained in Nordhausen, and then later I left for a camp in Bergen–Belsen. There we met a young man from Kamenetz who had been rescued from the camps; I don't recall his first or last name. He is living in Israel[40] now. In the camp he was with Averbuch (Baruch Averbuch, a friend[41] of Bertzik Schmidt). From Bergen–Belsen I went to the camp near Munich, and from there to Italy with the *Bricha*[42]. From Italy, *landsleit* [fellow–townsman] brought me over to Argentina in the year 1948. In 1954 I came to Israel as a tourist; here I got married to a woman from Kamenetz, Sara Harle (who perished in an automobile accident), and I have remained in Israel since.[43]

—[44] **taken down by Meir Bobrowski**[45]

Translator's Footnotes:

1.   From *Kamenetz–Litovsk, Zastavije and Colonies Memorial Book*, edited by S. Eisenstadt and M. Galbert, published by the Israel and America Committee of Kamenetz Litovsk and Zastavya, (Orly, Tel Aviv, Israel, 1970), pp. 534–539. A Hebrew–language version, appearing on pp. 183–188, is essentially identical, except where noted below. It was written as a translation of the Yiddish original (see Footnote 45 below).

2.   Pruzhany is located approximately 50km northeast of Kamenetz. *Map of Routes from Kamenetz-Litovsk to Death Camps*, p. 160 of this Yizkor Book.

3.   The edge of the Bialowieza Forest is about 30km north of Kamenetz.

4.   Probably Charnauchytsy, Belarus (20km south of Kamenetz)

5.   *beis medrash* = study house, often also used as a synagogue

6.   "Rad" may refer to the narrow row of shops off the town square. This sentence is omitted in the Hebrew version.

7.   Hebrew version refers to her as Sorke (a diminutive of Sara).

8.   Also known as Dov Schmidt (see below)

9.   *rebbe* = probable meaning here is a children's teacher of religious subjects

10.   "Rad" may refer to the narrow row of shops off the town square. This sentence is omitted in the Hebrew version.

11.   *melamed* = children's teacher

12.   Hebrew version adds: "He was a teacher and was active in community affairs in Pruzhany. They all died in Auschwitz."

13.   Brisk is the Jewish name for the city of Brest, located 35 km south of Kamenetz.

14.   Pruska or Prusky Forest is located on the outskirts of Kamenetz. See article on pp. 189-191 of this Yizkor Book, L. Aloni, "A Tear for the Loss of My Townspeople"; also article on pp. 77-79, P. Rudnicki, "The Gordonia Movement in Kamenetz-Litowsk". The latter gives the distance to the Prusky Forest as 10km.

15.   Hebrew versions adds: "Also among them were Yankl Fodbiler, and Yankl Sara Sheina Chaye's."

16.   *Judenrat* (German) = Jews appointed by the Germans to a council that represented the Jewish community in dealings with the German military.

17.   Hebrew version: "clandestinely"

18.   From the context it appears that this was a nickname indicating he hailed originally from Novitzkevitch

19.   In the Hebrew version Bertzik is here referred to as Dov Schmidt. See above, Footnote 8.

20.   Hebrew version: "Yehuda Rappaport, who was sent to Auschwitz together with the Jews of Pruzhany and miraculously survived."

21.   Hebrew version: "for a few days after the war ended" . See the more detailed narratives in the the following articles in this volume: A. Glezer, "Yehuda Rappaport", p. 143; Ben-Moshe, "Kamenetz in 1945", pp. 561-568.

22.   Hebrew version: "after much wandering"

23.   Linova, Belarus, is located 10km south of Pruzhany.

24.   Częstochowa, Poland, 400km southwest of Kamenetz, and 100km north of Birkenau.

25.   Hebrew version replaces "crematoria" by "gas chambers"

26.   Kobier (German) or Kobior (Polish), a work camp set up to clear forests for firewood. See the following link (retrieved July, 2018): http://auschwitz.org/en/history/auschwitz–sub–camps/kobier/

27.   Hebrew version adds: "The air there was saturated with a sharp smell of burning flesh, coming from the crematoria of Auschwitz."

28.   This sentence is omitted in the Hebrew translation. But see Footnote 27.

29.   *Appellplatz* (German) = area of daily roll call

30.   The name of the plant was "Buna Werke". See the following link (retrieved July, 2018), which describes the history of this camp: https://en.wikipedia.org/wiki/Monowitz_concentration_camp

31.   Hebrew version: "but work there was hard, very hard."

32.   Buchenwald, Germany, located ~5km north of Weimar.

33.   Hebrew version reads: "After we made our final decision to escape from the camp, my friend Budgash, who was staying behind, said that in any event we were going to die, so what difference would it make where we breathed our last? But I encouraged my friend and he came along."

34.   Hebrew version adds: "We didn't get any bread."

35.   Hebrew version: "They warned us to watch out for the foreman who was overseeing their work; they expected him to come along momentarily."

36.   Hebrew version adds: "to our camp transport"

37.   Hebrew version adds: "who were also armed"

38.   Hebrew version has instead: "In the end one or two men managed to get a piece of bread; the rest of the bread was crushed together with one of the escapees who lay there, dead."

39.   Hebrew version adds "armed"

40.   Hebrew version adds: "in Hadera"

41.   Hebrew version has instead "a relative"

42.   *Bricha* = Postwar underground Jewish movement to get Holocaust survivors out of Europe and bring them to Palestine. See the following link (retrieved July 2018): https://en.wikipedia.org/wiki/*Bricha*

43.   Hebrew version adds this paragraph: "These were twelve years of my life, a time of wandering, hunger, terror and suffering, until I was fortunate enough to attain some status in the State of Israel."

44.   Hebrew adds: "testimony"

45.   Hebrew version states here that Yiddish was translated [into Hebrew] by Leah Aloni–Bobrowski.

[Pages 540-549]

What I Lived Through
in the Ghettos and Concentration Camps[1]

By Dvora Rudnitzky-Singer (New York)

Translated by Allen Flusberg

Note by translator: *The original Yizkor Book contains 3 versions of this article: the first in Yiddish (the present article, pp. 540-549); a translation into Hebrew (pp. 174-182); and an English version (pp. 105-116 of the English section). The three versions are essentially identical. One discrepancy is the date on which the 3rd transport from Pruzhany arrived at Auschwitz. According to the Yiddish version (p. 544) and the Hebrew version (p. 177), it was February 23, 1943; the English version (p. 110) gives the date as February 3, 1943.*

The Yiddish version begins with the following dedication, not present in the other two versions:

Dedicated to the memory of my parents Yoel and Esther, my brother Zanvil, my grandfather Aharon, my aunt Bayla-Chashe with her husband and two sons, my aunt Leah, and all our family members who were put to death by the Nazi murderers.

For the remainder of this article, see the original English version on pp. 105-116 of the English section.

Translator's Footnotes:

1. From *Kamenetz-Litovsk, Zastavije and Colonies Memorial Book*, edited by S. Eisenstadt and M. Galbert, published by the Israel and America Committee of Kamenetz Litovsk and Zastavya, (Orly, Tel Aviv, Israel, 1970), pp. 540-549.

[Page 550]

The Kamenetz Ghetto
(A Testimony)[1]

by Dora Galpern

Translated by Allen Flusberg

Before the German occupation of Kamenetz began, we had no inkling that such a great calamity was in store for us, that they were going to put all the Jews to death. We could have run away with the Soviets [when they evacuated the town], but no one did.

The Germans entered Kamenetz on June 22, 1941, around noon. At that time people were still walking around in the streets freely. The first night they did not rob or beat anyone, nor were there any rapes, since the soldiers had continued onward right away. And at first, we had enough food.

But on the second day SS men arrived in an automobile and staged a *lapanka* [roundup] in the street: whichever Jews they happened to come across were put to death. The first victims were: Sholom Galperin, Simcha–Layzer Gewirtzman, Shimon Buchgalter[2], Reuven Mandelblatt (Shloimke Mandelblatt's son), Samek Rosenstein, Shmerl Jaffe and many others. So immediately we were overcome with great fear.

On the third day a German commissar [administrator] named Wisozik was already in place, as well as a commandant: a Ukrainian from Brisk[3] (Michal Akimov). They didn't treat us very badly at first, but that did not last very long. A second commissar (Neumann) arrived, as well as a second commandant (Stanislav Reisky). These two stayed on until the very end.

Commissar Neumann was a mad dog who beat people everywhere, wherever he turned. From the very beginning, from the day he had first arrived, he beat every passerby in the street, Jew and Christian alike. He did his beating with a whip. He got around riding in a *bryczka* [chaise carriage] drawn by two fine horses. One time he was riding very fast while forcing Alter Khasanovich to run behind him, running and falling, all the way to Zastavya[4] and back. By the time Alter Khasanovich got home he was more dead than alive. I was there and saw him. After this occurrence no one dared to let himself be seen by the commissar; the main streets became as deserted as a cemetery. The *bryczka* had iron wheels, so you could hear the commissar coming from far away; and whoever heard him coming would hide wherever he could.

[Page 551]

Every day the commissar would give everyone orders where to go to work. He also demanded many items: jewelry, fur coats and other valuables.

An order was given that all Kamenetz Jews would have to leave for Pruzhany[5]; but then the order changed a bit: whoever was a skilled worker would be allowed to stay. And so everyone began trying to find a way to stay. In Kamenetz there was a technician named Michalkevitch. He registered laborers in Stolarnia, Kachlarnia, Cegielnia, and in other workplaces. Whoever could arrange it stayed put. Back then everyone still had something they could give [in exchange]. At that time Commandant–Mayor Akimov was still there, and with him you could arrange anything. Not many Kamenetzers went to Pruzhany. I believe that 70% remained in Kamenetz when you include those who had gone to Pruzhany but came back afterwards.

With respect to the Judenrat, they weren't elected by a vote, they were nominated. In the Judenrat were Gedalya Shostakowski, Moishe Melnicki, Avrohom Bash, Zalman Zhitnicki, Shayke Stempnicki, Lipa Gurwitch and Boruch Gurwitch. Within the ghetto the militiamen were exclusively Jewish. Velvl Glezer was the commandant in the ghetto, and the militiamen were: David Zhitnicki, Shayke Stempnicki, Mordechai Bobrowski, Pesach Freier, Berl Reznik, Boruch–Layb Aronowski, Isaac Golubtchik and Chaim Grunt (Yisroel Grunt's son).

When the Germans had first come, they had given orders to the Judenrat that every Jew must wear a yellow patch or a Star of David. The ghetto was set up after the German Neumann arrived. In April, 1942 the ghetto was fenced off; and the Jews were brought to the train at Wysoke[6] on November 9, 1942.

[Page 552]

In Kamenetz there were about 450 families. The ghetto was located on Brisk Street, from Oizer Garbazh up to Michael Gelerstein's house; and on the opposite side, from Rachel Geier up to Yitzchok–Mordechai Hoichman, as well as the little lane where Chava the dairy–lady (the daughter–in–law of the mason Yaakov–Leib) once lived; also the little lanes that led to Shepsl's *beis–medresh*[7]; Kobryn Street, from Yitzchok Gewirtzman to the hospital; Litowsk Street, from Yisroel Grunt to Layzer's house, and on the opposite side, up to Yisroel Grunt's factory. All of this was surrounded by barbed wire. No one was allowed to go from one ghetto to the other. Anyone caught by a policeman was beaten. Only the Judenrat and the ghetto militiamen were allowed to go from one ghetto to the other.

We were given only a few days to move into the ghetto, and everyone rushed in to grab a better place to live. We were allowed to bring all our belongings, but by then we had very little, because every day we had to sell something in order to buy food. I was in the Brisk Street Ghetto and I lived at the home of Ben–Tziyon Zub (Bertchik Schmidt's uncle). My sisters Rayzl and Golda were living in the same ghetto, and my sister Sara was living at the *kotlyer* [coppersmith] on Litowsk Street.

The little lane of Mordechai Galman was not within the ghetto. Mostly Germans were walking around on that street, since the police station was located in Osowski's house; there were Germans living in our house and that of Shidlowski, as well.

No Germans came into the ghetto, they were present only on the other side [of the fence]. None of the Christian population was allowed to enter the Jewish side; the threat was that it would be punishable by death, and no one would risk it. No underground movement to help the ghetto Jews existed on the Christian side.

Every morning the militiamen would accompany the laborers to work, and then every afternoon they would bring them back to the ghetto. The laborers always came back, all of them. There was no pay for the work. Jews were beaten for any little infraction. The ghetto was kept lit up until 11pm every night.

Several weddings took place in the ghetto. Velvl Glezer got married to Aydl Wolfson, and Bayla Schmidt married Sholom Feldman, the son of Chaim Glikes. Velvl Glezer escaped from the ghetto, but no one knows what became of him.

There were ill people in the ghetto as well. Medications were brought from Osowski's pharmacy by the Judenrat.

Several people died in the ghetto. I still remember Pinye Wapniarski, of blessed memory. Those who died were buried in the Jewish cemetery, but none of their families could be present at the funerals, since it was forbidden. Still there was always someone from the Judenrat at the burial.

[Page 553]

They did not distribute any special rations in the ghetto; everyone supplied himself with food as well as he could. Whoever had more money managed better. I believe no one was starving in the ghetto. When Gedalya Shostakowski would receive a check for 40 measures of flour, he would come to me, and we used to doctor the number to 140 or 240 and even more; and then Grigorevski would distribute it without any trouble. The manager of the mill was a German who lived in Biala–Podlaska[8] and seldom came to Kamenetz, relying instead on Grigorevski, who had a good head on his shoulders. And for this reason there was no starvation in the ghetto.

The residents of Zastavya were brought to Kamenetz and were in the ghetto together with the Kamenetz townspeople.

By then we knew that in Brisk there were no longer any living Jews,[9] and yet we continued to go to work as usual. We commemorated the first and last days of the *Yom Toivim*[10] in great sorrow in the ghetto as we wept and cried, pleading with God for a miracle, that the murderers should not find the time to liquidate the Kamenetz Jews.

When the ghetto was liquidated the Germans took all our possessions away, bringing them to *Dom Ludowy*[11] on Szkolna [School] Street. The Jews were told that they need not take anything along, since they were going to be brought to the Black Sea; there each family would receive all that was needed, as well as work, and they would live well.

The better items, such as furs, feather–beds, pillows and machine–made products, were sent by the murderers to Germany, and the rest of the items they sold on the spot to Kamenetz Germans, some of whom were locals while others were from Germany itself. The Christian population of Kamenetz was also given the opportunity to buy some of it. An auction was conducted by Zofia Staszuk of Zastavya. Her mother was a teacher; Zofia worked in the commissary office as a secretary and translator. Her German was perfect and she despised Jews. She collaborated with the Germans and [later] escaped with them from Kamenetz.

I was at the home of my sister Rayzl, who lived at Mayer Fisher's house, and from there I watched through the window as they brought 155 people (Communists) to be shot. Zosza Staszuk was riding in the *bryczka* with the commissar to observe the execution in the Pruska Woods[12]. These were young people, and among them several women. The chairman of Kamenetz, Kuzka, as well as his secretary Cebulya, and the porters Chaim and Arye Waksman (Shlomo–Zelig's sons) dug the graves and buried them there.

[Page 554]

A German stood guard on our end of the ghetto, as did Russian and Polish militiamen. I escaped from the ghetto on November 3, 1942. My escape was planned by people who lived outside the ghetto. I escaped at a time when no Germans were standing guard, only Kamenetz militiamen. They didn't shoot because they had been bought off. The militiamen who were on guard were: Tadeusz Ruzicki and Rafael Liepskevicz, both of whom were Polish; and one Russian, Vitya Razdielnikow, at whose home I [later] hid for a long time. In 1944 Razdielnikow was shot by the Soviets; the Polish militiamen escaped to Poland, where the *Akowces* [Home Army, the Polish Underground] shot them.

The first house that I stayed in just after my escape from the ghetto was that of Pavel Kozlowski, right near the ghetto boundary. Kozlowski was already waiting for me, as he knew that the Germans had gone off to eat lunch. Right away he hid me in his barn. Afterwards the following people helped me: Michas Grigorevski and his family; the Kozlowski family; Razdielnikow; and also a Christian named Kolye Zhuk, from the Rozalin colony. I hid in this colony, which was located 12 km from Kamenetz.

Once during the winter, early in the morning, Germans arrived there in an automobile, and I barely managed to climb up to the attic. I lay there in terror; it was cold and there was nowhere to escape to. The owner of the house gave them whatever they wanted: schnapps, honey, goose and duck; he was just waiting for them to drive away. It did not end very badly: they left, and then I was brought back into the apartment. I was neither dead nor alive, traumatized by cold, terror and hunger: so much so that I was unable to speak to anyone. I was crying ceaselessly and was very frightened that they might come again and bring misfortune on the family that I was staying with. They, too were now afraid to keep me on; and so I experienced a new tragedy: where should I go now? Every day I had the feeling that they had had enough of me. From there I was brought back to Kamenetz, to the family Razdielnikow. I was brought lying on a sleigh, wearing old clothing, covered by a quilt, with my head bandaged. And this is how they brought me, as if I were ill and was being taken to a hospital. Fortunately no Germans stopped us along the way.

[Page 555]

Not far from Kamenetz there was a village called Liska. The murderers burned the entire village down with all its inhabitants: men, women, children, and old people. Nothing remained of them but ashes. This happened because it had been rumored that the village had been supporting partisans who had been coming there.

I left my hiding place on July 22, 1944. During all the time I had been in hiding, I was ill more than once, but I was never able to get any medical help; it would have been too great a risk to call a Christian doctor. And this has had an adverse effect on my health.

They did not bring refugees from the colony to Kamenetz. In the Kamenetz ghetto there were people from the colonies that lay just beyond the Zastavya mills.

Even after I left my hiding place I didn't go outside for a long time. My feet were swollen. I was still afraid and didn't feel good. It was so empty and lonely, because no one was glad to see me; no one asked me where I had been all this time, and how I had managed to survive. There were those Christians who said that one survivor was also one too many. So after having hidden out I didn't stay in

Kamenetz; there was nothing for me there. I left for Brisk and lived there, but on October 23, 1944 the Soviets arrested me. They tormented me for an entire year. I was incarcerated there almost without any bread or water under terrible conditions. The reason was that they wanted to arrest Wolodie Grigorevski, who was already then in Poland; but they believed that he was still in Brisk or in Kamenetz and that I knew where he was but was refusing to tell.

My landlord Razdielnikow was always compassionate to me, but troubles came from all sides. I survived it all, but it has left a mark on the state of my health.

[Page 556]

When they led our sisters and brothers out of Kamenetz it was already cold out. It was possible to dress warmly, but traveling 10 hours to Wysoke with little children and old people was intolerable. They brought them to the train in Wysoke and from there to Treblinka, where they were all put to death.

They didn't bring anyone from the Kamenetz ghetto to Wolkowysk[13]: of that I am certain. Every day I knew exactly what was going on in the ghetto from conversations I had with the militiamen, who came to the ghetto on a daily basis.

And this is how the bloody Nazi murderers murdered all of our Kamenetz Jews.

Lyusha Kalasowski worked in the Kamenetz hospital. She took a great deal of interest in Yossl Glezer, who had hidden out in a village with a Christian acquaintance. She didn't know which village he was in or the name of the peasant he was with. He hadn't wanted to tell her, although the Christian went to see her several times to bring Yossl several items from her. But we didn't hear anything about Yossl. I believe it was not the Germans who put him to death, but rather the man who had hidden him. And so the hope I had of meeting up with Yossl again did not come true.

Right after the war a man named Itzik Zhitnicki of Baku asked me to go to his house and search for his diploma that had been in a cupboard in his house. He had studied engineering in France. I went there but found nothing, because the cupboard with all its contents had been taken away. And later Zhitnicki came on a visit to Kamenetz with his wife and two daughters.

A couple of years ago Dvora Radieszc, a daughter of Babel the Tokerkes, was in Kamenetz. They lived near the *plump* [water pump] on Zamkowe Street. She had sold their house and gone away.

After I was already living in Poland I met up with Boris Paskewicz of Kamenetz. He told me that in Warsaw by chance he had run into Itche Gurinski, who told him that he was going to leave to join his brother in Cuba. And I believe that he did not ask him about other people from Kamenetz. For the Christians did not get very involved in the misfortune of the Jews.

Testimony taken by Meir Bobrowski

Translator's Footnotes:

1. From *Kamenetz–Litovsk, Zastavije and Colonies Memorial Book*, edited by S. Eisenstadt and M. Galbert, published by the Israel and America Committee of Kamenetz Litovsk and Zastavya, (Orly, Tel Aviv, Israel, 1970), pp. 550–556.
2. Likely a misprint for Shimon Buchhalter, a name appearing on p. 253 of the necrology.
3. Brisk was the Jewish name for Brest–Litowsk, currently (2019) Brest, Belarus. It is located 40km south of Kamenetz.
4. Zastavya was a village adjacent to Kamenetz, on its northwest.
5. Pruzhany, Belarus is located approximately 50km northeast of Kamenetz. See map on p. 160 of this volume.
6. Wysoke–Litowsk, currently (2019) Vysokaye, Belarus, 33km west of Kamenetz. See map on p. 160 of this volume.
7. *beis–medresh* = House of Study, where Jewish men studied religious books and held prayer services
8. Biala–Podlaska, Poland, about 70km southwest of Kamenetz
9. Yiddish: not a single Jewish heart beat anymore
10. *Yom Toivom* = Jewish holidays (in this case September–October, 1942)
11. Community or Town Hall (see article by Ben–Moshe, "Kamenetz in 1945", pp. 561–568 of this volume).
12. Prusk or Pruska Forest was located on the outskirts of Kamenetz. See article on pp. 189–191 of this Yizkor Book: L. Aloni, "A Tear for the Loss of My Townspeople".
13. Wolkowysk, now (2019) Vawkavysk, Belarus, is located ~80km north of Pruzhany and 100km northeast of Kamenetz. The Jews of Pruzhany, together with the Jews of Kamenetz who had been expelled from Kamenetz to Pruzhany, were taken to Auschwitz via Wolkowysk. See map on p. 160 of this volume for the routes taken by the Kamenetz Jews to the death camps.

[Pages 557-558]

Historical Questions and Answers on Kamenetz-Litowsk[1]

Mota Montag, Historical Committee, Schwandorf[2], April 30, 1947

Translated by Allen Flusberg

Question: How old was the Jewish community?
Answer: 300 years.

Question: How many Jews lived in this shtetl before the war?
Answer: 500 families.

Question: What were the main sources of income there?
Answer: 60% business, 30% artisan, 10% agriculture.

Question: What were the community institutions and social cultural establishments; and how many were there?
Answer: 1 synagogue; 5 houses of study; 1 large yeshiva; 2 cemeteries; 1 home for the elderly, *Linas-Hatzedek*; 2 libraries; 1 drama circle; 1 bank; 1 *gmilus-chesed* [charity] treasury; and all the political parties.

The most important events in the town, starting from the beginning of the war:

On Rosh Hashana[3] 1939 the German army marched into the town. After eight days they left, and the Russians then occupied the town.

On June 28, 1941 the Germans took the town again and immediately imposed a levy of 3 kg of gold. They robbed all the Jewish homes and confiscated all the Jewish property. Jews had to wear a yellow patch on their front and back. They were drafted into forced labor, and at the same time they received terrible beatings.

After three months all the Jews were locked up inside a ghetto. There was a great hunger in the ghetto, and many peopled died of starvation. At the beginning of the winter about 100 men were sent to forced labor in a camp in Wolkowysk.[4] At the end of 1942 the entire Jewish population was sent to Treblinka, where they were all put to death.

Question: What was the attitude and action of the non-Jewish population?
Answer: The Russian population didn't treat the Jews badly; in contrast the Poles caused them terrible troubles.

Question: Did the Jews of this area organize a resistance?
Answer: No.

Question: How many [Jews] of this town survived?
Answer: 3, survivors of the concentration camps.

Distinguished personalities: Yeshiva Head Boruch-Ber, who died of grief during the Russian occupation.

The person who provided these details is not known to us as someone from Kamenetz. Certain details don't fit. —The Yizkor Book Committee

Translator's Footnotes:

1.   From *Kamenetz-Litovsk, Zastavije and Colonies Memorial Book*, edited by S. Eisenstadt and M. Galbert, published by the Israel and America Committee of Kamenetz Litovsk and Zastavya, (Orly, Tel Aviv, Israel, 1970), pp. 557-558.
2.   Schwandorf is a town in Bavaria, Germany, that is located about 90km east of Nuremberg.
3.   September 14-15
4.   Wolkowysk, now (2019) Vawkavysk, Belarus, is located ~100km northeast of Kamenetz.

[Page 561]

Kamenets after the Holocaust

Kamenetz in 1945[1][2]

Ben–Moshe[3], Yafo–Tel Aviv

Translated by Allen Flusberg

After a good deal of travel, utilizing every means of transportation of that period, I stood at the intersection of Brisk and Bialystok Streets in Kamenetz on an autumn day of the year 1945.

Deep in my heart there still remained in me, just as in every survivor, a hope that perhaps there would still be someone left there[4]. I stood there as if paralyzed, actually unable to move, not wanting to believe that I was really standing on the ground where I was born and raised—in the very place where so many times I had, as a child, gone to *chayder*[5] and Talmud Torah[6], and afterwards, whether alone or with friends, gone for so many walks; and now—this intersection was quiet and empty. Where was the row of shops, where one could always hear the sound of peasants shouting as they bargained with the Jewish shopkeepers over the price of an item, a sound mingled with the continuous laughter of children? Today in this place there stands a monument in memory of the fallen members of the Red Army. Only the *plump*, the water pump from which half the town drew its water, has remained just as it was.

Approaching the street where our house had stood, Szkolna [School] Street, or as it was called in Kamenetz, "der Hoif', I became numb again. I was able to recognize the place where our beautiful house had stood thanks only to a small apple tree that by chance was still there. That tree, which my father z.l.[7]had planted, was standing in what had once been a small garden.

On both sides of the street all the houses up to the *Powszechna*[8] School, the *Dom Ludowy*[9] and the *Gmina*[10] had been dismantled, and the ground they had stood on had been leveled as if no one had ever lived there. And this was the fate of all the Jewish houses. The building material of all the [newer[11]] Jewish houses was taken away by the German murderers and sold to the peasants in the nearby villages. The older houses were burnt down, and the ground where they had stood was leveled so that no sign of them remained.

[Page 562]

I passed the Rabbi's house. As I found out later, the Germans had expelled the Jewish population from that area, transferring [most of] them to the Ghetto that was set up on Litowsk Street, and some to Kobryn Street. If memory serves me correctly, the following houses were still standing: the houses of Winograd, of Shlomo the Tanner, and of Moshe Layb Platendom; the Rabbi's large house[12], as well as the houses of Motye Reznik and of Binyomin Geier. On Apisk Street (the street that leads to Zastavya[13]) there has remained the house of the Szczytnickis and their mill, which had several co–owners: the Kuptsiks of Zastavya and Meir Fisher. The mill had been disassembled, just like the mill in Zastavya that belonged to Yankel Aliyer (Yankel Orlanski) with several co–owners: Chaim Schmid, Motye Aronowski and another Zastavya Jew. Shortly before the war the mill had burned down and had been rebuilt even better. This mill also was dismantled by the Germans. The only mill that remained standing was Shostakovski's, left intact because it generated all of the town's electric power. In addition there remained: Osowski's large house, where the pharmacy was located; Aharon Hersh's large house (Gorfayn's), Miretzki's large house, and the houses of Hershl Jankies (Hershl Friedman) up to that of Galpern, including Leah Gellerstein's house. (Further along Brisk Street there remained Manishe's house, Avrohom Kazanovich's big house, and Aharon–Moshe Galpern's big house (where in that period the NKVD Office[14] was located), Shidlovski's big house, Yosef Vigutov's and Zelig Glembovski's big house. The only Jewish institution that remained standing, the Talmud Torah, still bore the marble plaque with the inscription "Talmud Torah and Yeshiva" and the name of the builder and benefactors.[15] There I found a Christian living there who had once been a janitor in the *Powszechna* school. Only a skeleton of the *Beis Medresh*[16] building remained standing (the four walls and the roof). As the Christians told me, the Germans had used it as a warehouse for grain.

The building of the renowned Yeshiva "Knesses Bays Yitzchok", which had been headed by Rabbi Boruch Ber Leibovitch z.tz.l.[17] (who died in Vilna a short time after the yeshiva had left Kamenetz, 5 Kislev 5699 [sic][18] —1939), was converted into a club.

As I passed Binyomen Geier's house I saw through the window the wool–brushing machines turning; these machines had been made by my father, may he rest in peace. And not only for Binyomin Geier, but rather for all the wool–brushing machines that existed in Kamenetz, for he was the only expert in town.

[Page 563]

The purpose of my visit to Kamenetz was to find out where the Jews of Kamenetz were taken away to, where their last path had been, and how they were put to death. Unfortunately I was not successful. I would occasionally run into a Kamenetz Christian, who lived across from Lipman Katz (his sister worked in the courthouse and was one of Shlomo'ke Mandelblat's assistants). To my question, whether he knew where they had brought the Kamenetz Jews, he replied that the peasants who had transported the Jews had told him that they took all the Kamenetz Jews to Wysoke–Litowsk[19], where they were loaded into train cars and taken by train to Treblinka[20] or to Malkin[21], he didn't know which. I also tried to get to Wysoke, but unfortunately I could not because the Polish–Russian border has been established a couple of kilometers before Wysoke.[22]

Among the various letters that I sent to Kamenetz, only one letter to the Christian Grigorewski was actually answered. He gave my letter to Dora Galperin, the only Kamenetz Jew who had been rescued; and I met with her a short time afterwards[23].

From Dora I also found out that my uncle Yossl Glezer escaped from the ghetto one night before the German murderers liquidated the ghetto. He hid for a short time in one of the cellars of the Kamenetz hospital. When the Christian doctor of the hospital found out that Yossl Glezer was hiding out in one of the hospital cellars, he warned the midwife that he would turn both of them in if he [Yossl] did not leave the hospital. Then Yossl went away to a Christian he knew, who, according to later information, murdered him.

When I was with the Christians the subject came up about what had transpired in Kamenetz right after the Jews had been expelled. As is known, when the Jews were expelled each of them had been permitted to take along a small bundle. Everyone took along the best of what he still owned. As the Jews were being taken away, the German murderers also forcefully tore away their last bundles; they took out whatever was valuable, and whatever did not appeal to them they ordered taken to the *Dom Ludowy*[24] on Szkolna Street.

After there were no Jews left in Kamenetz, the Germans and the Christian population arranged a public sale of the Jewish belongings. The sale was headed by the young Christian Zosza Staszuk, a daughter of a Polish–language teacher in the *Powszechner* School[25], who was well known to many Kamenetz residents.

[Page 564]

According to what the Christians told me, during the public sale of the Jews' belongings this Zosza exhibited a hatred of the Jews that was as intense as that of the German S.S. murderers. As she would hold one of the Jews' items up in her hand, she would call out the price with an obnoxious laugh.

This Zosza Staszuk worked for the Germans as a translator in the Kamenetz commissary office that was in the *Powszechner* school. When they led the first victims to the Prusk forest[26] to be shot there, she came along with the German Commissar in order to be present at the executions. (Also present was the chairman of the Kamenetz City Council, named Kuska.) This was told [to the Christians I knew][27] by the Kamenetz Jew Arye Wachsman, who had been dragged along by the Germans to dig graves for the victims. (Later on he perished in the ranks of a group of partisans.)

Thus the Jewish possessions were sold, so that whatever objects the Germans hadn't stolen remained with the Christian population, leaving a telltale sign behind in every Christian home. There were also Christians who expected to return the Jewish property. Bronek Szidlowski's wife (who had a tavern right next to Yossl Vigutov's house) asked me several times to take from her a sewing machine that the sister–in–law of the barber Yitzchok Leib had given her to hide; she didn't want to have it on her conscience. The woman who left her the machine had been a seamstress, the sole provider [of her family]. I told her [Bronek] that it was quite nice of her to offer, but I had no need for the machine. She then asked me to write a short note in Yiddish, so that she would have the note available in the event that someone came, and she would show the note and return it. I did what she asked, although while writing it I knew that unfortunately no Jewish hand would ever hold it [the note] again.

After a few days I left Kamenetz, coming back again only a few weeks later to meet up with Yudl[28] Rappaport.

At that time I met in Zastavya a peasant from Plisiszc (a Jewish colony). From this village I recall only one [Jewish] family, consisting of a brother and two sisters. One of the sisters was named Malka, and the other was named Osne; the brother was named Boruch. They had a large family in America. The Jewish residents of this village apparently shared the fate of all the Jews of Kamenetz. But the peasant told me that Boruch had fled and had hidden out in the surrounding forests. (The entire village and the area nearby were surrounded by the Bialowieza Forest[29].) However, after he heard that they had taken all the Jews out of the village, including his sisters, he committed suicide. The peasants found him not far from the village, shot dead, with his gun beside him.

[Page 565]

*

While in Brisk[30] I was told by Kamenetz Christians that Yudl Rappaport was alive and was in Zastavya. This was at the beginning of January 1946. It is hard to describe in writing how I felt when I heard this news. But I didn't have the time to think about it very much; it was already afternoon, and outside a light rain mixed with some snow was coming down. Without thinking I took off to the outskirts of town to find some means of transportation that could get me to Kamenetz as quickly as possible. Going a couple of kilometers, I came across a half–drunk soldier who was driving a truck. After a little haggling he agreed to take me as far as Czernaptzitz[31]. After a great deal of difficulty I reached Zastavya via Kamenetz at 1:30 AM. There I found Yudl in a little house owned by a Christian.

It is hard to describe in words how we greeted each other. For a long time it was as if both of us were paralyzed. From the first conversation with Yudl it became clear to me that he had been in the Soviet army; he had been wounded in battle and captured by the Germans. While in the hospital he escaped, and after much wandering he arrived back in Kamenetz at the beginning of 1942. For a short time he hid in Kamenetz; afterwards he was expelled to Pruzhany[32] with all the Jews of Kamenetz. Jews from all the surrounding areas, not only those from Pruzhany, had been concentrated in the Pruzhany Ghetto. From Pruzhany he went to the forest with a group of Jewish partisans. There they came across a group of Christian partisans who did not want to take them in and instead confiscated their arms. They also took their shoes away and told them to go back to the ghetto. Back in the ghetto they built a bunker, and among the people in the bunker was Yossl Wolfson. After some time had passed, the bunker was blown up by the Germans, and Yudl was brought to Auschwitz in the last transport from the Pruzhany Ghetto.

[Page 566]

After being in Auschwitz for a long time, Yudl couldn't stand it anymore, and he asked that he be taken to the crematoria[33]. But then a miracle happened. On the night that they brought him in a group of Jews to the crematoria, the man in charge was dead drunk, and so he ordered the driver who had brought them to take them back and bring them again the next day. But the next day a selection took place, and Yudl was selected, together with some others who were still able to stand, as able–bodied enough to work; and they took him away to a coal mine in Zawieszewice[34]. In the mine there were prisoners of war from various countries. Among them were some French who kept him supplied with food. He stayed there for a long time. When the Russian front began approaching them, they [the Germans] evacuated them to Buchenwald (apparently in the year 1944). From Buchenwald they moved them out again; he continued on to Thüringen[35] and was freed by the American army in the city of Gera[36].

But the Yudl I met in Kamenetz was not the same Yudl whom I had remembered from our *chayder* years, nor from the later years when we would do things together. The residual traces of what he had gone through, particularly in Auschwitz, had a strong effect on the state of his emotional health. It was not possible to reach a definitive decision about our future paths. I, too, had gone through a lot, but our present situation and what our future course should be were both clear to me. Once, when I touched upon the issue of returning to Poland and continuing on from there, he angrily jumped up, making me truly frightened by the terrible look on his face. "What, wander again?" he shouted, "I've had enough of that. I'd rather be a shepherd and remain here."

[Page 567]

To me it became clear that I should not leave him alone in the state he was in. But I anticipated that something would happen that would make him think about our situation more calmly and would certainly make him change his mind; and my intuition did not deceive me. It came about as a result of the NKVD bureau chief.

Yudl, who wanted to remain in Kamenetz, had to apply for a passport; and in those days this meant filling out a form in the NKVD office, in the department that issues passports. Several days after we had gotten together (having stayed over with various Christians in Zastavya), he went over to the NKVD Bureau to get a passport. Apparently the NKVD bureau chief was not very fond of Jews. When Yudl was filling out the form and writing down his biography, he mentioned that he had been in Auschwitz. Hearing the word "Auschwitz", the bureau chief jumped up and turned to him with a sarcastic question: "Ha, you are a Jew; you were in Auschwitz and survived? You must have collaborated with the Germans."

As Yudl told me afterwards, he felt paralyzed by such an anti–Semitic accusation. It was already late afternoon, and just at that moment the room lights went out because of a sudden short circuit. Unable to turn the light back on to see the effect that his words had had on Yudl, the bureau chief told him to come back in three days. Since it was Thursday, Yudl was supposed to return on the following Sunday.

Meanwhile I had been waiting for Yudl in Zastayva. Seeing that it was taking him a long time, I started walking in his direction. It was already late in the evening when I ran into him on a bridge that separated Kamenetz from Zastavya. He was disheveled and upset, and was holding on to the handrail of the bridge. Finally he started talking on his own, as if to himself: "You see, they think it is too bad that I survived." Right away he sat down and told me everything that had happened to him in the room with the bureau chief of the NKVD. And now the change that made him think had taken place.

That night neither of us slept. My path was clear, and I told him that by Sunday, i.e., the day when he was supposed to go back to the NKVD bureau chief, neither of us should be here anymore. Fortunately he agreed with me.

[Page 568]

The next day I went to talk to a Christian man who worked in the appropriate department that could provide us with an authorization attesting that we were former Polish citizens. At first the Christian tried to talk me out of this plan. He was committed to the idea that as the only remaining Kamenetz Jews we should stay there. But finally he relented and gave me whatever I needed. And on the next day (Saturday morning) we left Kamenetz via back roads on our way to Brisk.

In Brisk I didn't leave him [Yudl] by himself until he filled out all the requisite papers, and then I accompanied him to Terespol Street, which led to the new Russian–Polish border crossing. He crossed into Poland, and after some time we met again in Germany.

Translator's Footnotes:

1. From *Kamenetz–Litovsk, Zastavije and Colonies Memorial Book*, edited by S. Eisenstadt and M. Galbert, published by the Israel and America Committee of Kamenetz Litovsk and Zastavya, (Orly, Tel Aviv, Israel, 1970), pp.561–568.
2. A translation of this Yiddish article into Hebrew is to be found on pp. 195–199 of this volume. Any additions in the Hebrew version are indicated below in footnotes to this translation of the Yiddish version.
3. Hebrew version: Asher Ben–Moshe. As indicated below in this article (p. 563), his original family name was Glezer. The Hebrew name "Ben–Moshe" (= son of Moshe) is consistent with the name of Asher Glezer's father, which was Moshe (see Necrology on p. 310 of this volume).
4. Hebrew version adds here: "that one of the Jews of Kamenetz had been saved."
5. *chayder* = school of religious studies for young children (usually written *cheder*)
6. Talmud Torah = school of religious studies for older children, through high school age
7. z.l. = of blessed memory (acronym for Hebrew *zichroinoi livrocho*)
8. *Powszechna* = universal or common (Polish), the name of the public elementary school (Grades 1–7). See the following article: Ch. Gurwitz–Goldberg, "The *Szkola Powszechna*", p. 450 of this volume.
9. Community or Town Hall (see Footnote 24 below)
10. *Gmina* = Commune (Polish)
11. Hebrew version adds "newer"
12. Yiddish *moyer* (= wall); Hebrew version: *beit choma* = a house surrounded by a wall, a mansion. Alternative meaning: a brick or stone house.
13. Zastavya was a village adjacent to (northwest of) Kamenetz and connected to it by bridges over the Leshna River.
14. NKVD = Soviet police
15. See p. 67 of this volume for a photograph of this marble plaque.
16. *Beis Medresh* = study house (where religious books are studied, and where prayer services are often conducted as well).
17. z.tz.l. is an acronym for *zaycher tzadik livrocho*, = may the memory of the righteous be a blessing
18. He died in Vilna shortly after the Soviet occupation began, on 5 Kislev 5700 (November, 1939). See the following article: Y.Edelstein, "Rabbi Baruch Dov Leibowitz, Head of the Yeshiva of Kamenetz–Litovsk", p. 67 of this volume.
19. Wysoke–Litowsk, currently (2019) Vysokaye, Belarus, 33km west of Kamenetz. See map on p. 160 of this volume.
20. Treblinka, Poland, is located 100km west of Wysoke–Litowsk.
21. Malkin = Malkinia–Gorna, Poland, 4km north of the village of Treblinka. There was a train station at the Malkinia Junction with a spur line running into the Treblinka camp. See the following link (retrieved June, 2019): https://furtherglory.wordpress.com/2011/10/07/malkinia–junction–where–the–trains–to–treblinka–stopped/
22. Hebrew version reads instead: this town is now on the border with Poland
23. Hebrew version adds "in Brisk".
24. Hebrew version: government town hall
25. See Footnote 8 above.
26. Prusk or Pruska Forest was located on the outskirts of Kamenetz. See article on pp. 189–191 of this Yizkor Book: L. Aloni, "A Tear for the Loss of My Townspeople".
27. Hebrew version adds those words
28. Yudl is called Yehuda in the Hebrew version, "Yudl" being the Yiddish diminutive for the Hebrew name "Yehuda".
29. The edge of the Bialowieza Forest is about 30km north of Kamenetz.
30. Brisk is the Yiddish acronym for Brest–Litovsk, a city 40km south of Kamenetz. It is presently (2019) the border crossing between Brest (Belarus) and Poland.

31.   Hebrew version: Czernapczitz. This is apparently Charnaŭchytsy, Belarus, which lies 20km north of Brest. Kamenetz is 25km north of Charnaŭchytsy (about a 5–hour walk).
32.   Pruzhany is located approximately 50km northeast of Kamenetz. See map on p. 160 of this volume.
33.   Hebrew version has "gas chamber" instead of "crematoria".
34.   Apparently Jawiszowice, Poland, in an area with a long history of coal mining. It lies about 10km southwest of Oswiecim, Poland (Auschwitz).
35.   Thüringen is a state of Germany.
36.   Gera, Germany is located 70km east of Buchenwald, Germany; it is in the state of Thüringen.

[Pages 569-578]

A Journey to the Past[1]
(Memories from the Period of the Second World War)

By D. (Bertchik) Shmida (Haifa)

Translated by Allen Flusberg

Note by translator: *This Yiddish article is nearly identical to a Hebrew-language version, by the same author, with the same title, on pp. 200-208 of this Yizkor Book. See the English translation of the Hebrew version, in which footnotes indicate any differences between the two, as well as differences from the English version in the original Yizkor Book (pp. 175-181 of the English section).*

Translator's Footnote:

1.   From *Kamenetz–Litovsk, Zastavije and Colonies Memorial Book*, edited by S. Eisenstadt and M. Galbert, published by the Israel and America Committee of Kamenetz Litovsk and Zastavya, (Orly, Tel Aviv, Israel, 1970), pp. 569–578

[Pages 579-584]

Activity of the
Kamenetz-Litowsk Memorial Committee in Israel[1]

By Leah Bobrowski-Aloni and Ḥaya Krakowski-Karabelnik

Translated by Allen Flusberg

Note by translator: *This Yiddish-language article is essentially identical with the Hebrew-language article, by the same authors, on pp. 216-222 of this Yizkor Book, entitled "Activities of the Organization of Former Residents of Kamenetz". See the English translation of the Hebrew version (pp. 216-222).*

Translator's Footnote:

1.   From *Kamenetz–Litovsk, Zastavije and Colonies Memorial Book*, edited by S. Eisenstadt and M. Galbert, published by the Israel and America Committee of Kamenetz Litovsk and Zastavya, (Orly, Tel Aviv, Israel, 1970), pp. 579-584.

[Page 587]

Kamenetser in America

The Establishment of the
Kamenetz-Litowsk Aid Society in America[1]

by Meir Mendel Visotzky (New York)

Translated by Allen Flusberg

Note by translator: a translation into English of this Yiddish article appeared in the original English section of this Yizkor Book, pp. 130-133. *The following paragraph (third-from-last paragraph on p. 589) had some additional information in the Yiddish article:.*

[Page 589]

While describing the Society's activity, we must mention the great personality of the late Jacob Hurvitz who was one of the first active members of our society. He was the son-in-law of Isaac Bazhes, the uncle of Chaya Krakowski, who is now in Israel.

Also, the following photograph that appeared at the end of the Yiddish article (p. 590) is reproduced here:

[Page 590]

From right to left: Bayla Krinsky, Michael Bontchik and Basha Visotzky,
founders of the Bontchik family circle

Translator's Footnote:

1.   From *Kamenetz-Litovsk, Zastavije and Colonies Memorial Book*, edited by S. Eisenstadt and M. Galbert, published by the Israel and America Committee of Kamenetz Litovsk and Zastavya, (Orly, Tel Aviv, Israel, 1970), pp. 587-590.

[Page 591]

Kamenets-Litowsk
Memorial Committee in America

Kamenetz-Litowsk *Malbush-Arumim* [Clothing Aid] Society in New York[1]
Activity Report by the Correspondence Secretary

by Sarah Hurwitz

Translated by Allen Flusberg

In the year 1923, the following individuals founded our society: R.[2] Binyomin Mostowsky, Mordechai[3] Simchowich, Rivka Lipshitz[4], Esther Dolinsky, Ḥaya Sara Mendelson and Fayge Radishitz. We had only a small number of ladies among the members. Gradually the society expanded and became a large undertaking. That was right after the First World War, when large numbers of people began immigrating to America. Our Kamenetz *lands-froyen* [ladies from our town] joined the society, and we already had more than 150 members then.

Our first activity was to send money for the Kamenetz Talmud Torah [beginning high school], clothing and food parcels for the children, and also monthly allowances for the teachers. These funds were sent to R. Yosef Vigutov, of blessed memory, who would distribute the money according to need[5].

Some time later we found out that some Kamenetz townspeople, together with the yeshiva, were now actually in Russia. Right away we started corresponding with them in writing, and we sent them money and parcels of food.

[Page 592]

The *Malbush-Arumim* [Clothing for the Poor] Ladies Society sent boat tickets for the yeshiva students to come to America, and so now we have a Kamenetz Yeshiva here (likewise in Jerusalem).

Thousands of dollars in charity have been spent for American and Kamenetz yeshivas, hospitals, *Hachnosas Kalla* [funding a wedding for a bride with limited means] and other institutions. We send aid to Israel, where we purchased a house through the United Jewish Appeal, as well as Israel Bonds. We purchased a room in the Kamenetz Yeshiva in Jerusalem and sent them a Torah scroll. We adopted a yeshiva student (a grandson of Rabbi Boruch-Ber[6], of blessed memory). Now they are constructing an additional building for the yeshiva in Jerusalem, and we have sent them a respectable sum of money for this project We also distribute *Mo'ois Ḥittin*[7] every year just before Passover.

We contributed to planting trees in Israel (through Yaakov Savitzky, of blessed memory) in the name of *Malbush-Arumim*. We contributed money to help rescue 4 orphaned sisters from a convent in France.

We contributed to Israel through the American Red Shield of David, sending shipments of various kinds of equipment: machines, building supplies, an ambulance, a blood-plasma centrifuge, oxygen tents and many medications, to the hospital and to the David Marcus Memorial Building.

More recently, we bought a clinic in Israel in Ofakim[8], near Beersheba, for $5,000, for which the Israeli government provided a contribution of $20,000.

On May 5th, 1963, we proudly and joyously celebrated our 40th anniversary. During the 40 years of its existence, our *Malbush-Arumim* Society has achieved a great deal of charitable work. It has also helped make the publication of the Yizkor Book possible.

The following ladies serve as our officers: Rivka Lifshitz—president; *Rebbitzin*[9] Bayla Tendler—vice president; Sarah Hurwitz—reporting and finance secretary; Nelly Federbush—treasurer. The following are vice presidents: Babel Serota, Ḥaya Rivka Sirota, Pearl Goldstein and Tema Goldman.

Translator's Footnotes:

1.   From *Kamenetz-Litovsk, Zastavije and Colonies Memorial Book*, edited by S. Eisenstadt and M. Galbert, published by the Israel and America Committee of Kamenetz Litovsk and Zastavya, (Orly, Tel Aviv, Israel, 1970), pp. 591-592. This article is mostly the same as the English-language article by the same author, Sarah Hurwitz, "The Kamenetz Society in America", on pp. 127-129 of the English section of this Yizkor Book (referred to in footnotes below as "the English-language version").

2.   R. = Reb, title similar to English "Mr." Or possibly in this case it stands for "Rabbi", as written in the English-language version.

3.   The English-language version has the name "Sarah" here instead of "Mordechai".

4.   In the English-language version her family name is spelled "Lifshitz".

5.   See the following article by Mendelson, "R. Yosef Vigutov," pp. 505-506 of this Yizkor Book.

6.   Rabbi Boruch-Ber (or Baruch Dov) Leibovitch (or Leibowitz), the last head of the Kamenetz Yeshiva. See the following article by Edelstein, pp. 64-67 in this Yizkor Book, "Rabbi Baruch Dov Leibowitz, Head of the Yeshiva of Kamenetz-Litovsk"

7.   *Mo'ois Ḥittin [Maot Ḥittin]* = charity for the needy to purchase Passover food

8.   Ofakim is located ~20km northwest of Beersheba.

9.   *Rebbitzin* is the title used for the wife of a rabbi. Bayla Tendler's husband was Rabbi Yitzḥak Tendler, who came from Kamenetz.

[Page 593]

Memorial Day on the 20th Yahrzeit, in New York, of the Destruction of Kamenetz-Litowsk: a Report[1]
Activity Report by the Correspondence Secretary

by Chatzkl Kagan, Recording Secretary of the Kamenetz Society in New York

Translated by Allen Flusberg

A banner with the slogan "Don't forget, don't forgive" is hanging over the stage. A menorah with six candlesticks is sitting on the table. The prominent *landsleit* [fellow townspeople] sit around the table: Rabbi Yitzchok Turetz, a son-in-law of Rabbi Boruch Ber, who headed the Kamenetz Yeshiva; Rabbi Yehuda Gershuni, a [former] student at the Kamenetz Yeshiva; Rabbi Yosef Dolinsky (a son of Koppl the tailor); vice-presidents Chaim Mendelson and Velvl Kustin. The following are sitting on the right side, next to a small table: the finance secretaries Mrs. Chaya Goldberg and Elvin Sheinfeld. Chatzkl Kagan, recording secretary, sits on the left side, next to small table.

The auditorium is full of *landsleit*, young and old, from various walks of life, who have come from near and far to pay their respects to the martyrs, and to shed a few tears communally.

Our honorable president, Avrohom Shudroff, who is chairing the memorial meeting, declares from the stage that the meeting has commenced. A hush falls over the auditorium as all eyes turn to the stage. The chairman calls up the *chazan* [cantor], Avrohom Aharon Weinberger, who recites a chapter of *Tehillim* [Psalms].

The correspondence secretary, Mrs. Sarah Hurwitz, reads a communication from the [Yizkor] Book Committee of Israel, written by Pinchas Rabinowitch. He describes the Kamenetz destruction, stating that it is the obligation of our *landsleit*, scattered across the globe, to establish a memorial to perpetuate the martyrs. The Yizkor Book will serve as such a memorial. The chairman, Avrohom Shudroff, thanks everyone for responding by coming to attend, especially Rabbi Yitzchok Turetz for coming to take part in our communal sorrow.

[Page 594]

Mr. Shudroff presents an overview of Kamenetz, which was famous for its scholars as well as skilled workmen from all walks of life—all of whom perished during the Hitler period. The Yizkor Book that we, the committee, are preparing for publication, will serve as the greatest and most significant monument to them.

He ends his speech by reading a "proclamation" that was published about the Warsaw Ghetto Uprising.

He then hands the floor over to Rabbi Yehuda Gershuni, who says:

"Friends and *landsleit*, being here with you I will present a review of Kamenetz. But first I wish to express our sorrow over the loss of Israel's President Ben-Tzvi[2], whom I knew personally. He was someone who incorporated the greatness of an individual not only from the perspective of Jews, but also from that of non-Jews. Let us now pay our respects to his memory by rising for a minute of silence.

"In the year 1943, when the sorrowful news of the Jewish annihilation reached us, we in Israel did not believe it—we could not take the events in. Even religious Jews were unable to grasp it; and there were instances of disillusionment with religion because of the catastrophe.

"The State of Israel has come into existence signifying a mirroring of the life of all the towns and shtetls.

"What comes back to me about Kamenetz is the warmth of the people, whom I liked so much.

"I stayed over with Dodye the butcher, a very warm and honest person, full of friendliness and goodness; Hershl Rudnicki, the owner of the hardware store, who was modern in thought, and had such great love for Israel, for worldliness; even Laybl Katz, the communist—he was such a good, warm person. All of them, without distinction, were such dear, good people.

"Rabbi Reuven Burstein, the rabbi of the small town, who was descended from a line of rabbis, was a wonderful, noble person—from examples in the Talmud he might be compared to King Solomon. The book that Rabbi Burstein published is very valuable. (Here Rabbi Gershuni cites an article from the book that was related to *kiddush hashem* [Sanctification of God's Name], as if he [Burstein] foresaw that such a time would come.) Rabbi Burstein was very tolerant, a quality that made him even greater."[3]

[Page 595]

In Rabbi Gershuni's speech, it has been interesting to hear the depiction of a splendid past.

The chairman thanks Rabbi Yehuda Gershuni for the warm speech about Kamenetz.

In the name of the committee, he appeals to the audience to provide funding for publication.

The response is certainly warm: there are contributors who respond very generously. The names of these contributors have been recorded in the account book. The appeal has brought in a large sum of money.

The chairman introduces Rabbi Yitzchok Turetz, who speaks lovingly about the people of Kamenetz, saying that the world and the Jews throughout the world did nothing to raise a hue and cry about the horrifying destruction. The Jews of Kamenetz certainly did cry out, demanding and calling upon their own relatives to remember. He turns to the chairman, squeezes his hand and says: "You are all to be commended—it is refreshing to be here with you!"

The six candles are lit—the symbol of the six million of our people who perished.

The first candle is lit by Dvorke Singer, the daughter of Yoel Rudnicki, one of the two survivors of the concentration camps (the second, Lyube Strashinsky, lives in Washington and is not present today). Others light candles: the president of *Malbush Arumim*[4], Mrs. Rivka Lipshitz from the Kamenetz Society; Mr. M. Visotzky and Mr. Miletzky of the Workmen's Circle; Chaim Rubin, Jack Joffe from the *Lapates Family Circle*; Isser Goldberg and Mrs. Siegel.

The sixth candle is lit by three rabbis: Rabbi Yitzchok Turetz, Rabbi Yehuda Gershuni, and Rabbi Yosef Dolinsky.

Vice-President Velvl Kustin is called up to read from his memoirs, which he has written for the Yizkor Book. In the middle of his reading, as he mentions his family members, his voice chokes up, and he is unable to continue reading. This incident brings tears to the eyes of many of those present. Vice-Chairman Ḥaim Mendelson is asked to read a poem, "Kamenetz", which he himself has written.

The chairman states that a resolution is read at every memorial. This time the resolution will be read by Recording Secretary Chatzkel Kagan:

[Pages 596-597]

Yiddish on sign at rear: "Kamenetz-Litowsk.
We honor the memory of our martyrs, whom we will never forget."[5]

[Page 598]

Kamenetz-Litowsk Memorial Committee in America

From right to left: Yehoshua Silbergleit (treasurer), Zeev Kustin, Shmuel Yitzchok Melnitzky
(vice-president), Mordechai Borenstein, Dov Appleman (president), Chaim Velvl Mendelson,
Shraga Feivl Tendler (finance secretary).
(Photograph from the year 1965.)

[Page 599]

"We, the *landsleit* of Kamenetz-Litowsk, Zastavya and Colonies, have assembled here on Sunday, 4 Iyar 5723—corresponding to April 28, 1963—in the Adelphi Building, 74 Fifth Avenue, New York, to remember the beloved dear members of our family. They were put to death as martyrs by the Germans Fascist murderers—with the help of Polish and Ukrainian Fascists—only because they were Jews.

"We promise not to forget and not to forgive the horrifying extermination."

"The Yizkor-Book Committee here in America, in partnership with the Israel Committee, will participate together in this monument with all we can, materially and spiritually, to honor our martyrs. We promise to keep the sacred oath of all the Jewish ghetto fighters and partisans—who have elevated the esteem of the Jewish people—with the promise to do everything we can to prevent such slaughters from ever taking place again."

"Hail to the martyrs! We will never forget you!"

The *chazan* chants the traditional *El Molei Raḥamim* ["God Full of Compassion", prayer for the souls of the dead].

As chairman, the president, Avrohom Shudroff, has contributed his esteem to carry out the mission of the Yizkor-Book Committee.

After the meeting ended the *landsleit* remain in the auditorium, conversing about their impressions of the memorial meeting.

These, then, are the proceedings of the third memorial meeting.

[Page 600]

Committee members of the Kamenetz Yizkor Book in America

Standing, right-to-left: Ḥ. Z. Mendelson, M. Visotzky, V. Kustin, Ḥ. Hurwitz, Goldberg, A. Kozak, Goldberg
Sitting, right-to-left: Y. Sheinfeld, S. Horowitz, President Avrohom Shudroff, P. LIptchik, Ḥ. Kagan
[Two other names are added here on the left, between the two lines of the caption, in a different font:] H. Gers, Ḥ. Rubin..
(Photograph from the year 1965.)

Translator's Footnotes:

1.   From *Kamenetz-Litovsk, Zastavije and Colonies Memorial Book*, edited by S. Eisenstadt and M. Galbert, published by the Israel and America Committee of Kamenetz Litovsk and Zastavya, (Orly, Tel Aviv, Israel, 1970), pp. 593-600.

2.   Ben-Tzvi died in office on April 23, 1963, five days before this gathering (April 28, 1963, as mentioned below).

3.   See article by Gershuni, "Rabbi Reuven David Hakohen Burstein", pp. 50-54 of this Yizkor Book, where Gershuni goes into these topics in detail.

4.   The *Malbush Arumim* Clothing Aid Society is described in the article by Hurwitz on pp. 591-592 of this Yizkor Book.

5.   Translator recognizes a small number of faces in the photograph, as follows: Third row from front, fifth from right: Harry Jaffe (a.k.a. Aharon Meir Yoffe), and left of him (on his right) his wife, Lilly (a.k.a. Leah'ke) Jaffe. Sixth row from front, starting from right: sisters Helyn Reichenthal (née Ḥaika Morgenstern) and Dorothy Flusberg (née Dobbe Morgenstern).

[English page 9]

ENGLISH SECTION

<u>The Old Home</u>

Foreword

by Abraham Schudroff

A memorial to our destroyed home town

Soon after the end of World War II, we set up a relief committee. We discovered the tragic fact that there was hardly anybody left whom we could help. No one will ever know exactly, but according to all reports, it is believed that all Jewish families in Kamenetz-Litvosk and its vicinity were put to death.

We could not rest, however. If it was not given to us to give material help, we decided to start a movement amongst our fellow-townsmen in America and in Israel to perpetuate the memory of the martyrs of Kamenetz-Litovsk by means of a Memorial Book.

Though there exists a synagogue in New-York, bearing the name of our town, and there are a number of "Landsmanschaft" organizations, unfortunately no initiative was taken to organize Memorial Assemblies or other meetings of similar character.

But this could not continue in such a manner and we, a closely-knit group of several fellow townsmen, took it upon ourselves to initiate the creation of a Committee for the Perpetuation of the Memory of the Martyrs of our town. Several attempts failed, but at the end of December 1960, when I was sent as delegate to the 25th Zionist Congress, I had a meeting with an active group of fellow-townsmen in the State of Israel.

During the reception which they organized in my honor, upon my arrival, and later on, at the Memorial Assembly to the memory of the Martyrs of our town, we talked over and elaborated the plan to publish a Memorial Book by the townsmen of Kamentz-Litovsk, which should consist of various memoirs, descriptions and pictures, reflecting the Jewish life in Kamenetz-Litovsk in the past and its destruction, and thus serving as a spiritual monument to our hallowed martyrs.

The above mentioned plan was brought to America and the first meeting of the Memorial Book Committee took place at my home. An executive committee was formed. At the first meeting there participated: Mrs. Sarah Horowitz, Secretary of the Committee, with many years of active work amongst the townsmen of Kamenetz-Litovsk behind her and her children Mr. and Mrs. Iser Goldberg; Mr. and Mrs. Haim Mendelson; Mr. and Mrs. Chatzkel Kagan; Mr. and Mrs. Itzhak Schoenfeld; Mr. Haim Rubin; Mr. and Mrs. Velvel Kustin; Mr. and Mrs. Harry Gers; Mr. and Mrs. Leizer Lifshitz; Mr. and Mrs. Joseph Post; Mr. and Mrs. Meyer Wisotzky; Mr. J. Jaffe; Mr. and Mrs. Benjamin Tendler; Mr. and Mrs. David Schudroff; Mr. and Mrs. Morris Siegel; Mr. and Mrs. Eli Chait; Mr. and Mrs. Golomb; Mr. and Mrs. Louis Horowitz; Mr. Alex Schudroff and Mr. M. Morgan.

In connection with the Memorial Book, I met together with the following fellow-townsmen in Israel: Y. Rimon, Simha Dubiner, Pinhas Rabi, Hayka Cracovsky, Mr. and Mrs. Alony, Yehudith Kostakevich, Pinhas Rabid-Rudnitsky and others.

We wish to note with great pride the fact that the fellow-townsmen in America responded very warmly to our undertaking. It was my lot to become the Chairman of the Kamenetz-Litovsk Memorial Committee, and to accomplish the project of creating the Memorial Book, together withmy faithful collaborators, and in cooperation with all Kamenetz-Litovsk organizations that raised the financial contribution for this purpose.

We also introduced the custom of arranging, on the 27th day of Nisan, a yearly Commemorative Assembly to the memory of the hallowed martyrs of Kamenetz-Litovsk, with the participation of well known rabbis, writers and people active in community affairs. A touching Memorial Meeting takes place, six candles to commemorate six million hallowed martyrs are kindled. All present recite publicly "Kaddish" Prayer for the Dead.

All of us should feel proud of having fulfilled our duty and of having erected a spiritual monument to our dearest and beloved, the Jewish men, women and children of the historic Jewish Community of Kamenetz-Litovsk, near Brest-Litovsk. I thank the Almighty God for having given me the physical and spiritual strength to build the bridge which united our fellow-townsmen in America and Israel and to publish this Memorial Book.

May our children and our children's children not forget the memory of the hallowed martyrs.

Blessed be their memory!

Abraham Schudroff
President and Initiator of
"Kamenetz-Litovsk Memorial Book
Committee in America"

[English page 12]

The Beginning of Jewish Settlement in Kamenetz

(till the middle of the 18th century)

by Leybl Goldberg (Sarid)

To the Memory of My Martyred Parents – Kalmen and Rachel Lea.
My Innocent Brothers Noah and Israel Itshack.

My Pure Sisters – the Hallowed Martyrs Shifra, Rivka and Brakha.
Who were put to death by the abominable murderers.

God will avenge their blood.

I walked on the roads of the places which will be mentioned later on; I was in the villages whose history will be told. I grew up in the town of Kamenetz. I was brought up there and I brought up others. Therefore everything, is so close to my heart – and so heart-breaking.

It is not easy to write the history of Jewish settlement in our town. It is made difficult by the lack of Jewish documentary sources, with the exception of several lines in Dubnov's "Notebook of the Council of Communities in Lithuania". I have not found any document about those distant years. It is a depressing fact that we are cut off from the sources and treasures including also Jewish documents, that can be found in the archives of Brest, Grodno and others, from which we are barred. Therefore, there was no other possibility, but to write the history of the Jewish settlement according to non-Jewish documents, mainly those belonging to Polish State institutions here.

Those documents throw very little light on Jewish life in those distant years. Informations about Jewish settlements in our region appear only at the end of the 14th Century.

As it had already been told, the Jews of Brest were, in 1388, granted a privilege by Witold, the Duke of Lithuania; but it may be assumed that Jewish settlement in Brest had existed earlier too. We have clear information about the region only from the end of the 15th century. But even in this case it is to be assumed that Jewish settlements had existed earlier. Kobryn appears as an organized community at the beginning of the 16th Century. It should be stressed that Jews were expelled from Lithuania in 1495, during the rule of the Lithuanian Duke and Crown Prince Alexander. However, after he had been crowned King of Poland, he allowed them to return in 1503 – and returned them their houses and property in exchange for an annual tax.

Thus it can be taken for granted that the Jewish settlement in Kamenetz began very early.

The Jews were for the first time mentioned in a document from the year 1525. We can conjecture that during the process of establishment of towns in backward Lithuania, when the Jews had the possibility not only to deal in trade and money but also to acquire land property and to exercise all professions, they lived in an important town, situated on a highway and close to such a big town as Brest-Litovsk.

In a collection of Lithuanian documents, published by the historian G. Bershadsky, the Kamenetz Jews are described as tavern-keepers. However, the above document is shrouded in obscurity and we do not know whether it referred to a Jewish population center in the town or to a few tavern-keepers. We may therefore assume that some Jews lived there; even if their number was not large, it reached at least ten men – the number prescribed for community prayer.

From this follows that there had been Jews in Kamenetz even before that date. The aforementioned document includes the following statement:

On February 26th 1525 the town Kamenetz received the rights of "Wojtowstwo" (administrative unit) in addition to the Magdeburg Rights (rights granted to newly established towns) of the "Starostwo" (district) of Kamenetz. The Christian townspeople received also licenses for keeping taverns, which had previously been leased by the Jews. The development of towns in Lithuania caused — just like in other countries — the growth of an urban class. The growth of the urban class in Lithuania, however, was slower than in other parts of Poland. At the beginning they were granted the status of a "Wojtowstwo", including a town-court headed by a "Wojt" (in German "Vogt"). The Starostwo of Kamenetz had received the Magdeburg Rights at an even earlier date. We may suppose that in the same period the Magdeburg Rights were also given to other towns in Lithuania such as: Brest, Grodno, Lutsk, Polotsk, Minsk etc. (1546). But it is interesting to note that the rights to lease the taverns were transferred to the Christian townsmen. The taking away of the taverns from the Jews was connected with granting the particular rights pertaining to the status of "Wojtowstwo" to the town's Christian inhabitants. It does not seem likely that the Jews had given up their means of livelihood of their own accord. Presumably, this came about as a result of the struggle of the town's Christian population against the Jewish inhabitants.

The Jewish settlement in Kamenetz and vicinity existed throughout the entire 16th century. A document from 1565, drawn up for the purpose of levying taxes in the region of the "Starostwo" of Kamenetz imposes the following taxes upon the Jews of Sarowka: Eliezer (Leyzer) —3 Zlotys; Nahum — 3 Zlotys; Bitschko — 3 Zlotys; Pesah — 2 Zlotys; Stopka — 3 Zlotys; altogether 14 Zlotys

We learn from the aforementioned document that Jews lived not only in Kamenetz but also in the townlets of the region.

The Kamenetz Jews were for the first time mentioned in Jewish documents when the Council of Lithuania was established. It had split from the all-Polish "Council of the Four Lands". In 1623 the Lithuanian Jews were required to pay a fixed sum of tax-money to the Lithuanian Treasury. This resulted in the establishment of the Lithuanian Council. At the beginning three communities and their surroundings were represented: Brest (the principal community), Grodno, and Minsk. Kamenetz belonged to the communities of the Brest region. Kamenetz did not attain the honor shared by its neighbors — Wysokie and Pruzhany — where the Council held its meetings. We read in the Register of the Lithuanian Communities that the Council, which met in 1670 at Seltz, imposed upon the Community of Kamenetz the tax of 600 Polish Zlotys to be paid to the landowner Yuditsky.

The historic document, dated December 11, 1635, and granting basic rights to the Jews of Kamenetz, was given to them by King Ladislaus (Wladyslaw) IV; it was ratified by his brother Yan Casimir (Jan Kazimierz) in 1661 and confirmed once again, for the third time, by King Michael Wisniowiecki in 1670. The above privilege included several advantageous additions:

1. One additional market day, except Saturday.
2. Permission to build a synagogue, subject to the condition that it should not be taller and more beautiful than the local Christian churches.
3. Permission to build a ritual bath on a plot belonging to the town.
4. Permission to establish a cemetery in the town or outside it.
5. Permission to engage in commerce and trade without limitations, as well as to buy real estate in the town and to build houses.

The Christian townsfolk were warned not to disturb the life and activities of the Jews, should the latter want to take advantage of the rights given to them in the royal privilege. Furthermore, says the privilege, if they do disturb them, they will be held responsible for it and have to pay fines. We must add that the scroll of King Michael Wisniowiecki's privilege specifies the amount to be paid as fine by the Christian townsfolk, in case they would cause damages to the Jews. Noting the decree of Wladyslaw IV, it includes a sentence missing in the text of Jan Kazimierz (Jan Casimir):

"Should the townspeople have the audacity to disturb the Jews, they will be fined 5000 Zlotys, which will be divided between the claimant and the Government."

The privilege is also based on the royal laws concerning the rights of the Lithuanian Jews. We may take it for granted that the reference was made here to the rights bestowed upon the Lithuanian Jews in 1629, according to which they were allowed to engage in crafts without belonging to the Christian guilds, and all this in addition to their commercial rights and permission to sell alcoholic drinks. Quite interesting is the discriminatory measure taken by Wladyslaw (Ladislaus) IV, whose friendly attitude towards the Jews was known: in 1633 he restricted the Jewish tailors to sew clothes for Jewish customers only; he permitted them to deal freely in ready-made clothes only and to engage solely in such trades in which the Christian craftsmen were not represented by an organization.

Therefore, attention should be drawn to the fact that Jewish craftsmen in Kamenetz were the first ones in Lithuania who received the privilege of unrestricted activity in trade at the same time when Jewish craftsmen in other Lithuanian townlets were limited in their rights.

The chapter on the relations between the Jews and the Christian inhabitants of Kamenetz brings to light the sentiments of hatred and jealousy felt by the Gentile townspeople towards the Jews. The Christian inhabitants of Kamenetz were arrogant and contemptuous and led a struggle against both the nobility and the Jews.

Just like in other towns of Poland and Lithuania, so did the Jews of Kamenetz enjoy the support of the nobility.

We had already taken note of the first document from 1525, which decreed that the Jewish taverns be transferred to the Christian inhabitants of the town. Let us pay attention to the sharp tone used by Ladislaus IV in the privilege granted by him in 1635:

"We let it be known by our Starosta in Kamenetz and other municipal offices: we declare that it is our desire to confirm the validity of everything put down in the privilege and we order not to disturb (in Latin: inviolabiter) the freedom of the Jews which had been given to them by us."

The disappearance, in the privilege of Jan Casimir, of the fine-clause, with which the townspeople had been threatened in case they would sabotage the rights of the Jews, bears witness to the sharp struggle of the Christians in the town against the Jews. It ought to be understood that the sentence appearing in the decree of King Michael Wisniowiecki bears witness to the obstacles put by the townspeople in the way of realizing the privilege. They doubtlessly fought with all their strength against the fulfilment of the terms of the privilege.

At the end of the 17th century (1693) a protest, signed by 40 citizens, was lodged by the Kamenetz Town Council, against the Councillor Andrej Piablewicz who had leased the tax on alcoholic drinks to the Jews, without having previously consulted the other Councillors and the entire town-council. It must be stressed that under the rule of King Jan Sobieski, in the years 1670-1696, the policy of the Central Government supported the Jews just like in the previous years. And so we see the Finance Minister Sapieha lease the taxes in Kamenetz to the Jews Isaac (Ajzyk) Nojgmowicz and Yeshayahu Jakubowicz.

At that time Kamenetz was still a district capital with a customs house to deal with the transit of goods from the Region of Brest to the Region of Podlasie.

Kamenetz was mentioned in the above document among the important towns Brest, Pinsk and Yalovo to which belonged a number of adjoining townlets. One of the townlets subordinate to Kamenetz was Mlitsytch.

The townspeople did not rest and, throughout the entire reign of Sobieski, they sought all conceivable pretexts to act against the privilege given to the Jews of the town. In 1684, the chief town official requests that the privilege granted to Kamenetz by King Jan III (Sobieski) be registered in the Book of Documents in Vilna, upon the request of the town-Council. In this document the King confirms the rights which the town has received from Alexander, Sigismund I (Zygmunt), Sigismund III and others. In the document notice is taken, too, of the accusation levelled by the Kamenetz Christians against the Wojewoda (Provincial Governor) Ostap Tyszkiewicz, owner of the villages Klepiez and Pasieki. The accusation had already been dealt with in 1631 and was concerned with privileges which had been granted long ago. Jan III confirms the rights of the town-council and orders the Jews to accept its authority and jurisdiction. In this decree, Sobieski compels the Jews to obey the municipal instances and fulfil all duties imposed upon every citizen of the town.

All this should not mislead us. From the lines of the aforementioned documents we learn about good relations between the Jews and their neighbours. The Jews lived in Kamenetz and its vicinity and presumably also in the villages. In documents from 1733 we read about Jews from the villages Holoborek as well as about a Jew dwelling in a church estate.

From the wills included among the documents deposited in the archives of the Kamenetz municipality we learn about commercial relations and negotiations between Christians and Jews.

Landlords and estate-owners from the surrounding area traded mainly with the Jews and there were no limits to the transactions. The Christians townsmen could not bear it.

At the beginning of the 18th century, during the rule of August II, King of Saxony, we already perceive a change in the conditions. The importance of Kamenetz decreases. Another "Starostwo" (administrative unit) exists beside it; it is located at Klacze, which was Tyskiewicz's property, and its authority extends over the entire region adjoining the Bialowieza Forest.

Hard times arrived for the Jews of Poland and Lithuania.

Blood-libels and other concocted charges became a frequent occurrence. The political reaction, headed by the clergy, spread all kinds of prejudices among the people who became afraid of Jewish witches who allegedly had made a pact with evil spirits. Anti-Jewish persecutions became a daily occurrence. Simple people were frightened by stories about the Jews casting an "evil eye" on crops in the fields. An echo of this period reaches us from Kamenetz too. A document from June 17th, 1718, tells us the following story: "Two Jewesses charged with witchcraft were arrested at Kamenetz. Hayka Shmulikha concealed in garbage a pot with strange objects, for example: flour, moon, eggs, oats etc. Hayka claimed she had done it upon the request of another Jewess Yospa. Yospa declared that she had hidden the objects in order to heal her daughter. The same Yospa, a musician's wife, cried and said she had visited a wise woman who had ordered her to prepare the mixture and hide it in order to protect it from an evil eye and the view of wicked people. Both of them were taken under guard to the fortress.

We know the end of the story of the two Jewesses, but this libel conforms to the false accusations spread about the Jews in Brest and its vicinity, who were flooded with blood libels and charged with having aided the Swedes in 1703 during their invasion.

Finally the struggle led by the townspeople against the Jews achieved its aim. The townspeople complain to King August II that in addition to the privilege from 1670 the Kamenetz Jews live comfortably, sell spirits, honey, beer and other drinks, trade quite freely, open shops in the market and in the town itself, buy and sell houses and property belonging to the nobility and the church, sell textile-wares at retail and at wholesale as well as haberdashery of various kinds, dump merchandise in the Old Town, cut down the prices of the houses, and with all this cause suffering to the citizens of Kamenetz".

King August II of Saxony replies to these accusations by an order which forbids the Jews to build flats in the courtyards, and to deal in alcoholic drinks. He also orders the "Starosta" to impose limitations upon the Jewish trade and shops. The above complaint of the townspeople is based on the privilege which the town received from Michael Wisniowiecki – the same king who had confirmed the old rights of the Kamenetz Jews and added to them new ones. We have already noted that in 1684 the townspeople lodged a complaint against giving the Jews priority rights, and they did so on the basis of the privilege granted to the town inhabitants.

The whole thing is somewhat puzzling. But the problem looks different when we investigate the manner in which the Jews in Lithuania received privileges from the Polish kings. The Jews used to obtain the privileges with great efforts and large amounts of money. Therefore they used to be called at that time: "hens that lay golden eggs", since every confirmation of a privilege or granting of a new one was connected with a delivery of "golden eggs" to the king, to his chancellery, to the provincial (voyvodship) authority and others.

We are familiar with the situation which arose in this manner. General and particular privileges were granted in addition to previous ones, given to the townspeople by the king and the principal aim of which was to restrict Jewish activity of a competitive character. Both sides would often reach agreement. The townsmen, however, could not abide by the terms of the agreement, for the life reality proved to be more powerful and so they used to apply for intervention of the authorities; and the Jews, in exchange for money, would procure new privileges. We learn from the above complaint that Kamenetz was divided into two parts – the Old Town and the New Town. It is easy to understand that the western part constituted the Old Town which included the Litevska Street and its neighbourhood. The Jewish Quarter was located in the center of Kamenetz and comprised all the lanes around the Great Synagogue, besides Leszno with the religious school (Talmud-Torah), and the ritual bath.

The Municipality of Kamenetz was a powerful and active institution which displayed remarkable arrogance, refused even to receive orders from the provincial governor(Wojwoda) and often appealed directly to the king. This explains the hard struggle for existence led by the Kamenetz Jews. It is easy to understand that the citizens fought against the Jews and Jewish peddlers who hawked in the villages, estates and in Kamentez itself without permission.

The taverns which were a source of livelihood for the Jews, galled the Christian inhabitants. The aforementioned documents re-echo the accusations brought forth by Polish anti-Semites, such as the well-known Jew baiter Stanislaw Macinski and others.

The Jewish population in Kamenetz reached the number of several hundred souls. We learn this from a document dated 1705:

"The Treasurer of the Synagogue, Shimon from the Community of Brest delivered a budget of the – head-tax imposed upon the Jewish Communities and townlets in the region of Brest. At the meeting the sum of 11084 Zlotys was imposed on Brest, on Kobryn – 315 Zlotys, on Pruzhany 485 Zlotys, on Kamenetz – 50 Zlotys, on Meltsch – 100 Zlotys etc.

At the beginning of the 18th century, during the period of the Central Jewish Autonomy, the Lithuanian Jews paid an annual head-tax amounting to 60.000 Zlotys. But after the autonomy had been abolished in 1764 the communities had to pay 2 Zlotys head-tax for every Jew over one year old.

Therefore it may be taken for granted that during the period of the counting the tax amounted to one Zloty per person. The Lithuanian Jews paid 60.000 Zlotys at that time. Hence, we shall not make an error if we estimate the number of Jews in Kamenetz, at the beginning of 18th century at 200 persons whose age exceeded one year. It follows that Kamenetz was a small Jewish center, but according to the standards of those times such a center was considered important.

The history of Jews in Kamenetz has not yet been written. As it had already been told the documents concerning the internal life of the community, its cultural life, its economic struggle, its rabbis and sages learned in the Law, were not in possession of the writer of this outline. But even these few lines expose to view a Jewish Community in its historic struggle for existence.

Translation of the Royal Privilege granted in 1661 by Jan Kazimierz, King of Poland, to the Jews of Kamenetz

Sixteen hundred and sixty years after the birth of Christ, the twentieth day in January, in the office of the Court of the Town of Brest, before the standard-bearer and under-Starosta Hieronim Casimir Olenski, with those who represent the Jews of Brest, Berek and Barukla, the heads of the Jews in Kamenetz. The Letter of His Grace Royal Excellency.

Letter of His Grace the Royal Excellency which is a privilege written on parchment in the Little Chancellery of the Grand Duchy of Lithuania, and which is given to the Jews in Kamenetz and is being copied in the books of the town of Brest, and this is its worded content:

Jan Kazimierz, King of Poland, with God's Grace etc. We announce in this letter: In order to bolster up and increase the prosperity and welfare of our subjects, we are concerned that our towns should have control not only over population but also over ramified trade. For this purpose markets have been set up in the towns.

Therefore we take the advice of our officials in the Royal Court who are together with us, and who have advised us that in conformity with the needs of people of religious and secular status, and also in conformity with the needs of our Jewish subjects who live in Kamenetz, we declare: In addition to the market-day which in our town Kamenetz, falls on every Saturday, every Tuesday in every week will be a market day, too, so that henceforth two market-days will be held in our town Kamenetz and so it will remain forever, without causing any damage to the adjoining towns.

Desiring to show our royal favour to the Jews in Kamenetz, and following the example of other towns and townlets in our Kingdom, we permit them to construct a synagogue and a Jewish religious School on the plot belonging to the Jew Baruch Szporzakowicz which is situated near the plot belonging to the citizen Chrustkowski, or in a different place, owned by a different man, but it should not equal in height and splendour the churches and mosques in town.

We also permit them to build a bath on a municipal plot of land, which has already been acquired by Jacob Kushnir whose name is famous and praiseworthy.

They are also entitled to establish a cemetery within or outside the town-limits. And finally, we grant them all freedoms to open shops, taverns and to engage in every trade and to acquire property and plots of land in the town.

And in order that they should not thereby sustain hardship and damages (praeditiones in Latin) at the hand of our townspeople, we impose a fine, in accordance with the letter of our brother, Wladyslaw IV whose memory we hallow, of the eleventh of December sixteen hundred and thirty five of our era. We declare and stress it again with all our strength and notify about it our citizen the Starosta, now and in the future; we also notify the town authorities and order them to protect the freedoms which we had conferred upon the abovementioned Jews and the rights of the Jews of the Grand Duchy of Lithuania, without any disturbance whatsoever.

Given in Warsaw in elected Crown Sejm (Parliament) on the sixteenth day in the month of June, in the year sixteen hundred and sixty-one, in the thirteenth year of the reign of our Polish and Swedish Lord King Jan Kazimierz.

The Chancellor of the Grand Duchy of Lithuania brought this letter to be recorded in the books of the town Brest.

Signed with my own hand

Jan Kazimierz

Историческій памятникъ Гродненской губ. XII в.

Бѣлая Каменецкая Вѣжа—„столпъ камень высотою 17 саженей, нодобенъ удивленію всѣмъ зря-
щимъ нань" (Инат. лѣт. 1275-6 г.), выстроенная
Волынскимъ княземъ Владиміромъ Васильковичемъ
для защиты основаннаго имъ г. Каменца отъ на-
паденія ятвяговъ.

(низъ башни отремонтированъ).

Изд. Кружка научнаго изученія
Гродненскаго губ. при С.-Петербургскомъ Университетѣ.

The historical "White Tower" of Kamenetz, erected in the
13th Century.

The historical "White Tower" of Kamenetz, erected in the 13ᵗʰ Century

vicinity of the town; three or four storekeepers sold aprons, kerchiefs, drapery etc.; the remaining ones were haberdashers, merchants of tar, pitch and others.

Only women and young, girls and maids ran the stores. All these women used to sit opposite one another, excited and flushed. Of course there were helpers around, girls or married women who dragged and pulled the prospective customers, mostly a villager or a peasant woman, to the shop, or call them in a loud voice.

But the "high class" customers, the Jews and the estate-owners had their own particular shopkeeper, and no one dared to pull, forcibly like a herring, such a customer to one's own store. Perhaps quietly, such a customer was accompanied by a curse which was addressed also at the merchant-woman who sold him the merchandise.

Actually, the turnover was very low, except on Sundays, because on other days the peasants hardly came to town. Therefore, the women used to sit idly in front of the shops. Sundays, however, were market days with the villagers coming in large numbers. They crowded and jostled near the doors of the shops like buzzing flies on a window pane covered with powdered sugar.

Inns were also among the more important establishments in town. They were quite numerous. The peasants could find a bite there: cheese, herring and cucumbers. But there was plenty of liquor, too. Only members of the gentry ("Szlachta") or at least small estate-owners could offer themselves such a treat. After they had a drink, they would not be satisfied, like the peasants, with a bit of cheese or herring, but ate a piece of goose-meat or fish. These inns, just like the shops, were also run by women. Only on Sundays, when business was brisk, and the turnover large, the menfolk helped out too.

This being so, what was the occupation of the men? They did not sit with folded hands either. In the vicinity of Kamenetz there were several hundred estate-owners. Each of them had several hundred or even more serfs. These serfs toiled and sweated by day and by night and were penniless; on the other hand the land owners, quite obviously, had to enjoy life. Each of the estate-owners had dealings with one or two Jews in the townlet, who profited from them to a lesser or greater degree.

If the noble man had two Jews in his entourage, one of them had to be a "nice Jew" and a respectable merchant, whereas the other one was less outstanding as regards both the outward appearance and the respectability of his commercial dealings. Both Jews were the estate owner's factotums. The "nice Jew" served him more with advice, the other one was more of a Jack-of-all-trades, whose occupations were of the shadier sort. Both of them, however, lived in great fear of their patron. Though they derived part of their livelihood from him, and he acted like a protecting Tsar in their dealings with the authorities, nevertheless we ought to praise God ten times a day hat this kind of relationship with the estate owners has disappeared from the scene of history.

If the squire fancied so, he might beat severely his Jew and then say to him "if you keep silent, you will stay with me, if not I shall give your job to another Jew". Just the same you will not be able to do anything to me, because both the magistrate and the police-chief are friends of mine."

The Jew kept silent thinking to himself "well, I got beaten. That is why he is a squire. But on the other hand, I eat my piece of bread thanks to him, and when I close my eyes forever my child will gain his livelihood from him."

His reasoning was quite correct. When a Jew serving a land-owner died, the squire took in his place the factotum's son or son-in-law, whomever he liked more. This was not unlike a marriage contract, and the Jew received the squire as a sort of inheritance. Perhaps it is worthwhile to mention here that the estate owner also had his own artisan in the townlet, to whom he would give all his work. There were numerous artisans in the townlet – cobblers, tailors, tinsmiths etc.

It is understandable that they found it more difficult to earn a living than the shopkeepers. Even though the rents were low and one had to pay only ten to twelve rubels a year for a flat, they could not afford to live by themselves in an apartment and the lodgings in a little house were shared by two or three families.

In those days the assessor and the district police-chief were the real rulers in the town. When a quarrel broke out between two Jews, they at once brought their case to the assessor. They appeared before him accompanied by their wives, children, helpful assistants, good friends and relatives. The assessor ruled in favour of the one who had bribed him with a larger sum or who had evoked greater sympathy in him. And if one of the litigants was daring enough to challenge the verdict and lodged a complaint, with the district police officer in Brest, against the assessor, it was seldom effective. On the contrary, the bold fellow was not worth a half penny afterwards, because the assessor tormented and persecuted him, as much as he could, and went as far as to beat and arrest the victim. As a rule the district police officer went hand in glove with the assessor.

At that time, the district police officer exercised full authority in the region. The notions people had about the provincial Governor were indeed strange. He was regarded as being on the same level as the Tsar, and nobody would ever conceive the idea of involving him in Jewish affairs.

The squire had a Jewish factotum who lived in his country estate. He also had a lease-holder, usually a Jew, and when he possessed several estates and several villages, a Jewish factotum and a Jewish lease-holder lived there too. It can be understood that such Jews trembled with fear before the squire.

At that time, when it was a mere trifle for the landowner to lash his peasants, men and women, young and old alike, what weight could such a little Jew carry?

One can imagine how the factotum, the lease-holder and their children lived in deadly fear of the estate-owner. If, God forbid, they had good-looking daughters, this was regarded as a terrible calamity. One had to fear lest the daughters should attract the squire's attention, because he had power to do whatever he fancied.

Pretty girls of the village-Jews were always dirty, unwashed, covered with soot and grime so that their good looks might remain unnoticed. Only when the girls went to town, and after they scrubbed and washed themselves with soap, did the people know that the village-Jew, had a pretty daughter.

The squire employed his Jews to handle most of his affairs, since he believed the Jew was a clever being, cunning but nevertheless honest. Every estate-owner regarded only his own Jews as honest, but the others were, in his opinion, swindlers and thieves.

He used to send his Jews on missions to his colleagues, the other land-owners. Though he had a Christian steward running the whole estate and giving orders to the peasants, he preferred to deal with the Jews. The squire who believed that a Jew could accomplish his task in a more skilful manner did not lift a finger without his "Moshke" and "Shmulke".

The majority of the estate owners who lived around Kamenetz were not very rich. The soil of the Kamenetz region is sandy and not particularly fertile.

The crop from one "morga" of land (two thirds acre) amounted to no more than four shocks of sheaves; each shock yielded about five-six wagon loads of corn. Not much wheat grows in the region of Kamenetz. Only here and there a patch of fertile land occupies several square miles and there the yield per acre amounts to eighteen to twenty shocks of sheaves.

The land owners, who lived two or three miles away from one another, arranged frequent balls, each time at the residence of another squire. These feasts were grandiose, with the best wines stored up for the occasion.

In fact, these balls drove quite a number of the estate-owners into financial straits, so that they were constantly short of money.

The Jews used to buy grain, alcohol and wool. The payments, which amounted to large sums of money, were made in advance. Often they exceeded the value of the bought goods.

Also merchants were not lacking, who would run to the estate-owner and try to cut the price offered by the steady buyer. Yet whatever the squire needed for himself, was bought from his "exclusive" Jews, with whom no one could compete.

As was fashionable at that time, the estate-owners were fond of dogs. Each squire had different sorts of dogs. There were hounds and beasts that would silently, without barking, fall upon a stranger and almost tear him to pieces. There was a third kind too – dogs that would only bark but not bite; but there was a fourth kind as well – dogs that barked and bit at the same time. Each estate-owner kept all these kinds of dogs in his courtyard, and the torments the Jews, who were on their way to the squire, had to suffer from them could fill quite an important page of the history of Jewish dispersion.

A Jew, who was on his way to the squire's residence, would first of all stop his horse-cart near the gate to the estate and wait till he saw a peasant man or a peasant woman. The man or woman would take him to the factotum, who usually sat in some corner, and from there someone would accompany him to the squire.

When the Jew had to leave, the estate-owner would send a servant to take the Jew to the front entrance. This applied only in case the Jew merited the honour of leaving through the front entrance.

If he did not possess this privilege, however, the Jew had to walk in deadly fear from the palace to the Jewish factotum, so that the latter might accompany him to the gate.

But not until he reached the gate was the Jew secure from the bad dogs. Should the estate-owner bear the slightest grudge against the Jew, the latter's life was not worth a dime. In such a case the Jew was left without an escort and had to undergo the methodically applied tortures of mockery and pain.

At first the squire sent out several dogs of the barking-but not biting kind. They were soon followed by the other kind and finally came the real "biters". The whole pack fell upon the Jew, not letting him budge from the spot; at the same time he received a considerable portion of bites.

While the cries of the Jew rent the air and he was frightened to death, the squire with all his family was standing on the porch and laughing heartily.

Sometimes, a land owner, to whom the Jew had caused the slightest displeasure, would tell a servant to accompany the Jew to the gate, at first, and then to have him alone in the Jew to the gate, at first, and then to have him alone in "privileged" one, would receive the same treatment as an ordinary Jew.

We cannot generalize however, and say that all squires acted in such a manner. There were others, more decent ones whose attitude toward the Jews was different.

The Jew was half dead when he returned home and many became sick as a result of the fright. The wife and particularly the children, who saw their father as he arrived tottering and pale, burst out crying and it seemed as if Yom Kippur (Day of Atonement) had arrived. But it often happened that, after a couple of days, the estate owner again sent for the Jew to come, because he, the squire, needed him urgently. And the Jew, to be sure – ran at once at full speed to the estate owner, because what will a Jew not do for title sake of gaining a livelihood?

The Jew used to console his wife constantly that basically the squire was not a bad fellow and that one could earn money from him; only when the "evil moment" overcame him things were bad – apparently all this comes from God. Nothing in the world happens without God's will. When God squire's head. May this expiation put an end to my troubles, and may God continue to protect me from the bad dogs.

[Yiddish page 380]

Melamdim [Schoolteachers]

Kamenetz-Litowsk[1]

By Yeḥezkel Kotik

Translated by Allen Flusberg

Note from translator: *This Yiddish article was already translated into English in the original Yizkor Book, in the article "My Reminiscences" appearing on pp. 29-37 of the English section of the Yizkor Book. However, the following section of the Yiddish article is absent in that English translation. The Hebrew version of the Yiddish article, which appears on pp. 39-43 of this Yizkor Book, does include this section. Differences between the Hebrew and Yiddish articles are indicated in the footnotes below.*

The Yiddish version also incorporates the photograph below of Yeḥezkel Kotik.

The *melamdim* [schoolteachers of religious studies] were the main educators of the town. The one who taught the youngest children was Yakov-Ber the *melamed*, whom nearly all the children of the town were taught by first. A child of age three, or even younger, would begin to learn the *aleph-bays* [Hebrew alphabet] with him, and he would continue to study with him for about two years, until he could *daven* [read the prayers out loud] well and rapidly. After that the children were handed over to the *melamdim* of *ḥumesh* [Pentateuch] and beginners' *Gemoro* [Talmud], the latter consisting of easy *Mishnas*[2] specifically selected for children, referred to as *Lekaḥ Tov*. The children were transferred from *melamdim* of this type to higher-level and still higher-level *melamdim*, until they reached the most advanced teachers who taught the adolescent boys—both unmarried and married.

There were two such highest-level *melamdim* in the town, both of whom had vicious tempers. They used to beat the children severely, give them lashes, and put them in the "*pekl*". The "*pekl*" was the worst punishment of all. The *melamed* would lower the boy's trousers and tuck the boy's shirt up over his jacket, folding or tying them into a *pekl* [bundle]. In that state the boy would begin reading and explaining the *Gemoro* section out loud, as the *rebbe* [teacher] would stand over him, holding a sturdy rod or leather strap in his hand. And if the boy came to something that he couldn't explain, the *rebbe* would deliver a powerful lash that immediately left a black-and-blue mark on his flesh. In this manner the boy would continue to read and explain for an entire hour. This test always took place on a Thursday, the day it was the boys' turns to orally explain the *Gemoro* themselves—the section the *rebbe* had been teaching them all week—because on *Shabbes* [Saturday] the *melamed* would have to go with each boy to the boy's father, to have the father hear the boy read and explain the *Gemoro*. A father who was not knowledgeable enough himself would already have asked a learned person to be there, so that the latter could hear the boy out as he explained the *Gemoro*. And if the boy didn't do a good job, the father would not hesitate to blame the *melamed*. Not taking this well, the *melamed* would channel all his ire onto that unmentionable part of the boy's anatomy.

[Yiddish page 381]

Of these two vile-tempered *melamdim*, one was called "Matted-Hair" Dovid, nicknamed after the full head of *koltenes* [matted, plaited hair][3] that he had. He also had a terrible temper, and—simply put—he was always beating the boys black-and-blue. Sometimes he would lift a boy up [and throw him down onto the floor in a rage].[4] And one time a boy actually died as a result. After this child's funeral, it did not even occur to his parents to challenge R. Dovid[5] and ask why he had killed their son. They thought it had probably been God's will that the *rebbe* should kill him—perhaps preordained. Nor did it occur to anyone else in the town that "Matted-Hair" Dovid had actually committed a murder. Even M.S. Zun, who was always seeking to expose crimes in the town to foment intrigue and division, was also silent in this case, and "Matted-Hair" Dovid continued on as usual in his profession. He was teaching young unmarried and married boys, and all of them were damaged by the time they left his class.

The other high-level *melamed*, called "Blind" Dovid because he was blind in one eye, was an even more advanced teacher than "Matted-Hair" Dovid. Many of his students emerged from under his tutelage well-educated in Talmud. But he had an outrageous temper and was always mercilessly beating and lashing the children. It was this very *melamed* that I, too, studied under—but more about that later.

As I said, both boys and girls used to get married very young: that is, from ages thirteen to seventeen. While they were still in school learning. the boys would get a dowry ranging from two hundred to a thousand rubles,[6] and the father-in-law contributed *kest* [board]. In the *tenoyim* [engagement agreement], the parents would stipulate that either the father-in-law or the father would have to pay for a *melamed* for the young married boy. And when the boy actually did get married and was receiving *kest* at the father's house, he would continue to study with the same *melamed* who had been teaching him before the wedding. Thus, the *rebbe* would still be lashing the groom after the wedding, just as he had before.

In my times it was no longer in fashion for the boys to continue studying in *hayder* [classrooms of the *melamdim*[7]] after the wedding. And my *rebbe*, "Blind" Dovid, was indeed pining away for those good old days, when he was still able to lash the married boys. He used to tell stories about specific incidents. For example, a student's mother once dropped by the *hayder* to congratulate her son on the birth of his newborn son; the birth had just taken place. But she couldn't get into the *hayder*, whose door had been barred while lashings were being administered. "At that time," recounted the *rebbe*, "the mother was tapping on the windowpane shouting *mazel tov* [congratulations] to her son, and I was congratulating him with the rod. Each time I struck him I said: '*Mazel tov* on your newborn boy! You *shaygetz*![8] *Mazel tov* on your a newborn boy!'"[9]

[Yiddish page 382]

In all of Kamenetz there were no writing teachers. The same *melamdim* used to teach us how to write Yiddish.

The only real subject was *Gemoro* with its commentaries. They taught *humesh* [Pentateuch], as well, but not the entire weekly section [read in synagogue on the Sabbath]—only half of it. As far as Bible [beyond the Pentateuch] was concerned, only one *melamed*, called Motke Melamed, taught it. He was teaching the nine- and ten-year olds *Gemoro* with a bit of *Toisfois*[10], and he would devote one hour a day to Bible and another hour to stories about wonders and miracles of the Geonim [7th-11th century scholars of Babylon]. He also described Gehenna so picturesquely that he brought it to life (but apparently he had barely any knowledge of Paradise). He even drew a picture of Gehenna on a sheet of paper, indicating what its dimensions were and on which side the door was located. But unfortunately he did not know the dimensions of Paradise or where its door was. And with respect to Bible, he didn't teach anything beyond First Prophets: Joshua, Judges, Samuel I and II, Kings I and II—and nothing more. But the other *melamdim*, who were teaching the bigger boys *Gemoro* with *Toisfois* and all the other commentaries, didn't teach any Bible at all. Teaching Bible was considered a kind of *apikorsus* [heresy].

A *melamed* typically earned between sixty and one hundred rubles from his students' tuition every school-term. A *melamed* who made just under four rubles a week could consider himself a wealthy *melamed*.[11]

The lowest-level *melamdim*, who taught the little children aleph-bays [Hebrew alphabet], had between sixty and eighty little boys in their class. The tuition for these little ones was one ruble per school-term. The wealthy paid ten gilden[12] per term. When a boy reached the age of five, he was transferred to a *humesh melamed*, who had twenty to thirty boys in his class, for whom tuition was three rubles per term.

When a boy began studying *humesh*, the fathers would make a party for the *melamed* and for all the boys who attended the *hayder*; and their families would also come. Each of the fathers decided for himself—based on his wealth—how elaborate to make the *humesh* party. For example, my grandfather, Aharon-Layzer, would have a small calf slaughtered for such a party to honor one of his children or grandchildren. And for drinks there was wine served with expensive dishes.

[Yiddish page 383]

The little boys learned *humesh* for a year or two: that is, the first subsection or at most three subsections of the *sidra* [the weekly section of the Pentateuch, read each week in synagogue]. And after that they would be transferred to the *melamdim* who taught beginners' *Gemoro*; these had fifteen to twenty boys in a class. The tuition was four rubles per term; the wealthy paid five.

There were also some *melamdim* who taught both *humesh* and beginners' *Gemoro*. They would begin to teach *Lekah Tov* to the better *humesh* students.

Once a boy had studied under a *melamed* who taught beginners' *Gemoro* for two or three years, his father would transfer him to a more advanced *melamed* who would teach the boys a page of *Gemoro* in the first term, and two pages in the second term. Such a *melamed* would have twelve boys in his class, for each of whom the tuition was six or seven rubles per term. After studying for three terms, the child was transferred to a more advanced *melamed*, who taught *Gemoro* with *Toisfois*. Such a *melamed* had about ten students in his class, each of whom brought in a tuition of eight rubles per term, etc.

Each *melamed* taught the children a different Talmudic *maseches* [volume] without asking the students which volumes they had already studied with other *melamdim*. Hence there was obviously no well-defined order in which the various volumes of *Gemoro* were studied. And since each *melamed* would switch volumes from one year to the next, or even more often, learning was discontinuous and fragmented.

Less capable students would continue studying in one *ḥayder* for a long time. However, less capable children of the more prominent townspeople were transferred to more advanced *melamdim* together with the better students. The father of a less capable student would ask the more advanced *melamed* to teach his son something he could fathom, rather than the material that he was teaching the better students. The prominent fathers were embarrassed to have their sons, bigger boys, continue to study with more elementary *melamdim*. In each *ḥayder* there were thus less capable, coarser boys, studying together with the better students. Nevertheless, no one embarrassed the bigger boys, for most of the better students came from the lower class, and so *yichus* [pedigree] wound up as the equalizer among these children. The good students didn't brag about their capability, and the bigger boys didn't brag about their pedigree. And as a result, it all balanced out.[13]

The children were in school from 9 AM until 2 PM, at which time everyone went home for an hour to eat lunch. At exactly 3 PM every boy had to be back in *ḥayder*, or else be delivered terrible blows, slaps, or even lashes.

Studies resumed at 3 PM. In summer they continued until sunset, when the *melamdim* had to leave to attend *minḥa* [afternoon prayer service] in the *bays medresh* [study house that doubled as a prayer hall]. During winter the younger boys were in school until 8 PM and the older ones until 9 PM. In the winter the *melamdim* would recite the *minḥa* and *maariv* [evening] services in the *ḥayder* together with their students. This was the schedule for the entire week, except for Friday. On Fridays the boys studied until 2 PM in the winter and until 3 or 4 PM in the summer.

Even on the Sabbaths the boys didn't get any respite from studies. First, each boy was tested orally by the *melamed* in front of either his father or someone else who was knowledgeable. In this oral test, the boy had to repeat whatever he had learned that week. And after that, he had to go to the *ḥayder* to study *Perek* [Ethics of the Fathers] or *Medresh* [Midrash = homiletical interpretation of the Bible].

The boys never had any free time, except on the holidays: Purim, Passover, *Shevuos* [Pentecost], Rosh Hashana [New Year], Yom Kippur [Day of Atonement] and *Sukkes* [Tabernacles]—all together twenty-six days a year.

And this was the regimen of life and education in my native town, Kamenetz-Litowsk, during my youth.[14]

(Excerpted from his book, *My Reminiscences*)

Translator's Footnotes:

1. From *Kamenetz-Litovsk, Zastavije and Colonies Memorial Book*, edited by S. Eisenstadt and M. Galbert, published by the Israel and America Committee of Kamenetz Litovsk and Zastavya, (Orly, Tel Aviv, Israel, 1970), pp. 376-385.
2. The Mishna is the core text of the Talmud, composed around 200 CE. The *Gemoro* (*Gemara*) of the Babylonian Talmud, completed around 500 CE, is an analysis of the Mishna and other early traditions. The Talmud incorporates both.
3. On *koltenes* in Poland see the following link (retrieved December, 2020): https://en.wikipedia.org/wiki/Polish_plait
4. These words [in brackets] are missing in the Yiddish version because of a printing error (a line from further below is substituted for the missing line, and that same line is printed again in its proper place further below). The words in brackets are translated from the Hebrew version.
5. R. stands for *Reb*, an honorific similar to English "Mr."
6. A ruble could be exchanged for US $0.78 in 1899, which in 2020 would be equivalent to US $24 after taking inflation into account. (The exchange rate was about the same in the 1880s, the period referred to in this article.) The average textile worker earned about 15 rubles per month. See the following links (retrieved July 2020): https://kehilalinks.jewishgen.org/lida-district/wages.htm, https://westegg.com/inflation/
7. A classroom was often located in the *melamed*'s home.
8. In this context, *shaygetz* connotes rascal.
9. This entire paragraph is missing in the Hebrew version of this article.
10. *Toisfois* (*Tosafot*), a 12th-century commentary on the Talmud is printed in the margin of the Talmud pages. It is a relatively difficult commentary that often brings up and attempts to resolve apparent contradictions between different volumes of the Talmud.
11. See Footnote 6 above.
12. Ten gilden = 1.5 rubles. There were 100 kopecks in a ruble, and the 15-kopeck coin was called a gilden (A. Harkavy, Yiddish-English-Hebrew Dictionary, 1925, Steven Spielberg Digital Yiddish Library, National Yiddish Book Center, Amhurst MA).
13. This entire paragraph was omitted in the Hebrew version of this article.
14. This sentence appears in the Hebrew version but is not present in the Yiddish version of this article.

[English page 38] [Yiddish page 384]

Yehezkel Kotik

Author of "My Reminiscences"

Yehezkel Kotik was born in April, 1847 in Kamentz-Litovsk in the Province of Grodno. His father was a Hassidic Jew. Yehezkel learned the Talmud until the age of 17. Then he married and was a lease-holder of estates in various villages for about two years. Later on he settled in Kiev. The anti-Jews pogroms which took place there made him move to Warsaw, where for many years he owned a coffeehouse in Nalewki Street. This coffee-house was a meeting place for Yiddish writers as well as for activists of the Jewish Labour Movement. Kotik was known in public affairs. He founded a number of philanthropic societies and institutions. He also published various pamphlets in Hebrew and Yiddish, and a book of Jewish stories. But he gained world fame thanks to his memoirs published in two volumes under the name "Meyne Zikhroynes".

Particular interest was evoked by the first volume where the author gives us a bright picture of Jewish life in Russia in the middle of the 19th century.

In this volumes Kotik depicts the social, economic and cultural conditions of that period. He drew a picture of the people who lived there and the struggle between the "Hassidim" and the "Mitnagdim",etc.

Except for its cultural-historical value, "Meyne Zikhroynes" has also purely literary values. The personages appearing on its pages are very vividly described.

Kotik died in Warsaw in 1921.

From "The Eternal Source"
(Morgen Journal New York)

[English page 39] [Yiddish page 386]

Sholom-Aleichem's Letter to Yehezkel Kotik

Lausanne (Switzerland), 10.1.1913

Very respected and unfortunately unknown colleague, Yehezkel Kotik!

At the same time that I wrote to you, I wrote to Nicrer that we should exchange the books. It turns out that you had sent to Niger the copy dedicated to the poet Abraham Reisin - and Reisin is now in no other place but in New York, in America! If this had happened a few years ago, when Sholom Aleichem was still light-footed, it would have been child's play for me to get up and take a trip to America. But since right now this is a bit more difficult, what was I do if I was dying to read your "Reminiscences?" I put the entire blame on you for committing the transgression, cut open Niger's copy and I feel no regrets. I began reading your "Reminiscences" and what shall I say? I do not remember a year when I experienced such great pleasure, such enjoyment – real spiritual enjoyment! That is not a book – that is a treasure, a garden, a paradise, full of flowers and singing of birds. It reminded me of my youth, my family, my "heder",my holidays, my dreams, my types. No! Compared with you, I, with my bunch of types and pictures, many of which I had known and many of which I had invented - I am a poor little boy and a beggar, and I say it without any flattery or false modesty.

If I had your experiences and family I would by now have flooded the world with them. For Heaven's sale, where have you been till now? A man possesses so many brilliant diamonds and pearls and nothing happens! A Jew "collects precious coins",as the pious ones from your hometown would say – without even mentioning to anyone that he possesses such a treasure.

I began to read and was unable to tear myself away from your book. It almost drove me crazy! Who is that Kotik? I had heard about someone whose name, I believe, is A. Kotik and who is a young man - and you are a Jew with a grey beard. What enchanted me in your book is the sacred, simple truth, unadulterated simpleness. And now the language! No, you are not only a good, honest, faithful watchman of a rich, an enormously rich treasure you have a talent blessed by God and an artist's soul which has no self-knowledge. There were not few Jews in your Kamenetz and in Zastavye, not few relatives in your noisy – as you call it – family. But why has none of them collected such reminiscences as you have? Why has none of them displayed anything like your imagination which flames?

I somehow feel that your family is my family, and every reader probably feels the same. I know your grandfather Aharon-Leyzer, and your grandmother Beyle-Rashe, and your father, the Hassid Moyshe, and all your uncles and aunts, and even the district police officer and the assessor, with all the estate owners, the good ones and the bad ones, and the religious teachers ("Melamdim"), and the Hassidic Jews with their opponents, the "Mitnagdim", and the doctors, and the rabbi, and that sceptical atheist, the writer from Brest, willing to write for a rubel, and both Israels, and Aharon-Leybele, and Hatzkele, and Moshke, and Berel-Bernt, the steward and just all of them! They are all alive. I know them all and I share the joys and sorrows of all of them. After all some force is necessary to make me not only laugh (there are spots in your book when I burst out in a side-splitting laughter), but also to extract tears from my eyes. I swear upon my word of honor that I was crying together with all of you, when your grandfather gave his blessing to you all, before the Day of Atonement, and when your pious and righteous Grandmother was lying, dead on the floor and your grand-father fainted a hundred times. Let us rejoice as much in a speedy deliverance of Israel as I shed my tears, and Oh Almighty God, I did not do it because a human being died. How many people are dying every day, at any time and at any hour!

But I was crying because your grandmother and your grandfather - they are mine, mine, mine! And because they are living, golden-hearted people, whom you had cherished and snuggled in your soul and whom you had invested with your entire fiery truth. I am really filled with pride that we possess such people, such Jews like you to whom we owe it that the "small coins",thrown aside and neglected – in nay opinion many of them are still lying around – have not been lost for our people. I am really proud that our still young Yiddish folk-literature has been enriched by such a book like your "Reminiscences".

Will you continue writing, your "Reminiscences"? Will they be as rich and as masterful as the first volume? Masterful? I am sure they will be. But rich? I do not know; I am afraid their contents will be poorer, thinner. Those Jews are no longer! It means they are, but not so much in the foreground; they are like a drop in the ocean, in particular in large towns.

11.1.1913.

Today, on a mountain called Leson, which is 4,500 feet high and tops Lausanne, I accidentally met a writer Izbicki (Michalowicz). I told him how much admiration was aroused in me by a book of a respectable Jew, Y. Kotik, which moved me to tears. It turned out that Izbicki knows you very well, that you are A. Kotik's father, that you are the owner of the coffee house on Nalewki Street and that everyone has known for a long time about some "Reminiscences" of yours. One must ask: "Where have they been all the time, the idiots?" Why did they keep silent, if they knew about it? And where was I, an idiot myself? Was I not myself in the Nalewki Street and did hot I drink coffee there - with Spector, I believe. Why was I unaware where I was and at whose place I had a coffee? Why is our book market being flooded with the worst of trash, at a time when treasures like yours are lying around in a crate, in a drawer or under a mattress. Murderous hatred rises up in me against our critics whenever I recall to mind how they praise every young scribbler who produces an obscenity taken from the "Goyim". I boil with indignation while reading the digested and spitted out obscenity of Artzibashev and similar filth, which enrage the good humorist – as I am called – and deprive me of the desire to write. I become a vicious criminal; do not imagine that it lasts long – I am just like the proverbial "Jewish robber".

Well, I have been chatting too much about myself. If you have time, answer this question, please. Are you still writing your "Reminiscences" and what period and what circles are you dealing with? Is it going as smoothly as previously? Are you dealing with the family? There are persons and characters whose stories you must carry on and on.

Live long, be healthy and cheerful and write! Your thankful reader, friend and pupil,

Sholom-Aleichem

[English page 43]

Yearning and Mourning for My Home Town

By Abraham Shudroff

Almost every one of us yearns for the small town or the "shtetl" where we were born. Wherever we may be, our hearts and minds are often drawn to it, and great is our longing for this place across the seas where our cradles once stood. It is of little importance that half a century or more has elapsed since we left it. Although we all know well that perhaps there is nothing to long for, the spell of the native land is so powerful that we cannot help feeling nostalgic about it. Perhaps it is the yearning for the bygone years of childhood and youth that makes us unceasingly discuss and reminisce, write and read about those points on the map with which our personal experiences are linked forever. This homesickness is made stronger by our knowledge that our own parents and forefathers lived for generations in those Central and East European towns and townlets and created a rich and complete Jewish life. Seldom in the history of Jewish wanderings on various continents has there been anything resembling it. After the First World War, when I was sixteen years old, I left Kamenetz for the United States. Though over forty years have gone by since then, I still have a clear picture before my eyes of my home town and its inhabitants. The town was neither large nor rich. Its Jews were poor but lovable and friendly. A considerable number of them were shopkeepers and small merchants. But the majority were independent craftsmen and tradesmen, shoemakers, tailors, furriers, etc. There were also a few rich men, according to the standards of that time. The overwhelming majority were religious, God-fearing Jews, many of them learned in the Law. They were all, without exception, devoted to their families and to their children. There were numerous parents, deeply rooted and long settled in Kamenetz, who, in the first decade of the 20th century, grieved deeply when they had to accompany their children to the railway station. The children set out on their way to the "Land of Columbus" and most of the parents knew that they would never see them again. Quite soon, however, they derived satisfaction when the sons and daughters, who settled down and established themselves in the faraway land, began sending material aid to their fathers and mothers to support them in their old age.

I was a little boy attending "heder", the traditional religious school, when the First World War broke out. A year later, in 1915, the German and Austro-Hungarian armies occupied Kamenetz-Litovsk. Difficult times full of hardships and sufferings began.

A fine generation of Jewish youth grew up in Kamenetz after World War I. Many of them emigrated, but a considerable part remained at home. Schools, libraries, and many educational circles were established. But on the whole, the Jews suffered under the anti-Semitic Polish administration.

The year 1939 came. The Second World War broke out and we were cut off from the townlet. And then came the accursed Hitler, the worst oppressor and enemy of our people in all times:

In 1941, when the Nazi murderers entered Kamenetz-Litovsk, they immediately shot the leaders of the Jewish community and locked all Jews in a ghetto. Later on the entire Jewish community, headed by the Rabbis Reuven Burstein and the Yeshivah-Principal, Hayim Garfinkel of blessed memory perished in the gas chambers and death camps of Treblinka and Auschwitz. The Jews of Kamenetz shared the tragic fate of their six million martyred Jewish brethren.

[English page 46]

Kamenetz as I Remember You

By Dvora Dolinsky-Pansky (New York)

In July, 1915, Kamenetz and the neighbouring townlets were captured by the German-Austrian army which had successfully marched forward. The Russian army was shattered; it was retreating in confusion and carrying out anti-Jews pogroms. Pools of blood, dead horses, wrecked wagons could be seen on the roads. People, with a look of despair in their eyes, were wandering on every highway. They lost the ground under their feet, the events dazed and confused them, driving them into utter desperation. Everybody saw clearly that a period of chaos was setting in. People were being driven out of their houses, all their property was being set on fire and destroyed. Every day, homeless, evacuated people entered the town, some of them on horse-drawn wagons, and others trudging along with tired, pale children by their sides. Hysterical cries could be heard everywhere. With bundles in their hands and on their backs, large crowds were standing and searching f or a way of escape. But how could they flee when no trains were leaving Kamenetz. The only thing to do was to march on one's own feet toward the horizon. When the Russian army began its retreat the situation deteriorated even more; during the last days of its stay Kamenetz and vicinity turned into a military center. The retreating Russian army enjoyed itself at the expense of the Jewish population and began robbing and destroying whatever they could. Everyone was seized by fear; people hid in the houses, fled to their neighbours or even sought refuge in the cellars and waited for one fighting army to supersede the other.

And when Kamenetz was finally occupied by the Germans, the people of the town felt sharply that they were really caught in a war and subjected to strict military laws. Life was even more restricted and hopeless. The food problem became more acute, the population hungered. After the Germans had come, parts of the defeated Russian army remained in hideouts, formed different gangs which used to rob and murder Jews in the area comprising the neighbouring towns and villages. As a result the Jews were forced to leave their homes and move into neighbouring towns where there was a larger Jewish population. Being herself one of the victims, the writer of these lines moved with her family to Kamenetz and became a permanent resident there. In that little town I lived during most of my youth, that is, in the years between the two world wars. I do not have to search for any materials in libraries or archives, but only to turn to my own memory, though the events and experiences could not be recorded when their impression was still recent and fresh. At that time there was no possibility – or rather no necessity – to do it. However, after they had lost some of their weight and can now be considered as belonging to the past, I am better able to arrange them in an orderly manner and to revise everything I had heard, seen or experienced personally, as a direct participant in the events, even though I can not recollect every detail.

Kamenetz-Litovsk lies in Byelorussia (White Russia) on the Lesna River, which flows into the Western Bug. Judging by the religious institutions, as, for instance, the beautiful Great Synagogue with its original Holy Ark, old synagogues, the Jewish cemetery with its old tombstones and many other sites, it is possible to state that Kamenetz was an old Jewish community which had existed for many centuries. An obelisk erected many centuries ago by a Lithuanian duke may be added to the list of the relics of ancient times. The obelisk provided Kamenetz with a special attraction which other little towns did not possess. Memories of wooden houses, of signs over shops, of old men with long beards, of visionary youth, of zest for life and above all, of tragedy, come back to my mind. Those images are enduring and unforgettable.

I find in my memory materials for a family chronicle, memoirs and in the main, recollections of a little town that was alive, a townlet with its images and human types. I remember bright and shady figures, a gallery of portraits of tailors, cobblers, smiths and other craftsmen; religious teachers, school teachers, cantors; the water-carrier, the bath-house 'attendant, the beadle. A popular saying, which stated that "every town has its madman" applied also to Kamenetz. We had our Alterke though it must be said that he was not completely crazy. In other words, he was harmless to the inhabitants of the town. Alterke was short, skinny and his face deathly pale; his eyes were dull; he always wore a stained, sweaty cap and a long coat; he used to hang out near the municipality building where he swept the rooms. He also performed another function in the town: whenever a circumcision ceremony took place he had to set the pillow on which the boy rested.

Each one of these types and figures had his own specific charm; each one of them cherished the traditional folklore and possessed hidden talents. There were religious Jews, though some of them had been tinged by the "Has kala" (Enlightenment) movement and were also partly interested in worldly affairs. And there were free-thinkers who derived their pleasure from reading the works of modern Jewish authors and dreamed about better days to come. Kamenetz was just one of the many towns and townlets spread all over White Russia and Poland where the majority of the Jewish population lived in hard and painful conditions; it embodied, in miniature, the whole Jewish national existence with all its shades – from the extreme right to the extreme left. Tradition and a profound Jewish religious feeling reigned supremely at home and in the sphere of social life. The synagogue was a meeting place for young and old. All problems, including the political, were solved there. On the other hand, it is a fact that the strict and fanatical adherence to tradition brought in its wake some petrifaction of Jewish life. In spite of it, Kamenetz was not an ignorant town belonging to the dark ages but adjusted itself to the modern world. There were parties and circles striving toward other aims; they had their own vision of a better future for the Jewish people and the working masses. All this added color and warmth to our existence.

I shall never forget the Saturday afternoons in our town. After eating "tscholent" (a Sabbath dish kept warm from Friday) the" Jews went to sleep and complete silence enveloped the town, with its closed shops and empty streets. This was a day of rest and the worries of the past week were shoved away into a distant corner of the mind. But gradually the whole town woke up from the deep slumber. The ordinary working days returned, with their grey reality and worries about the following day. This went on year in year out.

Kamenetz was surrounded by villages with a large population. They supplied bread, potatoes, dairy products, hides and wood. The regular fairs taking place in the market square full of stands, drew noisy crowds, milling about and buying and selling. Peasants from the neighbouring villages used to come to town to sell their products and to buy the necessary articles for the whole week.

There was hardly any industry in Kamenetz. There were a few rich Jews and there were some extremely poor ones. There were small and big Jewish merchants, middlemen, tradesmen, money-lenders and idle loafers; there was also a small number of salaried workers. Here and there the knocking of a shoe-maker's hammer could be heard.

There were some good craftsmen and some incompetent bunglers. I remember a cobbler who used to mend the shoes of my family. He lived on the Napiska Street in the house of Tsirel Dubiner; I do not remember his name. Before I had time to ask him about the price, he would tear off the soles and throw the shoes into a bucket filled with water; only then would he tell us the price, because by then he could be sure that I would not take the shoes away from him. Most of the workshops were small. Their proprietors usually worked alone or with an assistant. I can also remember Alter's tannery on the Napiska Street, Bershtig the shoemaker, David the miller and the brewery which belonged to Guterman and was then considered a large industrial enterprise. But the workers in that period did not manage to get organized in trade union. Through the thirst for knowledge and education was great, no systematic propaganda work was done and therefore the fields of trade unionism and social activity were somewhat neglected.

Notwithstanding the expanding number of employed Jewish workers and craftsmen, the majority of Kamenetz Jews were shopkeepers and merchants. The typical house in Kamenetz was built of wood with thatched or tiled roof. This was the cause of frequent big fires which devastated large parts of our town.

In the cultural sphere, Kamenetz was far from being a backward town. It is always the human material which can secure cultural advancement and we possessed such people. Our youth was very keen and sensitive to everything going on in the world. I should like to honor them by recording the good example they gave. Though our life was hard and hopeless, our town possessed a beautiful and intelligent young generation, which, in spite of the difficult conditions, was full of energy, zest for life and strove to accomplish its vision of a better future.

After World War I economic and social pressure was felt in many ways. From this resulted further impoverishment of the Jews — and the strengthened desire to emigrate, but the gates of the wide world were not open to everyone. Many young people were jealous of me since I had a chance to go to America. I shall never forget the day when I had to part with my parents, will my town and with all those close to me: I felt as if I had known that I would never see all of them again. Until the First World War there were mostly traditional, religious schools of the "heder" type in Kamenetz. At that time there were many teachers of religious subjects and special teachers for the very young. They taught the Hebrew alphabet and how to write letters in Yiddish and Russian. In that period it was important to know how to address letters to America because there was hardly anyone without relatives or friends there.

But all these institutions were not sufficient. Some of the well-off Jews used to send their children to larger cities to obtain secular education. The nearest city was Brest-Litovsk.

There was also a two-grade Russian State school. At that time the percentage of Jewish students in Russian state schools was very small; as far as I can remember there was not a single Jewish child in the Russian state school at Kamenetz. During the First World War, after the Tsarist administration had fled and the Germans occupied Kamenetz, a new type school was established. During the time of the German occupation changes took place in the entire educational system. The Germans established a school where German, of course, was the language of instruction and Hebrew one of the taught subjects. Hebrew was taught by Israel Unterman, Lea Bobrovsky, and Malca Poliakevitch. The school which existed until the end of 1918, when the Germans left Kamenetz was the fortuitous start of a new Jewish school net which was organized in the later years; it comprised Jewish elementary schools where modern methods of teaching were used under the supervision of well known pedagogues. With great desire and enthusiasm the Jewish children strove towards a brighter future; they were attracted by a free world away from the narrow confines of the "heder" with its old-fashioned teachers. The new school was directed by the Sapirstein brothers, Nahum Gelerstein and Israel Pomerantz. In the years 1919-1929, the writer of these lines herself opened a school, together with Lea Bobrovska, in the school building which remained empty since the German occupation. The building had previously been used as the municipal post-office, therefore the street in which it was located was named "Pocztowa"

(Post Street). The building was new, handsome and sunny – almost ideal for a school. The street, too, was very beautiful, in particular in the days of spring, when the lilac shrubs, full of white and violet clusters of flowers, and the blooming apple trees were caressed by the warm sun. And the street looked even more colourful and beautiful when the children rushed out of the school building and their young, delicate voices resounded in the open air. Hebrew and Russian were the languages of instructions. Several subjects were taught in Russian. Later on we were joined by the Sapirstein brothers, Nahum Gelerstein and Israel Pomerantz, and together we formed a kind of "teachers society". Only those few children whose parents were well-off paid school fees; the majority of parents could not afford to pay; therefore the school budget was not big enough to allow the school to function normally. The American Joint Distribution Committee helped us a lot; it sent clothes for the children and teachers. I shall never forget the "costumes" we received from America. The kids put on fancy brown dresses and black aprons and – if I am not mistaken – also shoes and caps. But we, the teachers, received pyjama jackets; since they looked very much like Russian shirts ("rubashkas") we adorned ourselves in the fancy pyjama jackets and paraded in them on a Saturday night thinking that the whole world was smiling together with us.

The school was a fine institution. We were a group of teachers who, in the course of our work, became a closely knit circle of personal friends sharing the same ideals. We thought that nothing in the world could ever separate us.

Our youth was strongly attracted by Jewish culture. They were avid readers of books in Yiddish and members of the Jewish library. The library at Kamenetz possessed a considerable number of books – ranging from fiction to works on social and economical problems. The library served also as a meeting place for the people who sought answers to their social problems.

In the period between the two world wars the spread of Jewish press made only little headway. "The Haynt" and "The Moment" were the two most popular Yiddish newspapers. I remember that in Kamenetz there were only few regular subscribers; they subscribed jointly for a paper. Quite often we used to talk in our circle about the need for our own dramatics section, stage players, singers and reciters, so that we might have our own cadres for the literary or other cultural evenings. Unfortunately, several attempts to organize such a circle failed. After it had finally come into existence it fell apart after several performances. Perseverance and endless patience were required. The Sapirstein brothers and Rahel Atlas had those qualities. Rachel Atlas, who died in America, had originally come from Brest and lived for many years in Kamenetz. It is worthwhile to mention her activity. She was a fine actress with deep understanding of her roles and a very cultured person. Selda Steinberg-Sapirstein, too, was quite talented and she contributed her share. After all, we were far from such great centres where good performances could be seen and serve us as examples. Despite the fact that the theatrical performances took place in the barn belonging to Motye Klepatcher, Kamenetz possessed a circle of quite good amateur actors who appeared on stage from time to time.

I should like to devote a few words to Velvel Sapirstein who was one of my intimate friends. Usually, after a friend dies, the memory of his personality becomes dimmer every year. Sometimes the memory disappears altogether but this did not happen in the case of our unforgettable Velvel. On the contrary – in the course of time his image has become even shaper and deeply impressed upon my memory.

Let us honor his shining memory!

Let us go back to the town with its cultural and spiritual life. In the years when the Jewish colonization in the Land of Israel was still young, economically weak and constantly endangered by Arab attacks, a pioneering (Halutz) movement came into existence in the towns and townlets also in Kamenetz. Till the outbreak of the last war, the Zionist organizations carried out a great national mission in every field of their varied activities. Thanks to them there was a cultural advancement. Most of the young people studied Hebrew. Kamenetz did not stay behind in this respect; it had a large Zionist youth organization.

Remembering the years of my youth, I recall those who were my friends during the largest part of that period. I remember my mother, my father, my family, my friends, neighbours and close friends; I shall never forget them. I see the torn threads which linked me with each one of them. How painful it is to realize that I shall never see them again. I had dreamed for many years that I would see my home town again. But my desire remained unfulfilled, my hopes were all in vain. One still does not want to accept the fact that everything is lost, that everything perished and nothing but a desert remained.

I recollect the Friday nights – or the Saturdays or the holidays; how joyful and heart-warming was our modest home! I remember so many happy moments. We thought that such idyllic life would last forever.

Everybody came to our home to sing and to rejoice. Until today the hearty melodies accompany me.

From our home we used to run down to the Napiska Street, to meet the remaining members of our circle and to take a walk past the Zastavye Bridge. The bridge served as a place for promenades and dates there we used to make new acquaintances and from there we went wherever we fancied.

[English page 56] [Yiddish pp. 389-399]

The Jewish Agricultural Colonies

By Velvel Kustin (New Jersey)

Three Jewish agricultural colonies lay in the vicinity of Brest-Lito: Abramovo, Sarovo, and Lotovo. These colonies, situated close to each other, were established approximately 160 years ago.

The first to be established was Lotovo; it was named after Lot. The other two were also named after Biblical personages: Sarovo, after Sarah; Abramovo, after our fore-father Abraham. The first of these colonies, Lotovo, was also known as Plisich.

The reason for these colonies being set up by the Jews is unknown to me. However, some people used to say that this was one way of avoiding military service, which in those days could last up to twenty-five years. Conscription in our sense of the term was not practiced. The military would seize young children and induct them for long periods. Only tillers of the land were exempt by law. Therefore, the Jews, it is believed, settled on the land and in that way protected their children. However, no one really knows the actual reason for the founding of the colonies.

At the time of its establishment, the colony of Sarovo consisted of 24 families, each of whom received 65 acres of land from the Russian government. All of the Jews of Sarovo originally came from Brest-Litovsk. They were tradesmen and merchants of various kinds. My great-grandfather, for example, was a manufacturer of candles. His name was Hershel Lichtzier-Kustin. I can recall the names of some other first colonists: Eliezer Ashkenazi, Yosef Sokolovsky, Hershel Seidinger, Mordecai Simhovich, Kravietsky, and Chorny.

The founders of the colonies tilled the soil year in and year out, but when their children grew up the enlarged families could not live off the land anymore. The profits from their labours were insufficient. Since there was no possibility of acquiring additional land, some of the colonists were forced to leave the settlement, and they moved back into town. The majority of these colonists went back to Brest and some of them went to Kamenetz Litovsk, the nearest small town. There they worked as coachmen and as millers. Meanwhile, their abandoned land was rented to the colonists who remained. I say rented because according to the laws of that period, the departing colonists were unable to sell their holdings to non-colonists. And since the colonists who did remain in the settlement had no money with which to buy the land, the best thing was to rent it. Among the second generation of settlers was Israel Ashkenazi, who did not want to return to Brest. Instead, he left for Palestine and became one of the founders of the colony of Yesod Hama'ala in Upper Galilee. Many stories are told about him; how he taught the first Jewish settlers of Yesod Hama'ala to plow and to sow. He brought his father and mother, Eliezer and Gittel Ashkenazi to Palestine.

Their numerous descendants settled in various parts of the country. They still live in Yesod Hama'ala and other parts of Israel. One of the descendants of Eliezer Ashkenazi, Zvi Ashkenazi fell in the defense of Kfar Giladi, in the year 1946. Their entire story is told in two Hebrew books which deal with the history of Yesod Hama'ala.

The Kustin family were the only ones whose descendants remained in the colony of Sarovo for the entire life span of four generations. My great-grandfather, Hershel Lichtzier-Kustin had an only son, my grandfather Velvel. Hershel bought 65 acres of land from a colonist who had gone back to town, and because of his large holdings, he was able to gain a livelihood from agriculture.

Grandfather Velvel had four sons and three daughters. One of his sons was my father, Moshe Yossel. The daughters grew up, married, and settled in adjoining small towns. The sons rented additional land from ex-colonists, but even so, it was difficult to earn a living. They began to migrate to America. My own father sailed to America twice. Returning home from his second trip in 1909, he bought an additional 32 acres, which doubled his original holding of 32 acres which he had inherited previously. He also acquired ten head of cattle. He bred horses, raised chickens and ducks and became an established colonist.[1]

Regarding our religious life, it is to the glory of the original settlers that once their homes were built and their colony established, they erected a Beth-Hamidrash. This is a synagogue and religious school combined. They built it in the center of the settlement so that it could be conveniently reached by everyone.

It was a square-shaped building with a thatched roof. It was distinguished from the surrounding houses by a sign over the enclosed porch displaying that it was the Beth-Hamidrash. Within the building itself, the Holy Ark containing two Torah Scrolls, was flanked by two lions and surmounted by the Tablets of the Law. The pulpit, located in the center of the Beth-Hamidrash, was surrounded by six columns. The ceiling was decorated with stars in a blue field and the signs of the zodiac.

Prayers were recited in the Beth-Hamidrash three times a day, and I can recall even as a boy we always had a "minyan" and that the prayers were conducted alternately by different members of the colony. After the prayer service, many remained to study Talmud.[2]

Religious instruction for the children was given in a room within the Beth-Hamidrash. School began at 7:00 in the morning and ended at 8: 00 in the evening. In my time, the teacher came from the town of Kalenkovich. He taught us the Five Books of the Law with Rashi's commentary, as well as Talmud with annotations. I can recall the names of other teachers, such as Reb Eliezer Rogoznitsky, Reb Pinya Rappaport, and Yosel Terk. But one name I can recall with particular joy, for his coming was not only a joy to me but a festive pleasure for the entire colony. He was Rabbi Leyser Velvel of Blessed Memory, the Rabbi and religious Judge from Zastavye, our neighbouring small town. Before the Passover festival he would arrive in a wagon and come to pray at the Beth-Hamidrash. On these visits he would take up a collection for the poor. It was my father's privilege to have the visiting Rabbi as a guest for dinner in our house, when I would be examined in chapters of Talmud that I had studied. At his leave taking, a committee of home owners would collect corn, wheat, rye, and even potatoes, and the Rabbi would leave with the wagon, in which he had arrived, fully loaded.

Although the children had the right to attend the village school where Russian was taught, the instruction there was not suited for Jewish children, and our parents, despite their great economic difficulties, maintained constant, regular Jewish instruction in the colony in the Beth-Hamidrash. They did not forget the reading from our Bible and repeated in our prayer book . . . "And ye shall instruct your children diligently." In the matter of hiring a teacher they never haggled for the cheapest. He had to be one of the best, not only a versatile scholar, but a good pedagogue as well and knowledgeable in secular subjects also. This was a standard of excellence not easy to maintain and I can recall that the majority of the parents whose children were attending our "Heder" were usually obliged to borrow money from the wheat merchants in Kamenetz against their next year's crop. The Rebbe (teacher) was not only well paid; he was provided with food and lodging.

The colonists paid no dues to the Religious Council (The Kehilla). Whatever business we had in connection with our religious life was carried out by an elected Community Council. This election took place on the night of Simchat Torah, when they would also elect their Gabay, (the chief officer). This honor was bestowed upon my father every year and he served as Gabay for his entire life. It was on Simchat Torah night that the Gabay used to make a statement to the assembled community as to the expenses for communal needs and the homeowners would promise to pay them in part. The colony had no cemetery of its own and the deceased would be buried in Kamenetz Litovsk. But there were other expenses. For the High Holidays a paid cantor was brought in from Kamenetz. For several years the cantor was Reb Shlomo Rudnitsky from Kamenetz. He was called Shlomo Lysker because he was an overseer in the village of Lyski, where he was in the service of a rich non-Jewish landowner. He was the farm manager. Part of his duty was to keep strange cattle from rambling into the landowner's fields at night when they might damage the crops. Due to this, some of the peasants aimed to kill him and so he left the village. Not wanting to become a Gemora teacher because this would deprive the teachers of Kamenetz of their livelihood he became a teacher for beginners. But during the High Holidays, he was the cantor in our colony.

There are other facets of our religious life that I can recall. Our Sabbaths were observed strictly, and only the necessary labours, which were forbidden to be done by Jews on the Sabbath and Holy Days, were performed by peasants from neighbouring villages. They milked the cows and fired up the stoves in winter. Our relationship with them was peaceful and at times even friendly. Naturally, they were paid extra for doing these chores. There was one among these gentile peasants, Ivan the Shepherd as we called him, whose job was to look after the herd as they roamed the fields. In addition to being the shepherd of the colony, he was also the colony's Shabbat-Goy. He would turn off the lamps in the Beth-Hamidrash and tend to the stove there during the winter. He was devoted to the colony and I remember that soon after the First World War, there was a shortage of "Ethrogim" (citrons) which were used for Succoth, the Feast of the Tabernacles. The neighbouring town of Zastavye had both a citron as well as a "Lulav" (ritual palm branch). Each day during the Feast of the Tabernacles, Ivan would run the distance of three miles from Zastavye to our colony holding the citron and palm branch as he ran, and after our services in the Beth-Hamidrash he would run back with them to Zastavye.

There is one more item concerning our religious life that needs to be recalled and that is the renovation of our Beth-Hamidrash.

In 1909, on my father's second return from America, the colony decided that our religious house was in need of refurbishing. It was my father's proposal that this be done and again he was chosen to be the Treasurer. Each member not only pledged a financial contribution but in addition, his own work to rebuild and to embellish the building.

The most active in the project of reconstruction were my father and his three brothers: Reuben Leyb, Hershel, and my favourite Uncle Ephraim Shimon. It was the last mentioned who was the permanent official representative of the colony in its dealings with the local authorities. He was the "Starosta". He was also the most accomplished "Reader" in the synagogue; that is, leader of prayers, a "Baal-Tefilla". To be sure, every member in the colony was able to do the same, but each had his own variations but none was quite as authoritative as my Uncle Ephraim Shimon. Another uncle, Manche Ashkenazi, a born artist, made his contribution to the rebuilding of the Beth-Hamidrash. All the fine wood work and carvings contained on the Ark and on the Bima were done by his God given talent to his hands.

*

Now, to return to the beginning The first generation of colonists found agricultural life difficult and strange. It became advisable to hire peasants from neighbouring villages, the nearest to our colony being the village of Bilyeve. This practice of hiring peasants continued well into our days. that is for the lifespan of four generations. At harvest time, when it was necessary to gather the yield rapidly, it was usually the Bilyeve peasants who were hired to help with the work. After a small part of the colonists had left the settlement, those who remained, the hearty and determined, lived a real good Jewish farm life. It was a hard life but well-organized, Winter was naturally the hardest period but during the summer months, our youth were busily engaged in the fields, and with the grazing of cattle. It was not unusual for young boys to be awakened at three O'clock in the morning to begin the farm chores, if there were no older brothers or sisters to do them. One should remember that "Heder" (Hebrew school) began at 7:00 A.M. But it was all in a day's work, including a watch on the herd to keep them from grazing too close to the borders of the corn fields. Usually a gentile would be hired for this purpose.

In my time, there remained fourteen families in the colony numbering over fifty people. Living conditions had improved, thanks to the help given by the Jewish Colonization Association. At the turn of the century, our colonists had applied for agricultural assistance to the JCA. This organization sent experts who gave instruction in modern methods of fertilization and the use of agricultural machinery for ploughing, threshing and harvesting. Some of the settlers put little trust in the new methods but those who began using them were successful according to the standards of that time.

One of these settlers was Zimel Simchovich. By a stroke of good luck, he had succeeded in acquiring additional land from several families. Employing the new methods of farming, he became a rich colonist, envied not only by his Jewish neighbours but also by gentile landowners who bought from him seed, hay, and straw in large quantities which he had accumulated before onset of winter. He also planted an orchard of some 250 fruit bearing trees, an achievement that was new in the entire region. He raised apples, pears, cherries, plums of the larger size, and gooseberries. Professional literature from the JCA on how to be a successful orchardist helped Zimel with his work. He also bought saplings from the same source.

Needless to say, Reb Zimel was the most outstanding member of our colony. While everyone in the colony was kind, generous, and hospitable, not to mention warm-hearted and agreeable, Reb Zimel, however, was the shining example of all these virtues. One of the best students of the "Mishmar Yeshiva" in Brest, Rev Yosel Soroka, who became his son-in-law, was sustained and maintained by him in the traditional manner of a rich man supporting a Talmud student who was to marry into the family. Reb Yosel Soroka was descendant of a "Hassidic" family and was himself a Hassid.

On the Sabbath he wore a silk coat with a silk woven belt (gartel) and a little Polish cap on his head.

But it was not all work in the colony, especially for the young people. In the summer, the young folks did put in their licks in the field, but winter was the time for entertainment. They would gather in large houses to dance and to sing love songs and Zionist songs. These gatherings generally took place on Saturday night when everyone was well rested. No one ever missed any affair or event that took place in the little town of Kamenetz.

As for the adults, they too had their fun. On Holidays, the settlers visited each other for "Kiddush" and housewives were afforded the opportunity to show off their cooking and baking arts. Such delicious cakes and pastries! The young fry, meanwhile, played parlour games, sang and danced and recited poems by Morris Rosenfeld, Abraham Raisin, S. Frug, Haim Nachman Bialik, and the stories of Sholom Aleichem and Peretz. As a lad, I too was among those who recited these works.

Then came the bad days!

During the First World War, almost three quarters of the colony, as well as the town of Zastavye, were burned down and completely destroyed. The people were driven out and most who returned found no place to live. The retreating Russian Army had burned all our crops and barns and stolen livestock and our farm tools. But miracle of miracles, the Beth-Hamidrash was not destroyed and three families moved in there temporarily. They hoped to settle elsewhere, but a man named Yankel and another called Jacob Hertsky Chorny died there.

Following the retreat of the Russian armies, bands of robbers formed and our colony suffered greatly from their criminal assaults. Then came the Germans. When they withdrew, the Poles set up their own State and occupied our region. But then the Poles and the Bolsheviks fought, and when that was over the Poles carried off everything they could lay their hands on in our colony. Not only live stock – but even children's shoes. However, after a while, order was established, and it was at about that time that my intended wife, Sarah Ashkenazi, and I, began to think about our future. This was shortly after her father, Chaim Itche, may he rest in peace, had passed away.

It was difficult everywhere.

More than half of Zastavye was destroyed during the First World War but the Jewish streets and the two synagogues bore the brunt of the destruction. Some of the Jewish people moved into Christian homes on Christian streets where the residents had fled although their homes had not been damaged. This was in marked contrast to what had befallen Jewish homes, for only a very few Jewish houses had been spared. These were the homes of Shaye Nahum, Yosel Nehemvas and Velvel Prohotsky. Among their first consideration was to find a place where a "Minyan" of 10 Jews could meet for congregational prayers. Reb Yankel Eliezer, a pious Jew living in the large house of Shaye Nahum, at once put his living room at the disposal of the congregation. It was there, until the house was sold, that prayers were recited. Then Velvel Prohotsky invited the congregation to pray in his three-room house. Part of this dwelling provided him with the means for marking a living, the part which was the bakery, where on market days people made a stopover for a bite and a purchase. Despite this, Velvel Prohotsky offered his home for several years, and it was used for religious services until the Beth-Hamidrash was rebuilt. The little town of Zastavye had such worthy Jews!

The horrors of the war brought a measure of relief from America with the creation of the Joint Relief Committee (JRC).

It sent food and clothing to Brest, which was the distribution center for our area, and we chose Reb Zimel to be Zastavye's and the colony's representative. In this capacity, he would go to Brest from time to time to settle matters pertaining to relief work and food distribution for the colony and Zastavye. Once while walking in the streets of Brest a Polish soldier from General Haller's army assaulted him and tore out a large part of his beard. I still can remember the painful impression and the grief this created in our colony and in Zastavye. Reb Zimel sat in mourning for his beard for seven days, and I may say that his grief and anguish were so great that he became ill and never completely recovered.

It was in and around these days that the Jews of Zastavye began to suspect that there was something unfair in the way the food relief from the JRC was being distributed. The amount that was being given to the individual families was constantly getting less.

One Saturday, after prayers were over, an assembly was held and it was decided to appoint a new committee. The proponents of this movement were simple, honest, upright workers – men like Itche "Klotz" (a nickname I do not employ in a derogatory manner but simply to identify him properly); Eli Yakir, son of Moshe; Gabriel, son of Yakir Moshe, Pesach Kaletsky, and several others. The people assembled at that meeting decided to elect young and energetic workers to the new committee. Shouts went up: "We want Velvel Toybe's!" (This was my name, – the Toybe part having been added when I became the husband of Sarah Ashkenazi, her mother's name being Toybe.) Two others were chosen, dear friends of mine who later were murdered by the accursed Germans. On was Moshe Savshitsky, an upright, intelligent young man; the second one was Mendel Caplan, the son of Heske, a miller and a neighbour of ours, a fine young man.

The new committee was formed but, the old committee refused to disband. However, the whole community went to the Kamenetzer Rabbi, who decided in favour of the new committee because it had been democratically chosen. This, I may say, is an example of the peaceful manner in which a simple people who had suffered and had been wronged, adjusted to its Grievances.

But life, as the Bible had taught us, is not by bread along.

Despite these hardships, the Jewish community in Zastavye remembered that their children also needed spiritual nourishment. Joint efforts in this direction produced some results. The children studied under very difficult conditions but those who wanted to broaden their education could not do so. There was no library in Zastavye.

It was at about this time that I saw the haplessness of the Jewish situation in Europe, and I decided to leave for America. Soon after my arrival in New York I received a letter from my wife's sister, Bracha, may she rest in peace written in an excellent Hebrew and requesting that we raise the money for the creation of a Jewish Library in Zastavye. My own circumstances then were indeed meagre. I took the matter up with several fellow townsmen and among us we dispatched to Zastavye for the purpose requested.[3]

There is much more that can be said and written, but in the briefest of summaries – this was the life as we lived it in the colony of Sarova and the town of Zastavye. The world knows that the German murderers exterminated one-third of our people, but we, from Sarovo and Zastavye, know and can remember the victims in our communities.

Josef Soroko

A colonist

Translator's Footnotes:

     1.   Yiddish version adds: My father's three brothers also remained in the colony. They purchased additional land and inventory. When their families got bigger, my uncles went to America—one of them once and another twice. There they worked very hard for several years. When they returned they didn't go to the town; instead they applied themselves to work the land even more energetically.

     2.   Yiddish version adds: Every day several of the men studied Mishna [the core text of the Talmud]. Reb Yudel Kravietzky and Reb Zimel Simchovitch used to teach these study groups.

     3.   Yiddish version adds: I consulted with several fellow townsmen, and we decided to purchase a performance. We sold tickets and made a profit of over sixty dollars, which we sent to start a Jewish library.

[English page 69]

The Day of Atonement in our Town

By H. Mendelsohn (New York)

Already in the morning hours of the eve of Yom Kippur (The Day of Atonement), certain disquiet could be felt among the Jews of our townlet. Everybody hurried to pray in public. The coming of the holiday was noticeable. The everyday hustle and bustle stopped suddenly, the usual gayety disappeared from everyone's face; everybody was seized by a feeling of gloom when the last preparations for receiving the Great Holy Day of Atonement (Yom Kippur) were finished. People became friendlier to one another; the enemies of yesterday reconciled; shop-keepers, bitter competitors, smiled at one another, wishing to forget the harm done by one to another, for the sake of a piece of bread, during the entire year.

Everybody walked hurriedly to the afternoon prayer (Minha), lest they might – God forbid – come late. The synagogues were packed. Right next to the entrance there stood long tables with plates belonging to various charitable institutions like "Meot Hitim for Orphans (Financial Aid given before the Passover Holiday), Interest Free Funds for the Poor" (Gmilat Hesed) etc.; it's impossible to remember all such institutions since there was no lack of needy persons in the town. Everybody dropped a coin some a large one and others a small one – but all made a contribution, requesting forgiveness for their sins, and was there anyone who had not sinned?

The prayers were ardent and everyone felt the earnestness of the coming hour. Immediately after the afternoon prayer people rushed home to eat the last meal before the Great Fast. My father, dressed in a white garment, blessed the children while my mother was lighting the candles.

This unforgettable picture is still in my memory. The room is shrouded in partial darkness. My God-fearing mother, slight in stature and with a delicate face, never failed to thank and praise the Almighty and to say the benedictions, as he stooped above the tallow candles and cried.

"Why is mother crying?", I asked my older brother. "She is thanking the Almighty for the kindness He has shown her till now, and she is asking Him for health and means of livelihood for father in America and for all of us," replied my brother.[1]

I knew, in fact, that father found it difficult to earn his living in America. Otherwise, we would not have to buy on credit and mother would not have to pluck feathers in the late winter-evenings, and to knit woollen table-cloths she did it with real artistic talent – as well as to work in gardens in the heat of the summer, in order to earn something. Therefore, her prayer asking for means of living for my father in America, was understandable to me; even then I could not grasp the meaning of her expressions of gratitude for the favours God had shown her, but my God-fearing mother thought differently.

Then we all went to the synagogue to "Kol Nidrei".

The Kamenetz Synagogue was a tall, circular building whose outward appearance reminded more of an ancient temple than of a modern synagogue. Inside it looked even larger and more beautiful. The blue-painted ceiling was so high that it could hardly be seen with a naked eye. Indeed, the ceiling represented the sky with sparkling stars exquisitely painted. But most striking was the hand-made woodcarving stretching along the entire height of the wall on both side of the Holy Ark. On one side were carved various wild animals living in the forest; their teeth were protruding and the beasts looked as if they were alive and always ready to defend the persecuted Jewish people against its attackers. On the other side various fruit trees were carved. They symbolized the time when the Jewish people would be in its own land and enjoy its own fruits. All this had been done by an artist endowed with great talent; it was told that he had succeeded to create only two such works and one of them was in our synagogue.

On the Yom Kippur night the synagogue was crowded and brightly illuminated by hanging lamps; a forest of burning wax candles cast dark shades; along the eastern wall the older men of our town, clad in white garments, were swaying slowly like old trees in a woods and murmuring prayers; complete silence reigned while everybody held his breath and waited for the cantor to been chanting the "Kol Nidrei".

The notables of the town also came to hear the cantor and they were standing on the pulpit with an expression of awe and reverence on their faces. As soon as the sounds of the "Kol Nidrei", chanted by the town cantor H. Yaffe and the choir, were heard, everyone was filled with awe and felt the approach of the hour of reckoning. Though many years have elapsed since those times, I still cannot forget the tremendous impression made on me by the sweet, soul stirring chant. The town-cantor H. Yaffe, rather short and with long white hair, was a man endowed with many talents. Besides being a cantor he also painted sign-boards for shop-keepers and was learned in the Law; though neither he, nor the local young people who sang in the choir had ever attended a conservatory, they all knew how to read musical notes and had to sing harmoniously. Whenever one of the young singers committed the slightest mistake, a glance of the cantor was sufficient to correct it at once. The cantor Yaffe possessed not only a powerful, wailing voice; he was an excellent interpreter of Jewish prayers. Even those who did not understand their text, could easily grasp their meaning. Who is able to forget his Rainfall Prayer and his other compositions – real pearls causing delight to everyone who heard them.

And in such a manner we were standing on the Yom Kippur evening and deriving pleasure from the soul-stirring prayers.

During the entire Day of Atonement hardly anyone was seen in the streets. Complete silence reigned over the whole townlet: only the chanting of prayers in the synagogues could be heard. The "Neilah" Prayer which concluded the services on the Day of Atonement was recited by the cantor with much heartfelt emotion. Every word expressed sorrow and supplication. Was it not the last hour in which the fate of everyone would be sealed? Who could know what one's own fate would be? But as soon as the cantor lifted his hands up to Heavens and cried our in his powerful voice: "Open the gate, for the day is almost gone!", all of us believed that the gates had really been opened, that our prayers had been accepted; with a light heart we uttered the phrase "Next Year in Jerusalem", and so the Yom Kippur service in our town came to an end.

When I reflect upon those bygone times and think about those Jews who are not with us anymore, I begin to realize how many talented people perished in our own town and how great their achievements would have been if they had lived in other places and in different circumstances.

There are no Jews and no synagogues left in Kamenetz. All that remained are the memories. Who can forget them?

Translator's Footnote:

1.   This paragraph and the one following it are not present in the Yiddish version of this article (pp. 412-415).

[English page 73]

The Years of my Youth in Kamenetz-Litovsk

By Hatzkel Kagan

Many images are engraved in my memory, and first among these are the religious teachers ("melamdim") of my youth who planted in my heart the desire to learn.

I remember Joseph Vigotov. A fine person, a scholar and active in communal work, he was a teacher at the "Talmud Torah" School, which was located in a side lane in the Christian quarter, where the court was later situated. His beautiful commentaries on the Book of Psalms still resound in my ears. It sounded poetic when he recited melodiously the chapter "Ashrei Haish" and when he exclaimed "Lama Ragshu Hagoyim"; all of us in the room felt as if it were a call to the whole Jewish people. We all loved learning together with him.

I remember also Ben-Zion, a more "modern" Rabbi, a teacher and a pedagogue. He taught us the Bible, the Talmud, the Grammar, arithmetic and writing. It is interesting to note that when we learned the Book of Esther his comments bore the character of a modern explanation. We could see vividly the events of the past. Every Saturday, instead of having an ordinary lesson with us, he would read us stories from the "Hagada". Their beauty captivated us, and this was largely due to the exciting manner in which they were read aloud by our teacher. As to the words of rebuke he directed at us, they sounded more or less like this: "Listen fellows. Now, at the time you are young, it is time for you to learn. You will have enough time in the future to stroll on the bridges and to wander in the streets. However, if you study, you will be respected by your fellowmen, no matter where you find yourselves".

Another memory is linked with my father who used to pay frequent visits to Rabbi Burstein. My father was active in the community's affairs and people from all walks of life praised his honesty and Willingness to help others. Once, on a Saturday, my father took me with him to be examined by the Rabbi, as was customary in those days. Noticing my nervousness, the Rabbi calmed me. I passed my "exam" well and smoothly, to the satisfaction of both the Rabbi and my father.

Every day the Rabbi honored the Main Street by walking along it on his way to the "Shepsel" Synagogue where he used to pray. He preached twice a year in the large brick synagogue – on the Saturday which falls between the Jewish New Year and the Day of Atonement and on the Saturday which precedes the Passover.

The Rabbi officiated at wedding ceremonies which usually took place outdoors near a synagogue and were attended by the majority of the town's inhabitants.

The Rabbi was respected in the town by all kinds of people for his wise advice given on various problems. He used to travel to North America to sell the books he wrote.

The members of his family were educated too. Rabbi Burstein's house was very near to the house of Motie "Klepechiner".

I should like to mention the name of Shlomke Mandelblatt, the permanent secretary of the municipality. He warmly responded to all those who applied to him for help and advice. He always had an encouraging word for them as he filled in questionnaires for those who were getting ready to emigrate or had received a call to military service. Another example of extending help to his fellow-men was given by "Little" Mendele Levin. Mendele, the Hassid, went around with a basket on Saturday afternoon to collect "halot" for the needy. I remember the joy of the housewives who carried the "halot" for him; they blessed him for he had enabled them to fulfil a religious precept (mitzvah).

My memory takes me to a winter day in 1927. On a frosty Sunday morning, we, a group of young boys, were walking in a street inhabited by Christians. Suddenly we heard a voice of crying children. It came from a Christian house with a thatched roof and tiny windows covered by snow. We entered the house and saw a number of huddled childish figures dressed in rags, and crying because of hunger and cold. It turned out that a weaver's family with many children lived in that little house. Shmerl Solnitze, Shaye, the Melamed's son, who was together with us, was the first to react. He exclaimed that in such terrible conditions the children would die of hunger and cold and he called us to act immediately. We entered the neighboring houses and recounted what we had seen. Soon, firewood, food and money were collected and each one contributed whatever he could.

A philanthropic organization carrying the Hebrew name "Linat Tzedek" (Hospice for the Poor) was active in the town. Its purpose was to aid the families of the sick. The "equipment" it possessed was very modest indeed. It included several thermometers to us in compresses, a clyster and a rubber container for holding ice. The ice was for use in compresses applied to the head. When the typhus epidemic was raging in Kamenetz a young man and a young girl from the "Linat Tzedek" organization used to visit the sick every night. They attended to the patients, gave them juice to drink, applied cold compresses to their heads and helped in other ways, thus bringing relief to numerous families.

The Great Yeshivah, with dozens of students from various towns and cities, played a great part in the life of our town. Many families drew their livelihood from the institution. The Yeshivah bordered on the Beit Hamidrash where the students learned avidly and ardently arguing vigorously about the Law. In the time between the afternoon and evening prayers the Yeshivah students would break into a song, whose moving, sad melody plunged the outside onlookers into gloom. But during the joyful celebrations of the Feast of Water Drawing (Simhat Beit Hashoevah) and Rejoicing of the Law (Simhat Torah) the students sang and danced joyfully.

On the Sunday preceding the Day of Atonement, with an orchestra playing, Kamenetz welcomed the arriving Head of the Yeshivah, Rabbi Barukh Baer. Young and old, men, women and children streamed to the highway. After a long wait they finally saw the arriving Head of the Yeshiveh and his assistants. The people of Kamenetz cheered the arriving guests who were welcomed with great honor by prominent town representatives.

An apartment had already been prepared for the Yeshivah Head and his assistants. It was located in the Main Street, in the house formerly occupied by a pharmacy.

The Yeshivah became an integral part of the town. It exercised great influence on its spiritual life, particularly in the earlier period when there were no secular Hebrew or Yiddish schools.

While dealing with the educational and cultural aspects of our life in Kamenetz I ought to mention the four Sapirstein brothers: Asher, Shlomke, Velvel and Hershel. They were well known in town as teachers, each one of them in a different field. I attended the class led by Asher Sapirstein. The lessons took place at his home in a side lane near the Kobrynska Street. Even today I still remember his lovely Biblical chants.

Shlomke taught a group of children including Yosel, the son of Ephraim Kotebe, Golde and Feigl, Rivele's sisters.

Shmelke taught my class geography, natural sciences and arithmetic. Velvel and Hershel worked as teachers in other towns.

Asher used to stage well-known theatrical plays like"The Sale of Joseph","Shulamit" and others. His three brothers Velvel, Hershel and Shlomke, as well as Shlomke's wife, Zelda, were the chief actors. Also Isaac Wolender and Sara Rudnitsky also played their parts exceedingly well.

Asher staged the well-known Goldfaden operetta"Di Kishefmacherin" ("The Sorceress"). The actors were a group of young workers – boys and girls – Sender (David Pasheker's son) played the role of "Babe Yakhne", the witch; a tailor's apprentice who played the role of the little"Duckling" sang very nicely. Bashka, Maya Golde's daughter, a pretty young girl who appeared in the main role as "Babkelech" acted and sang beautifully. The operetta was successfully performed several times. The public warmly applauded the actors.

The theatrical activity was a great contribution to the town's cultural life.

There were in the town three important cultural institutions. Those were the Shalom-Aleichem Library, the Children's Library and the Y. L. Peretz Library. The last one had a rich choice of books in Yiddish. The youth read avidly the books of our great classics: Mendele (Mokher Sfarim), Peretz, Shalom-Aleichem, Shalom Asch, Abraham Reisin and others. The literary critics Baal-Maha-shavot, Niger and Trunk were also widely read. But the world literature and its classics in Yiddish translations were not neglected either. During walks taken in the summer evenings we used to discuss and express our opinions on the books we had read.

In its premises in a little street in Odalina, the Y. L. Peretz Library arranged well frequented"box-evenings". Everyone who wanted to ask a question could do it by writing its contents on a piece of paper and dropping it into a box which stood on the table around which the organizers read out the question and asked whether anyone from the public could reply to it. Many of those present replied according to their knowledge and lively debates ensued. Our knowledge was enriched thanks to this collective learning. Literary evenings, where excerpts from books were read and anlyzed, also took place. The critical judgments were usually on a high level. Thus the Library was for us the key to knowledge which could be attained by everyone.

The Zionist Organizations. The Z. O. had its"headquarters" in Relken's house. It propagated the Zionist idea and its activity was most intensive among the youth of the town. The organization sold "shekels" which were the annual membership fee to the Z. O., collected money for the Jewish National Fund and the Jewish Foundation Fund. Speakers from the Central Organization would come frequently to stimulate the collections.

The Zionist organization was active in the cultural field, too, and organized on Saturday literary evenings with the participation of guest artists. I recall an interesting evening devoted to a trial of Shakespeare's"Shylock". The hall was crowded and the air stuffy, but complete quiet reigned when Lipa Horovitz, one of the local Zionist leaders and a talented speaker, was reading the contents of the play. The assembly followed with interest the proceedings of the trial and listened intently to the prosecutor's and defendant's speeches.

The right wing of the"Poalei Zion" Party was also active in Kamenetz. It was located in a house next to Beit-Hamidrash. The youth organization"Freiheit" ("Freedom") which was affiliated to it. had a self-education circle. Speakers from Brest used to visit us often. The comrades Rogzhansky and Sheinman organized propaganda meetings, whose theme was a Jewish homeland constructed on socialist principles. In 1927 a conference of Youth organizations took place in Brest in the hall of the artisans' union. I was one of the delegates. I received instructions from Israel Freier and Haya Krakowsky. The principal speaker at the conference was Shpizman from the Head Organization in Warsaw.

The youth in our townlet was searching for a purpose and a practical aim in life, but even learning a trade was a problem. There were excellent tradesmen and craftsmen in Kamenetz: shoemakers, tailors, furriers, carpenters, smiths, tanners, a cartwright, a potter, and three barbers. One or two of each trade possessed his own house.

Nevertheless, the earnings of the skilled workers were not sufficient to make ends meet. People worked long hours six days a week. Finally, trade unionism began to gain a foothold in the townlet. An organizer from the tailor's trade union arrived from Brest and a strike was declared in tailoring establishments. Tailors and sempstresses gained an 8 hour working day and better employment conditions. A strike broke out in shoemakers establishments too, but the employers put up strong resistance and did not give up. This time the strikers gained only shorter working hours.

A leftist underground organization was formed in the town to fight against lawlessness in the province of Polesie, to which Kamenetz belonged. Indeed, the Poles regarded Polesie as their colony and the Polish police maltreated the peasants. No wonder that the propaganda spread by the organization struck deep roots among the impoverished local peasantry.

Before May 1st, secret meetings were held to stress the importance of the Workers' Day. Every gathering assembled in a different place – in "Mogilki" in the nearby woods, in the "valley" past the Kobrynska Street or in homes of workers who lived in side lanes. Young boys were standing guard to warn the assembled of any possible danger.

On May 1st, 1928 a public demonstration took place. The demonstrators – mostly young peasants – arrived in their Sunday clothes. The men wore red ribbons, the women donned bright dresses and red kerchiefs. They gathered in the market square opposite the Russian Monastery. When one of them began making a speech, the police intervened, dispersing the gathering and arresting several demonstrators. The assembled peasants dispersed, throwing stones at the police. The townspeople refrained from taking part in the clash.

On a winter's night, plain-clothed and uniformed policemen, who had come from Brest, carried out a search in a dozen houses and dragged out of their beds youths suspected of revolutionary activity. These were the first arrests that occurred in town. The parents and other relatives cried helplessly while the young men were being taken to the Brest Prison.

For a long time afterwards the town remained gripped by fear and uneasiness. But the young people displayed political maturity, discussed social problems and hoped that in the future life would be more beautiful and just.

Our small town awakened to new life thanks to increased motor traffic, especially after buses had begun to run regularly on the Brest-Zhabinka-Kamenetz route. The bus station became an attraction for young and old. They used to wait for the arriving buses to meet the passengers, or receive greetings from Brest and Zhabinka and to take a look at the "new faces" of people from other towns who arrived in Kamenetz. People would also meet at the station to see the outgoing buses. Whoever wanted to have a bite could get it from Motke Kotek who sold foodstuffs of good quality. His kiosk was standing right next to the station in Brest Street opposite the row of stores.

This regular communication enabled the Kamenetz youth to visit Brest frequently, and enriched the cultural life in our town. Wandering theatrical groups often showed up in Kamenetz, particularly during the holidays of Passover, Shavuoth and Succoth, and performed many well known plays. The performances took place in Motye Klepecherer's barn or in a large building in Otzalina. The spectators enjoyed the shows which ended late at night.

On the whole the young people strove to leave for the wide world. Those who had an opportunity to emigrate to the United States were considered the most fortunate. Many left for Argentine, Cuba, Palestine, Australia and other countries. Our townsmen struck roots in and became citizens of many countries, and established families. Their children acquired higher education and became teachers, physicians, engineers, druggists, chemists, businessmen, skilled craftsmen, etc.

Though our life was restricted, it was nevertheless varied. After all, people learned in traditional religious schools ("heder"), continued in Talmud Torah, in the Yeshivah, had private teachers; they married, raised children, belonged to political parties and dreamed of a better future; they read books and newspapers. Several persons subscribed to one copy and it went from hand to hand.

I ought to devote a few lines to the shops. They provided the main source of livelihood for the Kamenetz Jews. Most of the stores were in two rows divided from one another by wooden partition walls.

On ordinary weekdays the shopkeepers used to wait for customers. On hot summer days the two rows of shops provided pleasant shade. In winter time, amidst frost and snow, one had to stamp one's feet to keep oneself warm. Women clutched little pots filled with charcoals to warm themselves. In winter, they wore hoods, long scarves and knee-high felt shoes.

The principal source of income was market-day. On every Thursday and on the fifth day of each month, peasants from the neighboring villages came to Kamenetz to do their shopping. There were also yearly fairs named after saints. Then shopkeepers hired boys and girls to keep an eye on the merchandise brought specially for market day. The young helpers received one and a half Zloty a day for their work. The merchandise usually came from Brest by wagons drawn by horse.

It must be said that the wagon-owners in Kamenetz, who were fathers of large families, were respectable people and made a decent living. Yeshivah students ate at their tables on fixed week days and on Sabbaths.

The coachmen of Kamenetz-Litovsk were considered as belonging to the merchant class. The wholesale merchants from Brest greatly respected them for their honesty and put faith in their word.

Those entering the town to sell their goods had to pay a special toll. The tax collectors were Jewish youths hired by the municipality. This led to dissatisfaction on the part of the peasants coming to town. They used to come from far and near in order to sell a horse, a caw, a calf, a lamb, a pig, chickens, ducks, geese, eggs, corn, fruits, hides, pig hair and wagon loads of timber. Horse merchants and cow merchants used to come too. When the intermediaries with their big sticks clapped their hands the deal was regarded as concluded.

Potters would display earthenware pots, bowls and dishes.

Shopkeepers displayed colored kerchiefs and nailed boots right at the entrance. Cheap ready-made clothes were, with a pull here and a squeeze there, made to fit the peasant who put them on. The cartwright prepared brand new cartwheels ready for sale. The smiths were very busy shoeing horses. The hardware merchants exhibited sickles, harrows, nails and other tools needed by the villagers. The bakers had been working hard to supply the stands with fresh breads, rolls, with garlands of large and small"beigeleich".

Beyle Hoch served soda-water from a copper container wrapped in ragged cloth and sold chocolate-colored ice-cream from a barrel. The look of halvah, various delicacies and even herring, tickled the palates of the onlookers. The villagers ate bread with herring which was kept in barrels. The pubs and taverns were full of men and women from the neighboring villages. They drank vodka and had a bite of fried fish. Curses of drunken peasants could be heard all the time. The crowds milled about, buying and selling or just looking around. An organ-grinder, with a parrot on the barrel-organ, was busy selling horoscopes. Peasant women paid a few groshes to learn about their fate. Ordinary swindlers and pickpockets, who had come from faraway to try their luck, had a field day. Cries and shouts of the victims who lost all their money were heard long afterwards.

The merchants and shopkeepers were busy trying to attract the attention of the peasants and persuade them to enter the shops. Then interminable, exhausting haggling ensued. Even those inhabitants of Kamenetz who did not engage in any buying or selling joined the crowds and watched the proceedings of the market day. With sundown the market ended and everyone left in all directions.

One of the simple pleasures we enjoyed was the stroll along the Main Street along Kobrynska Street which stretched to Napiski and to the bridges across the river. The river was the division between Kamenetz and the suburb Zastavye. The youngsters liked rowing on its waters. Sometimes they sang to the accompaniment of a musical instrument. In springtime the meadows on both sides of the river were covered with yellowish flowers and looked like golden carpets.

The stroll on Saturday night or on holiday was something of a tradition. Everyone put on his best clothes and went out into the Main Street, – married couples, lovers, groups of boys and girls. Some spoke softly, others expressed their opinions loudly trying to persuade the opponents with their arguments. The subjects of the talks were varied and included literature, politics, world and local events.

This went on for generations. I can still hear the youthful laughter in the streets of Kamenetz of Kamenetz that exists no longer...

[English page 85]

Kamenetz - The Memories of my Youth

By Itzhak Sheinfeld (Brooklyn, N. Y.)

Kamenetz – the little town where I was born after World War I, where I went to school and spent the years of my youth.

Our family lived in the Kobrynska Street, near the hospital. My father was a wood-merchant, who made trips to the adjoining townlets and country-side to buy plots of timber; the trees were cut and sold for use in building. When I was a little boy my father took me with him on some of his trips and I admired the village-Jews. My father used to mediate whenever differences arose between a Jewish villager and his White Russian, Christian neighbours.

Neighbours from the Kobrynska Street often gathered in our house to discuss local problems, to find ways and means of helping a needy person or of securing the water supply for the inhabitants of the street. That was quite a problem since the municipality refused to sink a new well and the management of the hospital did not allow us to use the well belonging to the hospital. The Jewish inhabitants of the Kobrynska Street had to supply the financial means and laborers to carry out the work, but the efforts were necessary and successful. I remember the Yeshivah students, walking in the streets and engaged in lively discussions on religious subjects.

During the winter-evenings we heard sounds of hammer-blows coming from the smithies of Pesah Gorinsky and Gedaha Rubinstein; at the same time the vanes of the wind-mills belonging to two old Jews, Rav Yeshayahu Ashkenazi and Rav Israel Timiansky were turning with a groan.

In the inclement wintry evenings the old religious teacher, Alter Velvel trudged in deep snowdrifts to teach the children the fundamentals of Jewish religion, the prayers and recitations like"Mode Ani" and"Kriat Shema".

There were many devoted Jews in Kamenetz. Asher Sapirstein, a private teacher, taught smaller groups and opened a"heder" which drew many pupils. The religious chants, the melodies of chanted prayers and biblical intonations can never be forgotten. Asher Sapirstein, a traditional religious teacher of the new type hired another teacher who gave lessons in the Polish language to anyone interested in it.

In 1928, the government decreed that all children between the ages of 6 and 14 must learn the Polish language. The Talmud-Torah employed a teacher from the Polish State elementary school to teach Polish as a regular subject. I should like to add that Jewish girls had learned in the Polish State elementary school before the Jewish boys.

Later on five Jewish boys registered to enter the Polish school. They were: Herzl Sapirstein, Mendel Szczytnicki; (Bezalel's son), Itzhak Sheinfeld, Shimon Wolfson and Israel Maretzky. We did it ignoring the fact that the majority of Kamenetz Jews frowned upon us. But we still learned Yiddish and Hebrew in the "heder" of Asher Sapirstein; later on our Hebrew teacher was Velvel Haim Kirshenbaum, an ardent Zionist.

The Jewish youngsters did not feel at ease ámong the Christian pupils. Therefore we were encouraged when two years later more Jewish boys enrolled in the Polish school. The majority of them finished their studies at the age of fourteen. Many went to other towns to enter religious learning institutes (Yeshivot).

The Zionist movement"Gordonia", under the leadership of Pinhas Rudnitsky, occupied the most important place among all youth organizations in Kamenetz, and was the most active one. When the Revisionist party – the "Beitar" – was founded in the town, Lipa Hurwitz and Binyamin Bogatin became its local leaders.

Members of the"Beitar" joined the Volunteer Fire Brigade; the municipal council and the mayor Piotrowski appreciated the abilities shown by the young fellows. When the town-orchestra was reorganized and named"The Firemen Orchestra" it included members of the"Beitar".

Kamenetz was the focal point for the surrounding townlets. Members of the "Gordonia" and"Beitar" from Wysokie Litewskie, Czemopczyce, Zhabinka, Szereszew and other localities, took part in the Lag Baomer celebrations. The Zionist Organization invited the local, higher officials to participate in the festivities. In addition to the town-mayor, the police-chief, the judge and the officials of the local council, all Jewish house-owners were invited.

In the thirties, with the approach of the elections to the World Zionist Congress, a festive atmosphere reigned in Kamenetz. The elections evoked great interest and almost every Jewish household bought a"shekel" in order to acquire the voting-right.

Pre-election propaganda campaigns were conducted by the various organizations. Public meetings were held in the synagogues, in the building of the old, Polish elementary school and in the theatre-hall. In addition to local speakers well-known public figures from others towns also came to Kamenetz to speak.

Despite differences of opinions on political matters friendly relations existed among the political organizations and party-leaders. Pinhas Rudnitsky, for example, who led the local"Gordonia", was a close friend of the "Beitar" leader Binyamin Bogatin.

In the years 1936-37 the activity of the Zionist Organization in Kamenetz weakened and almost ceased. There was, however, a group of young people who collected money for the Keren Kayemet (Jewish National Fund); the treasurer of the Fund in Kamenetz, Yosef

Grinblatt used to send the contributions to the Head Office in Warsaw. The group consisted of: Itzhak Sheinfeld, Yosef Feldman, Noah Goldberg, Reuven Szczytnicki and Yacov Weizhandler.

Our companion, Israel Goldshall, a native of Pinsk, was at that time teaching in the Pinsk Talmud-Torah Secondary School. In 1939 he became a teacher in Kamenetz and taught the children Hebrew.

Following discussions with him, on the subject of reviving the Zionist movement in Kamenetz, it was decided to establish a branch of the "Hashomer Hatzair". Yosef Feldman was named as the leader and Itzhak Sheinfeld as the secretary whose duties would include also correspondence with the Central Office in Warsaw. Noah Goldberg became the second-in-command and Reuven Szczytnicki the treasurer.

[Page 91]

The Holocaust

The Tragedy and Destruction of Kamenetz

by Dora Galperin

(The Letter of Dora to Lea and Dov Aloni)

At the Beginning of the Second World War

Soon after the outbreak of the Second World War, at the end of 1939, the Soviets occupied Kamenetz-Litvosk. The situation of the Jewish population changed for the worse. The local Communists, like Leybke Katz, Leyzer Dolinsky, Joseph Wolfson, Joseph Kupchik, the two Jacobson brothers from Zastavye, Malca Radisch and other such "prominent party-members" hastily assumed posts of authority under the new rulers. They were familiar with everyone and they knew well how and whom to oppress and persecute.

Three quarters of Kamenetz Jews had lived from commerce until then. They eked out their livelihood from their stores and stands. The stores were soon liquidated, commercial activity was severely punished and most houses were nationalized. The situation was very grave, almost hopeless. The synagogues were closed down. The Great Yeshiva was converted into a club which a cinema hall. Everybody was obliged to work on Saturday which also affected people badly. However, things were not so bad yet. Whoever knew some Russian obtained employment.

In 1940, the Russians simply threw us out of our house into the street. My sister Reyzel lived at Shidlovsky's home and I moved into the house of a Christian, Fyodor Fanasevich.

When the Germans arrived in our town he told me straight away that he would not hang out a Star of David on his house because of me. I understood from that, that I must look for another place to live.

With the German Murderers

On June 22, 1941, the wild German murderers marched in to our little town soon afterwards the SS arrived in Kamenetz and caught Jews in the streets.

I myself saw through the window how they caught David Rosenberg's son-in-law, who was going from the direction of Zastavye. The murderers beat him up cruelly, pushed him forward and kicked him with their boots. This affected me so badly that I was unable to calm myself. We learned afterwards that the murderers had caught a large number of Jews in the town and beat them up heavily. Then everyone was seized by strong fear.

I was afraid that Fedosevich might deliver me to the Germans, so I moved out of his house and lived together with Reyzel Gevirtzman and her family.

Once, 2 gendarmes came and took away from us whatever they fancied, even furniture, quilts, curtains and other things. Then they put on Reyzel's head and old black hat they had found in the cupboard; they also put a big pot on my head and forced us to dance and sing and on top of all this swung their whips and lashed us. That was a terrible experience. Insult was added to injury.

Before the war a woman physician lived in Kamenetz. Everyone knew she was a Christian. She used to go to church and always wore a cross on her breast. After the arrival of the Germans she worked for a long period at the Municipality office and also exercised medical practice. Her name was Halina Weidenberg. All of a sudden she disappeared. We found out that the Germans had taken everything away from her and killed her, because a postman, a Christian, had told them that she had been receiving letters and postcards written in Yiddish.

Miriam Pachter-Wapniarsky used to live next to Gevirtzman. The Germans occupied her house. She had previously concealed something in the garden. Once, when she came there and tried to dig it out, a gendarme ran after her. She began to run away and entered our house. The gendarme began beating her savagely, while we had to hold her by the hands and head. She was so faint that she had no strength to cry. This made us feel very broken-hearted. It was very difficult to bear all this.

When the Ghetto was set up in 1942, we thought that perhaps there would be a change for the better. In the Ghetto there lived 10 persons in a room. Everyday the murderers raised new demands through the "Judenrat" (the Ghetto Council appointed by the Germans) but at first they themselves did not enter the Ghetto.

Once, while on my way to buy some food for my sister's children, a gendarme seized me and beat me heavily.

I fell to the around. Then he kicked me in my belly with his boots several times and roared at me to get up, but I did not have sufficient strength to do it. My face remained swollen for two weeks. This happened near the house of Yosel Glezer, outside the Ghetto. The savage Nazi's name was Werbel. I can remember this scene even today. When I returned home, my sisters cried bitterly, but unfortunately they were unable to help me. Of course, I dared not go out of the Ghetto anymore. Our Reyzel's sister-in-law, a young and very pretty girl was staying with her. She dreaded the Nazi murderers so much that she lost her senses. One early morning she left the house and never returned. The Germans caught and shot her. In such a manner the situation got worse from day to day.

On January 1, 1942, the Ghetto area comprising Brzeska Street was encircled by guards. We were all transferred to another Ghetto area comprising the street Kobrynska and Litewska. The first victims fell in the early morning hours.

Simha Dubiner's mother was running in the fields adjoining Litevska street. A German halted her. She implored him to let her go back. Crying she said she only wanted to bring some food for her son who was working nearby; but the murderer was not moved by her tears and shot her. She fall near Kozlovski's barn. She was still alive and tried to get up again. She muttered her last words: "Woe to me", then the assassin shot at her once more and killed her.

Motke, one of the Kozlovski brothers, carried her body to the Jewish cemetery and buried her.

Several minutes later, more people were shot on the same spot. They were: Issachar Velvel Freizer [written "Freier" in Hebrew and Yiddish versions] from Kobrynska street, his daughter Beyla, Zina Porolska's [written "Zuna Pochalski's" in Hebrew and Yiddish versions] son-in-law, and a man from Warsaw, Dr. Gelberg's guest. Dr. Gelberg himself, his daughter Yanechka and her husband Ludwig escaped from the Ghetto and avoided being caught. Some time later, a Christian betrayed them and they were shot together in Demitrowiche Village, in the vicinity of Kamenetz. The doctor's wife, who remained in the Ghetto, lost her reason.

Quite a large number of Jews escaped from the Ghetto, but they had no place to hide; later on they requested from the members of the "Judenrat" to bring them back into the Ghetto.

Suffering, Courage and Escape from the Hands of Murderers

For three days I stayed in the heavily guarded Ghetto. On the third day at noon, a Christian, Joseph Golyak, with whom we were acquainted, approached the barbed wire fence and told me to escape. He said there were no German around – only local militiamen who would let me pass. I replied that it was impossible as there was an obstacle in the shape of a wooden fence above the ground. How could I possibly get out? He left but returned after a few minutes with another Christian friend. They brought an axe, smashed the wooden boards and simply pulled me out of the Ghetto.

Mrs. Kozlovsky who had been waiting nearby put a bed-cover on me and led me up to the attic in her house. Where I was lying quietly till seven o'clock. Later on they made me change my clothes and put on a long bright dress and a handkerchief. In such attire I was taken to Litevska street to an acquaintance, a Christian by the name of Joseph (Yuzhek) Grigorevsky.

I remained only one day in his house, because his wife's family, who were staying with him, were very frightened; they took the children and fled. This made me think that perhaps my escape was useless. I wanted to go back to the Ghetto. In the evening, another Christian, Nicolay Zhuk, arrived. He took me to a tiny settlement where there were only two houses – his and his brother's. It's difficult to describe what I felt during the journey. Miraculously, we arrived safely in the hamlet. The first few days were not bad, but in the course of time the situation grew worse and worse. They used to lock me up in the barn for the whole day.

Nobody would come to me and ask if I needed or wanted anything. Late in the evening I entered the house for a short while and soon went back to the barn. And yet such conditions could be considered as good.

One day, Nicolay went to Kamenetz and, upon his return told me that there was nobody left in the Ghetto. Everybody had been deported to Wysokie. This news depressed me greatly. I realised that the bitter end of the Ghetto had come. Sadness and despondency overcame me.

I cried and cried but unfortunately the flowing tears were of no help. The Christians began to fear more and more to keep me. I would not even leave the barn. It was dark and very cold inside and I felt indescribably disheartened. Under these circumstances I spent almost six weeks. Once, early in the morning, when I accidentally entered the house for a minute, some German arrived in a car. I do not know how I managed to rush out of the room and to climb up to the garret. The murderers stayed in the house all day long. I remained motionless in the attic in my dress only, though it was a very cold winter-day.

All the time I was thinking that the end of my life was near. I saw in my imagination how the savage German murderers seize, torture and torment me and I thought how much suffering they would inflict upon me before shooting me. This went on for a couple of hours, till I was unable even to think clearly. In the evening, after the Germans had left, Zhuk came up to take me down from the attic. He had to carry me on his hands for I was so frightened and frozen that I could not walk by myself. Nicolay's family looked scared when they saw me.

Several days later, Zhuk took me at night in a sledge back into Kamenetz. I was swathed in rags, my head bandaged. He intended to say he was taking a sick woman to hospital. We met no German on our way and arrived safely. Christian friends, who wanted to save me, requested that a Kamenetz policeman, who had had seen me leave the Ghetto, hide me at his house. He lived on Litevska Street together with his mother. After the policeman and his mother had agreed, I was taken to them at night. There I was better off. I remained there for 6-7 months, though they did not want to keep me so long; they simply had to; no other hiding place could be found. During the entire day, I used to lie on the stove which was partly screened by a curtain. No one knew that a living human being was hidden there, a being having no right to live. Friends used to visit my landlady. Sometimes they would sit for hours on end and chat; I could hear everything. Some of them even claimed to have seen me with their own eyes on a horse-drawn wagon together with my sisters, during the deportation of the Jews. Others said they had not seen me. Some had seen me crying together with the other deported.

None of them knew I was alive. In such a manner I used to lie for hours on the stove, completely motionless. I dared not move for fear lest someone might hear. Sometimes it was unbearably hot on the stove. But the worst was when a visitor arrived early in the morning, when I was still lying in bed. Then the landlady would cover me with an eiderdown, make the bed hastily, and though I was suffocating I refrained from coughing, waiting impatiently for the guests' departure.

This was not all. On one occasion, late at night, when we were already asleep, someone began knocking on the window and asked to open the door, for a gendarme had been inquiring about the landlady's address.

"God in Heavens! What am I going to do with myself?"

I thought feverishly. The woman wanted me to remain in bed and to cover me, like she usually did, but I leapt out quickly and hid myself on the top of the stove. To escape somewhere else was out of the question.

When she opened the door, a friend of hers, Mania Lacinska and a gendarme entered. The gendarme's name was Goetzke. The couple simply wanted to "have a good time"... Goetzke turned off the electric light and directed the light of his electric torch into every corner in the room, asking at the same time: "Are there any partisans here?" A few minutes later he was lying on the same bed in which I had been sleeping earlier.

There was another bed next to the stove. After Mania had gone, he lay down close to the stove. I was afraid I would not overcome the terror that struck me. But a miracle happened. The German was a bit drunk and he fell asleep immediately. When I heard him snore I felt somewhat relieved. This lasted till he got up in the morning and left the house. The landlady and I got high fever, and we were very sick as a result of the fright. I was unable to speak for several days. The woman did not want to keep me in her house any longer, though she could not easily throw me out. I told her I cared no more about my life, but that she might also lose her head, if it became known that she had been hiding a Jewess.

Thereupon, Mrs. Kozlovsky took me to her home. This surprised me for there was no place to hide in her house. Later on, it became known to me that the policeman, the son of the woman at whose house I had been hiding, confided to Mrs. Kozlovsky that he would kill me in my sleep and throw me into the river.

I could not stay at Mrs. Kozlovsky's house. The same night I was taken to a Christian who lived on Litevska Street.

One could say that the conditions there were relatively good. I was well aware of my plight. Till now, I do not understand how I survived. Food and comforts were of no importance under those circumstances, but whenever I heard the murderous Nazis marching in the street I began to shiver from terror and fear.

Several months passed by in this manner and it seemed there would be no end to the troubles. I had no alternative. I had to live in a cupboard full of various things. There I felt best. The cupboard was locked all the time.

I thought that no one would ever find me there. But even this good fortune came to an end pretty soon.

A priest's daughter, who was living in close neighbourhood, began to get interested in the family in whose house I was hiding. On one occasion she entered the house and went directly to the cupboard intending to open it, as one of the landlady's dresses aroused her admiration. Fortunately, the cupboard was locked. Since then I did not stay in the cupboard anymore but tried my luck in a cellar which was cold, dark and damp. But I never caught a cold and, fortunately, never had a cough, though I was ill many times. I recuperated without a doctor and without medicines. I washed myself seldom and this made me feel even worse. From time to time, I used to crawl out of the cellar, late at night, and warm myself up for a short while in the room.

Once, late in the evening while we were talking quietly in the room, the window-shutter went up suddenly. The proprietor of the house ran outside but found nobody.

We thought that the wind had opened the shutter. A couple of days later, the shutter went up again. The landlord, who had darted outside, found the priest's daughter next to the window. She told him she had heard my voice, though I had never spoken to her. I hid in the cellar at once. The landlord led the priest's daughter into the house asking her where I was and how could she make up such things. Her reply was that she had pity on him, as her neighbour; otherwise she would have called the gendarmes and they would surely find me. Thereupon they both left. I too left the place in a hurry.

Mrs. Kozlovsky took me to a good friend of hers, an elderly Christian, who lived in a side-street, not far from the Litevska Street. This was the only hide-out we could think of at the time. I was fairly well off there, but it did not last long. A German family had moved into one of the rooms and I had to run away once more. It is difficult to describe all I went through. I do not know till now what made me willing to accept so much suffering. I could have hanged myself or put an end to my life in another way, but the thought never entered my mind. Apparently, it was my fate to survive, so as to be able to tell a little about our pitiable life under the murderous Nazis.

In the meantime, I had no other way out but to return to the cold and damp cellar. I remained there till the frontline came nearer to us; it drew closer from day to day. Then a spark of hope made its appearance. One night I caught the sight of a burning airplane. The sky seemed to be on fire. The scene was frightening and the people began running away to find refuge out in the fields. I did not run away, in order to avoid being seen by the people and waited f or the end to come.

A few days passed by and it became common talk that the Germans would burn the town to the ground before giving it up. I could not help asking myself: "What is going to happen to me? Shall I be burned alive, when the house goes up in flames, after I have gone through so much suffering during the last two years? "

Nicolay Zhuk had a sister who lived in Oglyan Village near Kamenetz. She had hidden me in the past and was willing to take me to her. I rode in a horse-cart, covered by hay and other bundles. The heat was oppressive. My nerves were taut and I felt half-dead under the heavy burden of so many things. But at the same time I thought that within a few days I should be liberated from the Nazi murderers. Unluckily, it took several weeks. Zhuk's sister hid me in a cave which was used for dumping potatoes. The place was very dark and infested by mice that harassed me all the time. The place was insecure, because the front-line ran in its vicinity. There was a lot of shooting. People sought protection in the cellars. Only I lay crouched in the potato dump. The Germans made searches for horses, partisans etc. and my life was hanging by a thread. This situation, however, was of short duration.

In July 1944, the Germans withdrew and the first Russian partisans appeared. I did not even believe that the deliverance had come.

Soon I saw the first Jew. He was Feygi Meretzky's nephew. They used to live in Selz. At the time I saw him he was in a Russian Army unit.

Then the Russians left and my life was again in danger. While I was in the kitchen, the Germans showed, up unexpectedly. They were looking for the Russians. Nailed to the spot, I continued to stir the food in the pot with a spoon. The Germans did not search long and left because they were in a hurry. The murderers did not come to us anymore but I remained in the village for several days, fearing that they might return.

On July 22, 1944, I came back to Kamenetz. I could not walk. The feet hurt me terribly and I was swollen. For two years I had been living without fresh air, suffering from hunger, cold and filth. I lived in constant fear of death. It is difficult for me to describe the feeling of sadness and bitterness accompanying me where I saw Kamenetz again. The town was silent and desolate. Every stone seemed to be weeping after its inhabitants that were gone forever. So much blood of innocent people had been shed and no one worried about it. There were even some Gentiles in Kamenetz who were pleased by the fact. And if anyone, of them felt badly it was only because he regretted having acquired too little of Jewish property. I know only what it looked like when it became known that I had survived. It looked as if lightning had struck them. The ground started to burn under my feet. I could not breathe freely and felt I was in danger. I had to escape to Brest-Litovsk in a hurry.

Upon my arrival there I thought I was a human being leaving a right to live, just like everyone else, but I was mistaken. My troubles began afresh. One night two Russians knocked on my window and asked who was living in the flat. They asked me to open the door. I was still very naive, so I complied with their request. They immediately drew out a pistol and pointed its muzzle at me. At the same time they opened the cupboard and took away everything. When I asked them to leave me my coat they fired the pistol. I was so terrified that I fell. I was told not to leave the house during 20 minutes, otherwise they would shoot.

Soon, many arrests took place in Kamenetz. People were denouncing one another to the authorities. Fanasevich, in whose house I was living when the Germans marched in, was afraid I might venge myself upon him for having thrown me out. He got in touch with his cousin and the cousin's wife, whose sister, Aniuta, was a prominent Communist in Brest. The began intriguing against me.

Russians came to me and made an inquiry about G. W. a Christian, who hid me during the German occupation. I replied I did not know his whereabouts. In October, 1944 I was arrested.

Russian major asked me why the Germans had left me alive. Twice he gave me a real beating and claimed that I had not told him the truth. Therefore, he said, I must be imprisoned. I suffered very much. Every night they would drag me for an interrogation and beat me up badly. For several days they kept me in darkness, almost without food. All I received was a little piece of bread. Then I was told that I was not under arrest anymore – but imprisoned.

All is lost, I thought. The cup of my troubles is not yet filled.

One night I was taken for an interrogation. Fanasevich's cousin and his sister-in-law, Aniuta, the Communist, were present. They accused me of the worst crimes imaginable. They said that I had not been hiding from the Germans, that I was a liar, that I was a mistress of the German Commissar, that I had been living quite well under the Germans, that I used to change my hair-do everyday etc. Then she charged me that she had been my maid-servant and I had been treating her badly.

When I asked her where I had lived during the German occupation, she took off her shoe and hit me on my head with it. She seized the ink-pot, poured the ink on me and did not let me talk.

I spent six weeks in jail, very sick, lying on a hard, damp floor and suffering from hunger and thirst. At the end of the six weeks, the trial took place. Five militiamen led me into the court-room to prevent my escape. Three military judges judged me. I saw twelve witnesses for the prosecution.

This did not surprise me. I did not care anymore.

When the first witness was called to submit evidence, he said that everything he knew about me had already been set down in writing. "That which was written down is none of your business", one of the judges told him. His duty was to tell everything, the judge added, The witness remained silent. This encouraged me. The judge asked me if I had anything to say. I asked the witness if he saw me after the Jews had been deported and whether he knew that I was alive.

His answer was "No". The same happened with the remaining witnesses. Aniuta tried to say something but did not succeed. The prosecutor interrupted her by saying: "She is probably dissatisfied because she (Dora) survived".

I was fortunate that the judge's attitude to the case was correct. They decided to arrest Aniuta and the remaining witnesses for false charges and ordered to free me.

But the militiamen led me back to the prison and it took a long time till I was set free. For almost a year I was kept in prison though I was entirely innocent. We were 45 persons in a small cell, suffering from hunger, thirst and cold and lying on a cement floor.

On September 13, 1945, I was set free and officially acquitted. I went into the street, not knowing where to go. I was pretty desperate. All my belongings consisted of the old rags which I had on me during my stay in prison which lasted over a year.

Once more, the terrible scenes and experiences, the Kamenetz Ghetto and later events appeared in front of my eyes. I felt I must leave, as soon as possible, the places where so much Jewish blood had been shed. I was so desperate and lonely that I could not decide in which direction I should go. Together with a friend of mine I arrived in Poland.

Upon my arrival there I was very sick and run-down from hunger and misery.

After so much suffering I had to undergo two serious operations. Two toes of my left foot had to be amputated because gangrene had set in, as a result of my plight – my life in hideouts during the rule of the Nazi's and my stay in the terrible prison of Brest.

More than 20 years have elapsed since and I still cannot forget all this. The memory of our dearest, of our martyrs with whom I shared the life in the Ghetto is deeply engraved in my heart. I cannot forget the frosty winter morning when the murderers deported the entire Ghetto population.

Little innocent children cried from fear and shivered from cold. They clung to the parents, who were being driven on foot, beaten and shot at.

I can still see the terrible scene; I see them being tortured before being killed. Till now I can not be happy like other people.

This is the result of the bloody German occupation and the life in the Russian paradise.

[Page 105]

My Life in Ghettos and Concentration Camps

by Dvora Rudnitsky-Singer, New-York

As soon as the Russians temporarily occupied Kamenetz, at the beginning of World War II, all shops were closed. Even skilled tradesmen were forbidden to work independently; a sort of "Kolhoz" was established and they worked collectively in it, but the salaries they received were low. The only advantage that the workers enjoyed was that their passports did not bear the stamped paragraph: "Bourgeois". The above paragraph threatened the bearer of such a passport with being deported to Siberia. I remember how my late father, Yoel Rudnitsky, and others who had the "Bourgeois" paragraph went outside the town to shovel snow on the highroad; they did it to be able to show themselves with a spade at the militia-station, to prove that they were workers and perhaps thus to get rid of the paragraph.

The worker's wages were insufficient to earn a living a government store was opened; a remained closed most of the time for it had no merchandise; whenever there were wares available, first of all the government officials took their share and the long queue of waiting people received very little. The only way of survival was to carry out illegal trade with Christian acquaintances who smuggled in potatoes, butter, flour and onions in exchange for hidden goods.

The NKVD took over Aharon Moshe Galperin's house. They forced all party members and state officials to attend school on Saturdays. The Great Yeshiva was converted by the Russians into a cinema and a hall for Communist meetings and dances. It was the newly erected building of the Yeshiva. When its construction was finished the Yeshiva students formed a dancing ring round the Academy Head, the learned Rabbi Barukh Baer of blessed memory, and led the whole rabbinical procession across the town to the new Yeshiva.

We, too, had to vacate our flat in the house of Sara and Yoseph Spector, because the Police-Commander with his family who had come from Russia moved into it. We moved into the house of Meir Zabinker-Rimland.

But in spite of all this, we could still live; we did not realize how comparatively well off we were and what the fate had in store for us.

Real hell began when the German-Russian war broke out in 1941. Within a short time the Nazi murderers entered Kamenetz. The frontier near Brest was attacked before dawn at 2.30 a.m. and on the same day around 6 o'clock in the evening, a few armoured vehicles and tanks halted in the town-center, facing the shops at the end of Brest Street. There was no resistance; no Russian soldiers were on the spot; already in the morning the few remaining Russian party and government officials had sent away their families.

The streets were empty and an air of desolation hung over the entire townlet. The Germans demanded from the Jews to send a number of men who could serve as intermediaries. Shlomo Mandelblatt, a respected, intelligent man was chosen as representative. The Germans demanded toilet soap, chocolate, coffee and other items which were collected. They also demanded 100 men for work; nobody knew for what kind of work they were required.

Looking out from behind the curtain, we saw an army car with civilians in dark clothes. As it turned out later they belonged to the Gestapo. Also SS men with dog's arrived on the spot and soon sounds of blows and cries and screams of women and children could be heard. The Germans went from door to door, dragged out the Jewish men and assembled them all in the town-center near the water-pump. There was no place to hide.

The only man not taken away from our house was Meir Zabinker-Rimland. His son-in-law and my father had been taken away to work in the morning. Not knowing where to hide, he crawled under the kitchen-table which was covered with a large cloth. But neither the table nor the tablecloth would have saved him. What saved him from being taken at that time was the fact that the Germans simply forgot to enter our house. Later on I went from one courtyard to another, crossed the fences dividing between them and ran fast across the streets. Only in such manner was it possible to reach the house where one wanted to get. When the shouting and knocking stopped, I made my way, with difficulty, in this manner, to the extreme house on Brest Street from where there was a lookout on the water-pump.

The men assembled here had to kneel down. When a Jew with a long red beard who had been Head of the Little Yeshiva and the Rabbinical Judge's son-in-law raised his hands to heaven, probably after saying the Last Confession Prayer (Vidui), an SS man kicked him with his boot. Reuven Mandelblatt, the son of Shlomo, Samek Rosenshein, the Jewish pharmacist's son, Shalom Galperin, David Zisel's son, Simha Layzer Gevirtzman, Shimon Buchhalter, Alter Chazanovich and tens of others were all crowded into the truck and driven away from the town. In the evening, when the men who had been taken to work in the morning, returned, unaware of what happened during the day, they were greeted with joy.

A spark of hope flashed for a while. It seemed that perhaps the men seized during the day were also taken to work and would come back. Unfortunately they were never heard of again. The only news about them was brought by the peasants from the neighboring villages; they told that all the caught Jews had been taken to a place near a woods outside the town and shot. In the meantime, Shlomo Mandelblatt and Rosenshein, the pharmacist, requested the Polish priest to intervene on behalf of the seized men. His reply was that he could not help them at all, because they had been picked out by the Germans as Communists.

The days passed by full of uncertainty. Nobody knew what the next morning would bring. We were ordered to on yellow badges, so that a Christian could be distinguished from a Jew and so that pain and humiliation would be put inflicted upon us.

Christian peasants with whom we were on friendly terms used to smuggle in food for which we have them whatever we could. Then one day, the Jews from Kamenetz were deported. Only the families of those who were needed by the Germans for work were exempted from the deportation. Every Jew was permitted to take only 15 Kilogrammes baggage. Peasants from the adjoining villages swooped upon the abandoned Jewish houses and took away everything they could grab. Not all of the peasants were bad. I remember a forester's wife who brought us marmalade and butter in a pail and put a layer of salt on the top of the pail's contents in order to conceal them. We, too, gave her many things and all the remnants of the shop's stock. The same Christian woman endangered her life during the deportation of the Jews; she was standing on the road near the woods, and when the wagons with the deported were passing by she approached them and handed us a food parcel. The wagons were rolling along one after the another. The children were sitting on the bundles close to their mothers. Once in a while the men would get off and run, holding on to the wagons, in order not to tire the horses too much.

At that time no one knew what would happen to us. We had already heard about transports when men were forced to run and all those unable to keep running were shot.

The Rabbi of Kamenetz, Ruven Burstein of blessed memory, with his family, was in one of the wagons behind us. Each one of us dreaded for his fate. He sat hunched down, the collar of his coat raised up to hide his beard. Whenever the first wagon made a stop to allow those in retard to catch up, with them, we were seized by fear that the Germans were about to execute us. And so, filled with terror, we were brought to the Ghetto of Pruzhany and each one of us breathed relieved.

There, the "Judenrat" took charge of us. It was Friday night and at first we were put up in the synagogues. On the following day they began to place us in various houses. Whoever could work, went to work. Some were sent by the Judenrat to work for the Germans outside the Ghetto, and traded in food smuggled into the Ghetto. The Judenrat, as well as the Jewish police, were intent on helping every Jew in the Ghetto. But many of our fellow-townsmen left Pruzhany clandestinely and returned to Kamenetz stealthily and joined the few Jews who had remained there. My mother, too, left the Ghetto secretly in a horse-drawn wagon and accompanied by a Christian succeeded to return to Kamenetz. She also succeeded in bringing back with her a little food and a few things which she received from several Christian acquaintances. But the main purpose of her trip was to see whether we should return; what she witnessed made us resolve not to move from Pruzhany.

All the Jews in Kamenetz lived concentrated in several streets set apart for them. At that time there was no fence around them but the people were scared to move. My mother only saw a few Jews sweeping the streets. Upon her return she spoke very little, but she said one sentence emphatically: "We're not going". In Pruzhany we were fenced in but we could move freely among the Jews. We were not allowed to leave the houses at night but the streets of the Ghetto were guarded by Jewish police.

The Rabbi of Kamenetz with his family remained in Pruzhany; my grandfather Aharon Rudnitsky (Lysker) with my father's stepmother Leah and my aunt Bela Hasya, her husband and two sons remained there too.

Several weeks before we were deported from the Ghetto my grandfather had become ill and was unable to come to us. I used to run to him everyday bringing with me some hot food. Once, on a Saturday, when I was on my way to my grandfather and carrying for him some Sabbath food kept warm from Friday, I tripped in the deep snow and fell down; at that moment all my thoughts were concentrated solely on the basket with the warm food.

Several weeks before our deportation from the Ghetto of Pruzhany we heard that all the Jews had been removed from Kamenetz and murdered. That was the last news that reached us from Kamenetz. Then the liquidation of the Ghetto of Pruzhany began. Altogether four transports of deported left the Ghetto. We were in the third transport.

The night before our deportation my father assembled all of us in our room. With tears in his eyes he showed us four vials with a poisonous solution. He told us that he succeeded to obtain them from a pharmacist with whom he was acquainted. According to what my father heard we were going to be sent to a camp where we would work very hard; if we got sufficient food we might survive with God's help. We did not know about the gas-chambers and crematoria but we knew about the large pits where people were shot and buried-some of them still alive. Father told us to drink the poison only in case we would be wounded, so as not to be buried alive.

Being myself a mother of two children, I am even more amazed now at the strength and courage shown by my father in acting so. Each one of us packed into a bundle the things one was allowed to take; we put on additional clothes and got ready to move. This time we were not transported in horse-drawn wagons but in railway-cars used for transporting cattle, with a small grated window. From 50 to 75 persons were in each car. The doors were locked from the outside; that is how the dismal journey began.

There was no place to take care of the physiological needs. The urine oozed through a narrow opening in the wall, the excrements were packed in paper or in rags and pushed out through the grated window.

As soon as the doors opened, after the train had come to a halt, we could hear the murderers bellow: "Raus" (out). Everybody trudged out of the car, cramped after sitting on the bundles for several days and dressed heavily in as many clothes as one could put on. This was done purposely, so that if the bundles were taken away from us in the camp at least the things we had on should remain.

Immediately the men were separated from the women. We were ordered to form a line. The children remained with their mothers. SS men selected some of the people and told them to step aside. Others were told to go in a different direction. The little stick in the hand of the SS man, that pointed the direction in which everyone was to go, decided wether the fate of the people was life or death. The mothers of the children, no matter how young they were, hod to join the group of the old people and children. I remember how a mother of a 2 year old boy left him and hid herself. Elderly women wanted to take the child but the boy resisted. Until now I can hear the child cry: "Mame", "Mame"!

The mother was in fact selected, for work in the camp, but in short time she, herself, was taken to Block 25. Everyone could enter the block but not leave it, for the only way out of there led into the gas-chambers. My little brother Zavele was quite tall for his age and we decided he should stand next to my father. But our plan failed and my little brother was sent to the group of old people and children and my father to another group separated from them. We were looking at the scene shocked but we could not do anything. We, a group of women, were sent to the women's camp at Birkenau and the men went to the men's camp.

We were led to a bath-house; there our hair was cut, a number tattooed. Later on we were driven into a steam bath and from there to a shower-room; the flow of water could not be regulated and hot and cold water showered down alternately. Whoever uttered a cry was beaten with a stick by the "Kapos". The "Kapos" were Germans, Poles, Ukrainian criminals etc. In the steam-bath delousing took place and we received rags as clothing. In darkness we were driven into a brick-building with narrow passage-ways. Bunks made of bricks and covered with wooden boards served as beds. They were built in tiers. Those who got the upper bunks were considered lucky because up above the air was a bit fresher, in particular in the centre of the building where the roof-slopes were joined and formed a sharp edge. On the beds there were two sacks filled with straw and a couple of threadbare quilts. Each one received a large tin bowl and a little pot;

this was all our property. Four, five and sometimes six women lay on one bed stretched in all directions. One of the girls from our transport received a shirt full with lice. She wanted to throw it away but someone told her: "Don't do it, child. You won't get another one and you'll freeze. There are plenty of lice here, on every step – even in the clean things". We turned our heads toward the girl who had spoken and saw a half-naked woman delousing her things. She looked old and bony. From her we learned about the tall, protruding chimneys giving off smoke day and night. The smoke rose from the burning of the bodies of the Jews, the bodies of our nearest. Whenever, on our way to or back from work, we saw an arriving transport we knew that the fires would blaze again in the furnaces of the crematories and the chimneys would again give off smoke. At that time the transports came so often that the smoke rose unceasingly day and night.

Everyday before dawn we were wakened by whistles, lined up in front of the "block" (the building in which we lived) and waited in the dampness of the early morning for the German SS women who came through the gate and counted the people. They knew perfectly well that it was impossible to cross the electric wire fence surrounding the camp. Those who died during the night were also dragged outside and laid next to the lines of the prisoners. After making sure that the numbers were correct we were taken to work.

My first job was to pull down houses partly destroyed during the war. Ten girls were holding a wooden pole with iron edges, and, following an order, thrust it against the wall. This was a job for men, but it would not have been difficult even for us, had we not been surrounded by Kapos and the bellowing SS with dogs, who beat us. Once, while returning from work, one of our girls felt so sick and weak that she was unable to walk; however she had to be brought back to the camp, alive or dead. She was laid on a wooden stretcher and four girls had to volunteer to carry her. I was one of the four. The distance to the camp was several kilometers and after some time I felt tired; I asked the "Kapo" if she would be willing to exchange me for a while with someone else; thereupon the "Kapo" told the SS man to let his dog jump on me; he immediately did it but unloosened the dog so that the dog could tear only my clothes; then I forgot my fatigue and the fright carried me on my way.

Later on I was in a labour-gang (Kommando) employed in drying swamps. We took sand from one place and carried it on wooden wheelbarrows to the swamp to cover it. At that time I was quite ill with dysentery and fever; besides, my hands, nose and lips which were parched by the sun froze as a result of the frost and formed a hard crust.

It was enough to touch my hands or lips to see the raw flesh. I myself was unaware how terrible and inhuman my appearance was. One saw enough skeletons around and I was one of them. In the camp such people were called the "Musulmans". The only thing which kept me from going to Block 25, as many others had done, was the thought that my father was alive in the men's camp in Auschwitz. A man from Pruzhany who knew me told me that on the way to work.

At night I was unable to rest because of the high fever or the overexertion. Even in sleep I used to dream about the day of work and toe blows. Sunday, our day of rest, used to fill us with fear. When the well known shout "Juden heraus" (Jews out) was heard we knew what it meant. We were led out of our compound, under the escort of the SS men with dogs who used to guard us at work. This was called "The control of the numbers". In fact, a table with books in which all our numbers were registered was standing near the gate. The murderers, too, were standing there; one of them did the counting with a stick in his hand, and whenever he thought fit he selected several people to be gassed. In such a manner he created space for newcomers.

When the selection was over, we breathed with relief, not knowing how long it would last.

For the first time I met my father after three months in the camp. It is unbelievable how a human being can change during such a short period. My father was in a labour-gang that came to work in the women's camp. They had to carry out repairs in the barrack of the "Kapos". My father who knew, that I was in the women's camp was searching for me and looking at every woman. Two girls working in the camp carried a bed into the barrack in which he was working and he had an opportunity to ask them to find me.

In the evening the girls came into the block and after calling my name told me where my father was working. I rushed there but the girls stopped me and said that the men had already left, for they had to leave before the return of the women labour-gangs into the camp. My father had said, however, that if I could remain in the camp on the following day he would be on the same spot. I decided to pose as sick on the following day and to remain in the camp, without taking into consideration the possible results of such a step. From time to time, Germans used to come to the block for inspection and those who were not working were sent to the gas-chambers. We were also forbidden to enter the area where my father was working but my only thought was to see him. The first time I went out in the morning but did not see him. The second time I went at noon-time hoping that the men would be outside – but nobody was there. I went in the afternoon once more; on the side I saw my father Pushing a wheelbarrow with lime and escorted by an SS man with a rifle. Since the women were forbidden to talk to the men I did not take the risk of calling him. My father looked at me and kept on walking. Not knowing whether I would see him again after he entered the barrack. I called him: "Tate". The German asked my father what was going on. He told the German from the SS that three months passed since we separated in the camp and that I called him "Father" but he did not recognize me.

For a moment a humane emotion swept the young murderous SS man. He told me to wait until my father would empty the wheelbarrow and then return. My father and I entered one of the buildings while the German was on guard so that another German should not come in, because it was forbidden to let a father talk to his daughter. The German told my father that his father, too, had once upon a time not recognized his daughter and this incident reminded him of it. I stood face to face with my father, who recognized me only after having spoken with me about the family. Afterward I met my father many times on the way to work till his group finished their work in the women's camp. But even later on we used to send greetings to each other from time to time. Our meeting renewed our will to live. I lost touch with him when, as a result of the front drawing near, Auschwitz was evacuated. We were sent from one camp to another until we were liberated by a miracle. Then everyone began to search for relatives who survived. I wandered for some time and inquired in various Jewish Community Centres which were formed after the war but did not find my father or anyone else from our family. I knew that I had an uncle in Israel, so I got in touch with him through the help of the Jewish Brigade. In Italy I married a survivor of the holocaust and together we went to Israel. There I learned from a person who was together with my father in the last camp that my father, who had survived the hell of Auschwitz and other camps, died of hunger a month before the liberation when the rescue was so near.

[English page 117]

Spectres of War haunt the "Angel of Belsen"
Prison Camp Heroine Tries to Forget
Shielded Children from Nazi Terrors

One day in 1942 the Germans moved 10,000 Jews from a ghetto near Kamenetz-Litovsk Poland, to their Oswiecim (Auschwitz) Concentration camp. Oswiecim (Auschwitz) later became known around the world as the Nazi's most efficient death factory. At that time, however, it was just another place where helpless people suffered and died quickly or slowly, it didn't much matter which.

SS guards sorted out this group of new arrivals, piling the old and sick into trucks bound for the gas chambers, marching the rest to barracks, where they would live in squalor as long as they were capable of working. One of them grabbed the arm of a young woman holding her 3-year-old son by the hand.

"How old are you?"

She told him.

Flames Seared Her Heart

He said, "That's a lie." As he said the last word his fist smashed into her mouth. A few seconds later, when she came to her senses, she was lying on the ground, her mouth full of blood and broken bits of teeth. Her eyes focused just in time to see the guard throw her baby on the back of a gas chamber truck, already piled high with the wasted forms of other useless human beings. The truck drove away.

That was the last Luba Tryszynska saw of Isaac, only child of Hersch, the husband the Nazis had taken away the year before to work as a slave labourer. By the time she made her way to the crematorium, fire had done its work.

In the summer of 1944, they moved her to Belsen. She had survived typhus and two trips to the gas chambers door where, stripped naked, she won last-second reprieves from death. Briefly, pitifully, her path had crossed that of her husband. When they put her to work as a nurse in the camp's so-called hospital, he was caught trying to throw her a piece of bread over the wire fence surrounding the hospital compound. They punished him by making him work at the crematorium and shot him dead when he tried to escape.

Her life of torture seemed somehow to have caused the spirit to freeze inside her. She no longer reacted to anything. S lie could not cry or care.

But now, as a nurse, there were certain advantages for Luba Tryszynska. Wearing a long-sleeved jacket, she was able to conceal the small triangle beneath the identification number tattooed on her left arm – the mark of the Jew. She told the Belsen authorities she was

Russian and, because she spoke the language perfectly, they believed her. They put her into one of a number of little shacks in which nurses from the hospital were housed.

Always the Same

While Luba Tryszynska was trying mainly to sleep, on her first night in Belsen, she suddenly became obsessed with the idea that she heard children crying. She woke up the nurse sleeping next to her, another transfer from Oswiecim.

"Do you hear?" she said. "Children. They are crying."

"Go to sleep," said the woman. "It is always the same.

You imagine you hear your baby. Go to sleep."

But Luba Tryszynska could not sleep. Defying the regulations, she got up and went outside the shack.

In a dark corner of the road near-by, a large truck like a coal truck – was parked. The motor was running, the headlights cut a sharp swath in the darkness and she could see the driver in the cab. Suddenly there was the sound of whirring machinery. The carrying part of the truck tipped up steeply, and the back panel fell away. Thus, casually, the driver dumped his load, which piled up in the mud behind the truck.

Luba Tryszynska could not see what the load was, but she could hear. She ran as fast as she could toward that dark pile in the mud, from which the crying came. There – struggling, screaming, helplessly intertwined – were dozens of children.

She snatched a boy about 6 months old from the top of the heap and, with the baby in her arm, ran to the front of the truck.

"What are you doing with these children?" she asked the driver.

Comforts Children

"What do I care what they do with them? They will die, of course." The driver put the truck in gear. "They are Jews," he added. Then he drove away.

That night Luba Tryszynska went from one hut to another, waking the nurses, making them take some children in each room. There were 64 children. At least 17 of them, of which she took personal charge, seemed to be under 2 years of age. The oldest was 12. They were Dutch, but she found she could talk to some of them in German and through these she pieced together their story.

With their parents, part-Jewish Hollanders caught in Germany by the war, they had been living in a nearby camp waiting to be sent back to the Netherlands. The Germans had found three loaves of bread illegally hidden in the barracks. The parents had been sent to work in an ammunition factory. The children, for whom there was no room in the factory barracks, had been sent to Belsen.

Luba Tryszynska spent the night doing what she could to make the 17 babies in her hut clean and comfortable. When a German worker, the wife of an SS trooper, passed by in the early morning, she begged this woman to give her something for the children to eat. The woman refused, but later returned with some bread scraps, a little marmalade and a big jug of drinking water. The children ate, then slept.

Luba Tryszynska went to the hospital commandant, a Dr. Klein. She begged him to let her care for the children.

"He was a murderer," she said later, "but he spoke soft.

He said, "You are a nurse, you belong to the hospital, not to these Jewish kids."

The Simplest Way

Still she pleaded. She would keep them out of the way, she said. He would never know they were in the camp. At last he agreed to look at the children.

Dr. Klein stood for almost a minute in the doorway of Luba Tryszynska's hut, watching the sleeping infants. Then he said, "I will give you a barracks. You will have charge of all the children in the camp. There are 30 others here already."

"It was not," she explained late, "that he was a good man. He thought it was the simplest way. No one knew better than he how absurd it was to try keep all those children alive in Belsen."

Three days later, Luba Tryszynska had her barracks and her 94 children. The new ones were from Eastern Europe: A few Poles, some Czechoslovaks – 18 were Russian.

Of course, as Dr. Klein believed, it was an absurd attempt. The camp's basic diet, at the time, seemed to be one of turnips and saltpetre. She went first to some Russians who had jobs in the hospital's central kitchen. She told them she had charge of 94 children in the camp – all Russian.

Luba Tryszynska was no Communist, but she could lie for her charges as easily as she could steal for them. "Comrades," she told the Russian workmen, "I give you my word as a Bolshevist, if you get me food for these children – and if I am caught – they can kill me, but I will not tell where it came from."

Fought Cold and Hunger

From the kitchen to her barracks, she smuggled food she got from these Russians in the bottom of jars, the top half of which was filled with the regulation turnips. It was not much. A bit of flour for making tiny biscuits, a little sugar, some margarine, and now and then a small piece of horse-meat.

She cooked every night, all night long inside the barracks, feeding the children in groups of 20 while the rest slept. She did this to avoid calling attention to what was going on; in the daytime, the barracks were as quiet as though they had been deserted. At all times, the children stayed indoors.

Luba Tryszynska's hopeless attempts to keep the place and the children clean did not, of course, prevent them from becoming sick. Everybody was sick in Belsen. Like the others, the children – almost all of them – developed typhus and dysentery. She put bottles of hot water on their stomachs to try ease their terrible cramps. In winter she braved the guards to wander around the compound at night, endlessly searching for bits of wood with which to keep going the one stove in the barracks.

The youngest baby was obviously dying. She knew he could not be kept alive on little biscuits, ground horse-meat and water. One day, she told another nurse she was going to Joseph Kramer himself, the "Beast of Belsen," dread commandant of the camp. She said she would ask him for milk for the children.

The Beast Listened

"You are mad!" her friend said. "He will kill you".

It was a logical reaction. Kramer used to walk around Belsen with a whip in his hand, and it was his habit to use the whip on prisoners who approached him. In a bad mood, he would lash at anybody not quick enough to get our of reach.

Three time Luba Tryszynska made her way into his office. The first two times, he threw her bodily out of the room, but the third time she screamed at him that she would be paid whether he liked it or not. The squat, brutish sadist had not heard that kind of talk for a long time, and he hesitated for a moment. That opening was all she needed. She began to talk, so fast and loud that he listened in spite of himself.

He listened in silence for perhaps five minutes. Then, suddenly, he leaned forward and scribbled something on a piece of paper. He tore the paper from the pad, crumpled it in his hand and threw it in Luba Tryszynska's face.

"Get out!" he roared. "Take your G-- d-- Jew b-- and get out of here!"

The paper, she found, entitled her to five liters of milk from the camp stores.

Less than six quarts of milk for almost 100 children. Dr. Klein had been right, of course. The whole thing was obviously absurd.

Exhausted and Broken

Nine months after the children arrived at Belsen, the British Army arrived there. They were amazed by many things in that vast chamber of horrors. Nothing amazed them more than the children – exactly 94 of them – that they found alive in one ramshackle barracks building presided over by a Polish Jewess named Luba Tryszynska, exhausted, broken and fully middle-aged in her 28th year.

They made a good deal of her. They put her and the children in a special hospital and gave them the best care. An official of the British Red Cross began collecting material for a book about her. Incredulous doctors interviewed her, and came back to hear the story again.

Later, the Dutch Government provided a special airplane and she took the 64 Dutch children who had been dumped in the mud back to their homes in Holland. Queen Wilhelmina decorated her on behalf of the nation. "The Angel of Belsen," the Queen called her.

Luba Tryszynska took to Sweden those of the other children, who like herself, were in the category of displaced persons. There they were put in a fine state orphan asylum. Many were quickly adopted into families in Sweden and Finland. Some were sent to new homes in Palestine through Youth Aliyah, an organization connected with Hadassah.

In Sweden, Luba Tryszynska married a handsome young Pole named Sol Frederich, whom she met in a DP camp. He had spent five years in Oswiecim, but she did not know him there. He had relatives in the United States.

[English page 127]

Kamenetzers
in the United States

The Kamenetz Society in America

Activity Report by Sarah Hurwitz, Correspondence Secretary

Our Society was established in May 1923 by: Rabbi Benjamin Mostovsky, Sarah Simhovich, Rivkah Lifschitz, Ester Dolinsky, Haya Sara Mendelson and Feyge Radishitz.

There were only few ladies among its members.

Gradually, the Society grew larger and increased the scope of its activities. That was the period of large-scale immigration to America after the First World War. Many women from Kamenetz joined the Society which numbered over 150 members at that time.

Our activity began by sending money for the Kamenetz Talmud-Torah School, and a monthly allowance for the Rabbis. We also sent food and clothes for children. The money was sent to Reb Joseph Vigotov, May He rest in peace; he distributed it according to everybody's needs.

Some time later, we found out that some of our fellow countrymen from Kamenetz including some Yeshivah Students were in Russia. We lost no time in establishing contact with them by mail and we sent them money and food parcels.

The "Malbush Arumim Ladies Society" which provided clothes for the needy, financed the transportation to America of the Yeshivah students. We have a Kamenetz Yeshivah here and also in Jerusalem.

Many thousands of dollars have been spent for philanthropic purposes for American and Kamenetz "Yeshivot" (Institutions for religious studies), hospitals and other institutions. Funds were provided to enable brides from poorer families to get married.

New Ambulance presented to Magen David Adom
by Kamenetz Litovsker Women's Malbish Arumim League

We are sending help to Israel; we participate in the United Jewish Appeal and buy Israel Bonds. We financed the erection of a house in Israel and of a room in the Kamenetz Yeshivah. We also sent a Torah scroll there. One of the Yeshivah students (a grandson of Rabbi Baruch Ber of blessed memory) was adopted by us. Now we are erecting an additional building for the Yeshivah. The above institution received also a considerable amount of money.

Every year, before the Passover holiday, we send a special allocation ("Meot Hitin"). We planted trees in Israel with the help of Jacob Savitzky of blessed memory, in the name of the "Malbush Arumim" Society.

We contributed a fund for the rescue from a French convent of four orphaned girls.

We contributed to the American Magen David Drive for Israel and sent various equipment, machines, building supplies as well as an ambulance, a centrifuge for blood plasma, 2 oxygen tents and a large quantity of drugs, to the David Marcus Memorial Building, for use in the hospital.

Quite recently we provided 5000 dollars for the erection of a clinic at Ofakim, near Beersheba. The Israel Government allocated 20000 dollars for the same purpose.

On May 5, 1963, we celebrated our 40th anniversary with pride and joy.

Our "Malbush Arumim" Society has done much for the general good, during the 40 years of its existence; it also helped to make possible the publication of the Memorial Book.

The following ladies hold offices in our society: Rivka Lifshitz – President: Bella Tendler, the Wife of Rabbi Tendler - Vice-President; Sara Hurwitz - Protocol and Financial Secretary; Nelly Federbush – Treasurer; Vice-Presidents: Babel Serota, Haya Rivka Sirota, Pearl Goldstein and Tema Goldman.

[English page 130]

The Establishment of Kamenetz-Litovsk Aid Society in America

Activity Report by Meir Mendel Visotzky, New-York

In the 19th Century and at the beginning of the 20th Century, when the gates of America were widely open to the large stream of immigrants coming from Europe and other continents, our townlet, Kamentz-Litovsk, did not remain outside the stream.

Kamentz was not an industrial town and the possibilities of earning a living were very limited. As a result of the difficult economic conditions, many of our fellow townsmen from Kamenetz were forced to emigrate to America in search of happiness in the new land.

That is how many natives of Kamenetz settled down and because citizens in the new country where they hoped for a better future.

One of the Kamenetz townsmen died unexpectedly in a car-accident. The question where to bury him turned up. At that time there already existed the "Kokhav Ya'acov Anshei Kamenetz D'Lita" Synagogue, called also the Kamenetzer Shul, which possessed its own cemetery.

The Kamenetz people requested the permission of the management of the Synagogue to bury the victim Of the accident in their cemetery. Unfortunately, the request was refused on the grounds that the cemetery was only for strictly Orthodox Jews. This incident provided a stimulus for the more progressive Kamenetz townsmen to get organized in a separate organization.

Thereupon, in 1900, the Kamenetz-Litovsk Aid Society was established.

Beginning with a mere handful, the Society grew larger and in the course of time, counted 200 members.

The actions of the Aid Society have full justified the name it carries. During the years of its existence its doors were always open to the Kamenetz townsmen and to other institutions that needed help.

After the end of the First World War, the Society, the Synagogue Council and all other Kamenetz organizations, established a large Relief Committee to help all Kamenetz victims, wherever they might be; particular efforts were made to come to the assistance of the Kamenetz Talmud Torah, the only religious learning institution in Kamenetz.

During his visit to America, the Society honored the Late Kamenetzer Rov, Rabbi Burstein who was always guest at our meetings; we gave him the greatest possible measure of assistance. In this way our Society kept up contacts with our unforgotten townlet Kamenetz till the great Catastrophe.

Soon after the end of the Second World War, the Kamenetz Society, together with all other Kamenetz organizations, again set up a relief-committee, in the hope of helping the war victims of our town. Great were our pain and sorrow when we learned about the enormous proportions of the catastrophe.

Unfortunately, our hopes of being able to extend help to our fellow-townsmen did not materialize. Those few, fortunate persons from Kamenetz, who succeeded to survive the Nazi death-camps and came to America, were received by us like brothers and sisters.

On their first visit to our Committee, each one of them received 100 dollars. To our sorrow, there were no more people from Kamenetz whom we could help.

The sum of $ 2300, which was at our disposal for aid purposes, was transferred by us to the United Jewish Appeal, the only body which extended help to the holocaust survivors and to the State of Israel. The Relief-Committee was dissolved. Despite the dissolution of the General Relief Committee, the Aid Society, as an independent organization, did not give up its philanthropic activity.

The Society was instrumental in selling $ 5000 worth of Israel Bonds and continues to participate in various drives for Israel.

The Kamenetz Society was pleased to welcome our fellow townsman Abraham Shudroff who arrived from Israel with the proposal to publish a Memorial Book. The Society has been one of the active participants on the Memorial Book Committee. It gave both material and moral support to the project.

The following members direct the affairs of the Kamenetz-Litovsk Aid Society:

Velvel Miletsky – President; Hershel Bobrofsky – Vice President; Meir Visotzky – Financial Secretary; Harry Simon – Protocol Secretary; Jack Goldberg – Treasurer.

The author of this report is one of the Society's representatives on the Memorial Book Committee.

While describing the Society's activity, we must mention the great personality of the late Jacob Hurvitz who was one of the first active members of our society.

He was a great scholar learned in the Law. In spite of his great knowledge he was a very modest man without a trace of haughtiness in his relations with the humblest of men. It was he who drew up the Statute of the Society.

He was devoted with all his heart and soul to the Society's work. Whenever requested, he was always ready to lend his helping hand in cultural matters.

An Aramaic phrase of our forefathers: "Woe for those who are gone and cannot be replaced certainly applies to a man like him.

Blessed be His Memory!

Members of Aid Socierty
Sitting, from right to left: Mr. Babel Man; Mr. Harry Simon; Mr. Wiliam Miletsky; Mr. Jim Goldberg; Mr. Meyer Wisotzky
Standing from right to left: Mr. Louis Radish; Mr. Harry Bobrofsky; Mr. Izzy Silverman; Mr. Sam Melnitsky

Members of Lopata Family
Sitting, from right to left: Mrs. Esther Weinstein; Mr. Sam Weinstein; Mr. Iser Goldberg; Mr. Meyer Tendler; Mr. Meyer Wisotzky;
Mrs. Helen Wisotzky; Mrs. Hayke Goldberg; Mrs. Sylvia Tendler; Mrs. Shoshke Wisotzky; Mr. Moshe Segal

[English page 136]

The Kamenetzer Yeshivah of America

by Charles Raddock

Imprint of a Unique Personality – Baruch Baer of Kamenetz

Break up the cluster of the seven Slavo-Germanic regions that but a while ago comprised East-European Jewry, and you find that each had a character all its own, each gave birth to movements of no relation to one another and even opposed to one another.

At the western end, for example, there was Germany, where Reform Judaism was born under Moses Mendelsohn the wake of the European enlightenment, as historians describe the cultural transition of eighteenth to nineteenth centuries. In the south-eastern regions – that is, the Ukraine, Poland, Austria, Hungary, and Rumania – the Hassidic movement was sired by Israel Baal Shem. While at the north-eastern extreme, where north Poland links with western Russia, the yeshivah and kolel movement was founded by Hayim of Volozhin, disciple and colleague of the phenomenal Elijah of Wilno.

Of the first two movements only Hassidism still seems to show some sign of life, despite its old-world features, while Reform is dying, as its leaders frankly confess. And only the last – the yeshivah movement – appears to be gaining impetus, if we may gauge it by certain symptoms across the length and breadth of the land. What is particularly significant about yeshivah growth is its un-indigenous character (except for Yeshiva University). For the moment it seems rather to be gathering momentum in the tradition of the yeshivoth of Russo-Polish Lithuania and of points south.

This would never have happened if East European Jewry had survived, and it is with lingering sadness that we observe this unprecedented transplantation of European academic institutions that left their imprint on universal Jewry. The transplantation has been so complete in some instances as to carry along faculties and student bodies, often via circuitous routes as remote as Mongolia, Siberia and China from the heart of East-European Jewries. A case in point is the Kamenetzer Yeshivah of America which, if the term "wandering Jew" has any meaning, applies to this institution of higher learning. You may call Kamenetzer Yeshivah of America the most itinerant yeshivah of the century.

Founded sixty-one years ago as "K'nesseth Beth Yitzhak," it was forced to flee to Minsk at the outbreak of World War I. Then down again to Kremenchug, about five hundred miles south. Then to Wilno, about seven hundred miles north. And, shortly before the rise of Hitler, to Kamieniec Litewski (Kamenetz-Litovsk), about four hundred miles south-west, closer to the Polish border, a small settlement in Bielorussia founded in the thirteenth century. And, then, again, following the catastrophe of World War H, via the Far East, to Jerusalem and New York, where it is presently housed in a five-story brown-stone at 255 East Broadway, on the Lower East Side of Manhattan. Here, the heroic survivors pursue their studies, as in happier days under their late guide and mentor Rabbi B. B. Leibovitz, affectionately remembered by the scholarly world as "Rav Baruch Baer," and regarded by authorities as the greatest Talmudic savant of our time.

What sets apart Kamenetzer Yeshivah of America from other yeshivoth is that its disciples are competent to carry on in the absence of their late celebrated dean, hewing to the course laid down during the four creative decades of his regime. The first principle of his teachings was this, that the study of Talmud, Halachah and related subjects must be pursued for its own sake, without regard to material gain or reward. It is therefore at Kamenetzer Yeshivah that the Talmudic elite may be found, adult scholars from whose ranks are expected to emerge America's Talmudic authorities of the future.

Kamenetz, it seems, does not produce mere "rabbis" or other ecclesiastical functionaries. Its emphasis is on research and scholarship, as, in a sense, Princeton University's Institute for Advanced Study under the directorship of Prof. Robert Oppenheimer concentrates on scientific research for the enhancement of science. In this sense, you might say, too, Kamenetzer Yeshivah is not a "yeshivah" at all, as we have come to understand that word. But is rather a "kolel," in the tradition of nineteenth century "kolelim," whose fraternity included the greatest scholars of the old world. The term "yeshivah," as you know, has been bandied about indiscriminately in our country. In fact, what is usually described here as a "yeshivah" would have been classified abroad as a "talmud torah" that serves adolescents. Since the term "yeshivah" (for reasons we need not go into) is frequently a misnomer, it would be an understatement to call K.Y. other than a "kolel". A "kolel" serves advanced students exclusively.

Advanced students, as you know, cannot be mere undergraduates, so to say. The very nature of scholarly research involves long and arduous pursuit, often years of preparation far beyond the normal years of study for average students. Thus, in order to encourage research, Kamenetzer Yeshivah of America finances its Talmudic projects by stipends to keep its scholars going even after they have taken on the responsibilities of home and family. It may not be much from our standpoint of living, but it seems to be enough for these dedicated men who have made Jewish scholarship their life work.

This method of financing Talmudic projects was introduced by the above-mentioned Hayyim of Volozhin a century and a half ago, when on the outskirts of Wilno he founded the model yeshivah – or "kolel" – for the scholarly elite, a fraternity that produced the most learned halakhic spokesmen during, the whole range of the nineteenth century. And as informed readers know, too, Judaism is not a faith of mere form and rite. While form and rite are basic to our Faith, it is the study of that vast literature transmitted to us down the centuries that is an integral part of the Faith. Without it Judaism would long ago have been relegated to the limbo of dead antiquity.

It is no secret to those who have been exposed to it that to probe even into a minor section of that encyclopedic literature, a whole lifetime could not suffice. For it involves, among other things, a knowledge of Hebrew, Aramaic, etymology, philology, mathematics, architecture, astronomy, anatomy, physics, biology, medicine, criminology, theology, not to mention mysticism (as we Jews understand it). In short, merely to read the voluminous literature based on the twenty-four books of the "Old Testament" and particularly on the Five Books of Moshe – were humanly impossible, so vast is it so diversified, so intricate, so diffused.

The anthology just published by Kamenetzer Kolel en titled "Deggel Naphtali" and containing original monographs of the most abstruse rabbinic problems, attests to the scholarship of that learned fraternity. To my knowledge, this is the first instance of a student body showing up in print under the imprimatur of a yeshivah. Of course there are so-called "journals" and "annuals" published by various student bodies of American yeshivoth, but they have no more value, say, than journalism has to literature; they are featherweight stuff. Original "Deggel Naphtali" represent the original Talmudic findings of the scholars of K.Y. every one of whom gives promise of future creative endeavour, as each is expected to enrich that vast rabbinic treasure house of literature begun two millennia ago by our sages.

There were great minds in the past that traversed much of the range of that literature during a single lifetime. Among them we may include the above-mentioned Elijah of Wilno, for example, and perhaps his disciple, Hayyim of Volozhin. And in our own era, the late dean of Kamenetzer Yeshivah of America, the above-mentioned "Rav Baruch Baer." Their vast erudition was due to superior mentalities, of course, to devotion to projects that left them little time for normal day-to-day activity, as two or even less hours of sleep per day were common practice for them. Needless to say, for all their erudition, even the elite of Kamenetzer Yeshivah of America would not claim such superhuman effort. Suffice it to say in all fairness, though, that Elijah of Wilno, Hayyim of Volozhin and the late Rav Baruch Baer are their models and inspiration.

The story of Rav Baruch Baer's successors calls for a treatise by itself. But I have no room here for details, except to point out that it is to these men that K.Y. owes its survival and, above all, its transplantation to New York. Particularly to the late Rabbi Naphtali Ze'ev Leibowitz, Rav Baruch Baer's brother-in-law and colleague who, though granted leave to settle in the U.S.A., refused to abandon his disciples – and stayed behind to brave the Siberian wilds until he saw them safely to the 'States. The story of how this soft-spoken scholar, with his bare emaciated hands, buried students who perished in Siberia from cold and starvation, is blood-curdling. Suffice it to say that the survivors followed the late Rabbi Naphtali faithfully to the States, as he had indeed followed them loyally to Siberia.

Readers might well ask: What purpose does such dedicated scholarship serve? What good can it do the American community? Is the American environment conducive to such supreme scholarly efforts of an esoteric elite?

The answer to these questions, I believe, was given in the first century of our era. Then, as you may recall, the great Hillel's youngest and favorite pupil, Yohanan ben Zaccai – during the Roman siege of Jerusalem, as history tells us – managed an interview with Vespasian, and won the emperor's consent to continue the academy Jamniah south of Jaffa, which finally became the scene for the canonization of the "Old Testament". It was Zaccai's belief, apparently, that with a nucleus of scholars the Jewish people could be kept alive. As we see now, this is what happened. Had Zaccai's Jamniah been shut down, the lavish synagogues then planted everywhere across the Roman Empire would never have been able to hold the Jewish nation together from Jerusalem down through the Egyptian coastline and up to as far north as the primitive France that then bordered on a primitive Germany.

It is therefore not far-fetched to say that if Judaism is to hold its own in the face of a challenging modern environment, it can do so better with institutions like the Kameezer Yeshivah in our midst. Without it, without other institutions to emulate it, our synagogues might well remain nothing but beautiful edifices that manage to fill to capacity no more than twice a year. But that is not enough for historic survival.

There seem to be, as you know, quite a few institutions in our country today that produce rabbis and minor religious functionaries to serve an ever expanding Jewish community.

Who, you might ask, is going to teach our rabbis and teachers? Heaven knows, many have no time later for study! And, we are in need, it seems, of scholars to teach our future communal leaders. We also need scholars to whom our American-trained rabbis may turn when questions about the Faith arise that call for clear, authoritative answers based on sound and profound erudition. In this respect, I think, Kamenetz Yeshivah of America is a model institute for advanced study, setting pace and tempo for others, in the spirit of great European institutions of learning now, alas, gone forever!

This, I believe, it was what the illustrious Rav Baruch Baer must have had in mind when, two years after he transplanted his yeshivah to the town whose name it bears he visited New York, accompanied by the late Rabbi Reuben Grozowsky, to bear Torah tidings to an awakening American Jewry. That was thirty years ago.

[English page 143]

The Kokhav Ya'akov Anshey Kamenetz D'lita Society

by Velvel Kustin (New-Jersey)

Large-scale Jewish immigration from Eastern Europe to the United States began in the 17th century in the eighties. Jews from Kamenetz were among those coming to America's shores.

The first newcomers from Kamenetz were poor and quite miserable. They suffered common hardships and were homesick. This and the fact that the Jewish population in the U.S. was as yet small made them cling together.

When the number of Kamenetz townspeople in the "new country" grew up, they acquired a Torah-Scroll and established a society centred round their own synagogue which was named "Kokhav Ya'acov" (Jacob's Star) – The society, founded in 1891, in Suffolk Street, New York, became the oldest Kamenetz organization and one of the first Jewish societies of that kind in America.

The society's founders are no longer among the living. Let us recall their names: Joseph David Appelman, Moshe Silverman, Israel Zlotes, Abraham Luring and Abraham Yoel Radish. They drew up the constitution of the society and formulated its aims. One of the fixed rules states that meetings must be conducted in Yiddish. The society's aims included:

a)   Acquisition of a synagogue of its own for holding lectures and other cultural activities as well as services.

b)   Acquisition of cemetery plots where the members of the society would rest eternally "after 120 years".

c)   Help for the sick.

d)   The setting up of an Interest Free Loan Fund (Gemiluth Hesedim).

e)   The provision of aid to the needy Jews in Kamenetz.

f)   Participation in philanthropic activity carried out by institutions in the United States.

The Society has been active since its foundation but it flourished in particular in the thirties. At that time the number of its members rose to 250. Some of them were American-born and some were not even natives of Kamenetz. Today even the President of the 74-year-old Society is not a native of Kamenetz, but he is very devoted to its work. The vice-President, the Financial Secretary and the Treasurer, all Kamenetz-born, have many years of fruitful work behind them and we wish them many additional years.

These are the names of the Society's officers: Mr. David Appelman – President; Mr. Shmuel Itshak Melnitzky Vice-President; Mr. Joshua Silverblatt – Treasurer; Mr. Shraga Feivel Tendler – Financial Secretary.

The older members of the Society have introduced the custom of calling one another at meetings "Brother" and "Sister" and this custom reigns also in their private lives.

The Society participates in all local or national drives. In recent years it has contributed its share to the rebuilding of Israel. It has also made a contribution to the publication of the Kamenetz-Litovsk Memorial Book.

In 1917, a Kamenetz Ladies organization (Ladies Auxiliary) was formed. Its primary purpose was to aid the synagogue.

The late Esther Dolinsky was the first President of the Ladies Auxiliary and the late Ida Singer was the first Vice-President. At present Mrs. Sarah Melnitsky is the President and Mrs. Rose Bobrovsky the Vice-President.

Congregation Kochob Jacob Anshey Kamenetz, Lite

חברה כוכב יעקב אנשי קאמינעץ, דליטא

65 EAST 3rd STREET

[English page 149]

<u>Kamenetzers in Israel</u>

"Yad Vashem" Martyrs' and Heroes' Memorial Authority

Ceremony of Perpetuating the Memory of The Community Kamenetz-Litovsk-Zastavye

by Hayim Nahman Bialik State School in Tel Aviv on October 30th, 1963

Mr. Gorion: Today's date has neither been marked in our calendar as a holiday nor as a remembrance-day. Nevertheless, we have interrupted the studies, and yesterday we asked you to come in holiday-dress today, and we are assembled here to adopt a destroyed Jewish community. We are celebrating he beginning of a great undertaking. It is a work you took upon yourselves – the work of collecting information about that destroyed community.

The fact that it was decided to interrupt the studies at this moment, and that this step was approved by the Ministry of Education, underlines the great importance which we attach to this matter. An additional proof of the importance of this morning's gathering is the presence of people occupying very important and responsible positions. They took leave of their work and came to us in order to participate in this morning's celebration. I shall mention, first of all, Mr. Gideon Hausner, whose speeches during Eichmann's trial were heard by all of you here at the school; Mr. Kubovy, Director of "Yad Vashem"; Mr. Bar-Tana, our inspector whom all of you know, and the townsmen of Kamenetz-Litovsk (that is the community adopted by us) who are sitting here with you.

The question is – "For what reason?" What is the purpose of our morning gathering? The answer is simple. It can be defined in one word: "Remember!" That is the inscription on the badge which you all put on today: "Remember what the Nazi Amalekite did unto you!"

We are fulfilling a precept from the Torah, and we had better remember what Dr. Hayim Weizmann, the first President of the State of Israel, had to say on this subject. He said: "Our people was endowed with a good memory, and it is thanks to that good memory that our people exists. Other nations, which could not withstand the stress and strain of great suffering and forgot their homelands, disappeared and ceased to exist – but our people lives on. Thus we remember. We remember the Exodus from Egypt and the destruction of Jerusalem, and the heroes of Massada and a great many chapters of our long history.

Now, it is our duty to remember the Victims of the Holocaust – but to remember means to learn. There is no remembering without learning. However, we shall be unable to learn about all the destroyed communities. Upon the initiative of our friend, Mr. Aloni, we have chosen one community. We shall make a study of this community which until the outbreak of the Second World War was pulsating with life, hard work, happiness and a Halutzic (pioneering) spirit. Her sons settled in the Land of Israel. Many of them had always been under the spell of Zion and hoped to come there someday. This community was destroyed, just like many other communities were. It no longer exists. But it is in our power to bring it to life again by means of learning about it from the community's sons and daughters in Israel, some of whom are sitting with us right here. We shall hear them speak, learn from them, record their stories and summarize them. As the Holocaust and Heroism Remembrance Day approaches, we have taken upon ourselves the publishing of this summary in the form of a brochure.

Pupils, we are greatly honoured by the presence of such distinguished guests here. We now wish to avail ourselves of the opportunity to learn from them, from Mr. Hausner, from Mr. Kubovy and from Mr. Bar-Tana. They are familiar with the task which I presented to them. We shall be happy to listen to the words of instruction and advise which will direct us in this sacred task. We shall also listen to the words of the sons of this community, who today will begin to tell us their story. But we shall turn to them time and again and draw more and more information from them. And today, we shall all, willingly and gratefully, listen to their narratives.

"Fortunate is the match that was consumed after it had kindled the blaze
Fortunate is the blaze that burned in the recesses of the hearts
Fortunate are the hearts that knew how to stop beating and did it honourably
Fortunate is the match that was consumed after it had kindled the blaze". (Hana Senesh)
"Keep not thou silence O God: hold not thy peace and be not still O God.
For, lo, thine enemies make a tumult: and they that hate thee have lifted up the head.

They have taken crafty counsel against thy people, and consulted against thy hidden ones.
They have said, come and let us cut them off from being a nation: that the name of Israel
may be no more in remembrance.
For they have consulted together with one consent: they are confederate against thee."

(Psalm 83)

"Lift up thyself, thou judge of the earth: render a reward to the proud.
Lord, how long shall the wicked, how long shall the wicked triumph?
They break in pieces thy people 0 Lord, and afflict thy heritage.
They slay the widow and the strange and murder the fatherless."

(Psalm 94)

Mr. Bar-Tana: Dear townsmen of Kamenetz-Litovsk, dear pupils. With awe and respect, with pounding heart, faithful to the words of the lamenting poet "I shall remember…", we today commemorate the holy and splendid Jewish communities or, alien soil, which for milleniums and centuries were like ships driven by storm on wrathful waves till the savage oppressor exterminated them so that hardly anyone from them remained alive.

Dear children Today, in your presence, we shall commemorate the one million of our children, one million of pure, innocent Jewish children who were mercilessly put to death in Nazi Europe.

Setting out to the first exile, our ancestors commanded us to remember Jerusalem. "If I forget thee Jerusalem, let my right hand forget her cunning". Perhaps if in the day's of the exile we had remembered Jerusalem better, the great catastrophes would not have struck us, and surely had we, throughout the entire period of the Diaspora, always remembered the great catastrophes, we would not have been overtaken by the last, terrible disaster.

Let us, therefore, remember that our fortress is Israel and Jerusalem and, consequently, let us be stronger, better and more clever, so that we might be better able to withstand any storm threatening us; today we shall remember the martyred communities and among them the community of Kamenetz-Litovsk, the Lithuanian Kamenetz.

The Ministry of Education is sending its blessing to the project and to your participation in it.

Mr. Gorion: Children, as you all know, Mr. Aloni is the living spirit of this entire project. For this reason I requested that he be the chairman of this morning's ceremony… Mr. Aloni.

Mr. Aloni: Dear Mr. Hausner. The number of your friends in the entire world, in the entire Jewish diaspora exceeds twelve millions; this in addition to the six millions you represented at the trial. Your faithful friends, the pupils of the Bialik School had listened to you at the time of the trial, and they are very happy, indeed, as we all are, to have you here with us today. Mr. Gideon Hausner is the initiator of the idea that schools should perpetuate the memory of the communities, which once existed and are no more. For a long time he devoted his attention to this matter. He took it up with institutions, with important people and with directors of schools.

We are the first who have attained the honour of perpetuating the memory of the town Kamenetz-Litovsk-Zastavye, a community that existed for about five hundred years, was destroyed and does not exist more. It is with great honour that we welcome you, Mr. Gideon Hausner and Dr. Kubovy and we shall listen attentively, in an atmosphere of particularly great solemnity, to your address to the pupils of our school.

Mr. Gideon Hausner: Mr. Aloni, Dr. Kubovy, Principal of the School, children.

In the life of a nation there are generations, during which nothing seems to happen. Years of relative tranquillity pass by, layers of time accumulate successively one upon another and one generation follows another.

And it happens that the Lord of History concentrates all at once, in one generation, the powers of creation – and the powers of destruction, suffering and hope, anguish, torment and hopeful expectations. And only after some time has elapsed is it possible to say that it was a wonderful, unique generation – a generation which gained one of History's great prizes. The Principal of the School recalled the Exodus from Egypt; it was a generation when great slavery was interlaced with hopes of freedom. And the nation, during the course of its entire existence, from then on, carries with it the memory of that great event.

I believe that we are such a Generation. Two events the like of which had never before occurred in the history of the People of Israel, took place within our life-span, in this generation. A terrible catastrophe, that even we, a nation whose experience is full of sufferings, and whose history has from the beginning been drenched in blood, had never known – and a renaissance that no nation or language has ever achieved after its destruction. Our generation must prove itself equal to the task. This does not depend on us, but has been imposed upon us. We were born in those years and we have to carry out the orders of the Lord of History.

We already take for granted the existence of the State, but when I was a pupil in the 8th Grade, right here in Tel-Aviv, Jewish independence seemed a distant dream, and this was not such a long time ago…

The great catastrophe which befell us in the Diaspora was perhaps the root from which the tree has grown up. And it so happened that some time had to elapse before many of us dared to take a look at that vale of tears, to study it, to form a judgment on it and to relive it.

Perhaps it was not sheer coincidence that the trial of Eichmann was held after the State had become firmly entrenched and its foundations had been strengthened. As it is written in the Bible: "After the Lord had given rest unto Israel from all their enemies round about…" – Only then, many years after the event, the Lord told Saul, "Remember what the Amalekite did unto you." There had been earlier possibilities, many centuries of Israelite presence in the Land of Israel passed, but not till the country's foundations had become stronger were the People of Israel ordered to remember.

And we, too, after we had to some extent established ourselves, again devote our thoughts to what had been and is no more. We do it not only to remember, not only to pay a debt of honour – though that too is a precious thing – but we do it primarily for our own sake, so that we may know where we came from, who were our fathers and forefathers, how they lived, what they created and what they brought here with them.

We shall see the continuation of the communities, alive, active and making fertile the Land of Israel with thought, culture and creative work. And we shall be better Jews and better Israelis if we gain knowledge about our ancestors and know where our roots lay. Our tree will grow and bear fruit, for we shall know how to strike the roots deeper, and, perhaps, we need the perished communities more than they need us, because we descend from them, and they are the source.

For us this will not be a day of mourning or a day of sorrow. We shall remember with a shudder and holy reverence but also with the hope that we may be able to follow in their footsteps. The oppressor intended to wipe out the People of Israel and their memory, and this satanic undertaking encompassed a whole continent; the forces were tremendous. Never before in the history of Mankind has there been such an example of the might of evil. These forces outraged the West and the East. Hitler attacked the Western powers and Soviet Russia at the same time. He smashed them at first and penetrated deep into their territories.

He struck on the left and on the right and it seemed that nothing could withstand him. And the Jewish People were in his hand, defenceless, armless, without an army, with much faith in their hearts – and with nothing more. A scheme was hatched to annihilate them to the last man, to the last child. And they were persecuted with wrath. perished and are no more. The name of the oppressor was covered with shame and dreadful disgrace. His scheme was foiled and we are alive. That is the historic vengeance of the Jewish People. Therefore, conscious of the great task imposed upon us by History, we shall remember pridefully and joyfully.

I wanted to recount to you briefly an event or two. In the ghettoes, beset by fear and misery, two longings existed. One that someone should remain alive to tell what had happened, and the second one – to record. A fever of taking notes seized them. There were youth organizations which 6 volunteered to bring every piece of information, every note, the memory of every event, to those who were collecting the records. They tell us what happened on a certain day in a certain street, what took place in some cellar, where a search had been carried out, what did the Jews say, even jocular remarks – and they knew how to laugh even then. All this was taken down. And the children wrote: "I shall carry on, even if this will be my last deed, to hide the notes well, so that in the future the Jews will be able to read them and to know what happened."

And behold, those concealed documents were discovered and revealed to us. We have found a treasure of culture, hope, pain and sufferings. With us here is the man who is in charge of all these hidden treasures, Dr. Kubovy, Director of the Institution which gathers all this great heritage. He and his assistants, some of whom are here with us, will pass on these records to us and to the children of Israel and the life of the communities will continue within us.

The Jews of Kamenetz-Litovsk are no more. We are unable to return them to life. But we can erect a monument to them in our hearts, here, within the walls of this building. Here we shall learn about them, we shall talk and write compositions about them, we shall hang their pictures on our walls. We shall keep their records in our book-cases. And neighbouring schools will take care of nearby or distant communities. In this way, the diaspora, which exists no more, will perhaps in the near future not only continue its spiritual existence in us, its continuators, but will go on living in the hearts of the children of Israel. We shall bring the communities to us, to our schools. We shall study them and from this study and knowledge of the facts we shall love and respect them, and thus we shall gain self-respect and appreciate justly the path we are taking.

The pupil Carmela: In the presence of teachers and pupils in Israel, we commune with the memory of six millions of our people who were led to slaughter and perished at the hands of the Nazis and their helpers. We commune with the memory of communities, and Jewish homes which perished as a result of the wicked scheme to wipe out the name of Israel and its culture from under the sun.

We remember reverently the courage of our brethren who, together with their people, sacrificed their lives in purity and holiness; we remember the glorious struggle of the besieged Ghettoes and of fighters who rose up and kindled the fire of rebellion to save their nation's honour. We remember the wonderful and persevering struggle of the Jewish masses to uphold their human image and the Jewish culture. We remember the Just of the Nations who endangered their own lives to rescue Jews.

The Pupil Aviva: Remember, O God, the souls of our people, the Children of Israel, victims of the Disaster and its heroes, the souls of six millions Jews who were put to death, gassed and buried alive; and the Holy Communities which perished for the sake of "Kiddush Hashem" (Sanctification of the Holy Name).

May God remember their sacrifice together with the sacrifices of other martyrs and heroes of Israel in the past, and may He grant eternal life to their souls.

"They were lovely and pleasant in their lives, and in their death they were not divided. May they rest in peace".

Mr. Aloni: In the name of the Organization of Kamenetz-Jews in Israel, the Director of the School is honoured with kindling one of the six candles.

Rabbi Zadok is requested to kindle the second candle.

Mr. Simha Dubiner, Chairman of the Organization of Kamenetz-Jews in Israel, is requested to kindle the third candle.

Leah Bobrovsky-Aloni is requested to kindle the fourth candle.

Mr. Pinhas Ravi, Secretary of the Organization is requested to kindle the sixth candle.

We shall now hear the words of Dr. Kubovy, Chairman of "Yad Vashem" who has accomplished great and wonderful work for the perpetuation of the memory of the millions who once were and are no longer.

Dr. Kubovy: There is a verse in Psalms CII which depicts accurately the terrible fate which befell our nation in Europe during the period of Destruction and Heroism. It says: "For my days are consumed like smoke and my bones are burned as an hearth". An entire people went up in flames because there had risen an enemy who decided to wipe out the name of Israel from, under the sun.

What are we doing at "Yad Vashem" and what are you doing by starting to work on your project today? We are trying to thwart the enemy's intention. We are trying – you and we – not to let him fulfil his design.

How is it possible? Is such talk realistic? Can we bring back to life a murdered people? It certainly is not in our power to cover the dry bones – which no longer exist – with flesh and sinews, but we can – as has already been said today – guard their memory. We can maintain their image, we can revive the values and principles for the sake of which they died. We can learn to understand their mode of living which was admirable.

How to do this? How shall we approach this understanding? In what spirit shall we study the past of that little, not too well known town? You did well not to have chosen one of the large communities, because there is much to be learned from the features of this townlet, that are so characteristic of the mode of living of a large part of European Jewry. How shall we do this? In what spirit shall we approach the problem?

The great poet, after whom this school was named, will be our guide.

The same Hayim Nahman Bialik wrote with anger, with sorrow and with pain the most reproachful verses about the Jews who did not defend themselves:

"And there is no sense to your death
As there is no sense to your life
And very great is the pain
And very great is the shame".

The same Hayim Nahman Bialik, found beautiful words, precious words to speak about those Jews who, when there was no escape from death, received the inevitable with honour; and you all know the poem:

"If your soul desires to know the source from which your brethren, put to death, drew such courage in the days of evil such strength of their souls comfort from their belief in God, and self-assurance power, patience and iron-strength…"

Bialik attributed all these wonderful qualities to people who had been put to death, who had not fought with arms but who had known one thing: how to die and how to live a life of justice, culture and charity, to the end. He knew how to distinguish between two kinds of heroism – heroism in the use of arms and heroism in attitude, between heroism in applying force and heroism which expressed itself in receiving with honour the sentence of death and suffering.

When we begin to study the history of a small Jewish town, we must remember that this presents difficulties to those born in Israel. The notions and attitudes of most of the European Jewry are strange to them, even though their parents and Grandparents were very familiar with those notions. The majority of Europe's Jews, for example, did not rely upon force, since the Jews were a negligible minority, and did not believe that force could protect them. They also despised force. Although there were numerous manifestations of heroism during the uprisings in the ghettoes and camps, we must understand that facet of their life which was based upon ethics, and upon belief in God. Only when we have understood their attitude toward life, which was quite different from that of a people living on its own soil – only then will the great miracle of communication take place.

That is why we do not say "Disaster". We say "Disaster and Heroism" because they are interwoven. In this manner we must study the life of the little town, which you have decided to adopt, and to continually understand that those people were our own flesh and blood and – whether we want it or not – we are their descendents, and they deserve our respect and love. For unless we respect and love them, we cannot possibly respect ourselves. We are their sons and grandsons, and they are worthy of our respect and affection.

Mr. Goldberg Sarid: Children, distinguished guests. I shall digress a bit and say a few words. When I heard the recitation of the verses from the Psalms, I was reminded of a poem written by a medieval poet whose name was Rabbi David Meshulam:

"Do not keep silent and still
When my blood is crying out to you
Demand it from the hand of my oppressor Earth, do not cover it."

And in the following verse the poet gives us this description:

"The children are clinging convulsively to one another
The children are in the throes of agony
The parents are crying
They are crying and wailing."

The people of Kamenetz have to tell, you about their sisters and brothers who were your age; among them the sisters of the man before you.

The town Kamenetz, as Dr. Kubovy rightly said, was not a large Jewish center. It is a townlet, somewhere in Lithuania, that throughout most of its history, was attached to a Jewish "mother-city" Brest-Liovsk, one of the most important historic cities of Lithuania and Poland. Altogether there were four large cities and Jewish centres: Cracow, Brest, Lvov (Lemberg) and Lublin. Kamenetz was affiliated with Brest. Great Jewish men lived in Brest. A representative of the Jewish community was also a Rabbi in Cracow. It was no sheer coincidence that Rabbis from Brest usually moved to Cracow – the ancient Polish capital (as the representative, Rabbi Shalom Feibush etc.).

That townlet, a typical medieval little town had, according to its chroniclers, a romantic beginning. After the Tartar invasions, appeared Prince Vladimir the Philosopher, founder of the town Vladimir Volynski, which was also an important Jewish center. He climbed a hill and declared that a fortress destined to repulse the attacks of the Tartars would be erected there. He called the place "Album Ordi", and this Latin name, after it had been translated into the Polish Biala Wieza (White Tower), denoted the largest European forest which stretched for hundreds of miles.

Regarding its non-Jewish history that little town attained real greatness. The great period of its Jewish history starts only in the beginning of the 19th century. Its Gentile history tells us that Wladyslaw (Ladislaus) Jagiello, who brought about the union of Poland and Lithuania and became their king stayed at Kamenetz; it tells us about wars and quarrels between the Duke Witold and Jagiello for possession of this little town. The history also recounts that King Kazimierz (Casimir) IV used to visit the town in winter-time, just like Goering who went hunting in our forests.

Kamenetz was a crossroads, a meeting place between the north and the south, the west and the east. At that time here were no highways and railroads.

The history of the Jewish community becomes known to us from the beginning of the 16th century and it happened to be a Gentile who gave us information about Jews in the townlet. The name of that man who began to study the history of Lithuanian Jews was Worszecki. In his book, for the first time, we come across the name Kamenetz. But to our dismay the first information about the presence of Jews there, in the year 1525, relates to a restrictive measure which took away the taverns from the Jews and gave them to the Christians.

Later on we learn about the privileges conferred upon the Kamenetz Jews, in 1635, by King Jan Casimir who freed them from various taxes except the tax on alcoholic drinks. Then it seems as if a curtain had been drawn upon the townlet. We know nothing about this particular period. Nobody took pains to search for documents and none were found. We begin again to receive information on Kamenetz from the 18th century. By that time it had already become a large Jewish center from which a number of great men descended. The first one almost came to Palestine in 1803. Later on he established the foundations of geography of the Land of Israel; he was Menahem-Mendel of Kamenetz who in later years opened the "Kamenetz Hotel" in Jerusalem. Now let us refer to Dr. Kubovy who said, "it is these children's fortune that we possess excellent literature for youngsters – the writings of Yehezkel Kotik. They comprise a unique book of reminiscences, with a foreword by Sholem-Aleikhem himself; it is one of the wonderful books from which the children will be able to learn so much. It is not a collection of dry, historic documents but a thrilling, interesting story depicting a Jewish townlet and its customs.

In addition, we know other Jewish writers from Kamenetz. They are Natan Grinblatt and M. A. Zak. But real greatness came to Kamenetz close to its end, just as a candle whose light grows stronger before it dies out.

It came in the shape of the Great Yeshivah which spread the teachings of the Torah throughout all Poland's Jewry.

This little town exists no more. It was not so keen on guarding its medieval character as on preserving the positive values of the Middle Ages: internal organization, mutual help, medical assistance, religious schools, the custom of visiting the sick etc. This was a little town which retained the medieval structure of the religious community including all the elements of mutual help.

And finally I should like to conclude. I cannot, on this occasion, elaborate too much on this subject but I would like to say this. Let us draw a conclusion. Jews had lived in this townlet for over five hundred years. And their fate was so bitter that throughout the period of their settlement they did not acquire the citizens' rights to live, and the only right they did gain was to be murdered, killed and destroyed. This is the conclusion we ought to draw. There were communities that existed for nine hundred years; there were Jewish communities in Germany that existed for fifteen hundred years. But in spite of all this, the Gentiles said that the Jews had no right to live – only the right to die. From this we conclude. We have one right only – the right to live, just like everyone else, and there is only one land which assures us this – the Land of Israel and the State of Israel.

Teacher Leah Bobrovsky-Aloni: Dear pupils of the 8th Grade. Greetings to you all and to your friends. After an interruption of two years I am happy to meet you again at this gathering. This time I want to tell you how the children of my town, Kamenetz-Litovsk, and of its suburb Zastavye acquired knowledge and education.

The period I remember begins before World War I. Then, in the days of the Russian, Tsarist regime, a Russian state school existed in the town. We, Jewish children, were not accepted to this school. Our parents, of blessed memory, thought it their holy duty to provide education for their children. They took great pains to provide private teachers, graduates of high-schools and universities, and highly qualified Hebrew teachers for our town. We learned privately or in circles. Devotion to studies was great. The Bible, Hebrew and the Geography of Palestine were the favorite subjects. The Hebrew language was heard in the streets, to our parents' delight. But this situation did not last long. With the outbreak of World War I the town's cultural life was paralysed. Many teachers and parents were mobilized, either for army service or for compulsory work of erecting fortifications in the vicinity. Despite the numerous difficulties we continued to study with our own resources, with the help of text-books and we regarded our educational work as – very fruitful.

In 1916 there was a turning point in the cultural life of our town. The community, which was almost completely destroyed after the outbreak of the war, had not as yet reorganized itself. The only place serving public activities was one of the synagogues in town. After evening prayer the entire congregation discussed the affairs of the town and decisions were made on various subjects.

And so it happened that one evening, in the spring of 1916, the congregation decided to establish a Hebrew school where all the children form the town and from the suburb Zastavye would learn in a normal fashion. At the same gathering in the synagogue, three teachers (two women and one man) were chosen. I was one of them and my fellow teacher was Malca Polakevitch-Kurshansky, now residing in Mexico.

I worked in the above-mentioned school, in the capacity of teacher and pedagogue, for over three years. Even though, at that time, all of us were young teachers, we had no difficulties in regard to discipline. And this must be said in praise of the town's children. All of them had a very respectful attitude towards their school studies and followed instructions lovingly and willingly. Despite a shortage of textbooks, instruments, and financial means, the results of our work were good and encouraging.

After I had left my home town Kamenetz in order to come to Eretz-Israel, the work was carried on without interruption. Many youth organizations were formed, and some of their members underwent pioneer training (Hakhsharah) and settled in the Land of Israel – thus realizing their youthful dreams. The seeds sown at that time in Kamenetz sprouted here, in the revived Homeland.

Many fellow townsmen who managed to come to the Land of Israel are scattered all over the country – in kibbutzim, villages and towns.

They are all faithful citizens working in all fields of constructive work.

Dear children, blessing will come upon you for perpetuating the memory of my fellow townsmen.

Pinhas Rabinovich-Rabi: In our native town Kamenetz and Zastavye, there existed educational institutions and religious academies (Yeshivot) with thousands of scholars and rabbis who acquired their education there and who later spread the teachings of the Torah to many countries. This dear town, where many generations led an active life, based on the teachings of the Law and on charity, was completely destroyed by the accursed Nazis. Kamenetz and Zastave were wiped off. Old and young, women and children were murdered and burned in the crematories. The houses were set on fire and razed to the ground. The tombstones in the cemeteries were smashed and used for pavements. The Jewish community of Kamenetz-Zastavye was uprooted and perished with no remnant to remind of its existence.

Already 133 years ago, one of the first settlers in Palestine, Menahem Mendel from Kamenetz, left the town together with his family, and, braving mortal perils, made his way in a sailboat to the Land of Israel. He composed the Hebrew book "Korot Haetim" which served as the first useful guide to the immigrants who followed him. He also opened the first hotel for guests and newcomers in Jerusalem. From Kamenetz came Rabbi Zanvil Maccabi, called the Preacher from Kamenetz, who thrilled and inspired the Jewish masses in the lands of the Diaspora with his great sermons on the love of Zion and the redemption of Israel.

Rabbi Mohilever of blessed memory wrote about him: "With his fiery speeches he kindled in the hearts of the Children of Israel a love for their people, for their religion, for their land and for their heritage".

You have already been told about the writer Kotik. In Zastavye, which was a little suburb of Kamenetz, there lived a writer Falik Zolf who in several books depicted Jewish life in tiny Zastavye, its synagogues, its scholars and righteous men.

The great Gaon, Rabbi Barukh Baer was Head of the Kamenetz Yeshivah, "Knesseth Beit Itshak". Mr. Shmuel Warshaw, one of the Yeshivah-students who perished during the war catastrophe thus described the Yeshivah: "Even while you are standing outside the building you hear the voice of the Torah, bursting out vigorously from behind the high walls of the Yeshivah. When you enter you are greatly impressed by the passion and zeal of the students who became one body. Here the tradition of generations is being united. Here is the source which quenches their thirst, the words of Rabbi Hayim. Here the agitated emotions of the pure Jewish soul are flowing in a powerful, steady current. Youngsters from the entire Diaspora are in the Kamenetz Yeshivah. Students from Poland, the United States, Germany, Belgium, Denmark. Switzerland, Hungary and also from Palestine. How serious they all appear. Their eyes burning, they are immersed in the study of the Law and see it as their destiny.

My late father, Rav Moshe Itshak, of blessed memory, was active as rabbi in Kamenetz for twenty nine years. In the little wooden synagogue he studied all his life and prayed for peace and redemption for his people.

Before his death, he remarked that he had learned the six Talmudic Orders (Sha"s) 49 times over and over again. During the long winter nights when I woke up at midnight, I would see him pacing to and fro while he memorized the Talmudic chapters by heart.

The sons of Kamenetz and Zastavye, scattered in the Lands of the Diaspora and in Israel will, for the generations to come, revere and remember the martyrs and everything that was created by this beloved congregation that was beautiful and sublime.

Today, dear pupils, you are our partners in this sacred undertaking – the perpetuation of the memory of Kamenetz and Zastavye.

Dear pupils. You who were fortunate to have been born in Israel and who live here in our independent State, who are studying and progressing in an atmosphere of free Hebrew culture – you will have to face tests and problems that will require courage and devotion to the ideals of our new era. If you will draw from the deep sources of the past, from the history of Jewish Kamenetz and Zastavye and of thousands communities in the Diaspora that were destroyed by the cruel murderers, the accursed Nazis – you will know how to live and progress as proud Israeli citizens. You will know how to faithfully bear, as Jews, the burden of duties and obligations you owe to your people and to the State.

Mrs. Haya Krakovsky-Karabelnik: Honourable guests, dear children. You have heard an outline of the history of Kamenetz and Zastavye from the teacher Arieh Goldberg Sarid. I should like to add a few words concerning the last period in the life of our town, before its destruction, and about our fellow townsmen in Israel and in the lands of the Diaspora.

Before the Catastrophe thousands of Jews lived in our town. It was famous throughout the entire vicinity as a town steeped in the vision of the redemption and yearnings for Zion. Mr. Ya'acov Nir, the regional inspector, and native of Svislotsk, quite far from Kamenetz, bears witness to this fact.

I remember you, my little town, where I was born and spent the days of my childhood. I remember the Jews who lived there, within your limits, the various youth organizations, which instilled the pioneering spirit in the hearts of their members and prepared them for immigration to the Land of Israel. I remember the children's library, to which I dedicated much of my time and I remember the little houses pulsating with Jewish life. In almost every one of them was a Jewish National Fund box.

Every year, we regularly meet to commemorate our martyrs – our parents, brothers, sisters, old people and young children who were alive and are no more. Even their graves are unknown to us.

Some years ago we, the fellow townsmen from Kamenetz and Zastavye, formed our organizations in Israel and in the lands of the Diaspora.

Today, after the years of the Catastrophe, there remain four hundred of us, who have established our own families. About 120 persons live in Israel and over 300 are scattered all over the world. Practically all of them left our town before the Disaster. Only ten persons survived the horrors of that period. About a year ago, in the United States, I met many of our fellow townsmen from New-York and I attended several meetings organized by them. Those present decided to respond favourable to the proposal put forward by the Organizing Committee of the Kamenetz Jews in Israel and to participate, together with us, in the publication of the Memorial Book consecrated to the communities of Kamenetz-Litovsk and Zastavye. For this purpose they have already collected a fund to ensure the financing of the printing of the book in Israel. After we had informed our organization in the United States of the favourable response of the Ministry of Culture and Education and of the Management of the Hayim Nahman Bialik State School to the project of perpetuating the memory of the martyrs of our town, we were requested, by cable, to convey to you, at this gathering, the following message: "Please convey our profound emotion. We are moved to tears by the great news that the famous Bialik State School perpetuates the memory of the martyrs of our town Kamenetz-Litovsk and Zastavye. Thank you. Receive our blessings. Signed: On behalf of the Directing Board of the Organization – Abraham Shudroff."

In their name and in the name of our Organization in Israel be blessed forever!

The pupil Tsiporah: In the name of the pupils of the 8th Grade and in the name of all pupils of Bialik School I do solemnly declare that we are ready to take upon ourselves the holy task of perpetuating the memory of the community of Kamenetz-Litovsk and Zastavye. We shall try to do our utmost to remember the live image of the community as it existed until the Disaster, and the image of its martyrs, and also those who participated in the heroic struggle against the cruel enemy. We are proud of the honour bestowed upon us, namely that we, pupils of Bialik School, shall be the first to take part in this important undertaking and let us hope that our work will be crowned will success and be taken up by other schools all over the country.

Mr. Dubiner: Honourable assembly!

With deep awe and reverence we stand before you, educators and children of Israel. Together with you we have commemorated our brothers and sisters from Kamenetz-Litovsk and Zastavye who were murdered twenty-two years ago by the heinous, accursed Nazis. These martyrs, whom we commemorate today were greatly learned in the Law, steeped in culture and faithful to Zion. At first they sent their sons and daughters (over 100 young people) to participate in the rebuilding of the Land of Israel and to build a connecting bridge for those who were to follow them.

One of us even spent ten years with you, in this school, which bears the name of our greatest poet, the poet of resurrection Hayim Nahman Bialik. Everyone received with great respect and deep emotion the perpetuation project, which you have announced during this impressive gathering. On behalf of the Kamenetz organizations in the countries of the Diaspora, I thank you from the bottom of my heart for this activity and express our best wishes to all of you.

Mrs. Lily Seitmann: Honoured guests and dear pupils. Today's assembly is a very special occasion. This gathering evokes profound anxiety in our hearts. Millions of eyes, which will never open again, the eyes of the murdered Children of Israel, of our hallowed, martyred brethren are looking, at you, Israeli boys and girls, and they are crying out one mute question: "Shall you remember?". You have been entrusted with a sacred task today. An honourable and difficult task – to create a permanent bridge between you, young children of Israel, and the Jewish People of numerous communities which no longer exist. Thousands of Jewish communities, which had been scattered throughout the countries of the Diaspora, and had pulsated with love of the Torah, love for their people, are waiting to be redeemed and resurrected. They implore us: "Do not forget us, recall our memory! Let us tell about the life that sparkled amongst us." This redemption will come to them from you – from the thousands of boys and girls in Israel. You shall revive the memory of the missing. You shall tell the tale of their sufferings and of their silent heroism in the face of beastly, cruel hatred – a hatred which Satan himself had never before created. Let us not forget that from the ashes of the six millions burst forth the proud flame which became the State of Israel. Because in spite of all of our enemies who have set out to annihilate us, the People of Israel lives on. But we and they constitute one body and one soul and their soul must live forever.

You are the first to start the great undertaking – the undertaking of perpetuation. There is no clear path as yet, how to do it. But the way will be discovered through devotion and love of the idea. Representatives of the Kamenetz community in Israel and in the Diaspora will keep in touch with you and will provide information, recollections and stories about the community whose memory you must perpetuate. Great honour has been bestowed upon you and upon the entire Bialik School, in being the first to be entrusted with such a task. We shall fulfil it with humility and reverence.

What about the future?

It was decided, under the auspices of the Management of "Yad Vashem", Martyrs' and Heroes' Memorial Authority, and, under the guidance of Attorney Gideon Hausner and with the kind agreement of the School Director, Mr. Moshe Gorion, to create strong ties between the H. N. Bialik School and the townsmen of Kamenetz Litovsk-Zastavye in Israel and in the Diaspora.

The pupils should aim toward gathering the facts, data and dates relating to the history of the community, its personalities, rabbis, writers, youth organizations, communal workers and, in particular, information about the last twenty years before the catastrophe.

The pupils of the 7th and 8th Grades, participating in the project will write compositions on the theme "The Disaster and the Heroism in Israel and the Perpetuation of the Memory of the Destroyed Communities". The compositions will be published in the School Newspaper "Benetiv Hageulah" (The Road to Redemption) and partly in the Memorial Book that is about to be published.

In order to fulfil this purpose pupils will visit the homes of persons from Kamenetz who live in Tel-Aviv and its surroundings, and will exchange letters with the sons of the community who live in villages and kibbutzim, in order to acquire additional knowledge and facts about the life of the community that perished.

The pupils will begin corresponding with the three hundred families who originate from Kamenetz Litovsk-Zastavye and who reside in the United States, Mexico, Argentine, Poland etc. In school they will be hosts to tourists, new immigrants, and the townsmen of Kamenetz-Litovsk and chat with them.

The Organizing Committee of the Community will set up in the school a special book-case which will include the "Disaster and Heroism Library for Perpetuating the Memory of the Community Destroyed by the Nazis in the Years 1941-43." Till now books published by "Yad Vashem" have been delivered.

Let us hope that the Hayim Nahman Bialik State School in Tel-Aviv, which initiated the "Remember" movement, will not remain alone in perpetuating the memory of the communities which perished in the Disaster years.   **Dov Aloni**

[English page 175]

My Journey to Kamenetz in 1965

by Dov (Bertschik) Schmidt

In the summer of 1965, I was notified that I would be allowed to participate in a seminar on fishing which was to be held in the Soviet Union. My first thought following the news was that I would visit Dora Galperin, and then make a pilgrimage to my parents' and forefathers' graves in my hometown Kamenetz. Dora, whom I knew from early childhood, survived the war in Kamenetz and lives in Poland now. From her I expected to hear the whole terrible story of the catastrophe that befell the Jews of Kamenetz.

Although I knew that no remnants and no traces of their graves exist, I felt the urge to see it with my own eyes. After applying for a special visa at the Embassy of the Soviet Union, I was allowed to visit Brest and to receive there permission to travel to Kamenetz. I decided that on my way to the Soviet Union I would spend three days in Poland to visit Dora and to hear her personal account of the Disaster.

My hometown Kamenetz on September 20th, 1965

Kamenetz is in the Soviet Union now. It is situated close to the present Russian-Polish frontier which runs in a distance of five miles from the town, in the direction of Bialowieza, and cuts across the Bialowieza Forest.

At the edge of the Forest, in the village of Kamienyoki, the Soviets built a hunting centre, with hunting lodges and hotels, which serve the Soviet leaders who come there to hunt in the summer days. Kamenetz provides the necessary supplies for this center. Therefore, the town is barred to tourists, and those who do not live there need a special permit to travel from Brest to Kamenetz.

I explained to a N.K.V.D. official in Brest that the only reason I cared to make the trip from Israel to the Soviet Union was to visit my birth-place; thereupon I received a permit to stay in Kamenetz for five hours. That is how, on September 20th, 1965, I left Brest in a taxi and set out for Kamenetz. I was accompanied by Clara Sapir, a native of Kamenetz, Misha Serba, a, native of Brest, and a Jewish student from Bobruysk, whose acquaintance I made in Brest. The road which leads through Ciechanowczyce is wide and covered with asphalt. On my way I stopped at Ciechanowczyce, which I knew from the many trips I used to make from Kamenetz to Brest. Rahel Leah's inn is still standing and so are all the Jewish houses – only the Jews are in their houses no longer. In fact, nothing seems to have changed there, except the asphalt road. The wooden houses with thatched roofs looked as low and humble as ever and peasants with bored looks could be seen in the houses' backyards. I noticed only few changes in the villages adjoining the highway, but near Vidomla and Branka I saw tractor stations and collective farms ("Kolkhozes"). Here and there appeared chimneyed buildings. Those, I was told, were plants for agricultural products. At noon I arrived in Kamenetz from the direction of "Odalina". I could not recognize the entrance to the town and the Brest Street, which is much longer and runs alongside the main highway.

The windmills which used to greet you at the entrance to Kamenetz exist no longer. Residential houses, three stories tall, were built in their place and they occupy the entire length of the street. Only the mill of Shostokovsky has remained.

There is no trace of the Jewish cemetery in Brest Street. There, where once was the Catholic priest's courtyard, now stands a four-storied Government building, surrounded by a large square. Lenin's statue was erected in front of the building. On the place once occupied by Geier's house, the Soviets built a three stories high "Gum" Store, a kind of state-run supermarket.

The old Catholic church and the Municipality disappeared. They gave place to a spacious bus station provided with a large restaurant and good conveniences. Till then I found it difficult to reconstruct in my mind the image of Kamenetz I had cherished so long. Only when I got to the market place ("Rynek") I recognized a familiar sight and I knew I arrived in Kamenetz. But this was merely the outward, physical appearance of my hometown. Its living spirit was not there anymore.

My Kamenetz

The market square did not look the same either. A garden was planted in place of the shops and in its center stands a monument commemorating the Red Army soldiers who fell in the Second World War. The houses round the square, however, are all standing as they did once, as if I had returned to Kamenetz after a day's absence and as if nothing had happened in the meantime. The house of the ritual slaughterer (shochet) Reb Itshak, the houses of Halperin and Vigotov, the pharmacy and the Russian Orthodox church are still there. So are the houses of the religious Judge, of Shmuel Golobchick and David Rosenstock. Only Hayim Shayke and Hana Bobro are missing on the sidewalks; only the Jews are missing in their houses and Jewish children are not playing in the streets.

All the lanes and streets adjoining Kobrynska Street, with their wooden houses sustained no damage and were untouched by the Disaster.

Brest Street is now an asphalt road, leading to Bialostocka, through Zastavye to Kamienicki. But the other streets are paved with the same old cobblestones. The sidewalks are old and decrepit, the house-fronts unchanged. Only the front-porches disappeared.

I paid a short visit in Yuzek Grigorevsky's house. Yuzek had saved Dora by hiding her in various places. He did it endangering his own life and the life of his own family. When we met, Yuzek was even more moved than I. All the time he kept on repeating: "They murdered everybody and I could save only one with difficulty! Not a single one of 'you' remained!"

The Great Synagogue (Der Mayer) together with the Talmud-Torah were converted into a factory. The remnants of the ancient fortress ("Slup") were reconstructed and a museum consecrated to the history of the Bialowieza Forest and the antiquities of the region was set up. The adjoining houses were pulled down and gave their place to a parking lot and to a square which surrounds the museum.

I carried on my way, wandered in the narrow lanes, glanced at the windows of the houses I had known in the past, and just could not accept the fact that everything was left standing, but that life itself had been uprooted. It seemed to me that all the strangers did not realize what had happened there – or did not want to remind themselves of it. Either they lent their helping hands to the murderers or their consciences bothered them, because they did not lift up a finger to help the victims and only wanted to seize the inheritance of their Jewish neighbours.

The people I came across in the streets, in the supermarket, and in the stores, looked at me with curiosity at first, believing I was a tourist who had come there by mistake. However, upon learning I was a Jew, a native of the town, their attitude changed. Immediately, they seemed shocked and stepped aside, In the eyes of many of them I saw an expression of bad conscience, as if they were reminded of something unpleasant, as if I had brought them a message from the world of eternal truth. While I was walking in the streets in the company of Yuzek, people sometimes asked him: "Who's that man?" And he kept replying: "Don't you remember the son of Hayim. Schmidt?" Following his reply people reacted in various ways. One said: "Is that the truth?" Another one distorted his face as if this had reminded him of something bad. A third one expressed pity and uttered a loud "Bozhe Moy" (My God).

I shall never forget the only person who received me with tears during my visit to Kamenetz. While I was walking in Litevska Street with Yuzek's children, an old Christian woman went out from the yard of the house opposite Yuzek's and asked me: "Aren't you the son of Hayim Schmidt, the butcher?" When I said "Yes, that's right", she burst out in tears and flung herself at me to kiss me.

The woman wailed loudly: "How the wild beasts murdered you! Why was your fate so bitter! Your father and mother and all your family were good, upright people! Why did they murder you! Have any Jews from Kamenetz remained in the world?" So this simple, honest Christian woman lamented and cried together with me.

I also went to my house where I was born and lived for 19 years, I knocked softly on the door and opened it even before I heard an answer. An old woman went out of the second room which had been my parents' bedroom. Tears choked me. I felt paralysed and unable to utter a word. Apparently, the woman understood my feelings and she began whispering, as if she were talking to herself:

"Yes, I knew the owners of this house, Hayim and Rahel and their children and grandchildren. They were good people and did only favours to others. The Nazi beasts murdered them! I thought no one of you was left. Oh, my God, is it our fault if the authorities allocated the houses?"

I could stand it no longer… Dazed and heart-broken I went out and saw two children in white shirts playing in the yard of my house. Seeing me and my camera they asked me to photograph them. I took their picture, with my parents' house in the background… That was the only souvenir left.

For another hour I wandered in the Kobrynska Street, and the adjoining lanes, near the houses of my sister, my friends and acquaintances.

I calmed down, gathered strength and was bold enough to enter the Government House. Perhaps I could obtain some official information on the period of the catastrophe which befell my townlet.

Effacing the Memory and the Past

I entered the Secretariat and turned to the Soviet official who was sitting at the table. I told him about the purpose of my coming from Israel and about my desire to hear from him something about the fate of the 500 Jewish families, among whom were my parents, sister, uncles and aunts, who perished with other inhabitants of the town.

With marked coolness and reserve the trim official responded: "Citizen! You can see all there is, and what happened here in the past does not concern us anymore. You are allowed to see, to look around and to receive your own impressions. That is all."

With these curt, dry and smooth words, the representative of the regime of liberation effaced the past centuries, the ways of life of many generations – the entire Jewish small town! I left the Soviet Government office. It was five o'clock in the afternoon. The validity of my permit to stay in Kamenetz had expired. Feeling dizzy I entered the taxi, and without turning my head I said to the driver: "Go straight ahead!"

The life had been smothered and the stones are valueless. But I shall remember! We shall remember and tell the story to the generations to come!

I felt as if I were returning from a funeral. The funeral of my parents, my sisters, my uncles and aunts, my friends and acquaintances and all the Jews who had lived in Kamenetz, my home-town.

[English page 182]

Our Heritage

by Samuel Lipchick (New York)

Yes, Polish Jewry was the crown of the Jewish people, and our little Kamenetz-Litovsk, a shining gem in that brilliant crown. We had our own cultural and benevolent institutions and movements, synagogues and Hebrew schools,organizations and youth clubs, we had our own capable leaders and instructors, and, as I have already stated, our families were among the most recognized and cherished.

But all this altered with the coming of the Second World War, in the "night of the long blade". The black Nazi regime wrought upon us the worst destruction in our history, exterminating one third of our people, and all our achievements through the countless generations.

As one who has been fortunate enough to come to America, and thus avoid the tragic ending that befell the rest of our family, I feel it my duty to tell you about them, and inform you that you are their spiritual and moral inheritors.

You may have to answer our enemies that often ask: Why did your Polish cousins allow themselves to be led, passively, to their death, as do sheep? Why did they not fight to defend themselves?

Our nation is a nation of giants, and, even during the Nazi occupation, they showed unmatched courage and heroism; they fought in ghettos and concentration camps, they were partisans in the woods and forests and so took revenge. They fought in the armies of the Allies until victory was won.

The Jews were mostly from Poland, and among them those from Kamenetz-Litovsk.

It is understood that Israel needed, and still needs help from the Jews in the world. There was a vast desert, where cities had to be built to accommodate millions of Jews, displaced persons from Europe and other countries of exile. This can only be accomplished by our help.

No one will help us if we don't attempt to help ourselves. "If I am not myself, who will be for me, and if not now, then when?"

Kamenetz-Litovsk exists no longer as a Jewish town. All the Jews are gone. Our friends now reside in Israel and everywhere in the world. The memories in this book are all that remains of our "old country".

This is our heritage for the generations to come.

[English page 184]

To Their Memory

With deep emotion, we are setting our hands to the sacred undertaking – the publication of the Kamenetz Litovsk Memorial Book which will perpetuate the memory of the hallowed martyrs of our town.

WE SHALL NOT FORGET the simple people of our town, of the difficult burden of your everyday existence, means of living for their families.

WE SHALL NOT FORGET you, dear parents who, in spite who toiled in the sweat of their brows to obtain and despite the oppressive measures of the changing rulers of the town, spared neither efforts nor care to teach your children to perform good deeds. You sent your sons and daughters to the Land of Israel to build it and to build their home there. Large is your share in the establishment of the State of Israel, though the Nazi murderers prevented you from seeing it restored.

WE SHALL NOT FORGET our brothers and sisters and the pure, innocent souls of the children of the town who were led to slaughter.

WE SHALL NOT FORGET the teachers of our town, who despite difficult conditions took great pains to instil cultural values and knowledge among the youth and to prepare them for a life of work and creative toil in the restored homeland of our people.

WE SHALL NOT FORGET the many students of the Torah in our town and foremostly the Rabbis Reuven Burstein and Barukh Baer Leibovich who educated the young generations to live according to the precepts of the Law, to perform good deeds and to love the fellow-Jews.

WE SHALL NOT FORGET the community workers in Kamenetz who were driven by their concern for the welfare of the fellow townsmen and established charitable, cultural and social institutions.

WE SHALL NOT FORGET the youth organizations which in spite of the social and political differences existing among them, were faithful to their people and strove to come to the Land of Israel and to participate in the establishment and defence of the State.

We shall remember all of you!

Let us not pass over in silence over what the terrible Nazi Amalekite did to us!

This Memorial Book will provide historical documentation for the scientific researchers who will, in the course of time, explore the sources and will be able to learn about the characteristic features of the communities of Kamenetz-Litovsk and Zastavye that perished and will never rise again.

This book will serve as memorial candle and genealogical table to our sons and their descendants. From it they will gain knowledge about their forefathers, their origin, the circumstances in which they lived, worked and suffered in various periods. This book will tell them about the holocaust and the heroism, about the struggle against the savage Nazi beast and about the yearnings of the victims who longed, in the last moments of their lives, for a free life in Zion.

Let the future generations know about their origin and be proud of the deeds of their forefathers.

May their memory live forever.

Kamenets Necrology

[The Yizkor list from the book has been converted into a searchable, alphabetically arranged list of names.

A	B	C	D	E	F	G	H	I	J	K	L	M
N	O	P	Q	R	S	T	U	V	W	X	Y	Z

Surname	First Names	Maiden Name
ADLER	Josef	
AIZENSTEIN	Avraham Simcha	
AIZENSTEIN	Dvora Gitel	
AIZENSTEIN	Esther	
AIZENSTEIN	Gershon Moshe	
AIZENSTEIN	Mania	GELERSTEIN
AIZENSTEIN	Nechemia	
AIZENSTEIN	Nochim	
AIZENSTEIN	Reichel	
AIZNER	Blume	
AIZNER	Itche	
AIZNER	Sarah	
AIZNER	Zlata Bayle	
AKERMAN	Aharon	
AKERMAN	Chana -Gishes	
AKERMAN	Esther	
AKERMAN	Motel	
AKERMAN	Rivkah	
AKERMAN	Shalom	
ARONOVSKI	Baruch Leyb	
ARONOVSKI	Sirka (Baruch Leyb's wife)	GOLOVCHIK
ARONOVSKI	Bracha	TIMIANSKI
ARONOVSKI	Chava	
ARONOVSKI	Gitel	
ARONOVSKI	Leiba	
ARONOVSKI	Leiba	
ARONOVSKI	Matya	
ARONOVSKI	Moshe	
ARONOVSKI	Nache	
ARONOVSKI	Nissel	
ARONOVSKI	Shayna Chaya	
ARONOVSKI	Yehudit	
ARONOVSKI	Yehudit	MANDELBLAT

ARONOVSKI	Yudel	
ASHKENAZI	Bracha	
ASHKENAZI	Chaim Yitzchak	
ASHKENAZI	Ertche	
ASHKENAZI	Feige	
ASHKENAZI	Gitel	GRONET
ASHKENAZI	Iteh	
ASHKENAZI	Liptze (his wife)	SHOSTAKOVSKI
ASHKENAZI	Menche	
ASHKENAZI	Mirka	
ASHKENAZI	Toybe	
ASHKENAZI	Yakov - Ber	
ASHKENAZI	Yehoshua	
ASHKENAZI	Yitzchak Eizig	
BALGALAI	Chaya Sara	
BALGALAI	Modechai	
BALGALAI	Tuvia	
BAS	David	
BAS	Itzel	
BAS	Sara	
BASH	Avraham	
BASH	Blume	
BASH	David Shepsel	
BASH	Fraidl	SHOSTAKOVSKI
BASH	Leah	GRONET
BASH	Leah	
BASH	Yakov	
BASH	Zelig	
BECHZINSKI	Bayla Gitel	
BECHZINSKI	David	
BECHZINSKI	Itche	
BECHZINSKI	Raizel	
BECHZINSKI	Yakov	
BELFER	Sima	SAVITSKI
BELFER	Tzelya	
BERG	Eva	
BERG	Laibl	
BIALER	Alter	
BIALER	Chaim	
BIALER	Golda	

BIALER	Sara	
BIALER	Shaina Chaya	
BIALER	Shloime	
BIELKIN	Aharon	
BIELKIN	Bayla	
BIELKIN	Chana	
BIELKIN	Gitel	
BIELKIN	Itche - Leyb	
BIELKIN	Leah	
BIELKIN	Sara - Basha	
BIELKIN	Yona	
BILETSKI	Baruch Leyb	
BILETSKI	Bezalel	
BILETSKI	Chana	
BILETSKI	Chaya Sara	GORINSKI
BILETSKI	Laibl	
BILETSKI	Mordechai	
BILETSKI	Moshe	
BILETSKI	Naphtali	
BILETSKI	Rachel	
BILETSKI	Rachel	
BILETSKI	Sender	
BILETSKI	Shimon	
BILETSKI	Tzipa	
BIRMAN	Avraham	
BIRMAN	Esther	
BIRMAN	Raizel	RETEMPNITSKI
BLEICHBORD	Avraham - Shimon	
BLEICHBORD	Chaya	
BLEICHBORD	Leiba	
BLEICHBORD	Miriam - Rachel	
BLEICHBORD	Moshe	
BLEICHER	Bracha	
BLEICHER	Gedalya	
BLEICHER	Shaina (Gedalya's wife)	HAYAT
BLEICHER	Tzelya	
BOBROVSKI	Avraham	
BOBROVSKI	Babel	
BOBROVSKI	Beile	
BOBROVSKI	Esther	

BOBROVSKI	Leiba	
BOBROVSKI	Meir - Leyb	
BOBROVSKI	Mirme - Zlata	
BOBROVSKI	Mordechai	
BOBROVSKI	Moshe	
BOBROVSKI	Shmuel -Yossel	
BOBROVSKI	Sine	
BOBROVSKI	Yakov	
BOBROVSKI	Yenta	GRONET
BONTCHIK	Avraham	
BONTCHIK	Chassia	
BONTCHIK	Chaya	
BONTCHIK	Gitel	
BONTCHIK	Golda	
BONTCHIK	Moshe	
BONTCHIK	Raizel	
BONTCHIK	Shulamit	
BONTCHIK	Yudel	
BONTIN	Benyamin	
BUCHALTER	Shimon	
BUCHALTER	Sprince	
BURSTEIN	Alter	
BURSTEIN	Chaim	
BURSTEIN	Chana	
BURSTEIN	Chana	
BURSTEIN	Faigl	
BURSTEIN	Isne	
BURSTEIN	Lipche	
BURSTEIN	Mordechai	
BURSTEIN	The Rebbetzen (his wife)	
BURSTEIN RABBI	Rabbi Ruven- David	
CHAZANOVITCH	Alter	
CHAZANOVITCH	Avraham	
CHAZANOVITCH	Gitel	
CHAZANOVITCH	Hinda - Lipa	
CHAZANOVITCH	Israel	
CHAZANOVITCH	Moshe - Yakov	
DOLINSKI	Bracha	
DOLINSKI	Chaim - Shloime	
DOLINSKI	Chava	

DOLINSKI	Devorah	
DOLINSKI	Eliezer	
DOLINSKI	Esther	
DOLINSKI	Hershel	
DOLINSKI	Itka	TENDLER
DOLINSKI	Laibl	
DOLINSKI	Leizer	
DOLINSKI	Lipman	
DOLINSKI	Malka	
DOLINSKI	Malka	
DOLINSKI	Matya	
DOLINSKI	Shloime	
DOLINSKI	Shloime	
DOLINSKI	Shmuel	
DOLINSKI	Yakov	
DOLINSKI	Yakov - Koppel	
DOLINSKI	Yossel	
DOLITSKI	Sara	
DUBINER	Alter	
DUBINER	Bayla	
DUBINER	Doba	
DUBINER	Eizig	
DUBINER	Hershel	
DUBINER	Leizer	
DUBINER	Leizer	
DUBINER	Matya	
DUBINER	Moshe	
DUBINER	Raizel	
DUBINER	Sara	
DUBINER	Shaya	
DUBINER	Simcha	
DUBINER	Yosef	
EISENSTEIN	Avraham Simcha	
EISENSTEIN	Dvora Gitel	
EISENSTEIN	Esther	
EISENSTEIN	Gershon Moshe	
EISENSTEIN	Manya	GELERSTEIN
EISENSTEIN	Nechemia	
EISENSTEIN	Nochim	
EISENSTEIN	Reichl	

EISIGMAN	Anoushka	
EISIGMAN	Laibl	
EITES	Aharon	
EITES	Aharon Ben David	
EITES	Berl	
EITES	David	
EITES	Kalman	
EITES	Leiba	PATZNIK
EITES	Miriam	
EITES	Sara	BOBROVSKI
EPSTEIN	Berel	
EPSTEIN	Tzvia	
EPSTEIN	Zalman -Moshe	
FELDMAN	Alter	
FELDMAN	Avraham	
FELDMAN	Avraham - Zelig	
FELDMAN	Babel	
FELDMAN	Bayla - Raizel	SHMIDT
FELDMAN	Berl	
FELDMAN	Chaim	
FELDMAN	Chaya	WOHLHENDLER
FELDMAN	Dov	
FELDMAN	Isser	
FELDMAN	Leiba	
FELDMAN	Malka	
FELDMAN	Minda	
FELDMAN	Mitche	
FELDMAN	Raitze	
FELDMAN	Rivka	
FELDMAN	Shlomo	
FELDMAN	Shlomo	
FELDMAN	Tova	
FELDMAN	Yakov	
FELDMAN	Yosel	
FELDMAN	Zlata	
FISHBEIN	Daniel	
FISHBEIN	Josef	
FISHBEIN	Malka	
FISHBEIN	Malka	STRUSHEVSKI
FISHBEIN	Raizel	

FISHBEIN	Yehoshua	
FISHER	Berl	
FISHER	Chana	
FISHER	Chayele	HINKES
FISHER	Chinke	
FISHER	Meyer	
FISHER	Shimon	
FLAMENBOIM	Dinka	SAVITSKI
FLAMENBOIM	Shmuel	
FLAYSHETZ	Chana	
FLAYSHETZ	Devorah	RUDSKI
FLAYSHETZ	Israel	
FLAYSHETZ	Itche -Laizer	
FLAYSHETZ	Monish	
FLAYSHETZ	Rachel	
FLAYSHETZ	Sara	
FLAYSHETZ	Yente	
FLOMBOIM	Avraham -Meir	
FLOMBOIM	Rachel - Leiba	
FLOMENBOIM	Leiba	
FLOMENBOIM	Moshe	
FLOMENBOIM	Shmuel	
FREIDMAN	Avraham	
FREIDMAN	Avraham	
FREIDMAN	Chaim	
FREIDMAN	Chana	
FREIDMAN	Chana	
FREIDMAN	Chemke	
FREIDMAN	Eizik	
FREIDMAN	Hershel	
FREIDMAN	Osna	HAYAT
FREIDMAN	Rivka	
FREIDMAN	Sara	
FREIDMAN	Shimon	
FREIDMAN	Tema	
FREIDMAN	Zemel	
FREYER	Avraham - Yakov	
FREYER	Bayla	
FREYER	Beyamin -Laizer	
FREYER	Breine	

FREYER	Issachar - Velvel	
FREYER	Laizer	
FREYER	Melech	
FREYER	Miriam	
FREYER	Osna	
FREYER	Pesach	
FREYER	Raizel	
FREYER	Sara	BUCHALTER
FREYER	Sara	
FREYER	Shlomo	
FREYER	Velvel	
FREYER	Yudel	
GALPERIN	Chaya -Bayla	
GALPERIN	Itzik	
GALPERIN	Mira	
GALPERIN	Motel	
GALPERIN	Sara	
GALPERIN	Shalom	
GALPERIN	Zissel	
GANZITZKI	Moshe -Ber	
GANZITZKI	Tzipa	
GARBASH	Feigel	
GARBASH	Oizer	
GARBASH	Rachel	
GARBASH	Ravtze	
GARBASH	Yakov	
GELBERG	Azriel	
GELBERG	Gershon	
GELBERG	Sacha	
GELBERG DR.	Moshe (Michislav)	
GELERSTEIN	Asher	
GELERSTEIN	Leah	
GELERSTEIN	Rachel	
GERSHENGORN	Bracha	
GERSHENGORN	Chaim	
GERSHENGORN	Chaya - Sara	
GERSHENGORN	Esther	
GERSHGORN	Dvorah - Dina	
GERSHGORN	Dvorah -Bayla	
GVIRTZMAN	Berl	

GVIRTZMAN	Chana	
GVIRTZMAN	Chaya	
GVIRTZMAN	Chaya - Raizel	
GVIRTZMAN	Josef	
GVIRTZMAN	Leah	
GVIRTZMAN	Simcha -Laizer	
GEYER	Asher	
GEYER	Benjamin	
GEYER	Benjamin -Asher	
GEYER	Bentze	
GEYER	Berl	
GEYER	Beyla	
GEYER	Chaim	
GEYER	Chaya	
GEYER	Chaya	
GEYER	Dinah	
GEYER	Esther	
GEYER	Fraidel	
GEYER	Laibl	
GEYER	Mina	
GEYER	Miriam	
GEYER	Moshe	
GEYER	Moshe	
GEYER	Moshe	
GEYER	Moshe	
GEYER	Perel	WOLFSON
GEYER	Pinye	
GEYER	Rachel	
GEYER	Rivkah	
GEYER	Sheva	
GEYER	Shmuel	
GEYER	Shprinza	
GEYER	Simcha	
GEYER	Tuvia	
GEYER	Tzipa	
GEYER	Yitzchak	
GEYER RABBI	Tzvi	
GISHES	Alter	
GISHES	Chaskel	
GISHES	Chassia	

GISHES	Chava	
GISHES	Chaya	
GISHES	Henia	
GISHES	Itche	
GISHES	Josef - Mordechai	
GISHES	Laizer	
GISHES	Leiba	EPSTEIN
GISHES	Moshe	
GISHES	Rachel	
GISHES	Raizel	AKERMAN
GISHES	Riva	
GISHES	Rueben	
GISHES	Sara	
GISHES	Tzalel	
GLOMBOVSKI	David	
GLOMBOVSKI	Dinah	
GLOMBOVSKI	Ilya	
GLOMBOVSKI	Itche	
GLOMBOVSKI	Miriam	
GLOMBOVSKI	Sara	
GLOMBOVSKI	Yente	
GLAZER	Chayele	
GLAZER	Eidel	WOLFSON
GLAZER	Eliezer	
GLAZER	Esther - Breine	
GLAZER	Faigel	
GLAZER	Josef	
GLAZER	Laibl	
GLAZER	Malka	
GLAZER	Velvel	
GOLDBERG	Bracha	
GOLDBERG	Israel	
GOLDBERG	Kalman	
GOLDBERG	Noah	
GOLDBERG	Rachel - Ella	
GOLDBERG	Rivka	
GOLDBERG	Shifra	
GOLDFARB	Benya	
GOLDFARB	Chassia	
GOLDFARB	Itche	

GOLDFARB	Laibl	
GOLDFARB	Moshe	
GOLDFARB	Velvel	
GOLDIN	Manya	
GOLDMAN	Chesha	
GOLDMAN	Shaina	KATZ
GOLDMAN	Yakov	
GOLDSHEL	Israel	
GOLDSZTERN	Golda	
GOLDSZTERN	Heidel	
GOLDSZTERN	Josef	
GOLDSZTERN	Tzvi	
GOLNIK	Chana	
GOLNIK	Fishel	
GOLNIK	Gitel	
GOLNIK	Shmuel	
GOLNIK	Sima	
GOLNIK	Simcha	
GOLNIK - EISNER	Avraham	
GOLNIK - EISNER	Yoel	
GOLOMBURSKI	Gisia	
GOLOMBURSKI	Moshe - Tuvia	
GOLOMBURSKI	Shmuel	
GOLOVCHIK	Bayla	
GOLOVCHIK	Bayla	
GOLOVCHIK	Berl	
GOLOVCHIK	Chana	
GOLOVCHIK	Eizig	
GOLOVCHIK	Henia	
GOLOVCHIK	Leah	
GOLOVCHIK	Shaina	LINDENBAUM
GOLOVCHIK	Shloime	
GOLOVCHIK	Shmuel	
GOLOVERSKI	Avigdor	
GOLOVERSKI	Avraham	
GOLOVERSKI	Shmuel	
GOLOVSKI	Laizer	
GOLOVSKI	Noteh	RASHKOVTZER
GOLOVSKI	Raizel	
GORDON	Raizel	

GORENSKI	Mordechai	
GORINSKI	Aharon - Moshe	
GORINSKI	Chaim	
GORINSKI	Chana	
GORINSKI	Chaya - Sara	
GORINSKI	David	
GORINSKI	Dinah	
GORINSKI	Esther	STEMPNITSKI
GORINSKI	Gedalia	
GORINSKI	Gedalia	
GORINSKI	Henoch	
GORINSKI	Itka	
GORINSKI	Jospa	
GORINSKI	K.	
GORINSKI	Laibl	
GORINSKI	Liba	
GORINSKI	Matche	
GORINSKI	Meir	
GORINSKI	Miriam	
GORINSKI	Nechama	OLSHANSKI
GORINSKI	Nechemia	
GORINSKI	Note	
GORINSKI	Pesach	
GORINSKI	Rachel	
GORINSKI	Rachel	
GORINSKI	Raizel	
GORINSKI	Richa	KNOLIK
GORINSKI	Rivkah	
GORINSKI	Sara	
GORINSKI	Shaul	
GORINSKI	Shmuel - Chaim	
GORINSKI	Sossel	
GORINSKI	Yitzchak	
GORKI	Esther - Dvoshe	
GORKI	Laizer	
GORKI	Moshe - Hersh	
GORKI	Odel	
GORKI	Sara	
GORKI	Yekutiel	
GORNI	Asher - Lemel	

GORNI	Chava	
GORNI	Kayla	
GORNI	Pinchas	
GORNI	Shmuel	
GORNI DR.	Eizik (Dr.Mathematics)	
GREITBERG	Moshe	
GREITBERG	Sara - Faige	GARBASH
GRINBLAT	Aharon - Zev	
GRINBLAT	Alter	
GRINBLAT	Avraham	
GRINBLAT	Chaya - Malka	
GRINBLAT	Henia	BLEICHBARD
GRINBLAT	Isser	
GRINBLAT	Malya	
GRINBLAT	Malya	
GRINBLAT	Moshe	
GRINBLAT	Yerachmiel	
GRINBLAT	Yosel	
GRONET	Chaim	
GRONET	Chana	
GRONET	Elka	
GRONET	Israel	
GRONET	Leah	
GRONET	Malka	
GRONET	Meir	
GRONET	Meir	
GRONET	Miriam	
GRONET	Nochim	
GRONET	Yakov	
GRYNSPUN	Chana	
GRYNSPUN	Esther - Rivkah	
GRYNSPUN	Genendel	
GRYNSPUN	Gitel	
GRYNSPUN	Golda	
GRYNSPUN	Moshe - Eizik	
GRYNSPUN	Note	
GRYNSPUN	Sara	
GRYNSPUN	Shifra	
GRYNSPUN	Shifra	
GRYNSPUN	Yakov - Shaye	

GUREVITZ	Baruch	
GUREVITZ	Chaya	
GUREVITZ	Dinah	SHMIDT
GUREVITZ	Fraidel	
GUREVITZ	Gronya	GVIRTZMAN
GUREVITZ	Israel	
GUREVITZ	Laibl	
GUREVITZ	Lipa	
GUREVITZ	Lipa	
GUREVITZ	Mindel	
GUREVITZ	Shmuel	
GURFEIN	Aharon - Hersh	
GURFEIN	Chana	
GURFEIN	Moshe	
GURFEIN	Raizel	
GURFEIN	Shifra	
GURFEIN	Shmuel	
GURFINKEL	Aharon	
GURFINKEL	Eliezer	
GURFINKEL	Elyahu (Ilya)	
GURFINKEL	Hinda	
GURFINKEL	Israel	
GURFINKEL	Moshe	
GURFINKEL	Peshka	
GURFINKEL	Simcha	
GURFINKEL RABBI	Shlomo - Chaim	
GURVITZ	Faitche	
GURVITZ	Meir - Josef	
GURVITZ	Moshe	
GURVITZ	Rachel	
GUTBEITER	Raizel	
GUTBEITER	Tzvi	
GUTMAN	Avraham Yudel	
GUTMAN	Chaya	
HARLO	Aharon - Hersh	
HARLO	Alter	
HARLO	Chaya	
HARLO	Malka	
HARLO	Mordechai	
HARLO	Rachel	

HARLO	Rachel	
HARLO	Raizel	
HARLO	Sara	
HARLO	Shaina - Chaya	
HARLO	Shaul	
HARLO	Shmuelke	
HARLO	Yakov	
HARNIVITSKI	Doba	PACHALSKI
HARNIVITSKI	Shmuel	
HAYAT	Aharon	
HAYAT	Chana	
HAYAT	Chaya	
HAYAT	Chaya - Gitel	
HAYAT	Esther	
HAYAT	Ettel	
HAYAT	Freide	
HAYAT	Hershel	
HAYAT	Itzel	
HAYAT	Masha	STARKOVSKA
HAYAT	Mordechai	
HAYAT	Moshe	
HAYAT	Motel	
HAYAT	Pesel	
HAYAT	Rachel	
HAYAT	Rachel - Leah	
HAYAT	Rachel - Leah	
HAYAT	Rivka	
HAYAT	Rivka	
HAYAT	Rueven	
HAYAT	Shaina	
HAYAT	Shevach	
HAYAT	Yosel	
HAYAT	Zlata	
KAGAN	Chaya - Malka	
KAGAN	Doba	
KAGAN	Freida	
KAGAN	Garlihu	
KAGAN	Gitel	
KAGAN	Laizer	
KAGAN	Leib	

KAGAN	Moshe	
KAGAN	Noah	
KAGAN	Shaina	TENDLER
KAGAN	Velvel	
KAGAN	Yakov	
KAGAN	Yeshayahu Leyb	
KAGAN	Yoche	
KAMINSKI	Babel	
KAMINSKI	Chana	
KAMINSKI	Hodes	
KAMINSKI	Meir	
KAMINSKI	Shalom	
KAMINSKI	Yente	
KAMINSKI	Yitzchak	
KAMINSKI	Yosel	
KAPLAN	Bluma	
KAPLAN	Henia	
KAPLAN	Hershel	
KAPLAN	Hertzko	
KAPLAN	Mendel	
KAPLAN	Moshe - Sine	
KAPLAN	Reuven - Leyb	
KAPLAN	Rivka	
KAPLAN	Shaina	
KAPLAN	Shimon	
KAPLAN	Tema	
KAPLAN	Tzasha	
KAPLAN	Yente - Bayle	
KAPLAN	Yoche	
KAPLANSKI	Chaim	
KAPLANSKI	Chaim -Yitzchak	
KAPLANSKI	Esther	POPOVITCH
KAPLANSKI	Fraidel	
KAPLANSKI	Laibl	
KAPLANSKI	Leah	
KAPLANSKI	Nachman	
KAPLANSKI	Noske	
KAPLANSKI	Tzalik	
KAPLANSKI	Velvel	
KAPLANSKI	Yakov	

KAPLANSKI	Yitzchak - Fishel	
KAPLANSKI	Ze-ev	
KATZ	Asher	
KATZ	Avraham	
KATZ	Basha	
KATZ	Chana	
KATZ	Chaya - Taube	
KATZ	Dinah	
KATZ	Esther	
KATZ	Feige - Leah	
KATZ	Leiba	
KATZ	Leibke	
KATZ	Lipman	
KATZ	Pinye	
KATZ	Sara	SPEKTOR
KATZ	Sara - Breine	
KATZ	Shlomoi	
KATZ	Sonia	
KATZ	Yakov	
KATZ	Yakov Moshe	
KATZ	Yente	
KATZ	Zlatke	TCHERENSKI
KATZELZKI	Elyahu - Chaim	
KATZIZNA	Gutka	GISHES
KATZIZNA	Shmuel	
KATZKEVITCH	David	
KATZKEVITCH	Mordechai	
KATZKEVITCH	Shulamit	HAYAT
KATZKEVITCH	Zlata	
KAUFMAN	David	
KAUFMAN	Faige	
KAUFMAN	Rivka	
KAUFMAN	Shlomo	
KAUFMAN	Zelig	
KERSHENBOIM	Aharon -Hersh	
KERSHENBOIM	Noske	
KERSHENBOIM	Osna	
KERSHENBOIM	Shifra	
KERSHENBOIM	Zlata	
KIRSHENBOIM	Aryeh	

KIRSHENBOIM	Noche	
KIRSHENBOIM	Velvel - Chaim	
KIRSHENBOIM	Zlatke	
KLAVKOVITZ	Fruma	
KLAVKOVITZ	Fruma	TANKTON
KLAVKOVITZ	Leiba	
KLAVKOVITZ	Mania	KOZAK
KLAVKOVITZ	Sara	
KLAVKOVITZ	Shlomo	
KLAVKOVITZ	Yakov	
KLAVKUTS	Henia	
KLAVKUTS	Israel	
KLEINMAN	Bayle	GURFINKEL
KLEINMAN	Chana	
KLEINMAN	Elyahu	
KLEINMAN	Sara - Breine	
KLEINMAN	Shaina	ZUB
KLEINMAN	Tzvi	
KLUTZKI	Elyahu	
KLUTZKI	Elyahu	
KLUTZKI	Itche	
KLUTZKI	Itche	
KLUTZKI	Leiba	
KLUTZKI	Moshe	
KLUTZKI	Moshe	
KLUTZKI	Pesach	
KLUTZKI	Slova	
KLUTZKI	Tzvia	
KLUTZKI	Yoshiya	
KNOLIK	Avraham	
KNOLIK	Avraham - Hersh	
KNOLIK	Bracha	ASKENAZI
KNOLIK	Chaim -Yitzchak	
KNOLIK	Chana - Hinda	
KNOLIK	Chaya	
KNOLIK	Doba	
KNOLIK	Gitel	
KNOLIK	Gitel	
KNOLIK	Israel	
KNOLIK	Leiba	

KNOLIK	Moshe	
KNOLIK	Shaye	
KNOLIK	Shifra	
KNOLIK	Tzirl	
KNOLIK	Yosel	
KNOLIK	Yosel	
KOLITZKI	Laizer	
KOPCHIK	Chinke	
KOPCHIK	Frayda	
KOPCHIK	Golda	
KOPCHIK	Laibl	
KOPCHIK	Nachum	
KOPCHIK	Reuven	
KOPCHIK	Simcha	
KOPCHIK	Zelig	
KORNGOLD	Bayle	
KORNGOLD	Berl	
KORNGOLD	Pesia	
KORNGOLD	Raizel	
KOSTAVSY	Basia	SHAFIR
KOSTAVSY	Yakov	
KOTIK	Berl	
KOTIK	Ida	
KOTIK	Rachel	
KOTIK	Raya	
KOTIK	Sasha	
KOZAK	Menucha (his wife)	
KOZAK	Tuvia	
KRAKOVSKI	Chana - Rachel	
KRAMER	David	KACHUTZKI
KRAMER	Golda	KACHUTZKI
KRAMER	Gotleib	KACHUTZKI
KRAMER	Hershel	KACHUTZKI
KRAMER	Meir	KACHUTZKI
KRAMER	Sima	
KRASHINSKI	Itche	
KRASHINSKI	Laibl	
KRASHINSKI	Moshe	
KRASHINSKI	Pelta	
KRASHINSKI	Pelta	

KRASHINSKI	Raizel	
KRASHINSKI	Raizel	
KRAVSKI	Aharon -Josef	
KRAVSKI	Azriel	
KRAVSKI	Doba	EITES
KRAVSKI	Esther	
KRAVSKI	Frume	
KRAVSKI	Gitel	
KRAVSKI	Hershel	
KRAVSKI	Israel	
KRAVSKI	Kayla	
KRAVSKI	Kayla	
KRAVSKI	Malka	
KRAVSKI	Moshe - Sine	
KRAVSKI	Nechama	
KRAVSKI	Shaina	
KRAVSKI	Shlomo	
KRAVSKI	Yakov	
KRAVSKI	Yosel	
KRAVSKI	Zalman - Hersh	
KRAVTZIK	Chume	GISHES
KRAVTZIK	Elya	
KRAVTZIK	Moshe - Sine	
KRIVITITSKI	Azriel	
KRIVITITSKI	Babel	
KRIVITITSKI	Berl	
KRIVITITSKI	Betzalel - Mordechai	
KRIVITITSKI	Esther	
KRIVITITSKI	Laizer	
KRIVITITSKI	Leiba	
KRIVITITSKI	Masha	
KRIVITITSKI	Pesia	
KRIVITITSKI	Rivka	
KRIVITITSKI	Shmuel	
KRIVITITSKI	Yehoshua	
KROYN	Bely	
KROYN	Chana	
KROYN	David	
KROYN	Doba	
KROYN	Laizer	

KROYN	leah	
KROYN	Misha	
KROYN	Moshe	
KRUGMAN	Anshel	
KRUGMAN	Henoch	
KRUGMAN	Moshe -Zisel	
KRUGMAN	Nache	
KRUGMAN	Tova	
KRUK	Elyahu	
KRUK	Golda	
KRUK	Leiba	
KRUP	Baruch	
KRUP	Pasha	
KUPERSTEIN	Eizik	
KUPERSTEIN	Esther	
KUPERSTEIN	Israel	
KUPERSTEIN	Leiba	
KUSTIN	Berel	
KUSTIN	Blume	
KUSTIN	Chaim -Yitzchak	
KUSTIN	Chava	
KUSTIN	Chaya	
KUSTIN	Ephraim	
KUSTIN	Esther	
KUSTIN	Freida -Rachel	
KUSTIN	Heidel	
KUSTIN	Henia	
KUSTIN	Hershel	
KUSTIN	Laibl	
KUSTIN	Mired	
KUSTIN	Rachel	EITES
KUSTIN	Reuven	
KUSTIN	Reuven - Leyb	
KUSTIN	Sara - Fraida	
KUSTIN	Sara - Fraida	
KUSTIN	Sara - Rivka	
KUSTIN	Velvel	
KUSTIN	Yakov -Yishayahu	
KUSTIN	Yoel	
LEDER	Alte	

LEDER	Golda	
LEIBOVITZ	Faige	
LEIBOVITZ	Miriam	
LEIBOVITZ	Risha - Rivka	
LEIBOVITZ	Shaye	
LEIBSON	Henia	BOBROVSKI
LEIBSON	Tzelya	
LEMSON	Benyamin	
LEMSON	Doba	
LEMSON	Esther	
LEMSON	Riva	
LEV	Chana - Leah	
LEV	Lezach	
LEV	Shaina	
LEV	Yehoshua	
LEVIN	Aryeh	
LEVIN	Babel	
LEVIN	Bayle	
LEVIN	Breine	
LEVIN	Chana	
LEVIN	David	
LEVIN	Feivel	
LEVIN	Laizer	
LEVIN	Malka	
LEVIN	Meir	
LEVIN	Meir	
LEVIN	Mindel	
LEVIN	Pesia - Chaya	
LEVIN	Rachel	
LEVIN	Raizel	
LEVIN	Riva	
LEVIN	Shifra	GRYNSPAN
LEVIN	Tzvia	
LEVIN	Yitzchak	
LEVIN	Yitzchak	
LEVIN	Yosel	
LIBMAN	Chaim Yitzchak	
LIBMAN	Faigel	WEINSTEIN
LIBMAN	Hinda	
LIBMAN	Shaina - Chaya	KAGAN

LIBMAN	Yehezkel	
LINDENBOIM	Avraham - Meir	
LINDENBOIM	Betzalel	
LINDENBOIM	Chaya -Tzinke	
LINDENBOIM	Frima	
LINDENBOIM	Moshe -Hersh	
LINDENBOIM	Shlomo	
LINDENBOIM	Velvel	
LINDER	Aviezer	
LINDER	Moshe	
LINDER	Sara	
LINDER	Yerachmiel	
LIFSHITZ	Henia	
LIFSHITZ	Moshe	
LIFSHITZ	Rachel	FREIDMAN
LIFSHITZ	Riva	
LIFSHITZ	Sima	
LIFSHITZ	Simcha	
LOPATES	Benyamin	
LOPATES	Eizik	
LOPATES	Esther	
LOPATES	Josef	
LOPATES	Josef	
LOPATES	Mindel	
LOPATES	Shalom	
MANDELBLAT	Chaya - Iteh	
MANDELBLAT	Chaya - Sara	
MANDELBLAT	Chetka	
MANDELBLAT	Freida	
MANDELBLAT	Golda - Raizel	
MANDELBLAT	Henia	
MANDELBLAT	Reuven	
MANDELBLAT	Shlomo	
MATELMAN	Chaskel	
MATELMAN	Chaya	
MATELMAN	Faige	
MATELMAN	Minka	
MATELMAN	Miriam	
MATELMAN	Nechama	
MATELMAN	Shmuel	

MATELMAN	Simcha	
MATELMAN	Tuvia	
MATELMAN	Zeidel	
MAZOR	David	
MAZOR	Elyahu	
MAZOR	Moshe	
MAZOR	Pesia	
MAZOR	Raizel	
MAZOR	Yitzchak	
MAZOR	Yitzchak	
MAZOR	Yoshke	
MELNIK	Faigl	
MELNIK	Henia	
MELNIK	Laibl	
MELNIK	Nache	
MELNIK	Pesach	
MELNIK	Shmuel	
MICHAEL	Velvel	
MIKEY	Avraham - Meir	
MIKEY	Chaim	
MIKEY	Chaya	
MIKEY	Masha	
MIKEY	Mordechai	
MIKEY	Motel	
MIKEY	Tzvia	WIDOMLANSKI
MILETSKI	Avraham	
MILETSKI	Basha	
MILETSKI	Bayle	
MILETSKI	Chana	
MILETSKI	Chaya	
MILETSKI	Devorah	
MILETSKI	Eliezer	
MILETSKI	Elka	GOLOVSKI
MILETSKI	Ephraim	
MILETSKI	Israel	
MILETSKI	Mendel	
MILETSKI	Mindel	
MILETSKI	Moshe	
MILETSKI	Pesel	LINDENBOIM
MILETSKI	Pinye	

MILETSKI	Rachel	
MILETSKI	Raizel	
MILETSKI	Sara - Esther	
MILETSKI	Shaina	
MILETSKI	Shmuel	
MILETSKI	Shmuel	
MILETSKI	Velvel	
MILETSKI	Yakov	
MILGROIM	Hersh	
MILGROIM	Pesach	
MILGROIM	Pinye	
MILNITSKI	Israel	
MILNITSKI	Rachel	
MILNITSKI	Shlomo	
MILOVOVITZ	Avraham	
MILOVOVITZ	Chaya	
MILOVOVITZ	Faige	
MILOVOVITZ	Moshe - Meir	
MILOVOVITZ	Sara	
MINC	Matya	
MINC	Sara	GLEZER
MIRTSKI	Doba	
MIRTSKI	Faigel	
MIRTSKI	Israel	
MIRTSKI	Josef	
MIRTSKI	Polya	
MITELMAN	Blume	MONTSHER
MONCZAR	Israel - Aharon	
MONCZAR	Mordechai	
MONCZAR	Rivka - Glicke	
MORGENSTERN	Golda	
MORGENSTERN	Masha	
MORGENSTERN	Riva	
MORGENSTERN	Sara	
MOSTOVSKI	Chana	
MOSTOVSKI	Chayke	
MOSTOVSKI	Genia	
MOSTOVSKI	Josef	
MOSTOVSKI	Moshe	
MOSTOVSKI	Nachum	

MOSTOVSKI	Nutke	
MOVNITSKI	Chaya	
MOVNITSKI	Esther	
MOVNITSKI	Yakov	
MOVNITSKI	Yudel	
NEIMAN	Chana	
NEIMAN	Faige - Mirel	
NEIMAN	Rivka	
NEIMAN	Sara	
NEIMAN	Shaina - Rachel	
NERUSHTCHINSKI	Bayle -Fraydle	
NERUSHTCHINSKI	Chaya -Faigel	
NERUSHTCHINSKI	Elyahu	
NERUSHTCHINSKI	Menachem	
NERUSHTCHINSKI	Moshe -Zeidel	
NERUSHTCHINSKI	Pesia	
NERUSHTCHINSKI	Rachel	
NERUSHTCHINSKI	Yente	
NISELEVITCH	Avraham	
NISELEVITCH	Chana	
NISELEVITCH	Esther - Gitel	
NISELEVITCH	Josef	
NISELEVITCH	Meir -Laizer	
NISELEVITCH	Sara	
NITSELBEIN	Israel	
NITZBERG	Avraham -Leyb	
NITZBERG	Chaim	
NITZBERG	Rachel	
NITZBERG	Shmuel - Chaim	
NOVINSKI	Chana	
NOVINSKI	Laibl	
NOVINSKI	Moshe	
NOVINSKI	Pinye	
NOVINSKI	Rivka	LIPSHITZ
PACHALSKI	Abba	
PACHALSKI	Bashe	
PACHALSKI	Bashke	
PACHALSKI	David	
PACHALSKI	Eizik	
PACHALSKI	Hershel	

PACHALSKI	Leah	
PACHALSKI	Leiba	
PACHALSKI	Rafael	
PACHALSKI	Rivtche	
PACHALSKI	Shmuel	
PACHALSKI	Sima	
PACHALSKI	Vichna	
PACHALSKI	Zena	
PACHTER	Aharon -Moshe	
PACHTER	Blume	
PACHTER	Chana	
PACHTER	Ilya	
PACHTER	Josefa	
PACHTER	Kaziel	
PACHTER	Sara	
PACHTER	Shlomo - Hersh	
PACHTER	Zalman - Mechel	
PAPOVITCH	Rachel -Leah	
PATALYUK	Memel	
PATALYUK	Sara	
PAYKER	Chaim	
PAYKER	David	
PAYKER	Hinda	
PAYKER	Moshe	
PAYKER	Sima	HARLO
PIATEK	Itche -Meyer	
PIATEK	Perel	
PIATEK	Velvel	
PLATENDOM	Chaim	
PLATENDOM	Meir - Laizer	
PLATENDOM	Moshe -Leyb	
PLATENDOM	Rivka	
PLATENDOM	Sara - HInda	
POLYAKEVITCH	Aharon - Laizer	
POLYAKEVITCH	Arkeh - Yakov	
POLYAKEVITCH	Berl	
POLYAKEVITCH	Chaya	
POLYAKEVITCH	Fraidel	
POLYAKEVITCH	Hertzke	
POLYAKEVITCH	Hitzle	

POLYAKEVITCH	Itche	
POLYAKEVITCH	Kayla	
POLYAKEVITCH	Leiba	
POLYAKEVITCH	Mirka	
POLYAKEVITCH	Moshe	
POLYAKEVITCH	Moshe - Note	
POLYAKEVITCH	Motya	
POLYAKEVITCH	Naphtali	
POLYAKEVITCH	Rachel	
POLYAKEVITCH	Rachel	
POLYAKEVITCH	Raizel	
POLYAKEVITCH	Raizel	
POLYAKEVITCH	Sara - Gitel	
POLYAKEVITCH	Sara - Gitel	
POLYAKEVITCH	Shaye	
POLYAKEVITCH	Yakov	
POLYAKEVITCH	Yakov	
POLYAKEVITCH	Yente	
POMERANITZ	Faige -Chaya	
POMERANITZ	Israel	
POMERANITZ	Malka	
POMERANITZ	Rachel	
POMERANITZ	Rivka	
POMERANTCHIK	Feivel	
POMERANTCHIK	Golda	
POMERANTCHIK	Laibl	
POMERANTCHIK	Mordechai	
POMERANTCHIK	Rivka	
POMERANTCHIK	Sara	
POMERANTCHIK	Tzipa	LOPATA
POMERANZ	Chaim	
POMERANZ	Esther	
POMERANZ	Hillel	
POPOVITCH	Avraham	
POPOVITCH	Avraham	
POPOVITCH	Chaya - Yente	
POPOVITCH	Dinah	HAYAT
POPOVITCH	Fraidel	
POPOVITCH	Moshe	
POPOVITCH	Pesel	

POPOVITCH	Rachel	NERUSHTCHINSKI
POPOVITCH	Shomo	
POPOVITCH	Yakov	
PORTNOY	Chaya -Sara	
PORTNOY	Gitel	
PORTNOY	Itche	
PORTNOY	Liba	DOLINSKI
PORTNOY	Shmuel	
PRAGER	Pesach	
PRAGER	Yoche	
PROKOVSKI	Ettel	SAVITSKI
PUCHTENSKI	Alter	
PUCHTENSKI	Chaya	
PUCHTENSKI	Henia	
PUCHTENSKI	Meir	
PUCHTENSKI	Moshe	
PUCHTENSKI	Rishel	CHAZANOVITCH
RABINOVITCH	Leibke	
RABINOVITCH	Rusha	
RADISHETZ	Babel	
RADISHETZ	Devorah	
RADISHETZ	Josefa	
RAPOPORT	Asher	
RAPOPORT	Josef	
RAPOPORT	Leah	
RAPOPORT	Shepsel	
RAPOPORT	Vishki	
RAPOPORT	Yoche	
RATZEVSKI	Dinah	
RATZEVSKI	Feivel	
RATZEVSKI	Malka	
RATZEVSKI	Moshe	
RATZEVSKI	Simcha	
RATZEVSKI	Vishki	
RATZEVSKI	Yitzchak	
RESNIK	Bayle	GLIMBOVSKI
RESNIK	Berl	
RIMLAND	Chana	
RIMLAND	Meir	
RIVLER	Bashke	

RIVLER	David	
ROCH	Esther - Riva	
ROCH	Gitel	
ROCH	Malka	
ROCHAMES	Chaim	
ROCHAMES	Esther	
ROSENBERG	Nache	
ROSENBERG	Shmuel - David	
ROSENBLUM	Alter	
ROSENBLUM	Heshke	
ROSENSHEIN	Benyamin	
ROSENSHEIN	Samek	
ROSENSHEIN	Sara	
ROSENTHAL	Hershel	
ROSENTHAL	Malka	
ROSENTHAL	Yente	
ROTSTEIN	Chinke	
ROTSTEIN	Faige	
ROTSTEIN	Genendel	
ROTSTEIN	Pavel	
RUBINSTEIN	Chaya	
RUBINSTEIN	Yitzchak	
RUDNITZKI	Aharon	
RUDNITZKI	Esther	
RUDNITZKI	Hershel	
RUDNITZKI	Leah	
RUDNITZKI	Leiba	
RUDNITZKI	Malka	
RUDNITZKI	Mindel	
RUDNITZKI	Pesia	
RUDNITZKI	Raitsa	
RUDNITZKI	Reichel	
RUDNITZKI	Sara	
RUDNITZKI	Shmuel	
RUDNITZKI	Yoel	
RUDNITZKI	Zevel	
SABASHITSKI	Blume	
SABASHITSKI	Blume	
SABASHITSKI	Daniel	
SABASHITSKI	Elka	

SABASHITSKI	Elka - Dinah	
SABASHITSKI	Elya	
SABASHITSKI	Elyahu	
SABASHITSKI	Faige	
SABASHITSKI	Gedalyahu	
SABASHITSKI	Israel	
SABASHITSKI	Laibl - Hersh	
SABASHITSKI	Moshe	
SABASHITSKI	Pinye	
SABASHITSKI	Raizel	
SABASHITSKI	Riva	
SABASHITSKI	Roza	
SABASHITSKI	Shmuel	
SABASHITSKI	Yakov	
SABASHITSKI	Yitzchak	
SABASHITSKI	Zelda	
SAFIR	Bentze	
SAFIR	Esther	
SAFIR	Freida	
SAFIR	Henia	GRYNBLAT
SAFIR	Israel	
SAFIR	Leah	
SAFIR	Leah	
SAFIR	Leiba	
SAFIR	Matka	KRIVITITSKI
SAFIR	Michael	
SAFIR	Nachum	
SAFIR	Pinchas	
SAFIR	Sara	
SAFIR	Shmuel	
SAFIR	Simcha	
SAFIR	Yakov	
SAFIR	Zlata	
SAMUEL	Berl	
SAMUEL	Chana	GLEZER
SAMUEL	Chaya	
SAMUEL	Moshe	
SAMUEL	Yona	
SANCTON	Aharon -Leyb	
SANCTON	Breine	

SANCTON	Ephraim	
SANCTON	Faige - Leah	
SANCTON	Hershel	
SAPERSTEIN	Asher	
SAPERSTEIN	Avraham	
SAPERSTEIN	Michela	DEMITROVSKI
SAPERSTEIN	Simcha	
SAVITZKI	Berl	
SAVITZKI	Berl	
SAVITZKI	Chaim - Ber	
SAVITZKI	Devorah	
SAVITZKI	Devorah	
SAVITZKI	Fayeh	
SAVITZKI	Hershel	
SAVITZKI	Leiba	MILETSKI
SAVITZKI	Moshe	
SAVITZKI	Rachel	
SAVITZKI	Tuvia	
SAVITZKI	Yakov	
SHAFIR	Mordechai - Leyb	
SHAFIR	Sara	
SHALITZKI	Asher	
SHALITZKI	Berl	
SHALITZKI	Chana - Faigel	
SHALITZKI	Miriam - Yente	
SHALITZKI	Reuven	
SHALITZKI	Ziporah	
SHEDROVTZKI	Freide	
SHEDROVTZKI	Israel	
SHEDROVTZKI	Meir	
SHEDROVTZKI	Sara	GALPERIN
SHEDROVTZKI	Zalman	
SHEDROVTZKI	Zelig	
SHEDROVTZKI	Zissel	
SHEINFELD	Basia	
SHEINFELD	Chaim	
SHEINFELD	Freida	
SHEINFELD	Perel	
SHER	Chasia	
SHER	Chaya -Zisel	

SHER	Sara	
SHER	Velvel	
SHERMAN	Devorah	MANDELBOIM
SHERMAN	Esther	
SHERMAN	Moshe	
SHERSHEVSKI	Devorah	
SHERSHEVSKI	Motel	
SZCZYTNITSKI	Bat-Sheva	
SZCZYTNITSKI	David	
SZCZYTNITSKI	Dov	
SZCZYTNITSKI	Israel	
SZCZYTNITSKI	Mendel	
SZCZYTNITSKI	Mosheke	
SZCZYTNITSKI	Nache	
SZCZYTNITSKI	Reuven	
SZCZYTNITSKI	Sheva	
SZCZYTNITSKI	Yitzchak	
SZCZYTNITSKI	Yosel	
SZCZYTNITSKI	Yudel	
SZCZYTNITSKI	Zalman	
SZCZYTNITSKI	Zelig	
SZCZYTNITSKI	Zlate	
SHMERLOVITZ	Laizer	
SHMERLOVITZ	Rachel	
SHMERLOVITZ	Yoche	
SHMIDT	Chaim	
SHMIDT	Pesia	
SHMIDT	Rachel	
SHMIDT	Raizel	
SHMUKLER	Chaim	
SHMUKLER	Eizik	
SHMUKLER	Fayeh	
SHMUKLER	Malya	
SHMUKLER	Matye	
SHMUKLER	Mordechai - Leyb	
SHMUKLER	Moshe	
SHMUKLER	Mosheke	
SHMUKLER	Motel	
SHMUKLER	Pinye	
SHMUKLER	Sara	PATALYUK

SHMUKLER	Sara -Rachel	VOHLHENDLER
SHMUKLER	Shaina	
SHMUKLER	Simcha	
SHMUKLER	Tema	
SHMUKLER	Tema	
SHMUKLER	Yakov	
SHMUKLER	Yoche	
SHNIDER	Bayle	
SHNIDER	Golda	
SHNIDER	Rasha	
SHNIDER	Shalom	
SHNIDER	Vigdor	
SHOSTAKOVSKI	Charne	
SHOSTAKOVSKI	Chayele	
SHOSTAKOVSKI	Eizik	
SHOSTAKOVSKI	Gedalya	
SHOSTAKOVSKI	Gitel	
SHOSTAKOVSKI	Laibl	
SHOSTAKOVSKI	Mira	GOLDMAN
SHOSTAKOVSKI	Raya	
SHOSTAKOVSKI	Sonia	GRONET
SHOSTAKOVSKI	Yakov	
SHOSTAKOVSKI	Yakov Shmuel	
SHOSTAKOVSKI	Yakov Shmuel	
SHTEINGRAD	Betzalel	
SHTEINGRAD	Esther	
SHTEINGRAD	Fishel	
SHTEINGRAD	Rachel	DOLINSKI
SHTEINGRAD	Yente	
SHVARTZ	Chesha	RUDNITZKI
SHVARTZ	Josef	
SHVARTZ	Moshe	
SHVARTZ	Zisi	
SHVETSKI	Chemke	
SHVETSKI	David - Yakov	
SHVETSKI	Devorah	
SIMCHOVITZ	Mendel	
SIMCHOVITZ	Minka	
SIMCHOVITZ	Shaina	
SINGER	Elyakim	

SINGER	Pesach	
SINGER	Sine	
SINGER	Yitzchak	
SIROKA RABBI	Josef	
SIROTA	Asher	
SIROTA	Bracha	
SIROTA	Laibl	
SOCHOLITSKI	Asher	
SOCHOLITSKI	Bayla	
SOCHOLITSKI	Eizik	
SOCHOLITSKI	Nuske	
SOCHOLITSKI	Slava	
SOFER	Aharon	
SOFER	David	
SOFER	Gitel	
SOFER	Hartzik	
SOFER	Perel	
SOFER	Sara	
SOLNITZE	Chana	
SOLNITZE	David - Shlomo	
SOLNITZE	Ettel	
SOLNITZE	Golda - Raizel	
SOLNITZE	Sara	
SOLNITZE	Shmuel	
SOLNITZE	Yishayahu	
SOROKA	Josef	
SPEKTOR	Alter	
SPEKTOR	Bertche	
SPEKTOR	Breine	
SPEKTOR	Breine	
SPEKTOR	Chava	
SPEKTOR	Faige	
SPEKTOR	Itche	
SPEKTOR	Itka	
SPEKTOR	Josef	
SPEKTOR	Roza	
SPEKTOR	Sara	
SPEKTOR	Sara	
SPEKTOR	Shimon	
SPEKTOR	Simcha	

SPEKTOR	Simcha	
SPEKTOR	Yoche	
SPETKA	Mordechai	
STAVSKI	David	
STAVSKI	David	
STAVSKI	Moshe	
STEINBERG	Genendel	
STEINBERG	Nachman	
STEINBERG	Riva	
STEINBERG	Tuvia	
STEMPNITSKI	Aharon	
STEMPNITSKI	Avraham	
STEMPNITSKI	Betzalel	
STEMPNITSKI	Chana	
STEMPNITSKI	Chayka	TENDLER
STEMPNITSKI	Chinke	
STEMPNITSKI	Devorah	
STEMPNITSKI	Eizik	
STEMPNITSKI	Eshke	
STEMPNITSKI	Esther	
STEMPNITSKI	Faitche	
STEMPNITSKI	Genendel	
STEMPNITSKI	Itzik Leyb	
STEMPNITSKI	Moshe	
STEMPNITSKI	Motke	
STEMPNITSKI	Pichas	
STEMPNITSKI	Pinye	
STEMPNITSKI	Sara	
STEMPNITSKI	Shaina- Faigel	
STEMPNITSKI	Shalom Menashe	
STEMPNITSKI	Shaye	
STEMPNITSKI	Shimon	
STEMPNITSKI	Shmerel	
STEMPNITSKI	Shoshana	
STEMPNITSKI	Tuvia	
STOPITSEVSKI	Aharon - Hersh	
STOPITSEVSKI	Chasia	
STOPITSEVSKI	Chaya	
STOPITSEVSKI	Nachum	
STOPITSEVSKI	Sara	

STOPITSEVSKI	Sara	
STOPITSEVSKI	Shifra	
STOPITSEVSKI	Yitzchak	
STRUSHEVSKI	Benyamin	
STRUSHEVSKI	Sara	
STRUSHEVSKI	Yakov	
TARCHINSKI	Asher	
TARCHINSKI	Avraham	
TARCHINSKI	Chava	
TARCHINSKI	Laizer	
TARCHINSKI	Michla	
TARCHINSKI	Rueven	
TARCHINSKI	Vichna	
TARCHINSKI	Yudel	
TARTASH	Sara	
TAYBLUM	Chana	
TAYBLUM	Laizer	
TAYBLUM	Moshe	
TAYBLUM	Perel	
TAYBLUM	Velvel	
TCHERNETSKI	Gitel	
TCHERNETSKI	Hershel	
TCHERNETSKI	Lipman	
TCHERNETSKI	Malka	
TCHERNETSKI	Mendel	
TCHERNETSKI	Perel	
TCHERNY	Chaim	
TCHERNY	Faigel	
TCHERNY	Gitel	
TCHERNY	Henia	
TCHERNY	Shaina	
TCHERNY	Yakov	
TCHERNY	Yitzchak	
TCHERNY	Yitzchak	
TCHOR	Shprinze	
TENDLER	David - Yitzchak	
TENDLER	Sara	
TESSLER	Faigel	
TESSLER	Hershel	
TESSLER	Hinda	

TESSLER	Laizer	
TIMIANSKI	Aharon - Yitzchak	
TIMIANSKI	Bracha	
TIMIANSKI	Chana	
TIMIANSKI	Chaya -Sirka	
TIMIANSKI	Chesna	
TIMIANSKI	Chumke	
TIMIANSKI	Chuna	
TIMIANSKI	Eizik	
TIMIANSKI	Esther	
TIMIANSKI	Esther	KOPTZIK
TIMIANSKI	Esther	
TIMIANSKI	Faigel	
TIMIANSKI	Gishe	
TIMIANSKI	Gitel	
TIMIANSKI	Moshe -Hershel	
TIMIANSKI	Motel	
TIMIANSKI	Rivka	
TIMIANSKI	Shlomit	
TOPOLOVSKI	Basha	
TOPOLOVSKI	Chuna	
TOPOLOVSKI	Josef	
TOPOLOVSKI	Leah	
TOPOLOVSKI	Yitzchak - Yakov	
TRASTNITZER	Rachel	
TRASTNITZER	Zelig	
VICHNES	Chaim	
VICHNES	Henia	
VICHNES	Itche	
VICHNES	Shaine	
VICHNES	Sirka	
VICHNES	Yakov	
VIGOTOV	Berl	
VIGOTOV	David	
VIGOTOV	Eli	
VIGOTOV	Helka	
VIGOTOV	Henia	
VIGOTOV	Josef	
VIGOTOV	Laizer - Itche	
VIGOTOV	Pesia	

VIGOTOV	Shloime	
VIGOTOV	Taube	
VIGOTOV	Yente	
VOLHENDLER	Berl	
VOLHENDLER	Eizik	
VOLHENDLER	Glicka	
VOLHENDLER	Malka	ENGLANDER
VOLHENDLER	Miriam	
VOLHENDLER	Shloime	
VOLHENDLER	Tamar	
VOLHENDLER	Yehudit	
VOLHENDLER	Yosel	
VOLHENDLER	Zissel	
VOLVOLVITCH	Benyamin	
VOLVOLVITCH	Sara	
VOLVOLVITCH	Yehudit	
VOLVOLVITCH	Yosel	
WARBIN	Chana	
WARBIN	David	
WARBIN	Doba	
WARBIN	Dov	
WARBIN	Eizik	
WARBIN	Ettel	
WARBIN	Leah	
WARBIN	Motke	
WARBIN	Riva	
WARBIN	Shaina	
WARBIN	Shaya	
WAXMAN	Arieh	
WAXMAN	Chaim	
WAXMAN	Rachel	
WEIDERMAN	Chana	
WEIDERMAN	Laibl	
WEINERMAN	Aharon - Hersh	
WEINERMAN	Chaim	
WEINERMAN	Encel	
WEINERMAN	Kayla	
WEINERMAN	Mania	
WEINERMAN	Raizel	
WEINERMAN	Yochevet	

WEINSTEIN	Aharon	
WEINSTEIN	Benyamin	
WEINSTEIN	Eizik	
WEINSTEIN	Eliezer	
WEINSTEIN	Golda	GALPERIN
WEINSTEIN	Moshe	
WEISSMAN	Benyamin	
WEISSMAN	Chinke	
WEISSMAN	Laibl	
WEISSMAN	Tzipa	
WEISSMAN	Velvel	
WEISSMAN	Yakov	
WEITZHENDLER	Schalom	
WEITZHENDLER	Yakov	
WIDOMLANSKI	Chaim	
WIDOMLANSKI	Chaim David	
WIDOMLANSKI	Chana	
WIDOMLANSKI	Gitel	
WIDOMLANSKI	Malka	
WIDOMLANSKI	Pesia	
WIDOMLANSKI	Riva	
WIDOMLANSKI	Riva	
WIDOMLANSKI	Sara	
WIDOMLANSKI	Sender	
WIDOMLANSKI	Yeshaya	
WINOGRAD	Bendet	
WINOGRAD	Fraidel	
WINOGRAD	Kayla	
WINOGRAD	Malka	
WISCHENGRAD	Babel	
WISCHENGRAD	Eliezer	
WISCHENGRAD	Israel	
WISCHENGRAD	Miriam	
WISSOTSKI	Aharon	
WISSOTSKI	Babel	
WISSOTSKI	Babel	
WISSOTSKI	Bentze	
WISSOTSKI	Berl	
WISSOTSKI	Beyla	
WISSOTSKI	Bracha	

WISSOTSKI	Leah	
WISSOTSKI	Malka	
WISSOTSKI	Moshe	
WISSOTSKI	Moshe	
WISSOTSKI	Rachel	
WISSOTSKI	Raizel	
WISSOTSKI	Yitchak	
WOFFENSTEIN	Eizik	
WOFFENSTEIN	Kayla	
WOFFENSTEIN	Malka	
WOFFENSTEIN	Mendel	
WOFFENSTEIN	Shifra Iteh	
WOFNIRSKI	Chayele	
WOFNIRSKI	David	
WOFNIRSKI	Fishel	
WOFNIRSKI	Laibl	
WOFNIRSKI	Miriam	FECHTER
WOFNIRSKI	Pinye	
WOFNIRSKI	Shmuel	
WOFNIRSKI	Soya	
WOFNIRSKI	Zisa	
WOLF	Chana	
WOLF	Chana	
WOLF	Chinke	
WOLF	Moshe	
WOLF	Raizel	
WOLF	Sara	PAPAVITCH
WOLFSON	Babel	
WOLFSON	Esther	
WOLFSON	Esther	
WOLFSON	Heidel	
WOLFSON	Hinda	
WOLFSON	Josef	
WOLFSON	Leiba	GRYNBLAT
WOLFSON	Memel	
WOLFSON	Miriam	SHARSHEVITSKI
WOLFSON	Rachel	
WOLFSON	Shimon	
WOLFSON	Yosel	
WOLFSON	Ziska	

YAFFE	Chaim	
YAFFE	Gitel (wife of the Chazan)	
YAFFE	Moshe	
YAFFE	Shlomo	
YAFFE	Shmerel	
YAFFE	Tema	STEMPNITSKI
YAGODCHINSKI	Meir	
YAGODCHINSKI	Rivka	
YAGODCHINSKI	Shaina	
YAGODCHINSKI	Shimon	
YAGOLKOVSKI	Aharon	
YAGOLKOVSKI	Eizik	
YAGOLKOVSKI	Elka	SPEKTOR
YAGOLKOVSKI	Rachel	
YAGOLKOVSKI	Sara	
YAGOLKOVSKI	Sashke	
YAKUBOVITCH	Baruch	
YAKUBOVITCH	Elyahu	
YAKUBOVITCH	Gavriel	
YAKUBOVITCH	Moshe	
YAKUBOVITCH	Moshe Yudel	
YAKUBOVITCH	Risha	
YAKUBOVITCH	Shalom	
YOCHENIK	Chaya	
YOCHENIK	Perel	
YOCHENIK	Shlomo - Meir	
YUNGERMAN	Chana	
YUNGERMAN	Josef	
YUNGERMAN	Yakov -Velvel	
ZARETSKI	Shlomo	
ZAYENTS	Alteh	
ZAYENTS	David	
ZAYENTS	Devorah	
ZAYENTS	Miriam	
ZAYENTS	Pasha	
ZAYENTS	Rivka	
ZAYENTS	Sashke	
ZAYENTS	Tova	
ZAYNDMAN	Ephraim	
ZAYNDMAN	Raizel	KRIVIATITSKI

ZAYNDMAN	Shmerel	
ZAZASHVER	(His wife)	
ZAZASHVER	Asher	
ZAZASHVER	Eizik	
ZAZASHVER	Hershel	
ZAZASHVER	Laizer	
ZAZASHVER	Leah	KOOPERSTEIN
ZAZASHVER	Pesia	
ZAZASHVER	Shaina	
ZAZASHVER	Shevach	
ZAZASHVER	Yosel	
ZEIDENBERG	Bashe	
ZEIDENBERG	Bayle	
ZEIDENBERG	Charse	
ZEIDENBERG	David	
ZEIDENBERG	Henia	
ZEIDENBERG	Moshe	
ZEIDENBERG	Pesach - Laizer	
ZEIDENBERG	Sara	
ZEIDENBERG	Shaina	
ZEIDENBERG	Shimon	
ZEIDENBERG	Shmaryahu	
ZIGERMAN	Bashe - Raizel	
ZIGERMAN	Chaya	
ZIGERMAN	Hettel	
ZIGERMAN	Kalman	
ZIGERMAN	Leah	
ZIGERMAN	Pinye	
ZIGERMAN	Simcha	
ZIGERMAN	Yakov	
ZILBERBERG	Rachel	GRYNBERG
ZILBERBERG	Shmuel	
ZILBERSTEIN	Sara - Mindel	HOCHMAN
ZILBERSTEIN	Yitzchak	
ZLATES	Avraham - Moshe	
ZLATES	Chaya	
ZLATES	Chuna	
ZLATES	(Chuna's wife)	
ZLATES	Esther	
ZLATES	Fania - Doba	

ZLATES	Hinda	
ZLATES	Leiba	
ZLATES	Matteh	
ZLATES	Perel	
ZLATES	Sara	
ZLATES	Shalom	
ZLATES	Shloime	
ZLATES	Yakov	
ZLIBANSKI	Esther	
ZOLF	Leyb	
ZOLF	Mentche	
ZOLF RABBI	Yitzchak Eizik	
ZONENSHEIN	Aharon - Yitzchak	
ZONENSHEIN	Raizel	GALPERIN
ZONENSHEIN	Sima	
ZONENSHEIN	Simcha	
ZONENSHEIN	Yitzchak	
ZUB	Bela	
ZUB	Ben -Zion (Bentze)	
ZUB	Chaya - Sara	
ZUB	Eliyahu	
ZUB	Faige	
ZUB	Lipa	
ZUB	Sara	
ZUB	Shaina	
ZUB	Tzvia	
ZUBOVITCH	Alteh	
ZUBOVITCH	Gavriel	

Name Index

Chaye's, 178, 279
Chayet, 206
Chayit, 176
Chazanovich, 343
Chazanovitch, 380, 405
Chazanowitz, 163
Cholomowski, 15
Chorny, 323, 325
Chrostowski, 20
Chrustkowski, 307
Cohen, 121, 169
Collins, 131
Cracovsky, 302

D

Demitrovski, 408
Denishevski, 40
Dmitrewski, 262
Dolinski, 178, 196, 207, 238, 254
Dolinski, 380, 381, 405, 410
Dolinsky, 295, 296, 297, 320, 337, 351, 359
Dolitski, 381
Dov, 56
Dubiner, 6, 7, 9, 10, 50, 51, 121, 133, 134, 137, 140, 210, 211, 236, 254, 257, 302, 321, 338, 365, 369
Dubiner, 381
Dubnov, 303
Dubnow, 16, 26

E

Edelstein, 42, 65, 230, 289, 296
Ehrlich, 128, 129
Eichmann, 137, 362, 364
Eidels, 92
Eisendstadt, 1
Eisenstadt, 6, 7, 8, 25, 30, 31, 34, 37, 38, 40, 42, 45, 49, 50, 53, 56, 57, 62, 63, 65, 69, 71, 72, 73, 74, 77, 80, 83, 84, 85, 87, 88, 90, 91, 94, 95, 96, 98, 100, 101, 104, 105, 106, 107, 108, 110, 112, 114, 116, 119, 120, 122, 125, 129, 131, 133, 138, 149, 150, 160, 218, 219, 220, 221, 223, 225, 228, 230, 231, 232, 234, 236, 237, 239, 240, 241, 242, 245, 249, 252, 253, 254, 255, 257, 258, 259, 261, 262, 263, 264, 266, 268, 269, 271, 272, 273, 275, 278, 280, 283, 284, 289, 290, 293, 296, 300, 316
Eisenstein, 169, 204, 214
Eisenstein, 381
Eisigman, 382
Eisner, 88, 186
Eisner, 387
Eites, 382, 396, 397
Elboim, 31
Elchanan, 40, 44, 46, 121, 188
Englander, 415
Ephrati, 31
Epstein, 77, 78
Epstein, 382, 386
Ever, 196

F

Fabry, 272
Fanasevich, 337, 341
Faygenblum, 197, 198
Fechter, 417
Federbush, 295, 353
Felayev, 74, 151, 152
Feldman, 252, 281, 335
Feldman, 382
Finkel, 84, 85
Fishbein, 276
Fishbein, 382, 383
Fisher, 253, 282, 286
Fisher, 383
Flamenboim, 383
Flayshetz, 383
Flomboim, 383
Flomenboim, 383
Flusberg, 1, 3, 6, 7, 8, 9, 13, 29, 30, 31, 35, 38, 39, 40, 42, 48, 50, 51, 53, 56, 59, 62, 64, 65, 70, 71, 73, 74, 76, 78, 80, 83, 86, 88, 89, 90, 92, 94, 95, 96, 97, 98, 99, 101, 103, 104, 105, 106, 107, 109, 111, 112, 114, 115, 118, 119, 120, 125, 131, 132, 133, 139, 150, 151, 205, 218, 219, 220, 223, 224, 227, 229, 230, 231, 232, 234, 236, 238, 239, 240, 242, 243, 245, 249, 252, 253, 254, 256, 257, 259, 260, 261, 263, 264, 266, 267, 268, 269, 271, 273, 275, 276, 279, 280, 284, 286, 290, 292, 295, 296, 300, 313
Fodbiler, 279
Forer, 206
Frederich, 349
Freidman, 383, 399
Freier, 52, 275, 281, 331, 338
Freizer, 275, 338
Freyer, 383, 384
Friedman, 65, 286
Frug, 325

G

Galbert, 6, 7, 8, 25, 30, 31, 34, 37, 38, 40, 42, 45, 49, 50, 53, 56, 57, 62, 63, 65, 69, 71, 72, 73, 74, 77, 80, 83, 85, 87, 88, 90, 91, 94, 95, 96, 98, 100, 101, 104, 105, 106, 107, 108, 110, 112, 114, 116, 119, 120, 122, 125, 129, 131, 133, 138, 149, 150, 160, 218, 219, 220, 221, 223, 225, 228, 230, 231, 232, 234, 236, 237, 239, 240, 241, 242, 245, 249, 252, 253, 254, 255, 257, 258, 259, 261, 262, 263, 264, 266, 268, 269, 271, 272, 273, 275, 278, 280, 283, 284, 289, 290, 293, 296, 300, 316
Galin, 41
Galman, 281
Galperin, 119, 125, 127, 129, 138, 190, 275, 280, 287, 337, 342, 343, 371
Galperin, 384, 408, 416, 420
Galpern, 69, 71, 190, 251, 258, 271, 280, 286
Galprin, 121
Ganzitzki, 384
Garbash, 384, 389
Garfinkel, 158, 159, 186, 229, 231, 319
Gedimin, 14
Geier, 168, 172, 264, 281, 286, 372

www.ingramcontent.com/pod-product-compliance
Lightning Source LLC
Chambersburg PA
CBHW082006150426
42814CB00005BA/239